◆ PERSPECTIVES ◆ ON ARGUMENT

Fourth Edition

NANCY V. WOOD

University of Texas at Arlington

550

PEARSON
Prentice
Hall

Upper Saddle River, New Jersey 07458

Library of Congress Cataloging-in-Publication Data

Wood, Nancy V.
    Perspectives on argument / Nancy V. Wood.—4th ed.
      p. cm.
    Includes bibliographical references and index.
    ISBN 0-13-182374-4
      1. English language—Rhetoric. 2. Persuasion (Rhetoric). 3. College readers.
4. Report writing. I. Title.

PE1431.W66 2003
808'.042—dc21   2003048240

Editor in Chief: Leah Jewell
Senior Acquisitions Editor: Corey Good
Editorial Assistant: Steven Kyritz
VP, Director of Production and Manufacturing: Barbara Kittle
Senior Production Editor: Shelly Kupperman
Production Assistant: Marlene Gassler
Copyeditor: Kathy Graehl
Prepress and Manufacturing Manager: Nick Sklitsis
Prepress and Manufacturing Buyer: Mary Ann Gloriande
Marketing Director: Beth Gillette Mejia
Executive Marketing Manager: Brandy Dawson
Marketing Assistant: Christine Moodie
Creative Design Director: Leslie Osher
Interior and Cover Designer: Carmen DiBartolomeo, C2K, Inc.
Art Coordinator: Guy Ruggiero
Electronic Artist: Mirella Signoretto
Cover Illustration: Jim Frazier/SIS, Inc.
Senior Art Director: Anne Bonanno Nieglos

For permission to use copyrighted material, grateful acknowledgment
is made to all copyright holders listed on pages 707–710, which are
considered a continuation of this copyright page.

This book was set in 10/12 Meridien Roman by Lithokraft
and printed and bound by Courier Companies.
The cover was printed by Coral Graphics.

 © 2004, 2001, 1998, 1995 by Pearson Education, Inc.
Upper Saddle River, New Jersey 07458

Printed in the United States of America
10 9 8 7 6 5 4

ISBN 0-13-182374-4

Pearson Education LTD., London
Pearson Education Australia PTY, Limited, Sydney
Pearson Education Singapore, Pte. Ltd
Pearson Education North Asia Ltd, Hong Kong
Pearson Education Canada, Ltd., Toronto
Pearson Educación de Mexico, S.A. de C.V.
Pearson Education—Japan, Tokyo
Pearson Education Malaysia, Pte. Ltd
Pearson Education, Upper Saddle River, New Jersey

Brief Contents

Contents

➡ Part Two   Understanding the Nature of Argument for Reading and Writing   125

⟶ Part Three **WRITING A RESEARCH PAPER THAT PRESENTS AN ARGUMENT**   293

Part Four FURTHER APPLICATIONS: VISUAL AND ORAL ARGUMENT/ ARGUMENT AND LITERATURE   393

Alternate Table of Contents

ALPHABETICAL LISTING OF ISSUES IN THE ESSAYS

MAJOR ASSIGNMENTS

(Other assignments, in addition to those listed here, appear in the Exercises and Activities sections at the ends of the chapters.)

Issue Proposal, 27–28
Provides initial information about an issue and shows how to test it to see if it is arguable. Student example, 28.

Argument Style Paper, 47–48
Describes student's usual style of argument and analyzes the outside influences on this style.

Analyze the Rhetorical Situation, 83
Analyzes the elements of the rhetorical situation in a written essay.

Summary-Response Paper, 88
Summarizes an essay and provides the writer's response to its ideas.

Exploratory Paper, 123
Describes three or more perspectives on an issue and helps writers identify their own perspective. Exploratory paper worksheet, 123. Student example, 120–122.

Toulmin Analysis, 149–150
Analyzes the claim, support, and warrants in student-provided essays, cartoons, advertisements, or letters to the editor. Student example, 150–151.

Position Paper Based on "The Reader," 240–242
Develops a claim through research in "The Reader" and the employment of the Toulmin model, 146, the claim questions, 195–196, the types of proof, 229–230, and checks for fallacies, 240. Student example, 242–244.

Rogerian Argument Paper, 254–256
Restates the opposition's position before stating the writer's position to achieve common ground. Student examples, 256–259, 260–262, 263–264.

Rogerian Response Paper, 265
Applies Rogerian strategy to respond to a written essay with which the writer disagrees. Student example, 266–267.

CLASS PROJECTS

EXAMPLES OF ARGUMENT STRATEGIES IN "READER" ARTICLES

1. **Argument Papers.** Exploratory: Hawkins, 611; Brooks, 629; Mead (see paragraphs 1–3), 675. Rogerian: Wilson (see paragraphs 5–6), 652; James, 671; Ury, 692. Position: Powers, 542; Lewis, 601; Cohen, 614; Zakaria, 623; Rhodes, R., 696.

2. **Claims.** Fact: Wilson, 466; Moore, 539; Powers, 542. Definition: Gómez-Peña, 573; Shapiro, 588; Wiesel, 690. Cause: Weinberger, 555; Hanson, 680, Sarraj, 685. Value: Hewlett, 478; Bennett, 686. Policy: Rhodes, F., 496; hooks, 566; Majid, 585. Qualified claim: Hawkins, 611; Louria, 662; Hoffman, 700.

3. **Language and Style.** Language that appeals to logic: Wilson, 466; Rhodes, F., 496; Sollod, 503; Payne, 509. Language that appeals to emotion: Glaser, 463; Kozinski, 532; Goldberg, 617. Language that developes *ethos:* Rhodes, F., 496, Kozinski, 532; Powers, 542.

4. **Organizational Patterns.** Claim plus reasons: Will, 530; Kluger and Dorfman, 657. Cause and effect: Zernicke, 513; Wilson, 466; Louria, 662. Chronological or narrative: Gonshak, 506; Feuer, 559; Silver, 633. Comparison and contrast: Wilson, 466; Freire, 519; Kurzweil, 638. Problem-solution: Rhodes, F., 496; Majid, 585; Stolberg, 642; Wilson, 652.

5. **Proofs:** *Ethos.* Self as authority: Rhodes, F., 496; Majid, 585; Hendrix, 481; Gilligan, 526. Quoted authorities: Coontz, 472; Guernsey, 607; Hewlett, 487.

6. **Proofs:** *Logos.* Sign: Feuer, 559; hooks, 566; Zakaria, 623. Induction: Hendrix, 481; Mead (see paragraphs 4–8), 675; Hoffman, 700. Cause: Jones, 550; Weinberger, 555; Hanson, 680. Deduction: Payne, 509; Louria, 662; James, 671. Analogy: Adler, 458; Posner, 598, Kurzweil, 638; Dyer, 569. Definition: Hetherington, 489; Payne, 509; Freire, 519. Statistics: Coontz, 472; Hewlett, 478; Kluger and Dorfman, 657.

7. **Proofs:** *Pathos.* Motives: Rothstein, 557; Pan and Keene-Osborn, 581; Goldberg, 617. Values: Adler, 458; Kozinski, 532; Clemetson and Naughton, 622.

8. **Refutation.** Cain, 455; Posner, 598; Silver, 633; Wood, 646.

9. **Adaptation to Rhetorical Situation.** Gonshak, 506; Clemetson and Naughton, 622; Kozinski, 532, Sarraj, 685.

10. **Support.** Examples: Cain, 455; Adler, 458; Maas, 604. Facts: Will, 530; Moore, 539; Rhodes, R., 696. Narration: Hendrix, 481; Light, 516; Jones, 550; Silver, 633. Personal examples and narratives: Gonshak, 506; Kozinski, 532; Gómez-Peña, 573; Kondo, 576.

11. **Warrants.** Glaser, 463; Gilligan, 526; Jones, 550; Kondo, 576; Chang, 583; Wood, 646; Bennett, 686; Sarraj, 685.

Preface

PURPOSE

The most important purpose of *Perspectives on Argument* is to teach students strategies for critical reading, critical thinking, research, and writing that will help them participate in all types of argument both inside and outside of the classroom. A basic assumption is that argument exists everywhere and that students need to learn to participate productively in all forms of argument, including those they encounter in school, at home, on the job, and in the national and international spheres. Such participation is critical not only in a democratic society but also in a global society, in which issues become more and more complex each year. Students who use this book will learn to identify controversial topics that are "at issue," to read and form reactions and opinions of their own, and to write argument papers that express their individual views and perspectives.

A central idea of this text is that modern argument is not always polarized as right or wrong, but that instead it often invites a variety of perspectives on an issue. Another idea, equally important, is that not all argument results in the declaration of winners. The development of common ground and either consensus or compromise are sometimes as acceptable as declaring winners in argument. Students will learn to take a variety of approaches to argument, including taking a position and defending it, seeking common ground at times, withholding opinion at other times, negotiating when necessary, and even changing their original beliefs when they can no longer make a case for them. The perspectives and abilities taught here are those that an educated populace in a world community needs to coexist cooperatively and without constant destructive conflict.

SPECIAL FEATURES

Both instructors and students who pick up *Perspectives on Argument* have the right to ask how it differs from some of the other argument texts that are presently available. They deserve to know why they might want to use this book instead of another. This text, which is targeted for first-year and second-year students enrolled in argument or argument and literature classes in two-year and four-year colleges, is both a reader and a rhetoric. Within this reader and rhetoric format are a number of special features that, when taken together, make the book unique.

◆ **Reading, critical thinking, and writing** are taught as integrated and interdependent processes. Comprehensive chapters on the reading and writing processes show how they can be adapted to argument. Extensive instruction in critical reading and critical thinking appear throughout. Assignments and questions that invite critical reading, critical thinking, and original argumentative writing appear at the end of every chapter in "The Rhetoric" and at the end of every section of "The Reader."

◆ **Cross-gender and cross-cultural communication styles** are presented in a unique chapter that provides for a classroom in which every student can find a voice. Students learn to identify and develop their own unique styles of argument and to recognize how their styles may have been influenced by family background, gender, ethnic background, or country of origin. Also included are international students' perspectives on the argument styles of their countries. Many readings in the book are by authors of varied cultural and ethnic backgrounds.

◆ **Explanations of the elements and structure of argument** include the **Toulmin model of argument,** the **classical modes of appeal,** the **traditional categories of claims** derived from classical stasis theory, and the **rhetorical situation.** Theory is integrated and translated into language that students can easily understand and apply. For example, students learn to apply theory to recognize and analyze the parts of an argument while reading and to develop and structure their own ideas while writing.

◆ **Audience analysis** includes the concepts of the familiar and the unfamiliar audience as well as Chaim Perelman's concept of the universal audience.

◆ **Productive invention strategies** help students develop ideas for papers.

◆ **Library and online research is presented as a creative activity** that students are invited to enjoy. Workable strategies for research and note taking are provided along with criteria for evaluating all types of sources, including those found online. Students are taught to document researched argument papers according to the most up-to-date **MLA** and **APA styles.**

◆ **Exercises, class projects, and writing assignments at the ends of the chapters invite individual, small group, and whole class participation.** Collaborative exercises encourage small groups of students to engage in critical thinking, and whole class projects invite students to participate in activities that require an understanding of argument. Classroom-tested **writing assignments** include the **exploratory paper,** which teaches students to explore an issue from several different perspectives; the **position paper based on "The Reader,"** which teaches students to incorporate readily available source material from "The Reader" in their first position paper; the **Rogerian argument paper,** which teaches students an alternative strategy that relies on establishing common ground with the audience; and the **researched position paper,** which teaches students to locate outside research, evaluate it, and use it to develop an issue of their own choosing. **Examples of student papers** are provided for each major type of paper. The writing assignments in this book are models for assignments that students are likely to encounter in their other classes.

◆ **Summary Charts at the end of "The Rhetoric" present the main points of argument** in a handy format. They also integrate the reading and writing processes for argument by placing strategies for both side by side and showing the interconnections.

◆ **A total of 108 different readings** in "The Rhetoric" and "The Reader" provide students with multiple perspectives on the many issues presented throughout the book. Eleven of these readings are argument papers written by students.

◆ **The readings in "The Reader" are clustered under eighteen subissues** that are related to the seven major general issue areas that organize "The Reader." This helps students focus and narrow broad issues. Furthermore, the readings in each subissue group "talk" to each other, and questions invite students to join the conversation.

NEW TO THIS EDITION

◆ **Two new chapters** have been added:

Chapter 8, "The Fallacies or Pseudoproofs," is an expanded version of the material about fallacies that previously appeared in Chapter 7, "The Types of Proof," now itself a more manageable length. The new Chapter 8 teaches students not only to recognize fallacies but also to evaluate the support and eliminate the fallacies in their own argument.

Chapter 13, "Visual and Oral Argument," teaches students to analyze the argument they see and hear every day.

- **A color portfolio of ten visual arguments,** accompanied by **Questions for Discussion and Questions for Writing,** provides students with opportunities to practice analyzing visual argument.
- **Martin Luther King Jr.'s speech, "I Have a Dream,"** provides students with an opportunity to practice analyzing oral argument. It is accompanied by a Web site address that enables students to listen to the speech as it was first delivered.

◆ **WHERE IS IT? Major Writing Assignments and Sample Papers by Students** appears on the inside front cover of the book to help students locate frequently visited pages quickly.

◆ **Improved organization: Rogerian argument is now taught before the researched position paper** so that students may include Rogerian elements in the research paper as one possible strategy.

◆ **A worksheet and additional explanations to help students organize and write an exploratory paper** are added to Chapter 4.

◆ **Extended information and examples of plagiarism** in Chapters 4 and 12 teach students how to avoid it.

◆ **Two new examples of student writing** provide models for an **issue proposal** and a **Rogerian response paper.**

◆ **New essays for analysis** have been added to Chapters 1, 2, 6, 7, 8, 9, 13, and 14.

- ◆ **Recent updates on MLA and APA style along with new examples of how to cite electronic sources** appear in the Appendix to Chapter 12.

- ◆ **More than half (57) of the 108 essays in the book are new.** Three-fourths of the essays in "The Reader" are new, and one-third of the essays in "The Rhetoric" are new.

- ◆ **Three new issue areas** in "The Reader" explore issues associated with **freedom, the future,** and **war and peace.**

- ◆ **Fifteen new issue questions,** each **accompanied by sets of related essays** that provide different perspectives on the questions, appear in "The Reader." These questions include, "What Is the Status of the Traditional American Family? How Far Are We Willing to Go to Find Alternatives?" "What Are the Benefits and Pitfalls of Being Married?" "What Creates Successful Relationships? What Causes Them to Fail?" "What Should Colleges and Universities Teach? Is There Anything They Should Not Teach?" "What Helps Students Learn and Succeed in College? What Hinders Them?" "To What Extent Should Individuals Allow Their Cultural Heritage to Be Assimilated?" "How Rigorously Should We Protect Our Civil Liberties?" "How Can We Balance Security Against Privacy in a Technological Age?" "How Does Profiling Threaten Civil Liberties?" "What Are Some Possible Issues for the Future?" "What Might Affect the Future of Human Beings?" "What Might Affect the Future of the Planet?" "Is War Inevitable?" "How Do People Justify War?" "What Might Help Establish Peace?"

- ◆ **Questions to Consider Before You Read** now appear at the beginning of each issue question in "The Reader" to help students access their background knowledge.

- ◆ **Web Sites for Further Exploration and Research** are now provided for each issue area in "The Reader" to guide students to possible research sites.

ORGANIZATION

The book is organized into five parts and, as much as possible, chapters have been written so that they stand alone. Instructors may thus assign them either in sequence or in an order they prefer to supplement their own course organization.

 PART ONE: Engaging with Argument for Reading and Writing. This part introduces students to issues and the characteristics of argument, in Chapter 1; helps them begin to develop a personal style of argument, in Chapter 2; and provides them with processes for reading and writing argument, in Chapters 3 and 4. Writing assignments include the issue proposal, the argument style paper, the analysis of the rhetorical situation paper, the summary-response paper, and the exploratory paper.

 PART TWO: Understanding the Nature of Argument for Reading and Writing. This part identifies and explains the parts of an argument according to

Stephen Toulmin's model of argument, in Chapter 5; explains the types of claims and purposes for argument, in Chapter 6; presents the types of proofs along with clear examples and tests for validity, in Chapter 7; identifies the fallacies and teaches students to use reliable support in their own writing, in Chapter 8; and explains Rogerian argument as an alternative to traditional argument and as an effective method for building common ground and resolving differences in Chapter 9. Writing assignments include the Toulmin analysis, the position paper based on "The Reader," and Rogerian argument papers. A summary exercise in the Appendix to Chapter 9 invites students to review and synthesize argument theory as they analyze and respond to a well-known classic argument.

PART THREE: Writing a Research Paper That Presents an Argument. This part teaches students to write a claim, clarify purpose, and analyze the audience, in Chapter 10; to use various creative strategies for inventing ideas and gathering research materials, in Chapter 11; and to organize, write, revise, and prepare the final manuscript for a researched position paper, in Chapter 12. Methods for locating and using resource materials in the library and online are presented in Chapters 11 and 12. An Appendix to Chapter 12 provides full instruction for documenting sources using both MLA and APA styles.

PART FOUR: Further Applications: Visual and Oral Argument/ Argument and Literature. Chapter 13 teaches students to extend and apply in new ways what they have learned about argument to the analysis and critique of visual and spoken argument as they encounter it in all parts of their lives. Chapter 14 suggests ways to apply argument theory to reading and writing about literature. Assignments include creating a visual argument, creating an oral argument, and writing papers about argument and literature.

PART FIVE: The Reader. This part is organized around the broad issues concerning families, marriages, and relationships; education; crime and the treatment of criminals; race, culture, and identity; freedom; the future; and war and peace. Strategies and questions to help students explore issues and move from reading and discussion to writing are also included.

THE INSTRUCTOR'S MANUAL AND COMPANION WEBSITE

My co-contributors and I have included five chapters in the *Instructor's Manual*, three of them new, that provide syllabi, day-by-day teaching journals, and handouts to facilitate classroom management in five different types of argument classes that use *Perspectives on Argument* as the primary textbook. Since these five classes and syllabi have been classroom tested repeatedly, they may be followed or changed and adapted with confidence. One class follows the textbook closely, another employs a considerable amount of student discussion of issues, a third includes a number of effective ways for teaching visual argument, a fourth describes an argument class that can be taught in a computer classroom, and the fifth describes a class that can be taught online as a distance education class.

Another chapter in the manual provides descriptions of each chapter's contents and the exercises that accompany them. Instructors can save themselves considerable time by reading these descriptions before they read the chapters themselves. A set of class handouts ready for photocopying is also provided. Copies of this manual may be obtained from your Prentice Hall representative.

A Companion Website for *Perspectives on Argument* can be accessed at <http://www.prenhall.com/wood>. Beth Brunk is the original author of this site. It has been updated for the fourth edition by Heath Diehl.

ACKNOWLEDGMENTS

My greatest debt is to my husband, James A. Wood, who has also taught and written about argument. He helped me work out my approach to argument by listening to me, by discussing my ideas, and by contributing ideas of his own. He was particularly generous in providing his expertise with communication theory as we discussed the ideas for the new Chapter 13 on visual and oral argument. The process renewed my faith in peer groups and writing conferences. Most writers, I am convinced, profit from talking through their ideas with someone else. I have been lucky to work with someone so knowledgeable and generous with his time and insights.

I also owe a debt to the first-year English program at the University of Texas at Arlington. When I joined the department a number of years ago, I found myself caught up in the ideas and challenges of this program. It provided me with much of the interest and motivation to write this book.

For the past several years, I have participated in the training of the graduate teaching assistants in our department who teach argument. An exceptionally alert group of these students volunteered to meet with me and recommend revisions for this fourth edition. They include Teri Gaston, Toni Manning, Kevin Pajak, Robert Leston, Sandi Hubrik, Judy Donaldson, and Lynn Atkinson. I hope they will be pleased when they see that I followed most of their suggestions for improvement.

Graduate students, many of whom are now faculty members elsewhere, who have contributed recommendations for revisions in earlier editions and that remain a part of the fourth edition include Nicole Siek, Christine Flynn Cavanaugh, Vera Csorvasi, Martha Villagomez, Barbara Saurer, Sara Latham, Vannetta Causey, Donna Brown, Kody Lightfoot, Beth Brunk, Chris Murray, Leslie Snow, Samantha Masterton, J. T. Martin, Brad McAdon, Kimberly Bessire, Cheryl Brown, Mathew Levy, Alan Taylor, and Deborah Reese. Many other graduate teaching assistants in our program have also taught with this book and have made useful recommendations and suggestions. I am always grateful to them for their insights and enthusiasm.

I am also indebted to other colleagues and friends who have helped me with this book. The late James Kinneavy is the originator of the exploratory paper as it is taught in this book. Audrey Wick, Director of First Year English at our university and a seasoned teacher of argument, has provided me with much counsel and advice. My colleague Tim Morris helped me think through some of the ideas in Chapter 14, and he provided me with many excellent examples of poems and other literary works that make arguments. I owe a special debt of gratitude to Robert Leston who spent hours locating and reading articles and then helping to assemble them for "The Reader." I have only included those articles that survived our joint scrutiny. Robert Leston also provided the new elements in "The Reader" that encourage students to question what they already know and that direct them to specific Web sites for further research. Beth Brunk, Samantha Masterton, Sarah Arroyo, and Robert Leston have all provided chapters in the *Instructor's Manual*. Robert Leston formatted and typed it. It has been a constant pleasure to work with these bright, energetic, and creative colleagues, and I am grateful to all of them for the contributions they have made to this fourth edition.

I wish I had the space to acknowledge by name the many undergraduate students from argument classes, including my own, who read the first three editions and made recommendations for this fourth edition. Some of them also contributed their own essays to be used as examples, and their names appear on their work. I paid particularly close attention to these students' comments, and I know their suggestions and contributions have made this a better book for other argument students throughout the country.

At Prentice Hall, my greatest debt is to Phil Miller, former President, Humanities and Social Sciences, who got me started with this project. I also thank Leah Jewell, Editor in Chief, and Corey Good, Senior English Editor, who helped me plan positive changes for this fourth edition and then provided me with support and encouragement throughout the revision process. Thanks also to Brandy Dawson, Executive Marketing Manager, who has always encouraged me with her good cheer and positive outlook. Shelly Kupperman, Senior Production Editor, once again has done her usual impressive and conscientious job of seeing the book through all phases of production. Barbara DeVries also provided her seasoned expertise with some of the early phases of production. Kathy Graehl provided outstanding editorial expertise. Judy Kiviat, cheerful and persistent, found the errors that had escaped everyone else and also made suggestions that improved the general appearance and readability of the book. I have felt fortunate to work with such conscientious, reliable, and capable professionals.

Colleagues around the country who have provided additional ideas and recommended changes that have helped improve all four editions of this book include Margaret W. Batschelet, University of Texas at San Antonio; Linda D. Bensel-Meyers, University of Tennessee; Gregory Clark, Brigham Young University; Dan Damesville, Tallahassee Community College; Alexander Friedlander, Drexel University; William S. Hockman, University of Southern Colorado; James Kinneavy, University of Texas at Austin; Elizabeth Metzger, University of South Florida; Margaret Dietz Meyer, Ithaca College; Susan Padgett, North Lake College; Randall L. Popken, Tarleton State University; William E. Sheidley, United States Air Force Academy; Diane M. Thiel, Florida International University; Jennifer Welsh, University of Southern California; Shannon Martin, Elizabethtown Community College; Keith Rhodes, Northwest Missouri State University; Kim Donehower, University of Maryland; Lynce Lewis Gaillet, Georgia State University;

Carol David, Iowa State University; Sue Preslar, University of North Carolina, Charlotte; John Schaffer, Blinn College; Bob Esch, University of Texas at El Paso; Richard Grande, Pennsylvania State University; Kim Stallings, University of North Carolina, Charlotte; Julie Wakeman Linn, Montgomery College; Raquel Scherr Salgado, University of California, Davis; Perry Cumbie, Durham Technical Community College; and Claudia Milstead, University of Tennessee. I am grateful to them for the time and care they took reviewing the manuscript.

I also want to acknowledge the many instructors and students around the country who have e-mailed observations and suggestions for improvement. It is a special treat to receive e-mail from people who are using the book and have ideas for improving it. In fact, I thank all of you who use this book. I like to hear about your experiences with it, and I am especially interested in your ideas for improving the chapters and readings. My e-mail address is <woodnv@uta.edu>.

This book has been a genuinely collaborative effort, and I expect that it will continue to be. I hope students will profit from the example and learn to draw on the expertise of their instructors and classmates to help them write their papers. Most writing is more fun and more successful when it is, at least partly, a social process.

N. V. W.

Part One

ENGAGING WITH ARGUMENT FOR READING AND WRITING

THE STRATEGY IN PART ONE IS TO INTRODUCE YOU TO ISSUES AND THE SPECIAL CHARACTERISTICS OF ARGUMENT, IN CHAPTER 1; TO HELP YOU BEGIN TO DEVELOP A PERSONAL STYLE OF ARGUMENT, IN CHAPTER 2; AND TO HELP YOU DEVELOP YOUR PROCESSES FOR READING AND WRITING ARGUMENT, IN CHAPTERS 3 AND 4. THE FOCUS IN THESE CHAPTERS IS ON YOU AND HOW YOU WILL ENGAGE WITH ARGUMENT BOTH AS A READER AND AS A WRITER. WHEN YOU FINISH READING PART ONE:

- You will understand what argument is and why it is important in a democratic society.

- You will have found some issues (topics) to read and write about.

- You will have analyzed your present style of argument and considered ways to adapt it for special contexts.

- You will have new strategies and ideas to help you read argument critically.

- You will have adapted your present writing process to help you think critically and write argument papers.

- You will have experience with writing an issue proposal, a summary-response paper, and an exploratory argument paper.

Chapter 1

A Perspective on Argument

You engage in argument, whether you realize it or not, nearly every day. Argument deals with *issues,* topics that have not yet been settled, that invite two or more differing opinions, and that are consequently subject to question, debate, or negotiation. Pick up today's newspaper and read the headlines to find current examples of issues, such as the following: Should the Internet be censored? Has the quality of health care declined? Should same-sex and transgendered couples have the same legal rights as heterosexual couples? Should one government participate in solving the problems of other governments, or should it limit itself to solving its own problems? How can population growth best be controlled in third-world countries? Should politicians be held to higher ethical standards than everyone else? Do we need better gun laws? Or think of examples of issues that may be closer to your daily experience: Why are you going to college? What close relationships should you form, and how will they affect your life? Which is the more important consideration in selecting a major: finding a job or enjoying the subject? How can one minimize the frustrations caused by limited campus parking? Is it good or bad policy to go to school and work at the same time?

All of these issues, whether they seem remote or close to you, are related to the big issues that have engaged human thought for centuries. In fact, all of the really important issues—those dealing with life and death, the quality of life, ways and means, war and peace, the individual and society, the environment, and others like them—are discussed, debated, and negotiated everywhere in the world on a regular basis. There are usually no simple or obvious positions to take on such important issues. Still, the positions we do take on them and ultimately the decisions and actions we take in regard to them can affect our lives in significant ways. In democratic societies, individuals are expected to engage in effective argument on issues of broad concern. They are also expected to make moral judgments and to evaluate the decisions and ideas that emerge from argument.

The purpose of this book is to help you participate in two types of activities: evaluating other people's arguments and formulating arguments of your own. The book is organized in parts, and each part will help you become a more effective participant in the arguments that affect your life. Part One will help you engage with argument personally as you begin to identify the issues, the argument styles, and the processes for reading and writing that will work best for you; Part Two will help you understand the nature of argument as you learn more about its essential parts and how certain strategies operate in argument to convince an audience; Part Three will provide you with a process for thinking critically and writing an argument paper that requires both critical thought and research; Part Four will teach you to analyze visual and oral argument and alert you to uses of argument in literature; and Part Five will provide you with many good examples of effective argument to analyze and draw on as you create original arguments of your own.

WHAT IS YOUR CURRENT PERSPECTIVE ON ARGUMENT?

You may never have been in an argument class before. If that is the case, as it is with most students, you will have a few ideas about argument, but you will not have a totally clear idea about what you will be studying in this class. It is best to begin the study of any new subject by thinking about what you already know. Then you can use what you know to learn more, which is the way all of us acquire new knowledge.

What does the word *argument* make you think about? The following list contains some common student responses to that question. Place a check next to those that match your own. If other ideas come to mind, add them to the list.

_____ 1. It is important to include both sides in argument.

_____ 2. Argument is angry people yelling at each other.

_____ 3. Argument is a debate in front of a judge; one side wins.

_____ 4. Argument takes place in courtrooms before judges and juries.

_____ 5. Argument is what I'd like to be able to do better at home, at work, or with my friends so that I'd get my way more often.

_____ 6. Argument is standing up for your ideas, defending them, and minimizing the opposition by being persuasive.

_____ 7. Argument requires one to keep an open mind.

_____ 8. Argument papers are difficult to write because they require more than a collection of personal feelings and opinions about a subject.

_____ 9. Argument, to me, is like beating a dead horse. I have done papers in high school about subjects I'm supposed to care about, like abortion, homosexuality, drugs, capital punishment. They're old news. They no longer spark my imagination.

_____ 10. Argument is something I like to avoid. I see no reason for it. It makes things unpleasant and difficult. And nothing gets settled anyway.

Whether your present views of argument are positive, negative, or just vague, it's best to acknowledge them so that you can now begin expanding on them or even modifying some of them in order to develop a broad perspective on argument.

A definition of argument at this point should help clarify the broad perspective we are seeking. There are many approaches to and views of argument, and consequently various definitions have been suggested. Some focus on identifying opposing views, providing evidence, and declaring winners. Others emphasize reasoning, understanding, agreement, and consensus. Both types of definition are useful, depending on the context and the purpose of the argument. Chaim Perelman and Lucie Olbrechts-Tyteca, respected modern argument theorists, provide the definition that we will use in this book. They suggest that the goal of argument "is to create or increase the adherence of minds to the theses presented for [the audience's] assent."[1] In other words, the goal of argument is at times to reach agreement on controversial issues among participants and at other times merely to increase the possibility of agreement. This definition is broad enough to include both argument that focuses on opposing views and sometimes the declaration of winners and Rogerian argument that emphasizes understanding and results in consensus; both approaches to argument are taught in Part Two of this book. This definition further invites argument participants either to agree to the best position on a matter of dispute or to carve out a new position that all participants can agree on. Using this definition as a starting point, we can now add to it and consider argument in its broadest sense.

DEVELOPING A BROAD PERSPECTIVE ON ARGUMENT

Think about the implications of this idea: *Argument is everywhere.*[2] It can be written, spoken, sung, or chanted, or it can be read, heard, or observed in pictures that are either still or moving. It is not only found in obvious places such as courts of law, legislative assemblies, or organized debates. Indeed, it is a part of all human enterprise, whether at home, at school, at work, or on the national or international scene. Home argument, for example, might center on spending money, dividing the household work, raising the children, and planning for the future. School argument might include such issues as increasing student fees, finding parking, understanding grades, or selecting classes and professors. Work argument might focus on making hiring decisions, delegating responsibility, or establishing long-term goals. National argument might deal with providing health care, abolishing crime, or electing leaders. International argument might deal with protecting human rights, abolishing hunger, or negotiating international trade agreements. Thus argument appears in virtually any context in which

---

[1]Chaim Perelman and Lucie Olbrechts-Tyteca, *The New Rhetoric: A Treatise on Argumentation* (Notre Dame, Ind.: University of Notre Dame Press, 1969), p. 45.

[2]I am indebted to Wayne Brockriede for this observation and for some of the other ideas in this chapter. See his article "Where Is Argument?" *Journal of the American Forensic Association*, 11 (1975): 179–182.

human beings interact and hold divergent views about topics that are at issue. Furthermore, argument is a perspective, a point of view that people adopt to identify, interpret, analyze, communicate, and try to reach settlements or conclusions about subjects that are at issue.

If we accept the idea that argument can indeed be found anywhere, we discover that it can also appear in different guises and involve varying numbers of people. In fact, argument can take eight forms, as in the following list. Some, like organized debate and courtroom argument, will not surprise you. Others may.

FORMS OF ARGUMENT

Argument, in its most basic form, can be described as a **claim** (the arguer's position on a controversial issue) which is **supported by reasons and evidence** to make the claim convincing to an audience. All of the forms of argument described below include these components.

1. *Debate, with participants on both sides trying to win.* In a debate, people take sides on a controversial issue that is usually stated as a proposition. For example, the proposition "Resolved that health care be affordable for all Americans" might be debated by an affirmative debater arguing in favor of this idea and a negative debater arguing against it. A judge, who listens to the debate, usually selects one of the debaters as the winner. The debaters do not try to convince one another but instead try to convince the judge, who is supposed to be impartial. Debates are useful for exploring and sometimes resolving issues that have distinct pro and con sides. Debates on television often feature people who hold conflicting views. The judge for these programs is the viewing public, who may or may not pick a winner.

2. *Courtroom argument, with lawyers pleading before a judge and jury.* As in a debate, lawyers take opposing sides and argue to convince a judge and jury of the guilt or innocence of a defendant. Lawyers do not try to convince one another. Also as in debate, someone is designated the winner. Television provides opportunities to witness courtroom argument, particularly on cable channels devoted exclusively to televising real trials. You can also visit courtrooms, since trials are open to the public.

3. *Dialectic, with people taking opposing views and finally resolving the conflict.* In dialectic, two or more people argue as equals to try to discover what seems to be the best position. A questioning strategy is often used to test the validity of each opposing view. The ancient philosopher Plato used this form of argument in his *Dialogues* to examine such questions as What is truth? What is the ideal type of government? and What is more important: honesty and justice or political power? Dialectic is used by some professors to help students think about and finally arrive at positions that can be generally accepted, by most of the class. For example, dialectic might be used to ascertain students' views on the roles men

and women might assume in a family or whether religion should or should not be taught in school. Participants explain and justify their own positions and test others' positions. The object is to discover a common bedrock of ideas that everyone can agree on. There are no winners. There is instead a consensual discovery of a new position on the issue that is agreeable to everyone.

4. *Single-perspective argument, with one person arguing to convince a mass audience.* We encounter argument in single-perspective form constantly on television and in newspapers, journals, books, and public speeches. It is usually clear what the issue is and what position is being taken. Opposing views, if referred to at all, are usually refuted. Specific examples of such argument range from a politician trying to influence voters to change their ideas about taxes, to an environmentalist trying to influence management to eliminate toxic waste, to an advertiser trying to sell sportswear. The arguer does not usually know what immediate effect the message has had on the audience unless a poll or vote is taken, unless there is an opportunity for the readers to write letters to the editor, or unless there is a publicized change in policy or behavior. It is not clear, in other words, whether anyone "wins."

5. *One-on-one, everyday argument, with one person trying to convince another.* Convincing another person, one on one, is very different from convincing an impartial outside judge or a large unspecified audience. In the one-on-one situation, one person has to focus on and identify with the other person, think about what he or she wants and values, and be conciliatory if necessary. Each person either wins, loses, or succeeds in part. An example of this form of argument might include convincing a partner to sell the business, convincing an employment officer to hire a favored candidate, or convincing a potential customer to buy a car.

6. *Academic inquiry, with one or more people examining a complicated issue.* The purpose of academic argument is to discover new views, new knowledge, and new truths about a complex issue. For example, physicists engage in academic inquiry about the nature of gravity, historians about the causes of major wars, and political scientists about the benefits of a strong state government. There are no clear-cut pro and con positions, no judges, and no emphasis on winning. Anyone can participate, and there are potentially as many views as there are participants. Inquiry is a common form of argument that you will encounter in many of your college classes, where you will also be assigned to write inquiry papers. Virtually every discipline includes matters that are still open to inquiry, matters that people are still thinking and arguing about. Many professors expect their students to be able to identify the issues for inquiry in an academic discipline and also to participate in the ongoing search for answers. Imagine, for example, people reasoning together in a sociology class about whether war is ever justified or in a psychology class about whether discrimination can ever be eliminated from society. These are not simple questions with yes or no answers. Inquiry can, however, produce insight into very difficult questions, with each new participant contributing a new reason, a new example, or a new angle that the other participants may not have considered. As the conversation progresses, participants achieve better understanding through mutual feedback, and some may even change their minds in order to bring their ideas in line with those of other participants. The inquiry form

of argument is appropriate for the complex issues that one can find in every area of study and in every field of human endeavor. Like other forms of argument, it focuses on an issue and examines evidence. It is conducted through a cooperative search for knowledge, however, rather than focusing on finding a winning position at the expense of others. Its result, ideally, is a consensus theory of truth that may take some time to emerge.

7. *Negotiation, with two or more people working to reach consensus.* This is an important form of argument that is used to formulate plans of action that solve problems. Both the Palestinians and the Israelis, for example, could not claim ownership of the same land, so other solutions had to be negotiated. One country could not kill sea life that another country depended on, so rights to the sea had to be negotiated. Closer to home, people negotiate who gets the car, who picks up the check, or who takes out the newspapers. Negotiation most often takes place between two people, one on one, or in a group meeting. Individual negotiators often represent constituencies of people not present at the negotiating table who must ultimately be as satisfied with the final agreements as the negotiators themselves. Negotiation involves both competition and cooperation, and for it to be successful, all involved must state their positions, including those of the individuals they represent, and support them with reasons and evidence. Everyone must also be willing to listen to alternative views and reasons and modify their original views in order to reach consensus and satisfy all parties involved.

8. *Internal argument, or working to convince yourself.* We all use internal argument for individual decision making and to increase motivation. New Year's resolutions are one example of internal argument and decision making. As in other forms of argument, different possibilities are identified, reasons both for and against are considered, and conclusions are finally reached.

Now reconsider some of the student perspectives on argument listed at the beginning of this chapter. Most of those ideas fit into one of the eight forms of argument just described. The exception is item 2, argument with angry people yelling at each other. No argument can be effective if people stop listening and stop thinking and engage in vocal fighting, so "having an argument" of this sort is not part of the broad perspective on argument defined in this chapter. Look back also at item 8 (argument is difficult to write because it requires more than opinion), item 9 (I'm tired of some of the topics for argument), and item 10 (argument makes me uncomfortable). If you found yourself initially in sympathy with those responses, you may now have discovered forms of argument that could be acceptable vehicles for your ideas. Here is the list again: debate, courtroom argument, dialectic, single-perspective argument, one-on-one argument, academic inquiry, negotiation, and internal argument. Which have been successful forms for you in the past? Which others are you drawn to? Why?

These examples and explanations of forms of argument demonstrate that effective argument does not take place automatically. Special conditions are necessary if argument is to be effective. Let's look at some of those conditions to expand our perspective on argument even further.

UNDER WHAT CONDITIONS DOES ARGUMENT WORK BEST?

To work best, argument requires (1) an arguable issue, (2) a person who will argue, (3) an audience that will listen, (4) some common ground between the arguer and the audience, (5) a forum in which the argument can take place, and (6) some changes in the audience. Let's look at some optimal requirements for each of these important elements.

1. *An issue.* An argument needs to have as its central focus an issue that has not yet been settled. Furthermore, there must be the potential for at least two or more views on that issue. For example, some people seem to think that the handgun issue has only two sides—everyone should, by constitutional right, be allowed to own handguns, or no one should be allowed to own them. Between these two extreme views, however, people can and do take a variety of positions, including the view that owning and using handguns may be acceptable under certain conditions but not others or that handguns themselves can be modified to limit their use.

2. *An arguer.* Every argument requires an arguer who is motivated to take a position on an issue, get information and think about it, and communicate it to others. This person needs to develop expertise on an issue and be willing to take a risk to express his or her own ideas about it. Furthermore, the arguer should seek to go beyond the "current wisdom" about an issue and find fresh perspectives and approaches that will suggest original insights to the audience. For example, an individual arguing for tougher handgun laws needs to present fresh reasons and evidence to get people's attention and agreement.

3. *An audience.* Every argument needs an audience that is willing to listen or read and consider new views or perspectives. The audience should also be capable of understanding, thinking, questioning, discussing, and answering. It may be composed of one or more people who are personally known to the arguer, or it may be unknown, in which case the arguer must imagine and invoke its background, motives, and values. The arguer should want to communicate with this audience. It should not be composed of people who are usually ignored or who are not respected by the arguer. It is a compliment to draw someone into discussion on an issue, so the audience should be valued, and to be effective, the arguer must show that he or she cares about the audience, its interests, and its state of mind. This approach will ensure an audience that listens and does not shut the arguer out or otherwise try to escape. Receptive audiences are potentially willing to change their minds, a desirable outcome of argument.[3] Consider, for example, an audience member who favors handgun ownership, who is a parent of school-children, and who is willing to listen to an opposing view because a respectful fellow parent has described the problem of children carrying handguns to school.

4. *Common ground.* Effective argument requires a community of minds that is achieved through common language and the establishment of some common

---

[3]Some of the observations in this chapter about the special conditions for argument, especially for the audience, are derived from Perelman and Olbrechts-Tyteca, *The New Rhetoric,* pt. 1.

ground that is relevant to the issue. People from different countries obviously need a common language, but they also need an understanding and respect for one another's cultural differences in order to argue effectively. People from different disciplines must be able to understand one another's technical jargon and other words and concepts central to the understanding of a particular field of study. In addition, they need to share some background, values, and views to make communication possible. Three situations are possible when one works to establish common ground in argument. First, if two parties agree totally, they do not argue. For example, two parents who agree that their child should go to college do not argue about that part of the child's future. Second, if two parties are too far apart, they usually do not understand one another well enough to argue. The United States did not have enough common ground with Iraq in 1991 to work out differences, and the two countries went to war. There were several causes for this war. Iraq had invaded Kuwait, and the United States was committed to helping this country maintain its independence. Kuwait's independence was important to the United States because Kuwait was a major source of U.S. oil. Finally, Iraq was developing a powerful military with nuclear potential, so it seemed important to the United States to stop that military growth. In 2002 and 2003, the United States again expressed its concern about Iraq's alleged military growth and convinced the United Nations to send weapons inspectors to Iraq to search for evidence of the development of weapons of mass destruction. In 1991, common ground virtually did not exist; as a result, reasoned argument gave way to "an argument," and many people were killed. In 2002 and 2003, common ground again was lacking, and a standoff resulted that allowed almost no opportunity for productive argument, leading to yet another war. The third possible situation for establishing common ground creates more effective conditions for argument than the first two. Common ground may be established through the discovery of common interests—common ideas, motives, or values—or even through recognizing common friends or enemies. As soon as two parties realize they have something in common, they can more easily achieve identification, even if it is minimal, and engage in constructive argument. Imagine, once again, two parties who disagree on handgun ownership. One party believes handgun ownership should be forbidden to stop random killing. The other party believes people should own handguns to protect themselves from random killers. Both agree that random killing is bad and must be stopped, and this basic agreement provides the common ground they need to begin to engage in constructive argument about handgun ownership. Figure 1.1 diagrams these three possible situations.

5. *A forum.* People need safe forums for argument where they can feel creative and know they will be heard. Such widely available forums include magazines and journals, newspapers, books, letters and reports, television programs of all sorts, courtrooms, legislative assemblies, motion pictures, art, drama, fiction, poetry, advertisements, and music. College is another safe forum for argument. Professors and students argue in class, at meals, and in dorms and apartments. Outside speakers present argument. The argument class, with its discussions, papers, and other assignments, can be a safe forum for practicing argument, particularly if both the students and the instructor work to create an environment in which all students participate and are respected.

THE ISSUE: SHOULD LIMITS BE PLACED ON HANDGUN OWNERSHIP?

Possibility 1: *Complete agreement and no argument.* Two individuals believe that all private citizens should be allowed to own one or more handguns to protect themselves from random shooters. They agree totally and share the same common ground. They have nothing to argue about.

Possibility 2: *Total disagreement, no common ground, and no argument.* One individual believes private citizens should have the right to own handguns to protect themselves from random shooters, and another believes that no private citizen should own handguns for any purpose. They disagree totally, and there is no common ground. Productive argument is nearly impossible.

Possibility 3: *Two parties discover something in common, and there is a possibility of argument.* The two parties discover they each hold their positions because of their fear of random shooters. One wants to own a handgun to kill a random shooter in self-defense. The other wants to banish handguns so that random shooters will have trouble obtaining them. They have an important point in common: they both want to stop random shootings. They share common ground on that point, even though they may disagree on other points. The common ground creates the possibility for productive argument about what can be done to stop random shooting, the ultimate goal.

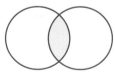

FIGURE 1.1   Establishing Common Ground.

6. *Audience outcomes.* Successful arguments should produce changes in the audience. These changes will vary with the audience and situation. At times the audience becomes convinced and decides to change its mind. Or a successful negotiation is achieved, people find themselves in consensus, a decision is reached, and a plan of action is proposed. Other arguments may not have such clear-cut results. A hostile audience may be brought to a neutral point of view. A neutral audience may decide to take a stand. Sometimes it is a significant accomplishment to get the audience's attention and to raise its level of consciousness. This success can lay the groundwork for a possible future change of mind.

At times an event can create a massive change in the way that people view issues. The Million Man March held in Washington, D.C., in the fall of 1995 changed many peoples' perceptions about the size, commitment, and solidarity of the black male community. The Stand for Children demonstration held in Washington the following summer also changed public perceptions about the issues that are of major concern to women. As private American citizens and public organizations prepared to assemble at the Stand for Children demonstration, Betty Friedan wrote in the *New Yorker* that the probable outcome of the Stand for Children rally would be "to bring out some new thinking." The demonstration, she predicted, would help identify the "most urgent concerns of women today." These would not be the "gender issues" (abortion, date rape, sexual harassment, pornography, and the like) that engaged women in the past but rather issues associated with "jobs and families." Women will not abandon their concern for gender issues, she contended, but the Stand for Children demonstration would largely refocus their attention on a concern for children and their future. Friedan concluded that a major shift in thinking would come about as a result of the demonstration.[4] And indeed, in the months that followed this gathering of some 200,000 people, in the writing and discussion about women's issues that appeared in the press, there did seem to be a new interest and concern for children, including adequate family and public resources for their care and their future. The event seemed to cause the change in focus that Friedan predicted.

In 1999, an e-mail blitz on Washington created new interest in the resolve to settle the problems associated with Social Security. The heightened awareness generated by what was known as the Internet March for Social Security made that issue a major theme in the president's State of the Union Address that year, and the issue later became a focus for political debate by politicians. Finally, the media reports on the terrorist attacks in New York City on September 11, 2001, created a renewed spirit of patriotism and changed most citizens' ideas about what is needed to maintain national security.

How much can you expect to change people's thinking as you discuss and write about the issues that are important to you? Some students in argument class wonder if they must convince their teachers along with their classmates of their point of view in every paper they write if they are to get good grades. This demand may be too great, since audiences and the outcomes of argument vary so much. Convincing the teacher and your fellow students that the argument paper is effective with a particular audience is probably the best possible outcome in argument class. As one professor put it, "My ambition is to return a paper and say that I disagreed with it completely—but the writing was excellent—A!"[5]

UNDER WHAT CONDITIONS DOES ARGUMENT FAIL?

We have just examined the optimal conditions for argument. Now let's look at the conditions that can cause it to flounder or fail. No argument, we have seen, can take place when there is no real disagreement, no uncertainty, or no possibility

---

[4]Betty Friedan, "Children's Crusade," *New Yorker*, June 3, 1996, pp. 5–6.
[5]Hilton Obenzinger, "The Israeli-Palestinian Conflict: Teaching a Theme-Based Course," *Notes in the Margins*, Winter 1994, p. 12.

for two or more views. Also, neutral people who do not have enough interest in an issue to form an opinion do not argue. For example, some young people do not want to argue about possible retirement plans because they are neutral on this issue. Argument also cannot take place unless people perceive an issue as a subject for argument. An example might be a college orientation session where various department representatives argue in favor of their areas as majors. This is not an issue for students who have already decided, and thus they will not identify issues or perceive this session as a forum for argument.

Big problems or risky problems that may require radical change are difficult for some people to argue about. Finding a new career or dissolving a longtime relationship may fit into this category, and many people, wisely or not, tend to leave such difficult issues alone rather than argue about them. Religious issues or issues that threaten global disaster are also sometimes too big, too emotional, or too scary for many people to argue about. At the other extreme, some issues may be perceived as low-risk, trivial, boring, or even ridiculous. Some family arguments fall into this category, like what to eat for dinner or who should take out the trash. One person may care, but the rest do not.

Arguments that lack common ground among participants do not work well. It is sometimes difficult to establish common ground and argue constructively with "true believers," for example, who have made up their minds on certain issues and will not listen, budge, or change. Racial bigots fall into this category. It is also difficult to argue with some religious people who take certain issues on faith and do not perceive them as subjects for argument. In fact, argument often fails when one participant perceives a topic as an issue and the other does not. Again, there is no common ground. Finally, argument cannot take place when one party is not motivated to argue. "Don't bring that up again" or "I don't want to discuss that" puts an end to most argument. The cartoon in Figure 1.2 provides a similar example.

We have already described the audience outcomes of effective argument. When argument is not working, as in the situations just described, the outcomes are negative also. Sometimes poor argument results in a standoff: both parties

CALVIN AND HOBBES

FIGURE 1.2 When Argument Fails.

agree to keep their original views and not to cross the line. Or emotions run strong, verbal fighting breaks out, and extreme views are expressed. No one agrees with anyone else. People shake their heads and walk away, or they become hurt and upset. Some individuals may become strident, wanting to debate everyone to demonstrate that they are right. When classroom argument results in such negative outcomes, some students drop the class, others fall silent and refuse to participate, and everyone becomes confused.

One important aim of this book is to provide you with the insight and skill to manage these negative situations so that more constructive argument can take place. Students are in an excellent position to overcome some of the fear, resistance, and aversion associated with difficult issues and, by using evidence and good sense, get to work and face some of them. Understanding audience members, especially their attitudes, needs, and values, is an important first step. Another useful idea to keep in mind is that most arguers have more success with some audiences than with others, depending on the amount of common ground. Even in the most difficult situations, some common ground can usually be found among people who seem to disagree on almost everything else. Recent research suggests that one vehicle for establishing common ground is through narratives, with each side relating personal experiences and stories. Even the most hostile adversaries can usually relate to one another's personal experiences and find some unity in the common villains, heroes, or themes in their stories. What sometimes also happens in this process is that the issues themselves change or are transformed in ways that make them easier for both parties to argue.[6]

Arguing effectively in difficult situations requires a conscious effort to avoid both stereotypical reactions and entrenched behavioral patterns. Past habits must be replaced with new strategies that work better. It is sometimes difficult to make such changes because habits can be strong, but it is possible to do so, and the stakes are often high, especially when the choice is constructive argument or verbal fighting and standoffs.

ENGAGING WITH ISSUES

To summarize, the most easily arguable issues are those that invite two or more views, that are perceived by all parties as issues, that are interesting and motivating to all participants, and that inspire research and original thought. They also promise common ground among participants, and they do not appear too big, too risky, too trivial, too confusing, too scary, or too specialized to discuss profitably. But you may also find yourself drawn to some of the more difficult issues that do not meet all of these criteria, and you should not necessarily shun them just because they are difficult. You will need to work with your audience in creative ways and consider the entire context for argument, regardless of the nature of the

---

[6]Linda Putnam, in the keynote speech at the Texas Speech Communication Association Conference, October 1993, reported these results from her study of negotiations between teachers and labor union leaders.

issues you select. Most important is that you now identify some issues that are arguable and important to you and to your classroom audience. Identifying issues will help you keep a high level of motivation and receive the maximum instructional benefits from argument class. Finding your own arguable issues is much better than accepting assigned issues as writing topics.

So now the search begins. What will help you find your arguable issues? Issues exist in contexts, and the issues most engaging to you will probably emerge from the parts of your life that demand your greatest attention and energy. For example, people who are compellingly engaged with their professions think about work issues, new parents think about child-rearing issues, dedicated students think about the issues raised in class, and many teenagers think about peer-group issues. To begin the search for your issues, examine those parts of your life that demand your most concentrated time and attention right now. Also, think about some of the special characteristics of issues in general. Here are a few of them.

▲ *Issues Are Compelling.* People get excited about issues, and they usually identify with a few in particular. In fact, most people can quickly name one or more issues that are so important to them that they think about them often. Some people even build careers or change careers because of issues that are vital to them. James Watson, for example, resigned his post as head of the Human Genome Project because companies were patenting humans genes for future profit, and he believed human genes should not be patented or owned by private parties. People who devote large amounts of time and study to particular issues become the "experts" on those issues. Can you think of some of your own issues that are particularly compelling to you?

▲ *Issues Often Originate in Dramatic Life Situations.* Things happen—a teenager gets shot at school, several major companies decide to downsize and lay off workers, a doctor helps a terminally ill patient die, an oil spill pollutes a beach and kills wildlife. To understand these occurrences better, people react to them intellectually, and issues emerge. Should teenagers (or anyone) be allowed to purchase guns? Are companies making too much money at the expense of employee morale? Should doctors help patients die, or should they be required to let nature take its course? Which is more important, economic growth or environmental protection? Because of their dramatic origins, many issues are intensely interesting to many people. Pay attention to the stories that are newsworthy this week, and identify the issues associated with them. Select the ones that interest you the most.

▲ *Current Issues Are Related to Enduring Issues.* Current issues can be linked to enduring issues, those that have engaged people for ages. For example, recurrent questions about military spending have their roots in age-old issues that are associated with war: Is war ever justified? Should a country be constantly prepared for war? The capital punishment issue has its roots in enduring issues about life: Should life be protected at all costs? Should anyone ever have the right to take the life of another human being? Think about the enduring issues that engage you. They may help you find your arguable issues.

▲ *Issues Go Underground and Then Resurface.* Public concern with particular issues is not constant. Experts may think about their issues continuously, but the public usually thinks about an issue only when something happens that brings it to public attention. How to deal with increasing population is an example of such an issue. Experts on that issue may think about it daily, but the general public may think about it only when new information is released. For example, in 1999 the world population reached six billion people. It had doubled in forty years, a fact that prompted a considerable amount of argument from the media, particularly about future population growth and the ability of the planet to sustain it. As one TV commentator noted, the media often make arguments out of the news. Persistent issues are, of course, always lurking in the background, always important. But we do not think about all of them all of the time. Think back. Are there some issues that used to concern you that you have neither thought about nor read about for a long time? What are they?

▲ *Issues Sometimes Get Solved, but Then New Ones Emerge.* Some issues command so much public attention that the people who can do something about them finally perceive them as problems and pass laws or take other measures to solve them. As soon as an issue is solved, however, other, related issues spring up in its place. For example, for many years, people argued about what to do about health care. As soon as health maintenance organizations became widely accessible, new issues emerged that focused on the quality of care patients received in these organizations and how physicians could profit economically from these changes in the delivery of health care. Are there any new issues of this type that might interest you? Think of problems that now seem solved but probably aren't fully solved.

▲ *Issues Seem to Be Getting More Complex.* Issues seem to become more and more complex as the world becomes more complex. In an interview, the actress Susan Sarandon, who has always been engaged with social issues, stated that in the mid-to-late 1960s, when she was in college, the issues seemed simpler, more black and white. The issues at that time, for example, centered on civil rights and the Vietnam War. "We were blessed with clear-cut issues," she says. "We were blessed with clear-cut grievances. Things were not as gray as they are now."[7]

Because issues are now more complex, people need to learn to engage with them in more complex ways. The word *perspectives* as used in this book refers not only to a broader perspective on issues and argument itself but also to the variety of perspectives that individuals can take on particular issues. Few issues are black and white or can be viewed as pro or con anymore. Most invite several different ways of looking at them.

As you develop your own perspectives on the complex issues that engage you, keep in mind that it takes many years to become an expert. You will want to look at what the experts say. But you will not have the background and information to write as comprehensively as they do. When you write your own argument, you will want to research and write on a limited aspect of your issue, one that you can learn enough about. Limiting your topic will permit you to get

---

[7]Ovid Demaris, "Most of All, the Children Matter," *Parade*, March 1, 1992, pp. 4–5.

the information and gain the perspective to be convincing. Suggestions to help you limit your approach to a complex issue will be made in future chapters.

EXAMPLES OF ARGUABLE ISSUES

Looking at examples of issues that many people find engaging should help you select ones that will interest you. Intervention in the internal affairs of other countries, the justification of war, the future of genetic engineering, the effect of violent video games on their users, the treatment of criminals (particularly young ones), environmental protection, gay rights, men's and women's family roles and responsibilities, Internet censorship, and privacy issues often interest students. In presidential campaigns, a number of public issues emerge that in the past have included welfare reform, taxation policies, gun control, immigration, clean air and water, and drug control. Such issues do not change radically from one election to the next, although certain issues may receive more attention in some years than in others. In Box 1.1 (pages 18–19), some contemporary public issues have been linked with enduring issues to demonstrate the timeless quality of most of them. See if you can add examples of your own as you read through those in the "current" column.

Box 1.2 (page 20) illustrates some of the issues you are likely to encounter in your other classes in college. These are examples of issues that your professors argue about, the subjects for academic inquiry. You may be expected to take positions and develop arguments yourself on these or similar issues if you take classes in some of these subjects. As you read, try to add examples from your own classes.

HOW SHOULD YOU ENGAGE WITH ISSUES?

Boxes 1.1 and 1.2 represent only a sampling of issues. When you start focusing on issues, you will identify many more. Here are some final suggestions to help you engage with issues.

- ◆ Listen for issues in all of your classes, and identify them with a circled *I* in the margins of your lecture notes. Ask your professors to identify the major issues in their fields.
- ◆ Read a newspaper daily, if possible, or at least three or four times a week. If you do not subscribe to a newspaper, read one in the library or set up a newspaper circulation system in class. You will find stories about issues throughout the paper. The opinion and editorial pages are especially good sources.
- ◆ Read a newsmagazine, like *Time* or *Newsweek*, on a regular basis, and look for issues.
- ◆ Watch television programs where issues are discussed: newscasts as well as such programs as *The News Hour with Jim Lehrer, To the Contrary, Crossfire, CNN Presents, Nightline, Larry King Live, Meet the Press,* or *60 Minutes.* Some of these programs focus mainly on debate and pro and con argument, and others explore an issue from several perspectives.

BOX 1.1   **Examples of Current and Enduring Public Issues.**

WHAT ARE SOME PUBLIC ISSUES?

CURRENT ISSUES	ENDURING ISSUES
WAYS AND MEANS ISSUES	
Should everyone pay taxes? In what proportion to their income?	Where should a government get money, and how should it spend it?
Should free trade be limited?	
How much business profit can be sacrificed to keep the environment clean and safe?	
Should scholarships and fellowships be taxed?	
How should we finance health care?	
QUALITY OF LIFE ISSUES	
Should more resources be directed to protecting the environment?	What is a minimum quality of life, and how do we achieve it?
Are inner cities or rural areas better places to live?	
How can we improve the quality of life for children and senior citizens?	
PERSONAL RIGHTS VERSUS SOCIAL RIGHTS ISSUES	
Should individuals, the government, or private business be responsible for the unemployed? Health care? Day care? The homeless? Senior citizens? Drug addicts? People with AIDS? Race problems? Minority problems? Dealing with criminals? Worker safety? Deciding who should buy guns?	Can individuals be responsible for their own destinies, or should social institutions be responsible? Can individuals be trusted to do what is best for society?
WAR AND PEACE ISSUES	
How much should the government spend on the military?	Is war justified, and should countries stay prepared for war?
Should the United States remain prepared for a major world war?	
Should you, your friends, or your family be required to register for the draft?	

(continued)

Box 1.1 (continued)

CURRENT ISSUES	ENDURING ISSUES
SELF-DEVELOPMENT ISSUES	
What opportunities for education and training should be available to everyone?	What opportunities for self-development should societies make available to individuals?
How well are job-training programs helping people get off welfare and find employment?	
Should homosexuals be allowed the same opportunities to participate in society as heterosexuals?	
HUMAN LIFE ISSUES	
Should abortions be permitted?	Should human life be protected under any conditions?
Should capital punishment be permitted?	
Is mercy killing ever justifiable?	
Should stem cell research be allowed?	
FOREIGN AFFAIRS ISSUES	
Which is wiser, to support an American economy or a global economy?	In world politics, how do we balance the rights of smaller countries and different ethnic groups against the needs of larger countries and international organizations?
How much foreign aid should we provide, and to which countries?	
Should college graduates be encouraged to participate in foreign service like the Peace Corps?	
Should the United States defend foreign countries from aggressors?	
LAW AND ORDER ISSUES	
Is the judicial system effective?	What is an appropriate balance between the welfare and protection of society as a whole and the rights of the individual?
Does the punishment always fit the crime?	
How serious a problem is racial profiling?	
How can international terrorism be eradicated?	

BOX 1.2   **Examples of Academic Issues across the Disciplines.**

WHAT ARE SOME ACADEMIC ISSUES?

In Physics—Is there a unifying force in the universe? Is there enough matter in the universe to cause it eventually to stop expanding and then to collapse? What is the nature of this matter?

In Astronomy—What elements can be found in interstellar gas? What is the nature of the asteroids?

In Biology—What limits, if any, should be placed on genetic engineering?

In Chemistry—How can toxic wastes best be managed?

In Sociology—Is the cause of crime social or individual? Does television have a significant negative effect on society?

In Psychology—Which is the better approach for understanding human behavior, nature or nurture? Can artificial intelligence ever duplicate human thought?

In Anthropology—Which is more reliable in dating evolutionary stages, DNA or fossils?

In Business—Can small, privately owned businesses still compete with giant conglomerate companies? Are chief executive officers paid too much?

In Mathematics—Are boys naturally better than girls at math? Should the use of calculators be encouraged? Should calculators be allowed in testing situations?

In Engineering—How important should environmental concerns be in determining engineering processes? To what extent, if any, are engineers responsible for the social use of what they produce? How aggressive should we be in seeking and implementing alternative sources of energy? Should the government fund the development of consumer-oriented technology to the same extent that it funds military-oriented technology?

In History—Have historians been too restrictive in their perspective? Does history need to be retold, and if so, how? Is the course of history influenced more by unusual individuals or by socioeconomic forces?

In Political Science—Where should ultimate authority to govern reside: with the individual, the church, the state, or social institutions? Is power properly divided among the three branches of government in the United States?

In Communication—How can the best balance be struck between the needs of society and freedom of expression in the mass media? How much impact, if any, do the mass media have on the behavior of individuals in society?

In English—Is the concept of traditional literature too narrowly focused in English departments? If yes, what else should be considered literature?

◆ Browse at the newsstand or in the current periodicals in the library and look for issues.

◆ Browse among the new arrivals at the library looking for books that address issues.

◆ Listen for issues in conversations and discussions with other students. If you get confused, ask, "What is at issue here?" to help focus an argumentative discussion.

◆ Study the table of contents of this book, and sample some of the issues in the various readings at the ends of chapters and in "The Reader." Notice that "The Reader" is organized around broad areas and issues related to them. The articles have been selected to provide various perspectives on many specific current and enduring issues.

◆ Begin discussing and writing about some of the ideas you get from reading and listening to other people's arguments.

REVIEW QUESTIONS

1. Provide three examples of your own to illustrate the statement "Argument is everywhere."
2. What are some of the defining characteristics of debate, courtroom argument, academic inquiry, and negotiation?
3. What are some of the conditions necessary for argument to work best?
4. What are some of the conditions that may cause argument to fail?
5. Describe some of the special characteristics of issues.
6. What are some examples of enduring issues?
7. What are some examples of current issues?
8. What are some of the issues you will probably encounter in your other classes this semester?
9. What did you think of when you encountered the word *argument* before you read this chapter? What do you think now?

EXERCISES AND ACTIVITIES

A. CLASS PROJECT: "ARGUMENT IS EVERYWHERE"

Test the idea that argument can be found everywhere. Each member of the class should bring in an example of an argument and explain why it can be defined in this way. Each example should focus on an issue that people are still arguing about and on which there is no general agreement. Each example should also present a position on the issue, and the position should be supported with reasons and evidence. Look for examples in a variety of contexts: newspapers, magazines, the Internet, television, motion pictures, music, sermons, other college classes, conversations, and printed material you find at work, at school, and at home. Bring in actual examples of articles, letters to the editor, bumper stickers, advertisements, or other easily transportable arguments, or bring in clear and complete descriptions and explanations of arguments from sources you cannot bring to class, like lectures, television shows, or billboards. Students should give two- to three-minute oral reports on the arguments they select that include a description of the issue and some of the reasons and evidence. This is most easily achieved by completing the statement "This arguer wants us to believe . . . , because . . ." The class should decide whether all examples described in this activity are indeed examples of argument.[8]

B. READING, GROUP WORK, AND CLASS DISCUSSION: WHAT MAKES A GOOD ARGUMENT?

Read the following two argumentative essays. Then, in small groups, answer the following questions for each of them.

1. What is the issue?
2. What is the author's position on the issue?
3. What reasons and evidence are given to support the author's position?
4. What makes each of these arguments successful?
5. What are the weaknesses in the arguments, if any?

Then compile a class list of the best argumentative features of each essay, as well as a list of the weaknesses. Keep a copy of this list. It is a starting point. You will add to it as you learn more about what it takes to make a good argument.

PAY YOUR OWN WAY! (THEN THANK MOM)*

Audrey Rock-Richardson

The author, who lives in Utah, wrote this essay in 2000 after she had completed her college education. She wonders why more students don't do what she did.

1   Is it me, or are students these days lazy? I'm not talking about tweens who don't want to do their homework or make their bed. I'm referring to people in legal adulthood who are in the process of making hugely consequential life decisions. And collectively, their attitude is that they simply cannot pay for college.

2   Don't get me wrong. I realize that there are people out there who pay their own tuition. I know that some cannot put themselves through school because of disabilities or extenuating circumstances. But I have to say: the notion that parents must finance their children's education is ridiculous.

3   During college I consistently endured comments from peers with scholarships and loans, peers who had new Jeeps and expensive apartments, all who would say to me, eyes bulging, "You mean your parents didn't help you at *all?*"

---

[8]I am indebted to Cedrick May for the basic idea for this project.

*From *Newsweek*, September 11, 2000, p. 12. All rights reserved. Reprinted by permission.

4 I resented my fellow students for asking this, first because they made it sound like my parents were demons, and second because they were insinuating that I wasn't capable of paying my own way. "How did you pay tuition?" they'd ask. My response was simple: "I worked." They would look at me blankly, as though I had told them I'd gone to the moon.

5 As an undergrad (University of Utah, 1998), I put myself through two solid years of full-tuition college by working as a day-care provider for $4.75 an hour. I then married and finished out seven more quarters by working as an interpreter for the deaf and a tutor in a private school.

6 I didn't work during high school or save for years. I simply got a job the summer following graduation and worked 40 hours a week. I didn't eat out every weekend, shop a lot or own a car. I sacrificed. I was striving for something bigger and longer-lasting than the next kegger.

7 Looking at the numbers now, I'm not sure how I managed to cover all the costs of my education. But I did. And I bought every single textbook and pencil myself, too.

8 I remember sitting in a classroom one afternoon during my senior year, listening to everyone introduce themselves. Many students mentioned their part-time jobs. There were several members of a sorority in the class. When it came to the first girl, she told us her name and that she was a sophomore. "Oh," she added, "I major in communications." After an awkward silence, the teacher asked, "Do you work?"

9 "Oh, no," she said emphatically, "I go to school full time." (As if those of us who were employed weren't really serious about our classes.)

10 The girl went on to explain that her parents were paying tuition and for her to live in a sorority house (complete with a cook, I later found out). She was taking roughly 13 credit hours. And she was too busy to work.

11 I, on the other hand, was taking 18, count 'em, 18 credit hours so I could graduate within four years. I worked 25 hours a week so my husband and I could pay tuition without future loan debt. And here's the kicker: I pulled straight A's.

12 I caught a glimpse of that same girl's report card at the end of the quarter, and she pulled C's and a few B's, which didn't surprise me. Having to juggle tasks forces you to prioritize, a skill she hadn't learned.

13 I'm weary of hearing kids talk about getting financial help from their parents as though they're entitled to it. I am equally tired of hearing stressed-out parents groaning, "How are we going to pay for his/her college?" Why do they feel obligated?

14 I do not feel responsible for my daughter's education. She'll find a way to put herself through if she wants to go badly enough. And (I'm risking sounding like my mom here), she'll thank me later. I can say this because I honestly, wholeheartedly thank my parents for giving me that experience.

15 I'm not saying that it's fun. It's not. I spent the first two years of school cleaning up after 4-year-olds for the aforementioned $4.75 an hour and taking a public bus to campus. My husband and I spent the second two struggling to pay out our tuition. We lived in a cinder-block apartment with little privacy and no dishwasher.

16   Lest I sound like a hypocrite, yes, I would have taken free college money had the opportunity presented itself. However, because my parents put themselves through school they expected me to do the same. And, frankly, I'm proud of myself. I feel a sense of accomplishment that I believe I couldn't have gained from 50 college degrees all paid for by someone else.

17   Getting through school on our own paid off in every way. My husband runs his own business, a demanding but profitable job. I write part time and work as a mother full time. I believe the fact that we are happy and financially stable is a direct result of our learning how to manage time and money in college.

18   So, kids, give your parents a break. Contrary to popular belief, you can pay tuition by yourself. And you might just thank your mother for it, too.

For Discussion: What are your opinions about who should pay the bills for a college education? What are the advantages of doing it yourself? What are the disadvantages? If your parents had saved money and were intent on paying for your education, what would you say to them?

◆◆◆

THE LAPTOP ATE MY ATTENTION SPAN*

Abby Ellin

The author lives in New York and writes a regular column, "Preludes," for the *New York Times* about starting out in business.

1   [What is] the latest issue on business school campuses? It's not whether to start your own dot-com before graduation, but whether you should be allowed to use your laptop in the classroom as you please.

2   While more and more schools—especially business schools—provide Internet access in class and require students to lug their laptops with them, some are imposing rules on what their students can and cannot do with them in class.

3   But why, in the sedate hallways of graduate schools, is there need for debate on rules of discipline? It seems that some students, although smart enough to earn M.B.A.'s, have not figured out how the old, generally unwritten rules of conduct apply to the wired classroom. More and more students are sending instant messages to one another (chatting and note-passing, 21st century–style), day trading (as opposed to daydreaming) and even starting their own companies, all in class.

4   The resulting commotion has annoyed many students. Jen McEnry, 28, a second-year M.B.A. student at the University of Virginia's Darden Graduate School of Business Administration, recalled that a classmate once downloaded an e-mail attachment during a finance lecture. The attachment automatically turned

---

New York Times, April 16, 2000, p. B15.

on the sound on the student's computer, which then delivered a booming message: "Oh my God, I'm watching porn!" Everyone roared at the practical joke, but the problem was clear.

5   "It's distracting when people are day trading, checking their e-mails or surfing the Web," Ms. McEnry said. All the more distracting because Darden relies heavily on classroom participation.

6   At Columbia University, the business school's newspaper reported that a student-run "chat room" ended up on the overhead projector in the middle of class. University officials denied the report. But by January, cyberspace had so intruded on classroom space at Columbia that a committee of professors and students came up with a code of professional conduct. "We're trying to find ways professors and students can use technology effectively and appropriately to create leaders," said Jeff Derman, a second-year M.B.A. student who heads the panel.

7   Yet how can M.B.A. students, whose average age is about 28 nationally, not know that it's rude to click away in class? After all, they presumably know not to walk out in the middle of a lecture, however boring. The rules of etiquette shouldn't change just because of technology.

8   Still, some business schools have gone beyond issuing rules. Two years ago, Darden officials installed a switch in each classroom; a professor can program it to shut down the students' Net-surfing at fixed times. The students, however, found that they could override the teacher's decision by sneaking over before class and flicking the switch back on. It became a kind of game, the Battle of the Button.

9   The students spent hours arguing the broader issues. Should computers be banned from class? (No, we're adults! We pay to be here!) Should networks be shut off? (Of course not! Web access is an inalienable right!) Should professors be able to turn off the systems? (That's, like, so 1984!)

10   Blood started to boil: Students got mad at professors, professors got mad at students, students got mad at each other and everyone cursed technology. Why should they have to deal with all this when all they really wanted to do was learn how to be a millionaire?

11   Ms. McEnry proposes a standard of reasonable necessity. "If I'm expecting something important, like news about a job or something, then it's O.K. to go online," she said. "There are really pressing issues in people's lives, and they need to have access."

12   She's not kidding. Ms. McEnry found out that she had been elected president of the Student Association after her friends found the news on the school's Web site and told her. In class.

◆◆◆◆

13   At the Columbia business school, Safwan Masri, vice dean of students and the M.B.A. program, takes a temperate tone. "These kids have grown up with computers; they can multitask," he said, explaining why Columbia decided against a Web shutdown switch. "We don't want to act as police. They're adults. We'd like to think they can control themselves."

14   I agree. Let them control themselves. And if they can't, here's my suggestion to them: Take a computer to the Metropolitan Opera. Log on. Write e-mail. Check your portfolio. At the end of the night, you'll be lucky to still have a computer.

FOR DISCUSSION: Does this article describe a problem that you have experienced in your classes or labs? What do you think instructors should do? Do you think that students ever talk on cell phones or answer their beepers at inappropriate times? Elaborate. How do you think instructors should respond to that?

◆◆◆

C.   BEFORE YOU WRITE: FINDING COMPELLING ISSUES FOR FUTURE ARGUMENT PAPERS

The objective is to make a list of the issues that interest you so that you can draw possible topics from this list for future argument papers. You will need topics for the exploratory paper on page 122, the position paper based on "The Reader" on page 240, the Rogerian argument paper on page 254, and the researched position paper on page 366.

1. *Get acquainted with the issues in "The Reader."* Turn to the table of contents for "The Reader". Eighteen issue questions organize the essays in the seven issue sections. Check all of the issue questions that interest you.
2. *Report on the issues in "The Reader."* This exercise will provide all class members with a preview of the issues and articles in "The Reader." Individuals or pairs of students should select from the eighteen issue questions in "The Reader" until they have all been assigned. Then follow these instructions to prepare a report for the class.
   a. To understand the content, read "The Issues" at the beginning of each issue section.
   b. Read "The Rhetorical Situation" for the issue section.
   c. Read the questions at the end of the issue section.
   d. Read the issue question you have selected and the articles that accompany it.
   e. Give a two-minute oral report in which you identify the issue question, briefly describe the articles, and identify at least two issues that these articles have raised for you.
3. *Find "your" issues.* Most students have issues that they really care about. What are yours? Think about what has affected you in the past. Think about your pet peeves. Think about recent news items on television or in the newspaper that have raised issues for you. Make a class list of the issues that concern you and the other students in your class.
4. *Identify campus issues.* What issues on campus concern you? What could be changed at your college to improve student life and learning? Make a class list.

D.   BEFORE YOU WRITE: APPLYING THE TWELVE TESTS

Before you write about an issue, apply the twelve tests of an arguable issue that appear in Box 1.3 to make certain that it is arguable. If all of your answers are yes, you will be able to work with your issue productively. If any of your answers are no, you may want to modify your issue or switch to another one.

BOX 1.3   **Twelve Tests of an Arguable Issue.**

DO YOU HAVE AN ARGUABLE ISSUE?   ◆◆

If you cannot answer yes to all of these questions, change or modify your issue.

Your issue (phrased as a question): _____

Yes _____ No _____ 1. Is this an issue that has not been resolved or settled?

Yes _____ No _____ 2. Does this issue potentially inspire two or more views?

Yes _____ No _____ 3. Are you willing to consider a position different from your own and perhaps even modify your views on this issue?

Yes _____ No _____ 4. Are you sufficiently interested and engaged with this issue to inspire your audience to become interested also?

Yes _____ No _____ 5. Do other people perceive this as an issue?

Yes _____ No _____ 6. Is this issue significant enough to be worth your time?

Yes _____ No _____ 7. Is this a safe issue for you? Not too risky? Scary? Will you be willing to express your ideas?

Yes _____ No _____ 8. Will you be able to establish common ground with your audience on this issue—common terms, common background and values?

Yes _____ No _____ 9. Can you get information and come up with convincing insights on this issue?

Yes _____ No _____ 10. Can you eventually get a clear and limited focus on this issue, even if it is a complicated one?

Yes _____ No _____ 11. Is it an enduring issue, or can you build perspective by linking it to an enduring issue?

Yes _____ No _____ 12. Can you predict some audience outcomes? (Think of your classmates as the audience. Will they be convinced? Hostile? Neutral? Attentive? Remember, any outcomes at all can be regarded as significant in argument.)

E. WRITING ASSIGNMENT: WRITING A SHORT ARGUMENT ON A CAMPUS ISSUE

Select the campus issue that interests you the most, apply the twelve tests in Box 1.3, and write a 250- to 300-word argument about it. Use the two short arguments on pages 22–24 and 24–25 as models. Write a title that identifies your issue. Then make a statement (a claim) that explains your position on the issue, and add reasons and evidence to convince a college official to accept your views and perhaps take action to improve the situation.

F. WRITING ASSIGNMENT: WRITING A ONE-PAGE ISSUE PROPOSAL

Issue proposals help you organize and develop your thoughts for longer argument papers. Once you have selected an issue, test it with the twelve tests, do some background reading as necessary, and write a proposal that responds to the following four items:

1. Introduce the issue, and then present it in question form.
2. Explain why it is compelling to you.
3. Describe what you already know about it.
4. Explain what more you need to learn.

The following issue proposal was written by a student.*

Lada Carlisle
Issue Proposal
Professor Wood
English 1302
15 October 2003

Censoring the Internet

Introduce the issue.

1   The Internet contains all kinds of information, and some of it is objectionable or even dangerous to certain people. The First Amendment protects the Internet from censorship and guarantees freedom of speech in that environment. However, the Internet can still be used for illegal purposes. Crimes are still crimes no matter how they are committed, and criminal laws are applicable to an individual's activity on the Internet. It is illegal, for example, to publish child pornography and hate material on the Internet. Yet it is difficult to catch the illegal or harmful information and still protect all of the other material that is not illegal. What should be censored on the Internet, and what is the best way to control access to such unwanted and objectionable material?

Present it in question form.

Explain why it is compelling to you.

2   We discussed this problem recently in a computer ethics class, and many people in the class did not have any knowledge of this issue. Some thought that censoring is the right thing to do, and others disagreed. The students had very little evidence to support their positions. I personally found the issue compelling because I am from Uzbekistan, and this year all of our e-mail messages are monitored. It has not been a pleasant feeling knowing that somebody is reading my family's personal mail. I have felt this year that I was being censored, and I did not like that feeling.

Describe what you already know about it.

3   I spent some time researching this issue for my computer ethics course. I found out that monitoring and filtering software that is supposed to block the reception of objectionable information on the Internet is ineffective.

Explain what more you need to learn.

4   I need to learn more about why monitoring and filtering software does not work and whether or not it could be made to work better. I also need to learn more about other possible solutions to this problem, and I need to decide which one is best and why it is the best.

*The format shown in this paper and similar student papers throughout this book is reflective of MLA documentation style but has been modified to accommodate space limitations. All MLA-style student papers are double-spaced throughout. For actual MLA guidelines and a sample student paper showing the correct MLA format, see the Appendix to Chapter 12.

Chapter 2

Developing Your Personal Argument Style

S ome students resist the idea of finding issues and participating in argument because they think they will be required to take an opposing view, to debate, or to be contentious or aggressive in class, and they feel that they do not do these things well. This chapter will develop the important idea that everyone can and should participate in argument but not everyone may participate in the same way. You already have a personal style of argument, developed by several influences in your background. Many of the students who read and commented on this chapter in earlier editions of this book identified family and cultural backgrounds as particularly potent forces in influencing the ways in which they argue. In addition, some researchers think that men tend to argue differently from women, that some Asians argue differently from Europeans and Americans, and that blacks and Hispanics may have distinctive styles that are influenced by their cultures. We will look at some of these causes for differences in this chapter, and you may want to argue about them. They are controversial. This chapter invites differing views on the issues it raises.

The final purpose of this chapter is to encourage you and your classmates to become aware at the outset of how each of you argues best. Thus you will learn to recognize, rely on, and perhaps even improve your existing style of argument. You will also learn from others how to modify or change to another style in certain situations when your preferred style may not be working well. This process will help you learn flexibility. Finally, you will learn to recognize and adapt to other people's styles, and you will therefore become a more sensitive and persuasive arguer, more likely to establish the common ground essential for the give-and-take of argument.

Individual tendencies and preferences in argument are present in many but not all argumentative situations. If you discover, for example, that you prefer reaching consensus over winning the argument in most instances, this discovery does not mean that you should always argue for consensus. Furthermore, if you discover that you are reluctant to participate in argument, your reluctance does not mean that you cannot find a way to participate. An awareness of individuals' predominant styles should reduce the dissonance and discomfort experienced by some people in argument classes where a single argument style or perspective may seem to dominate. By acknowledging instead that individualistic and preferred perspectives and styles not only exist but also are valued, everyone in class should feel empowered to join the ongoing conversation about issues with confidence and skill. The goal is to create and maintain an inclusive classroom where everyone has a voice and where every approach and style is tolerated and understood. This is a worthy real-life goal as well for a world in which cultural, racial, and gender diversity often influences the nature and special characteristics of the ongoing conversations about issues.

THE ADVERSARIAL AND CONSENSUAL STYLES OF ARGUMENT

Most argument classes contain a mix of students who favor either the adversarial or the consensual style of argument. Some students exhibit a combination of these styles. The adversarial approach to argument is the traditional approach. The arguer is intent on changing the other person's mind. Further, the arguer usually tries to refute the opponent by showing what is wrong or invalid with the opponent's view. The views of the person doing the arguing are supposed to prevail. You are familiar with this form of argument. You observe it, for example, when political candidates debate public issues to impress voters with their analysis and ability to win.

Some modern authors now amend this view of argument. In *The Argument Culture: Moving from Debate to Dialogue*, sociologist Deborah Tannen states that all topics and all occasions do not call for the same approach to argument.[1] She claims that in our culture, we typically approach issues as though there were only one approach: we present them as a fight between two opposing sides. We look at many issues in an adversarial frame of mind since our assumption is that opposition is the best way to solve problems or to get anything done.

The three groups in our society who are most likely to engage with issues as conflicts are politicians, lawyers, and journalists. When an issue comes to public attention, journalists, for example, often set up a debate between politicians and then jump in themselves to keep the debate going. Journalists look for politicians who are willing to express the most extreme, polarized views on an issue with the ostensible objective of presenting both sides.

Our culture also likes to settle issues with litigation that pits one party against the other. We have frequent opportunities to watch trial argument on television

---

[1]Deborah Tannen, *The Argument Culture: Moving from Debate to Dialogue* (New York: Random House, 1998).

and to read about it in the newspaper. The objective is always to declare a winner. The argument culture as exhibited in the media, in the courts, and in the political arena carries over to the classroom, according to Tannen. Often students learn to start essays with opposition, and some students are quick to criticize and attack most of what they read. Sometimes these approaches are necessary, as in court-room argument or in public and collegiate debate. These forums for argument very often require rebuttal and a declaration of winners. But if this is regarded as the only approach to controversial issues, we often create more problems than we solve.

Tannen claims that as a society, we have to find constructive and creative ways of resolving disputes and differences. It is better, she says, to make an argu-ment for a point of view than to have an argument, as in having a fight. She also notes the value of studying argument in other cultures, because some cultures work for agreement more than others. Her subtitle, *Moving from Debate to Dialogue*, suggests an alternative to the win-lose model of argument. She points out that other ways exist for dealing with issues: negotiating disagreement, mediating conflicts in an effort to find agreement, and resolving differences in order to get things done. The old culture of conflict has the potential at times of becoming de-structive to families, workplaces, communities, or even the world. The culture of conflict can be replaced in some situations with other possibilities, including working for consensus.

Which style is more typical of you, the adversarial or the consensual? You probably use both at times, but which are you more likely to turn to first in argu-ment? Which style are you more comfortable with? The checklist on page 47 will help you find out. Now consider the influences in your life that may have caused you to prefer one style over the other.

INDIVIDUAL STYLES OF ARGUMENT

When students are asked to describe their styles of argument—that is, what they do when they have to be convincing—individual differences in style and strategy surface right away. Some of these differences seem to be related to home train-ing and role models, others may be related to gender, and others seem to be attributable to the background and experience provided by different cultures or nationalities. Modern research indicates that men and women describe different approaches to argument often enough to suggest that gender may contribute to differences in argument style. African American, Asian American, Hispanic American, and Native American cultures may also produce recognizably distinct styles and approaches. And students from non-Western cultures sometimes de-scribe approaches to argument that strike Americans as distinctive and even unique.

These differences among styles are usually neither consistent nor strong enough for typecasting. In fact, in some studies, a sizable minority of men indicate they prefer the styles that some researchers have identified as predominantly female.[2] Also, a particular style may be more convincing in some contexts than in others, so that students who have a preferred style find that they vary it at times to meet the demands of particular argumentative situations. Thus no single style emerges as best for all occasions for anyone. For example, one student in the group that test-read this book reported that when he argues with close friends about baseball players, he always wants to be right, he is very contentious and argumentative, and he expects to win. On the job, however, where he has low status in an office of four women, he never argues to win but rather tries to achieve agreement or consensus. Another student said she argues most aggressively when she is secure in her knowledge about the subject. She is tentative or even silent when she is not sure of her facts. Students also point out that there is a difference between home or "kitchen" argument and argument that takes place in school or on the job. Home argument may be more emotional and less controlled, especially in some cultures, than the reasoned discourse that one associates with school or work. Now let us look at some of the factors that may influence the ways in which you prefer to argue.

INFLUENCE OF BACKGROUND, EXPERIENCE, AND ROLE MODELS

Students often identify their upbringing or early experience as an influence on their argument style. Some students from military families, for example, say that argument was not encouraged at home. Instead, orders were given in military fashion, and opposing views were not encouraged. These students, out of habit, may spend more time listening than talking in an argument class. Other students, such as those whose parents are teachers, lawyers, or politicians, have reported that arguing about issues occurred frequently in their households. These students may be the ones who speak the most in class. All of these students, whether they speak frequently or prefer to listen, still participate in the critical thinking that enables them to write productively about issues.

U.S. Supreme Court justices are brilliantly skilled in argument. Yet all of them do not participate in argument in exactly the same way. When Justice Clarence Thomas was asked by high school students in a televised session why he did not ask more questions that would initiate oral argument on the Supreme Court, he described aspects of his background and experience that have influenced the way in which he typically participates in argument.

> There's no reason to add to the volume. I also believe strongly, unless I want an answer, I don't ask things. I don't ask for entertainment, I don't ask to give people a hard time. I have some very active colleagues who like to ask questions. Usually, if you wait long enough, someone will ask your question. The other thing, I was on that other side of the podium before, in my earlier life, and it's hard to stand up by yourself and to have judges who are going to rule on your case ask you tough questions. I don't want to give them a hard time. But I'm going to give

---

[2]Carol S. Pearson, "Women as Learners: Diversity and Educational Quality," *Journal of Developmental Education*, 16 (1992): 10.

you a more personal reason, and I think this is probably the first time I ever even told anybody about it. How old are you? You're 16. When I was 16, I was sitting as the only black kid in my class, and I had grown up speaking a kind of a dialect. It's called Geechee. Some people call it Gullah now, and people praise it now. But they used to make fun of us back then. It's not standard English. When I transferred to an all-white school at your age, I was self-conscious, like we all are. It's like if we get pimples at 16, or we grow six inches and we're taller than everybody else, or our feet grow or something; we get self-conscious. And the problem was that I would correct myself midsentence. I was trying to speak standard English. I was thinking in standard English but speaking another language. So I learned that—I just started developing the habit of listening. And it just got to be—I didn't ask questions in college or law school. And I found that I could learn better just listening. And if I have a question I could ask it later. For all those reasons, and a few others, I just think that it's more in my nature to listen rather than to ask a bunch of questions. And they get asked anyway. The only reason I could see for asking the questions is to let people know I've got something to ask. That's not a legitimate reason in the Supreme Court of the United States.[3]

Students also sometimes account for their argument styles by identifying the well-known arguers who are most like themselves as the role models they like to imitate as they develop their styles. Those students watch such individuals on television or in the movies, and when the students find themselves in argumentative situations, they tend to imitate the styles of the people they admire. If you find it difficult to initiate argument in class or to talk as much as some of the other students, Justice Thomas may be a role model who will appeal to you.

INFLUENCE OF GENDER

Some people think there are differences in the ways that men and women argue and that the basis for these differences lies in the power relationships that exist between the sexes in certain situations. Advocates of this view point out that men are often able to dominate an argument, while women tend to remain silent. Men are thus perceived to have more personal power in these situations. In an essay titled "The Classroom Climate: Still a Chilly One for Women," Bernice Sander describes the results of some unequal male-female power relationships.[4] Even though most people think that women talk more than men in everyday situations, she says, a number of studies show that in formal situations, such as a class, a meeting, or a formal group discussion where argument is conducted, the stereotype of talkative women does not hold up. In these situations, men often talk more than women. Men, Sander claims, talk for longer periods, take more turns, exert more control over what is said, and interrupt more often. Furthermore, their interruptions of women tend to be trivial or personal, and thus they often get women off the track and cause the focus of the discussion to change.

Deborah Tannen, in *You Just Don't Understand: Women and Men in Conversation*, also provides detailed descriptions of some differences between the argument

---

[3]Justice Clarence Thomas, "In His Own Words," *New York Times*, December 14, 2000, p. A17.
[4]In *Educating Men and Women Together*, ed. Carol Lasser (Urbana: University of Illinois Press, 1987), pp. 113–123.

styles of men and women.[5] Tannen asserts that many men make connections with one another primarily through conflict. (She qualifies this assertion because she realizes that she cannot generalize about *all* men.) Tannen quotes Walter Ong, a scholar of cultural linguistics, who claims that men see the world as competitive, and the competition can be either friendly and involved or unfriendly. Men, furthermore, like self-display and achieve it often by reporting what they see and what they know. According to Ong, typical male behavior is centered on "the idea of contest, including combat, struggle, conflict, competition, and contention."[6] Ong further reminds us that many men enjoy ritual combat such as rough play and sports. Friendship among men often takes the form of friendly aggression. Ong also asserts, according to Tannen, that in daily argument, men expect the discussion to stick to the rules of logic. They expect argument to be adversarial, to include clash, to take the form of debate, and to rely primarily on logic.

Here is what one young man in an argument class wrote about his argument style.

> My head is as hard as a rock, and if I choose to disagree with you, I have the capability of tuning you out without you ever knowing it. I see things my way and tend to disagree with most people, even if they're right. Being wrong is a hard pill for me to swallow, and if I can avoid it, I will.[7]

For the checklist on page 47, this young man marked every item in the adversarial column and no items in the consensual column as being most typical of him.

Tannen says that most women do not like ritualized combat. They do not like conflict, either, and will often try to avoid it at all costs. Women tend to be the peacemakers and to want to work for the general good. They are as interested in making connections with other people as men are in competing. Making connections and keeping the peace are such strong tendencies in women's argument that even when women are being competitive and critical, they often mask their actual intentions with apparent cooperation and affiliation. Women, in fact, are often less direct than men in argumentative situations, and their indirect style sometimes causes men to think that women are trying to be devious and to manipulate them.

To summarize Tannen, men's power comes from acting in opposition to others and to natural forces. Women's power comes from their place in a community. For women, in fact, life is often a struggle to keep from being cut off from the group and to stay connected with the community.

Linguistics professor Susan Herring has conducted research on men's and women's styles in electronic argument on the Internet.[8] She identifies some differences in style that she claims are gender-related. Slightly more than two-thirds of the men she studied are much more aggressive than women in their electronic

---

[5]Deborah Tannen, *You Just Don't Understand: Women and Men in Conversation* (New York: Ballantine Books, 1990), esp. ch. 6, "Community and Context."
[6]Ibid., p. 150.
[7]From a student paper by Tucker Norris; used with permission.
[8]Susan Herring, "Gender Differences in Computer-Mediated Communication" (speech to the American Library Association panel titled "Making the Net *Work*: Is There a Z39.50 in Gender Communication?" Miami, June 27, 1994).

messages. Men write longer posts, are adversarial, and do not seem to mind criticism or ridicule since they say they do not take insults and "flaming" personally. Women, by contrast, say they dislike this type of interaction; either they avoid participating and "lurk" silently or, when they do participate, they hedge, apologize, or ask questions rather than making assertions.

Recent studies of the leadership styles of men and women confirm some of the generalizations about gender differences made by Tannen, Herring, and other researchers. Male leaders, for instance, tend to be more authoritarian and hierarchical than women, who tend to be more democratic and affiliative. In one study, researchers surveyed more than one thousand male and female leaders from a variety of cultures and backgrounds and discovered that the men were more interested in competing for rank and achieving status in their groups. The women were most interested in creating a sense of social equality and building a consensus of opinion in their groups.[9]

Another effort to study some of the possible differences between men and women identifies additional characteristics that could affect their argument styles. Mary Belenky and her associates conducted in-depth interviews of 135 women who were either students in universities or clients in social service agencies.[10] Interviewees were asked about preferred types of classrooms for the exchange of ideas. These researchers discovered that debate—the style of argument that has dominated Western education and that is typically associated with the "masculine adversary style of discourse"—was never selected by women as a classroom forum for exchange and discussion. Instead, women students more typically gravitated toward the class in which there was a sense of community as opposed to a sense of hierarchy. In hierarchical groups, some people possess more power and consequently more ability to be heard than others. In groups that favor community, equality is favored, and power relationships become less important.

Critics of this study point out that Belenky and her associates asked only women about their preferences and did not include any men in this study. Men, if provided the chance, might well have expressed the same preferences as the women—that is, they too would have preferred "connected" classrooms with a sense of community to adversarial, doubting classrooms where debate is favored over collaboration.[11]

The requirements of a particular situation may be more influential than gender in determining the argumentative style that an individual or a group prefers at a particular time. In some cases, males find they prefer connection and consensus over contention and winning, and many females like the excitement and energy associated with winning debates. In fact, generalizations about male and female styles of argument do not always hold up. If you feel you are an exception, you will find many other students who are also.

---

[9]William F. Allman, "Political Chemistry," *U.S. News & World Report*, November 2, 1992, p. 65.
[10]Mary Field Belenky, Blythe McVicker Clinchy, Nancy Rule Goldberger, and Jill Mattluck Tarule, *Women's Ways of Knowing: The Development of Self, Voice, and Mind* (New York: Basic Books, 1986), esp. ch. 10, "Connected Teaching."
[11]Richard Fulkerson, "Transcending Our Conception of Argument in Light of Feminist Critique" (paper presented at the Rhetoric Society of America Conference, Tucson, Ariz., May 1996).

Here is the way one young woman in an argument class characterized her style of argument:

> My parents have played a major role in influencing my argument style. Both of my parents have always been very opinionated and vocal in regard to issues that they feel strongly about. I am also very aware of the lack of respect that females receive while they are speaking. Females are often not taken as seriously [as men], and much of what they have to say is disregarded. I refuse to be ignored. I make it a point to express my feelings on issues that are of importance to me.[12]

This young woman has a distinct style, and she can describe it. She tends toward the adversarial. Her boyfriend, who attended class with her, described himself as a consensual arguer. He was influenced, he said, by his mother, who also favored the consensual approach.

A young male student in an argument class, when asked to describe his style of argument, said that it was important to him to keep the peace, to negotiate, to work things out, and to gain consensus in argument. When he discovered that some of these qualities may be associated with female styles of argument, he quickly changed his description of himself, saying instead that he liked to win at any cost. Apparently, this young man did not want his classmates to question his masculinity, so he switched his description of himself to something less accurate. Actually, however, when questioned, a number of the male students in class admitted they preferred negotiation over winning at any cost. And the women in the class, even those who preferred to think of themselves as winners, still strongly supported the idea of men as negotiators rather than aggressive winners.

The tendency to prefer the consensual style of argument, sometimes associated with women, is often evident among real-world groups of men, including those in business and politics. One manager, for example, describes himself in the *Harvard Business Review* as a "soft" manager.[13] He explains that this description does not mean he is a weak manager. As a soft manager, he welcomes argument and criticism from subordinates, is often tentative in making difficult decisions, admits his own human weaknesses, and tries to listen to employees and understand them. In other words, he stresses connection over conflict and negotiation over winning. He believes that these qualities make him more human, more credible, and more open to change than the classic leaders of business with their "towering self-confidence, their tenacity and resolution, their autocratic decision making, and their invulnerable lonely lives at the top."[14]

As you analyze your own argument style and the styles of your classmates, you may discover that the people who break the hypothetical male-female stereotypes are some of the most effective arguers in class. In a recent discussion about argument, one woman commented that she disagreed so totally with an anti–gay rights group in her part of the country that she absolutely did not want to cooperate with it in any way or try to reach consensus. Instead, she wanted to argue and win. In another discussion, a businessman made the point that if he

---

[12]From a student paper by Jennifer M. Hart; used with permission.
[13]William H. Peace, "The Hard Work of Being a Soft Manager," *Harvard Business Review*, November–December 1991, pp. 40–42, 46–47.
[14]Ibid., p. 40.

didn't work for consensus in his business, he wouldn't get anywhere with his fellow workers, and nothing would ever be accomplished. Deborah Tannen makes a plea for the flexibility that can come from adapting features of both adversarial and consensual styles. Both men and women, she says, could benefit from being flexible enough to borrow one another's best qualities: "Women who avoid conflict at all costs," she suggests, "would be better off if they learned that a little conflict won't kill them. And men who habitually take oppositional stances would be better off if they broke their addiction to conflict."[15] It is also useful to realize that what may sometimes seem like an unfair or irrational approach to argument may simply be a manifestation of a particular individual's style. Such a realization makes it less frustrating, usually, to argue with such an individual.

INFLUENCE OF CULTURE

Now consider the possibility that members of different cultural groups in America may exhibit distinct styles of argument and that individuals learn these styles through affiliation with their groups. Here are some differences that may be influenced by cultural identity, as well as by experience.

Some people think that many African Americans tend to focus strongly on issues and that even though they make effective use of logical and ethical appeal, they sometimes also make superior use of emotional appeal. African American students report that much of their experience with argument styles comes from family interactions and also from the broad American cultural backdrop for the African American culture. The many African American magazines and publications on modern bookstore shelves attest to this group's strong interest in the issues that affect African American culture. Two other distinctly black forums for argument are available to many African Americans: rap music, which is relatively new, and the black church, which is old and traditional. Both provide African Americans with the opportunity to observe and imitate distinctive black styles of argument.

Contemporary issues, presented forcefully and emotionally, form the main content of much rap music, as Sister Souljah, the New York rapper, recognized in 1992. "I think it would be a good idea," she said, "for members of Congress and the Senate and all people who consider themselves policy makers to listen to the call of help that is generated by rap artists."[16] At that time she saw rap music as a deliberate effort to organize black people to think about issues and to engage in social action. She and other rap artists in fact organized a ten-point program to engage African Americans in such issues as African life, economics, education, spirituality, defense, and how not to support racism. Nearly ten years later at a "Hip-Hop Summit" held in 2001 in New York City, the attendees, including artists, politicians, music executives, and civil rights and religious leaders, identified a number of new initiatives and agreements regarding the future of rap

---

[15]Tannen, *You Just Don't Understand*, p. 187.
[16]Sheila Rule, "Rappers' Words Foretold Depth of Blacks' Anger," *New York Times*, May 26, 1992, p. B1.

music. One of these initiatives echoes the remarks made by Sister Souljah ten years earlier. An important goal for the hip-hop community in the future will be to work with civil rights organizations "to educate and address issues such as freedom of speech and racial profiling."[17]

The black church is regarded as another potent forum for argument. In an article describing a protest against a questionable court decision, the author observes that the African American church was at the forefront of the protest, "stepping into its time-honored role in politics and advocacy for social change."[18] Some of the most influential African American leaders who have addressed black issues have also been preachers in black churches. Included in this group are Martin Luther King Jr., Malcolm X, and Jesse Jackson.

The following description of his argument style was provided by a black student in an argument class. As you can see, he attributes some of his preferences and characteristics as an arguer to the fact that he is young, black, and male.

> What influences my style of argument the most is the fact that I am a young black male. The fact that I am young makes me want to be fair and direct with my opponent. That is, I attempt to be free of vagueness, ambiguity, and fallacies. Also, the fact that I am black affects the way I approach my audience. For instance, I tend to use emotional language, and my language is sometimes racially manipulative. I think that blacks tend to see people's race before they see people's attitudes and feelings. Finally, the fact that I am a male probably influences my argument. I think that males tend to be a bit more harsh in their argument. They tend to want to "rock the boat" and stir some emotions. I think that this is a strong tendency in my argument style. The use of facts, emotions, fairness, and strong language is very typical of black argument.[19]

Some Asian American students, according to recent research, may be more reluctant than other students to participate in argument because of their cultural background. Students who have spent a portion of their school years in Japan, China, or other Far Eastern countries or whose parents or grandparents come from these countries may regard argument class as an odd environment that has little to do with them. This statement may be particularly true if they view these classes as places where pro and con issues are debated and winners are declared. The reason is that argumentation and debate are not traditionally practiced in some of the countries in the Far East. Carl Becker, a professor of Asian curriculum research and development, explains some of the reasons for the lack of argumentation in the Far East. For these Asians, sympathetic understanding and intuition are more important means of communication than logic and debate. Furthermore, many Asians do not like to take opposite sides in an argument because they do not like becoming personal rivals of those who represent the other side. They value harmony and peace, and argument, as they perceive it, has the potential to disturb the peace.[20] An instructor who taught for a brief period in Japan reported

---

[17]Kevin Chappell, "Hip-Hop at the Crossroads," *Ebony*, September 2001, p.110.
[18]Gracie Bonds Staples and Anjetta McQueen, "Ministers Lead Prayers in Call for Awakening," *Fort Worth Star-Telegram*, March 27, 1993, p. 1.
[19]From a student paper by Kelvin Jenkins; used with permission.
[20]Carl B. Becker, "Reasons for the Lack of Argumentation and Debate in the Far East," *International Journal of Intercultural Relations*, 10 (1986): 75–92.

that he could not get his Japanese students to take pro and con sides on an issue and debate it. Instead, they all insisted on taking the same side.[21] In 1999, the Japanese Parliament decided to introduce British-style confrontational debate into its sessions. The objective was to conduct weekly forty-minute debates, but this was difficult for the Japanese debaters. The first question one member of Parliament asked the prime minister to get the exchange going was, "What did you eat for breakfast this morning?" Commentators noted, "Blunt confrontation, it seems, does not come any more easily to Japanese politicians than it does to ordinary Japanese, whose national language is a maze of well-practiced protocols and polite indirection."[22] A book published a few years ago in Japan teaches the Japanese how to say no to Americans. Taking an opposing stance and defending it is a skill that must be learned in Japan. It is not part of the traditional culture. Read the article provided in Exercise E at the end of this chapter for examples of what the Japanese really mean when they say yes to people outside their culture.

Here is the self-reported argument style of a young Asian American student in an argument class. This account was written at the beginning of the semester.

> My style of argument is to avoid argument as much as possible. I think that I argue more with other men than I do with women. I think the reason I don't argue a lot is because I analyze the situation a bit too much, and I can pretty much tell what the outcome is going to be. During argument I usually blank out what the other person is saying and think about when they are going to stop talking.[23]

He was more comfortable and skilled with argument at semester's end. He credited argument class, finally, with teaching him to listen more, argue more, and be less self-centered.

An Asian international student who petitioned to be excused from argument class said that for her, the idea of such a class was very confusing because she could not understand why she or any other student should spend time arguing and trying to convince others to agree with their points of view. She associated such activity with advertising and selling and could not envision it as useful in other contexts. Ironically, this student went on to write a convincing argument about why she should not have to take an argument class. This was an important issue for her, and she wrote a good argument in spite of her reluctance to participate in the class.

The Asian students who test-read this book warned that not all Asian cultures are the same and that the reluctance to argue may be stronger in some Asian cultures than others. For example, a Sri Lankan student pointed out that in her country, as well as in India and Bangladesh, argument is encouraged. Students also observed that there is a tradition of lively, contentious, and even combative kitchen arguments among close family members in some Asian cultures. This, they say, is typical of the Korean culture. Amy Tan, in her books about her childhood in a Chinese immigrant household, gives examples of the lively home

---

[21]Interview with Clyde Moneyhun.
[22]Howard W. French, "Hear, Hear, Please! 'Question Time' in Japan," *New York Times*, November 22, 1999, p. A8.
[23]From a student paper by Jim Lui; used with permission.

argument in that culture as well. Outside of the home, however, Asians may tend to be reluctant to enter into argument. For students reluctant to speak out, argument class is a safe place for developing and practicing that special ability.

Since Hispanic cultures promote strong family ties and group values, many Hispanic students seem to favor connection over contention and negotiation over winning. Female Hispanic students describe their styles of argument variously. One student says she tries to listen and understand others' points of view. Another says she likes the fact that she can express her feelings without hurting other people, while yet another says she likes a negotiated solution even though she would at times like to be more assertive.

The descriptions of argument style that you have read in this chapter were written by students enrolled in argument classes who responded to an assignment that asked them to describe their current argument styles. These students, along with more than six hundred others, also completed a questionnaire about their argument styles and were asked to reveal their gender and their cultural background. The idea was to see if the links between style and gender and background characteristics already discussed in this chapter seemed to have any validity.

The students were questioned in three areas. First, they were asked how they viewed the outcomes of argument. Then they were asked to report on their personal participation in argument. Finally, they were asked about their present style of argument. Several possible answers were provided for each of the three items, and students were asked to identify one item under each question that best described them and then to identify two others that also described them, but perhaps not quite so forcefully. The questions appear in Box 2.1. As you read them, answer them yourself. Under each question, identify the item you agree with most as number 1. Then number the additional items that also describe your opinions and practices as 2 and 3.

You may now want to compare your own answers to the questions with those reported by other students. Of the 647 argument class students who completed this questionnaire one week after classes started, 69 percent were second-semester freshmen, 19 percent were sophomores, and 12 percent were juniors and seniors. Also, 53 percent were male and 47 percent female. Of the males, 69 percent were white, 9 percent were black, 12 percent were Asian, and 10 percent were Hispanic. Of the females, 64 percent were white, 15 percent were black, 13 percent were Asian, and 8 percent were Hispanic. The percentages were weighted to indicate the relative strength of preference for each group in order to make more accurate comparisons.

One of the most interesting results of this study was that no items on the questionnaire were rejected by all students. Every item on the questionnaire was marked by at least a few students as being typical or somewhat typical of themselves. These students' responses suggest the wide diversity of attitudes and preferences among them.

In answer to the first question, about argument outcomes, both male and female students overwhelmingly favored the response that the best outcome of argument is to help them "understand others." Scoring highest in this area, however, were Asian men. "Changing minds" and "resolving conflict" were in second

BOX 2.1   **Student Questionnaire on Attitudes and Style in Argument.**

WHAT IS YOUR ARGUMENT STYLE?   ◆◆◆

How would you answer these questions? Identify as number 1 the item with which you agree most. Then identify as 2 and 3 the additional items that also describe you.

1. How would you describe the usual outcomes of argument?
_____ Argument helps people understand each other's points of view.
_____ Argument separates and alienates people.
_____ Argument causes conflict and hard feelings.
_____ Argument resolves conflict and solves problems.
_____ Argument can change people's minds.
_____ Argument rarely changes other people's minds.

2. How would you describe your personal participation in argument?
_____ Argument makes me feel energized, and I like to participate.
_____ Argument makes me uncomfortable, and I dislike participating.
_____ I participate a lot.
_____ I participate sometimes.
_____ I never participate.
_____ I think it is fun to argue.
_____ I think it is rude to argue.

3. What is your style of argument at present?
_____ I am contentious and enjoy conflict.
_____ I am a peacekeeper, and I value conflict resolution.
_____ I try to win and show people I am right.
_____ I try to listen, understand, make connections, negotiate solutions.
_____ I tend to use reason and facts more than emotion.
_____ I tend to use emotion more than reason and facts.

and third places among the preferences of the entire group. Clearly, more students thought argument resolves conflict than thought argument causes it. Only a few students indicated that argument separates and alienates people. There was essentially no difference between male and female responses to this first question.

Male and female students were also very similar in their assessment of their participation in argument. Most students reported that they "participated sometimes" instead of "never" or "a lot." Both women and men reported that they are energized by argument, they like it, and they find it "fun to argue." Asian women were the largest identifiable group among students who said they found argument "uncomfortable" so that they disliked participating. Not all of them, however, responded in this way. African American men and women ranked themselves slightly higher than the other groups in perceiving argument as energizing and enjoyable. Only a few students, and about the same number of males as females, thought it was "rude to argue" and said they "never participated."

Male and female students differed more in their responses to question 3, "What is your style of argument at present?" than they did in their responses to the other two questions. "Listening and connecting" was the style favored over the others by both men and women of all groups, but more women than men identified themselves with this style. More females than males also reported that they use emotion in argument more than reason, and more males than females favored reason and facts over emotion. White males said they "try to win" more than the other groups. Asian males and females identified themselves as "peace-keepers" somewhat more than the other groups, even though a significant number of the students in the other groups saw themselves this way as well. Finally, only a few of the men and even fewer of the women said they were "contentious" and that they "enjoyed conflict."

Although no Native American students participated in this study, research concerning Native American culture and values suggests that Native American students value community and cooperation more than rivalry and competition. Furthermore, in traditional Native American culture, young people are expected to agree with authority figures, especially with those seen as older and wiser. Consequently, Native American students are often reluctant to debate, particularly with the teacher.[24]

We concluded that the differences among these groups of students are certainly not great enough to create stereotypes. College students, in fact, often break stereotypes because of their close association with one another, which often results in greater flexibility, adaptability, and increased tolerance, and because of their common goal to become educated. The strongest tendencies among these students that seem to confirm the notion that gender and cultural background may have influence over them as arguers were that Asian students were less enthusiastic about argument than the others, that white males liked to win more than any of the other groups, and that more females than males said they typically try to listen and connect.

Some findings, however, are not typical of some of the tendencies described by recent researchers. For instance, listening, understanding, making connections, and negotiating solutions was a preferred style for nearly as many men as for women, and the contentious, conflictive style was less popular with both groups. Also, it seems clear that these students as a group value knowing the facts; are suspicious of too much emotion, particularly if it results in anger and loss of control; and have positive opinions about the outcomes and uses of argument.

The study mainly emphasizes the many differences in argument style that can be found in argument classrooms. The study confirms the importance of the goals for argument class listed at the beginning of this chapter: students need to learn to value one another's styles, to develop flexibility by extending their own styles and learning to borrow from others, and to adapt to styles other than their own.

---

[24]B. C. Howard, *Learning to Persist/Persisting to Learn* (Washington, D.C.: Mid-Atlantic Center for Race Equity, American University, 1987).

INFLUENCE OF NATIONALITY

Argument class can often be thought of as a microcosm of the larger world, particularly when the students in it represent a variety of countries and cultures. Cultural backgrounds outside of the United States can sometimes exert a powerful influence over the way in which individuals view and practice argument. Studying argument across cultures is a complicated field, and most of its findings are tentative because of the vast individual differences in people from culture to culture. Still, even tentative findings are important for the argument classroom. Hypothesizing about how argument differs according to nationality helps students focus on the preferences in argument styles that may be typical of certain groups and cultures. Developing an awareness of these characteristics and preferences and learning to adapt to them not only helps students achieve the goals of the inclusive argument classroom but also helps prepare students for lifelong communicating and negotiating with people from other countries and cultures.

Here are some examples of some possible differences. Deborah Tannen claims that argument in some societies is a way of coming together, a pleasurable sign of intimacy, a kind of game that people play together. This observation is particularly true of Italy, Greece, and Eastern Europe. To outsiders, the argument in these countries may seem to be conflictual rather than a reasoned inquiry into issues. Italian *discussione* strikes outsiders as loud, contentious arguing, but to Italians it is a friendly game. Greeks and Eastern Europeans may appear bossy and overbearing. In their view, however, they are showing friendly caring.[25]

In the following account, a student from Vietnam describes a different attitude and style of argument in his country.

> The Vietnamese are taught not to argue with their elders. When I was a little child, my parents always told me that it is bad to argue with your parents and elders. Since the first grade, my teachers told us that it is bad to argue, even among friends. That is why I did not like to argue. I did not want to be disrespectful to another person. When I came to the United States and attended school, I learned that in this society you are encouraged to argue for your opinion.[26]

Here is another example of a student, this time from Israel, who attributes his predominant style of argument to his country of origin.

> I am an Arab and a Palestinian, and my argument style is different from other styles used here in the United States. In my country children are taught not to argue with what their elders tell them. This is not only taught at home, but at school too. In school teachers come second to parents when it comes to advice. Parents are considered to be wiser and more experienced in life, and it is considered disrespectful to argue with them. Arguing, in fact, can lead to certain punishment.[27]

International students in your class may be able to provide additional examples that represent predominant styles of argument in their countries and cultures, along with an analysis of what causes them.

---

[25]Tannen, *You Just Don't Understand*, pp. 160–162.
[26]From a student paper by Lan Mai; used with permission.
[27]From a student paper by Edward Stephan; used with permission.

Some researchers have speculated about the reasons for the differences in argument styles among different cultures. *Preferred cultural values* and *preferred patterns of thinking* may be the two major factors that differentiate argument styles across cultures.[28] Differences in value systems from culture to culture are often particularly obvious. For example, Americans who relocate to Saudi Arabia are sometimes surprised when they receive copies of newspapers from outside the country. Before the newspapers are delivered, the Saudi censors use wide felt-tipped ink pens to obliterate visual material that is offensive to their cultural values. Pictures of a ballerina's legs and arms may be colored over, as well as other parts of the female anatomy usually kept covered in Arab countries.

You may want to discuss with your classmates, particularly if some of them come from other countries or have lived in another country for a while, what values and patterns of thinking are preferred in their cultures since these are believed to have an effect on the common ground that is established in cross-cultural argument.[29] For example, according to some researchers, Americans value individual achievement, hard work, and independence, and in their patterns of thinking, they tend to prefer generalizations backed by examples and experience to pure reasoning unaccompanied by examples. The Japanese, like Americans, also value achievement, but they also value serenity and self-confidence. Characteristic of their thinking patterns are the preferences to make suggestions, to give hints, and to communicate indirectly. Researchers who have studied Japanese argument claim that the Japanese like ambiguity, or saying one thing and meaning something else. They often use understatement. Their communication can seem incomplete to outsiders because they often omit logical links, expecting others to infer them. The Japanese dislike contention and debate.[30]

You see that understanding the value systems and preferred patterns of reasoning of other cultures can be very important in establishing the common ground necessary for productive argument across cultures. As you read newspaper accounts of intercultural communication and argument, watch for the problems and misunderstandings that can arise from an absence of shared values and shared ways of thinking. Here are two examples.

1. *Japan.* In an article concerning deliberations in Japan about whether or not that country should have a permanent seat on the United Nations Security Council, David Sanger wrote in the *New York Times*:

> The Tokyo Government has not wanted to appear to be openly seeking the Security Council seat, even though countries with far less economic power sit there

---

[28]Gregg B. Walker, "Assessing Multicultural Argument in the Law of the Sea Negotiations: A Rationale and Analytical Framework," in *Spheres of Argument: Proceedings of the Sixth SCA/AFA Conference on Argumentation*, ed. Bruce E. Gronbeck (Annandale, Va.: Speech Communication Association, 1989), pp. 600–603.

[29]Ibid. Walker summarizes the results of considerable cross-cultural research into the values and patterns of thought preferred by different cultures. See his article for additional sources and information. Pearson, "Women as Learners," also summarizes some of the cultural values included here.

[30]Michael David Hazen, "The Role of Argument, Reasoning and Logic in Tacit, Incomplete and Indirect Communication: The Case of Japan," in *Spheres of Argument: Proceedings of the Sixth SCA/AFA Conference on Argumentation*, ed. Bruce E. Gronbeck (Annandale, Va.: Speech Communication Association, 1989), pp. 497–503.

today. But there is also an underlying fear that Japan, if given a bully pulpit, may have little to say. "We might be ashamed to raise our hand," Seiki Nishihiro, a former Deputy Defense Minister, said during a recent conference.[31]

Nishihiro's comment is puzzling unless one recalls the Japanese reluctance to participate in contentious debate, which is a regular feature of the Security Council.

2. *Russia.* A human interest story about an international student from Russia says she was confident she would do well on her first exam. She studied hard, memorized the material, and wrote it well in the exam booklet. She was surprised, however, when she received a D grade. Her professor had penalized her for writing only what the book said and for not including her own opinions.[32]

This incident can be puzzling unless one realizes that not all countries and cultures encourage critical thinking, evaluative opinion, and argument. Totalitarian governments like the former Soviet Union, in fact, discouraged or even forbade diversity of opinion in public forums.

Argument is fundamental to democracy, and it flourishes in democratic societies. In totalitarian societies, however, if it exists at all, it must usually go underground. Thus argument in such countries may be heard only in the secret meetings of opposition political groups or in private meetings of citizens. Written argument may appear in underground newspapers or in material written by dissidents or political exiles. Forums for argument in such societies are severely limited compared to those in democratic societies. Students from such countries may at first find it difficult to participate in argument.

All participants in argument, whether they come from democratic or totalitarian societies, need to work to establish common ground if argument across cultures and gender boundaries is to be successful. This effort can be difficult and time-consuming. An issue that has been argued and debated through the ages is the fishing, navigation, and territorial rights to the oceans of the world. In the 1970s, the United Nations Conference on the Law of the Sea was charged with the task of reaching agreement among nations on access to and use of the seas. This group spent nine years engaged in intercultural argument and negotiation, finally reaching agreement on some, but not all, of the issues.[33]

When Boris Yeltsin was president of Russia, he made an effective attempt to achieve common ground on his visit to Japan in late 1993, when there was considerable tension between the two countries. Unlike some of his predecessors, Yeltsin was accomplished in building common ground. Soon after arriving in Japan, he apologized for Russia's treatment of thousands of Japanese prisoners of war who were sent to Siberia after World War II. More than sixty thousand of them died, and many Japanese believed an apology was long overdue. Later, Yeltsin repeated this apology to the Japanese prime minister and bowed deeply to

---

[31]David E. Sanger, "Toyko in the New Epoch: Heady Future with Fear," *New York Times,* May 5, 1992, p. A1.
[32]David Wallechinsky, "This Land of Ours," *Parade,* July 5, 1992, p. 4.
[33]Walker, "Assessing Multicultural Argument," pp. 599–600.

express his remorse, a gesture that is valued in the Japanese culture.[34] His efforts, according to reports, relieved a considerable amount of tension between the two countries because of the common ground he established. When common ground is not established, the consequences can be devastating. Wars are a frequent alternative to productive argument and negotiation, especially when the differences among the arguing parties are extreme.

The concept of all people knowing how to argue effectively to resolve differences in personal, national, and international relationships is potentially a very powerful idea. Think of a country and a world where major problems are resolved through profitable argument instead of through confrontation, shouting, fighting, or war. You will often fervently disagree with other people; in fact, life would be boring if you never disagreed. Yet even when you disagree, even when you decide to enter an ongoing argument, you can learn to use a style that is comfortable and natural for you. And that approach is preferable to the alternatives: either remaining silent or becoming involved in destructive arguments that solve nothing and may even cause harm.

REVIEW QUESTIONS

1. What are some of the possible influences on individual styles of argument? Which of these are the most potent for you?
2. What are some of the differences researchers have identified between men's and women's styles of argument? Do you agree or disagree? What in your own experience has influenced your answer to this question?
3. Why might it be important to be aware of different argument styles in international or cross-cultural argument? Give some examples of problems that might arise along with some ideas of how to deal with them.

EXERCISES AND ACTIVITIES

A. SELF-EVALUATION: IS YOUR PREDOMINANT ARGUMENT STYLE CONSENSUAL OR ADVERSARIAL?

Box 2.2 provides a summary of some of the characteristics of consensual and adversarial styles of argument. As you read the lists, check the items that are most typical of you. Does one list describe your style of argument better than the other? Or can your style best be described by items derived from both lists? From this analysis, how would you say you prefer to argue?

---

[34]David E. Sanger, "Yeltsin, in Tokyo, Avoids Islands Issue," *New York Times*, October 14, 1993, p. A5.

BOX 2.2   Two Styles of Argument.

WHICH STYLE DESCRIBES YOU?

Check all that apply in both columns. Does one style tend to predominate, or do you have a mixed style?

CONSENSUAL STYLE	ADVERSARIAL STYLE
_____ I prefer to be indirect.	_____ I am direct and open.
_____ I like to give reasons.	_____ I like to reach conclusions.
_____ I prefer cooperation.	_____ I prefer competition.
_____ I favor group consensus.	_____ I favor individual opinions.
_____ I like affiliation.	_____ I like conflict.
_____ I hate to fight.	_____ I like to fight.
_____ I prefer to avoid confrontation.	_____ I like confrontation.
_____ I dislike contentious argument.	_____ I like contentious argument.
_____ I am nonaggressive.	_____ I am aggressive.
_____ I solicit many views on an issue.	_____ I tend to see issues as two-sided, pro and con, right or wrong.
_____ I am both logical and emotional.	_____ I am primarily logical.
_____ I try to make connections.	_____ I tend to be adversarial.
_____ I prefer negotiating.	_____ I prefer winning.
_____ I favor the personal example, story, or anecdote.	_____ I favor abstract ideas.
_____ I want to keep the community strong.	_____ I want to keep the individual strong.

B.   WRITING ASSIGNMENT: THE ARGUMENT-STYLE PAPER

Think about the last time you had to argue convincingly for a certain point of view. Write a 300- to 500-word paper in which you describe your predominant argument style. Include the following information.

1. When you argued, what was the issue, what were you trying to achieve, and what did you do to achieve it?
2. Was that typical of your usual style of argument? If yes, explain why; if no, explain why and describe your usual style.
3. What has influenced your style of argument? Consider home training, role models, gender, culture, nationality, national heritage, or any other life experiences that have influenced you.
4. How would you describe your ideal arguer, and how would you like to be more like this person in your own arguing?

5. What do you like best about your current style of argument? What would you like to change? How can you become more flexible in your style?

C. CLASS PROJECT: A CLASSROOM ENVIRONMENT FOR ARGUMENT AND YOUR CLASS AS AN AUDIENCE

1. Read aloud the argument-style papers written by class members for Exercise B. Discuss the different styles described in these papers and some of the influences that have helped create them.

2. Discuss creating a classroom environment that can accommodate all of these styles. Jürgen Habermas, a modern European rhetorician, described an ideal environment for argument.[35] Read each item, indicate by raising your hand whether you agree or disagree, and explain why. What would you eliminate? Why? What would you add? Why?

   a. Each person should have the freedom to express ideas and critique others' ideas directly, openly, and honestly.

   b. The use of force and personal power that tend to inhibit some participants should be eliminated.

   c. Arguments based on an appeal to the past and tradition are to be exposed. These arguments superimpose the past on the present, and everyone does not share the same past.

   d. The aim of argument is to arrive at truth through consensus and an adherence of minds.

   What are the implications of accepting or rejecting these statements for your classroom?

3. Characterize your class as an audience as a result of reading the argument-style papers. Write for five minutes about the characteristics your class holds in common and also about the types of diversity that are evident in your class. What generalizations can you finally make about your class as an audience? Discuss the results.

D. GROUP WORK AND CLASS DISCUSSION: USING GENDER, NATIONALITY, AND CULTURAL BACKGROUND TO STRENGTHEN ARGUMENT

The following five essays are written by authors who have drawn on the unique experiences of themselves or others as members of a particular culture or gender. When you have read the essays, discuss them in small groups of four or five students. Appoint a scribe to record your findings and report them to the class. The following questions will help organize your discussion.

1. What experiences associated with a culture or a gender do these authors draw on to strengthen their arguments?

2. What is effective in their arguments as a result? Be specific.

3. What can you conclude about drawing on experiences associated with a culture, gender, or nationality to strengthen an argument?

---

[35]Habermas's ideas are summarized by James L. Golden, Goodwin F. Berquist, and William E. Coleman in *The Rhetoric of Western Thought*, 4th ed. (Dubuque, Ia.: Kendall Hunt, 1989), p. 438.

4. Would drawing on personal experiences of your own, as these authors have done, be consistent with your personal argument style? If your answer is yes, what experiences associated with your culture, gender, or nationality might you use to develop an issue that is important to you?

WE KNEW WHAT GLORY WAS*

Shirlee Taylor Haizlip

Shirlee Taylor Haizlip is also the author of *The Sweeter the Juice: A Family Memoir in Black and White.*

1   When I was growing up in the 40's and 50's, my father would pack up the car every August and squeeze in my mother, four children, several dolls and a picnic lunch. It was the time before air-conditioning, and the drive was hot, dusty and, after New York, without bathrooms.

2   We left long before dawn, because for a dark-skinned man driving a large shiny sedan holding a white-looking wife, the journey from Connecticut to the South was not without peril. It was essential that each leg of the trip be made before nightfall. We knew that safety lay within the homes and the churches of my father's friends and colleagues, the black ministers we would visit. They were our underground railroad.

3   My father was a Baptist pastor who ministered to a medium-sized black church in a Connecticut mill town. His father was a minister who had founded a major black Baptist church in Washington. At the beginnings of their careers, both had led small country churches in North Carolina, Virginia and West Virginia. Later, as popular officers of the National Baptist Convention and known for their dramatic oratory, the two were frequent guest preachers at rural churches throughout the South.

4   Traditionally, my father and his father before him preached a week of revival services at these houses of worship. After my grandfather died, my father continued to return to the South each year. For him, the churches were touchstones of faith, of culture, of triumph over slavery. For him, they were living, breathing links to the past and an indestructible foundation for the future.

5   There was more than a spiritual connection. When they were in college, my four uncles, all of whom played musical instruments and had glorious voices, would sometimes join my father and present musical programs of spirituals and the light classics to appreciative Southern congregations, all too often deprived of other cultural experiences.

6   At other times, my dad, resplendent in a white suit, would offer solo recitals. When he crooned "Danny Boy" or "When I Grow Too Old to Dream" in his high tenor vibrato and with exquisite diction, the fans moved a little faster, the backs

*New York Times, June 23, 1996, p. A13.

sat up a little straighter and the shouts of "Sing it, Rev!" were as heartfelt as they were for his renditions of "Amazing Grace" or "His Eye Is on the Sparrow."

7   I cannot hear the Three Tenors sing without thinking of my father standing in the pulpit of a spare little church, singing like a melancholy angel.

8   To reach many of the churches, we drove up deserted dirt roads covered by gracefully arching kudzu-fringed trees. Just when we thought we would never get there, a clearing materialized. There at its edge stood the church, often the only building for miles around, plain as a line drawing in a children's coloring book, more often than not in need of a fresh coat of paint. Never lonely looking, it seemed instead a natural part of the landscape, splendid in its simplicity.

9   Before the service, with admonitions of keeping our "best" clothes clean fading in our ears, my siblings and I would play with other children, running and jumping, catching fireflies, hiding and seeking in the darkening silver twilight. Each night, the revival crowd would get bigger and livelier. By the end of the week, the church was full, the room was hot and the penitents were saved.

10   During every service, I watched as my father, in high Baptist style, "picture painted" the stories of Moses and Job, Ruth and Esther. I listened as he moaned and hummed and sang the tales of W. E. B. Du Bois and Frederick Douglass, the Scottsboro Boys and Emmett Till. I clapped for joy as he brought the worshipers to their feet with promises of survival now and salvation later. In that place, at that time, we knew what glory was.

11   After the service, in the pitch blackness of a muggy summer night, we would drive back to our host's house, listening to parish gossip and ghost stories, accept offers of freshly made iced tea and every once in a while homemade ice cream. Sweetly, another church night had ended.

12   The best was yet to come. At the close of the week, we celebrated the homecoming, the end of the weeklong revival, behind the church, where picnic benches were felicitously placed among sweet-smelling pines. We ate miles of delicious food and drank lakes of sweet punch.

13   Usually there was a modest graveyard somewhere near the picnic grounds. We did not play there. Our parents had taught us better than that. Mold-covered gravestones barely hinted at the life stories they marked. The bones of slaves lay side by side with the bones of their emancipated children. All of their spirits were free to be free, at last.

14   As I grew older, I would learn about the lives of the church members from the comfort of my mother's side. I would grow to understand that there, in that place, every single church member was *somebody*.

15   In God's house, if nowhere else, they were C.E.O.'s and presidents, directors and chairmen, counselors and managers. In God's house, if nowhere else, they were women of infinite grace and men of profound dignity. Forever, amen.

16   With traditions that began in slavery, the parishioners carried forward, bit by precious bit, the dreams of their forebears. In their roles as deacons, trustees, missionaries and choir members, those domestics, handymen, cotton and tobacco farmers and teachers sang and prayed on hard, scrabbly benches, validating and celebrating themselves and one another, warmly and well, week after week, year after year, generation after generation.

17   Surely their oils and essences seeped into the well-worn pews. Surely the whorls of their fingertips left lovely striations in the wood, at which their grand-babies would stare before they fell off to sleep.

18   Not only did they tend to the church's business, they looked after the elderly and the infirm, encouraged the young to learn, learn, learn and rallied their communities in times of economic stress, natural disaster or social crisis. It did not escape my understanding that the church encompassed all. Seldom were there outcasts.

19   For me as a child, those beautiful little structures were places beyond enchantment. As an adult, I understood that the churches were indeed the collective soul of black folks.

20   I never thought that this particular reality could end. Although I have visited the South as an adult and know that some of those churches have been abandoned, enlarged or modernized, in my mind's eye all of them remain storybook sanctuaries, testament to my own faith, the faith of my father, his father and the larger black community.

◆ ◆ ◆

21   Heartsick now, my soul's light has been dimmed. Church after church in the South has been destroyed by fire, torched by arsonists. I watch the television images as long as I can. Then I hide my eyes behind my fingers, peeking at the screen as if it were a horror film, while hellish flames consume the heavenly places of my youth.

22   I ask my father across the void, Who will put out the flames, Dad? Where can we go now to be safe?

FOR DISCUSSION: What makes this an effective argument? What do you visualize? How do you participate in this essay and identify with its characters?

◆ ◆ ◆

A VIEW FROM BERKELEY*

Chang-Lin Tien

The late Chang-Lin Tien was chancellor of the University of California at Berkeley when he wrote this article.

1   When the debate over affirmative action in higher education started to simmer, the stance I took as the chancellor of the University of California at Berkeley seemed to surprise many people.

2   To be sure, my view—that we *should* consider race, ethnicity and gender along with many other factors in admissions—has put me at odds with some constituencies, including the majority of the Regents of the University of California. Last July, these officials voted to end affirmative action admission policies.

New York Times, March 31, 1996, Special Education Section, p. 30.

3   And with California voters to decide later this year whether to end all state affirmative action programs, silence might seem a more prudent course for the head of a major public university. We already have enough battles to fight, my staff sometimes reminds me: declining public funding, for example.

4   A few students and friends have hinted that it might make more sense for me, as an Asian-American, to oppose affirmative action.

5   Asian-Americans, who are not considered underrepresented minorities under affirmative action, have divergent views. Some are disturbed by the "model minority" stereotype; they say it pits them against other minorities and hides the discrimination they still face. Others—including the two Asian-American Regents who voted to end affirmative action—believe the only fair approach is to base admissions on academic qualifications. That also opens the door to more Asians.

6   So why do I strongly support affirmative action? My belief has been shaped by my role in higher education. And by my experience as a Chinese immigrant. I know first-hand that America can be a land of opportunity. When I came here, I was a penniless 21-year-old with a limited grasp of the language and culture. Yet I was permitted to accomplish a great deal. My research in heat transfer contributed to better nuclear reactor safety and space shuttle design. My former students are professors and researchers at some of America's best schools and business concerns.

7   But as I struggled to finish my education here, I also encountered the ugly realities of racial discrimination. This, too, is part of America's legacy and it is inextricably connected to the need for affirmative action.

8   When I first arrived in this country in 1956 as a graduate student, for example, I lived in Louisville, Ky. One day I got on a bus and saw that all the black people were in the back, the white people in the front. I didn't know where I belonged, so for a long time I stood near the driver. Finally, he told me to sit down in the front, and I did. I didn't take another bus ride for a whole year. I would walk an hour to avoid that.

9   I served as a teaching fellow at Louisville for a professor who refused to pronounce my name. He addressed me as "Chinaman." One day he directed me to adjust some valves in a large laboratory apparatus. Climbing a ladder, I lost my balance and instinctively grabbed a nearby steam pipe. It was scorchingly hot and produced a jolt of pain that nearly caused me to faint. Yet I did not scream. Instead, I stuffed my throbbing hand into my coat pocket and waited until the class ended. Then I ran to the hospital emergency room, where I was treated for a burn that had singed all the skin off my palm.

10   Outwardly, my response fit the stereotype of the model-minority Asian: I said nothing and went about my business. But my silence had nothing to do with stoicism. I simply did not want to endure the humiliation of having the professor scold me in front of the class.

11   Of course, four decades later, there have been major civil rights advances in America. But serious racial divisions remain. That's why colleges and universities created affirmative admissions programs. The idea was to open the doors to promising minority students who lacked educational and social opportunities.

12   As Berkeley's chancellor, I have seen the promise of affirmative action come true. No racial or ethnic group constitutes a majority among our 21,000 undergraduates. And Berkeley students enter with higher grades and test scores than their predecessors. They graduate at the highest rate in our history.

13   I think that affirmative action should be a temporary measure, but the time has not yet come to eliminate it. Educational opportunities for inner-city minority students, for example, still contrast dramatically with those of affluent students in the suburbs, where many white families live.

14   And as a public institution, the university needs to look at broader societal needs, including greater leadership training of California's African-American and Hispanic population.

15   I try to explain this when, as occasionally happens, Asian-American or white friends complain to me that their child, a straight-A student, didn't get into Berkeley because we give spaces to others. I also say that we use admission criteria other than test scores, grades and ethnicity, including a genius for computers, musical talent, geographical diversity.

16   Besides, a straight-A average wouldn't guarantee admission to Berkeley even if there were no affirmative action. For a freshman class with 3,500 places, we get about 25,000 applicants. This year, 10,784 of them had a 4.0 high school record.

17   What's more, helping minority students may not be the most compelling reason for preserving affirmative action.

18   Every time I walk across campus, I am impressed by the vibrant spirit of this diverse community. In teeming Sproul Plaza, the dozens of student groups who set up tables represent every kind of social, political, ethnic and religious interest. In the dorms, students from barrios, suburbs, farm towns and the inner city come together.

19   When there are diverse students, staff and faculty (among whom there are still too few minorities), everybody stands to gain.

20   Of course, interactions between students of different backgrounds can bring misunderstanding. Some white students tell me they feel squeezed out by black and Latino students they believe are less deserving, as well as by overachieving Asian-American students. Some African-American and Latino students confide they sometimes feel their professors and white classmates consider them academically inferior, a view that's slow to change even when they excel.

21   Still, the overall message I get time and again from students and recent graduates is that they have valued the chance to challenge stereotypes.

22   So I was stunned by the Regents' decision to end affirmative action admissions policies, which goes into effect by 1998. I even debated whether to resign.

23   In Chinese, however, the character for "crisis" is actually two characters: one stands for danger and the other for opportunity. And I took the Chinese approach. Noting that the Regents had reaffirmed their commitment to diversity when they discarded affirmative action, I decided to stay to try to make a difference.

24   Recently, I joined the superintendents of the major urban school districts of the San Francisco Bay area to announce a campaign: The Berkeley Pledge.

25   Under this program, Berkeley is deepening its support for disadvantaged youth trying to qualify for admission. One way will be to provide educational expertise for teachers; another will be to create incentives for pupils at selected school "pipelines" that begin in kindergarten. We also are stepping up our recruitment of exceptional minority students.

26   America has come a long way since the days of Jim Crow segregation. It would be a tragedy if our nation's colleges and universities slipped backward now, denying access to talented but disadvantaged youth and eroding the diversity that helps to prepare leaders.

FOR DISCUSSION: What are the major reasons Chancellor Tien provides for retaining affirmative action in higher education? Do you share his views? Give reasons for your answer, and use some of your own experiences to support your reasons, just as he does.

◆◆◆

GIVING PEOPLE A SECOND CHANCE*

Ernest Martinez

Ernest Martinez writes about his experience as an instructor in inmate vocational education at Wasco State Prison in Wasco, California.

1   I am very proud of being Mexican American and am both privileged and honored to have been blessed with a career as an educator. Yet, I sometimes think that when discussing the many Hispanic issues that we often attribute to a fractured American society, I believe we often do to ourselves what we don't want others to do to us: ostracize ourselves. On the one hand, we rally together as Hispanics to seek out equal opportunity and revel in the triumphs of our unity. But on the other hand, when we hear of our many Hispanic brethren who are ex-convicts who need employment avenues for reentry into society, we close our eyes and ears to their cry for assistance. We blame society for their plight and thrust the burden of our people on the very government we condemn for lack of opportunity.

2   For the past several years, I have been part of the lives of inmates by teaching them vocational studies. These inmates are an example to us all that it is only by the grace of God that we are not in their place. We can all attest to the fact that we have done something for which we have simply not been caught—for example, drinking alcoholic beverages as minors, or driving without a license, or hanging around with the wrong people and being at the wrong place at the wrong time, or telling little "white lies" while filing our taxes. These are all examples of "crimes" that we've gotten away with. And instead of being imprisoned, we are known as

---

Hispanic, June 1996, p. 64.

law abiding citizens. The inmates of Wasco State Prison have not been so lucky, graced or blessed.

3   I believe many of the inmates with whom I work are persons like you and me. Unfortunately, they took "the road less traveled," and found themselves in a situation that was beyond their ability to handle or solve. This is not only "man as the problem," but the "problems of man." There are many parallels that we can draw between ourselves—those of us in the professional and business communities in need of not only able but willing people—and the backgrounds, personalities, character traits, abilities, needs, and yes, even aspirations, of the many prison inmates wanting and asking for a "Chapter Two" in their lives.

4   The business environment today is not solely based on equipment, products, or services. It's dependent on the skills, talents, and savvy of people. We're not only in an information age today; we are in an Age of Man, whereby sales can only be made and increased through the interpersonal relationships that we create between provider and consumer, between our companies and our customers. The world-respected organization, business, and management guru Dr. Peter Drucker has said, "Show me an organization or business that does not believe people are their greatest resource and I'll show you an organization with built-in limits to its success, and perhaps one destined for certain failure." Remember the old saying, "*El ojo del amo engorda el caballo.*" [The literal meaning is, "The eye of love fattens the horse"; the metaphorical meaning is, that "anything seen through the eyes of love seems better"]. Only if we can secure our fiscally solvent present can we launch into a more expansive tomorrow. And, again, we can only do this if we focus on people as our greatest asset today.

5   I am of the ardent belief that many prison inmates are highly functional, tremendously skilled, fabulously talented, and often technically gifted. Some are inordinately intelligent, while others are blessed simply with the extraordinary ability to work diligently. I've learned over the years working as educator of vocational studies with inmates that their crime was more a matter of poor judgment rather than of faulty character. And while not so naive as to believe that all inmates are worthy of a "Chapter Two," I can empathize with how hard it is to take a breath when one is in a whirlwind. The momentum of the moment is a tremendous force in this "survival of the fittest" society.

6   This is not to mean that we are to be guilt-driven, but rather people-motivated. This is not to promote philanthropy, but to be responsible in not overlooking a pool of prospective employees that is often not considered in the equation. This is not to say that every prison inmate is right for our companies, but to instead entertain the financial and accessible feasibility of hiring persons (both men and women) who want to work hard and need the opportunity to do so. And, this is not about hiring the "lessor among us," but to seek the "gold hidden behind and beneath a bushel."

7   Yes, many among the prison population are the very best of people, both in skill and desire, and in character and spirit. These people represent a select group who did the crime and served their time. They possess abilities, skills, and talents that range from refined artistic propensities, technical adeptness, and computer literacy, to management skills, professional polish, and interpersonal qualities.

And, while they may need the power of your push or the compassion of your pull, they are people who can and will show a watching world that it is possible to "turn a large ship in a harbor."

8   If they can turn their lives around from the dungeons of prison to the epic of hope, they can also be a tremendous testimony to what is possible in the world of Hispanic business and to society at large.

FOR DISCUSSION: Do you think this article might persuade businesspersons to hire ex-convicts? Would you be persuaded if you could hire? Why or why not? Give a detailed explanation of your views about hiring individuals who have been through a vocational training program in prison.

◆◆◆

ONE OF OUR OWN: TRAINING NATIVE TEACHERS FOR THE 21ST CENTURY*

Suzette Brewer

The author, a Cherokee, explains how Native American children can benefit from being taught by native teachers.

1   As a first-grader in Farmington, New Mexico in 1980, Regine Brown was excited about the traditional Navajo dress her grandmother had made for her and couldn't wait to wear it to school. That day, she also wore a beaded necklace that had been given to her by her great-great-great grandmother.

2   When she got to school, rather than admiring her attire, a non-Indian teacher with no evident cultural understanding of the dress or the necklace derided her for not wearing "normal clothes." The teacher tore off the beaded necklace in front of Brown's classmates as the little girl stood in embarrassed silence, watching all 150 beads of the necklace sprinkle to the floor.

3   "I got down on my hands and knees and picked up each and every bead, because I knew how many there were," remembers Brown, now 27. "When I picked them up, I gave myself 150 reasons why I was a good person. It showed me not to treat kids that way because it ruins them mentally."

4   It was an incident that she would never forget, a scene that seared itself permanently into her heart and mind—and one that would ultimately serve to motivate Brown as an educator to change the world in her own way: teaching Navajo children the importance and pride of their heritage while preparing them with a solid base of academics.

5   She is not alone. It is the kind of experience that Indian children have faced since the beginning of European colonization: the destruction of their culture and sense of self in the very school systems that had been set up to educate them. As a result, many Indian adults have bad memories of school and are not motivated to let their own children be subjected to the same treatment. This, say experts,

Native Peoples, March–April 2002, pp. 52–53.

contributes to the low educational attainment and retention rates among the nation's K–12 Native students.

6   Today, however, Brown and many like her are attending tribal colleges to become teachers in their own home communities, filling a critical need in local tribal K–12 schools where Indian children have very few role models to look to in their education. Brown, who wants to teach bilingual elementary education on the Navajo reservation, will graduate from Diné College in Tsaile, Arizona in May.

7   Diné College's teacher training program—unofficially referred to as "grow your own"—is one of the few in the country that is geared specifically toward tribal culture, and Diné is one of a handful of tribal colleges that are now offering teaching degrees. Others, like Sinte Gleska University in South Dakota and Salish-Kootenai Community College in Montana, are also offering four-year teaching degrees. Some of the two-year tribal colleges, like Ft. Berthold in New Town, North Dakota and Lac Courte Oreilles Ojibwa Community College in Hayward, Wisconsin, have matriculation agreements with state colleges so students may finish their degrees and become teachers.

8   It is a trend that many involved in Indian education feel is necessary, not only for the role modeling, but also for improving student retention rates and test scores. And in areas of the country where the Native language is spoken as a first language, experts say that bilingual, bicultural education is the key to success in preserving unique Indian cultures that may be endangered while giving Indian children the tools to navigate mainstream society.

9   "We know that dealing with two languages is a lot easier in a school setting, teaching both at the same time," says Ben Barney, a professor and cultural specialist at Diné College. "Cognitive thought and language in terms of reading, writing and comprehension are more sophisticated when a person is proficient in multiple languages, because it forces the person to think on a number of different levels at the same time."

10   Therefore, says Barney, bilingual instruction enhances a person's education because it increases their ability to think, read and write in two languages, which is a significant focus of Diné's teacher training program. It is a teaching method that is just as valid and important, he says, as for those children who attend private schools with language programs that focus on Western European languages, such as French and German.

11   Bilingual Navajo-English teaching is why he believes the Diné program is so successful, with nearly all of the students being recruited for teaching positions prior to graduation. It is clearly filling a sorely needed gap in tribal education. "We didn't want the standard teacher education program at Diné," Barney says. "The mainstream program does not fit here."

12   Many times, he says, teachers who have been trained at mainstream universities come to the reservation and have to be retrained to suit the needs, culture and atmosphere of the Indian population. By using teaching methods that have been proven to work among Indian students, Barney says the success rates for both students and teachers increase.

13   "The teacher education program here is a core-language program that can be fitted to suit any tribe—not just the Navajo," Barney says. "But the language

element and culture are both very important because they work in tandem with who these children are as Native people and how they view the world."

14   Many Indian people believe, in fact, that the survival of their Native languages is crucial because much of their culture lies within their language and loses some of its meaning when translated into English.

15   "English is the dominant language of the United States, and as soon as you put a Native person in their traditional dress they become a toy to mainstream culture, which is diminishing to them," says Barney. "But in our program, you don't have to take off your 'Navajo-ness' at the door to be a teacher—self-identity and acceptance of oneself are an important part of our mission in training teachers for elementary education."

16   For students like Regine Brown, being able to reverse the trend of centuries of governmental policies and to give children on the Navajo reservation a sense of pride and self-esteem in their education is the happy outcome of a childhood incident that might have turned her away from education for good.

17   "This was something I promised myself," she says. "The kids on the rez need someone of their own to teach—someone who understands them, their backgrounds and where they're coming from culturally. And it's something that I'm looking forward to when I graduate."

FOR DISCUSSION: In your opinion, should teachers serve as role models for the students they teach? Why or why not? Do you favor bilingual education for children who speak a language other than English when they start school? Why or why not? Would you like to be taught by teachers who represent your culture or gender? Why or why not?

◆◆◆

WHY I WANT A WIFE*

Judy Brady

Judy Brady's famous essay first appeared in *Ms.* in 1971.

1   I belong to that classification of people known as wives. I am A Wife. And, not altogether incidentally, I am a mother.

2   Not too long ago a male friend of mine appeared on the scene fresh from a recent divorce. He had one child, who is, of course, with his ex-wife. He is looking for another wife. As I thought about him while I was ironing one evening, it suddenly occurred to me that I, too, would like to have a wife. Why do I want a wife?

3   I would like to go back to school so that I can become economically independent, support myself, and, if need be, support those dependent upon me. I want a wife who will work and send me to school. And while I am going to school I want a wife to take care of my children. I want a wife to keep track of the

---

*Reprinted by permission of the author.

children's doctor and dentist appointments. And to keep track of mine, too. I want a wife to make sure my children eat properly and are kept clean. I want a wife who will wash the children's clothes and keep them mended. I want a wife who is a good nurturant attendant to my children, who arranges for their schooling, makes sure that they have an adequate social life with their peers, takes them to the park, the zoo, etc. I want a wife who takes care of the children when they are sick, a wife who arranges to be around when the children need special care, because, of course, I cannot miss classes at school. My wife must arrange to lose time at work and not lose the job. It may mean a small cut in my wife's income from time to time, but I guess I can tolerate that. Needless to say, my wife will arrange and pay for the care of the children while my wife is working.

4   I want a wife who will take care of *my* physical needs. I want a wife who will keep my house clean. A wife who will pick up after my children, a wife who will pick up after me. I want a wife who will keep my clothes clean, ironed, mended, replaced when need be, and who will see to it that my personal things are kept in their proper place so that I can find what I need the minute I need it. I want a wife who cooks the meals, a wife who is a *good* cook. I want a wife who will plan the menus, do the necessary grocery shopping, prepare the meals, serve them pleasantly, and then do the cleaning up while I do my studying. I want a wife who will care for me when I am sick and sympathize with my pain and loss of time from school. I want a wife to go along when our family takes a vacation so that someone can continue to care for me and my children when I need a rest and change of scene.

5   I want a wife who will not bother me with rambling complaints about a wife's duties. But I want a wife who will listen to me when I feel the need to explain a rather difficult point I have come across in my course of studies. And I want a wife who will type my papers for me when I have written them.

6   I want a wife who will take care of the details of my social life. When my wife and I are invited out by my friends, I want a wife who will take care of the babysitting arrangements. When I meet people at school that I like and want to entertain, I want a wife who will have the house clean, will prepare a special meal, serve it to me and my friends, and not interrupt when I talk about things that interest me and my friends. I want a wife who will have arranged that the children are fed and ready for bed before my guests arrive so that the children do not bother us. I want a wife who takes care of the needs of my guests so that they feel comfortable, who makes sure that they have an ashtray, that they are passed the hors d'oeuvres, that they are offered a second helping of the food, that their wine glasses are replenished when necessary, that their coffee is served to them as they like it. And I want a wife who knows that sometimes I need a night out by myself.

7   I want a wife who is sensitive to my sexual needs, a wife who makes love passionately and eagerly when I feel like it, a wife who makes sure that I am satisfied. And, of course, I want a wife who will not demand sexual attention when I am not in the mood for it. I want a wife who assumes the complete responsibility for birth control, because I do not want more children. I want a wife who will remain sexually faithful to me so that I do not have to clutter up my intellectual life

with jealousies. And I want a wife who understands that *my* sexual needs may entail more than strict adherence to monogamy. I must, after all, be able to relate to people as fully as possible.

8   If, by chance, I find another person more suitable as a wife than the wife I already have, I want the liberty to replace my present wife with another one. Naturally, I will expect a fresh, new life; my wife will take the children and be solely responsible for them so that I am left free.

9   When I am through with school and have a job, I want my wife to quit working and remain at home so that my wife can more fully and completely take care of a wife's duties.

10   My God, who *wouldn't* want a wife?

FOR DISCUSSION: What is Brady really saying when she says she wants a wife? What solutions would you propose for the problem of who should be responsible for all of the tasks and duties described in this essay?

E. CLASS DISCUSSION AND WRITING ASSIGNMENT: INTERNATIONAL ARGUMENT

Read the following article, in which the author explains what "yes" (*hai*) means in Japanese. Are there other examples of words, gestures, customs, beliefs, or values like this one that could create confusion or distrust among people from different cultures? Draw on the experiences of international students both in and outside of class and on international news reports. Write a paper in which you explain one of the differences you have identified, along with what would be required to achieve common ground and better understanding.

A SIMPLE "HAI" WON'T DO*

Reiko Hatsumi

Reiko Hatsumi writes novels as well as essays.

1   Having spent my life between East and West, I can sympathize with those who find the Japanese *yes* unfathomable. However, the fact that it sometimes fails to correspond precisely with the Occidental *yes* does not necessarily signal intended deception. . . . It marks a cultural gap that can have serious repercussions.

2   I once knew an American who worked in Tokyo. He was a very nice man, but he suffered a nervous breakdown and went back to the U.S. tearing his hair and exclaiming, "All Japanese businessmen are liars." I hope this is not true. If it were, all Japanese businessmen would be driving each other mad, which does not seem

---

New York Times, April 15, 1992, p. A12.

to be the case. Nevertheless, since tragedies often arise from misunderstandings, an attempt at some explanation might not be amiss.

3   A Japanese *yes* in its primary context simply means the other has heard you and is contemplating a reply. This is because it would be rude to keep someone waiting for an answer without supplying him with an immediate response.

4   For example: a feudal warlord marries his sister to another warlord. . . . Then he decides to destroy his newly acquired brother-in-law and besieges his castle. Being human, though, the attacking warlord worries about his sister and sends a spy to look around. The spy returns and the lord inquires eagerly, "Well, is she safe?" The spy bows and answers "*Hai,*" which means "yes." We sigh with relief thinking, "Ah, the fair lady is still alive!" But then the spy continues, "To my regret she has fallen on her sword together with her husband."

5   *Hai* is also an expression of our willingness to comply with your intent even if your request is worded in the negative. This can cause complications. When I was at school, our English teacher, a British nun, would say, "Now children, you won't forget to do your homework, will you?" And we would all dutifully chorus, "Yes, mother," much to her consternation.

6   A variation of *hai* may mean, "I understand your wish and would like to make you happy but unfortunately . . ." Japanese being a language of implication, the latter part of this estimable thought is often left unsaid.

7   Is there, then, a Japanese *yes* that corresponds to the Western one? I think so, particularly when it is accompanied by phrases such as *sodesu* (It is so) and *soshimasu* (I will do so). A word of caution against the statement, "I will think about it." Though in Tokyo this can mean a willingness to give one's proposal serious thought, in Osaka, another business center, it means a definite *no*. This attitude probably stems from the belief that a straightforward *no* would sound too brusque.

8   When talking to a Japanese person it is perhaps best to remember that although he may be speaking English, he is reasoning in Japanese. And if he says "I will think about it," you should inquire as to which district of Japan he hails from before going on with your negotiations.

FOR DISCUSSION: Give some examples of what Japanese persons may really mean when they say yes as described in this article. Do you ever say one thing and mean something else? Give an example. What effect does this have in your communication with others?

◆◆◆

Chapter 3

A Process for Reading Argument

This chapter focuses on how to identify an argumentative purpose in a text and also on how to employ active reading strategies to help you read argument. The next chapter focuses on employing active writing strategies to help you write argument. Reading and writing are artificially separated in these two chapters for the sake of instruction. In actual practice, however, they should be integrated activities. To get you started using reading and writing together, the "Write While You Read" box contains a simple idea that can have a huge impact on improving the quality of your reading. Look for other connections between the reading and writing processes while you read this chapter and the next.

You will need a variety of strategies to help you do the reading and writing required by your college courses. These strategies will be most useful to you if you approach them as *processes*. You will usually adapt your reading process to the level of difficulty and to your purpose for reading specific materials. For example, much of what you read in college will be *academic writing* assigned by your professors and found in textbooks, academic journals, and other scholarly sources such as the library and certain Internet sites. Such material may seem complex and unfamiliar, especially at the beginning of the class: it is new to you, it contains specialized vocabulary, it is dense with many new ideas, and, compared with easier material, it will often contain fewer examples and transitions. Its sentences and paragraphs are often longer as well.

You will be able to use the information you are learning about reading argument to help you read such material; because the ideas you encounter in academic reading are often controversial, the authors take positions on them. Your purpose in reading such material is not only to understand it but also to analyze the issues, to evaluate the positions taken on them, and perhaps to take positions yourself and write about them. You will need a well-developed and strategic reading and writing process to help you meet the requirements of these demanding tasks.

WRITE WHILE YOU READ

You are probably willing to admit, along with most students, that you sometimes read without thinking. You may begin a reading assignment by counting the pages. Then you go back to stare at the words (or the computer screen) until you reach the end. During this process, your mind is blank or focused elsewhere. The best and quickest way to change this blank reading pattern is to *write while you read*. As soon as you begin reading with a pencil or pen (not a highlighter) in hand—underlining, writing ideas in the margin, summarizing, writing responses—everything changes. *You have to think to write.*

Furthermore, writing while you read helps you with two types of thinking. First, you will *think about* the material you read and perhaps even rephrase it so that it makes better sense to you. Second, you will *think beyond* the material you read and use it to help you generate ideas for your own writing. Your reading, in other words, becomes a springboard for your original thoughts and ideas. So pick up a pencil now and begin to write as you read. This process may take a little more time, but you will end up knowing far more than you would by "just reading," and your book with your annotations and ideas in it will be a valuable addition to your personal library.

At other times, you will use a simpler process to read simpler writing. The material you read in most newspapers and popular magazines has shorter sentences and paragraphs, simpler vocabulary, and fewer ideas. Important ideas are also often set off with transitions and explained through examples or pictures. You will use a simpler process when reading material of this type. For examples of both types of material, see "The Marriage Problem: How Our Culture Has Weakened Families" by James Q. Wilson in "The Reader" (pages 466–472). It is more scholarly than "The Mystery of Attraction" by Harville Hendrix (pages 481–487). As you sample these essays, notice that you adapt your reading process to the level of difficulty they present. Before we look at possible reading processes, however, let us consider how you can recognize an argumentative purpose in the material you read.

RECOGNIZING WRITTEN ARGUMENT

Some texts are obviously intended as argument, and others conceal their argumentative purpose, making it more difficult to recognize. You will recognize an argumentative purpose more easily if you think of a continuum of six types of writing that ranges from obvious argument at one extreme to objective writing at the other. Each of the six types exhibits not only a different authorial intention but also a different relationship between the author and the audience.

1. *Obvious argument.* The author's purpose is clearly and obviously to take a position and to change minds or to convince others. The author's point of view and purpose are clearly expressed along with reasons and supporting details that appeal to a wide audience.

2. *Extremist argument.* Authors who are "true believers" and who write about causes or special projects sometimes use strong values and emotional language to appeal to narrow audiences who already share their views. The aim is to strengthen these views. Imagine a labor union leader, for example, who is writing to workers to convince them to strike. The author's purpose is clearly to persuade.

3. *Hidden argument.* An argumentative purpose is not always obvious. Some ostensibly objective texts, on close examination, actually favor one position over another, but not in an obvious, overt manner. One sign that the text is not totally objective is the presence of selected supporting material that favors a particular point of view. Also, the presence of emotional language, vivid description, or emotional examples can be another sign that the author has strong opinions and intends not only to inform but also to convince the audience. For example, an author who actually favors reducing student financial aid writes an "objective" report about students who have received aid. However, all the students described in the article either left college early or defaulted on their loans, and they are described as dropouts and parasites on society. No examples of successful students are reported. Even though the author does not state a position or write this article as an obvious argument, it is still clear that the author has a position and that it manifests itself in biased reporting. The intention, even though concealed, is to convince.

4. *Unconscious argument.* Sometimes an author who is trying to write an objective report is influenced unconsciously by strong personal opinions about the subject, and the result is an unconscious intent to change people's minds. Imagine, for example, a strong pro-life newspaper reporter who is sent to write an objective expository article about an abortion clinic. It would be difficult for this individual to describe and explain the clinic without allowing negative perceptions to influence the way the facts are presented. Again, stacked or selected evidence, emotional language, quotations from authorities with well-known positions, or even pictures that establish a point of view may attest to an argumentative purpose while the author is unaware of it.

5. *Exploratory argument.* The author's purpose in exploratory articles, which are commonly found in newspapers and magazines, is to lay out and explain all of the major positions on a controversial issue. The audience is thus invited to view an issue from several perspectives and to understand all of them better. If the author has a position, it may not be revealed.

6. *Objective reporting.* Sometimes authors simply describe, explain, or report facts and ideas that everyone would accept without controversy. The author's own point of view, opinions, or interpretations are deliberately omitted. This is a pure form of expository writing. Examples include almanacs, data lists, weather reports, some news stories, and government, business, science, and technical reports. The audience reads such material to get information.

When you read and analyze argument, you will be studying and interpreting all these types of material with the exception of the last, objective reporting, and sometimes even there opinion creeps in. Now let's examine what you do at present when you read argument.

HOW DO YOU READ NOW?

You already have a reading process, but you may not have consciously adapted it to reading argument. What can you do to improve your present process for reading argument? Consider the following:

What do you do . . .
- ◆ Before you read argument?
- ◆ While you read argument?
- ◆ When the argumentative material is difficult?
- ◆ When you finish reading argument?

Many students describe their usual reading process by saying that they do nothing before they read, they then just read, they reread when the material is difficult, and they do nothing when they finish reading. If they add particular strategies for reading argument, these strategies are likely to include trying to identify both sides of the issue, trying to keep an open mind, deciding whether to agree or disagree with the author, or deciding what stand to take. Now consider what else you can do to help you read argument.

PREREADING STRATEGIES

Prereading helps you access what you know about a subject to help you interpret new, incoming material. If you know nothing about a subject, you will need to take special steps to learn more. Otherwise the new material will seem too difficult to read. Here we examine five prereading strategies to help you organize your prior knowledge about a subject, build background when you need it, and begin to analyze the material and make some predictions.

READ THE TITLE AND EXAMINE YOUR BACKGROUND ON THE ISSUE

Read the title and the first paragraph quickly to find out what is at issue. If you do not discover the issue there, read the last paragraph, where it is often stated, or read rapidly through the essay until you discover it. Then access your background on the issue by writing, in phrases only, eveything that comes to mind when you think of that issue. For example, suppose you read the article "Pay Your Own Way! (Then Thank Mom)" (pages 22–24). You are in college yourself, so you have some background on paying college costs. Your background on this subject might lead you to the following ideas.

> Working and saving money in high school
> Costs going up; need more money each year
> Getting a part-time job
> Parents helping some

You can already imagine what this article might be about, and you have created a context for reading it by thinking about what you already know.

Evaluate and Improve Your Background Information

When attempts to discover your background on an issue are unsuccessful and it is clear that you lack information, use some special strategies to help you build background. Find and read some other material on the subject that you can easily understand. An encyclopedia or easier books may be good sources of such information, or you can talk with someone who does understand the material, like a professor or a fellow student. Identify words that are used repeatedly and that you do not understand. Look them up in the glossary or dictionary, or figure them out from context.

Survey the Material

Survey a book or an article before you read it to get an introduction to the major ideas and a few of the supporting details.

Books. To survey a book (not a novel), follow these six steps in this order.

1. Read the *title*, and focus on what it tells you about the contents of the book.
2. Read the *table of contents*. Notice how the content has been divided into chapters and organized.
3. Read the *introduction*. Look for background information about the subject and author and also for information to help you read the book.
4. Examine the special *features* of the book. Are there headings and subheadings in boldface type to highlight major ideas? Is there a glossary? An index? A bibliography? Are there charts? Other visuals?
5. Read the title and first paragraph of the *first* and *last chapters* to see how the book begins and ends.
6. Read the title and first paragraph of the *other chapters* to get a sense of the flow of ideas.

This procedure should take about half an hour. It will introduce you to the main issue and approaches in a book, and reading will then be much easier.

Articles and Chapters. To survey an article or a chapter in a book, follow these six steps in this order.

1. Read the *title*, and focus on the information in it.
2. Read the *introduction*, which is usually the first paragraph but can be several paragraphs long. Look for a claim and any forecasts of what is to come.
3. Read the *last paragraph*, and look for the claim.
4. Read the *headings* and *subheadings*, if there are any, to get a sense of the ideas and their sequence. Read the first sentence of each paragraph, if there are no headings, to accomplish the same goal.
5. Study the *visuals:* pictures, charts, graphs. Read their captions. They often illustrate major ideas.
6. Identify the *key words* that represent the main concepts.

Surveying an article or chapter takes ten to fifteen minutes. It introduces you to the issue, the claim, and some of the subclaims and support. Survey before you read to make reading easier; survey when you do research to get a context for the material you quote; and survey when you review to help focus on the important ideas.

WRITE OUT YOUR PRESENT POSITION ON THE ISSUE

When you finish backgrounding and surveying, jot down your own current ideas and positions on the issue. This strategy will help guarantee your active interest as you read and will also promote an interaction between your ideas and the author's. Here is an example of an initial position statement in response to "Giving People a Second Chance" (pages 54–56).

> I favor the idea of a second chance for most people—unless they really do not deserve it because they have committed a particularly horrible crime.

MAKE SOME PREDICTIONS, AND WRITE ONE BIG QUESTION

Reading is a constant process of looking back at what you know and looking ahead to predict what you think may come next. Facilitate this natural process by linking what you know with what you predict will be in the text. Write your predictions and one big question to help focus your attention. Change your predictions as you read if they are off target and also stay open to the new ideas you did not predict. Finally, try to answer your big question when you finish reading. You might make a prediction like this about the article about giving people a second chance.

> This article will be in favor of giving the people he is writing about a second chance in life.

Here is a big question you might ask before you read.

> Who are these people, and why do they deserve a second chance?

READING STRATEGIES

You have been asked to describe how you read now. Did you indicate that you just read without doing anything in particular to improve your focus and concentration? You can often just read and understand enough, but you will usually need some special reading strategies to help you understand your college reading assignments and other complicated reading materials. Here are some suggestions to help you read such materials.

USE A PENCIL TO UNDERLINE AND ANNOTATE IMPORTANT IDEAS

As you begin to read, underline with a pen or pencil and write notes in the margin to help you concentrate and understand. These notes will also help you review and find information later. The key to marking a text is to do it selectively. Do not color an entire paragraph with a yellow highlighter. Instead, underline only the words and phrases that you can later reread and still get a sense of the whole. Then jot the major ideas in the margins, or summarize them at the ends of sections. Write the big ideas along with your personal reactions on the flyleaves of a book or at the ends of chapters or articles. If you do not own the book, write on self-stick notes and attach them to the book pages, or write on separate sheets of paper and keep them organized in a folder or in a section of your notebook.

Here is an example. This essay about girls and computers has been underlined and annotated as recommended. A brief summary has been added at the end to capture the main point. Note that this material is now very easy to understand and review.

GIRLS AND COMPUTERS*

girls behind

A <u>new report</u> by the American Association of University Women shows that a troubling <u>gender gap</u> in <u>computer use</u> exists in <u>high schools</u>. Girls make up only a <u>small percentage of students</u> who take high-level <u>computer courses</u> that might lead to technology careers. Yet they are <u>more likely</u> than boys to take <u>data-entry classes</u>, the high-tech equivalent of <u>typing</u>.

girls think boys better

The report also found that <u>girls</u> tend to use <u>computers in limited ways</u>, such as for word processing, while <u>boys</u> are more likely to use computers to <u>solve problems</u> or to develop their own programs. In one study, <u>girls</u> consistently <u>rated themselves</u> as <u>less competent</u> in computers than boys. This suggests that many girls are starting to see the <u>high-tech world</u> as a <u>masculine domain</u>.

games for boys

Some of the gender gap is created outside the classroom. <u>Computer toys</u> are more heavily marketed to <u>boys,</u> and most computer <u>games</u> and even educational software have more <u>male</u> characters than female characters. But <u>teachers</u> sensitive to these issues <u>could help</u> turn the situation around.

close gap-math

In 1992, the association raised the nation's awareness of a <u>gender gap</u> in enrollment in <u>math</u> and <u>science</u> courses in high school. In less than a decade, that gap has been narrowed because educators worked to <u>increase girls' participation</u>. Now educators must insure that <u>girls</u> are <u>not</u> inadvertently <u>left out</u> of the <u>computer</u> revolution.

girls behind with computers. Need to bring up to speed like did with math.

*New York Times, October 19, 1998, p. A20.

IDENTIFY AND READ THE INFORMATION IN THE INTRODUCTION, BODY, AND CONCLUSION

The organization of ideas in argumentative texts is not very different from other texts. Much of what you read, for example, follows the easily recognizable introduction, main body, and conclusion format. The introduction may provide background information about the issue and the author, get attention, state the main point, define important terms, or forecast some of the ideas to be developed in the main body. The main body will explain and develop the author's main point by giving reasons and support to prove it. The end or conclusion either summarizes by restating important points or concludes by stating the most important point, whatever it is that the author wants you to believe. Not all texts follow this pattern exactly, but enough of them do to justify your checking what you read against it.

LOOK FOR CLAIMS, SUBCLAIMS, SUPPORT, AND TRANSITIONS

All arguments have the structural components you are familiar with from other kinds of reading and writing. The main difference is their names. The special characteristics of the components of argument will be described when the Toulmin model is discussed in Chapter 5. We start using Toulmin's terms here, however, to help you get used to them. The thesis of an argument, which shapes the thinking of the entire text and states what the author finally expects you to accept or believe, is called the *claim*. The main ideas or *subclaims* are assertions, reasons, or supporting arguments that develop the claim. They are in themselves almost meaningless without further explanation. *Support* in the form of facts, opinions, evidence, and examples is the most specific material that provides additional information and further explanation. Support makes the claim and subclaims clear, vivid, memorable, and believable. *Transitions* lead the reader from one idea to another and also sometimes state the relationships among ideas. Furthermore, there is a constant movement between general and specific material in all texts, including argumentative texts, and this movement becomes apparent when the ideas are presented in various types of outline form.

UNDERSTAND THE KEY WORDS

Sometimes figuring out the meaning of one word in a difficult passage will suddenly make the whole passage easier to understand. For example, if you read the title of "A Simple 'Hai' Won't Do" (pages 60–61), you may be baffled by it until you learn that *hai* means "yes" in Japanese. Once you have that information, the article makes much more sense.

Unfortunately, many of us simply ignore words we do not know. Our eyes slide over unfamiliar words because there is nothing in our background to help us make sense of them. More thorough readers may stop when they see a strange word, discover they are stumped, and either dismiss the word or make an effort to puzzle it out.

When reading material suddenly seems difficult, go back and look for words you do not understand. Try to identify the key words, those that represent major concepts. In this chapter, *survey, claim, subclaim,* and *rhetorical situation* are examples of key words. First, read the context in which you find the word to help you understand it. A word may be defined in a sentence, a paragraph, or even several paragraphs. Major concepts in argument are often defined at length, and understanding their meaning will be essential to an understanding of the entire argument. If the context does not give you enough information, try the glossary, the dictionary, or another book on the subject. Remember that major concepts require longer explanations than a single synonym. Synonyms are useful for other minor words that are less critical to the understanding of the entire passage.

Analyze the Rhetorical Situation

Rhetorical situation is a term coined by Professor Lloyd Bitzer to describe the elements that combine to constitute a communication situation.[1] To understand these elements as they apply to argument helps us understand what motivates the argument in the first place, who the author is, who the intended audience is, how the audience might react to it, and how we as readers might also respond. By analyzing and understanding the rhetorical situation, we gain critical insight into the entire context as well as the parts of an argument, and this insight ultimately helps us evaluate its final success or failure. Analyzing the rhetorical situation is an important critical reading strategy that can be initiated during the prereading stages but should continue to be used as a tool for analysis throughout the reading process.

According to Bitzer, a rhetorical situation has five elements. Use the acronym TRACE, from the initial letters of these five elements, to help you remember them: the *Text*, the *Reader* or audience, the *Author*, the *Constraints*, and the *Exigence* or cause. Now look at each of them to see how they can help you understand and evaluate argumentative writing.

The *text* is the written argument, which has unique characteristics of its own that can be analyzed. These include such things as format, organization, argumentative strategies, language, and style.

The potential *reader* or audience for the text must care enough to read and pay attention, to change its perceptions as a result, and perhaps to mediate change or act in a new way. A rhetorical situation invites such audience responses and outcomes. Most authors have a targeted or intended reading audience in mind. You may identify with the targeted audience, or you may not, particularly if you belong to a different culture or live in a different time. As you read, compare your reactions to the text with the reactions you imagine the targeted or intended reading audience might have had.

The *author* writes an argument to convince a particular audience. You can analyze the author's position, motives, values, and varying degrees of expertise.

Constraints include the people, events, values, beliefs, and traditions that constrain or limit the targeted audience and cause it to analyze the situation and react to it in a particular way. They also include the character, background,

---

[1] Lloyd Bitzer, "The Rhetorical Situation," *Philosophy and Rhetoric* 1 (January 1968): 1–14.

available resources, and style of the author that limit or influence him or her to write in a certain way. The limits inherent in the type of text being produced, whether written, spoken, or visual, can also provide constraints. Constraints may bring people together or drive them apart. They influence the amount of common ground that will be established between an author and an audience. Here are some examples of constraints: an audience feels constrained to mistrust the media because it thinks reporters exaggerate or lie; reporters believe it is their responsibility to expose character flaws in candidates running for office, so they feel constrained to do so at every opportunity; candidates think voters want to hear rousing platitudes, so they deliver rousing platitudes; voters have lost their faith in public leaders, so they do not want to vote; people are too disturbed by the severity of the environmental crisis to want to listen to information about it, so they shut it out; people are too angry about destroyed property to consider peaceful solutions, so they threaten war; some welfare recipients fear that new changes in the system will deny food and shelter to them and their children, so they do not respond to training opportunities that may benefit them. Or, to continue with closer examples, you parked your car in a no-parking zone because you were late to class, but the police feel constrained by law to give you a ticket; you get a notice that you owe the bursar more money, but you thought you paid your tuition; you believe everyone should share the household chores, and your partner disagrees; you value the courses you took at another college, and you are told your present college will not accept them; you don't have reliable child care, so you cannot always attend classes; you do not particularly value college athletics, and you wish the money used to support them could be spent on something else; you are told a class is full, so you will have to take it next year; you see a banner in the cafeteria stating that the average student drinks one to four alcoholic beverages at a party, but you do not know whether to consider that amount good or bad since there are no other details. These constraining situations and circumstances will influence the way you react to the issues you encounter both in the material you read and in your life.

Exigence is the real-life dramatic situation that signals that something controversial has occurred and that people should try to make some sense of it. Exigence is a problem to be solved, a situation that requires some modifying response from an audience. Here are some examples of exigence for argument: people become suspicious of genetically engineered foods because of newspaper reports; several parents report that their children can access pornography on the Internet; a high school student shoots and kills several fellow students; too many homeless people are living in the streets and subways; a third-world country threatens to resume nuclear testing; politicians refuse to sign a nuclear test ban treaty; a football player is badly injured in a game and the fans of the opposing team cheer in delight; human rights are being violated in another country. In all cases, something is wrong, imperfect, defective, or in conflict. Exigence invites analysis and discussion, and sometimes also a written response to encourage both individual public awareness and discourse about problematic situations.

The following set of questions will help you analyze the rhetorical situation and get insight into its component parts.

1. *Text.* What kind of a text is it? What are its special qualities and features? What is it about?
2. *Reader or audience.* Who is the *targeted audience?* What is the nature of this group? Can it be convinced? What are the anticipated outcomes? How do *you as a reader* compare with the targeted audience? What are your constraints? How much common ground do you share with the author? What is your initial position? Are you motivated to change your mind or modify the situation? How?
3. *Author.* Who is the author? Consider background, experience, education, affiliations, and values. What is motivating the author to write?
4. *Constraints.* What special constraining circumstances will influence the audience's and author's responses to the subject? What beliefs, attitudes, prejudices, people, habits, events, circumstances, or traditions are already in place that will limit or constrain their perceptions?
5. *Exigence.* What happened to cause this argument? Why is it perceived as a defect or problem? Is it new or recurring?

Here is an analysis of the rhetorical situation for "We Knew What Glory Was" (pages 49–51).

Example

1. *Text.* This is an argumentative essay that uses narrative and description to convince the readers that it is wrong to burn African American churches.
2. *Reader or audience.* The targeted readers are people who have religious values and who enjoy reminiscing about the past. The author expects the readers to identify with her and to be horrified by the burning of the churches.
3. *Author.* The author is an African American woman whose father was the Baptist minister of a traditional black church in Connecticut. Every August he took his family to visit the South and the churches there. The author recalls these trips.
4. *Constraints.* Both the author and most readers are constrained by tradition, which includes the idea that churches should provide safety and sanctuary for their congregations. Churches and their members should automatically be protected from harm.
5. *Exigence.* Arsonists were deliberately burning black churches throughout the South at the time that the author wrote this article.

READ WITH AN OPEN MIND, AND ANALYZE THE COMMON GROUND BETWEEN YOU AND THE AUTHOR

Suppose you now begin to read the article on affirmative action, "A View from Berkeley" by Chang-Lin Tien (pages 51–54). Consider some typical responses that readers of argument sometimes make at this point. If you happen to agree with this author's ideas, you might read carefully, marking the best passages and insisting on reading them aloud to someone else. But if you believe that affirmative action provides unfair and unnecessary advantages for minorities, you may be tempted not to read at all or to read hastily and carelessly, dismissing the author as wrongheaded or mistaken. If you are neutral on this issue, with opinions on neither side, you might read with less interest and even permit your mind to wander. These responses, as you can see, will distract you and interfere in negative ways with your understanding of the article. Once you become aware of such unproductive responses, however, you can compensate for them by analyzing the common ground between you and the author and using this information to help you read more receptively and nonjudgmentally. What common ground do you have with Tien? When you have established that, try to generate interest, read with an open mind, and suspend major critical judgment until you have finished reading his article. Finally, reassess your original position to determine whether you now have reason to modify or change your perspective.

As you assess the common ground you think you share with the author, you can use written symbols to indicate how much or how little of it may exist: ◯ can mean you and the author are basically alike in your views and share common ground; ◯◯ can mean you are alike on some ideas but not on others and share some common ground; ◯◯ can mean your ideas are so different from the author's that there is no common ground; and *X* can mean that you are neutral in regard to the subject, that you consequently have little or no interest in it, and that you are not likely to agree, disagree, or establish common ground with the author. To avoid reading problems, you will now need to compensate for common ground differences that might interfere with comprehension. The symbols ◯ ◯, for disagreement and no common ground, and *X*, for neutral and no common ground, should signal that you will have to use all of the active strategies for reading that you can muster to give authors with whom you have no common ground a fair hearing.

STRATEGIES FOR READING DIFFICULT MATERIAL

Read a difficult text all the way through once, to the end, without stopping. You will understand some of it, but not all. Give yourself a comprehension score on a scale of 0 to 10, with 10 high. Now write brief lists of what you do and do not understand. Identify the words that are used repeatedly that you do not understand. Look them up in the glossary or dictionary, and analyze how they are used in context. Next, reread the material, using active reading strategies to help you get meaning. Add more items to the list of material that you can understand, and assess what you still do not understand. Give yourself a new comprehension score. You may want to reread again to gain even better understanding of what you could not understand on the first two readings. As a final step, get together with a fellow classmate or someone else who has read the material, and discuss it until you both understand it better. Consider how you would rate your comprehension now.

POSTREADING STRATEGIES

Postreading strategies help you think about the ideas in your reading and understand them better. They also improve your memory of what you have read. Here are several postreading strategies that will work for you.

MONITOR YOUR COMPREHENSION, CHECK THE ACCURACY OF YOUR PREDICTIONS, AND ANSWER YOUR QUESTIONS

At this point, insist on understanding. The results of reading are very much a private product that belongs to you and no one else. Only you can monitor and check your understanding of what you have read. One way to check is to look away to see if you can recite from memory the claim and some of the subclaims and support. If you cannot do this right after you have finished reading, you will probably not be able to do it later in discussion or on an exam. Reread, actively using reading strategies, and try again. Comprehension checks of this type help you concentrate and understand. Check your prereading predictions to see if they were accurate. You may need to change them. See if you can now answer the question you posed before you started reading.

DISCOVER THE ORGANIZATION, AND WRITE OUTLINES OR SUMMARIES

Outlines lay out ideas in a visual form and show how they are related to each other. Outlines also help you see the organization of ideas and remember them. Summaries condense and restate material in a briefer form that helps you understand and demonstrate to others that you have understood.

To make an outline, write the claim, the most general idea, at the left-hand margin; indent the subclaims under the claim; and indent the support—the specific facts, opinions, examples, illustrations, other data, and statistics—even further. You may not always need to write an outline. Sometimes you can make a simple mental outline to help you remember the claim and some of the ideas that support and develop it. Here is an outline of the essay "Why I Want a Wife" (pages 58–60).

OUTLINE OF "WHY I WANT A WIFE"
  Claim: I would like to have a wife.
    Subclaims: I could go back to school.
           My wife would work and run the household.
    Support (examples): She would take care of the children,
                 keep the house clean,
                 put my things away,
                 fix good meals,
                 listen to me,
                 take care of my social life, and
                 be sensitive to my sexual needs.
  Subclaim: My wife could be replaced if she didn't work out.

Support: If so, she gets the children and I start a new life.
Subclaims: When I finish school, my wife quits her job, stays home,
and becomes a better wife.
"Who *wouldn't* want a wife?"

To write a summary, you will need to answer the questions "What was this about?" and "What did the author say about it?" To help you answer those questions, follow these steps.

1. Read the title along with the beginning and ending sentences of the material you are summarizing. Jot down, in your own words, what you think it is about. You are identifying the issues and the claim.
2. Read and underline the subclaims that develop the claim. Now write, in your own words, a brief list of words or phrases that represent the subclaims, or the main points the author makes about the claim.

Two types of summaries can be useful to you. One is written only in words and phrases and is useful for your own quick review. The steps just outlined help you create such a summary. An example appears on page 68 in the margins and at the end of the annotated article about girls and computers.

A second type of summary, written in paragraph form with complete sentences, helps you understand an article and demonstrate to others that you have understood it. When you have completed steps 1 and 2 above, you will add step 3: using the words and phrases you have jotted down to guide you, write a summary in your own words that includes the claim and the most important ideas that develop it. The following is such a summary of "Why I Want a Wife."

SUMMARY OF "WHY I WANT A WIFE." Judy Brady's newly divorced friend wants a wife, which makes Brady reflect on why she, herself, might also like a wife. A wife could take care of the children and run the household while Brady goes back to school. Even though the wife also works, she will be expected to take care of the home as well. A wife could cook, clean, take care of the clothes, never complain, and listen to Brady when she wants to talk. A wife could arrange all of the family's social life and also provide a great sex life. If the wife does not perform adequately, the wife could be replaced with a better one. Brady concludes, "Who *wouldn't* want a wife?"

MAKE A MAP

As an alternative to outlines or summaries, make a map of the ideas in a text. For many students, maps are the preferred way to reduce and reorganize the material they read. To make a map, write the most important idea, the claim, in a circle or on a line, and then attach major subclaims and support to it. Make your map in very brief form. Figures 3.1 and 3.2 (page 76) are possible maps of the essays "Why I Want a Wife" and "Girls and Computers." You can be creative with map formats. Use whatever layout will give you a quick picture of the major ideas.

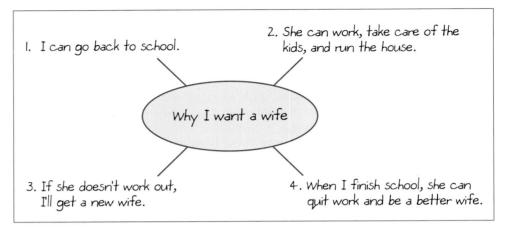

FIGURE 3.1   Map of Ideas for "Why I Want a Wife."

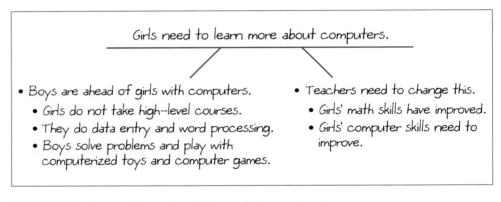

FIGURE 3.2   Map of Ideas for "Girls and Computers."

THINK CRITICALLY AND WRITE A RESPONSE

By the time you have written an outline, a summary, or a map to help you understand the ideas in an argumentative essay, you will also have formed some opinions of your own on the issue. Write a response to the essay to help you capture
some of your ideas in writing. These ideas can be starting points for future essays.
Here are some ideas and suggestions for what you might include in a response.

◆ Write your position now.
◆ Compare it with your initial position before you read the essay.
◆ Compare the author's position with your own. Do you agree or disagree?
◆ Add examples, suggestions, or other ideas of your own that the essay made
   you think about.
◆ What do you finally think about the essay? Is it convincing or not?

Your assessment of whether an essay convinces you or not, backed up with some reasons for this judgment, constitutes one kind of evaluation. Your professor may also want you to evaluate the quality of what you have read. (Criteria for evaluation, particularly for Internet sources of uneven quality, appear on pages 332–334.)

Here is an example of a response to the essay "Why I Want a Wife."

This essay is a condemnation of men who expect their wives to work and take care of the house without any help. This essay has not changed my mind. I agreed with Brady before I read it, and I agree even more strongly now. The essay is humorous, but it is also an angry response to the division of labor issue that exists in many households. Every household needs a housewife to do the chores and keep the family's life running smoothly. Some, but certainly not all, women take on these responsibilities with a reasonable degree of contentment. Others do not, either because of outside work or because they hate this type of work. Families have to solve this problem to avoid constant conflict. A division of labor exists in every other workplace. Why can't a reasonable division of labor also be created at home? I favor an equal division of chores for all members of the household so that everyone gets fair and equal treatment.

ORGANIZING A PROCESS FOR READING ARGUMENT

The reading process for argument explained in this chapter and summarized in Box 3.1 (pages 78–79) integrates prereading, reading, and postreading strategies and incorporates writing at every stage. Before you embark on this process, however, here are three cautionary notes.

1. Read as you usually do, using your own reading process for most reading. Add strategies either when you are not getting enough meaning or when your comprehension is breaking down altogether.
2. Be advised that no one uses all of the reading strategies described in this chapter all of the time. Instead, you should select those that are appropriate to the task, that is, appropriate for a particular type of material and for your reading purpose. You need to practice all of the strategies so that you are familiar with them, and you will be given an opportunity to do so in the exercises and activities. Later, in real-life reading, you will be selective and use only strategies that apply to a particular situation.
3. Even though the strategies will be laid out in an apparent order under the various headings, there is no set order for employing them. You may find yourself stopping to do some prereading in the middle of a difficult text, or you may stop to summarize a section of material, a postreading strategy, before you continue reading. The order of presentation simply makes the strategies easier to explain and use.

BOX 3.1   **A Summary of the Reading Process for Argument Explained in This Chapter.**

READING ARGUMENT

PREREADING STRATEGIES

Read the title and first paragraph; check your background on the issue. Identify the issue. Free-associate and write words and phrases that the issue brings to mind.

Evaluate and improve your background. Do you know enough? If not, read or discuss to get background. Look up a key word or two.

Survey the material. Identify the claim (the main assertion) and some of the subclaims (the ideas that support it); notice how they are organized. Do not slow down and read.

Write out your present position on the issue.

Make some predictions, and write one big question. Jot down two or three ideas that you think the author may discuss, and write one question you would like to have answered.

READING STRATEGIES

Use a pencil to underline and annotate the ideas that seem important. Write a brief summary at the end.

Identify and read the information in the introduction, body, and conclusion.

Look for the claim, subclaims, and support. Box the transitions to highlight relationships between ideas and changes of subject.

Find the key words that represent major concepts, and jot down meanings if necessary.

Analyze the rhetorical situation. Remember TRACE: text, reader, author, constraints, exigence.

Read with an open mind, and analyze the common ground between you and the author.

STRATEGIES FOR READING DIFFICULT MATERIAL

Read all the way through once without stopping.

Write a list of what you understand and what you do not understand.

Identify words and concepts you do not understand, look them up, and analyze how they are used in context.

Reread the material, and add to your list of what you can and cannot understand.

Reread again if you need to.

Discuss the material with someone who has also read the material and get further clarification and understanding.

POSTREADING STRATEGIES

Monitor your comprehension. Insist on understanding. Check the accuracy of your predictions, and answer your question.

(continued)

Box 3.1 (continued)

Analyze the organization, and write either a simplified outline or a summary to help you understand and remember. Or make a map.

Write a response to help you think.

Compare your present position with your position before you read the argument.

Evaluate the argument, and decide whether it is convincing or not.

The reading strategies described in this chapter—assessing your background, predicting, asking questions, surveying, analyzing the rhetorical situation, summarizing, writing simple outlines, making maps, and writing responses—all work. They help you access what you already know, relate it to new material, see the parts as well as the whole, rephrase the material in your own words, reduce it to a manageable size, and think critically about it. Research studies have demonstrated that these activities help readers understand, analyze, remember, and think about the material they read.

REVIEW QUESTIONS

1. What are some of the signs of a hidden argumentative purpose in an ostensibly objective essay?
2. What are the five elements in the rhetorical situation? Use TRACE to help you remember.
3. What are some prereading strategies that you will now want to use?
4. What are some reading strategies that you will now want to use?
5. What are some postreading strategies that you will now want to use?
6. What can you do when the material is difficult to understand?

EXERCISES AND ACTIVITIES

A. CLASS DISCUSSION: RECOGNIZING WRITTEN ARGUMENT

The following newspaper article was published on the front page of the *New York Times* as an objective story about some people in Los Angeles after riots in 1992 that were a reaction to the acquittal of four police who beat an African American man named Rodney King. First, identify what seems to be the main issue in this article. It is not directly stated. Then read the article carefully to see if you can recognize the author's attitudes, feelings, and opinions toward the subject at issue. What is the author's intention in this article? To explain? To convince? Or both? What does the author hope you will think when you finish reading? Justify your answer with specific examples from the article.

JOBS ILLUMINATE WHAT RIOTS HID: YOUNG IDEALS*

Sara Rimer

1   When Disneyland came two weeks ago to the First A.M.E. Church in South-Central Los Angeles to hold interviews for 200 summer jobs, it was a good-will gesture born of the riots.

2   When more than 600 young men and women, many in coats and ties or dresses showed up, the Disney officials were taken aback.

3   America has been bombarded with television images of the youth of South-Central Los Angeles: throwing bricks, looting stores, beating up innocent motorists. The Disneyland staff who interviewed the applicants, ages 17 to 22, found a different neighborhood.

4   "They were wonderful kids, outstanding kids," said Greg Albrecht, a spokesman for Disneyland. "We didn't know they were there." Nor, Mr. Albrecht added, had they known that the young people of South-Central Los Angeles would be so eager to work at Disneyland.

5   Joe Fox, a spokesman for the First A.M.E. Church, said that had there been time to better publicize the Disneyland jobs, thousands would have applied. "People just want to work, period," he said. With hundreds of small businesses destroyed during the riots, jobs are harder to find than ever.

6   One of the 600 who wanted to work at Disneyland was Olivia Miles, at 18 the youngest of seven children of a nurse's aide and a disabled roofer. "My friend Lakesha's mother told us Disneyland was hiring," said Miss Miles, who has worked at McDonald's and Popeye's since she was 15. "I said: 'Disneyland! C'mon, let's go!'"

7   Miss Miles will graduate on June 30 from one of South-Central Los Angeles's public high schools, Washington Preparatory, where she has earned mostly A's and B's and was the co-captain of the drill team. Next fall, she will attend Grambling University in Louisiana.

8   Washington has 2,600 students; 70 percent are black, 30 percent are Hispanic. The principal, Marguerite LaMotte, says that as impressive as Olivia Miles is, she is not exceptional. "I have a lot of Olivia's," she said. Indeed, 118 seniors plan to attend four-year colleges and 131 will go to two-year colleges.

9   The world knows about the gang members; estimates put the number at 100,000 across Los Angeles County, and last year there were 771 gang-related homicides. No one has tried to count the young people like Olivia Miles. They are among the invisible people of South-Central Los Angeles.

10 In some ways, Miss Miles is just another high school senior. One of her favorite shows is *Beverly Hills 90210*. She admires Bill Cosby and Oprah Winfrey. She enjoys reading books by Maya Angelou. And shopping. She loves soft-spoken, 17-year-old Damon Sewell, the defensive football captain at nearby Hawthorne High School. He will go on to Grambling with her.

New York Times, June 18, 1992, pp. A1, A12.

11   Miss Miles and Mr. Sewell and their friends who live in the neighborhood pay a terrible price because of geography. They have to worry about simply staying alive. They have friends who have been shot and killed. They can't even get dressed in the morning without thinking, red and blue are gang colors; wearing them is dangerous. Then they have to confront the stigma that comes with being young and black and from Los Angeles.

12   "The neighborhood is famous now," Miss Miles said on Saturday as she and Mr. Sewell gave a tour of the devastation. They were just 15 minutes away from Beverly Hills and Hollywood. Miss Miles's tone was plaintive. "Why did it have to be famous for a riot? Why couldn't it be famous for people getting up in the world, or making money, or being actors?"

13   Getting ahead, despite enormous obstacles, is the story of the Miles family. Her parents, Aubrey and Willie Mae Miles, grew up in the South and migrated to Los Angeles. They started their lives together in an apartment in Watts and eventually bought a two-bedroom on 65th Street, in the heart of South-Central Los Angeles.

14   Olivia remembers playing softball on the block with another little girl, LaRonda Jones, who became her best friend and who will attend Santa Monica Community College next year. She also remembers how scared she was at night.

15   "I would lie in bed and hear the police helicopters overhead," she said.

16   Her four sisters and two brothers are all high school graduates. Except for 22-year-old Tracy, who is home with a 2-year-old daughter, they are all working. Shirley has a job in a school cafeteria. Cynthia is a mail carrier. Jacqueline is a cashier at Dodger Stadium. William is a custodian at police headquarters. Masad drives a school bus. Olivia visited Disneyland once, when she was 8. Jacqueline took her.

17   Mrs. Miles said she had never been there. Admission is $28.75 for adults, $23 for children 3 to 11. "Disneyland's a little high for me," she said.

18   Olivia Miles is tall and slim and walks with her head held high. "My mama tells me: 'Be the best of everything; be proud, be black, be beautiful,'" she said.

19   Miss Miles knew some white people when her family lived briefly in Long Beach, but that was years ago. She says she wishes there were white students at her high school. "I want to learn about different cultures," she said. She believes a job at Disneyland will give her that chance.

20   Aubrey Miles, who is 45, says he has taken pains to tell his daughter that there are good white people. They saved his life, he told her. He was putting a roof on an office building seven years ago when a vat of hot tar exploded. He was severely burned.

21   "The guys on the job, who were white, helped me," he said. "I was on the ground, on fire. They put the fire out. One guy sat me up and put his back against my back. I could feel the connection. Then, afterward in the hospital, it was the same thing with the doctors."

22   Mr. Miles was speaking by telephone from Gautier, Miss. He and his wife moved there last year to care for Mrs. Miles's mother. Olivia remained in Los Angeles with her sister Shirley so she could graduate with her friends.

23   By last September, she and Mr. Sewell were already talking about the prom. It was set for May 1 in Long Beach. To save money for the big night, Mr. Sewell, whose father was recently laid off from his machinist's job at McDonnell-Douglas, worked as many hours at McDonald's as he could get.

24   Two days before the prom, Miss Miles still needed shoes. After school, she caught the bus to the Payless store at Crenshaw Plaza. It was April 29, the day the four policemen who beat Rodney G. King were acquitted.

25   "This lady on the bus told me, 'Baby, you better hurry up and get in the house,'" she said. "I said, 'Why, what's going on?' She said, 'The verdict was not guilty.'"

26   Miss Miles bought her shoes—"two pairs for $24.99"—and went home. The prom was postponed because of the riots. Watching the images of fire and violence engulf her neighborhood on television, she wept. "It hurt me when they beat that man in the truck up," she said. "I didn't know people could be that mean."

27   Her parents kept telephoning. "I was asking my Daddy, 'Why did this happen, why are they doing this?'" Miss Miles said. "He told me some people were just using it as an excuse, and some people were hurt that those cops didn't get any time."

28   Mr. Miles said the acquittal shattered his daughter. "She was about to lose it," he said. "She kept saying: 'Why am I working so hard? Why have you been telling me that I can achieve?' She had been sheltered. This was reality."

29   Mr. Miles, who grew up in a segregated Louisiana, said he had agonized over how to comfort her. "I didn't want her to just use it to sit on the curb and say, 'I'm black so I can't achieve,'" he said. "I told her: 'Don't let this stop you. You're going to college. Keep going on, even though you will be met with discrimination.'"

30   "I was praying, and talking to her," he said. "I was worried. I'm still worried. The summer's not over. . . ."

31   His daughter plans to be a lawyer. So does Mr. Sewell.

32   The riots presented Olivia Miles with the biggest ethical quandary of her life. "I saw people on television coming out with boxes of shoes and pretty furniture," she said. Her smile was embarrassed. "It was like Christmas. I wanted to get some. I was asking my sister if we could go. She said, 'No, you can't go out.' I thought: 'She's going to go to work. Should I get it, or shouldn't I get it? It's not fair that I can't. Everyone else is going to get stuff.'"

33   This, too, her father had foreseen. "I told her, 'There are going to be a lot of opportunities for you to get things, so just stay in the house,'" Mr. Miles said. "She knew automatically that stealing was a no-no. . . ."

34   That Sunday, Olivia was in her regular pew at the Mt. Sinai Baptist Church. "The pastor was saying, 'If you took something, shame on you. That's a sin,'" she said. She looked relieved all over again. "I was so happy."

35   Three weeks later, she and Mr. Sewell went to the prom in Long Beach. "We loved it," Mr. Sewell said. "We loved it." He was surprised, he said, when his classmates voted him prom king.

36   "I felt like a queen," Miss Miles said. Last Friday, Disneyland telephoned: She got the job. This summer, she will be selling balloons and popcorn at the

amusement park, about 30 miles from her home, that calls itself "the happiest place on earth."

37   The job, which includes transportation furnished by Disneyland, will also be hers on holidays during the year. The pay is $5.25 an hour.

38   Miss Miles had made herself familiar with Disneyland's grooming code. "Good-bye, nails," she said exuberantly, holding out her long, manicured ones. "A job's a job! Disneyland's Disneyland. It's not like Popeye's or McDonald's. It's like 'Hey, girl, how'd you get that job at Disneyland?'"

FOR DISCUSSION: How does the description of "the kids" in South-Central Los Angeles in this essay contradict the usual stereotypes? What is the author trying to make you think about these young people? What new stereotypes are being developed? What do you think about these young people as a result of reading this essay? Have you modified any of your previous opinions?

◆◆◇

B. WRITING ASSIGNMENT: ANALYZING THE RHETORICAL SITUATION

Read "Don't Know Much about History." Then write a 300- to 400-word paper in which you explain the rhetorical situation for this essay. Answer the following questions using TRACE.

1. How would you describe the text itself?
2. How would you characterize the reader or audience that the author may have had in mind when she wrote this essay?
3. What do you learn about the author?
4. What are some of the possible constraints that might have influenced the author? What constraints influence you as you read this essay?
5. What is the exigence for this essay?

DON'T KNOW MUCH ABOUT HISTORY*

Roberta Israeloff

1   East Northport, [Long Island]. Though I vowed, on graduation from high school in 1969, that I was leaving the suburbs forever, I now live in a town that is just 20 minutes from the one I grew up in. For all its problems and faults, suburbia offered me a superior public education, and I wanted my sons to have one, too.

2   Yet no sooner did we enroll them than I began to have misgivings. Their work did not seem to engage them, to challenge them as much as I remembered being challenged. It wasn't until last month that I was able to confirm my suspicions.

---

*New York Times, June 15, 1996, p. A11.

3   My eighth grader brought home a research paper assignment for his American history course. Thirty-one years ago, I took a similar course—and I saved my
papers. Comparing the two assignments left no doubt: the older assignment was
vastly superior.

4   Back in 1965, we were given this quotation—from a turn-of-the-century
commentator named Lloyd, in a book called *William Jennings Bryan and the Campaign of 1896*—and asked to agree or disagree with it:

5   "The Free Silver movement is a fake. Free Silver is the cow-bird of the reform
movement. It waited until the nest had been built by the sacrifices and labour of
others, and then laid its eggs in it. . . . The People's Party has been betrayed. No
party that does not lead its leaders will ever succeed."

6   It took mind-splitting work just to decipher the quotation. And then, to fulfill
the assignment, my classmates and I had to explore and understand three distinct
phenomena. First, we had to digest gold and silver monetary standards. We had
to research the reform movement, tracing the evolution of the People's Party
from its origins. We had to sift through the politics of 1896, in which the Populists
had to decide whether to field their own candidate and risk losing the election, or
join the Democrats and risk annihilation.

7   After all this, we still had to figure out for which cause Lloyd was the mouth-
piece. The passage, I finally realized, was an attempt to rally the Populists to take
their own course—advice not taken. They nominated Bryan, who lost to William
McKinley, thereby destroying the People's Party.

8   I concluded by urging Lloyd to grow up. The point is to have your issue prevail even if your party doesn't. The People's Party may have fallen on its sword,
but it did so in a good cause.

9   In their assignment, my son and his classmates had to answer three questions. To the first, "Did we have to drop the bomb on Japan?" my son argued that
Harry S. Truman, as well as many others, had no idea of the full devastation the
atomic bomb would cause. On the second, whether it hastened a Japanese surrender, he equivocated. To the final question—"Is it fair to use the knowledge we
have in 1996 to judge decisions made nearly 50 years ago?"—he wrote, "The simple answer is no."

10   We both received the same grade on our papers—100.

11   I do not intend to disparage my son, who has always been a highly conceptual thinker and an A student, or to exalt myself, for I was not alone in my high
grade. But I think these two assignments illustrate a profound diminution of educational expectations.

12   When my classmates and I fulfilled our assignment, we couldn't help but
learn that the world was much more complex than we could imagine; that we
had to absorb reams of information before staking claim to an opinion; that objective "information" existed only within a context and issued from a point of
view, both of which had to be fully understood.

13   From my son's paper, I see no evidence that he has absorbed any of these lessons. The newer assignment—three straightforward questions positing three answers—is premised on the modern view that we are all entitled to an opinion, no
matter how little we may know.

14   To be honest, the ins and outs of the election of 1896 have not stayed with me. What has endured is the value I place on scholarship, argument and critical thinking. My teacher's high hopes for us, which at the time seemed far too ambitious to be fair, became the scaffolding upon which we built our careers and the ways we define ourselves.

15   As for my son and his classmates—the class of 2000—I'm not as hopeful. We expect terrifyingly little of today's students, and they are responding in kind.

FOR DISCUSSION: Agree or disagree with the author's final statement, "We expect terrifyingly little of today's students, and they are responding in kind." Provide an example, just as the author did, to support your view.

◆◆◇

C. CLASS PROJECT: CREATING A COMPOSITE OF THE CLASS'S READING PROCESS

When all class members contribute their usual strategies to a composite reading process, the result is usually a very complete description of a possible reading process. Focus on developing a process for reading argument, and write the title "Reading Argument" on the board. Under it write the four headings "Prereading," "Reading," "Reading Difficult Material," and "Postreading." Class members should contribute both the strategies they use and those they would like to use to each of the four lists. When the activity is completed, students may freewrite for a few minutes on the reading process that they intend to use to read argument. Freewriting is described on page 97.

D. GROUP WORK: PRACTICING THE READING PROCESS

Practice the active reading strategies described in this chapter as you work with "The Road to Unreality," which follows.

PREREADING

The whole class should preread together and discuss the results of prereading as follows:

1. Read the title and the first two or three paragraphs for one minute. What is the issue? What is your present position on the issue?
2. What ideas do you predict might be discussed in this essay? What question might be answered?
3. Survey the article for two minutes. Read the first sentence in each of the remaining paragraphs. Read the last paragraph. Look through the notes at the end to see what they contribute. What do you now think the essay is about?
4. How much do you understand at this point? What do you still want to find out? Give yourself a comprehension score from 0 to 10, with 10 high.

READING

Each class member should read, underline, and annotate the essay, including the notes, and then discuss the following questions.

1. How would you describe the rhetorical situation? Use TRACE.
2. Was your prereading accurate? Did the issue turn out to be what you thought? How would you describe the issue now?
3. What is the claim? What are subclaims? What are examples of support?
4. What is the author's conclusion?
5. What common ground, if any, exists between you and this author?
6. How much do you understand now? Give yourself a new score from 0 to 10.

POSTREADING

Work in pairs to write a summary-response. Share your results with the rest of the class.

1. Discuss the essay, decide what should be in a summary, and write a summary.
2. Discuss your summaries, and write a response.
3. Read your summary-response to the class.
4. How much do you understand now? Give yourself a final score from 0 to 10. How much have your scores improved since your prereading score?

THE ROAD TO UNREALITY*

Mark Slouka

1   In 1990, a reporter for the *New York Times*, following the famous case of a man accused of murdering his pregnant wife and then blaming the assault on an unknown black assailant, asked a neighbor of the couple for her thoughts on the tragedy. Do you accept his story? she was asked. Does it seem possible to you, knowing this man, that he made up the whole thing? "I don't know," the woman said, "I'm dying for the movie to come out so I can see how it ends."[1]

2   I don't think this woman was joking. Or being cynical. Or even evasive. I think she simply meant what she said. For her, a TV movie about the tragedy would tell her—more accurately than her own experience—what to believe. It would settle for her what was real. Less than a year later, the made-for-television movie *Good Night, Sweet Wife: A Murder in Boston* presumably did just that.

3   I bring up this episode for the light it sheds on an important cultural trend, a trend so pervasive as to be almost invisible: our growing separation from reality.[2] More and more of us, whether we realize it or not, accept the copy as the original. Increasingly removed from experience, overdependent on the representations of reality that come to us through television and the print media, we seem more and more willing to put our trust in intermediaries who "re-present" the world to us.

4   The problem with this is one of communication; intermediaries are notoriously unreliable. In the well-known children's game of telephone, a whispered message is passed along from person to person until it is garbled beyond

*Mark Slouka, *War of the Worlds: Cyberspace and the High-Tech Assault on Reality* (New York: Basic Books, 1995), pp. 1–4.

recognition. If we think of that original message as truth, or reality, we stand today at the end of a long line of interpreters. It's a line that's been growing longer throughout the century. And now, accustomed to our place at the end of that line, we've begun to accept the fictions that reach us as the genuine article. This is not good news. For one thing, it threatens to make us stupid. For another, it makes us, collectively, gullible as children: we believe what we are told. Finally, it can make us dangerous.

5   When did we start accepting abstractions for the real thing? Most answers point roughly to the beginning of this century. Before 1900, daily life for the majority of individuals was agrarian, static, local—in other words, not that different from what it had been for centuries. The twentieth century, however, altered the pace and pattern of daily life forever. Within two generations, the old world (for better or worse) was gone. Its loss meant the loss of two things that had always grounded us: our place within an actual community and our connection to a particular physical landscape.[3]

6   What started us on the road to unreality? Though the catalog reads like a shopping list of many of the century's most dramatic trends—urbanization, consumerism, increasing mobility, loss of regionality, growing alienation from the landscape, and so on—technology, their common denominator, was the real force behind our journey toward abstraction.

7   A single example may make my point. As everyone knows, unreality increases with speed. Walking across a landscape at six miles an hour, we experience the particular reality of place: its smells, sounds, colors, textures, and so on. Driving at seventy miles an hour, the experience is very different. The car isolates us, distances us; the world beyond the windshield—whether desert mesa or rolling farmland—seems vaguely unreal. At supersonic speeds, the divorce is complete. A landscape at 30,000 feet is an abstraction, as unlike real life as a painting.

8   It's an unreality we've grown used to. Habit has dulled the strangeness of it. We're as comfortable with superhuman speed—and the level of abstraction it brings with it—as we are with, say, the telephone, which in a single stroke distanced us from a habit as old as our species: talking to one another face-to-face. We forget that initial users of the telephone (our grandmothers and grandfathers) found it nearly impossible to conceptualize another human being beyond the inanimate receiver; in order to communicate, they had to personify the receiver and speak to it, as to some mechanical pet, rather than *through* it to someone else. Today, that kind of instinctive attachment to physical reality seems quaint.

9   We've come a long way, very quickly. What surprises us now, increasingly, is the shock of the real: the nakedness of face-to-face communication, the rough force of the natural world. We can watch hours of nature programming, but place us in a forest or a meadow and we don't know quite what to do with ourselves. We look forward to hanging out at The Brick with Chris on *Northern Exposure* but dread running into our neighbor while putting out the trash. There has come to be something almost embarrassing about the unmediated event; the man or woman who takes out a musical instrument at a party and offers to play is likely to make everyone feel a bit awkward. It's so naked, somehow. We're more comfortable with its representation: Aerosmith on MTV, Isaac Stern or Eric Clapton on CD.

10   And now, as we close out the century, various computer technologies threaten to take our long journey from reality to its natural conclusion. They are to TV or videoconferencing what the Concorde is to the car. They have the capacity to make the partially synthetic environments we already inhabit complete—to remove us, once and for all, from reality.

NOTES

1. Constance L. Hays, "Illusion and Tragedy Coexist after a Couple Dies," *New York Times*, 7 January 1990.
2. I am aware, of course, that the term *reality*, problematic since Plato, has lately become a political minefield. So as not to be misunderstood, then, let me be as clear as possible. I have no problem with those who argue that reality, like taste, is subjective—a product of one's race, gender, economic class, education, and so on. These qualifications strike me as good and true. At the same time, however, I believe that under the strata of subjectivity, of language and perspective, lies a bedrock of fact: neo-Nazis in Köln or California may define the Holocaust differently than I do, yet the historical *fact* stands firm. It is *this* kind of reality— immutable, empirical, neither historically nor culturally relative—that I refer to here.
3. The rapid acceleration of cultural change in the twentieth century, of course, is a historical truism. One of the most vivid documents recording this transformation in American culture (it originally appeared in 1929) is Robert S. Lynd and Helen M. Lynd, *Middletown: A Study in Contemporary American Culture* (New York: Harcourt Brace Jovanovich, 1959).

FOR DISCUSSION: Provide at least one example of your own to support the author's view that human beings are losing touch with reality and another example to support the opposing view. Do you agree or disagree with this author? Provide some reasons for your answer.

◆◆◆

E.   WRITING ASSIGNMENT: THE SUMMARY-RESPONSE PAPER

1. Select the issue area in "The Reader" that interests you the most. Read the "Rhetorical Situation" section for that issue. Then select one of the issue questions in that area, and read the set of essays related to that question. Using your own words, write a one-page summary-response paper for each essay: divide a piece of paper in half, and write a summary on the top half and your response on the bottom half. Refer to the instructions and sample summary on page 75 and the sample response on page 77 to help you.
2. Find an article related to your issue, and write a one-page summary-response paper about it.

F.   GROUP WORK: CLASS MAPS

Figure 3.3 is a map of the issue area *race* that was made by some of the students who test-read this book. They made this map after they had surveyed the articles about race, culture, and identity in "The Reader." The map answers the question "What are the issues related to race?"

ISSUES RELATED TO RACE

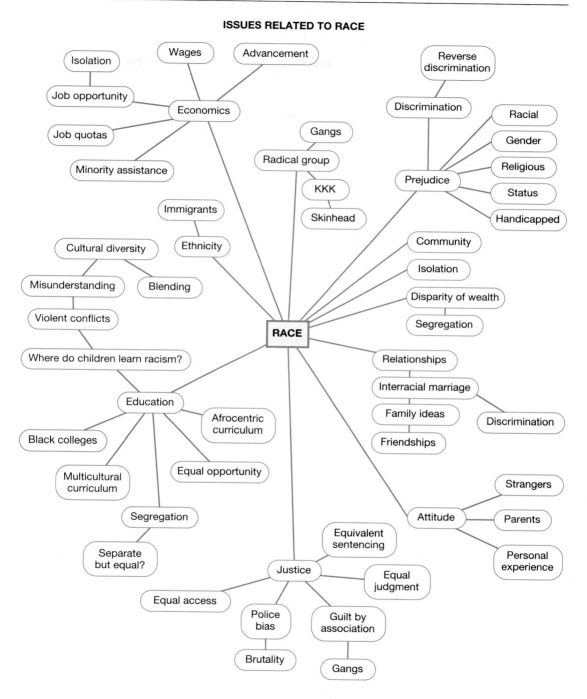

FIGURE 3.3 **A Map Can Help You Discover Specific Related Issues for Paper Topics.**

SOURCE: Designed by Eric West, Patricia Pulido, Ruby Chan, and Sharon Young. Used with permission.

Some classes select an issue that all students will write about, others form groups around four or five issues that are selected by the groups, and some classes decide that each student will write on individual issues. Whether you are working with a group or alone, a map can often help you focus and clarify your issue, see its various aspects, and provide ideas for developing it.

To make a map, write the broad issue in a circle in the center of a page. Think of as many related aspects of that issue as you can, and attach them to the broad issue. When you have completed the map, identify the aspect or aspects of the issue that interest you or your group. See if this aspect of the broad issue area can now be narrowed, expanded, or modified in some other way as a result of seeing it in this larger perspective.

❖ Chapter 4 ❖

A Process for Writing Argument

T his chapter will provide you with the expertise, confidence, and motivation that you will need to write arguments of your own on issues that are compellingly important to you. This chapter parallels Chapter 3, which covers the reading process, except that here the focus is on the writing process. You will be invited to analyze and describe your present process for writing argument and then to consider ways to improve this process. You will also practice the process by writing an exploratory paper in which you describe several perspectives on a single issue.

Chapter 3 introduced the concept that reading and writing should be integrated processes, and you were advised to write as part of your reading process. Writing while you read helps you understand a text better, and it helps you think beyond a text to develop ideas of your own. The "Read While You Write" box contains a corollary idea that can have a similarly powerful impact on the quality of your writing.

READ WHILE YOU WRITE

You may at times write without thinking very much. You find an idea, write something off the top of your head, and turn it in, perhaps without even reading it over. Or you may try to write and find that you have nothing to say. One of the best ways to convert this blank writing to thoughtful writing is to read as part of your writing process. Reading while you write will provide you with background on your subject, new ideas to write about, fresh perspectives on your issue, and evidence and supporting details for your paper. It will at the same time suggest ways to solve writing problems as you read to understand how other writers have solved them.

You will usually adapt your writing process to the specific writing tasks at hand. When you are expected to write academic argument as described on page 62, you will often write long, complicated papers that rely on research in outside sources and present complicated concepts explained with the specialized vocabulary of the discipline. You will need a well-developed writing process composed of a variety of thinking and writing strategies to write academic argument. At other times you will need a less elaborate process for simpler papers. A writing process makes the most difficult writing tasks seem less difficult. It also helps you avoid procrastination and the discomforts of writer's block.

HOW DO YOU WRITE NOW?

You already have a writing process, and to make it useful for writing argument, you will need to adapt it to that purpose. Begin by thinking first about what you do when you write argument.

What do you do . . .

◆ Before you write the draft of an argument paper?
◆ While you are writing the draft of an argument paper?
◆ When you get stuck?
◆ When you finish writing the draft of an argument paper?

What can you add to your present process to improve your ability to write argument? One idea is to write at all stages of the process, since writing helps you learn and also helps you think. Start writing ideas as soon as you begin thinking about your issue. Most people are especially creative and insightful during the early stages of a new writing project. Continue writing while you are thinking and gathering materials, organizing your ideas, and writing, rewriting, and revising your final copy. Notes and ideas on sheets of paper, on cards, and in notebooks are useful, as are lists, maps, various types of outlines, responses to research, drafts, and rewrites.

You must also be prepared to jot down ideas at any time during the process. Once your reading and thinking are under way, your subconscious mind takes over. At odd times you may suddenly see new connections or think of a new example, a new idea, a beginning sentence, or a good organizational sequence for the main ideas. Insights like these often come to writers when they first wake up. Plan to keep paper and pencil available so that you can take notes when good ideas occur to you.

Now consider what else you might do to improve your present process for writing argument. Focus on what you can do before you write, while you write, when you are stuck, and when you are working to finish your paper.

PREWRITING STRATEGIES

Prewriting is creative, and creativity is delicate to teach because it is individual. Still, like most writers, you will need directed prewriting strategies from time to time, either to help you get started on writing or to help you break through writer's block. Here are some suggestions to help you get organized, access what you already know, think about it, and plan what more you need to learn. You will not use all of these suggestions. Some, however, may become your favorite prewriting strategies.

GET ORGANIZED TO WRITE

Some people develop elaborate rituals like cleaning house, sharpening pencils, laying out special pens, putting on comfortable clothes, chewing a special flavor of gum, or making a cup of coffee to help them get ready to write. These rituals help them get their minds on the writing task, improve their motivation to write, and help them avoid procrastination and writer's block. A professional writer, describing what she does, says she takes a few moments before she writes to imagine her work as a completed and successful project. She visualizes it as finished, and she thinks about how she will feel at that time.[1]

Creating a place to write is an essential part of getting organized to write. A desk and a quiet place at home or in the library work best for most students. Still, if ideal conditions are not available, you can develop alternative places like a parked car on a quiet street, an empty classroom, a coffee shop, the kitchen or dining room table, or a card table in an out-of-the-way corner of a room.

Writing projects usually require stacks of books and papers that, ideally, one can leave out and come back to at any time. If you cannot leave them out, however, use a folder, briefcase, or box to keep everything in one safe place. You can then quickly spread your work out again when it is time to write. You will need a system to keep these writing materials organized. You may have idea notes, research notes, lists and outlines, and drafts at various stages of completion to keep track of. Categorize this material, keep it in stacks, and arrange the material in each stack in the order in which you will probably use it.

Finally, make a decision about the writing equipment you will use. The major choices will be the computer or paper and pens or pencils, or some combination of these. Experiment with different methods, and decide which is best for you. Most students prefer using computers to writing by hand for the same reasons that many professional writers like using them: typing is faster, and the copy is easier to read and revise. A disadvantage of using computers is that some people write too much. They literally write everything that occurs to them, and some of it is undeveloped, poorly organized, or off the subject. If you tend to write too much, you can solve your problem by cutting ferociously when you revise.

---

[1] Barbara Neely, "Tools for the Part-Time Novelist," *Writer*, June 1993, p. 17.

Understand the Assignment and Schedule Time

You will need to analyze the writing assignment and find time to do it. Divide the assignment into small, manageable parts, assign a sufficient amount of time for each part, set deadlines for completing each part, and use the time when it becomes available. Below is an example.

Assignment. Write a five- to six-page, typed, double-spaced argument paper in which you identify an issue of your choice, take a position, make a claim, and support it so that it is convincing to an audience of your peers. Do as much reading as you need to do, but plan to draw material from at least five sources when you write your paper. Use MLA style (explained in the Appendix to Chapter 12) to document your sources and prepare your bibliography.

Analysis of Assignment

Week 1

Select an issue from "The Reader," and write down some ideas.	2 hours Tuesday night
Read the articles on your issue in "The Reader," think, and take notes; write a first draft.	3 hours Thursday night
Read the draft to a peer group in class to get ideas for additional research.	Friday's class
Do research in the library and on the Internet to fill in the needs of the first draft.	3 hours Saturday

Week 2

Incorporate research and write a second draft.	3 hours Thursday night
Read it to the peer editing group in class.	Friday's class

Week 3

Rewrite, revise, and prepare final copy.	4 hours Tuesday night Hand in on Wednesday

Notice that the work on this paper has been spread out over two full weeks and is broken down into manageable units. A student would be able to complete this paper successfully, on time, and without panic and discomfort if this schedule were followed. A total of fifteen hours have been set aside for the various stages. The time is available even though the student may not need all of it. The student's focus should now be on finishing the paper as quickly as possible, not on simply using all of this time.

Here is a professional writer who cautions about the importance of working to finish rather than working to put in time: "Don't set your goal as minutes or hours spent working; it's too easy to waste that time looking up one last fact, changing your margins, or, when desperate, searching for a new pen." Instead, she advises, set a realistic writing goal for each day and work until you complete it.[2] Another author advises that you avoid creating units of work that are so large or unmanageable that you won't want to do them, such as writing an entire paper in one day. It may sound good on the surface to write a whole paper in one day or one night, "but you'll soon feel overwhelmed," and "you'll start avoiding the work and won't get *anything* done." Remember, she says, "it's persistence that counts" in completing writing projects.[3]

IDENTIFY AN ISSUE AND DO SOME INITIAL READING

You may start with a broad issue area such as crime, education, health care, or tax reform. You will need to find a more narrow and specific issue within this broad area to write about, however. The map in Figure 3.3 shows one way to find more specific issues related to a broad issue area. Reading about your issue can also help you discover a particular aspect that you want to explore. When you have an issue you think you can work with, write it as a question, and apply the twelve tests of an arguable issue presented in Box 1.3. You may also take a position on the issue and write a tentative claim. Additional information on how to write claims appears in Chapters 6 and 10.

ANALYZE THE RHETORICAL SITUATION

In Chapter 3, you learned to apply the elements of the rhetorical situation to help you read critically and analyze other authors' arguments. As a writer, you can now use the rhetorical situation to help you think critically and make decisions about your own writing.

All five elements of the rhetorical situation are important considerations for writers. Three elements of the rhetorical situation are in place before you begin to write. They are the *exigence,* the *reader* or *audience,* and the *constraints.* When you begin to write, two additional elements are added: you, the *author,* and the *text* that you create. Figure 4.1 (page 96) provides a diagram of these five elements to suggest some of the relationships among them.

Now consider the five elements from the writer's point of view. Use TRACE to help you remember the elements. As a writer, however, you should think about them not in the order presented in the mnemonic but in the following order.

▲ *EXIGENCE.* The exigence of the situation provides the motivation to write about the issue in the first place. Issues often emerge from real-life events that signal something is wrong. One student found a topic when a local jury appeared to have made a mistake because it assigned probation to a murderer instead of prison time. Another student developed an exigence to write when she visited a national forest and discovered that acres and acres of trees had been cut down since the last time she was there. Yet another student discovered an exigence when he read a newspaper article about the assisted death of an old woman who was very ill, and he began to compare her situation with his grandmother's. Such

---

[2]Peggy Rynk, "Waiting for Inspiration," *Writer,* September 1992, p. 10.
[3]Sue Grafton, "How to Find Time to Write When You Don't Have Time to Write," *The Writer's Handbook,* ed. Sylvia K. Burack (Boston: Writer, 1991), p. 22.

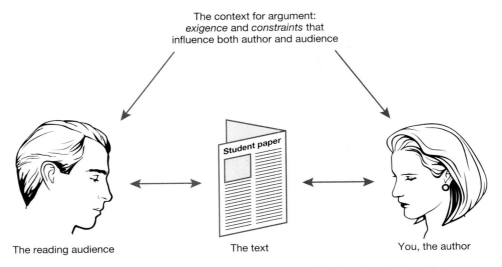

The context for argument:
exigence and *constraints* that
influence both author and audience

The reading audience   The text   You, the author

FIGURE 4.1 The Five Elements of the Rhetorical Situation That the Writer Considers While Planning and Writing Argument.

occurrences can cause the writer to ask the questions associated with exigence: What issue is involved in each of these incidents? Are these new or recurring issues? Do they represent problems or defects? How and why?

▲ *READER OR AUDIENCE.* Now think about how potential readers might regard the issues that emerge from these situations. Who are these people? Would they perceive these situations as problems or defects, as you do? Would they agree or disagree with you on the issues, or would they be neutral? What do they believe in? What are their values? Will you need to make a special effort with them to achieve common ground, or will you already share common ground? What audience outcomes can you anticipate? Will you be able to get the audience to agree and reach consensus, to take action, to agree on some points but not on others, or to agree to disagree? Or will they probably remain unconvinced and possibly even hostile?

▲ *CONSTRAINTS.* Remember that constraints influence the ways in which both you and your audience think about the issues. What background, events, experiences, traditions, values, or associations are influencing both you and them? If you decide to write for an audience of lawyers to convince them to change the nature of jury trials, for instance, what are the constraints likely to be? How hard will it be to change the system? Or if you are writing for forest service employees whose job it is to cut down trees, what constraints will you encounter with this group? If you are writing for a group of doctors who have been trained to preserve human life as long as possible, what constraints will you encounter with them? And how about you? What are your own constraints? How are your training, background, affiliations, and values either in harmony or in conflict with your audience? In other words, will your respective constraints drive you and your audience apart, or will they bring you together and help you achieve common ground?

▲ *AUTHOR.* Other questions will help you think like an author of argument. Why am I interested in this issue? Why do I perceive it as a defect or problem? Is it a new or old issue for me? What is my personal background or experience with this issue? What makes me qualified to write about it? Which of my personal values are involved? How can I get more information? Refer to your direct experience if you have some. You may, for instance, be planning to go to law school, and you are interested in trial results; or you may have spent many happy childhood vacations camping in forests, which led to your conservation outlook; or maybe one of your relatives suffered for many years before she died, so you have strong feelings about hospice care. Or you may have no direct experience, just an interest.

▲ *TEXT.* At this point, you can begin to plan your paper (the text). What strategies should you use? Will you favor an adversarial or a consensual style? How will you build common ground? What types of support will work best? Should you state your claim right away or build up to it? What will your argumentative purpose be? What will your original approach or perspective be?

As you can see, the rhetorical situation can be employed to help you get ideas and plan, and you should actually keep it in mind throughout the writing process. It will be useful to you at every stage.

FOCUS AND FREEWRITE

Focus your attention, write a tentative title for your paper, and then freewrite for ten or fifteen minutes without stopping. Write about anything that occurs to you that is relevant to your title and your issue. Freewriting must be done quickly to capture the flow of thought. It may be done sloppily, using incomplete sentences and abbreviations. Don't worry about making errors.

Go back through your freewriting, and find a phrase or sentence that you can turn into a claim. This freewriting is also your first partial manuscript. Later you may use some or none of it in your paper. Its main value is to preserve the first creative ideas that flood your mind when you begin to work on a paper. Its other value is to focus and preserve your ideas so that they won't get lost when you later read the thoughts and opinions of others. If you start to freewrite and you find you do not have very many ideas, do some background reading in your issue area, and then try to freewrite again.

BRAINSTORM, MAKE LISTS, MAP IDEAS

Brainstorming is another way to get ideas down on paper in a hurry. The rules for brainstorming are to commit to a time limit, to write phrases only, to write quickly, and to make no judgments as you write. Later you may go back to decide what is good or bad, useful or not useful. Brainstorming is like freewriting to the extent that it helps you get some ideas on paper quickly. It differs from freewriting in that it usually produces only words and phrases and it is often practiced as a group activity.

Listing is related to outlining. Insights may come at any time about how to divide a subject into parts or how to set up major headings for your paper. Write these ideas in list form. Or map your ideas (Figure 3.3) to get a better sense of what they are and how they relate to each other. You may also use a flowchart. Flowcharts are good for laying out processes or ideas and events that occur chronologically, over a period of time.

TALK IT THROUGH

Many people find it easier to speak the first words than to write them. Typical audiences for an initial talk-through may include a peer editing group, which is a small group of students in your class who will listen to and read your paper at all stages; your instructor, who, in conference, may ask a few questions and then just listen to you explore your ideas; or a writing center tutor, who is trained to ask questions and then listen. Friends or family members can also become valued listeners. Some people like to tape-record the ideas they get from such sessions. Others prefer to end them with some rapid freewriting, listing, or brainstorming to preserve the good ideas that surfaced. If you do not tape-record or write, your good ideas may become lost forever. A sense of security comes from writing your paper with a stack of notes and ideas at hand and ready to use.

KEEP A JOURNAL, NOTEBOOK, OR FOLDER OF IDEAS

Instead of talking to others, some authors talk to themselves on a regular basis by writing in a journal or notebook or simply by writing on pieces of paper and sticking them in a folder. To help you gather material for an argument paper, you may clip articles, write summaries, and write out ideas and observations about your issue as they come to you. These materials will provide you with an excellent source of information for your paper when it is time to write it.

A professional writer describes this type of writing as a tool that helps one think. This author sets out some suggestions that could be particularly useful for the writer of argument.

> Write quickly, so you don't know what's coming next.
> Turn off the censor in your head.
> Write from different points of view to broaden your sympathies.
> Collect quotations that inspire you and jot down a few notes on why they do.
> Write with a nonjudgmental friend in mind to listen to your angry or confused thoughts.
> When words won't come, draw something—anything.
> Don't worry about being nice, fair, or objective. Be selfish and biased; give your side of the story from the heart.
> Write even what frightens you, *especially* what frightens you. It is the thought denied that is dangerous.
> Don't worry about being consistent. You are large; you contain multitudes.[4]

---

[4]Marjorie Pellegrino, "Keeping a Writer's Journal," *Writer,* June 1992, p. 27.

You can write entire sections of material, ready to incorporate later into your paper. Or you can jot down phrases or examples to help you remember sudden insights. The object is to think and write on a regular basis while a paper is taking shape. Writing at all stages helps you discover what you know and learn about what you think.

Mentally Visualize

Create mental pictures related to your issue, and later describe what you see in your mind's eye. For example, if you are writing about preserving forests, visualize them before any cutting has been done and then later after clear-cutting, which removes all trees in an area. Use these descriptions later in your paper to make your ideas more vivid and compelling.

Do Some Directed Reading and Thinking

Continue reading, thinking, and writing notes and ideas throughout the prewriting process. Read to get a sense of other people's perspectives on the issue and also to generate ideas of your own. As you read, you may find that you need to narrow and limit your issue even more, to one aspect or one approach. Try to think of an original perspective or "take" on the issue, a new way of looking at it. For example, the personal examples in "Why I Want a Wife" (pages 58–60) present an original approach to the household responsibilities issue. As you continue reading and thinking, clarify your position on the issue, decide on your argumentative purpose (Chapters 6 and 10 will help), and revise your claim if you need to. When you have written your claim, write the word *because* and list some reasons. Or list some reasons and write the word *therefore,* followed by your claim. This will help you decide, at least for now, whether your paper would be stronger with the claim at the beginning or at the end. Decide which words in your claim will need defining in your paper.

Use Argument Strategies

You will learn more about these in future chapters. The Toulmin model (Chapter 5) will help you plan the essential parts of your paper. Later, when you are revising, you can employ the Toulmin model to read and check the effectiveness of your argument. The claim questions in Chapter 6 will help you discover and write claims to focus your purpose for argument. The list of proofs from Chapter 7 will provide you with a variety of ways to develop your paper.

Use Reading Strategies

Use what you know about analyzing the organization of other authors' essays to help you organize your own paper. For example, you can plan an introduction, main body, and conclusion. You can make an outline composed of a title, claim, subclaims, support, and transitions to help you visualize the structure of your paper. When you have finished your draft, you can try to summarize the claim and subclaims to test its unity and completeness. Or you can survey it. If you have problems with summarizing or surveying and discover, for example, that you cannot describe precisely what your paper is about or what you are trying to prove, you will need to revise more. Much of what you learned about reading in Chapter 3 can now be used not only to help you write argument of your own but also to read and evaluate it.

USE CRITICAL THINKING PROMPTS

You can get additional insight and ideas about your issue by using some well-established lines of thought that stimulate critical thinking. The "Critical Thinking Prompts" list in Box 4.1 provides some prompts that will cause you to think in a variety of ways. First, write out your issue, and then write your responses. You will be pleased by the quantity of new information these questions will generate for your paper.

PLAN AND CONDUCT LIBRARY RESEARCH AND AVOID PLAGIARISM

To help you plan your research tasks, make a brief list or outline of the main sections of your paper. This list will guide your research. Research takes a lot of time, and you will want to read only the materials in the library or on the Internet that are most relevant to the items on your research outline. Read and take notes on the materials you locate, and relate them to your outline. Search for additional materials to fill in places on the outline where you need more information.

Throughout the note-taking process, differentiate between your own words and the words and passages you have copied from your sources. Always place copied material in quotation marks, whether the source is printed material or the Internet. At the same time, write down detailed information about where the material first appeared. To help you do this, refer to pages 328–330. When you write your draft, remember to place borrowed material in quotation marks and also to let your reader know where you originally found it. You will avoid plagiarism by being careful when you use sources.

Lynne McTaggart, a professional writer whose work was recently plagiarized by a well-known author and commentator, explains plagiarism in this way: "Plagiarism is the dishonorable act of passing someone else's words off as your own, whether or not the material is published." She continues, "Writers don't own facts. Writers don't own ideas. All that we own is the way we express our thoughts. Plagiarism pillages unique expressions, specific turns of phrase, the unusual colors a writer chooses to use from a personal literary palette." She concludes, "In this age of clever electronic tools, writing can easily turn into a process of pressing the cut-and-paste buttons, . . . rather than the long and lonely slog of placing one word after another in a new and arresting way."[5] McTaggart was shocked to read a book by a best-selling author that included material from her

---

[5]Lynne McTaggart, "Fame Can't Excuse a Plagiarist," *New York Times*, March 16, 2002, p. A27.

| BOX 4.1 | Use These Prompts to Help You Think Critically about Your Issue. |

CRITICAL THINKING PROMPTS

What is your issue? _____

Use some, but not all, of these prompts to help you think about it.

1. **Associate it.** Consider other, related issues, big issues, or enduring issues. Also associate your issue with familiar subjects and ideas.
2. **Describe it.** Use detail. Make the description visual if you can.
3. **Compare it.** Think about items in the same or different categories. Compare it with things you know or understand well. Compare what you used to think about the issue and what you think now. Give reasons for your change of mind.
4. **Apply it.** Show practical uses or applications. Show how it can be used in a specific setting.
5. **Divide it.** Get insight into your issue by dividing it into related issues or into parts of the issue.
6. **Agree and disagree with it.** Identify the extreme pro and con positions and reasons for holding them. List other approaches and perspectives. Say why each position, including your own, might be plausible and in what circumstances.
7. **Consider it as it is, right now.** Think about your issue as it exists, right now, in contemporary time. What is its nature? What are its special characteristics?
8. **Consider it over a period of time.** Think about it in the past and how it might present itself in the future. Does it change? How? Why?
9. **Decide what it is a part of.** Put it in a larger category, and consider the insights you gain as a result.
10. **Analyze it.** Break it into parts, and get insight into each of its parts.
11. **Synthesize it.** Put it back together in new ways so that the new whole is different, and perhaps clearer and better, than the old whole.
12. **Evaluate it.** Decide whether it is good or bad, valuable or not valuable, moral or immoral. Give evidence to support your evaluation.
13. **Elaborate on it.** Add and continue to add explanation until you can understand it more easily. Give some examples to provide further elaboration.
14. **Project and predict.** Answer the question "What would happen if . . . ?" Think about further possibilities.
15. **Ask why, and keep on asking why.** Examine every aspect of your issue by asking why.

book, exactly as she had worded it, in passage after passage throughout the work without proper acknowledgment.

Avoid plagiarism on principle because it is dishonest. However, if you are ever tempted to plagiarize, you should also know there are Web sites where your instructors can submit your papers for an "originality analysis." These Web sites access huge databases of print materials and can report any passages that you have drawn word for word from other sources. If the passages you have used are reasonably short, support your own ideas, and are placed in quotation marks along with citations to show your reader where you found them, then you have done the right thing. If the passages are copied into your paper as though you had written them yourself, then you could receive a poor grade in the course or be expelled from college. Professors take plagiarism very seriously. It is a form of stealing. And, of course, you don't learn to improve your own writing when you copy other people's words instead of writing your own.

Make an Extended List or Outline to Guide Your Writing

A written outline helps many people see the organization of ideas before they begin to write. Other people seem to be able to make a list or even work from a mental outline. Still others "just write" and move ideas around later to create order. There is, however, an implicit outline in most good writing. The outline is often referred to metaphorically as the skeleton or bare bones of the paper because it provides the internal structure that holds the paper together. An outline can be simple—a list of words written on a piece of scrap paper—or it can be elaborate, with essentially all major ideas, supporting details, major transitions, and even some of the sections written out in full. Some outlines actually end up looking like partial, sketchy manuscripts.

If you have never made outlines, try making one. Outlining requires intensive thinking and decision making. When it is finished, however, you will be able to turn your full attention to writing, and you will never have to stop to figure out what to write about next. Your outline will tell you what to do, and it will ultimately save you time and reduce much of the difficulty and frustration you would experience without it.

Talk It Through Again

When you have completed your outline and are fairly satisfied with it, you can sharpen and improve it even more by reading it aloud and explaining its rationale to some good listeners. It is more and more common to organize peer editing groups in writing classes to give students the opportunity to talk through outlines and to read drafts to fellow students who then act as critics to make recommendations for improvement. Reading and talking about your outline in the early stages helps clarify ideas, making it easier to write about them later. At this stage, your student critics should explain to you what is clear and unclear and also what is convincing and not convincing.

WRITING THE FIRST DRAFT

The objective of writing the first draft is to get your ideas in some kind of written form so that you can see them and work with them. Here is how a professional writer explains the drafting process.

Writing a first draft should be easy because, in a sense, you can't get it wrong. You are bringing something completely new and strange into the world, something that did not exist before. You have nothing to prove in the first draft, nothing to defend, everything to imagine. And the first draft is yours alone, no one else sees it. You are not writing for an audience. Not yet. You write the draft in order to read what you have written and to determine what you still have to say.[6]

This author advises further that you "not even consider technical problems at this early stage." Nor should you "let your critical self sit at your desk with your creative self. The critic will stifle the writer within." The purpose, he says, is "not to get it right, but to get it written."[7]

Here is another writer, Stephen King, who advises putting aside reference books and dictionaries when concentrating on writing the first draft.

Put away your dictionary. . . . You think you might have misspelled a word? O.K., so here is your choice: either look it up in the dictionary, thereby making sure you have it right—and breaking your train of thought and the writer's trance in the bargain—or just spell it phonetically and correct it later. Why not? Did you think it was going to go somewhere? And if you need to know the largest city in Brazil and you find you don't have it in your head, why not write in Miami or Cleveland? You can check it . . . but *later.* When you sit down to write, *write.* Don't do anything else except go to the bathroom, and only do that if it absolutely cannot be put off.[8]

You will be able to follow this advice if your outline and notes are available to guide you and keep you on track. If you occasionally get stuck, you can write some phrases, freewrite, or even skip a section that you cannot easily put into words. You will have another chance at your draft later. Right now, work only to capture the flow of ideas that is on the outline. You will discover, as you write, that many of the ideas that were only half formed on your outline will now become clear and complete as you get insight from writing.

SPECIAL STRATEGIES TO USE IF YOU GET STUCK

Everyone suffers from writer's block from time to time, and there are a number of ways to get going again if you get stuck while writing your first draft. Many people read and take more notes at times like this. Since reading will make you think, you should write out all of the ideas and insights that come to you as you read. Soon you will have plenty of new material to add to your paper. You can also go back and reread your outline, lists, and other idea notes, rearrange them into new combinations, and add more information to them.

---

[6]John Dufresne, "That Crucial First Draft," *Writer,* October 1992, p. 9.
[7]Ibid., pp. 10–11.
[8]Stephen King, "Everything You Need to Know about Writing Successfully—in Ten Minutes," *The Writer's Handbook,* ed. Sylvia K. Burack (Boston: Writer, 1991), p. 33.

If you are so blocked that you simply cannot make yourself write the next words, try freewriting—writing fast, in phrases or sentences, on your topic without imposing any structure or order. Then do some more reading, and follow that with additional freewriting. You may end up with a lot of material that doesn't make much sense and with a lot of unrelated bits and sentence fragments. That's fine—you can go back through it later, crossing out what you can't use, changing phrases to sentences, adding material in places, and soon you will find that you are started again. Getting words on the page in any form is what it takes for some writers to break out of a block.

It is also extremely useful to talk about your ideas for your paper with someone else to get fresh insights and solve some of your writing problems. Or ask someone else to read a draft of your paper and to write some comments on it. This will provide you with insights and ideas to get you moving again. Finally, give yourself permission to write a less than perfect first draft. You can paralyze yourself by trying to produce a finished draft on the first try. Lower your expectations for the first draft, and remind yourself that you can always go back later and fix it.

POSTWRITING STRATEGIES

Resist the temptation to put your paper aside when you have finished drafting and declare it finished. Now is your opportunity to improve it in significant ways, and here are some suggestions for doing so.

READ YOUR DRAFT CRITICALLY AND SUBMIT IT FOR PEER REVIEW

If you can, put your draft aside for twenty-four hours, then read it critically and make all of the changes you can to improve it. It helps to read the paper aloud at this point to get an even better perspective on what can be improved. Then you can seek the opinion of other students in a class peer review session. The usual procedure for a peer editing session on a draft is to read the paper aloud to the group or to do a round robin reading session, in which group members read all of the papers silently and make some notes before they discuss the papers one by one.

Peer groups make the writing task more sociable and provide immediate feedback from a real audience. They also help you become a more sensitive critic of your own and others' work. Most professional writers rely heavily on other people's opinions at various stages of writing. Look at the prefaces of some of the books you are using this semester. Most authors acknowledge the help of several people who read their manuscript and made suggestions for improvement. Many individuals recommended improvements for this book. Some of these people were teachers, some were editors, some were friends and family members, some were colleagues, and some were students. The students who test-read this book wrote many good suggestions for improvement. In fact, these students were responsible for several of the major changes and special features in the book that make it easier to read and use. One student commented that she liked being a part of the writing process for this textbook because it helped her read her other textbooks more critically. If peer review groups are not part of your writing class, try to find someone else to read your draft. You need someone to make suggestions and give you ideas for improvement.

REWRITE AND REVISE

Working with a rough draft is easier than outlining or drafting. It is, in fact, creative and fun to revise because you begin to see your work take shape and become more readable. Skillfully revised material, incidentally, makes a good impression on the reader. It is worthwhile to finish your draft early enough so that you will have several hours to read and revise before you submit it in its final form to a reader.

Most writers have some ideas and rules about writing that come to their aid, from an inner voice, when it is time to revise. Listen to your inner voice so that you will know what to look for and what to change. If you do not have a strongly developed inner voice, you can strengthen it by learning to ask the following questions. Notice that these questions direct your attention to global revisions for improved clarity and organization, as well as to surface revisions for details.

1. *Is it clear?* If you cannot understand your own writing, other people won't be able to, either. Be very critical of your own understanding as you read your draft. Make your writing clearer by establishing some key terms and using them throughout. Add transitions as well. Use those that are associated with the organizational patterns you have used. (You can find more information about these in Chapter 12.) Or write a transitional paragraph to summarize one major part of your paper and introduce the next. If you stumble over a bad sentence, begin again and rewrite it in a new way. There are a dozen possible ways to write one sentence. Also, change all words that do not clearly communicate exactly what you want to say. This is no place to risk using words from the thesaurus that you are not sure about. Finally, apply this test: Can you state the claim or the main point of your paper and list the parts that develop it? Take a good look at these parts, and rearrange them if necessary.

2. *What should I add?* Sometimes in writing the first draft you will write such a sketchy version of an idea that it does not explain what you want to say. Add fuller explanations and examples, or do some extra research to improve the skimpy parts of your paper.

3. *What should I cut?* Extra words, repeated ideas, and unnecessary material find their way into a typical first draft. Every writer cuts during revision. Stephen King, who earns millions of dollars each year as a professional writer, describes how he learned to cut the extra words. His teacher was the newspaper editor John Gould, who dealt with King's first feature article as follows:

> He started in on the feature piece with a large black pen and taught me all I ever needed to know about my craft. I wish I still had the piece—it deserves to be

framed, editorial corrections and all—but I can remember pretty well how it looked when he had finished with it. Here's an example:

> Last night, in the ~~well-loved~~
> (gymnasium ~~of~~) Lisbon High School, partisans
> and Jay Hills fans alike were stunned by
> an athletic performance unequalled in school
> history: Bob Ransom, ~~known as "Bullet" Bob~~
> ~~for both his size and accuracy,~~ scored
> thirty-seven points. He did it with grace
> and speed . . . and he did it with an odd courtesy
> as well, committing only two personal fouls
> in his ~~knight-like~~ quest for a record which
> has eluded Lisbon's *basketball team* ~~thinclads~~ since 1953 . . .

When Gould finished marking up my copy in the manner I have indicated above, he looked up and must have seen something on my face. I think he must have thought it was horror, but it was not: it was revelation.

"I only took out the bad parts, you know," he said. "Most of it's pretty good."

"I know," I said, meaning both things: yes, most of it was good, and yes, he had only taken out the bad parts. "I won't do it again."

"If that's true," he said, "you'll never have to work again. You can do *this* for a living." Then he threw back his head and laughed.

And he was right: I *am* doing this for a living, and as long as I can keep on, I don't expect ever to have to work again.[9]

4. *Are the language and style consistent and appropriate throughout?* Edit out all words that create a conversational or informal tone in your paper. For example:

Change: And as for target shooting, well go purchase a BB gun or a set of darts.[10]

To read: For target shooting, a BB gun or a set of darts serves just as well as a handgun.

Also, edit out all cheerleading, slogans, clichés, needless repetition, and exhortations. You are not writing a political speech. For example:

Change: Violence! Why should we put up with it? Violence breeds violence, they say. America would be a better place if there were less violence.

---

[9]King, pp. 30–31.
[10]From a student paper by Blake Decker; used with permission.

To read: Violent crime has begun to take over the United States, affecting everyone's life. Every day another story of tragedy unfolds where a man, a woman, or a child is senselessly killed by someone with a gun. Under the tremendous stress of this modern society, tempers flare at the drop of a hat, and people reach for a gun that was bought only for defense or safety. Then they make rash, deadly decisions.[11]

You will learn more about language and style in Chapter 7. In general, use a formal, rational style in an argument paper unless you have a good reason to do otherwise. Use emotional language and examples that arouse feelings only where appropriate to back up logical argument.

5. *Is there enough variety?* Use some variety in the way you write sentences by beginning some with clauses and others with a subject or even a verb. Vary the length of your sentences as well. Try to write not only simple sentences but also compound and complex sentences. You can also vary the length of your paragraphs. The general rule is to begin a new paragraph every time you change the subject. Variety in sentences and paragraphs makes your writing more interesting to read. Do not sacrifice clarity for variety, however, by writing odd or unclear sentences.

6. *Have I used the active voice most of the time?* The active voice is more direct, energetic, and interesting than the passive voice. Try to use it most of the time. Here is a sentence written in the active voice; it starts with the subject.

Robotics is an exciting new technology that could enhance nearly every aspect of our lives.[12]

Notice how it loses its directness and punch when it is written in the passive voice.

Nearly every aspect of our lives could be enhanced by robotics, an exciting new technology.

7. *Have I avoided sexist language?* Try to avoid referring to people in your paper as though they were either all male or all female. Using such expressions as "he or she" or "himself or herself" sounds inclusive but comes across as awkward. Ways to solve this problem are to use plural nouns and pronouns and perhaps occasionally to rewrite a sentence in the passive voice. It is better to write, "The pressure-sensitive glove is used in virtual reality," than to write, "He or she puts on a pressure-sensitive glove to enter the world of virtual reality."

8. *Have I followed the rules?* Learn the rules for grammar, usage, and punctuation, and follow them. No one can read a paper that is full of errors of this type. Make the following rules a part of that inner voice that guides your revision, and you will avoid the most common errors made by student writers.

◆ Write similar items in a *series,* separated by commas, and finally connected by *and* or *or.*

---

[11]Ibid.
[12]From a student paper by Greg Mathios; used with permission.

Example: The National Rifle Association, firearms manufacturers, and common citizens are all interested in gun control.[13]

◆ Use *parallel construction* for longer, more complicated elements that have a similar function in the sentence.

Example: Parents who fear for their children's safety at school, passengers who ride on urban public transit systems, clerks who work at convenience stores and gas stations, and police officers who try to carry out their jobs safely are all affected by national policy on gun control.

◆ Keep everything in the same *tense* throughout. Use the present tense to introduce quotations.

Example: As Sherrill *states,* "The United States is said to be the greatest gun-toting nation in the world." Millions of guns create problems in this country.

◆ Observe *sentence boundaries.* Start sentences with a capital letter, and end them with a period or question mark. Make certain they express complete thoughts.

◆ Make subjects agree with verbs.

Example: Restrictions on gun control *interfere* [not *interferes*] with people's rights.

◆ Use *clear and appropriate pronoun referents.*

Example: The *group* is strongly in favor of gun control, and little is needed to convince *it* [not *them*] of the importance of this issue.

◆ Use commas to set off long initial clauses, to separate two independent clauses, and to separate words in a series.

Example: When one realizes that the authors of the Constitution could not look into the future and imagine current events, one can see how irrational and irresponsible it is to believe that the right to bear arms should in these times still be considered a constitutional right, and according to Smith, the groups that do so "are short-sighted, mistaken, and ignorant."

CHECK FOR FINAL ERRORS, ADD OR ADJUST THE TITLE, AND TYPE OR PRINT YOUR PAPER

Just before you submit your paper, check the spelling of every word you are not absolutely sure about. If spelling is a problem for you, buy a small spelling dictionary that contains only words and no meanings, or use the spell checker on the computer. If you use a spell checker, you should still read your paper one last time since the computer might not find every error. At this point you should also correct all the typographical errors that remain and format your paper. Now

---

[13]The examples presented here are drawn from a student paper by Blake Decker. I have revised his sentences for the sake of illustration.

either add a title or adjust your existing title if necessary. Be sure that your title provides information that will help the reader understand what your paper is about.

Complete your revision process by reading your paper aloud one more time. Read slowly and listen. You will be surprised by the number of problems that bother your ears but were not noticeable to your eyes. Your paper should be ready now to submit for evaluation. Print it so that it is easy to read.

ORGANIZING A PROCESS FOR WRITING ARGUMENT

The writing process for argument explained in this chapter and summarized in Box 4.2 (pages 110–111) integrates reading and writing at every phase. The strategies are presented in categories similar to those used for the reading process in Chapter 3. As you think about how you can adapt and use these ideas for writing argument, remember to keep the process flexible. That is, use your own present process, but add selected strategies as needed. It is unlikely that you will ever use all these strategies for one paper. Also, even though these strategies are explained here in an apparent order, you will not necessarily follow them in this order. You might write an entire section of your paper during the prewriting stage or do some rewriting and revising while you are working on the initial draft. The strategies are not steps. They are suggestions to help you complete your paper. By integrating them with your present writing process, you will develop an effective way of writing argument papers that is uniquely yours.

The bare bones of the process can be stated simply.

◆ Select an issue, narrow it, take a tentative position, and write a claim.
◆ Do some reading and research.
◆ Create a structure.
◆ Write a draft.
◆ Revise and edit it.

You can practice the writing process by understanding and learning to write an exploratory paper.

THE EXPLORATORY PAPER

In the exploratory paper,[14] the arguer identifies not just one position but as many of the major positions on an issue as possible, both past and present, and explains them through summaries and an analysis of the overall rhetorical situation for the issue. The analysis of the rhetorical situation in these papers explains what caused the issue and what prompted past and present interest and concern with it, identifies who is interested in it and why, and examines the constraints of the

---

[14]I am indebted to the late Professor James Kinneavy of the University of Texas at Austin for the basic notion of the exploratory paper.

BOX 4.2 **A Summary of the Process for Writing Argument Explained in This Chapter.**

WRITING ARGUMENT

PREWRITING STRATEGIES

Get organized to write. Set up a place with materials. Get motivated.

Understand the writing assignment, and schedule time. Break a complicated writing task into manageable parts, and set aside the time you need to write.

Identify an issue, and do some initial reading on it.

Analyze the rhetorical situation, particularly the exigence, the audience, and the constraints. Then think about you, as the author, and the text you will create.

Focus on your issue and freewrite.

Brainstorm, make lists, map ideas.

Talk things through with a friend, your instructor, or members of a peer editing group.

Keep a journal, notebook, or folder of ideas.

Mentally visualize the major concepts.

Do some directed reading and thinking.

Use argument strategies.

Use reading strategies.

Use critical thinking prompts.

Plan and conduct library research.

Make an expanded list or outline to guide your writing.

Talk things through again.

WRITING STRATEGIES

Write the first draft. Get your ideas on paper so that you can work with them. Use your outline and notes to help you. Either write and rewrite as you go, or write the draft quickly with the knowledge that you can reread or rewrite later.

STRATEGIES TO USE WHEN YOU GET STUCK

Read more, and take more notes.

Read your outline, rearrange parts, add more information.

Freewrite on the issue, read some more, and then freewrite some more.

Talk about your ideas with someone else.

Lower your expectations for your first draft. It does not have to be perfect at this point.

(continued)

Box 4.2 (continued)

> ## POSTWRITING STRATEGIES
>
> **Read your draft critically, and have someone else read it.** Put it aside for twenty-four hours, if you can, to develop a better perspective for reading and improving.
>
> **Rewrite and revise.** Make changes and additions until you think your paper is ready for other people to read. Move sections, cross out material, add other material, rephrase, as necessary.
>
> **Check your paper** for final grammar and punctuation errors. Spell check. Write the final title. Read your paper aloud one more time, make final changes, and print it.

inquiry and the various views in the ongoing conversation associated with it. The summaries of the positions not only explain each of the different perspectives on the issue but also provide the usual reasons cited to establish the validity of each perspective. The writer's own opinions are not expressed at all or are withheld until later in the paper.

There are a number of advantages to writing and reading exploratory papers. When writers and readers view an issue from many perspectives, they acquire a greater depth of understanding of it. They also acquire information—both facts and opinions—on the various views. All these are beneficial because both the arguer and the reader become better educated and more fluent in their discussions of the issue. Exploratory papers also help establish common ground between writers and readers. Writers, by restating several opposing positions along with the usual reasons for accepting them, are forced to understand several opposing views. The reader is also interested because the exploratory paper explains all views, which usually include the reader's as well. The reader is consequently more willing to learn about the other positions on the issue. Exploratory papers provide the mutual understanding and common ground essential for the next stage in argument, the presentation of the writer's position and reasons for holding it. The exploratory paper thus paves the way for the writer to enter the conversation on an issue with a single-perspective argument.

Exploratory papers are a common genre in argumentative writing. You will encounter them in newspapers, newsmagazines, other popular magazines of opinion, and scholarly journals. They are easy to recognize because they take a broad view of an issue, and they explain multiple perspectives instead of just one.

The following is an example of a short exploratory paper about single-sex classes in the public schools. The rhetorical situation, particularly the motivation for placing boys and girls in separate classes, is explained in the first paragraph. The author of this article then summarizes the different positions associated with this issue, including the reasons some schools give for separating the sexes, the arguments given by those who oppose this practice, and the requirements of federal law on the subject. Notice that the author does not take a side or express personal opinions directly. The reader gets a sense of the complexity of the issue and also of some new perspectives on it.

A ROOM OF THEIR OWN*

LynNell Hancock and Claudia Kalb

ESSAY

1

What is the rhetorical situation?

Who can forget the pubescent pain of junior high? Boys sprout pimples, girls sprout attitude and both genders goad each other into a state of sexual confusion. Teachers in Manassas, Va., figured that all these colliding hormones were distracting students from their academic tasks. So officials at Marsteller Middle School decided to try something old: dividing girls and boys into separate academic classes. Eighth-grade girls say they prefer doing physics experiments without boys around to hog the equipment. Boys say they'd rather recite Shakespeare without girls around to make them feel "like geeks." An eerie return to the turn of the century, when boys and girls marched into public schools through separate doors? Yes, say education researchers. But will it work—and is it legal?

What is the issue?

2

What is the position of the schools that have set up single-sex classes?

In districts across the country, public schools are experimenting with sexual segregation, in the name of school reform. There is no precise tally, in part because schools are wary of drawing attention to classes that may violate gender-bias laws. But, researchers say, in more than a dozen states—including Texas, Colorado, Michigan and Georgia—coed schools are creating single-sex classes. Some, like Marsteller, believe that separating the sexes will eliminate distractions. Others, like Robert Coleman Elementary in Baltimore, made the move primarily to get boys to work harder and tighten up discipline.

3

What is the position of those who oppose single-sex classes?

The great majority of the experiments are designed to boost girls' math and science scores. The stimulus for these efforts was a report four years ago from the American Association of University Women, which argued that girls were being shortchanged in public-school classrooms—particularly in math and science. The single-sex classroom, however, is not what the gender-equity researchers involved with AAUW had in mind as a remedy. Their report was meant to help improve coeducation, not dismantle it. Research shows single-sex schools tend to produce girls with more confidence and higher grades. But single-sex classrooms within coed schools? There are no long-term studies of that approach, only a smattering of skeptics and true believers. "It's a plan that misses two boats," charges David Sadker, coauthor of *Failing at Fairness*—the education of boys, and the reality that children need to learn how to cope in a coed world. In short, says University of Michigan researcher Valerie Lee, "these classes are a bogus answer to a complex problem."

Newsweek, June 24, 1996, p. 76.

4   Critics worry that segregated classes will set back the cause of gender equity just when girls are finally being integrated into all-male academics. Half a century ago, boys in advanced science classes learned, for example, that mold is used for penicillin while girls in home economics learned that mold is the gunk on the shower curtain. "It's not an era we're eager to return to," says Norma Cantu of the U.S. Office of Civil Rights.

Miracles Happen

5   As a general principle, federal law doesn't permit segregation by sex in the public schools. (Exceptions can be made for singing groups, contact sports and human-sexuality and remedial classes.) Some schools have survived legal challenges by claiming that their all-girl classes fill remedial needs. A middle school in Ventura, Calif., faced down a challenge by changing the name of its all-girl math class to Math PLUS (Power Learning for Underrepresented Students). Enrollment is open to boys, though none has registered yet.

What is the position of the federal law?

6   Despite the skeptics, single-sex experiments continue to spread. Teachers and students believe they work. At the high school in Presque Isle, Maine, members of the popular all-girl algebra class go on to tackle the sciences. University of Maine professor Bonnie Wood found that girls who take the algebra course are twice as likely to enroll in advanced chemistry and college physics [as] their coed counterparts. Michigan's Rochester High School turns away 70 students every year from its girls-only science and engineering class. Marsteller boys raised their collective average in language arts by one grade after a single term. Girls boosted their science average by .4 of a point.

What is the current trend?

7   For the teachers involved, the progress is no mystery. Sheryl Quinlan, who teaches science at Marsteller, knows single-sex classes let her kids think with something besides their hormones. Impressing the opposite sex is a 14-year-old's reason for being. Take away that pressure, and miracles happen. Quinlan recalls the girl who took a "zero" on her oral report rather than deliver it in front of her boyfriend. Those days are over. Now, says Amanda Drobney, 14, "you can mess up in front of girls, and it's OK." We've come a long way, babies—or have we?

What is the authors' perspective as indicated in their final question?

FOR DISCUSSION: Recall when you were in junior high school. Do you think you would have learned more effectively in a single-sex classroom? Why or why not? What do you think should be done to help junior high and high school students learn in public schools?

◆◆◆

HOW TO WRITE AN EXPLORATORY PAPER

Now write an exploratory paper of your own. An exploratory paper will help you look at your issue from several angles, which will help you decide what position you want to take. Exploratory papers pave the way for position papers (taught in Parts Two and Three). If you write an exploratory paper before you write a position paper, you will find the position paper much easier to write. Not only will you have discovered your own position, but you will also understand some of the other views that you may want to refute. Explanations and examples in the Exercises and Activities for this chapter will set up the exploratory paper assignment. To complete it successfully, follow these general suggestions.

1. *Select an issue, and do some research and reading on it.* You will need a controversial issue to write about, one that invites several different perspectives. You may have an issue list you can refer to (see page 26). Or you may already have an issue, especially if you have written an issue proposal (pages 27–28) and several summary-response papers (page 88). If you do not have an issue, either read a set of related articles in "The Reader" to become acquainted with several perspectives on an issue, or select an issue of your own and read about it on the Internet and in the library. Refer to "How Should You Engage with Issues?" (pages 17–21) to help you find an issue, and then refer to "Suggestions to Help You with Library and Online Research" (pages 323–328) to help you locate information about it. Either take notes on the different perspectives you identify in this material, or make copies of the material you locate so that you can quote it later in your paper.

2. *Make an outline, a list, or notes to help you plan your draft.* Review other suggestions for prewriting made in this chapter to help you with this phase of your paper (see pages 93–102). At the very least, however, do the following things.

First, sketch out answers to the three parts of the rhetorical situation for your issue that are already in place before you begin to write: the exigence, the reading audience, and the constraints. What happened to arouse your interest in the first place? Who shares your position on the issue, who takes other positions, and why? What are some of the constraints for these various groups of people?

Second, identify at least three different ways that particular groups of people might think about your issue. For example, three perspectives on handgun control might be stated as follows: some people believe there should be no restrictions on personal handgun ownership; other people believe possession of handguns should be banned for everyone except police officers and military personnel; a third group believes people have a right to own handguns, but with restrictions including background checks, special training, and licensing. Notice that these are three different ways of looking at this issue, not three separate ideas about the issue. As you plan the perspectives for your paper, you can think about perspectives that are for, against, or in the middle; perspectives that represent three (or more) possible approaches or "takes" on an issue; perspectives that describe three (or more) possible ways to solve an issue; perspectives that provide three (or more) ways of interpreting an issue; and so on. These perspectives may be yours or other people's. Your objective, finally, is to identify at least three distinctly different ways to think about your issue.

3. *Write a draft, and include transitions.* Draw on some of the ideas for drafting a paper that are discussed in this chapter (pages 102–104). As you write your draft, include transitions to separate and emphasize the different perspectives on your issue. You might use transitions like "some people believe," "others believe," and "still others believe"; "one perspective on this issue is," "another perspective is," and "a final perspective is"; or "one way to look at this issue is," "another way is," and "a third way is."

4. *Work summarized ideas and quotes from your research into your draft.* You will mainly summarize, in your own words, the positions you describe in an exploratory paper. If you decide to add direct quotations to make these summaries clearer or more interesting, work the quotations smoothly into your draft so that they make sense in context and are easy to read. Tell your reader where the summarized ideas and quotations came from by introducing them with the authors' names and citing the page numbers of the original sources in parentheses at the end of the citations in the text.

Here is an example of research worked into a student exploratory paper. The paper is about different perspectives concerning the contributions men can make to family life. This student is summarizing the perspective that men can contribute in positive ways to child care. He draws ideas from the article by Jerry Adler that appears on pages 458–463 of "The Reader." Notice that he follows the MLA documentation style (see the Appendix to Chapter 12), including page numbers in parentheses to reference both his summaries of Adler's ideas and the direct quotations from Adler.

Some people believe that men are doing an admirable job of establishing strong family ties, particularly in their relationships with their children. Jerry Adler, author of "Building a Better Dad," shows that despite statistics that suggest few fathers actually take major responsibility for child care (459), there is still reason to believe that fathers have come a long way in having more influence over their children's lives. Seven out of every ten American fathers spend more time with their children than their own fathers did (460). Adler quotes Andrew Cherlin, a Johns Hopkins sociologist who studies American families. According to Cherlin, "Men today are better fathers when they're around--and worse when they're not" (460). Adler also shares some compelling stories that give hope to the whole situation, stories of a father like Robert Blumenfield who gets up every morning at 6:30 to make his son's breakfast, or a dad like Michael Greene who cranks up the radio and dances with his daughter (462). What an inspiration men can be when we apply ourselves.[15]

For further information on how to incorporate source material into your draft, see "Incorporating Research into Your First Draft" on pages 358–363. For further advice on how to cite these sources in the text itself, see the Appendix to Chapter 12.

---

[15]From a student paper by Tucker Norris; used with permission.

5. *Revise your paper, and include a list of works cited or references at the end.* Follow the suggestions for revision that appear on pages 105–109. At the end of your paper, list the works you have quoted in the text of your paper so that your reader can see where your citations came from. Refer to the Appendix to Chapter 12 for help with this. To cite articles that appear in "The Reader" in this book, show where they were published originally and also where they are published in this book. Follow example 20 on page 375. To create these citations, notice also that original publication information for each article in this book is provided in a footnote at the bottom of the first page of the article.

This is how the student who wrote the paragraph about fathers cited the Adler source on his Works Cited page.

Works Cited

Adler, Jerry. "Building a Better Dad." <u>Newsweek</u> 17 June 1996: 58-64. Rpt. in
    <u>Perspectives on Argument</u>. Nancy V. Wood. 4th ed. Upper Saddle River:
    Prentice, 2004. 458-63.

REVIEW QUESTIONS

1. What are some of the benefits of including reading as part of the writing process?
2. What are some of the decisions writers need to make when they get physically organized to write?
3. How can the writer use the rhetorical situation during the prewriting phase of a paper?
4. What are some of the prewriting strategies you will use?
5. Describe your method for writing a first draft.
6. What would help you if you got stuck in the process of writing a paper?
7. What would you need to pay particular attention to in the rewriting and revising phase of the writing process?

EXERCISES AND ACTIVITIES

A. CLASS PROJECT: CREATING A COMPOSITE OF THE CLASS'S WRITING PROCESS

When all class members contribute their usual strategies to a composite writing process, the result is usually a very complete description of a possible writing process. Focus on developing a process for writing argument, and write the title "Writing Argument" on the board. Under it write the four headings "Prewriting," "Writing," "Writing When You Get Stuck," and "Rewriting." Class members should contribute both the strategies they use and those they would like to use to each of the four lists. When the activity is completed, students may freewrite for a few minutes on the writing process they intend to use to write argument.

B. GROUP WORK: ANALYZING AN EXPLORATORY PAPER FROM A MAGAZINE

Analyze the exploratory paper "Coming and Going," which follows.

PREREADING

The whole class should preread and discuss the results.

1. Read the title and the first paragraph. What is the issue? What is your present position on the issue? (30 seconds)
2. What ideas do you predict in this essay? What question might be answered? (1 minute)
3. Survey the article by reading the first sentence in each paragraph and the final paragraph. What more have you learned about the essay? (1 minute)

READING

Each class member should read, underline, and annotate the essay and then discuss the results as a class. (5 minutes)

1. Describe the rhetorical situation from the point of view of the reader, using TRACE: Text, Reader, Author, Constraints, and Exigence.
2. Circle the transitional words and phrases.
3. What are the perspectives on the issue that the author identifies? Make a class list on the board.
4. What is the author's own perspective?
5. What common ground, if any, exists between you and this author?

POSTREADING

Working in pairs, discuss your responses to this article. Do you favor any of the perspectives in the article? Or do you have another perspective of your own? If so, what is it? Report some of these perspectives to the class. (3 minutes)

COMING AND GOING*

Nathan Glazer

1   Americans remain divided over immigration, because they are divided over the moral issues behind the question of how many people we should admit into this country. There are those—wilderness enthusiasts, conservationists, and others alarmed at population growth—who believe America already has enough

---

New Republic, November 17, 1997, pp. 13–14.

people; they worry about Census projections that, if present immigration trends continue, there will be about 400 million Americans by 2050.

2   For others, immigration is a matter of economics. The debate between those who say immigration is good for the economy (University of Maryland economist Julian Simon and journalist Ben Wattenberg) and those who say it is not (Harvard University economist George Borjas) seems to be swinging in the direction of the pessimists. A recent study by Kevin McCarthy and Georges Vernez of the RAND Corporation concludes that for California, the state with the most immigrants, economic costs outweigh the benefits. Highly educated immigrants, about half the total, do well; in time, they reach income parity with natives. Poorly educated immigrants, however, do not.

3   Less-skilled immigrants also hurt the earnings of less-skilled natives. McCarthy and Vernez estimate that between one and one-and-a-half percent of the adult native-born population in the U.S. has become unemployed or left the labor force because of competition from immigrants. In addition, unskilled immigration has contributed to a declining migration rate to California by native-born Americans from other parts of the country, and to an exodus of natives from California. But then there is Silicon Valley, which believes the U.S. should skew immigration policy to favor those with the education and skills that high-tech industry needs.

4   Yet another value that influences immigration policy is "diversity." A while back, it became clear that the current emphasis on promoting the immigration of close family members of current residents was hurting potential Irish immigrants: their family members in this country were too distantly related to qualify as sponsors for new immigrants. Hence the remarkable "diversity" lottery in which persons from "underrepresented" countries may apply for immigrant visas by lottery. By now, the lottery mostly benefits not the Irish, but Africans.

5   Finally, there are those for whom the dominant value in setting immigration policy is compassion. Admitting large numbers of refugees is their desideratum—though it does not solve the problem of deciding who among the refugees deserves entry most; nor does it limit the role of foreign policy and domestic political considerations in making such determinations.

6   So, when we debate immigration, we are really debating which of these competing and sometimes incompatible values should predominate. Keeping America's population small, or making it bigger? Making America—or certain segments of America—richer? More "diverse"? Compassion, for refugees and for families, for families separated, and for those trying to create one? I would vote for compassion, primarily for refugees and close family members of residents.

7   But moral intuition rarely withstands the messy realities of policymaking. When Congress debated a new immigration law in 1996, it seemed easy to agree that the new law should deal only with illegal immigrants. While then Wyoming Senator Alan Simpson also wanted to review and revise laws that permit about 800,000 legal immigrants to enter each year—a number, the polls say, that most Americans consider excessive—Congress was more responsive to the views of those who feel most strongly about immigration. Thus, pro-immigrant groups and high-tech industries were able to block any major changes in the law affecting legal immigrants.

8   The legislation that emerged, then, seemed to link toughness (a crackdown on illegals) with compassion (hands off legal immigrants). But the new law has led to a spate of heart-breaking, and seemingly illogical, situations in which illegal immigrants, who are long-settled U.S. residents, married, with children and jobs, have run afoul of the law. Some have been seized by immigration authorities upon returning from trips abroad for seemingly minor infractions of immigration law, and whisked back to their countries of origin. The new laws often mean alleged illegals have less opportunity for a hearing before they are deported.

9   One change that is having drastic consequences is the requirement that applications for legal immigrant status be made from abroad. And now if you are illegal for more than six months and leave the country for any reason you can be barred from returning for three years—ten years if you were in the country illegally for more than a year. According to *The New York Times,* some immigrants without green cards are giving up jobs as waiters and chefs—even closing businesses that employ scores of workers—in order to go home to escape penalties. How can that possibly help the American economy?

10   So, while we can all agree in principle that there should be no illegal immigration, when we begin to act on that principle, it turns out that the illegal immigrant is the person who works for us, or runs the restaurant we eat at, or takes care of the garden, and has a spouse and children and parents from whom he or she will be separated if the law is enforced. Then our principled position crumbles before human realities.

FOR DISCUSSION: Have you or any of your ancestors immigrated from another country? Or do you know someone outside of your family who is an immigrant? How have your experiences affected your perspective on this issue? Which of the positions discussed in this article do you personally identify with? Why?

◆◆◆

C. PAIRED STUDENT ACTIVITY: ANALYZING A STUDENT EXPLORATORY PAPER

The following is an example of an exploratory paper written by Tanya Pierce, a student in an argument class. Her position paper on the same subject appears at the end of the Appendix to Chapter 12 (pages 379–385). Take a few minutes to read Tanya's paper. Then work in pairs to answer the following questions. Report your answers to the class.

1. What is the issue?
2. Describe the parts of the rhetorical situation that were in place when Tanya started to write. What is the exigence? Who are the groups of people interested in this issue? What are their positions? What are some of the constraints of these groups? Now, finally, decide what kind of text this is and who the author is.

3. What are the perspectives on the issue that the author identifies? Make a list.
4. What transitions does the author use? Underline them.
5. What is the author's own perspective? Why does she hold it?
6. What is her claim? Underline it.

You may want to use Tanya's paper as a model for your own exploratory paper.*

Tanya Pierce
Exploratory Paper
Professor Snow
English 1302
10 February 2003

Trial by Jury: A Fundamental Right and a Flawed System

1

Explain the issue.

The right to a trial by jury is a fundamental part of the U.S. legal system. It is a right firmly entrenched in our democratic tradition. The jury system provides a buffer between the complex and often inflexible legal system and the average citizen on trial. The right to be judged by a jury of one's peers is a right that most Americans are willing to defend. However, due to a number of well-publicized jury decisions, some critics are questioning the value of this institution.

2

Describe the rhetorical situation:
• Exigence
• Interested parties
• Constraints

Our jury system is by no means flawless. It is subject to constant scrutiny and debate concerning its merit and its downfalls. As is true in all institutions, juries are capable of making mistakes. Psychological studies have been done on many aspects of jury behavior. Political scientists are also intrigued by juries and the manner in which they arrive at important decisions. Although I believe most Americans support the jury system, there has been considerable controversy surrounding it in recent years. One controversial decision was in the case of Lionel Tate, who was twelve years old when he killed a playmate in 2000, and thirteen when he was prosecuted as an adult in Florida. Tate was sentenced to life in prison without parole and with no opportunity for rehabilitation. Other recent cases of children tried and sentenced as adults in Florida were those of Nathaniel Brazill, who was thirteen when he was accused of shooting his teacher, and brothers Derek and Alex King, who were twelve and thirteen when they were accused of killing their father in 2001. Controversy over the jury decisions in these cases centered around whether or not individuals this young should be tried and sentenced as adults

*See the Appendix to Chapter 12 for the actual MLA format guidelines for student papers.

(Canady 1A). Earlier examples of public concern about jury decisions occurred in the Los Angeles trials of Rodney King, O. J. Simpson, and the Menendez brothers. The outrage following certain jury decisions highlights examples of instances when the jury system has come under fierce attack. From the public reaction to such decisions and others like them, it is very clear that the way in which juries reach their decisions is often as important to the American people as it is to the specific person on trial. Many people believe that the average jurist is not equipped to make the kinds of decisions jurors face. These critics' suggestions range from restructuring the system to totally eliminating it.

First perspective 3

Most average Americans, I believe, think that the right to a jury trial is a fundamental one, and its guarantees should be honored. These people would argue that laws are inflexible. Statutes cannot deal with the individual circumstances in each case, but juries can take these into account. Still others believe that juries are favorable because they reflect the morals and values of the community they come from. Indeed, many proponents of the jury support the system because of a particular kind of jury bias, the tendency for jurors to place justice above the law (Goldberg 457).

Second perspective 4

Opponents of the system argue that juries are uneducated in legal procedures and should not be given the type of responsibility they have traditionally had. These people also argue that juries are biased. In fact, the psychological literature provides many examples of this bias. Jurors are less likely to punish a sad or distressed defendant, as opposed to a joyful one, apparently because the defendant is already being punished emotionally (Upshaw and Romer 162). Some opponents say that although juries are instructed not to pay attention to the media, they are more easily influenced by the news than by the presiding judges. Critics of the jury system also point out that juries are expensive and are often unable to reach a consensus. They argue that the decision making should be left up to the people who know the law, the judges and the lawyers.

Third perspective 5

In between these two extremes are those people who agree with the jury system as a whole but believe that some changes need to be implemented to improve its effectiveness. These people suggest that juries receive instruction prior to hearing testimony as well as before they begin deliberations. They argue that this would improve the system by providing some working legal knowledge for the jurors as well as giving them an idea of what they are to listen for. Research has shown that in laboratory mock jury situations, exposing jurors to the laws involved in their decision making resulted in significantly fewer verdicts of guilty when compared to not exposing jurors to the relevant laws (Cruse and Brown 131). This finding suggests that lawyers and judges should have the responsibility of ensuring that the jury is adequately informed of the legal issues at hand and the laws and statutes available to handle those issues.

6

Author's perspective
• **Why she holds it**

As a prospective law student, I am fascinated by this topic. I think it is incredible that juries, made up of ordinary citizens, make some of the most profound legal decisions in the world. I decided to write on this particular issue because of my recent study of a decision by a jury in Texas that recommended probation instead of prison for a man who shot his wife several times, killing her, and also shot and injured her lover. Jury members did not want to send this individual to jail because they claimed his own remorse would punish him sufficiently over the years (Korosec 1A). This example forced me to evaluate the positive and negative aspects of jury trials.

7

Author's claim

The rise in crime in this country and the question of what to do with the offenders makes the role of juries even more compelling. As a whole, though, I believe that the American guarantee of trial by jury is a valuable one. I do think, however, that in order to improve its utility, judges and attorneys need to accept the responsibility for educating the jury on relevant legal issues. That is my claim. I will define the problem in detail and then explain how my solution of jury training can be implemented.

Works Cited

Canady, Dana. "As Florida Boy Serves Life Term, Even Prosecutor Wonders Why." New York Times 5 Jan. 2003, 1A+.

Cruse, Donna, and Beverly A. Brown. "Reasoning in a Jury Trial: The Influence of Instructions." Journal of General Psychology 114 (1987): 129-33.

Goldberg, Janice C. "Memory, Magic, and Myth: The Timing of Jury Instructions." Oregon Law Review 59 (1981): 451-75.

Korosec, Thomas. "Brosky Probation Stirs More Protests." Fort Worth Star-Telegram 26 Mar. 1993, Tarrant ed.: 1A+.

Upshaw, Harry S., and Daniel Romer. "Punishments of One's Misdeeds as a Function of Having Suffered from Them." Personality and Social Psychology Bulletin 2 (1976): 162-69.

FOR DISCUSSION: What jury trial have you followed in recent years? Did you think the jury made a fair judgment? If you had been on the jury, would you have agreed or disagreed? Why? Do you think the present jury system needs improvement? If so, what could be done to improve it?

◆◆◇

D. WRITING ASSIGNMENT: THE EXPLORATORY PAPER

Review "How to Write an Exploratory Paper" (pages 114–116) to help you complete this assignment. Then write a 750- to 900-word exploratory paper. Use the worksheet below to help you plan your exploratory paper. Follow MLA style (see the Appendix to Chapter 12) unless you are advised otherwise.

EXPLORATORY PAPER WORKSHEET

1. Write your issue in a complete sentence. Explain it, and include information that provides background and makes the issue interesting to your readers.
2. Explain the parts of the rhetorical situation that are already in place as you begin to write. Describe the exigence or context for your issue, including what happened to make people interested in it. Identify the groups of people interested in this issue, with a brief introduction to their positions, and mention some of the constraints of these groups.
3. Describe at least three different positions on your issue, say who holds them, and give some of their reasons for holding them. You may explain more than three positions if you want to. Jot down the positions.

   a. Position 1: _____

   b. Position 2: _____

   c. Position 3: _____

4. Explain your personal interest in the issue and the position you favor.
5. In your last paragraph, make a claim about your issue that sets forth your position. This is your starting point for the next paper you will write.

Part Two

UNDERSTANDING THE NATURE OF ARGUMENT FOR READING AND WRITING

THE PURPOSE OF THE NEXT FIVE CHAPTERS IS TO EXPLAIN THE ESSENTIAL PARTS OF AN ARGUMENT AND SHOW HOW THEY OPERATE TO CONVINCE AN AUDIENCE. CHAPTER 5 IDENTIFIES THE PARTS OF AN ARGUMENT AS EXPLAINED BY STEPHEN TOULMIN IN WHAT HAS COME TO BE KNOWN AS THE TOULMIN MODEL. CHAPTER 6 DESCRIBES THE TYPES OF CLAIMS AND PURPOSES IN ARGUMENT. CHAPTER 7 DESCRIBES HOW SUPPORT AND WARRANT COMBINE TO PROVIDE PROOF FOR ARGUMENT AND ALSO DISCUSSES LANGUAGE AND STYLE. CHAPTER 8 ALERTS YOU TO FALLACIES OR FALSE PROOFS, AND CHAPTER 9 PRESENTS ROGERIAN ARGUMENT AS AN ALTERNATIVE STRATEGY TO TRADITIONAL ARGUMENT. WHEN YOU FINISH READING PART TWO:

- ◆ You will understand and be able to identify the essential parts of an argument.

- ◆ You will know the key questions that arguments attempt to answer.

- ◆ You will be able to identify types of claims and purposes in argument.

- ◆ You will understand how argument employs proof, language, and style to appeal to your reason, your emotions, and your sense of values about people's character.

- ◆ You will know how to recognize and avoid using fallacies.

- ◆ You will know how to write a traditional position paper and make it convincing.

- ◆ You will know how to write a Rogerian argument paper and make it convincing.

Chapter 5

The Essential Parts of an Argument: The Toulmin Model

The purpose of the chapters in Part Two is to present some ideas from argument theory that will help you add strategies for reading and writing argument with confidence and expertise. Because people have been analyzing argument and writing theories of argument for twenty-five hundred years, there is a considerable tradition of theory to draw on to help with this task. A theoretical background is useful because theory describes argument, and once you possess good descriptions, argument will be more familiar and consequently easier for you to read and write yourself.

As you acquire new understandings of argument, you will be adding to what you already know and gradually building a stronger and larger body of knowledge and comprehension. Eventually, you will achieve "all-at-onceness," a quality Ann E. Berthoff describes in her book *The Sense of Learning* to describe the use of many ideas, bits of information, and strategies about reading and writing that finally come together so that you are able to use them unconsciously, simultaneously, and automatically.[1]

For now, however, you are still expanding your knowledge. Your goals in this chapter will be to get a better understanding of the usual anticipated outcomes of argument and to identify its component parts as they are identified by Stephen Toulmin in his model for argument.

THE OUTCOMES OF ARGUMENT: PROBABILITY VERSUS CERTAINTY

In Chapter 1 you learned that arguable issues require the possibility of at least two different views. It is the nature of argument to invite differing views and perspectives on issues. Outcomes can include achieving a closer agreement with a

---

[1]Ann E. Berthoff, *The Sense of Learning* (Portsmouth, N.H.: Boynton/Cook, 1990), pp. 86–91.

friendly audience or getting the attention of and even perhaps some consensus from a neutral or hostile audience. Notice that these outcomes of argument are usually not described as establishing certainty or truth in the same sense that mathematics and science seek to establish certainty and truth. We do not argue about the fact that $2 + 3 = 5$ or that the area of a circle is πr^2. Mathematical proofs seek to establish such truths. Argument seeks to establish what is probably true as well as what might be expedient or desirable for the future. Arguers tell you what they think for now along with what they think should be done, given their present information. On that basis, you decide what you think for now, given your present information.

Throughout history, some thinkers have been drawn more to the idea of establishing truth and some have been drawn more to the idea of establishing probabilities. In ancient times the Greek philosopher Plato was interested in establishing truth. He employed dialectic, the question-and-answer method used in his dialogues, to help participants discover the Platonic ideas about truth. Aristotle, another Greek philosopher, was interested in probabilities. His *Rhetoric,* written somewhere between 360 and 334 B.C., is a key book in the history of argument theory, and its purpose is to train persuasive speakers to be convincing to audiences. Aristotle observed the orators of his time and described what they did. He noted that they were mainly concerned with matters and views concerning both the present and the future that were probably true rather than certainly true. The reason for their perspective lay in the audience. The ancient audience, like modern audiences, would disagree with many views that were stated as absolutely true. Those audiences could think of exceptions and reasons why certain views might not be true. Responsible persuaders, to communicate effectively, had to modify and qualify their views to make them acceptable to their audiences. They had to present probabilities instead of absolute truths. Thus views that are probably true comprise the realm of argument. To understand that realm better, it is useful to understand the parts that contribute to the whole argument.

THE PARTS OF AN ARGUMENT ACCORDING TO THE TOULMIN MODEL

Stephen Toulmin, a modern English philosopher, developed a six-part model of argument in his book *The Uses of Argument,* and this model has been useful to many people for explaining the essential parts of an argument.[2] At the time Toulmin wrote his book, his colleagues were logicians who were interested in discovering truth rather than probabilities. Toulmin tells us that his book had a chilly welcome among those English colleagues. His graduate adviser at Cambridge, he tells us, "was deeply pained by the book, and barely spoke to me for twenty years." Another colleague described it as "Toulmin's *anti*-logic book."[3] After that,

---

[2]Stephen Toulmin, *The Uses of Argument* (Cambridge: Cambridge University Press, 1958). I have adapted and added applications of the model to make it more useful for reading and writing.
[3]"Logic and the Criticism of Arguments," in James L. Golden, Goodwin F. Berquist, and William E. Coleman, *The Rhetoric of Western Thought,* 4th ed. (Dubuque, Ia.: Kendall Hunt, 1989), p. 375.

Toulmin expected his book to be a failure. But his editors assured him that people were buying it, and Toulmin found out who many of these people were when he visited the United States some time later. Professors in speech departments and departments of communication all over the United States were using his book to teach students to become better argumentative speakers. If you have ever taken a speech class, you may have already encountered the Toulmin model of argument. As time went by, the model was picked up by English departments to help students improve their reading and writing of argument. The Toulmin model has also been used in schools of law to help students learn to present legal argument. You will find that you can employ the model to help you write essays, reports, letters of application, proposals, legal memos, or any other document intended to convince others. The Toulmin model is also useful in designing or interpreting visual argument, such as photos, television, or motion pictures, and in writing or analyzing persuasive speeches. The Toulmin model is a very natural and practical model because it follows normal human thought processes. You have had experience with all its parts either in the everyday arguments you carry on with your friends and family or in the arguments that you see on television.

The Toulmin model has six parts. The first three parts are essential to argument, including both traditional and Rogerian argument. They are (1) the *claim;* (2) the *data,* including subclaims and specific supporting details, which we are calling *support;* and (3) the *warrant.* Arguments may also contain one or more of three additional elements: (4) the *backing,* (5) the *rebuttal,* and (6) the *qualifier.* Figure 5.1 shows Toulmin's diagram of these six parts of the model.

Here is an example to illustrate how these parts work together in an actual argument: The narrator of a television program makes the *claim* that critical thinking is more important now than it was seventy years ago. This is followed by *support* that includes pictures of modern scientists launching space shuttles and air traffic controllers directing airplanes to land. These individuals seem intent and busy. It appears to be clear that if they do not think critically, there will be trouble. Then the camera switches to children riding on an old-fashioned school bus

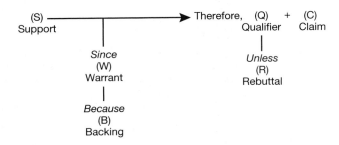

FIGURE 5.1   A Diagram of the Toulmin Model of Argument Showing the Three Essential Parts (Claim, Support, and Warrant) and the Three Optional Parts (Backing, Rebuttal, and Qualifier).

SOURCE: Adapted from Stephen Toulmin, *The Uses of Argument* (Cambridge: Cambridge University Press, 1958), p. 104.

of seventy years ago. One is saying that he wants to grow up and be a farmer like his dad. This youngster is relaxed and bouncing along on the bus. He doesn't look like he is thinking critically or that he will ever need to. The unspoken part of this argument, the assumption that the author of this program hopes the audience will share, is the *warrant*. The author hopes the audience will agree, even though it is not explicitly stated, that farmers of seventy years ago did not have to think critically, that modern scientists and engineers do have to think critically, and that critical thinking was not so important then as now. The author hopes that the audience will look at the two bits of support, the scientist and the farmer's son, and make the leap necessary to accept the claim. That's right, the audience will think, those scientists and that young boy don't seem to share the same demands for critical thinking. Times have changed. Critical thinking is more important now than it was seventy years ago. Those three parts, the *claim,* the *support,* and the *warrant,* are the three essential parts of an argument.

The other three parts, if present, might go like this: Suppose the camera then shifts to an old man, who says, "Wait a minute. What makes you assume farmers didn't think? My daddy was a farmer, and he was the best critical thinker I ever knew. He had to think about weather, crops, growing seasons, fertilizer, finances, harvesting, and selling the crops. The thinking he had to do was as sophisticated as that of any modern scientist." This old fellow is indicating that he does not share the unstated warrant that farmers of seventy years ago had fewer demands on their thinking processes than modern scientists. In response to this rejoinder, the author, to make the argument convincing, provides *backing for the warrant.* This backing takes the form of additional support. The camera cuts to the narrator of the program: "At least two out of three of the farmers of seventy years ago had small farms. They grew food for their families and traded or sold the rest for whatever else they needed. The thinking and decision making required of them was not as complicated and demanding as that required by modern scientists. Your father was an exception." Notice that this backing takes the form of a smaller unit of argument within the argument. It is linked to the main argument, and it is used to back up the weakest part of the main argument. Furthermore, this smaller argument has a claim-support-warrant structure of its own: (1) the *claim* is that most farmers did not have to think; (2) the *support* is that two out of three did not have to think and that the old man's father was an exception; and (3) the *warrant,* again unstated, is that the old man will believe the statistics and accept the idea that his father was an exception. If he accepts this backing for the new warrant by asking, "Hey, where did you get those statistics? They're not like any I ever heard," then another argument would need to be developed to cite the source of the figures and to convince the old man of their reliability. As you can see, the requests for backing, for more information to serve as further proof, can go on and on. But let's leave the old man and the narrator and look at what else might appear in this argument.

Suppose the camera now shifts to a modern science professor who wants to take exception with the claim itself by making a *rebuttal*. She makes her own claim: "The critical thinking required seventy years ago was demanding and sophisticated. Critical thinkers of that time had to figure out how to get the country out of a severe recession, and they had to develop the technology to win World War II." These opinions are then supported with factual evidence that includes pictures of individuals thinking.

After all of these challenges, exceptions, and requests for more information, the author at this point finds it necessary to *qualify* the original claim in order to make it acceptable to more of the audience members. Qualifying involves adding words and phrases to the claim like *sometimes, seems to be, maybe,* or *possibly* to make it more acceptable to the audience. In this case, the narrator now restates the qualified claim: "Critical thinking, because of modern science, seems to some people to be more important now than it was seventy years ago." Compare this with the original claim that critical thinking is more important now than it was seventy years ago. Figure 5.2 diagrams this argument according to the Toulmin model. You have probably never systematically used this or any other model to read or write argument. The model can serve as a kind of guide for reading and analyzing arguments and also for writing them. Authors do not usually use the model as an exact formula for writing, however. Rather, it describes what can be but is not necessarily always present in an argument. Consequently, when you read argument, you will at times easily recognize some parts of the model and at other times you will not. Some arguments, in fact, may not contain one or more of the parts at all, like a rebuttal, for example. You are not getting it wrong if you read and do not find all of the parts. When you write, you do not need to make all

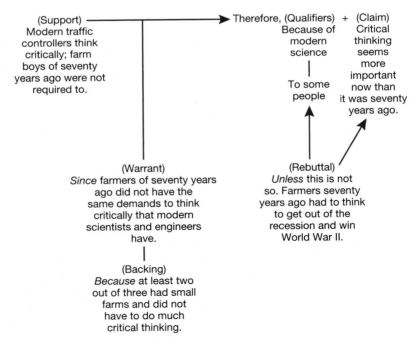

FIGURE 5.2   An Example of the Six Elements in the Toulmin Model.

parts explicit either. The following sections provide some details about each of the six parts that will help you understand them better.

CLAIM

Discover the claim of an argument by asking, "What is the author trying to prove?" Or plan a claim of your own by asking, "What do I want to prove?" The claim is the main point of the argument. Identifying the claim as soon as possible helps you focus on what the argument is all about.

Synonyms for *claim* are *thesis, proposition, conclusion,* and *main point.* Sometimes an author of an argument in a newspaper or magazine will refer to the "proposition," or an individual arguing on television will ask, "What is your point?" Both are referring to the claim. When someone refers to the claim as the conclusion, don't confuse it with the idea at the end of an argument. The claim can appear at the end, but it can also appear at other places in the argument. The claim is sometimes stated in a sentence or sentences called the *statement of claim.* This sentence can also be called the *thesis statement,* the *purpose sentence,* the *statement of focus,* or the *statement of proposition.*

The terms used in this text to describe the main elements in argument, along with some of their synonyms, appear in Box 5.1 (page 132). Become familiar with them so that you will understand other writers on the subject who may vary the terminology.

To locate the claim, what should you look for? The claim may be explicitly stated at the beginning of an argument, at the end, or somewhere in the middle. Or it may not be stated anywhere. It may sometimes be *implied,* in which case you will be expected to *infer* it. To infer an implicit claim, you will need to use what you already know about the subject along with what you have just read to formulate your own statement of it. In this case, the author is paying you a kind of compliment. The assumption is that you are smart enough to figure out the claim for yourself. You should probably make your own claims in your written arguments clear and explicit, however, at least at first.

Another interesting variation on the claim occurs in the case of irony. In irony the author says one thing but means something else. Usually the stated claim in irony is exaggerated, outrageous, or odd in some way. An example is the claim in "The Modest Proposal" (pages 430–436). You may read it and think to yourself, "Surely the author doesn't *mean* this." What does the author really mean? Again, you are expected to use your background and judgment to figure that out.

Authors often make conscious decisions about where to place a claim and whether to make it explicit or implicit. Their decisions are related to their notions about the audience. A claim at the beginning is straightforward and draws the reader in right away, like the claim in "A View from Berkeley" (pages 51–54) in paragraph 2: "We *should* consider race, ethnicity and gender along with many other factors in [college] admissions." Both parties are thinking along the same lines, together, from the outset. Or an author may decide to lead up to the claim, in which case it may appear either in the middle or at the end. For example, the claim in "Pay Your Own Way! (Then Thank Mom)" (pages 22–24) appears near

---

BOX 5.1   **Argument Terminology: Terms Used in This Book and Some of Their Synonyms.**

WHAT TERMS ARE USED IN ARGUMENT?

TERMS	SYNONYMS	
Claim	Thesis Proposition Conclusion	Main point Macro-argument Controlling idea
Statement of claim	Thesis statement Purpose sentence	Statement of focus Statement of proposition
Subclaims	Reasons Main ideas Micro-arguments Arguments	Lines of argument Supporting arguments Specific issues
Support	Evidence Opinions Reasons Examples Facts Data Grounds	Proof Premise Statistics Explanations Information Personal narratives
Warrants	Assumptions General principles Widely held values Commonly accepted beliefs Appeals to human motives	Cultural values Presuppositions Unstated premises Generally accepted truths

the beginning of the essay, at the end of paragraph 2: "The notion that parents must finance their children's education is ridiculous." And the claim in "The Laptop Ate My Attention Span" (pages 24–25) appears at the end, in the final paragraph: "I agree. Let them control themselves," the author says, agreeing with college officials, but then she qualifies her claim with what ought to happen to students who log on to their laptops at inappropriate times.

Delaying the claim pulls the audience in and increases interest and attention. "What is this author after?" the audience wonders, and reads to find out. The end of an essay is the most emphatic and memorable place for a claim. Many authors prefer to put the claim there to give it as much force as possible. There is some risk involved in putting the claim at the end. Students who use this strategy must be careful to insert cues along the way so that readers understand where the argument is headed and do not feel they are being led through a random chain of topics. Both the unstated claim and the ironic claim require special attention on the part of the reader, who has to make an inference to figure them out. As a result of this effort, the reader may find an inferred claim especially convincing and memorable.

The claim, whether implied or explicitly stated, organizes the entire argument, and everything else in the argument is related to it. The best way to identify it, if it is not obvious or easy to locate, is to complete the following statement as soon as you have finished reading: "This author wants me to believe that . . ." When you have finished that statement, you have the claim. As a writer, you can check your own claim during revision by completing this statement: "I want my audience to agree that . . ." Can you do it? If you can, you understand the concept of the claim, and you will be able to recognize the main point in the arguments you read and to use a claim to articulate the main point in any argument you write.

SUPPORT

Discover the support in an argument by asking, "What additional information does the author supply to convince me of this claim?" Or if you are the author, ask, "What information do I need to supply to convince my audience?" You can summarize the most essential elements of an argument as a *claim with support.* Aristotle wrote in his *Rhetoric* that the only necessary parts of an argument are the statement of proposition (the claim) and the proof (the support). There has been general agreement about those two essential parts of an argument for more than twenty-three hundred years.

The synonyms that Toulmin uses for *support* are *data* and *grounds,* the British equivalents. In the United States you will often read arguments in which the author claims to be "grounding" a claim with particular support, and *data* is sometimes used as a synonym for *facts and figures.* Other synonyms for support are *proof, evidence,* and *reasons.* Sometimes authors refer to major evidence as *premises.* When you encounter that term in your reading, remember that premises lead to and support a conclusion (a claim). Don't confuse premises with the claim.

SUBCLAIMS. Most arguments contain two levels of support. At the first level of support are the subclaims, which are the supporting arguments or reasons for the claim. We will present two examples that illustrate the relationships among the issues, related issues, claims, and subclaims in argument. Included are the following:

- ◆ *Two issue areas, racism* and *the environment,* that are at the most general level in these examples
- ◆ *Two of many possible specific related issues* in these issue areas that represent ideas *about* the general issue areas
- ◆ *Examples of claims* made in response to the specific related issues that are even more specific
- ◆ *Examples of some subclaims* used to support the claims (The subclaims are at the most specific level in this example because they represent ideas about the claims.)

Example 1

ISSUE AREA: RACISM

Specific related issue: Where do racist attitudes come from?
   Claim: People are not born with racist attitudes; they have to be taught them.
      Subclaims: 1. Some parents transmit racist attitudes.
                   2. The press can reinforce racist attitudes.
                   3. Peer groups can also strengthen racist attitudes.
                   4. Segregated schools and neighborhoods contribute to racist attitudes.

Example 2

ISSUE AREA: THE ENVIRONMENT

Specific related issue: How serious are the world's environmental problems?
   Claim: The environment is the single most serious problem the world faces today.
      Subclaims: 1. The rain forests are being destroyed, causing global warming.
                   2. Increasing population is depleting resources in some parts of the world.
                   3. Many important water sources are being polluted by industry.
                   4. The ozone layer, which protects us from harmful sun rays, is being destroyed by chemicals.

SPECIFIC SUPPORT. The second level of support is the specific support. Specific support provides the evidence, opinions, reasoning, examples, and factual information about a claim or subclaim that make it possible for us to accept it. Look back at the claims and subclaims in the examples above. If you are to take these claims seriously, you will want some additional specific support to make them convincing.

To locate such support, what should you look for? One bit of good news: support is always explicitly stated, so you will not have to infer it as you sometimes have to infer the claim. Thus an understanding of the types of support is all you really need to help you recognize it. Let us look at some of the most common types.

FACTS. In a court of law, factual support (the murder weapon, for example) is laid out on the table. In written argument, it must be described. Factual support can include detailed reports of *observed events;* specific *examples* of real happenings; references to *events*, either *historical* or *recent;* and *statistical reports*. Factual support is vivid, real, and verifiable. Two people looking at it together would agree on its existence, and what it looks like. They might not agree on what it *means* to each of them—that is, they might interpret it differently. But essentially they would agree on the facts themselves.

OPINIONS. When people start interpreting the facts, opinion enters the picture. The following quotation is an example of some statistics that have been interpreted. The author is a wildlife scientist who has studied wolves and other wild animals in Alaska for many years, and he is arguing against a plan by the state of Alaska to shoot wolves in order to protect herds of caribou. The issue continues to be debated in the twenty-first century in Alaska.

> The state is portraying the wolf kill as an emergency measure to boost the size of what is called the "Delta caribou herd," which ranges east of Denali. But the herd's population decrease since 1989—from 11,000 to 4,000—represents little more than a return to the numbers that prevailed for decades until the mid-80's. The short-lived increase to 11,000 probably resulted largely from a temporary shift of caribou from a neighboring herd.
>
> The Delta herd didn't even exist until about 60 years ago; it is probably an offshoot of a much larger herd farther to the east. There is no major caribou-hunting tradition in this area, so the plan is not a matter of restoring something that hunters had enjoyed for generations. Over the past 12 months, most of the Delta herd has spent most of its time well outside the wolf-control area.
>
> In fact, the state's view that this and other caribou herds should be managed at stable or minimum sizes is a mistake. Virtually all of Alaska's caribou belong to a single population within which, over the span of decades, there are shifting centers of abundance. Thousands of caribou may abandon a range they have inhabited for decades and move to an area where numbers have traditionally been low. Despite recent declines in the Delta herd and in several nearby areas, other herds have increased dramatically. Statewide, the number of caribou has more then tripled over the past 15 years to about a million animals and is continuing to increase rapidly.[4]

Note that the raw data, the herd's decrease in numbers from 11,000 to 4,000, have been interpreted and explained. The author says the decrease in the caribou population has probably been caused by the herd's moving around and that actually there are now more caribou statewide than fifteen years ago. Thus there is no need to slaughter wolves to protect caribou. State officials had interpreted the same data to indicate that wolves should be killed to save the caribou. You need to distinguish between facts everyone would agree on and interpret in the same way and facts that are open to interpretation and opinion. We do not argue with the facts, as the saying goes, unless of course they are lies or they omit important information. We do, however, argue with interpretation and opinion.

Opinions may be the personal opinions of the author or the opinions of experts the author selects to quote. The author may use direct quotations, set off in quotations marks, or summaries or paraphrases of what someone else thinks or has said. Furthermore, opinions may be informed, based on considerable knowledge and excellent judgment, or they may be ill-founded, based on hearsay and gossip. The most convincing opinions are those of experts, whether they be those of the author or of another person. Experts possess superior background, education, and experience on an issue. Contrast in your own mind the opinions of experts with the uninformed opinions of people on the evening news who are frequently cornered in the streets by reporters to give their opinions. Informed personal opinions and the opinions of experts can be more interesting and convincing than the facts themselves. Ill-founded, baseless opinion is boring and rarely convincing.

---

[4]Gordon C. Haber, "The Great Alaska Wolf Kill," *New York Times*, October 2, 1993, p. A23.

Examples. Examples can be real or made up, long or short. They are used to clarify, to make material more memorable and interesting, and in argument particularly, to prove. Examples that are real, such as instances of actual events or references to particular individuals, function in the same way that fact does in an argument. They are convincing because they are grounded in reality. Made-up or hypothetical examples are invented by the writer and, like opinions, can only demonstrate probabilities. Personal experience is one type of example that is frequently used in argument. Writers often go into considerable detail about the experiences that have influenced them to think and behave as they do. Combining personal experience with the opinions and reasoning derived from it is a common way to develop a claim.

There are no set rules about the placement of support in an argument. Support can appear before the claim, as in the following example: "The caribou have moved around and are alive [the subclaim]; in fact, there are about a million of them [specific support]; *therefore,* we do not need a wolf-kill policy [claim]." Or support can appear after the claim: "The wolf-kill policy should be abandoned [claim] *because* the caribou have moved around [subclaim], and there exist three times as many of them as fifteen years ago [specific support]."

Different authors manage support in different ways depending on the requirements of the subject, their purpose, and their audience. When the issue is an abstract idea and the audience is informed, the author may present mainly opinions and few, if any, facts or examples. Such arguments include a claim and blocks of logical reasoning organized around subclaims to develop and prove the claim. If you were to outline the argument, you might not need more than two levels, as in the claim and subclaim examples on pages 133–134. When the subject requires more specific support or the audience needs more information to be convinced, specific materials at lower levels on an outline are required to ground the subclaims in facts, figures, quotations from others, or author opinions.

Here is an example that illustrates these levels.[5] It includes (1) a general issue area, (2) one of many specific issues that could be generated by it, (3) a claim, (4) some subclaims, and (5) some support.

Example

Issue Area: Cities
Specific related issue: How should cities be planned so that people will live happily in them?
  Claim: Inner cities can be made more inhabitable.
    Subclaim: One way is to ban automobiles and encourage walking.
      Support: With no cars, people are forced to walk and interact, and interacting is pleasant. (opinion)
    Subclaim: Another way is to eliminate public housing projects.
      Support: More than half the poor live in public housing. (fact)
      Support: Warehousing the poor is destructive to the neighborhood and occupants. (opinion)

---

[5]The items in the example are from Witold Rybczynski, "How to Rebuild Los Angeles," *New York Times,* June 6, 1992, p. A15.

To summarize, support comprises both the subclaims and all the explicitly stated explanations, information, facts, opinions, personal narratives, and examples that authors use to make their claims and subclaims convincing and believable. Notice that support may be true, as in the case of facts and real examples, or probable, as in the case of opinions and made-up stories and examples.

Readers and writers of argument should require that the support in an argument be acceptable and convincing. Subclaims should clearly advance the argument and be convincing. Factual evidence needs to be true and verifiable. All evidence needs to be clear, relevant, and understandable. It also should represent all of the significant information available; it must, in other words, be an adequate sample. The experts whose opinions are quoted should be real experts, and their credentials should, when necessary, be stated by the author to establish their degree of expertise. Personal opinion, to be convincing, should be original, impressive, interesting, and backed by factual knowledge, experience, good reasoning, and judgment. Support that meets these requirements is not only accepted but often shared by the audience because they have had similar experiences and ideas themselves. Such quality support helps build common ground between the arguer and the audience. Rantings, unfounded personal opinions that no one else accepts, or feeble reasons like "because I said so" or "because everyone does it" are not effective support. Audiences usually do not believe such statements, they do not share experiences or ideas suggested by them, and they lose common ground with the arguer when they read or hear them.

When reading argument, to help you focus on and recognize the support, complete this sentence as soon as you finish: "The author wants me to believe that . . . [the claim] because . . . [list the support]." When you read to revise your own writing, you can complete this statement: "I have convinced my audience to believe [the claim] because [list your support]."

WARRANTS

Warrants are the assumptions, general principles, conventions of specific disciplines, widely held values, commonly accepted beliefs, and appeals to human motives that are an important part of any argument.[6] Even though they can be spelled out as part of the written argument, usually they are not. In many instances it would be redundant and boring if they were. For example, an argument might go as follows: *Claim:* The president of the United States is doing a poor job. *Support:* The economy is the worst it has been in ten years. The unstated *warrants* in this argument might include the following *generally accepted beliefs:* the president is responsible for the economy; when the economy is weak, it is a sign that the president is doing a poor job; or even though the president may be doing well in other areas, a robust economy is the main index to overall performance. You

---

[6]Toulmin's warrants are somewhat similar to Bitzer's treatment of audience as a constraint in the rhetorical situation. Bitzer, however, extends the concept of constraints to also include the resources available to the writer and the type of text being produced, whether written, spoken, or visual. Thus constraints is a broader concept than warrants.

may be able to think of some other ways of expressing the warrants in this argument. Since individual audience members vary in their backgrounds and perspectives, not everyone will state the warrants in exactly the same way.

Here is another example, and this one relies on a *value warrant. Claim:* Business profits are adversely affected by environmental protection laws. *Support:* Obeying environmental protection laws that call for clean air, for example, costs industry money that could otherwise be realized as profit. The unstated *warrants* in this argument involve the relative value individuals place on the environment and on business profit and might be stated thus: profit is more important than clean air, businesses must make a profit to survive, or environmental protection laws are threatening the capitalistic system.

Finally, here is an example of a warrant that relies on a *commonly accepted convention* of a specific discipline, which in this case is the discipline of writing. *Claim:* You have received a failing grade on this paper. *Support:* You have several sentence fragments and subject-verb agreement errors in your paper. The unstated *warrants* could be stated as follows: these types of errors result in a failing grade in college papers, or the conventions of writing college papers do not allow fragments and subject-verb agreement problems. When you encounter argument in your other college courses, try to identify the warrants that are implicit in these arguments and that are also part of the generally accepted knowledge or the conventions that inform these particular disciplines. Such warrants could include laws in physics, equations in mathematics, or theories in philosophy. Such information is not always spelled out in every argument, particularly if the people who are arguing share the same background information about these conventions, laws, equations, or theories. A physicist, for example, would not have to state the law of gravity to fill in the argument that an object dropped from a bridge will fall into the water below. Instead, the arguer assumes that the audience knows about the law of gravity and will mentally fill it in to complete an argument. Toulmin called the warrants that are specific to particular disciplines *field-dependent* because they are understood and accepted by individuals who have background and expertise in specific fields of knowledge. They can be differentiated from *field-independent* warrants that cut across disciplines and would be accepted by most people. The belief that the president should improve the economy is an example of a field-independent warrant.

Warrants originate with the arguer. Note, however, that the warrants also exist in the minds of the audience. They can be *shared* by the arguer and the audience, or they can be *in conflict.* Furthermore, if the audience shares the warrants with the arguer, the audience will accept them, and the argument is convincing. If the warrants are in conflict and the audience does not accept them (they believe private enterprise, not the president, is responsible for improving the economy, or they believe sentence fragments are acceptable in academic writing because many widely admired writers have used them), the argument is not convincing to them.

Here is another example. A politician arguing that crimes are caused by a lack of family values expects the audience to supply the warrant that people with family values do not commit crimes. The argument is strong and convincing for audiences who happen to share those values and who thus share the warrant. It is not so convincing for audience members who believe there are other causes for crime that have nothing to do with family values. A conflicting warrant might be the belief that peer groups, not families, cause people to turn to crime.

Notice how warrants themselves, when they are recognized by the audience as either acceptable or not, can themselves become claims for new arguments. The examples of the two warrants about what causes crime can each be stated as new claims and supported as new arguments. Developing warrants as subjects for new arguments is called *chaining arguments.* The process can go on indefinitely and can help move an argument in a variety of interesting directions. For example, if one claims that peer groups cause crime and then supports that claim with the evidence that gangs are notorious for committing crimes, the shared warrant would be that gang members are criminals. That warrant could then become a claim for a new argument about the criminal records of gangs. A conflicting warrant, that many gang members are law-abiding citizens, could become the claim for a different argument that would provide an entirely different view of gang members.

Besides being related to what people commonly believe, value, want, or accept as background knowledge in a discipline, warrants are also culture-bound. Since values, beliefs, and training vary from culture to culture, the warrants associated with them also differ from culture to culture. Tension between Japan and the United States was caused by a Japanese official's claim that American workers are lazy and do not work hard enough. American workers were angry and countered with a rebuttal about how hard they think they work. Japanese and American workers have different work schedules, attitudes, and experience with leisure and work time. Consequently, the part of both arguments that was unstated, the warrant, described hard work in different ways for each culture. The lack of a shared warrant caused the tension. Furthermore, neither side was convinced by the other's argument.

You may be wondering at this point, "How am I going to be able to understand warrants when they usually are not printed on the page, they exist in the minds of the author and the audience, and they may even differ from one individual or culture to another?" You will not have the difficulty with warrants that you may be anticipating because you already know a great deal about people and the opinions and beliefs they are likely to hold. You may have never noticed warrants before, but once you become aware of them, you will recognize them in every argument you read. Warrants are one of the most interesting features of argument. They represent the psychology of an argument in the sense that they reveal unspoken beliefs and values of the author and invite you to examine your own beliefs and make comparisons.

Finding warrants is not very different from "psyching people out" or trying to discover their real reasons for saying things. Here is an example that might make finding warrants easier. Suppose your spouse or roommate makes the claim that you really should start sleeping at night, instead of staying up to study, because it is more beneficial to study in the daytime. As support, you are reminded that sunshine keeps people from getting depressed, that people sleep more soundly at night than in the day, and that you need to build daytime work habits because you will probably not get a nighttime job when you graduate.

To understand the warrants in this argument, you must try to figure out what else your roommate believes, values, and wants but has not said directly. The warrants might include these: Daytime people are better than nighttime people; you should be like other people and change your work habits to conform; you will get more done in the daytime because other people do; and you will have trouble switching from night to day if you ever have to. You might go a step further and ask, "Why else is my roommate trying to change my work habits? What is the hidden agenda?" Maybe it is because you leave the lights on and music playing all night. We figure out the subtexts or hidden agendas in our conversations with other people all the time. Warrants and hidden agendas are not the same, as you can see from these examples, but they are similar in the sense that neither are usually spelled out and that discovering them requires looking for what is left unstated in our communications with other people.

Some of the synonyms for warrants are *unstated assumptions, presuppositions of the author,* and *unstated premises.* Warrants are also sometimes described as general truths that the audience will accept as true.

Warrants provide critical links in argument. For instance, they link the support to the claim by enabling an audience to accept particular support as proof of a particular claim. Without the linking warrant, the support may not be convincing. Here is an example.

Claim:	The appeal process for criminals should be shortened . . .
Support:	because the appeals for criminals on death row can cost more than $2 million per criminal.
Expected warrant:	Spending more than $2 million to keep a convicted criminal alive a little longer is a waste of money. *(This individual shares the author's warrant, the link is made, and the argument is convincing.)*
Alternative warrant:	We are dealing with human life here, and we should spend whatever is necessary to make certain we have a fair conviction. *(This individual supplies an opposing warrant, the link between claim and support is not made, and the argument is not convincing.)*

Supply your own warrant in the following argument.

Claim:	The government should abolish loan funds for college students . . .
Support:	because many students default on their loans, and the government cannot tolerate these bad debts.
Warrant:	*(Do you believe that evidence supports that claim? If yes, why? If no, why? Your answer provides the warrant. Is the argument convincing for you?)*

These examples demonstrate that the warrant links the evidence and the claim by justifying particular evidence as support for a particular claim. Notice also, however, that the warrant attempts to establish a link between the author and the audience as well. Shared warrants result in successful arguments. When the warrant is not shared or when there are conflicting warrants, the audience will question or disagree with the claim. When American workers argued with the Japanese about whether they are lazy or hardworking, a shared warrant was missing.

Japanese claim:	American workers are lazy . . .
Support:	because they work only 40 hours a week.
Japanese warrant:	People who work only 40 hours a week are lazy.
American rebuttal:	American workers are hardworking . . .
Support:	because they work 40 hours a week.
American warrant:	People who put in 40 hours a week are industrious and hardworking.

Perhaps now you can begin to appreciate the importance of shared warrants in argument. Shared warrants are crucial to the success of an argument because they are the most significant way to establish common ground between reader and writer in argument. Shared warrants and common ground, as you can imagine, are particularly important in international negotiations. Skillful negotiators take time to analyze warrants and to determine whether or not both parties are on common ground. If they are not, communication breaks down and argument fails.

At this point, you may wonder why authors do not spell out the warrants, since they are so essential to the success of the argument. There are two reasons for usually leaving warrants unstated, so that the audience has to supply them. First, an audience who supplies the warrant is more likely to buy in to the argument through a sense of participation. If there is potential for agreement and common ground, it will be strengthened by the audience's supplying the warrant. Second, remember that audiences differ and that their views of the warrant also vary somewhat, depending on their past experiences and present perceptions. A stated warrant negates the rich and varied perceptions and responses of the audience by providing only the author's interpretation and articulation of the warrant. Less active participation is then required from the audience, and the argument is less powerful and convincing to them.

To help you discover warrants, ask questions like the following:

What is left out here?
What does this author value? Do I share those values?
What is causing this author to say these things?
Do I believe that this evidence supports this claim? Why or why not?

As the author of argument, you should consider your audience and whether or not it will accept your warrants. More information will be provided in Chapter 10 to help you do so. Now let's look at the other three parts of the Toulmin model, the optional elements. All or none might appear in a written argument.

BACKING

You should have a sense by now that warrants themselves may require their own support to make them more acceptable to an audience, particularly if the audience does not happen to share them with the author. An author may provide backing, or additional evidence to "back up" a warrant, whenever the audience is in danger of rejecting it. When you are the author, you should provide backing also. In exchanges like debates or rebuttal letters to the editor, the author is sometimes asked to prove the warrant with additional support. Or the author may analyze the beliefs and values of the audience, anticipate a lack of common ground, and back the warrant with additional support explicitly in the text, just in case. For example, in the criminal appeals argument, the author might back the warrant that it is a waste of time to spend $2 million on a criminal appeal with additional statistical evidence that shows these appeals rarely result in a changed verdict. This additional backing would improve the likelihood that the audience would accept the claim.

Here is another example of backing for a warrant.

Claim: All immigrants should be allowed to come into the United States . . .

Support: because immigration has benefited the U.S. economy in the past.

Warrant: Current economic conditions are similar to past conditions.

Backing: Now, as in the past, immigrants are willing to perform necessary low-paying jobs that American citizens do not want, particularly in the service areas. *(Statistics could be supplied to show how many jobs of this type are available.)*

Look for backing in an argument by identifying the warrant and then determining whether or not you accept it. If you do not, try to anticipate additional information that would make it more acceptable. Then look to see if the author supplied that or similar additional support.

REBUTTAL

A rebuttal establishes what is wrong, invalid, or unacceptable about an argument and may also present counterarguments, or new arguments that represent entirely different perspectives or points of view on the issue. To attack the validity of the claim, an author may demonstrate that the support is faulty or that the warrants are faulty or unbelievable. Counterarguments start all over again, with a new set of claims, support, and warrants.

Here is an example of a rebuttal for the argument about immigration.

Rebuttal 1: Immigrants actually drain more resources in schooling, medical care, and other social services than they contribute in taxes and productivity.

Rebuttal 2: Modern immigrants are not so willing to perform menial, low-skilled jobs as they were in past generations.

Here is an example of a counterargument for the immigration argument.

Claim: Laws should be passed to limit immigration . . .

Support: because we have our own unskilled laborers who need those jobs.

Warrant: These laborers are willing to hold these jobs.

Rebuttals may appear as answers to arguments that have already been stated, or the author may anticipate the reader's rebuttal and include answers to possible objections that might be raised. Thus an author might write a rebuttal to the claim that we should censor television by saying such a practice would violate the First Amendment. Or if no claim has been made, the arguer could anticipate what the objections to television violence might be (violence breeds violence, children who see violence become frightened, etc.) and refute them, usually early in the essay, before spelling out the reasons for leaving television alone.

Here is another example. In an advertisement published in the *New York Times*, members of the National Rifle Association ask, "What kind of Mom puts a political agenda ahead of a child's safety?" They then answer their question.

> Not the American moms we know.
> Last week we offered a million-dollar incentive to put politics aside and put lifesaving gun safety education in every elementary classroom in America—ours or any equivalent program.
> Our invitation was categorically rejected by march organizers in league with the antigun lobby and this Administration.
> Their scolding refusal admitted their goal is instead "the licensing of handgun owners and the registration of handguns to protect our children . . . similar to that required for drivers and cars."
> That's preposterous. Thinking moms know that licensing drivers and registering cars doesn't make kids safer. What makes kids safe from cars is teaching them to look both ways before crossing the street.
> Despite their claims, the effect won't be safer kids. Just a political agenda masquerading as motherhood.[7]

Notice the two positions described here, that of the National Rifle Association and that of the antigun lobby. Most of this passage is a rebuttal of the position held by gun-control proponents.

Look for a rebuttal or plan for it in your own writing by asking, "What are the other possible views on this issue?" When reading, ask, "Are other views represented here along with reasons?" Or when writing, ask, "How can I answer other views?" Phrases that might introduce refutation include *some may disagree, others may think,* or *other commonly held opinions are,* followed by the opposing ideas and your reasons and evidence for rejecting them.

QUALIFIERS

Remember that argument is not expected to demonstrate certainties. Instead, it establishes probabilities. Consequently, the language of certainty (*always, never, the best, the worst,* and so on) promises too much when used in claims or in other parts of the argument. It is not uncommon for an author to make a claim and in

---

[7]*New York Times*, May 12, 2000, p. A27.

the midst of writing to begin revising and qualifying it to meet the anticipated objections of an audience. Thus words like *always* and *never* change to *sometimes; is* or *are* change to *may be* or *might; all* changes to *many* or *some; none* changes to *a few;* and *absolutely* changes to *probably* or *possibly.* Qualified language is safer for demonstrating the probabilities of an argument. Look to see if the author has stated the claim in other parts of the argument in probable or absolute terms, and then read the entire argument to figure out why.

The following is a qualified version of the claim that all immigrants should be allowed to come into the United States. These qualifications would make the original claim more acceptable to the people who offered the rebuttals and counterargument.

> Immigrants should be allowed to enter the United States only if they can prove that they already have jobs yielding sufficient income to offset social services and that no American citizens are currently available to perform these jobs.

VALUE OF THE TOULMIN MODEL FOR READING AND WRITING ARGUMENT

The Toulmin model has some advantages that make it an excellent model for both reading and writing argument. Its most essential advantage is that it invites common ground and audience participation in the form of shared warrants, increasing the possibility of interaction between author and audience. The three optional parts of the model also encourage an exchange of views and common ground because they require an arguer both to anticipate other perspectives and views and, at times, to acknowledge and answer them directly. The backing, for instance, requires additional evidence to satisfy audience concerns. The rebuttal requires answers to different or opposing views. The qualifier requires a modification of the claim to gain audience acceptance. The backing, rebuttal, and qualifier in the Toulmin model invite audience participation. They encourage dialogue, understanding, and agreement as argument outcomes. These features make the model valuable for examining the multiple perspectives likely to be expressed in response to complex modern issues.

The model works for reading or writing not only in debate and single-perspective argument but also in academic inquiry, negotiation, dialectic, Rogerian argument (explained in Chapter 9), or any other form of argument that requires exchange and attempts to reach agreement. It can even be a useful tool for one-on-one argument or personal decision making.

Writers of argument find the Toulmin model useful as both an invention strategy and a revision strategy. It can be used to help an author come up with the essential parts of an argument in the first place, and later it can be used to check and evaluate the parts of a newly written argument. See pages 151–152 for a writing assignment that uses the Toulmin model as a tool to help the writer think about the parts of a position paper. See pages 150–151 for an example of a student-written position paper with its Toulmin elements labeled in the margins.

Readers of argument find the model useful for analyzing and describing the essential parts of a written argument. Listeners find it just as useful for analyzing and describing the essential parts of an argumentative speech. Viewers find they can use the model to analyze visual argument whether it appears on television, in film, or in photographs, charts, graphs, and drawings accompanying printed text. It can be used to write or to analyze both consensual and adversarial arguments. It accommodates all of the various forms of arguments. The model is summarized in a handy chart for quick reference for the use of both readers and writers in the Summary Charts (page 440).

REVIEW QUESTIONS

1. Name and describe the three essential parts of the Toulmin model. Do the same for the three optional parts.
2. What are some synonyms for each of the three essential parts of the Toulmin model? Consult Box 5.1.
3. What are subclaims? What are some types of specific support?
4. Define warrants. Why does argument work better when warrants are shared by the arguer and the audience?
5. Give some examples of qualifiers.

EXERCISES AND ACTIVITIES

A. GROUP WORK AND CLASS DISCUSSION: TRUTH VERSUS PROBABILITY

This activity invites you to compare topics that are true and therefore not arguable with topics that are probable and thus open to argument. Think about one other course you are taking this semester, and write down one example of something you have learned in that course that is absolutely true or untrue and that you would not argue about. Then write one example of something you have learned in that course that is only probably true or untrue and that you might argue about. Make a class list of these examples. Think carefully about everything you put in the true and untrue columns. These must be topics that no one would argue about because they have been proved to be true or untrue. Here are some key words to help you think about these two types of information.

True: certain, fact, exact statement, right, correct, valid; wrong, incorrect, invalid

Probable: possible, opinion, qualified, reasonable, sound; unreasonable, unsound

You will be learning both types of information in college. Which topics on the probable list might be good topics for argument papers?

B. GROUP WORK AND CLASS DISCUSSION: USING THE TOULMIN MODEL TO ANALYZE AN ADVERTISEMENT

Study the advertisement that appears on the next page. Answer the following questions. *The first three parts will be present.*

1. *What is the claim?* Complete the sentence, "The author wants me to believe that . . ." Is the claim stated or implied?
2. *What is the support?* Complete the sentence, "The author wants me to believe that . . . [the claim] because . . . [support]." Look for subclaims (*reasons*) and specific support (e.g., *facts, opinions, examples*).
3. *What are the warrants?* Ask, "What does this author value or believe regarding the claim? Are these values or beliefs stated or implied? Do I agree or disagree with them?" Recall, also, that the warrants supply a link between support and claim. Ask, "Can I accept this evidence as support for this claim? Why or why not?" If you do not see how the evidence supports the claim, the argument will not be convincing to you.

The next three parts may or may not be present.

4. *Is there backing for any of the warrants?* Ask, "Does the author supply any additional information that would make it easier for me to accept the warrants, whether they are stated or implied? What is it?"
5. *Is there a rebuttal?* Ask, "Are other views on the issue represented here along with reasons? What are they?"
6. *Is there a qualifier?* Ask, "Is the claim stated in absolute terms (e.g., *always, never, the best, the worst*) or in probable terms (e.g., *sometimes, probably, possibly*)?"
7. *Do you find this ad convincing?* Why or why not?

C. GROUP WORK AND CLASS DISCUSSION: USING THE TOULMIN MODEL TO READ AND ANALYZE A SHORT ESSAY

Read the essay that follows. Then answer the questions and discuss your answers with the class. You can expect some disagreement because of your differing backgrounds and experiences. If you disagree on some of these answers, try to figure out what is causing your differences.

1. What is the claim? Is it explicitly stated, or did you have to infer it?
2. What are some examples of support?
3. What are the author's warrants? Does the author back the warrants? If yes, how?
4. Do you share the author's warrants, or do you have conflicting warrants? If you have conflicting warrants, what are they?
5. Is there a rebuttal in the article? If yes, what is it?
6. Is the claim qualified? How?
7. Do you find this argument convincing? Why or why not?

Will your

heart pound any

less because

it's safe?

Will your

goose bumps care that it's practical?

Find your own road:

900CS Turbo

Will that giddy feeling deep in your stomach diminish because the 9000 was ranked the safest car in Sweden three times in a row?* Will your exhilaration be dampened by the turbo's fuel efficiency? Will the guilty pleasure of driving it be compromised by its large interior and 56 cubic feet of cargo space? We don't think so. Experience turbo rush in the Saab 9000 CS. **For a free Saab Excursion Kit, call 1-800-582- SAAB, Ext. 222. www.saabusa.com**

*For years: 1990, 1992 and 1994. Based on a study of injuries sustained in auto accidents in Sweden. Data compiled by Folksam Insurance Institute between 1985 and 1993 maximize safety benefits, you must wear seat belts ©1996 SAAB CARS USA, INC.

SOURCE: Courtesy Saab Cars USA Inc.

WHAT'S HAPPENED TO DISNEY FILMS?*

John Evans

1   Many of today's over-30 adults who grew up on a diet of Disney movies are now responsible, God-honoring parents. They want their children to experience the same magic in films and videos that they once enjoyed.

2   Does the name "Disney" still mean the same in the '90s that it did in the '60s? Not at all. Disney is now a huge conglomerate with such diverse subsidiaries as Miramax Films, Hollywood Pictures, and Touchstone Pictures. The films they produce range from the violent, degrading *Pulp Fiction,* a Miramax film, to the delightful *Beauty and the Beast,* a Walt Disney Co. film. In between these two extremes are a myriad of movies of varying degrees of decency and offensiveness.

3   Listed below are descriptions which illustrate the undesirable content included in some Walt Disney Pictures films intended for young children. These comments are based on reviews from the *Preview* Family Movie and TV Guide.

4   *The Little Mermaid* (1989), G-rated animated film. While Disney's villains in the past have simply been mean and nasty, Ursula, the wicked sea witch, is downright evil. Her bizarre appearance and morbid undersea abode exude images of witchcraft, and some scenes are likely to frighten small children. Also, offensive, sexually suggestive dialogue is uncalled for. In one scene the evil Ursula intimates that the mermaid will have to "let her body do her talking." In romantic song, Ariel sings to Eric, "You know you want to do it." Even more disturbing, however, is the picture on the video box that includes a very obvious phallic symbol.

5   *Aladdin* (1992), G-rated animated film. The panther head entrance to the cave and a volcanic eruption are violent, jolting, and intense. The Genie transforms the evil Jofar into a sorcerer who violently manipulates others. Jofar changes into a giant snake to fight Aladdin. Again, the evil characters are more than scary—they attack. Also, the video tape includes some suggestive dialogue whispered in the background during a balcony scene between Aladdin and Jasmine. The words, "Take off your—" can be heard, implying that the muffled word is "clothes."

6   *Lion King* (1994), G-rated animated film. New Age and occultic concepts appear to be introduced when it's said that the father lion is living on in the son. Also, a remark is made that dead kings are looking down on the young lion. These can be interpreted literally as the Hindu concept of the universality of the soul. Also, when the young lion talks to his dead father, this violates the biblical admonition against communicating with the spirits of the dead.

7   *Lion King* also includes intense violence, including a graphic stampede and clawing and biting among animals. This continues the trend to show hand-to-hand combat that inflicts severe injuries.

8   *Pocahontas* (1995), G-rated animated film. This brand new feature film favorably depicts Indian animism, the belief that every natural object, such as rocks and trees, have spirits. Also, it portrays communication with spirits of the dead as

---

*Dallas/Fort Worth Heritage, August 1995, p. 12.

acceptable. "The producers give an exaggerated picture of the white colonists as greedy, bloodthirsty monsters who just want to rid the land of 'those savages.'"

9   The Walt Disney Pictures company continues to produce Disney's G-rated films as well as its more family oriented movies, such as *Iron Will, Angels in the Outfield, White Fang,* and the *Mighty Ducks* series. However, several years ago, the Disney organization decided to produce more "mature" films and established two wholly owned companies to produce them, Hollywood Pictures and Touchstone Pictures. Also, a few years ago, Disney acquired Miramax Films, which distributes some very offensive films, most of them produced in foreign countries.

10   A few examples of the most offensive films these companies have produced or distributed are given below.

11   *Pulp Fiction* (1994—Miramax Films). Disgusting R-rated adult film which contains over 320 obscenities and profanities, ongoing graphic and gratuitous violence, a homosexual rape, and much bizarre behavior.

12   *Color of Night* (1994—Hollywood Pictures). Gruesome R-rated murder mystery with bloody killings, stabbings, an impaling, and choking. Also, a sexual affair with graphic sexual content and nudity, and over 100 obscenities and profanities.

13   *Priest* (1995—Miramax Films). This controversial R-rated film sympathetically portrays a homosexual priest and depicts other Catholic priests as disreputable characters. Contains scenes of graphic homosexual lovemaking. Catholics nationwide protested the film.

14   *Who Framed Roger Rabbit* (1998—Touchstone Pictures). Suggestive, violent PG-rated cartoon film in which some characters are boiled in toxic waste and flattened by a steam roller. Also, features an implied extramarital affair, crude language, sexually suggestive humor, and a voluptuous, seductive female character.

15   For parents who want to select only wholesome, decent entertainment for their families, the *Preview* Family Movie and TV Guide publishes reviews of all current films twice a month. The reviews contain information on the desirable elements in a film as well as a detailed description of any offensive material.

FOR DISCUSSION: What was the first Disney film that you saw? Did it have a disturbing effect on you? Drawing on your own experiences and those of other people you know, how important do you think it is for parents to screen the movies and television shows that their children watch? Where would you draw the line if you were doing the screening? That is, would you agree with the author of this essay, or would you apply different criteria?

◆◆◆

D. WRITING ASSIGNMENT AND CLASS PROJECT: WRITING A TOULMIN ANALYSIS AND REPORTING ON IT IN CLASS

1. Clip a short article, an advertisement, a cartoon, or a letter to the editor, and use the Toulmin model to analyze it.
2. Write a 250- to 300-word paper in which you identify and explain the claim, support, and warrants in your example. Provide further information about backing, rebuttals, or qualifiers if they are present.

3. In class, circulate the item you clipped among your classmates. Either read your paper or give a two- to three-minute oral report in which you describe the parts of the argument to the class.

A student-written Toulmin analysis of "What's Happened to Disney Films?" follows. Read it to help you write your Toulmin analysis paper. Also, see if you and your classmates agree with this analysis. Everyone does not apply the Toulmin model in exactly the same way. There are no absolutely correct answers because different readers' interpretations vary.*

Beth Brunk
Toulmin Analysis
Professor Bartlett
English 1302
15 September 2003

Toulmin Analysis of "What's Happened to Disney Films?"

Identifies claim and support	1

In "What's Happened to Disney Films?" John Evans claims that Disney is not making the same caliber of movies that it was in the past; the majority of recent Disney films are not suitable for young audiences. Evans supports his claim through specific scenes and lines from recent Disney movies. The Little Mermaid and Aladdin contain sexual innuendoes. The Lion King presents New Age and occultic concepts and contains graphic violence. Pocahontas "favorably depicts Indian animism" and portrays the white settlers in a bad light. Evans also frowns on Disney's ownership of Touchstone Pictures, Miramax Films, and Hollywood Pictures, which have produced movies such as Who Framed Roger Rabbit, Pulp Fiction, and Color of Night, all of which he believes tarnish the once wholesome Disney image.

Analyzes warrants   2

Evans's argument has two warrants: Disney should only be making movies suitable for children regardless of the name they are produced under. Also, movies that are suitable for children are those that are based strictly on Christian ideologies and portray "the white man" in a positive light.

Identifies rebuttal   3

Evans prepares for rebuttal by naming some Disney movies such as Iron Will, Angels in the Outfield, and The Mighty Ducks that are considered suitable for children.

Identifies backing   4

The backing for his warrants is Christian doctrines and the Bible. Although he does not appeal to either explicitly throughout much of the article, he does say that Simba's conversation with his

---

*See the Appendix to Chapter 12 for the actual MLA format guidelines for student papers.

dead father in <u>The Lion King</u> "violates the biblical admonition against communicating with the spirits of the dead." This worldview underlies his entire argument.

Analyzes
qualifiers

5   His qualifier is a subtle one and is found at the end of the piece, where he claims that there is information available "for parents who want to select only wholesome, decent entertainment for their families." He allows that there may be some parents who do not care what their children watch and would therefore disagree with his claim.

For Discussion: Do you agree with this student's analysis of Evans's article? Look at the warrants spelled out in paragraph 2. Would you supply these same warrants? If not, what warrants would you supply? Why do you agree or disagree with this author's explanation of the warrants?

◆◆◆

E. PREWRITING: USING THE TOULMIN MODEL TO GET IDEAS FOR A POSITION PAPER

You have used the Toulmin model in Exercises B through D to read and analyze other people's argument. Now use it to identify the main parts of an argument you will write. You may use the model to help you plan any argument paper. If, however, you have written an exploratory paper based on an issue in "The Reader" for Exercise D in Chapter 4, you have already written a tentative claim for a position paper. Your claim appears at the end of your exploratory paper. Use the Toulmin model as a prewriting exercise to help you develop ideas for a position paper. (The assignment for the "Position Paper Based on 'The Reader'" appears as Exercise D in Chapter 8.)

1. Write the claim. All of the rest of your paper will support this claim.
2. Write the support. Write two or three subclaims that you will develop in the paper. To help you do this, write the word *because* after your claim, and list reasons that support it. Also jot down ideas for specific support for these subclaims, such as examples, facts, and opinions, that come from your reading of the essays or from your own experience.
3. Write the warrants. Decide whether to spell out the warrants in your paper or to leave them implicit so that the reading audience will have to infer them.
4. Decide on the backing. Assume that your classmates are your audience. They may be reading drafts of your paper. In your judgment, will some of them require backing for any of your warrants because they will not agree with them otherwise? If so, how can you back these warrants? Write out your ideas.

5. Plan rebuttal. Think about the positions others may hold on this issue. You identified some of these positions in your exploratory paper. Write out some strategies for weakening these arguments.

6. Decide whether to qualify your claim to make it more convincing to more people. Write one or more qualifiers that might work.

Read what you have written, and make a note about additional information you will need to find for your paper. Save what you have written in a folder. You will use it later when you complete your planning and write your position paper.

F.   GROUP DISCUSSION: UNDERSTANDING VALUE WARRANTS

Warrants often come from the systems of values that people hold. The values will not be spelled out in an argument, yet they will still influence the arguer and be present as warrants in the argument. The following essay describes six American value systems. These systems are somewhat oversimplified, and they do not identify all American value systems. They are useful, however, to help you understand some of the values that people hold. Read the essay, and then answer the questions for discussion at the end.

AMERICAN VALUE SYSTEMS*

Richard D. Rieke and Malcolm O. Sillars

1   By careful analysis individual values can be discovered in the arguments of ourselves and others. There is a difficulty, however, in attempting to define a whole system of values for a person or a group. And as difficult as that is, each of us, as a participant in argumentation, should have some concept of the broad systems that most frequently bring together certain values. For this purpose, it is useful for you to have an idea of some of the most commonly acknowledged value systems.

2   You must approach this study with a great deal of care, however, because even though the six basic value systems we are about to define provide a fair view of the standard American value systems, they do not provide convenient pigeon-holes into which individuals can be placed. They represent broad social categories. Some individuals (even groups) will be found outside these systems. Many individuals and groups will cross over value systems, picking and choosing from several. Note how certain words appear as value terms in more than one value system. The purpose of this survey is to provide a beginning understanding of standard American values, not a complete catalog.[1]

---

*Richard D. Rieke and Malcolm O. Sillars, *Argumentation and the Decision Making Process,* 2nd ed. (Boston: Allyn & Bacon, 1984), pp. 118–124. Copyright © 1984 by Pearson Education. Reprinted with permission of the publisher.

The Puritan-Pioneer-Peasant Value System

3   This value system has been identified frequently as the *puritan morality* or the *Protestant ethic*. It also has been miscast frequently because of the excessive emphasis placed, by some of its adherents, on restrictions of personal acts such as smoking and consuming alcohol.[2] Consequently, over the years, this value system has come to stand for a narrow-minded attempt to interfere in other people's business, particularly if those people are having fun. However, large numbers of people who do not share such beliefs follow this value system.

4   We have taken the liberty of expanding beyond the strong and perhaps too obvious religious implications of the terms *puritan* and *Protestant*. This value system is what most Americans refer to when they speak of the "pioneer spirit," which was not necessarily religious. It also extends, we are convinced, to a strain of values brought to this country by Southern and Eastern European Catholics, Greek Orthodox, and Jews who could hardly be held responsible for John Calvin's theory or even the term *Protestant ethic*. Thus, we have the added word *peasant,* which may not be particularly accurate. Despite the great friction that existed between these foreign-speaking immigrants from other religions and their native Protestant counterparts, they had a great deal in common as do their ideological descendants today. On many occasions after describing the puritan morality we have heard a Jewish student say, "That's the way my father thinks," or had a student of Italian or Polish descent say, "My grandmother talks that way all the time."

5   The Puritan-Pioneer-Peasant value system is rooted in the idea that persons have an obligation to themselves and those around them, and in some cases to their God, to work hard at whatever they do. In this system, people are limited in their abilities and must be prepared to fail. The great benefit is in the striving against an unknowable and frequently hostile universe. They have an obligation to others, must be selfless, and must not waste. Some believe this is the only way to gain happiness and success. Others see it as a means to salvation. In all cases it takes on a moral orientation. Obviously, one might work hard for a summer in order to buy a new car and not be labeled a "puritan." Frequently, in this value system, the instrumental values of selflessness, thrift, and hard work become terminal values where the work has value beyond the other benefits it can bring one. People who come from this value system often have difficulty with retirement, because their meaning in life, indeed their pleasure, came from work.

6   Likewise, because work, selflessness, and thrift are positive value terms in this value system, laziness, selfishness, and waste are negative value terms. One can see how some adherents to this value system object to smoking, drinking, dancing, or cardplaying. These activities are frivolous; they take one's mind off more serious matters and waste time.

7   Some of the words that are associated with the Puritan-Pioneer-Peasant value system are:

Positive: activity, work, thrift, morality, dedication, selflessness, virtue, righteousness, duty, dependability, temperance, sobriety, savings, dignity

Negative: waste, immorality, dereliction, dissipation, infidelity, theft, vandalism, hunger, poverty, disgrace, vanity

The Enlightenment Value System

8 America became a nation in the period of the Enlightenment. It happened when a new intellectual era based on the scientific findings of men like Sir Isaac Newton and the philosophical systems of men like John Locke were dominant. The founders of our nation were particularly influenced by such men. The Declaration of Independence is the epitome of an Enlightenment document. In many ways America is an Enlightenment nation, and if Enlightenment is not the predominant value system, it is surely first among equals.

9 The Enlightenment position stems from the belief that we live in an ordered world in which all activity is governed by laws similar to the laws of physics. These "natural laws" may or may not come from God, depending on the particular orientation of the person examining them; but unlike many adherents to the Puritan value system just discussed, Enlightenment persons theorized that people could discover these laws by themselves. Thus, they may worship God for God's greatness, even acknowledge that God created the universe and natural laws, but they find out about the universe because they have the power of reason. The laws of nature are harmonious, and one can use reason to discover them all. They can also be used to provide for a better life.

10 Because humans are basically good and capable of finding answers, restraints on them must be limited. Occasionally, people do foolish things and must be restrained by society. However, a person should never be restrained in matters of the mind. Reason must be free. Thus, government is an agreement among individuals to assist the society to protect rights. That government is a democracy. Certain rights are inalienable, and they may not be abridged; "among these are life, liberty and the pursuit of happiness." Arguments for academic freedom, against wiretaps, and for scientific inquiry come from this value system.

11 Some of the words associated with the Enlightenment value system are:

Positive: freedom, science, nature, rationality, democracy, fact, liberty, individualism, knowledge, intelligence, reason, natural rights, natural laws, progress
Negative: ignorance, inattention, thoughtlessness, error, indecision, irrationality, dictatorship, fascism, bookburning, falsehood, regression

The Progressive Value System

12 Progress was a natural handmaiden of the Enlightenment. If these laws were available and if humans had the tool, reason, to discover them and use them to advantage, then progress would result. Things would continually get better. But although progress is probably a historical spin-off of the Enlightenment, it has become so important on its own that it deserves at times to be seen quite separate from the Enlightenment.

13   Richard Weaver, in 1953, found that "one would not go far wrong in naming progress" the "god term" of that age. It is, he said, the "expression about which all other expressions are ranked as subordinate. . . . Its force imparts to the others their lesser degrees of force, and fixes the scale by which degrees of comparison are understood."[3]

14   Today, the unmediated use of the progressive value system is questioned, but progress is still a fundamental value in America. Most arguments against progress are usually arguments about the definition of progress. They are about what "true progress is."

15   Some of the key words of the Progressive value system are:

Positive: practicality, efficiency, change, improvement, science, future, modern, progress, evolution
Negative: old-fashioned,[4] regressive, impossible, backward

The Transcendental Value System

16   Another historical spin-off of the Enlightenment system was the development of the transcendental movement of the early nineteenth century. It took from the Enlightenment all its optimism about people, freedom, and democracy, but rejected the emphasis on reason. It argued idealistically that there was a faculty higher than reason; let us call it, as many transcendentalists did, intuition. Thus, for the transcendentalist, there is a way of knowing that is better than reason, a way which *transcends* reason. Consequently, what might seem like the obvious solution to problems is not necessarily so. One must look, on important matters at least, to the intuition, to the feelings. Like the Enlightenment thinker, the transcendentalist believes in a unified universe governed by natural laws. Thus, all persons, by following their intuition, will discover these laws, and universal harmony will take place. And, of course, little or no government will be necessary. The original American transcendentalists of the early nineteenth century drew their inspiration from Platonism, German idealism, and Oriental mysticism. The idea was also fairly well limited to the intellectuals. By and large, transcendentalism has been the view of a rather small group of people throughout our history, but at times it has been very important. It has always been somewhat more influential among younger people. James Truslow Adams once wrote that everyone should read Ralph Waldo Emerson at sixteen because his writings were a marvel for the buoyantly optimistic person of that age but that his transcendental writings did not have the same luster at twenty-one.[5] In the late 1960s and early 1970s, Henry David Thoreau's *Walden* was the popular reading of campus rebels. The emphasis of anti-establishment youth on Oriental mysticism, like Zen, should not be ignored either. The rejection of contemporary society and mores symbolized by what others considered "outlandish dress" and "hippie behavior" with its emphasis on emotional response and "do your own thing" indicated the adoption of a transcendental value system. Communal living is reminiscent of the transcendental "Brook Farm" experiments that were attempted in the early nineteenth century and described by Nathaniel Hawthorne in his novel *The Blithedale Romance.*

17   In all of these movements the emphasis on humanitarian values, the central-
ity of love for others, and the preference for quiet contemplation over activity
has been important. Transcendentalism, however, rejects the common idea of
progress. Inner light and knowledge of one's self is more important than material
well-being. There is also some tendency to reject physical well-being because it
takes one away from intuitive truth.

18   It should be noted that not everyone who argues for change is a transcendentalist. The transcendental white campus agitators of the late 1960s discovered
that, despite all their concern for replacing racism and war with love and peace,
their black counterparts were highly pragmatic and rationalistic about objectives
and means. Black agitators and demonstrators were never "doing their thing" in
the intuitive way of many whites.

19   It should also be noted that while a full adherence to transcendentalism has
been limited to small groups, particularly among intellectuals and youth, many of
the ideas are not limited to such persons. One can surely find strains of what we
have labeled, for convenience, transcendentalism in the mysticism of some very
devout older Roman Catholics, for instance. And perhaps many Americans become transcendental on particular issues, about the value to be derived from hiking in the mountains, for example.

20   Here are some of the terms that are characteristic of the Transcendental value
system:

Positive: humanitarian, individualism, respect, intuition, truth, equality,
sympathetic, affection, feeling, love, sensitivity, emotion, personal
kindness, compassion, brotherhood, friendship, mysticism

Negative: science,[6] reason, mechanical, hate, war, anger, insensitive,
coldness, unemotional

The Personal Success Value System

21   The least social of the major American value systems is the one that moves people toward personal achievement and success. It can be related as a part of the
Enlightenment value system, but it is more than that because it involves a highly
pragmatic concern for the material happiness of the individual. To call it selfish
would be to load the terms against it, although there would be some who accept
this value system who would say, "Yes, I'm selfish." "The Lord helps those who
help themselves" has always been an acceptable adage by some of the most devout in our nation.

22   You might note that the Gallup poll . . . is very heavily weighted toward personal values. Even "good family life" rated as the top value can be seen as an item
of personal success. This survey includes only a few social values like "helping
needy people" and "helping better America," and even those are phrased in personal terms. That is, the respondents were asked "how important you feel each of
these is to you." The personal orientation of the survey may represent a bias of
the Gallup poll, but we suspect it reflects much of American society. We are personal success–oriented in an individual way which would not be found in some
other cultures (e.g., in the Japanese culture).

23   Here are some of the terms that tend to be characteristic of the Personal Success value system:

> *Positive:*   career, family, friends, recreation, economic security, identity,
>   health, individualism, affection, respect, enjoyment, dignity,
>   consideration, fair play, personal
> *Negative:*   dullness, routine, hunger, poverty, disgrace, coercion, disease

The Collectivist Value System

24   Although there are few actual members of various socialist and communist groups in the United States, one cannot ignore the strong attachment among some people for collective action. This is, in part, a product of the influx of social theories from Europe in the nineteenth century. It is also a natural outgrowth of a perceived need to control the excesses of freedom in a mass society. Its legitimacy is not limited to current history, however. There has always been a value placed on cooperative action. The same people today who would condemn welfare payments to unwed mothers would undoubtedly praise their ancestors for barnraising and taking care of the widow in a frontier community. Much rhetoric about our "pioneer ancestors" has to do with their cooperative action. And anti-collectivist presidents and evangelists talk about "the team." At the same time many fervent advocates of collective action in the society argue vehemently for their freedom and independence. Certainly the civil rights movement constituted a collective action for freedom. Remember the link in Martin Luther King, Jr.'s speech between "freedom" and "brotherhood"?

25   But whether the Collectivist value system is used to defend socialist proposals or promote "law and order" there is no doubt that collectivism is a strong value system in this nation. Like transcendentalism, however, it is probably a value system that, at least in this day, cannot work alone.

26   Here are some of the terms that tend to characterize the Collectivist value system:

> *Positive:*   cooperation, joint action, unity, brotherhood, together, social
>   good, order, humanitarian aid and comfort, equality
> *Negative:*   disorganization, selfishness, personal greed, inequality

27   Clearly, these six do not constitute a complete catalog of all American value systems. Combinations and reorderings produce different systems. Two values deserve special attention because they are common in these systems and sometimes operate alone: *nature* and *patriotism*. Since the beginning of our nation the idea has prevailed that the natural is good and there for our use and preservation. Also, since John Winthrop first proclaimed that the New England Puritans would build "a city on the hill" for all the world to see and emulate, the idea has endured that America is a fundamentally great nation, perhaps God-chosen, to lead the world to a better life. This idea may be somewhat tarnished in some quarters today, but there is no doubt that it will revive as it has in the past. Linked to other value systems we have discussed, it will once more be a theme that will draw the adherence of others to arguments.

NOTES

1. The following material draws from a wide variety of sources. The following is an illustrative cross section of sources from a variety of disciplines: Virgil I. Baker and Ralph T. Eubanks, *Speech in Personal and Public Affairs* (New York: David McKay, 1965), pp. 95–102; Clyde Kluckhohn, "An Anthropologist Looks at the United States," *Mirror for Man* (New York: McGraw-Hill, 1949), pp. 228–261; Stow Persons, *American Minds* (New York: Holt, Rinehart and Winston, 1958); Jurgen Ruesch, "Communication and American Values; A Psychological Approach," in *Communication: The Social Matrix of Psychiatry,* eds. Jurgen Ruesch and Gregory Bateson (New York: W. W. Norton, 1951), pp. 94–134; Edward D. Steele and W. Charles Redding, "The American Value System: Premises for Persuasion," *Western Speech,* 26 (Spring 1962), pp. 83–91; Richard Weaver, "Ultimate Terms in Contemporary Rhetoric," in *The Ethics of Rhetoric* (Chicago: Henry Regnery, 1953), pp. 211–232; Robin M. Williams, Jr., *American Society,* 3rd ed. (New York: Alfred A. Knopf, 1970), pp. 438–504.
2. It is ironic that the original American Puritans did not have clear injunctions against such activity.
3. Weaver, p. 212.
4. Note that "old-fashioned" is frequently positive when we speak of morality and charm but not when we speak of our taste in music.
5. James Truslow Adams, "Emerson Re-read," in *The Transcendental Revolt,* ed. George F. Whicher (Boston: D. C. Heath, 1949), pp. 31–39.
6. It is interesting to note, however, that one of the major organizations in the United States with transcendental origins, the Christian Science Church, combines transcendentalism with science.

FOR DISCUSSION:

1. Can you find your own system of values in this article? Of the six value systems described, which do you most closely identify with?
2. Which value systems do you find operating in the selections listed below that you have analyzed in this and earlier chapters? What value warrants are implicit in each of these selections? Provide reasons for your answers. There are no correct answers. Use your imagination, and have some fun with this exercise.

> The Saab automobile ad (page 147)
> "What's Happened to Disney Films?" (pages 148–149)
> "We Knew What Glory Was" (pages 49–51)
> "A View from Berkeley" (pages 51–54)
> "Giving People a Second Chance" (pages 54–56)
> "One of Our Own: Training Native Teachers for the 21st Century" (pages 56–58)
> "Why I Want a Wife" (pages 58–60)

3. When your system of values does not match the system of values implicit in an argumentative essay, what happens? How does a difference in value systems influence your acceptance of the author's argument?

◆◆◇

Chapter 6

Types of Claims

This chapter and the one that follows it expand on and develop some of the ideas in Chapter 5. In Chapter 5 the claim, the support, and the warrants were identified as the three essential parts of an argument. This chapter, along with Chapter 7, provides additional information about these three parts. Claims are the subject of this chapter. Support and warrants, which constitute the proofs of an argument, are the subject of the next chapter.

Argument theorists categorize claims according to types, and these types suggest the fundamental purposes of given arguments. Knowing possible categories for claims and the special characteristics associated with each of them will help you understand more fully the purposes and special features of the arguments you read and will also improve your writing of them. When reading, as soon as you identify the type of claim in an argument, you can predict and anticipate certain features of that type of argument. This technique helps you follow the author's line of thought more easily. When writing, knowing the types of claims can provide you with frameworks for developing your purpose and strategy.

When you begin to read argument with the idea of locating the claim and identifying it by type, your ability to identify and understand all the parts of an argument will increase. An understanding of proofs, the subject of Chapter 7, will improve your understanding further. Chapters 6 and 7, taken together, will teach you how to recognize and use both claims and proofs, the major components of argument. But first, here is a strategy for analyzing an argument to get a preliminary sense of its purpose and to identify its parts.

GETTING A SENSE OF THE PURPOSE AND PARTS OF AN ARGUMENT

▲ *SURVEY.* Follow the procedures for surveying a book or an article on page 66. Your objective is to find the claim and some of the main subclaims or parts.

▲ *DIVIDE THE ARGUMENT INTO ITS PARTS.* Draw a line across the page (or make a light mark in the margin) each time the subject changes. This physical division of a written argument into its parts is called *chunking.* For example, in a policy paper that proposes a solution to a problem, the explanation of the problem would be a major chunk, as would be the explanation of the solution.

▲ *ASK WHY THE PARTS HAVE BEEN PLACED IN THAT PARTICULAR ORDER.* Try to determine if the parts have been placed in a logical order to facilitate understanding, for instance, or whether they have been placed in a psychological order, leading up to the conclusion or action step at the end. There are other possibilities as well. Try to get a sense of how the author thought about and organized the parts.

▲ *ANALYZE THE RELATIONSHIPS AMONG THE PARTS.* When you have speculated about why the author put the parts in a particular order, go a step further and think about the relationships among these parts. Do they all contribute to a central idea, such as a specialized definition? Or are other relationships apparent, such as causes for effects or solutions for problems?

When you begin to write argument, write a claim, list a few supporting reasons that represent the tentative parts, and then think about the best sequence for these parts. The relationships among them will become clearer to you as you rearrange them in an order that is logical to you.

Once you have a sense of the overall purpose and shape of an argument, you can then identify the type of claim that predominates in it.

FIVE TYPES OF CLAIMS

Virtually all arguments can be categorized according to one of five types of claims. You can identify each argument type by identifying the questions the argument answers. In general, certain types of organization and proof are associated with certain types of claims, as you will see in the following discussion. There are no hard-and-fast rules about using specific organizational strategies or types of proof to develop specific types of claims. Knowing common patterns and tendencies, however, helps readers make predictions about the course of an argument and helps writers plan and write their own arguments.

Here are the five categories of claims, along with the main questions that they answer.

1. *Claims of fact:* Did it happen? Does it exist?
2. *Claims of definition:* What is it? How should we define it?
3. *Claims of cause:* What caused it? Or what are its effects?
4. *Claims of value:* Is it good or bad? What criteria will help us decide?

5. *Claims of policy:* What should we do about it? What should be our future course of action?

The sections that follow provide additional explanations of the five types of claims, along with the general questions they answer, some examples of actual claims, a list of the types of proof (explained more fully in the next chapter) that are most typically associated with each type of claim, the organizational strategies that one might expect for each type, and a short written argument that illustrates each type as it appears in practice.

CLAIMS OF FACT

When you claim that you turned a paper in on time even if the professor can't find it, or that you were not exceeding the speed limit when a police officer claims that your were, you are making claims of fact.

QUESTIONS ANSWERED BY CLAIMS OF FACT. Did it happen? Is it true? Does it exist? Is it a fact?

EXAMPLES OF CLAIMS OF FACT. (Note that all of the "facts" in these claims need to be proved as either absolutely or probably true in order to be acceptable to an audience. All of these claims, also, are controversial.) The ozone layer is becoming depleted. Increasing population threatens the environment. American drivers are becoming more responsible. America's military is prepared for any likely crisis. The abominable snowman exists in certain remote areas. Women are not as effective as men in combat. A mass murderer is evil and not insane. The American judicial system operates successfully.

TYPES OF SUPPORT ASSOCIATED WITH CLAIMS OF FACT. Factual support, as you might guess, is especially appropriate for claims of fact. Such support includes both past and present *facts, statistics, real examples,* and *quotations from reliable authorities. Inductive reasoning,* which cites several examples and then draws a probable conclusion from them, is also a common type of argument for claims of fact. *Analogies* that establish comparisons and similarities between the subject and something else that is commonly accepted as true are useful. *Signs* that present evidence of a past or present state of affairs are also useful to establish claims of fact. *Expert opinion,* when used to support claims of fact, is usually based on fact.

POSSIBLE ORGANIZATIONAL STRATEGIES. Chronological order, which traces what has occurred over a period of time, usually in the order in which it occurred, can be used to develop claims of fact. For example, the history of the increase in population might be provided to show how it has happened over a period of time. Or *topical order* may be used. In topical order a group of reasons to support a fact may be identified and developed topic by topic. Thus reasons might be given for the existence of the abominable snowman, with each of them developed at length. This chapter is organized according to topics: the five types of claims.

The claim of fact itself is often stated at or near the beginning of the argument unless there is a psychological advantage for stating it at the end. Most authors make claims of fact clear from the outset, revealing early what they seek to establish.

An Example of an Argument That Contains a Claim of Fact. The following selection is from a longer article that argues that the "digital divide," a concept that predicted computer use would be unevenly distributed between the rich and the poor, did not, in fact, take place, and that the opposite has occurred. This article aims to disprove one fact and establish a more accurate one in its place.

DEBUNKING THE DIGITAL DIVIDE*

Robert Samuelson

Claim of fact

1   It may turn out that the "digital divide"—one of the most fashionable political slogans of recent years—is largely fiction. As you will recall, the argument went well beyond the unsurprising notion that the rich would own more computers than the poor. The disturbing part of the theory was that society was dividing itself into groups of technology "haves" and "have nots" and that this segregation would, in turn, worsen already large economic inequalities. It's this argument that's either untrue or wildly exaggerated.

2   We should always have been suspicious. After all, computers have spread quickly, precisely because they've become cheaper to buy and easier to use. Falling prices and skill requirements suggest that the digital divide would spontaneously shrink—and so it has.

Facts and statistics

3   The Census Bureau's latest survey of computer use reports narrowing gaps among different income and ethnic groups. In 1997 only 37 percent of people in families with incomes from $15,000 to $24,999 used computers at home or at work. By September 2001, that proportion was 47 percent. Over the same period, usage among families with incomes exceeding $75,000 rose more modestly, from 81 percent to 88 percent. Among all racial and ethnic groups, computer use is rising. Here are the numbers for 2001 compared with similar rates for 1997: Asian-Americans, 71 percent (58 percent in 1997); whites, 70 percent (58 percent); blacks, 56 percent (44 percent); Hispanics, 49 percent (38 percent).

4   The new figures confirm common sense: many computer skills aren't especially high tech or demanding. The point-and-click technology allows computers to be adopted to many business and home uses without requiring people to become computer experts. Just as you can drive a car without being a mechanic, you can use a computer without being a software engineer.

Analogy

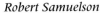

5   As a slogan, the "digital divide" brilliantly united a concern for the poor with a faith in technology. It also suggested an agenda: put

*Newsweek, March 25, 2002, p. 37.

Facts and statistics

computers in schools; connect classrooms to the Internet. Well, the agenda has been largely realized. By 2000, public schools had roughly one computer for every four students. Almost all schools were connected to the Internet, as were about three quarters of classrooms. Some students get computer skills that they might miss. Among 10- to 17-year-old students from homes with less than $15,000 of income, about half use computers only at school, reports the Census Bureau.

6   But whether education and students' life prospects have improved is a harder question. As yet, computers haven't produced broad gains in test scores. As for today's computer skills, they may not be terribly important, in part because technology constantly changes. Frank Levy, an economist at the Massachusetts Institute of Technology who studies how computers alter work, emphasizes the importance of basic reading and reasoning abilities. Often, new computer skills can be taught in a few weeks. But people have to be able to read manuals and follow instructions.

7   The "digital divide" suggested a simple solution (computers) for a complex problem (poverty). With more computer access, the poor could escape their lot. But computers never were the source of anyone's poverty and, as for escaping, what people do for themselves matters more than what technology can do for them.

FOR DISCUSSION: What was some of the evidence that the author presented to support his view that the predicted digital divide did not, in fact, take place? What evidence might someone use to refute this position? What is your own position? What evidence would you use to support your position?

◆◆◆

CLAIMS OF DEFINITION

When you claim that an athlete who receives compensation for playing a sport is "professional," and therefore loses "amateur" status, you are making a claim of definition.

QUESTIONS ANSWERED BY CLAIMS OF DEFINITION. What is it? What is it like? How should it be classified? How should it be interpreted? How does its usual meaning change in a particular context?

EXAMPLES OF CLAIMS OF DEFINITION. (Note that here we are looking at definition claims that dominate the argument in the essay as a whole. Definition is also used as a type of support, often at the beginning, to establish the meaning of one or more key terms.) We need to define what constitutes a family before we talk about family values. To determine whether an art exhibit is pornography or art, we need to define what we mean by pornography in this context. To determine whether the police were doing their job or were engaging in brutality, we need to establish what we mean by police brutality. To determine whether a person is mentally competent, we need to define what we mean by that designation. If we have established the fact that a young man killed his wife, shall we define this killing as self-defense, a crime of passion, or premeditated murder?

Types of Support Associated with Claims of Definition. The main types of support used to prove claims of definition are *references to reliable authorities and accepted sources* that can be used to establish clear definitions and meanings, such as the dictionary or a well-known work. Also useful are *analogies* and other comparisons, especially to other words or situations that are clearly understood and that can consequently be used to shed some light on what is being defined. *Examples,* both real and hypothetical, and *signs* can also be used to clarify or develop definitions.

Possible Organizational Strategies. *Comparison-and-contrast organization* can dominate the development of a claim of definition and serve as the main structure. In this structure two or more objects are compared and contrasted throughout. For example, in an essay that expands the notion of crime to include white-collar crime, conventional crime would be compared with white-collar crime to prove that they are similar.

Topical organization may also be used. Several special qualities, characteristics, or features of the word or concept are identified and explained as discrete topics. Thus in an essay defining a criminal as mentally competent, the characteristics of mental competence would be explained as separate topics and applied to the criminal. Another strategy is to *explain the controversy* over the term and *give reasons* for accepting one view over another.

An Example of an Argument That Contains a Claim of Definition. The following article suggests the confusion that can result if people do not agree on a definition for a term. Dr. Michael S. Gazzaniga, the author, writes about his experience serving on a board that was charged to advise President George W. Bush on cloning policy. Gazzaniga shows that the definition of cloning is crucial in such an assignment and should influence its outcomes.

ESSAY 2

Author establishes his authority

ZYGOTES AND PEOPLE AREN'T QUITE THE SAME*

Michael S. Gazzaniga

1   When President Bush convened his advisory panel on bioethics in January, he told those of us serving on it to engage in that age-old technique of intellectual exploration called debate. "That's what I want," he said. "You haven't heard a debate until you have heard Colin Powell and Don Rumsfeld go at it."

2   So it was a surprise when, on April 10, the president announced his decision to ban cloning of all kinds. His opinions appeared fully

---

New York Times op-ed, April 25, 2002, p. A35.

formed even though our panel has yet to prepare a final report and will be voting on the crucial point of biomedical cloning—which produces cells to be used in researching and treating illnesses. While it is true that the president's position is one held by some of the members of the panel, not all agree.

Two definitions of cloning

3   Most people are now aware that medical scientists put cloning in two different categories. Biomedical cloning is distinct from reproductive cloning, the process by which a new human being might be grown from the genetic material of a single individual. At this point, no scientist or ethicist I know supports reproductive cloning of human beings. <u>The debate is solely about biomedical cloning for lifesaving medical research.</u>

Claim based on definition

4   Scientists prefer to call biomedical cloning somatic cell nuclear transfer, because that is what it is. Any cell from an adult can be placed in an egg whose own nucleus has been removed and given a jolt of electricity. This all takes place in a lab dish, and the hope is that this transfer will allow the adult cell to be reprogrammed so that it will form a clump of approximately 150 cells called a blastocyst. This will be harvested for the stem cells it contains.

5   At this point we encounter a conflation of ideas, beliefs and facts. Some religious groups and ethicists argue that the moment of transfer of cellular material is an initiation of life and establishes a moral equivalency between a developing group of cells and a human being. This point of view is problematic when viewed with modern biological knowledge.

Comparison

6   We wouldn't consider this clump of cells even equivalent to an embryo formed in normal human reproduction. And we now know that in normal reproduction as many as 50 percent to 80 percent of all fertilized eggs spontaneously abort and are simply expelled from the woman's body. It is hard to believe that under any religious belief system people would grieve and hold funerals for these natural events. Yet, if these unfortunate zygotes are considered human beings, then logically people should.

Deduction

7   Second, the process of a single zygote splitting to make identical twins can occur until at least 14 days after fertilization. Also, divided embryos can recombine back into one. How could we possibly identify a person with a single fertilized egg?

8   Modern scientific knowledge of the fertilization process serves as the basis for the British government's approval of biomedical cloning and embryo research. Britain does not grant moral status to an embryo until after 14 days, the time when all the twinning issues cease and the embryo must be implanted into the uterus to continue developing.

Comparison

9   The blastocyst, the biological clump of cells produced in biomedical cloning, is the size of the dot on this i. It has no nervous system and is not sentient in any way. It has no trajectory to becoming

Comparison

a human being; it will never be implanted in a woman's uterus. What it probably does have is the potential for the cure of diseases affecting millions of people.

10

Reliable authorities silenced for now

When I joined the panel, officially named the President's Council on Bioethics, I was confident that a sensible and sensitive policy might evolve from what was sure to be a cacophony of voices of scientists and philosophers representing a spectrum of opinions, beliefs and intellectual backgrounds. I only hope that in the end the president hears his council's full debate.

For Discussion: What are the two definitions of cloning described in this article? Why is it important to distinguish between them before deciding on policy regarding the future of cloning? Speculate on why the president may have decided to ban all cloning even before he received the report from his committee. What does Gazzaniga seem to think might be one of the reasons for the president's decision?

◆◆◆

Claims of Cause

When you claim that staying up late at a party caused you to fail your exam the next day or that your paper is late because the library closed too early, you are making claims of cause.

Questions Answered by Claims of Cause. What caused it? Where did it come from? Why did it happen? What are the effects? What will probably be the results over the short and the long term?

Examples of Claims of Cause. The United States champions human rights in foreign countries to further its own economic self-interests. Clear-cutting is the main cause of the destruction of ancient forests. Legalizing marijuana could have beneficial effects for medicine. DNA testing is causing courts to review some of their death penalty decisions. The long-term effect of inadequate funding for AIDS research will be a disastrous worldwide epidemic. A lack of family values can lead to crime. Censorship can have good results by protecting children.

Types of Support Associated with Claims of Cause. The argument must establish the probability of a cause-and-effect relationship. The best type of support for this purpose is *factual data,* including *statistics* that are used to prove a cause or an effect. You can also expect *analogies,* including both *literal* and *historical analogies* that parallel cases in past history to show that the cause of one event could also be the cause of another similar event. You can furthermore expect *signs* of certain causes or effects, and you can also expect *induction.* Several examples cited as a cause will invite the inductive leap to a possible effect as the end result. *Deduction* is also used to develop claims of cause. Premises about effects are proposed, as in the Sherlock Holmes example in Chapter 7 (page 203), and a conclusion about the possible cause is drawn.

POSSIBLE ORGANIZATIONAL STRATEGIES. One strategy is to describe *causes and then effects.* Thus clear-cutting would be described as a cause that would lead to the ultimate destruction of the forests, which would be the effect. Or *effects* may be described and then *the cause or causes.* The effects of censorship may be described before the public efforts that resulted in that censorship. You may also encounter refutation of other actual or possible causes or effects.

AN EXAMPLE OF AN ARGUMENT THAT CONTAINS A CLAIM OF CAUSE. The following article suggests that many of the world's economic problems stem from the way women are treated in some of the relatively impoverished nations of the world. Facts, quotations from authorities, and comparisons are used to establish that if women were treated differently, economic improvement would be the effect. Not all people in these countries would agree with this cause-and-effect argument.

PAYING THE PRICE OF FEMALE NEGLECT*

Susan Dentzer

Facts

1   Call it the case of the missing women—*more than 100 million of them,* to be exact. It's a curiosity of human biology that women are hardier than men and thus outnumber their male counterparts in the United States, Europe and Japan. But in much of Asia, North Africa and parts of Latin America, the opposite is true: In all of South Asia, for example, females constitute less than 47 percent of the population, versus 52.2 percent in industrialized countries. The complex reasons, including poor health care and outright violence against women and girls, add up to pervasive neglect of females in many heavily populated nations. Harvard economist Amartya Sen concludes that well over 100 million women are in effect "missing" from the planet—the presumed victims of premature and preventable deaths. . . .

Quotation from authority

2   The consequences for social justice are self-evident, but less well understood in the West are the global economic costs of such widespread female deprivation. Of the 1.3 billion people living in poverty worldwide, a staggering 70 percent are women, notes a recent report by the United Nations Development Program. Thus, the surest route to propelling nations out of poverty is to end the cycle of female neglect. . . . It may well be that giving women a leg up in education, entrepreneurship and political power could pay off in priceless benefits—ranging from slower population growth and higher incomes to healthier families.

Claim of cause

Effects if claim were adopted

U.S. News & World Report, September 11, 1995, p. 45.

Vicious Cycle

Statistics

3   Women in developing nations clearly face a host of social and cultural obstacles, but they are also hurt by a simple economic calculus. On average, women worldwide earn 30 to 40 percent less than men; because their daughters will earn less, parents in poor countries often invest in them less than they do in their sons, especially in education and health care. The resulting vicious cycle of underinvestment exacts a huge toll, since research clearly shows that better-educated women are more likely to have fewer children, seek health care when needed, earn more money and plow more resources into educating their offspring. One recent World Bank analysis suggests that providing 1,000 girls in India with an extra year of primary schooling would cost a mere $32,000, yet would prevent the premature deaths of two women and 43 infants, as well as avert 300 births. Another concludes that if women in Kenya, who make up the majority of the nation's farmers, were educated on a par with Kenyan men, food-crop yields would increase by more than a fifth. . . .

Authority

4   Most crucial may be increasing women's capacities to be agents of change rather than merely recipients of greater help from others, says economist Sen. He points to the Indian state of Kerala, where property inheritance among an elite group passes through the female line. Perhaps it is no coincidence that the state also has

Comparison

the most developed school system in India, and that the ratio of females to males approaches that of the United States and Europe. That lesson in the apparent consequences of women assuming more power may translate even to the United States, which ranks well down the roster of major industrialized countries in the number of women in the national legislature. And women themselves may owe it to the memories of more than 100 million of the missing to attempt no less.

FOR DISCUSSION: Why is it important not to neglect women in a society? What are some examples in the article of efforts to change the trend of neglect in some countries? What else might be done? What would the results be?

◆◆◆

CLAIMS OF VALUE

When you claim that sororities and fraternities are the best extracurricular organizations for college students to join, you are making a claim of value.

QUESTIONS ANSWERED BY CLAIMS OF VALUE. Is it good or bad? How bad? How good? Of what worth is it? Is it moral or immoral? Who thinks so? What do those people value? What values or criteria should I use to determine its goodness or badness? Are my values different from other people's values or from the author's values?

EXAMPLES OF CLAIMS OF VALUE. Computers are a valuable addition to modern society. Prayer has a moral function in the public schools. Viewing television is a wasteful activity. Mercy killing is immoral. The contributions of homemakers are as valuable as those of professional women. Animal rights are as important as human rights.

TYPES OF SUPPORT ASSOCIATED WITH CLAIMS OF VALUE. *Appeals to values* are important in developing claims of value. The arguer thus appeals to what the audience is expected to value. A sense of a common, shared system of values between the arguer and the audience is important for the argument to be convincing. These shared values must be established either explicitly or implicitly in the argument. *Motivational appeals* that suggest what the audience wants are also important in establishing claims of value. People place value on the things that they work to achieve. Other types of support used to establish claims of value include *analogies,* both *literal* and *figurative*, that establish links with other good or bad objects or qualities. Also, quotations from *authorities* who are admired help establish both expert criteria and judgments of good or bad, right or wrong. *Induction* is also used by presenting examples to demonstrate that something is good or bad. *Signs* that something is good or bad are sometimes cited. *Definitions* are used to clarify criteria for evaluation.

POSSIBLE ORGANIZATIONAL STRATEGIES. *Applied criteria* can develop a claim of value. Criteria for evaluation are established and then applied to the subject that is at issue. For example, in arguing that a particular television series is the best on television, criteria for what makes a superior series would be identified and then applied to the series to defend it as best. The audience would have to agree with the criteria to make argument effective. Or suppose the claim is made that toxic waste is the worst threat to the environment. A list of criteria for evaluating threats to the environment would be established and applied to toxic waste to show that it is the worst of all. Another possibility is to use *topical organization* by developing a list of reasons about why something is good or bad and then developing each of the reasons as a separate topic. You may also expect that *narrative* structure will sometimes be used to develop a claim of value. Narratives are real or made-up stories that can illustrate values in action, with morals or generalizations noted explicitly or implicitly along the way. An example of a narrative used to support a claim of value is the New Testament parable of the good Samaritan who helped a fellow traveler. The claim is that helping one another in such circumstances is valued and desirable behavior.

AN EXAMPLE OF AN ARGUMENT THAT CONTAINS A CLAIM OF VALUE. The following article examines the value of standardized tests. Notice the author's conclusion and his major reasons for reaching this conclusion.

WHAT'S WRONG WITH STANDARD TESTS?*

Ted Sizer

Claim of value

1   One of American educators' greatest conceits is the belief that people can be pigeonholed, in effect sorted by some scientific mechanism, usually the standardized test.

Appeals to data and values

2   The results of even the most carefully and sensitively crafted tests cannot be used fairly for high-stakes purposes for individuals; the belief that they can persists stubbornly in the educational community, in spite of an avalanche of research that challenges the tests' precision—and in spite of parents' common sense.

3   All of us who have taught for a while know "low testers" who became wonderfully resourceful and imaginative adults and "high testers" who as adults are, sadly, brittle and shallow people. We cringe as we remember how we so unfairly characterized them. . . .

Induction: examples

4   Danny Algrant's writing and directing of the 1994 film *Naked in New York* certainly was not completely evident when I taught him. Danny was an ebullient itch, even as a high school senior, a trial— but a worthy one—for his teacher. All that ebullient itchiness I gather now has been focused in successful film making. And so on: the awkward adolescent who now juggles the myriad demands of an inner-city school as principal, or the "low tester" who is now a successful writer. . . .

Appeal to values

5   There is tremendous public reluctance to question the usage and values of such tests. Being against conventional "testing" makes one appear to be against "standards." Test scores both give those in charge a device to move large numbers of students around and provide a fig leaf to justify labeling and tracking them in one way or another. How can we, they say, accept each little person as complicated, changeable, special? Impossible. It would take too much time. (Then privately, But not for *my* child. Let me tell you about her.)

Signs of adequacy and inadequacy

6   It would be silly, however, to dismiss all standardized testing. If carefully crafted and interpreted, these tests can reveal certain broad trends, even if they tell us only a bit about individual children. Such testing is helpful at the margins: it can signal the possibility of a troubled or especially gifted or otherwise "special" youngster. It can signal competence at immediate and comparable work if the classroom task to be completed (effective close reading of a text) is similar to the test (made up of prose passages and related questions) and if the task is attempted shortly after taking the test.

7   But none of the major tests used in American elementary and secondary education correlates well with long-term success or

---

*New York Times Magazine, January 8, 1995, p. 58.

failure. S.A.T. scores, for example, suggest likely grades in the freshman year at college; they do not predict much thereafter.

8   On the contrary, conventional tests can distort and thereby corrupt schooling. Most do not measure long-term intellectual habits. Indeed, many undermine the value of such by excessively emphasizing immediate, particular facts and skills considered out of context.

9   Those characteristics that we most value fail to be "tested": the qualities of mind and heart upon which we count for a healthy culture.

10   And a competitive work force. Send me, says the business leader, young employees who know something about using important knowledge, who learn readily and independently, who think for themselves and are dependable in the deepest sense. The college teacher says much the same, perhaps describing the qualities somewhat differently. Unfortunately, when classifying students, schools still peg kids by brief paper records and scores. "If the combined S.A.T. scores are below 1100, we will not consider the student," the admissions staff says, knowing full well that some high scorers are less worthy potential students than some low scorers.

Comparison

FOR DISCUSSION: How and why does the author address the question of the value of standardized tests? What does he consider their strengths? What does he consider their weaknesses? What experiences have you had with these tests? Do you think they are or are not a good measure of your abilities? Give reasons for your answer.

 ◆◆◆

CLAIMS OF POLICY

When you claim that all new students should attend orientation or that all students who graduate should participate in graduation ceremonies, you are making claims of policy.

QUESTIONS ANSWERED BY CLAIMS OF POLICY. What should we do? How should we act? What should future policy be? How can we solve this problem? What concrete course of action should we pursue to solve the problem? (Notice that policy claims focus on the future more than the other types of claims, which tend to deal with the past or present.)

EXAMPLES OF CLAIMS OF POLICY. The criminal should be sent to prison rather than to a mental institution. Everyone should be taught to recognize and report sexual harassment in the workplace. Every person in the United States should have access to health care. Small business loans must be made available to help people reestablish their businesses after a natural disaster. Both filmmakers and recording groups should make objectionable language and subject matter known to prospective consumers. Battered women who take revenge should not be placed in jail. Genetic engineering should be monitored and controlled. Parents should have the right to choose the schools their children attend.

TYPES OF SUPPORT ASSOCIATED WITH CLAIMS OF POLICY. Data and *statistics* are used to support a policy claim, but so are moral and commonsense appeals to what people value and want. *Motivational appeals* are especially important for policy claims. The audience needs to become sufficiently motivated to think or even act in a different way. To accomplish this degree of motivation, the arguer must convince the audience that it wants to change. *Appeals to values* are also used for motivation. The audience becomes convinced it should follow a policy to achieve important values. *Literal analogies* sometimes support policy claims. The arguer establishes what other similar people or groups have done and suggests the same thing can work in this case also. Or a successful effort is described, and the claim is made that it could work even better on a broader scale. This is another type of literal analogy, because it compares a small-scale effort to a large-scale, expanded effort. *Argument from authority* is also often used to establish claims of policy. The authorities quoted, however, must be trusted and must have good credibility. Effort is usually made to establish their credentials. *Cause* can be used to establish the origin of the problem, and *definition* can be used to clarify it. Finally, *deduction* can be used to reach a conclusion based on a general principle.

POSSIBLE ORGANIZATIONAL STRATEGIES. The *problem-solution* structure is typical of policy claims. The problem is first described in sufficient detail so that the audience will want a solution. Then the solution is spelled out. Furthermore, the solution suggested is usually shown to be superior to other solutions by anticipating and showing what is wrong with each of the others. Sometimes the problem and solution sections are followed by a *visualization* of how matters will be improved if the proposed solution is accepted and followed. Sometimes problem-solution arguments end with an *action* step that directs the audience to take a particular course of action (vote, buy, etc.).

AN EXAMPLE OF AN ARGUMENT THAT CONTAINS A CLAIM OF POLICY. The following article concerns the degree to which colleges should serve *in loco parentis* ("in the place of parents") by supervising the behavior of college students. The author presents her solutions to this problem in her article.

Signs of freedom

CAMPUS CLIMATE CONTROL*

Katie Roiphe

1   I remember the butter pats that covered the soaring ceiling of my freshman dining hall. They were the first sign that I had entered a world utterly devoid of adults. I remember my best friend passing out from inhaling nitrous oxide. I remember someone I know

*New York Times, March 5, 1999, p. A25.

falling drunkenly off a fire escape and ending up in the hospital. I remember groups of us breaking into the pool at night and swimming naked. This was not 1967. This was 1990.

Comparison with 1960s 2   By the time I arrived at college, the idea of adult authority had been chipped away and broken down by a previous generation—by Watergate and Vietnam and drugs. And though we would have died rather than admit it, without it some of us were feeling lost. We had the absolute, shimmering freedom that had been dreamed up for us during the 60's. We had the liberating knowledge that no one cared what we did.

Problems 3   But it wasn't making us as happy as it was supposed to. I remember moments of exultation walking though the pink campus at dawn, but I also remember moments of pure terror.

4   During a particularly wild period of my senior year, a professor looked up from my essay on Robert Lowell's falling-out-of-love poetry, glanced at the violet circles under my eyes and said, "You really need to get some sleep." I stood there in my ripped jeans. I felt suddenly reassured. The adult world, where people wake up in the morning, pay their bills and take out the trash, was still intact.

Authority

Solutions 5   It therefore does not surprise me that students now want universities to act *in loco parentis* again, and that slightly perplexed baby-boom administrators are trying to find ways to accommodate them. Some of the practical ideas being floated around campuses seem absurd. Alcohol-free adult-supervised student centers? Students will mock them. But they may serve a function by their mere existence.

Signs 6   Parents of teen-agers are always embarrassing to adolescents, and institutions acting *in loco parentis* will also be embarrassing. The alcohol-free, adult-supervised student centers (or trips to the theater with professors, or more resident advisers) are simply signs of an adult presence. They offer tangible monuments to an authority that you can avoid or rebel against, but that nonetheless exists. You can find it on a campus map.

Literal analogy 7   I remember the stories my mother told of climbing into her dorm room, wedging open the window, when she got back after curfew. Part of the thrill of rules, the perverse allure, is that they can be broken. Even when students are deliberately ignoring them, the fact of their existence is comforting. Rules give order to our chaos; they give us some sort of structure for our wildness so that it doesn't feel so scary.

Definition of rules

8   At the heart of the controversy over whether colleges should act *in loco parentis* is the question of whether college students are adults or children, and of course they are neither. They are childish and sophisticated, naive and knowing, innocent and wild, and in their strange netherworld, they need some sort of shadow adult, some not-quite-parent to be there as a point of reference.

Literal analogy

9   That said, some new rules being considered on campuses seem extreme—like the rule at Lehigh that there can be no campus parties without a chaperone. Surely there must be a way of establishing a benign and diffuse adult presence without students having to drink and dance and flirt and pick people up around actual adults.

Historical analogy

10   Many students . . . seem to like the superficial wholesomeness of the 50's. But what about the attitudes that informed it, like the sexism that tainted any college girl who enjoyed sex?

Solution   11   There must be a way to create some sort of structure without romanticizing or fetishizing the 50's. There must be a way of bringing back an adult presence on college campuses without treating students like children, a way of correcting the excesses of the sexual revolution without throwing away all of its benefits.

Claim of policy   12   <u>Americans are always drawn to extreme ideologies, to extremes of freedom or repression, of promiscuity or virginity, of wildness or innocence, but maybe there is a middle ground, somewhere closer to where people want to live their actual lives: a university without butter pats on the ceiling or 10 o'clock curfews.</u>

FOR DISCUSSION: How much common ground do you share with the author? Have your experiences with student life been similar to or different from hers? To what extent does your college act *in loco parentis?* If you had the power to change college policy, would you place more or fewer restrictions on student behavior on your campus? Why?

◆◆◇

CLAIMS AND ARGUMENT IN REAL LIFE

In argument, one type of claim may predominate, but other types may be present as supporting arguments or subclaims. It is not always easy to establish the predominant claim in an argument or to establish its type. You may find some disagreement in your class discussions when you try to categorize a claim according to type. The reason for this disagreement is that often two or more types of claims will be present in an argument. But close reading will usually reveal a predominant type, with the other types serving as subclaims. For example, a value claim that the popular press does harm by prying into the private lives of public figures may establish the fact that this is a pervasive practice, may define what should be public and what should not be public information, may examine the causes or more likely the effects of this type of reporting, and may suggest future policy for dealing with this problem. All may occur in the same article. Still, the dominant claim is one of value, that this practice of newswriters is bad.

It is useful when reading argument to identify the predominant claim because doing so helps you identify (1) the main purpose of the argument, (2) the types of support that may be used, and (3) the possible organizational strategies. It is also useful, however, to identify other types of subclaims and to analyze why they are used and how they contribute to the argumentative purpose. When planning and writing argument, you can in turn identify a predominant claim as well as other types of subclaims, support, and organization. The types of support and the organizational patterns that are particularly appropriate for developing different types of claims are explained and illustrated in this chapter. For quick reference, a chart of the types of support that can best be used for each type of claim appears in Table 11.1 (page 322). A second chart that shows the organizational patterns that can best be used to develop each type of claim appears in Table 12.1 (page 352). Refer to these tables for a quick summary of the suggestions to help you develop your claim and purpose for the argumentative papers you write.

As you read and write argument, you will also notice that claims follow a predictable sequence when they originate in real-life situations. In fact, argument appears most vigorous in dramatic, life-and-death situations or when a person's character is called into question. We see claims and rebuttals, many kinds of support, and every conceivable organizational strategy in these instances. For example, as juvenile crime in this country increased in recent years, the issues that emerged included these: What is causing young people to commit crimes? What can be done to protect the family unit? Is the educational system adequate? Should the criminal justice system treat young offenders differently from older criminals? Does racial discrimination contribute to juvenile crime? How can we make inner cities more livable? How can we improve social programs?

Such real-life situations, particularly when they are life-threatening as juvenile crime often is, not only generate issues; they also usually generate many arguments. Interestingly, the types of arguments usually appear in a fairly predictable order. The first arguments made in response to a new issue-generating situation usually involve claims of fact and definition. People first have to come to terms with the fact that something significant has happened. Then they need to define what happened so that they can understand it better.

The next group of arguments that appear after fact and definition often inquire into cause. People need to figure out why the event happened. Multiple causes are often considered and debated. Next, people begin to evaluate the goodness or badness of what has happened. It is usually after all of these other matters have been dealt with that people turn their attention to future policy and how to solve the problems.

The issues and claims that emerged from the September 11, 2001, terrorist attacks on the World Trade Center in New York City follow this pattern. Again, people were caught off guard, and the first questions that emerged as people watched their television sets were questions of fact: "What is happening? Is this a bomb? Are we being attacked?" Definition arguments followed. The issue was how to define what had happened, which would help determine the country's response. The president and his advisers defined the situation as an act of terrorism and then declared a war on terrorism.

Causal arguments engaged people for a long time after the initial event. Possible causes of the attacks included the presence of evil in the world, the terrorists' desire for power, religious conflicts, the uneven opportunities between developed and developing nations, hatred of America, even biblical prophecy. At the same time many value arguments appeared in the media. The questions were, "How bad is this?" and "Can any good be discovered?" Pictures of grieving survivors and of the excavation work at Ground Zero, along with obituaries of the dead, forcefully demonstrated the bad effects. Some good was found in the heroic efforts of passengers on one of the planes who attacked the terrorists and died with them, as well as in the selfless efforts of New York police officers and firefighters, many of whom died in the rescue effort in the buildings.

Deliberations about policy followed. Many American citizens, on their own initiative, decided to fly the American flag and to donate money to the survivors. Government officials set policy on how to conduct a war on terrorism. Many additional arguments about policy followed: how to get the donated money to the deserving victims, how to identify the terrorists and then how to find and kill them, how to know when the war was over, and how best to protect the country from future attack.

We can use the issue that emerged from the Columbine High School shootings in Littleton, Colorado, as a second example of this typical sequence of claims. The shootings occurred quite suddenly in late spring of 1999. Two male students entered Columbine High School while it was in session, shot twelve of their classmates, injured several more, and then shot themselves. Everyone was caught off guard by the sudden chaos in Littleton, and the first question that was asked both at the scene and in the media was, "What happened?" The facts had to be established before people were prepared to examine other issues. There were also some early attempts to define what had happened, to give it a name. Was this revenge, a demonstration of some sort, evidence of mental illness, or wanton killing?

The initial concerns about fact and definition were soon followed by questions about the causes of this incident. A possible cause, examined early on, was the quality of parental supervision in the boys' homes. Some people argued that the supervision these parents provided seemed no better or worse than in many other homes. Others argued that since the boys prepared for the shooting over a long period of time, their parents should have been more aware of what the boys were doing. The cause that emerged as the most potent, however, was the boys' interest in violent video games, which they both played frequently, and violence on the Internet, which also seemed to fascinate them. A number of argumentative articles were written at the time that explored the effects of such games on their users.

After much speculation about cause, people turned their attention to value and to arguing about whether any good could be found in these killings. One mother wrote an article about how her daughter professed her belief in God just before she was shot and killed. This was viewed as positive, even though the girl's death was certainly negative. The general opinion, however, was that the shooting was a terrible occurrence and that similar incidents must absolutely be avoided in the future.

It was not until most of these initial matters were analyzed and debated that discussion of future policy began to surface. Articles about censoring the Internet versus preserving First Amendment guarantees appeared. Other articles discussed the issue of parental supervision and control and suggested policy for monitoring the behavior of teenagers. Still other articles presented ways to make schools safer and included suggestions that ranged from the installation of metal detectors in schools to requiring the wearing of school uniforms. These articles demonstrated how dramatic events that capture widespread attention can also generate issues for argument.

You may be able to think of other issues that have inspired a variety of arguments and claims in this same roughly predictable order. It is useful to pay attention to the issues that come out of dramatic events, the types of claims that are generated by them, and the order in which these claims appear. Such analysis will help you anticipate the course an issue will take. It will also help you determine at what point in the ongoing conversation about an issue you happen to be at a given moment. You can then speculate about the aspects of the issue that have already been argued and that are likely to be argued in the future.

VALUE OF THE CLAIMS AND THE CLAIM QUESTIONS FOR READING AND WRITING ARGUMENT

Readers of argument find the list of the five types of claims and the questions that accompany them useful for identifying the claim and the main purpose in an argument: to establish fact, to define, to establish cause, to assign value, or to propose a solution. Claims and claim questions can also help readers identify minor purposes in an argument, those that are developed as subclaims. When a reader is able to discover the overall purpose of an argument, it is much easier to make predictions and to follow the argument.

Writers of argument find the list of the five types of claims and the questions that accompany them useful for analyzing an issue, writing a claim about it, and identifying both the controlling purpose for a paper and additional ideas that can be developed in the paper. Here is an example of how this can work. The author writes the issue in the form of a question, as in the example "Should high schools be safer places?" Then the author asks the claim questions about this issue and writes a paragraph in response to each of them: Is it a fact that high schools are unsafe places? How should we define *unsafe*? What causes a lack of safety in high schools, and what are the effects? Is a lack of safety good or bad? What criteria could be established to judge the goodness or badness of safety in high schools? What can be done to make high schools safer places? Finally, the author reads the paragraphs and selects the one that is most promising to form the major claim and purpose in the paper. For example, suppose the author decides to write a policy paper, and the claim becomes "Parents, students, teachers, and administrators all need to cooperate to make high schools safer places." To show how that can be done becomes the main purpose of the paper. The information generated by asking the other claim questions, however, can also be used in the paper to provide reasons and evidence. The claim questions, used in this way as part of the prewriting process, can generate considerable information and ideas for a paper.

REVIEW QUESTIONS

1. What are the five types of claims?
2. What are the questions associated with each type?
3. What is a predictable sequence that claims follow when they originate in a dramatic, real-life situation?
4. How do claims typically appear in written argument? That is, do writers usually limit themselves to a single purpose and claim or not? Discuss.

EXERCISES AND ACTIVITIES

A. CLASS DISCUSSION: PREDICTING TYPES OF CLAIMS

Bring in the front page of a current newspaper. Discuss headlines that suggest controversial topics. Predict from each headline the type of claim that will be made.

B. GROUP WORK: READING AND ANALYZING TYPES OF CLAIMS

The class is divided into five groups, and each group is assigned one of the five articles that follow. Prepare for group work by reading the article assigned to your group. Then get in your group and apply the new reading strategies described in this chapter by answering the following questions. Assign a person to report your answers to the class.

1. Which sentence is the claim? Remember it can appear at the beginning, in the middle, or at the end of the essay. Underline it.
2. What type of claim is it? Decide which of the five types of claims this claim represents.
3. What are one or two examples of support used in the essay? To help you identify support, review the marginal labels that identify the support in the five sample readings in the chapter.
4. How would you summarize the argument in the essay in two or three sentences?
5. What is your reaction to the author's position?
6. Where might you position this argument in an ongoing conversation about the issue? At the beginning, the middle, or the end? Why?

GENE TESTS: WHAT YOU KNOW CAN HURT YOU*

Barbara Koenig

Barbara Koenig is associated with the Stanford University Center for Biomedical Ethics. She codirects the program in genomics, ethics, and society.

---

*New York Times, April 6, 1996, p. A15.

1   Last year, it was discovered that 1 percent of Ashkenazi Jewish women, those of Central or Eastern European ancestry, carry a mutated form of a gene that might predispose them to breast and ovarian cancer.

2   After this discovery, a surgeon who operates on women with breast cancer told me that a day rarely passes when a patient does not ask about "the gene test."

3   Even with this demand, however, almost all leading scientists and two major commercial testing laboratories agreed informally not to offer the test for the mutation to the general public because widespread testing would do more harm than good.

4   That consensus was broken recently by Dr. Joseph D. Schulman, director of the Genetics and I.V.F. Institute in Fairfax, Va. The doctor, who advertised the service on the World Wide Web, says it will give women access to valuable information. But in genetic testing, what you know won't necessarily help you—indeed, it might even hurt you.

5   As Alice Wexler points out in *Mapping Fate,* her book about genetically determined Huntington's disease, Americans' strong bias for information leads them to believe in genetic testing. Doing something, anything, to counter illness is considered the brave and correct approach.

6   But testing for the 185delAG mutation does not help most women. A positive test does not mean that you will get cancer, and a negative test does not mean that you won't.

7   Most scientists agree that the mutation occurs in families in which many members have suffered from breast and ovarian cancer. But leaping to the conclusion that a mutation inevitably leads to cancer, especially for women without a family history, reflects a naïve genetic determinism and ignores the possible effects of the environment and other genes on one's health.

8   But let's assume that a woman from a high-risk family tests positive. What then? There is no guaranteed way to prevent cancer or detect it early. Some desperate women do resort to drastic measures such as surgically removing their breasts.

9   Paradoxically, this isn't the recommended treatment for many women already diagnosed with cancer. For a decade, more doctors have recommended and more women, especially those with small tumors, have chosen instead to have lumpectomies.

10   Knowing your genetic makeup can also create profound emotional and financial problems. For example, a spouse might use this information in a custody dispute. Or a woman might decide not to have children for fear of passing on the gene. But if she decides to adopt, will she be approved by an agency? And should a 9-year-old girl be tested for the mutation?

11   The test brings up other thorny questions that may be better left unexplored. For instance, with current technology, a woman could test a fetus for the gene and then abort it. In his ad, Dr. Schulman suggests that his Genetics and I.V.F. Institute may be able to screen embryos for the gene mutation.

12   There are also real economic repercussions. Women could face discrimination from employers and health insurers. And most physicians have little experience

with ordering and interpreting genetic tests that determine a woman's cancer risk (and in guiding families through the turmoil generated by the results).

13   Until basic research on the clinical significance of the 185delAG mutation is complete, there is no justification for widespread screening. Unfortunately, nothing prevents laboratories from offering genetic tests, nor are there any regulations to insure the quality of the tests.

14   In March, a Federal task force on testing suggested possible regulatory strategies, from requiring Food and Drug Administration approval for new tests to strengthening the laws that govern labs.

15   Either approach would slow down the premature commercialization of testing. Strict regulation may be unpopular among those who believe that women have a right to this information. But extreme caution should be the order of the day.

FOR DISCUSSION: What is the problem described in this article? What is the proposed solution? Can you think of other examples of information that might be controversial in the way that gene tests are? What is your opinion about communicating information of this sort to the people who are affected by it?

◆◆◇

WITHOUT A SAFETY NET*

Barbara Ehrenreich and Frances Fox Piven

Barbara Ehrenreich is an author and columnist who has written extensively about people on welfare. Frances Fox Piven is professor of political studies and social studies at the City University of New York.

1   Just four years ago, Kimberly Hill was a poster child for welfare reform. A tall, strikingly attractive mother of two, she had been on welfare off and on for several years until, in 1995, a caseworker urged her to get computer training. Her first job—for which she rated a mention in a 1998 *San Francisco Chronicle* story titled "Firms Find Talent Among Disabled, Welfare Recipients"—was no prize. "People knew I was off welfare," she told us, "and they treated me like I had the plague." Hired as an administrative assistant, she found herself being asked to clean the rest room. She got luckier with her next job, at a staffing agency, where, after a series of promotions, she was earning $65,000 a year. Then, on December 20, 2001, just as the recession became official, she was laid off.

2   Hill meets us at Starbucks because she doesn't think the neighborhood where she lives is a good place for us to be wandering around. She is confident and direct, but admits to feeling the stress of being out of work. She has found one part-time

Mother Jones, May–June 2002, pp. 35–41.

office job and is about to add another, but neither offers health insurance. We ask if she would go back on welfare if things got bad enough. "No," she says, thrusting her chin out for emphasis. "It's too horrible, a horrible experience—demeaning."

3   Beverly Ransom was another welfare-to-work success story. We met her in Miami's Liberty City—site of the 1980 riot—at the storefront office of Low Income Families Fighting Together, a community organization that works for welfare rights and affordable housing. A bright-eyed, straight-backed woman of 50, with gray hair pulled back into a small ponytail, she speaks with pride about the catering job she found after years on welfare. But lately the work has fallen off; the catering companies that used to give her more work than she could handle just haven't been calling anymore. "Catering is based on tourism," she says. "Last year at this time I had so much work I had to beg for days off. Now I need food stamps." She gets $118 a week from unemployment insurance, but rent for herself and her children, who are 12 and 14, is $500 a month. Her biggest fear is that she'll end up in a shelter: "What do I do? My kids are at an age where they would be traumatized."

4   In 1996, when welfare reform was enacted, a recession seemed about as likely as the destruction of the World Trade Center by a handful of men armed with box cutters. The assumptions behind welfare reform were, one, that a job could lift a family out of poverty and, two, that there would always be enough jobs for anyone plucky enough to go out and land one. The first assumption was shaky from the start; women leaving welfare ended up earning an average of less than $8 an hour, hardly enough to support a family. Now the second assumption has crumbled as well: More than 2 million people lost their jobs last year, and single mothers have been especially hard hit. According to the Federal Bureau of Labor Statistics, the employment rate of women who head families fell far more sharply last fall than overall employment, by three percentage points in just three months.

5   There is, of course, a venerable New Deal program to protect laid-off workers—unemployment insurance—but it is, perversely enough, designed to offer the least help to those who need it the most. People in temporary, part-time, or very low-wage jobs—the kind most often available to someone leaving welfare—often don't qualify for benefits. According to the Economic Policy Institute, about 70 percent of former welfare recipients who have lost their jobs during the current recession are not eligible for unemployment.

6   In the past, poor single mothers had their own form of unemployment insurance—welfare. Contrary to the stereotype, most welfare recipients worked, at least intermittently, falling back on public assistance when a child got sick or a car broke down. But in their zeal to save the poor from their supposed sins of laziness, irresponsibility, and promiscuity, the reformers entirely overlooked the role of welfare as a safety net for working mothers. Temporary Aid to Needy Families (TANF), which is what the new version of welfare is called, has just one aim: to push the poor into the job market to become "self-sufficient." Whatever sense this made in the boom years when welfare reform was devised, it makes none now. As a poster at an East Harlem community organization put it, the acronym has come to stand for "Torture and Abuse of Needy Families."

7   Of course, pre-reform welfare was never adequate: Grants were low (an average of $550 a month nationwide), and recipients were routinely hassled and humiliated by the bureaucracy. Still, under the old system, if you were demonstrably poor and had children to support, you were entitled to cash assistance. The new system, legislated in 1996 with the passage of the Personal Responsibility and Work Opportunity Reconciliation Act, ended that entitlement. The law set strict time limits on assistance (no more than five years in a lifetime for most people), encouraged private companies to bid on contracts to administer welfare, and gave states wide discretion to cut people from the rolls.

8   Under the current system, someone who applies for welfare is lucky to get any benefits. More likely, the family will be "diverted"—sent to a food bank, told to apply for child support from an absentee parent, or assigned to a training program designed to keep them searching for a job. Those who make it through this process may see their benefits cut for any of a multitude of infractions (including, in some cases, having a child who regularly skips school).

9   These practices, often characterized as part of an effort to endow the poor with "self-esteem," have been extremely effective—at least at cutting the welfare rolls. A report by the National Campaign for Jobs and Income Support shows that welfare caseloads rose as unemployment went up in the recession of 1990–1991, but that this time, caseloads actually fell in 14 of the 47 states where unemployment rose between March and December 2001. In Wisconsin, the state that pioneered a particularly draconian version of welfare reform under the leadership of former governor and current Health and Human Services Secretary Tommy Thompson, unemployment rose by 0.6 percentage points during the same period, but the welfare rolls just kept on dropping—by 29 percentage points. And changes now being debated could make the program even less accessible to poor families: With TANF up for reauthorization in Congress by September 30, the Bush administration is pushing measures that would make benefits more difficult to get, and even harder to keep.

10   So what do you do when there are few jobs available and the safety net lies in tatters? We talked to former welfare recipients who recently lost their jobs in five states—New York, Oregon, California, Florida, and Illinois. Some had already exhausted their five-year lifetime benefit limit; others remained potentially eligible for welfare. None of them were having much luck. While the media tends to focus on displaced dot-commers and laid-off Enron executives, these women represent the hidden underside of the recession. In the scary new world of post-welfare America, their experience has been like that of someone who looks out an airplane window on a bright, clear day and sees nothing at all below.

◆◆◆◆

11   Janet Cook is one of the many who have gone from welfare to work to nothing in a few short years. We talked to her by phone at a residential motel in Portland, Oregon, where she was paying more than $300 a week for the single room she shared with her husband and their four children. Cook, who is in her late 30s, held a job with a truck manufacturer for six years until she was laid off last April. Her husband is a construction worker, and they used to live in the houses that his company was working on, moving on as each was completed. Then, last fall, the

company relocated to another city, and the couple decided to stay rather than yank their kids out of school. With no jobs in sight and their savings soon eaten up by the motel bills, there was nothing to do but apply for welfare.

12   It's "murder to get through the process," Cook says. "You have to be flat broke so you can't function. They want you to land a job, so they make you wait. They don't give you cash for the first two weeks. The first week they make you attend a job workshop. The second week is job search. If you miss one hour, you start over for the whole two weeks." On the day we spoke to her, the family was leaving the motel and moving to a shelter. (Cook ultimately did get benefits, but not until a Legal Aid attorney intervened on her behalf.)

13   All of the former welfare recipients we interviewed described the maze of obstacles that now lies between a needy family and even a paltry amount of cash assistance—a set of hurdles far more daunting than the pre-reform bureaucracy. There are long lines in welfare centers with waits, one New York woman told us, of up to nine hours. In a Latino neighborhood, there may be no Spanish-speaking caseworker on duty. In the 1960s, a federal regulation required that welfare offices accept oral applications. Now, you may have to fill out the same form three times, just to save the agency photocopying expenses.

14   "They close your case for any small thing now," reports Dulce Severino, a mother of two who lives in Brooklyn. "You can't speak to a social worker—you have to wait a whole day to see them. And they speak badly to people when they finally see them. There are ugly words, almost fights with the social workers." Another Brooklyn woman reports that "some days there are almost riots"—and there really would be, she believes, if it weren't for the heavy police presence inside the welfare centers.

15   Applicants who aren't turned away at the welfare office often face another obstacle—the private companies that increasingly contract with states and municipalities to administer welfare programs. The 1996 law allows governments to contract with churches and community groups, but most contracts have gone to such distinctly non-faith-based entities as Maximus, Unisys, and Lockheed Martin. Some companies specialize in "job readiness" services; others do everything from conducting interviews to determining recipients' eligibility, often under contracts that reward them for any funds they do not spend.

16   Sharon Bush, a mother of four who lives in the East New York section of Brooklyn, applied for welfare in November after medical problems forced her to quit her job. After she filled out the paperwork, two caseworkers paid her a visit to investigate her claim; next, she was sent to Curtis and Associates, a private, for-profit job placement firm. There she was given a lengthy test, shown to a desk with a phone, and told to start cold-calling companies in search of a job. "They don't help, they don't provide contacts," she says. "Meanwhile there are all these people sitting there, waiting, who need back rent." She would have to report to Curtis, she was told, from 9:30 to 4:30 daily for four weeks. In the meantime she'd receive some emergency assistance—a total of $156.60.

17   The sheer hassle of "reformed" welfare is enough to discourage many people from even applying. But the best-known and most clear-cut way that TANF

keeps the rolls down is through the five-year lifetime limit on benefits. The clock started ticking with the passage of the welfare reform law in 1996, with the consequence that 120,000 families exhausted their benefits just as the recession hit in 2001. Dulce Severino's family is one of them, although she has worked most of the time since 1992, packing clothes in the sweatshop factories that have sprung up in her Brooklyn neighborhood of Bushwick. Because her earnings were so low—her best wage was $5.15 an hour—Severino received a welfare wage supplement, so the clock on her lifetime limit was running even as she worked. If she had been paid better, she would still be eligible for welfare today.

◆◆◆◆

18   With six years' hindsight, it's hard to fathom why no one, back in 1996, seems to have thought ahead to a time when jobs would be in short supply and millions of Americans might sorely need cash assistance. We talked to Mary Jo Bane, a Harvard professor who left her post as the Clinton administration's assistant secretary for children and families in 1996 to protest the direction of reform. "People mumbled about it," she says, "but the economy was so good then." David Ellwood, who along with Bane co-chaired Clinton's welfare reform task force and who also teaches at Harvard, told us, "Many people thought about the possibility of a downturn. The real question is why the people who drafted the bill, and signed it, willfully didn't."

19   Part of the answer may lie in the peculiar economic euphoria of the mid- and late '90s, when bearishness began to seem unpatriotic and prosperity looked like a permanent entitlement. The emphasis, even among liberals, was on "making work pay" and expanding benefits such as child care and the Earned Income Tax Credit, which provides low-income working families with up to $4,000 a year in cash. Hardly anyone, welfare recipients included, wanted to see welfare-as-we-knew-it restored.

20   But the main problem, says Ellwood, was sheer irresponsibility—the very flaw the reformers aimed to eliminate among welfare recipients. "There was just enormous pressure to reduce welfare, and the attitude toward a possible economic downturn was basically, 'We'll cross that bridge when we come to it.'" According to Ellwood, Clinton believed the money that states saved as a result of welfare reform could be used to help people in case of a recession; he did not foresee that a downturn would find states strapped for funds and eagerly slashing programs like Medicaid and child care.

21   The result has been that America entered its most recent recession as defenseless as if we had to face a terrorist attack without firefighters or emergency rescue workers. The safety net that sustained millions of the poor through previous downturns, however inadequately, has been torn to shreds.

22   We could see the current crisis, whose effects on unemployment will persist long after the recession technically ends, as an opportunity for genuine reform—including meaningful assistance for those who cannot find work, and reliable help, such as child care, for those who can. But instead, the Bush administration and Congress, like the welfare reformers who preceded them, seem poised to look the other way.

FOR DISCUSSION: Respond to the authors' position on welfare reform. Do you agree or disagree? Why? If you had the authority to solve the problems associated with welfare reform that are described in this article, what would you do, and why?

❖❖❖

READING, WRITING, NARCISSISM*

Lilian G. Katz

Lilian G. Katz is a professor of early childhood education at the University of Illinois. This article first appeared in *American Educator* and was later adapted for the *New York Times*'s op-ed page.

1   Developing and strengthening children's self-esteem has become a major goal of our schools. Although it is true that many children, especially the youngest students, have low self-esteem, our practice of lavishing praise for the mildest accomplishments is not likely to have much success. Feelings cannot be learned from direct instruction, and constant reminders about how wonderful one is may raise doubts about the credibility of the message and the messenger.

2   A project by a first grade class in an affluent Middle Western suburb that I recently observed showed how self-esteem and narcissism can be confused. Working from copied pages prepared by the teacher, each student produced a booklet called "All About Me." The first page asked for basic information about the child's home and family. The second page was titled "what I like to eat," the third was "what I like to watch on TV," the next was "what I want for a present" and another was "where I want to go on vacation."

3   The booklet, like thousands of others I have encountered around the country, had no page headings such as "what I want to know more about," "what I am curious about," "what I want to solve" or even "to make."

4   Each page was directed toward the child's basest inner gratifications. Each topic put the child in the role of consumer—of food, entertainment, gifts and recreation. Not once was the child asked to play the role of producer, investigator, initiator, explorer, experimenter or problem-solver.

5   It is perhaps this kind of literature that accounts for a poster I saw in a school entrance hall. Pictures of clapping hands surround the title "We Applaud Ourselves." While the sign's probable purpose was to help children feel good about themselves, it did so by directing their attention inward. The poster urged self-congratulation; it made no reference to possible ways of earning applause—by considering the feelings or needs of others.

6   Another common type of exercise was a display of kindergartners' work I saw recently that consisted of large paper-doll figures, each having a balloon containing a sentence stem that began "I am special because . . ." The children completed the sentence with the phrases such as "I can color," "I can ride a bike," and "I like to

New York Times, July 15, 1993, p. A25.

play with my friends." But these children are not likely to believe for very long that they are special because they can color or ride a bike. What are they going to think when they discover just how trivial these criteria for being special are?

7   This overemphasizing self-esteem and self-congratulation stems from a legitimate desire to correct previous generations' traditions of avoiding compliments for fear of making children conceited. But the current practices are vast overcorrections. The idea of specialness they express is contradictory: If everybody is special, nobody is special.

8   Adults can show their approval for children in more significant ways than awarding gold stars and happy faces. Esteem is conveyed to students when adults and peers treat them with respect, ask for their views and preferences and provide opportunities for decisions and choices about things that matter to them. Children are born natural and social scientists. They devote much time and energy to investigating and making sense of their environments. During the preschool and early school years, teachers can capitalize on this disposition by engaging children in investigations and projects.

9   Several years ago, I saw this kind of project at a rural British school for 5- to 7-year-olds. A large display on the bulletin board read: "We Are a Class Full of Bodies. Here Are the Details." The display space was filled with bar graphs showing birth dates, weights and heights, eye colors, number of lost teeth, shoe sizes and other data of the entire class. As the children worked in small groups to take measurements, prepare graphs and help one another post displays of their analyses, the teacher was able to create an atmosphere of a community of researchers looking for averages, trends and ranges.

10   Compare this to the American kindergarten I visited recently in which the comments made by the children about a visit to a dairy farm were displayed on the bulletin board. Each sentence began with the words "I liked." For example, "I liked the cows" and "I liked the milking machine." No sentences began "What surprised me was . . ." and "What I want to know more about is . . ."

11   Of course, children benefit from positive feedback. But praise and rewards are not the only methods of reinforcement. More emphasis should be placed on appreciation—reinforcement related explicitly and directly to the *content* of the child's interest and effort. For example, if a child poses a thoughtful question, the teacher might come to class the next day with a new reference book on the same subject. It is important that the teacher show appreciation for pupils' concerns without taking their minds off the subjects at hand or directing their attention inward.

12   When children see that their concerns and interests are taken seriously, they are more likely to raise them in discussion and to take their own ideas seriously. Teachers can strengthen children's disposition to wonder, reflect, raise questions and generate alternative solutions to practical and intellectual problems. Of course, when children are engaged in challenging and significant activities, they are bound to experience failures and rebuffs. But as long as the teacher accepts the child's feeling and responds respectfully—"I know you're disappointed, but you can try again tomorrow"—the child is more likely to learn from the incident than be harmed by it.

13   Learning to deal with setbacks and maintaining the persistence and optimism necessary for childhood's long road to mastery are the real foundations of lasting self-esteem. Children who are helped to develop these qualities will surely respect themselves—though they probably will have better things to think about.

FOR DISCUSSION: What values does the author believe are communicated through school assignments and programs designed to improve students' self-esteem? How would she assess the final value of these assignments? What types of assignments might she consider more valuable? What is your position on teaching self-esteem as a major goal for public schools?

◆◆◆

DEVISING NEW MATH TO DEFINE POVERTY*

Louis Uchitelle

Louis Uchitelle conducted much of the research for this article in Indianapolis, Indiana. The 2000 census finally set the poverty line at $17,600.

1   The Census Bureau has begun to revise its definition of what constitutes poverty in the United States, experimenting with a formula that would drop millions more families below the poverty line.

2   The bureau's new approach would in effect raise the income threshold for living above poverty to $19,500 for a family of four, from the $16,600 now considered sufficient. Suddenly, 46 million Americans, or 17 percent of the population, would be recognized as officially below the line, not the 12.7 percent announced last month, the lowest level in nearly a decade.

3   A strong economy has undoubtedly lifted many families, but not nearly as many as the official statistics suggest.

4   "It is certainly our opinion, and the opinion of every researcher we have talked to, that something should be done to update the poverty measure," said Edward Welniak, chief of the Census Bureau's Income Statistics Branch.

5   Fixing a poverty line has always been a subjective endeavor. The current formula was created for President Lyndon B. Johnson to keep score in his "war on poverty" and has remained unchanged since 1965 except for adjustments for inflation. It is based on a minimal food budget that no longer represents American eating habits or spending. The Census Bureau's new Experimental Poverty Measures are an effort to determine what poor people must spend on food, clothing, housing and life's little extras.

6   "There is no scientific way to set a new poverty line," said Rebecca M. Blank, dean of the School of Public Policy at the University of Michigan. "What there is

*New York Times, October 18, 1999, pp. A1, A4.

here are a set of judgment calls, now being made, about what is needed to lift people to a socially acceptable standard of living."

7   Sociologists and economists who study what people must earn to escape poverty in the United States place the line even higher than the Census Bureau's experimental measures, which were published in July and are now the focus of a growing debate. They put the threshold for a family of four somewhere between $21,000 and $28,000. That is partly because the bureau's criteria, based largely on a study by the National Academy of Sciences, do not allow extra cash for emergencies—to fix a car, say, or repair a leaky roof, or to buy health insurance.

8   Ordinary Americans, in opinion polls, draw the poverty line above $20,000, saying it takes at least that much, if not more, to "get along in their community," to "live decently" or to avoid hardship.

9   But a higher threshold means government spending would rise to pay for benefits tied to the poverty level, like food stamps and Head Start. That would require an incursion into the budget surplus that neither Republicans nor Democrats seek.

10   Not surprising, the White House, which would have to authorize a change in the poverty formula, is proceeding cautiously. "We have at least a couple of years more work to do," an Administration official said, passing the decision for redefining poverty to the next administration. . . .

11   The new thinking has several facets. It redefines income to include for the first time noncash income like food stamps and rent subsidies. It puts child care and other work-related expenses in a separate category because they vary so much from family to family. And it tries to determine what a low-income family must spend in the 1990's not only to survive, but to preserve a reasonable amount of self-respect.

12   A telephone is considered essential. So is housing in good repair. Clothing is no longer just to keep warm or covered; looking decent is a critical status symbol. That is why Isaac Pinner, 16 and in ninth grade, and his sister, Lea, 12 and in seventh grade, insist they are not poor. Sitting in the living room of their run-down rented home with their mother, Julie Pinner, 35, a receptionist and clerk, they resent her decision to talk to a reporter about poverty. "I get what I want," Lea said, and Isaac agreed. "Why talk to us?" he asked.

13   Judging by their clothes, they do not seem poor, although their mother's income of $15,500, including a rent subsidy, while higher than the official poverty line for a single mother of two, puts the Pinners right at the dividing line in the Census Bureau's experimental measures.

14   "They think I am richer than I am," said Ms. Pinner, who noted that the gas was turned off recently when she could not pay the bill. She also lacks money to fix her car.

15   "But," Ms. Pinner said of her children, "he wears the latest Nike brand shoes and she the latest Levi's. I like them to look nice, and here in the ghetto there are standards of dress. If they don't dress up to the standards, other kids tend to pick on them. I am not the only poor person who dresses her kids."

16   Most proposed definitions of poverty include a car—an old one—which is deemed necessary not only for work but for the odd outing, or the supermarket.

"Not having a car is a big dividing line between the poor and the not so poor," said Christopher Jencks, a sociologist at Harvard's Kennedy School of Government.

17   More often than not, poor Indianapolis families own used cars, but they are often at risk. Austin Johnson, for example, says he cannot afford car insurance. Neither can Nevada Owens, who is also short of money to fix a flat tire. She drives her 1985 Delta Oldsmobile with a spare doughnut tire permanently on a rear wheel. The car was a gift from her church, but the cost of gasoline for this guzzler eats up 7 percent of her $17,300 in annual income.

18   Her income, from welfare, food stamps, rent and tuition subsidies and a $3,000 gift from her mother, puts Ms. Owens, a single mother, and her three children just above the official poverty line. But at 21, studying to be a licensed practical nurse, she needs the car. The course work requires her to travel from her school to two different hospitals, about 25 miles a day.

19   Then there is the Saturday outing in Ms. Owens's old car, which she drives to her grandfather's home in a rural area outside the city—the one family luxury. "We have a cookout," she said, "and the kids play on the swings and my mother comes over—she lives two doors away. We have a good time."

20   In a 1993 study of impoverished single mothers, published as the book *Making Ends Meet*, Kathryn Edin, a sociologist at the University of Pennsylvania, reported that the mothers found themselves forced to spend more than their acknowledged incomes. They got the difference from family members, absent boyfriends, off-the-books jobs and church charity.

21   "No one avoided the unnecessary expenditures," Ms. Edin said recently, "such as the occasional trip to the Dairy Queen, or a pair of stylish new sneakers for the son who might otherwise sell drugs to get them, or the cable subscription for the kids home alone and you are afraid they will be out on the street if they are not watching TV."

FOR DISCUSSION: What is the issue in this article? How does definition intensify this issue? What is your opinion about drawing the poverty line? Where should it be drawn? Who would benefit from your solution? Who would be burdened?

◆◆◆

BRINGING UP ADULTOLESCENTS*

Peg Tyre

This article is about a new phenomenon that is being studied by experts with $3.4 million of funding. Does it describe you or anyone you know?

1   When Silvia Geraci goes out to dinner with friends, she has a flash of anxiety when the check comes. She can pay her share—her parents give her

*Newsweek, March 25, 2002, pp. 38–40.

enough money to cover all her expenses. It's just that others in her circle make their own money now. "I know I haven't earned what I have. It's been given to me," says Geraci, 22, who returned to her childhood home in suburban New York after graduating from college last year. "It's like I'm stuck in an in-between spot. Sometimes I wonder if I'm getting left behind." Poised on the brink of what should be a bright future, Geraci and millions like her face a thoroughly modern truth: it's hard to feel like a Master of the Universe when you're sleeping in your old twin bed.

2   Whether it's reconverting the guest room back into a bedroom, paying for graduate school, writing a blizzard of small checks to cover rent and health-insurance premiums or acting as career counselors, parents across the country are trying to provide their twentysomethings with the tools they'll need to be self-sufficient—someday. In the process, they have created a whole new breed of child—the adultolescent.

3   For their part, these overgrown kids seem content to enjoy the protection of their parents as they drift from adolescence to early adulthood. Relying on your folks to light the shadowy path to the future has become so accepted that even the ultimate loser move—returning home to live with your parents—has lost its stigma. According to the 2000 Census, nearly 4 million people between the ages of 25 and 34 live with their parents. And there are signs that even more moms and dads will be welcoming their not-so-little-ones back home. Last week, in an online survey by MonsterTRAK.com, a job-search firm, 60 percent of college students reported that they planned to live at home after graduation—and 21 percent said they planned to remain there for more than a year.

4   Unlike their counterparts in the early '90s, adultolescents aren't demoralized slackers lining up for the bathroom with their longing-to-be-empty-nester parents. Iris and Andrew Aronson, two doctors in Chicago, were happy when their daughter, Elena, 24, a Smith graduate, got a modest-paying job and moved back home last year. It seemed a natural extension of their parenting philosophy—make the children feel secure enough and they'll eventually strike out on their own. "When she was an infant, the so-called experts said letting babies cry themselves to sleep was the only way to teach them to sleep independent of their mother," says Iris. "But I never did that either." Come fall, Elena is heading off to graduate school. Her sister, who will graduate from Stanford University this spring, is moving in. Living at home works, Elena explains, because she knows she's leaving. "Otherwise, it'll feel too much like high school," says Elena. "As it is, sometimes I look around and think, 'OK, now it's time to start my homework.'"

5   Most adultolescents no longer hope, or even desire, to hit the traditional benchmarks of independence—marriage, kids, owning a home, financial autonomy—in the years following college. The average age for a first marriage is now 26, four years later than it was in 1970, and childbearing is often postponed for a decade or more after that. Jobs are scarce, and increasingly, high-paying careers require a graduate degree. The decades-long run-up in the housing market has made a starter home a pipe dream for most people under 30. "The conveyor belt that transported adolescents into adulthood has broken down," says Dr. Frank

Furstenberg, who heads up a $3.4 million project by the MacArthur foundation studying the adultolescent phenomenon.

6   Beyond the economic realities, there are some complicated psychological bonds that keep able-bodied college graduates on their parents' payroll. Unlike the Woodstock generation, this current crop of twentysomethings aren't building their adult identity in reaction to their parents' way of life. In the 1960's, kids crowed about not trusting anyone over 30; these days, they can't live without them. "We are seeing a closer relationship between generations than we have seen since World War II," says University of Maryland psychologist Jeffrey Jensen Arnett. "These young people genuinely like and respect their parents."

7   To some, all this support and protection—known as "scaffolding" among the experts—looks like an insidious form of codependence. Psychiatrist Alvin Rosenfeld says these are the same hyperinvolved parents who got minivan fatigue from ferrying their kids to extracurricular activities and turned college admission into a competitive sport. "They've convinced themselves they know how to lead a good life, and they want to get that for their kids, no matter what," says Rosenfeld.

8   By the time those children reach their 20s, says market researcher Neil Howe, their desires for the future are often indistinguishable from the desires of their parents. "The Me Generation," says Howe, "has simply turned into the Mini-Me Generation."

9   Trying to guarantee your children the Good Life, though, can sometimes backfire. A few years ago, Janice Charlton of Philadelphia pressured her daughter, Mary, then 26, to get a master's degree, even agreeing to cosign two $17,000 school loans if she did. Mary dropped out, Janice says, and the loans went into default. "I'm sorry I ever suggested it," says Janice. "We're still close but it's a sticky issue between us."

10   Many parents say they're simply ensuring that their kids have an edge in an increasingly competitive world. When Tom D'Agnes's daughter, Heather, 26, told him she was thinking about graduate school, D'Agnes, 52, flew from their home in Hawaii to San Francisco to help her find one. He edited the essay section of her application and vetted her letters of recommendation, too. While Tom's wife, Leona, worried about creating a "dependency mentality," Tom was adamant about giving his daughter a leg up.

11   Parents aren't waiting to get involved. Campus career counselors report being flooded with calls from parents anxious to participate in their college senior's job search. Last fall the U.S. Navy began sending letters describing their programs to potential recruits—and their parents. "Parents are becoming actively involved in the career decisions of their children," says Cmdr. Steven Lowry, public-affairs officer for Navy recruiting. "We don't recruit the individual anymore. We recruit the whole family."

12   The steady flow of cash from one generation of active consumers to another has marketers salivating. These twentysomethings are adventuresome, will try new products and have a hefty amount of discretionary money. "They're willing to spend it on computers and big-screen TVs, travel and sports cars, things that other generations would consider frivolous," says David Morrison, whose firm,

Twentysomething Inc., probes adultolescents for companies like Coca-Cola and Nokia.

13   Jimmy Finn, 24, a paralegal at the Manhattan-based law firm of Sullivan & Cromwell, made the most of his $66,000 annual income by moving back to his childhood home in nearby Staten Island. While his other friends paid exorbitant rents, Finn bought a new car and plane tickets to Florida so he could see his girl-friend on the weekends. He had ample spending money for restaurants and cabs, and began paying down his student loans. "New York is a great young person's city but you can't beat home for the meals," says Finn.

14   With adultolescents all but begging for years of support after college, many parents admit they're not sure when a safety net becomes a suffocating blanket. "I've seen parents willing to destroy themselves financially," says financial planner Bill Mahoney of Oxford, Mass. "They're giving their college graduates $20,000, $30,000, even $40,000—money they should be plowing into retirement." And it might only buy them added years of frustration. Psychiatrists say it's tough to con-vince a parent that self-sufficiency is the one thing they can't give their children.

15   No matter how loving the parent-child bond, parents inevitably heave a sigh of relief when their adult kids finally start paying their own way. Seven months ago, when Finn's paralegal job moved to Washington, D.C., he left home and got an apartment there. The transition, he said, was hard on his mother, Margie. Mom, though, reports that she's doing just fine. She's stopped making plates of ziti and meatballs for her boy and has more time for her friends. "The idea all along was that he should be self-sufficient," she says. It just took a little while.

FOR DISCUSSION: This article will raise most of the claim questions in your mind: What are adultolescents? Do they really exist? What has caused this situation? How good or bad is it? What should we do about it? The author deals with all these questions. Which of these questions, however, seems to dominate the arti-cle? What are your experiences with the trend described in this article? Compare your experiences with those of your classmates.

◆◆◆

C. GROUP WORK: READING AND ANALYZING CLAIMS AND SUBCLAIMS

The following essay uses several types of claims and associated purposes. One type of claim, however, predominates in the essay, and the other claims sup-port and develop it. First divide the essay into "chunks" by drawing a line across the page each time the author changes the type of claim and purpose. Label the type of claim and predominant purpose of each chunk (*example:* fact, to establish the facts). Then underline the predominant claim and describe the purpose of the entire essay. Speculate about the reasons the author had for placing the parts of this essay in this particular order. Discuss the relationship between the parts.

Much argumentative writing combines claims in this way, and you may want to study the pattern of claims used here as a possible model for one of your own argument papers.

HOLD YOUR HORSEPOWER*

Lyla Fox

Lyla Fox writes from the point of view of a high school English teacher.

1   Folks in the small Michigan town where I grew up revere the work ethic. Our entire culture lauds those who are willing to work their tails off to get ahead. Though there's nothing wrong with hard work, I suggest that our youngsters may be starting too young—and for all the wrong reasons.

2   Increasingly I identify with Sisyphus trying to move that stone. There are more mornings than I would like to admit when many of my students sit with eyes glazed or heads slumped on their desks as I try to nurture a threatening-to-become-extinct interest in school. These are not lazy kids. Many are high-achieving 16- and 17-year-olds who find it tough to reconcile 7:30 A.M. classes with a job that winds down at 10:30 P.M. or later.

3   "What's wrong?" I asked a student who once diligently completed his home-work assignments. He groggily grunted an answer. "I'm tired. I didn't get home until 11 P.M." Half the class nodded and joined in a discussion about how hard it is to try to balance schoolwork, sports and jobs. Since we end up working most of our adult life, my suggestion to the class was to forgo the job and partake of school—both intra- and extracurricular.

4   "Then how do I pay for my car?" the sleepy student, now more awake, asked. Click. The car. That's what all these bleary eyes and half-done papers are about. My students have a desperate need to drive their own vehicles proudly into the school parking lot. The car is the teenager's symbolic club membership. I know because I've seen the embarrassed looks on the faces of teens who must answer "No" to the frequently asked "Do you have a car?" National Merit finalists pale in importance beside the student who drives his friends around in a shiny new Ford Probe.

5   My own son (a senior at the University of Michigan) spent a good part of his high-school years lamenting our "no car in high school" dictate. When he needed to drive, we made sure he could always borrow our car. Our Oldsmobile 88, however, didn't convey the instant high-school popularity of a sporty Nissan or Honda. Our son's only job was to do as well as he could in school. The other work, we told him, would come later. Today I see students working more than the legally permitted number of hours to pay for their cars. I also see once com-mitted students becoming less dedicated to schoolwork. Their commitment is to their cars and the jobs that will help them make those monthly car payments.

6   Once cars and jobs enter the picture, it is virtually impossible to get students focused on school. "My parents are letting me get a car," one of my brightest stu-dents enthused a few months ago. "They say all I have to do is get a job to make the payments." *All.* I winced, saying nothing because parents' views are sacrosanct

---

*Newsweek, March 25, 1996, p. 16.

for me. I bit my cheeks to keep from saying how wrong I thought they were and how worried I was for her schoolwork. Predictably, during the next few months, her grades and attitude took a plunge.

7   I say attitude because when students go to work for a car, their positive attitude frequently disappears. Teachers and parents are on the receiving end of curved-lip responses to the suggestion that they should knuckle down and do some schoolwork. A job and car payments are often a disastrous combination.

8   These kids are selling their one and only chance at adolescence for a car. Adults in their world must help them see what their children's starry eyes cannot: that students will have the rest of their lives to own an automobile and pay expenses.

9   Some parents, I know, breathe a sigh of relief when their children can finally drive themselves to orthodontist appointments and basketball practice. This trade-off could mean teens' losing touch with family life. Having a car makes it easy for kids to cut loose and take part in activities far from home. Needing that ride from Mom and Dad helps to keep a family connection. Chauffeuring teens another year or two might be a bargain after all.

10   What a remarkable experience a school day might be if it were the center of teens' lives, instead of that much-resented time that keeps them from their friends and their jobs. Although we may not have meant to, parents may have laid the groundwork for that resentment. By giving kids permission to work, parents are not encouraging them to study. Parents have allowed students to miss classes because of exhaustion from the previous night's work. By providing a hefty down payment on a $12,000 car and stressing the importance of keeping up the payments, they're sending a signal that schoolwork is secondary.

11   The kids I'm writing about are wonderful. But they are stressed and angry that their day has too few hours for too much work. Sound familiar? It should. It is the same description adults use to identify what's wrong with their lives.

12   After reading this, my students may want to hang me in effigy. But perhaps some of them are secretly hoping that someone will stop their world and help them get off. They might also concede that it's time to get out of the car and get on mass transit. For students in large metropolitan areas, public transportation is the only way to get around.

13   Adults should take the reins and let teens off the hook. We must say "no" when we're implored to "Please let me get a job so I can have a car." Peer pressure makes it hard for kids to turn away from the temptation of that shiny four-wheeled popularity magnet. It's up to the grown-ups to let kids stay kids a little longer.

14   The subject of teens and cars comes up in my home as well as in my classroom. My 15-year-old daughter gave me some bone-chilling news yesterday. "The Springers got Suzi her own car!" she announced. "All she has to do is make the payments."

15   I smiled and went back to correcting the essays that would have been lovely had their authors had some time to put into constructing them. The payment, I told myself after my daughter went grudgingly to begin her homework, may be greater than anyone in the Springer family could possibly imagine.

FOR DISCUSSION: How people use their time is often controversial. How is it controversial in this essay? Can you think of other examples where the use of time is controversial? In your opinion, is the problem the author identifies significant or not? Why do you think so?

◆◆◆

D. WRITING ASSIGNMENT: TYPES OF CLAIMS

Write a 250- to 300-word paper that is organized around a single type of claim. Use the following claims about campus issues as starter sentences for your paper. Use the information about types of support and organizational strategies for each type of claim in this chapter to help you plan and write. Work in pairs to generate ideas and support for your papers.

1. Is it true? Does it exist? *Claim of fact: In loco parentis* (is or is not) an important policy on our campus. (*In loco parentis* means "in place of parent." Colleges with this policy believe they are responsible for monitoring students' behavior much as their parents might if they were still at home.)
2. How should we define it? *Claim of definition:* Not everyone defines dangerous levels of drinking alcohol in exactly the same way.
3. What caused it? What are the effects? *Claim of cause:* Too much socializing contributes to the student dropout problem in college.
4. Is it good or bad? *Claim of value:* Sororities and fraternities (do or do not) contribute significant positive value to the college experience.
5. What is the problem and what should we do to solve it? *Claim of policy:* Students do not always know their academic standing in all of their courses during a semester, and measures should (or should not) be taken to correct this lack of information.

E. PREWRITING: USING THE CLAIM QUESTIONS TO GET IDEAS FOR A POSITION PAPER

The claim questions can be used to invent ideas for any argument paper. If, however, you are gathering ideas for the assignment for the "Position Paper Based on 'The Reader'" (Exercise D in Chapter 8), you may want to use the claim questions to generate additional material for this paper. (You may have already completed other prewriting activities for this paper, including an issue proposal, Chapter 1, Exercise F; summary-response papers, Chapter 3, Exercise E; an exploratory paper, Chapter 4, Exercise D; and a Toulmin analysis, Chapter 5, Exercise E.) Now use the claim questions to refine or revise the tentative claim you have written for your paper.

1. Write your issue in the form of an issue question. *Example:* Is parking a problem on campus?
2. Apply the claim question to the issue questions, and write a paragraph in response to each question.
   a. *Fact:* Did it happen? Does it exist?

    b. *Definition:* What is it? How can we define it?

    c. *Cause:* What caused it? What are the effects?

    d. *Value:* Is it good or bad? What criteria will help us decide?

    e. *Policy:* What should we do about it? What should be our future course of action?

3. Read the paragraphs you have written, and select the one that interests you the most and that also seems most promising as the focus for your paper. Now look at your tentative claim and revise it, if necessary, to bring it in line with your new purpose and focus. You may also, of course, use information from the other paragraphs you have written to develop subclaims and support for your paper. Save what you have written in a folder. You will use it later when you plan and write your position paper.

Chapter 7

Types of Proof

You learned in Chapter 5 that the claim, the support, and the warrants are the three essential parts of an argument. Chapter 6 helped you understand claims, and this chapter will help you understand the support and warrants that provide proofs for the claim. This chapter introduces you first to the different types of proof, then to the language and style associated with each of them. Chapter 8 will alert you to some of the fallacies or pseudoproofs that sometimes occur in argument.

As you understand and begin to work with the proofs, you will discover that they are not simply uniform patterns that are obvious and easy to recognize. Rather, slippery and imperfect as they are, they represent an attempt to describe what goes on in the real world of argument and in the minds of writers and readers of argument. Understanding them can put you closer to an author so that you may better understand how that individual thought about, interpreted, and developed a particular subject. Then, when you switch roles and become the author yourself, your knowledge of what can happen in argument will help you develop your own thoughts and create your own effective arguments.

THE TRADITIONAL CATEGORIES OF PROOF

The traditional categories of proof, like much of our most fundamental argument theory, were first articulated by classical theorists, and they are still useful for describing what goes on in real-world argument today. Recall from Chapter 5 that Aristotle, in his *Rhetoric,* said that an arguer must state a claim (or a proposition) and prove it. He also went into detail about the broad categories of proof that can be used to establish the probability of a claim. Aristotle's categories of proof are still useful both because they accurately describe what classical arguers did then and what modern arguers still do and because they have become such an accepted part of our intellectual heritage that, like generations before us, we learn these methods and use them to observe, think about, and interpret reality. Aristotle's ideas and observations still provide accurate descriptions of what goes on in argument.

Aristotle distinguishes between proofs that can be produced and laid on the table, so to speak, like a murder weapon, fingerprints, or a written contract, and proofs that are invented and represent the creative thinking and insights of clever and intelligent people.

Aristotle divides this second category of proof into three subcategories: proofs that appeal to logic and reason, proofs that establish the credibility of the source, and proofs that appeal to the emotions. The Greek words used to refer to the proofs are *logos* (logic), *ethos* (credibility), and *pathos* (emotion).

Logical proof appeals to people's reason, understanding, and common sense. It is consistent with what we know and believe, and it gives us fresh insight and ideas about issues. As proof, it relies mainly on such support as reasoned opinion and factual data and also on warrants that suggest the soundness and truth of such support. Aristotle declared that logical proof is the most important type of proof in argument, and most modern theorists agree with him. Richard M. Weaver, a well-known modern rhetorician, for example, says that argument has its primary basis in reasoning and that it appeals primarily to the rational part of man. Logical proof, he says, provides the "plot" of argument.[1] The other two types of proof are also present and important, however.

Proof that establishes ethos appeals to the audience's impressions, opinions, and judgments about the individual stating the argument. Arguers who demonstrate competence, good character, fair-mindedness, and goodwill toward the audience are more convincing then people who lack these qualities. Individuals who project such favorable qualities to an audience have established good *ethos*. Audiences are more likely to trust and believe individuals with good *ethos* than those without it. At times, arguers also need to establish the *ethos* of the experts whom they quote in their arguments. They usually accomplish this purpose by providing information about them so that audiences will appreciate these individuals' degree of expertise and consequently be more willing to accept what they say.

Emotional proof is used to appeal to and arouse the feelings of the audience. The audience's feelings are aroused primarily through emotional language, examples, personal narratives, and vivid descriptions of events that contain emotional elements and that arouse strong feelings in other people. Emotional proof is appropriate in an argument when it is used to develop the claim and when it contributes to the sense of logical conviction and agreement that are argument's intended outcomes. A well-reasoned set of logical proofs contributes to such outcomes. But emotion can also contribute to a strong acceptance of a logical conclusion. Imagine, for example, an argument in favor of increasing taxes to build housing for homeless people. The logical argument would describe reasons for these taxes, methods for levying them, and recommendations for spending them.

---

[1]Richard M. Weaver, "Language Is Sermonic," in Richard L. Johannesen, ed., *Contemporary Theories of Rhetoric: Selected Readings* (New York: Harper & Row, 1971), pp. 163–179.

The argument would be strengthened, however, by a few vivid and emotional examples of homeless people who lead miserable lives.

The next three sections will introduce you to seven types of logical proof, one type of proof that builds *ethos,* and two types of emotional proof. All are commonly used in argument. The number and variety of logical proofs is greater than the others because logical thinking dominates and provides the "plot" for most argument. Most arguments rely on a variety of proofs because offering several types of proof usually makes a stronger argument than relying on only one.

Each type of proof will be explained according to the following format so that you can understand each type as quickly and easily as possible.[2]

> *Examples:* Examples follow a brief general description of each proof.
>
> *Claim and support:* You are then told what to look for, or what types of support you can expect to find on the printed page and how to find the claim.
>
> *Warrant:* You are told what you are expected to assume to make logical connections between the support and the claim. The warrants associated with types of proof suggest specific ways of thinking about support and its function in an argument.
>
> *Tests of validity:* You are provided with questions to ask to help you test the reliability and validity of the proof. These questions will focus your attention on both support and warrant and how they do or do not function together as effective proof. They will also help you locate the weaknesses in an argument, which can help you plan rebuttal and formulate argument of your own.

In Exercise B at the end of the chapter, you will have the opportunity to identify and analyze the proofs in a short essay so that you can see how they operate in written argument. Other exercises show you how to use the proofs in your own writing.

TYPES OF LOGICAL PROOF: *LOGOS*

Logical proofs (also called substantive proofs) include facts, reasons, and opinions that are based on reality. They rely on factual information, statistics, and accounts of actual events, past and present. The support used in logical proof is real and drawn from experience. Logical (or substantive) warrants guarantee the reliability and relevance of this support. Logical proofs represent common ways of thinking about and perceiving relationships among the events and data of the real world and then using those ideas and relationships as support for a line of argument.

---

[2]In this chapter I have drawn on some of Wayne Brockriede and Douglas Ehninger's ideas in "Toulmin on Argument: An Interpretation and Application," *Quarterly Journal of Speech* 46 (1969): 44–53. I have expanded and adapted these authors' analysis of proofs to make it apply to the reading and writing of argument as explained in this book.

A Mnemonic Device

It is handy to be able to remember the full range of logical proofs both when you are reading and when you are developing a paper so that you can use them more readily. Figure 7.1 provides a mnemonic device that will help you remember them. It shows the first letter of each proof rearranged to make a nonsense word, SICDADS, and a picture to help you remember it. You can run through this mnemonic mentally when you are thinking about ways to develop the ideas in your paper.

Sign
Induction
Cause
Deduction
Analogies (historical, literal, figurative)
Definition
Statistics

"SICDADS" refuted by logical proof.

FIGURE 7.1   The Seven Logical Proofs: Their Initials Spell Out SICDADS.

We now present the seven logical proofs in the order provided by the mnemonic SICDADS.

Argument from Sign

A specific visible sign is sometimes used to prove a claim. A sign can be used to prove with certainty: someone breaks out in chickenpox, and the claim, based on that certain sign, is that the person has chickenpox. Or a sign can be used to prove the probability of a claim: a race riot, someone argues, is probably a sign of the claim that people think they are treated unfairly. Or the sign may turn out to be a pseudoproof, the "proof" of a false claim: a child asks, "Why should I believe in Santa Claus?" and the parent answers, "Look at all the toys under the tree that weren't there yesterday." That support is used as a sign for the claim that Santa Claus exists.

Example of Sign. Here is an example of an argument from sign used in the essay "Campus Climate Control" (pages 172–174). Would you say that the claim based on this sign is a certain or probable claim?

Claim:	There is no adult supervision in the dormitory dining hall.
Support (sign):	There are butter pats on the ceiling of the dining hall.
Warrant:	Adults do not flip butter pats onto the ceiling.

Claim and Support. Look for visible clues, symptoms, and occurrences that are explained as obvious and clear signs of a certain belief or state of affairs. Look for the conclusion or claim that is made on the basis of these signs.

Sign Warrants. You are expected to assume that the sign is actually a sign of what the author claims it to be.

Tests of Validity. Is this really a sign of what the author claims it to be? Is there another explanation for the sign?

Argument from Induction

Inductive argument provides a number of examples and draws a claim, in the form of a conclusion, from them. The audience is expected to accept the group of examples as adequate and accurate enough to make the inductive leap to the claim. Inductive argument is also called argument from generalization or argument from example because the claim is a generalization made on the basis of the examples. To help you remember the special features of inductive argument, learn its prefix *in-,* which means "in" or "into," and the root *duc,* which means "lead." *An inductive argument uses examples to lead into a claim or generalization about the examples.*

Examples of Induction. Here is an example of induction. Four different people take their cars to the same car repair shop and are overcharged. The claim is then made that anyone who takes a car to that repair shop will probably be overcharged.

Inductive reasoning is the basis of the scientific method. Most scientific conclusions are reached inductively. When a sufficient number of phenomena are observed repeatedly, a generalization is made to explain them. Here is another example.

Claim (generalization):	The sun always comes up.
Support:	For example, the sun has come up every day of recorded history.
Warrant:	Every day provides a sufficient number of days to make the claim that the sun always comes up.

Here is a third example. This inductive reasoning appears in the article "What's Wrong with Standard Tests?" (pages 170–171).

Examples:	Danny Algrant was a difficult student who became famous.
	An unpromising adolescent became a school principal.
	A low tester became a successful writer.
Claim (generalization made on the basis of the examples):	
	These unpromising students did well later, so others may also.
Warrant:	These three examples are enough to make us accept the claim.

Induction demonstrates probability rather than truth when there is the possibility of an example that would prove an exception. For instance, an unpromising student may become an unpromising adult. But an apple always falls from a tree, thereby demonstrating gravity, and the sun always comes up, demonstrating that law of nature. No one has been able to find exceptions to disprove these last two generalizations.

To be effective, inductive argument requires a sufficient number of examples. When a generalization is made on the basis of only one or a few examples, it is called a *hasty generalization*. To claim, for instance, that an office worker should always be able to enter a certain amount of data because he did it once may not be accurate. To make a broad generalization, such as *all* office workers ought to be able to enter a certain amount of data because *one* employee was able to, is called a *sweeping generalization*. An inadequate sample of cases weakens or invalidates an inductive argument.

CLAIM AND SUPPORT. Look for a group of examples followed by a generalization (claim) based on the examples; or the generalization (claim) may be stated first and then be followed by several examples.

INDUCTIVE WARRANTS. You are expected to assume that the list of examples is representative and that it shows a definite trend. You are also expected to assume that if you added more examples of the same general type, the conclusion would not change.

TESTS OF VALIDITY. Is the sample adequate? Would more examples continue to show the trend? Are there examples that show an opposite trend, that provide an exception? (Was someone charged a reasonable amount at the repair shop?) Can we make the inductive leap from the examples to the generalization to demonstrate that it is probably true?

ARGUMENT FROM CAUSE

Argument from cause places the subject in a cause-and-effect relationship to show that it is either the cause of an effect or the effect of a cause. It is very common in argument to explain or to justify a claim with cause-and-effect reasoning.

EXAMPLE OF CAUSE. The argument used in "Bringing Up Adultolescents" (pages 189–192) provides an example of argument from cause.

Warrant:	Adultolescents are postponing the responsibilities of adulthood.
Support:	Many college graduates in their twenties and thirties return home to be supported by their parents.
Claim:	Parents are turning many of their adult children into adultolescents in an effort to ensure that they get good jobs and become as successful as they are.

CLAIM AND SUPPORT. Look for examples, events, trends, and people that have caused certain things to happen. Look for the effects. For example, "Video games cause children to become violent." Or turn it around and look for the effects first and then the causes: "Many children are violent as a result of playing too many violent video games." Look also for clue words such as *cause, effect, resulted in, as a result, as a consequence,* and *because* to indicate that cause-and-effect reasoning is being used. Finally, the claim states what you are expected to conclude as a result of this cause-and-effect reasoning: "Too much time on the Internet may cause depression," or "Fewer job opportunities and overly indulgent parents together are causing the phenomenon of adultolescents."

CAUSAL WARRANTS. You are expected to assume that the causes really do create the identified effects or that the effects really are the results of the named causes.

TESTS OF VALIDITY. Are these causes alone sufficient to create these effects? Could these effects result from other causes? Can I think of exceptions to the cause-and-effect outcome that is claimed here?

ARGUMENT FROM DEDUCTION

Deductive argument is also called argument from principle because its warrant is a general principle. Remember that the warrant may or may not be stated explicitly in an argument. Etymology can help you remember the special features of deductive argument. The prefix *de-* means "from" and the root *duc* means "lead." *A deductive argument leads from a general principle,* which is the warrant, applies it to an example or specific case, which is described in the support, and draws a *conclusion,* which is the claim.

EXAMPLES OF DEDUCTION. In Chapter 6 you learned that argument deals with matters that are probably rather than certainly true. People do not argue about matters that are certainly true because they already agree about them. Here is an example of a deductive argument based on a general principle that people would agree with and accept as true. Thus they would not argue about it.

General warrant:	Every person has a unique DNA sequence.
Support:	The accused is a person.
Claim:	The accused has a unique DNA sequence.

This example might be used as a minor argument to support a claim that someone is guilty of a crime. It would never be the main issue in an argument, however, because it is not arguable.

Most of the deduction you will encounter in argument is arguable because it deals with probabilities rather than with certainties. Fictional sleuth Sherlock Holmes used deduction to reach his sometimes astonishing conclusions. Holmes examined the supporting evidence—footprints, for example—and deduced that the man who left them walked with a limp. The general principle, that most uneven footprints are left by people who limp, is an assumption that is important in Holmes's deductive thinking even though it is not stated in the argument. It does not need to be spelled out for readers who are able to supply that warrant themselves as they accept Holmes's conclusion. The Holmes deduction can be summarized as follows. The purpose of this argument is to establish the type of person who left these footprints.

Unstated warrant:	Most uneven footprints are left by people who limp.
Support:	These footprints are uneven.
Claim:	The person who left these footprints walks with a limp.

Is there any part of that argument that you might challenge as only possibly or probably rather than as certainly true? If so, you can argue about it.

Claim and Support. Identify the claim by answering this question: "On the basis of a general principle (warrant), implied or stated, what does the author expect me to conclude about this specific example or case?"

Deductive Warrants. You are expected to assume that a general principle about a whole category of phenomena (people, places, events, and so forth) has been stated or implied in the argument and that it is accurate and acceptable. You are expected to decide that since the general principle, or warrant, and the support for the specific case are both accurate and acceptable, the conclusion is also acceptable and probably true.

Tests of Validity. Is the warrant acceptable and believable? Does the warrant apply to the example or case? Is the support for the case accurate? How reliable, then, is the conclusion?

If the reader has a problem with either the warrant or the example in a deductive argument, the conclusion will not be acceptable. Consider Holmes's warrant that uneven footprints are left by people who limp. That may be convincing to some readers but not others. For instance, a reader might reflect that a person who is pretending to limp or is carrying a heavy valise in one hand could also leave uneven footprints. This reader would then question the warrant and decide that the proof is not even probably true.

Here is another example of a deductive argument that would not be equally successful with all audiences.

Unstated warrant:	Families cannot be happy when the mother works outside the home.
Support:	The mother in this family works outside the home.
Claim:	This is an unhappy family.

For readers who come from happy homes with working mothers, the warrant in this example would seem faulty.

In the next example of a deductive argument, the support could be a problem for some readers who might have trouble accepting it because they think children's stories are not literary and do not have deep symbolic levels of meaning. Another reader might disagree and argue for the opposite point of view, providing examples of children's stories that have such literary qualities and thus refute the other readers' claim. Whether or not a reader accepts the conclusion depends entirely on whether or not the reader also accepts the warrant and support.

Warrant:	All literary stories have deep symbolic levels of meaning.
Support:	Children's stories are literary stories.
Claim:	Children's stories have deep symbolic levels of meaning.

All parts of a deductive argument need to be accurate and acceptable to an audience for it to be convincing.

ARGUMENT FROM HISTORICAL, LITERAL, OR FIGURATIVE ANALOGY

Historical and literal analogies explore similarities and differences between items in the same general category, and *figurative analogies* do the same, only with items in very different categories. In drawing analogies, we show how something we may not know much about is like something we know in greater detail. In other words, we interpret what we do not know in the light of what we do know. We then supply the warrant that what happened in one case will happen in the other, we draw conclusions, and we make a claim based on the comparisons in the analogy.

HISTORICAL ANALOGIES. These explain what is going on *now* in terms of what went on in similar cases *in the past.* Future outcomes are also often projected from past cases. The idea is that what happened in the past will probably repeat itself in the present. Also, the two events are so similar that the results of the former will surely be the end result of the latter.

EXAMPLE OF A HISTORICAL ANALOGY. The following example compares a present event with a past event.

Claim:	Many people will die of AIDS.
Support:	Many people died of the Black Death.
Warrant:	AIDS and the Black Death are similar.

LITERAL ANALOGIES. These compare two items in the same category: two school systems, two governments, two religions, two individuals. Outcomes are described as in historical analogies—that is, what happened in one case will happen in the other because of the similarities or the differences.

EXAMPLE OF A LITERAL ANALOGY. Two similar items are compared in this example.

Claim:	The state should spend more money on education.
Support:	Another state spent more money with good results.
Warrant:	The two states are similar, and the results of one will be the results of the other.

FIGURATIVE ANALOGIES. These compare items from two different categories, as in metaphor, only the points of comparison in a figurative analogy are usually spelled out in more detail than they are in a metaphor. Many figurative analogies appeal to the emotions rather than to reason. Figurative analogies are effective as logical proof only when they are used to identify *real qualities* that are shared by both items and that can then be applied to help prove the claim logically. When the items in a figurative analogy are compared to add ornament or to stir up an emotional response, the analogy functions as emotional proof. It engages the emotions rather than the reason.

EXAMPLES OF FIGURATIVE ANALOGIES. Here are some examples of figurative analogies used as logical proof. To prove that reading a difficult book should take time, Francis Bacon compares that activity with taking the time to chew and digest a large meal. The qualities of the two activities, rather than the activities themselves, are compared. Since these qualities are not spelled out, the audience must infer that both take time, and understanding, like digestion, benefits and becomes a permanent part of the individual. Here is this argument laid out so that you can see how it works.

Claim:	Reading a difficult book should take time.
Support:	Digesting a large meal takes time.
Warrant:	Reading and eating are sufficiently alike that they can be compared.

In another example of a figurative analogy used as logical proof, the human fossil record is compared to an apple tree in early winter that has only a few apples on it. The quality that the fossil record and the tree have in common, which the reader must infer, is that both tree and fossil record have a complicated system of branches and limbs. Also, the few apples on the tree are like the few available fossils. At one time there were many of both. The qualities compared in these two instances improve a rational understanding of the fossil record.

Here is a third example of a figurative analogy. This analogy comes from an ad sponsored by the Sierra Club, a group that works to protect the environment. Two pictures are placed side by side. The first is of the Statue of Liberty, which is 305 feet high, and the second is of a giant sequoia tree, which is 275 feet high. A question is posed: "Would you destroy the Statue of Liberty for scrap metal?" We are expected to reason by analogy and compare destroying the Statue of Liberty for scrap metal with destroying the tree for lumber or sawdust. The individual who created this ad hopes this analogy will encourage people to want to protect the trees as much as they want to protect the Statue of Liberty. Would you say that this figurative analogy appeals mainly to the emotions or to reason?

Claim and Support. Look for examples of items, events, people, and periods of time that are being compared. Whether these items are drawn from the past or the present, as in the case of historical or literal analogies, they must be drawn from the same category: two types of disease, two types of school systems, two types of government, and so on. Look for the clue words *compare, contrast, like, similar to,* and *different from* to signal that comparisons are being made.

In the case of figurative analogies, look for two items being compared that are from totally different categories. Identify the qualities that they have in common. Look for the clue words *like, as, similar to,* or *compare.* Discover claims that are made as a result of comparing similarities or differences.

Comparison Warrants. You are expected to assume that the items being compared are similar as described and that what happens in one case will probably occur in the other. For figurative analogies you are expected to assume that the qualities of the two items are similar and significant enough so that reference to one will help explain the other and will serve as convincing proof.

Tests of Validity. Are the two items similar as claimed? Can I think of ways they are not similar or of other qualities they share that would change the claim? Are the outcomes really likely to be the same in both cases? Why or why not?

For figurative analogies: Are the qualities of these two items similar, significant, and real enough to help prove a logical argument? Or are they so dissimilar, so far-fetched, or so trivial that the comparison does not prove anything? Does the analogy serve as an ornament, an emotional appeal, or a logical proof?

ARGUMENT FROM DEFINITION

Definition is extremely important in argument. It is difficult to argue about any subject unless there is general agreement about the meanings of the key terms, especially when they are part of the claim. Sometimes an entire argument is based on the audience's acceptance of a certain meaning of a key term. If the audience accepts the definition, the arguer says that the claim should be accepted "by definition."

EXAMPLES OF DEFINITION. The argument in "Reading, Writing, Narcissism" (pages 185–187) can be laid out as deduction. Notice that if self-esteem is defined as narcissistic, then by definition educational goals that aim to teach self-esteem also end up teaching narcissism, or extreme self-centeredness.

> *Warrant:* Self-esteem is narcissistic.
> *Support:* An educational goal is to teach self-esteem.
> *Claim:* This educational goal also teaches narcissism.

Here is another example.

> *Warrant:* Family values characterize the good citizen.
> *Support:* Radical feminists lack family values.
> *Claim:* Radical feminists are not good citizens.

We will accept the claim that radical feminists, by definition, are poor citizens only if we also accept the warrants that define the good citizen as one who possesses family values and radical feminists as people who lack these values.

Even though argument by definition takes the form of deductive argument, it is listed separately here to emphasize the important function of definition in arguments that depend on it as major proof.

CLAIM AND SUPPORT. Look for all definitions or explanations of words or concepts. These may be a sentence, several paragraphs, or an entire essay in length. Notice if the definition is used simply to define a word or if it is used as part of the proof in the argument, as in the case of "Reading, Writing, Narcissism." Look for a claim that you are expected to accept as a result of the definition.

DEFINITION WARRANTS. You are expected to assume that the definition describes the fundamental properties and qualities of the term accurately so that it can be used to prove the claim.

TESTS OF VALIDITY. Is this an accurate and complete definition? Is it convincing in this context? Are there exceptions or other definitions for this term that would make the final claim less reliable?

Argument from Statistics

Like other forms of logical proof, statistics describe relationships among data, people, occurrences, and events in the real world, only they do so in quantitative terms. Modern readers have considerable faith in numbers and statistics. They seem more "true" than other types of support to many people. It is more convincing to some people, for example, to make the claim that we should end draft registration because it costs $27.5 million per year than simply to claim that we should end it because we no longer need it.

Read statistical proofs carefully to determine where they come from and how reliable, accurate, and relevant they are. Note also whether the original figures have been altered or interpreted in some way. Figures are often rounded off or stated in different terms, such as percentages or plots on a graph. They are also sometimes compared to other material that is familiar to the audience to make them more interesting or memorable.[3] Various types of graphs or charts also make data and statistics visual and easier to grasp and remember.

Example of Statistics. Here is an example of a typical use of statistics in an article titled "Child-Killing Increases in Rio."[4]

Claim:	Child-killing is increasing in Rio de Janeiro.
Support:	Forty percent more children may be killed this year than last year.
Warrant:	Forty percent represents an increase.

The source for these statistics is cited only as "preliminary statistics." On close reading, one realizes that 424 people under 18 were killed in one year in Rio, compared with 348 who were killed in seven months of the following year. Thus the claim of a 40 percent increase is qualified to read "may be killed," since it is based on a projection of what might occur in the next five months. The figures are also converted to percentages. The author goes on to compare these figures with one that is more familiar to the reader, the number of child killings in the United States. It is claimed that 6,000 to 7,000 children, or 20 a day, died from gunshot wounds during the comparable period of time in the United States. Notice that these figures, too, are rounded off. The source for these last figures is cited as a news conference interview with the executive director of UNICEF. You might have to read other sources on this subject to test the validity of these figures.

Claim and Support. Look for numbers and data, in both their original and their converted form, graphs and charts of figures, and interpretations of them, including comparisons. Look for a claim based on the data.

Statistical Warrants. You are expected to assume that the data have been gathered and reported accurately by competent people, that they are representative and complete unless stated otherwise, and that they have been interpreted fairly and truthfully.

---

[3]James Wood, *Speaking Effectively* (New York: Random House, 1988), pp. 121–127.
[4]James Brooke, "Child-Killing Increases in Rio," *Fort Worth Star-Telegram*, January 3, 1994, p. 7.

TESTS OF VALIDITY. Where did these statistics come from? To what dates do the statistics apply? How reliable is the source? How accurate are they? How are they presented? Have they been rounded off, changed, or converted? How has the change affected their accuracy? Do they prove what they are supposed to prove? Have they been interpreted fairly, or are they exaggerated or skewed? Has enough backing been provided to prove their reliability? What are they compared to, and how does this comparison contribute to their final significance? Is any significant information left out?

TESTS OF VALIDITY FOR STATISTICS PRESENTED AS GRAPHS. Statistics are sometimes presented in graph form. The tests of validity in this case include these: Where did the information come from? What information is included in the sample? How was it gathered? Is anything significant left out or ignored because it didn't fit? Are the charts and graphs labeled accurately? Are there any exaggerations?

PROOF THAT BUILDS CREDIBILITY: *ETHOS*

The materials provided in argument that help the audience gain a favorable impression of the arguer, the group the arguer represents, or the authorities and experts the arguer cites or quotes help create *ethos,* or the credibility of the author. The author may build credibility by referring to experience and credentials that establish his or her own expertise. Another way is to quote others or to use arguments from authority.

ARGUMENT FROM AUTHORITY

We are usually inclined to accept the opinions and factual evidence of people who are authorities and experts in their fields.

EXAMPLES OF AUTHORITY. In an article that claims California will have another earthquake, the author describes and provides the credentials for several professors of geology from the major universities in Southern California as well as scientists from the U.S. Geological Survey Office before quoting their opinions as support.

Claim:	California will have an earthquake.
Support:	Professors and scientists say so.
Warrant:	These experts are reliable.

Authors themselves sometimes establish their own credentials by making references to various types of past experience that qualify them to write about their subject. They also sometimes establish the *ethos* of the group they represent, like "the great Republican Party."

CLAIM AND SUPPORT. Look for all references to the author's credentials, whether made by the author or by an editor. Look for references to the author's training, education, professional position, background, and experience. Notice, also, references to the audience's concerns, beliefs, and values that demonstrate the author's effort to establish common ground and to show fairness and goodwill toward the audience. Look for references to groups the author may represent, and notice how they are described. Look for direct or paraphrased quotations from experts. Differentiate between facts and statements of opinion. Look for credential statements about these experts. Look for claims that are made more valid as a consequence of this expert opinion.

Authoritative Warrants. You are expected to assume that the information provided about the author, the group, or the expert is accurate, that these authorities are honorable, fair, reliable, knowledgeable, and experienced, and that they also exhibit goodwill toward the audience.

Tests of Validity. Is there enough information to establish the true character and experience of the author? Is this information complete and accurate? Is there enough information about the group to believe what the author says about it? Are the credentials of the experts good enough to make their contributions reliable? Also, are the credentials relevant to the issue? (A star athlete may not be the best judge of soft drinks or fast food.) If a source is quoted, is it reliable? Argument based on authority is as good as the authorities themselves.

TYPES OF EMOTIONAL PROOF: *PATHOS*

Some argument theorists would say that there should be no appeals to emotion or attempts to arouse the emotions of the audience in argument. The idea is that an argument should appeal only to reason. Emotion, they claim, clouds reasoning and judgment and gets the argument off course. Richard M. Weaver, quoted earlier in this chapter, would disagree. Weaver points out that people are not just austerely unemotional logic machines who are interested only in deduction, induction, and cause-and-effect reasoning. People also use language to communicate feelings, values, and motives.[5]

Furthermore, when we consider that the source of much argument lies in the dramatic, emotionally laden occurrences of everyday life, we realize how impossible it is to eliminate all emotion from argument. As you read the many argumentative essays in this book, study the emotional material that professional writers use. Try to develop a sense of when emotion contributes to argument in effective and appropriate ways and when it does not. In general, emotional proofs are appropriate in argument when the subject itself is emotional and when it creates strong feelings in both the writer and the reader. For writers of argument, emotion leads to positions on issues, influences the tone of the writing, and informs some of the interpretations. For readers, emotion leads to a stronger engagement with the issue and influences the final outcomes. Emotional proof is appropriate when the occasion justifies it and when it strengthens logical conviction. It is inappropriate when it merely ventilates feelings, serves as an ornament, or distracts

---

[5]Weaver elaborates on some of the distinctions between logic and emotion in "Language Is Sermonic."

the audience from the logical conclusion of the argument. Types of emotional proof focus on *motivation,* or what all people want, and on *values,* or what we consider good or bad, favorable or unfavorable, acceptable or unacceptable.

MOTIVATIONAL PROOFS

Some proofs appeal explicitly to what all audiences are supposed to want, such as food, drink, warmth and shelter, sex, security, belongingness, self-esteem, creativity, or self-expression. The purpose of motivational proof is to urge the audience to take prescribed steps to meet an identified need.

EXAMPLES OF MOTIVATIONAL PROOFS. Advertisements and speeches by political candidates provide obvious examples of motivational proof. Drink a certain beer or buy a brand of blue jeans, and you will be irresistible to others. Or support a particular candidate, and you will gain job security and safe neighborhoods.

Claim:	You should support this candidate.
Support:	This candidate can help you get job security and safe neighborhoods.
Warrant:	You want job security and safe neighborhoods.

CLAIM AND SUPPORT. To find the claim, look for what you are asked to believe or do to get what you want.

MOTIVATIONAL WARRANTS. Look for references to items or qualities that you might need or want.

TESTS OF VALIDITY. What am I supposed to need? Do I really need it? What am I supposed to do? Will doing what is recommended satisfy the need in the ways described?

VALUE PROOFS

Some proofs appeal to what all audiences are expected to value, such as reliability, honesty, loyalty, industry, patriotism, courage, integrity, conviction, faithfulness, dependability, creativity, freedom, equality, and devotion to duty.

EXAMPLE OF A VALUE PROOF. Here is an example that claims that a school curriculum can contribute to the values of equality and acceptance if it is multicultural.

Claim:	The curriculum should be multicultural.
Support:	A multicultural curriculum will contribute to equality and acceptance.
Warrant:	You value equality and acceptance.

CLAIM AND SUPPORT. Look for value statements that are generally accepted by everyone because they have been proved elsewhere many times. Examples include "Freedom of speech is our constitutional right," "There should be no freedom without responsibility," and "Individuals who have the courage of conviction are to be trusted." Look for slogans that display such values as "Honest

Abe," "The home of the free and the brave," and "Honesty is the best policy." Or look for narratives and examples that display values, such as the story of an industrious, thrifty, and ambitious mother who is on welfare. When the values are not directly stated, ask, "What values or beliefs are causing the author to say this?" Look for a claim that shows what will result if the recommended values are accepted.

Value Warrants. You are expected to assume that you share the author's values and that they are as important as the author says they are.

Tests of Validity. What are the values expressed or implicit in this argument? Do I share these values with the author? If not, how do we differ? What effect do these differences have on my final acceptance of the claim?

A Mnemonic Device

The mnemonic VAM (for *value, authority,* and *motivation*) may help you remember and use the proofs involving *ethos* and *pathos.*

LOGOS, ETHOS, AND *PATHOS* COMMUNICATED THROUGH LANGUAGE AND STYLE

You can learn to recognize logic, *ethos,* and emotion in argument not only by the use of proofs but also by the language and style associated with each of these types of appeal. Actually, you will not often encounter pure examples of one of these styles, but instead you will encounter a mix, with one of the styles predominating. The same is true of writing. You may plan to write in a logical style, but emotion and *ethos* creep in and actually help you create a richer and more varied style for your argument.

Language That Appeals to Logic

The language of logical argument, which is the language associated with reason, is sometimes called rational style. Words that carry mainly denotative meaning are favored in rational style over connotative and emotionally loaded language. The denotative meaning of a word is the commonly held meaning that most people would agree on and that is also found in the dictionary. Examples of words that have predominantly denotative meanings and that are emotionally neutral include *introduction, facts, information,* and *literal meaning.* Most people would agree on the meanings of those words and could produce synonyms. Words with strong connotative meaning may have many extra, unique, and personal meanings or associations attached to them that vary from person to person. Examples of words with connotative meaning include *rock star, politician, mugger, family values,* and *human rights.* Asked to define such words, different people would provide personal meanings and examples that would not be exactly alike or match the denotative meanings of these words in a dictionary.

For support, rational style relies on opinion in the form of reasons, literal or historical analogies, explanations, and definitions and also on factual data, quotations, and citations from experts and authorities. Furthermore, the reader is usually not required to make as many inferences as for other, more informal styles of writing. Most parts of the argument are spelled out explicitly for the sake of agreement and a better adherence of minds.

Slogans that elicit emotional response, such as "America is the greatest country," "The American people want change," or "Now is the time for healing," are also usually omitted in rational style. Slogans of this type substitute for logical thinking. Readers think better and draw better conclusions when provided with well-reasoned opinion, quotations from authorities, and facts.

For example, in the opening paragraph of an essay titled "The Lost Art of Political Argument," Christopher Lasch argues in favor of argument and debate.

> Let us begin with a simple proposition: What democracy requires is public debate, not information. Of course it needs information too, but the kind of information it needs can be generated only by vigorous popular debate. We do not know what we need to know until we ask the right questions, and we can identify the right questions only by subjecting our own ideas about the world to the test of public controversy. Information, usually seen as the precondition of debate, is better understood as its by-product. When we get into arguments that focus and fully engage our attention, we become avid seekers of relevant information. Otherwise, we take in information passively—if we take it in at all.[6]

Rational style, you can see, evokes mainly a cognitive, rational response from its readers.

LANGUAGE THAT DEVELOPS *ETHOS*

Authors who seek to establish their own credentials and good character use language to provide a fair-minded view of reality that is restrained and accurate rather than exaggerated or overly opinionated. When language is used to create positive *ethos,* an audience will trust the author as a credible source of information and opinion.

Language that develops *ethos* has several specific characteristics. To begin with, the writer exhibits a consistent awareness of the audience's background and values by adopting a vocabulary level that is appropriate for the topic and the audience. The writer does not talk down, use technical jargon for an audience unfamiliar with it, or use slang or colloquial language unless the context allows for that. Rap music, for example, invites a different vocabulary level than a scholarly paper does.

Writers intent on establishing *ethos* are sensitive to different audiences and what they will admire, trust, and accept. They try to use language precisely and to say exactly what they mean. They project an honest desire to communicate by avoiding ranting, filler material that gets off the subject, or anything that the audience would perceive as offensive or repugnant.

---

[6]Christopher Lasch, "The Lost Art of Political Argument," *Harper's,* September 1990, p. 17.

As you have probably figured out, an author can destroy *ethos* and alter an audience's favorable impression by changing the language. A student who uses colloquial, everyday expressions in a formal essay written for a professor, a commencement speaker who shouts obscenities at the audience, a father who uses formal, abstract language to talk to his five-year-old—all have made inappropriate language choices for their particular audiences, thereby damaging their *ethos* with those audiences.

When you read argument, notice how an author uses language to build connections and trust and also to establish reliability with the audience. When you write argument, use language that will help your audience regard you as sincere and trustworthy. Appropriate language is important when you write a college paper. The use of slang, slogans, and street language and expressions in otherwise formal writing damages your credibility as a serious thinker. Writing errors, including mistakes in spelling, punctuation, and grammar, also destroy *ethos* because they indicate a lack of concern and goodwill for your readers.

Here is an example of language that builds effective *ethos* with an audience. These excerpts come from Martin Luther King Jr.'s "Letter from Birmingham Jail." An explanation of the rhetorical situation for this letter and the full text of the letter appear in the Appendix to Chapter 9. Briefly, however, King was jailed because of his involvement in the civil rights movement in Birmingham, Alabama, and he had been criticized publicly for his participation by eight of his fellow clergymen in that city. He wrote this letter to those clergymen. Notice that he deliberately uses language that is sincere and honest and that establishes his credibility as a trustworthy and responsible human being with values that his audience is likely to share. He does not come across as a crackpot, a troublemaker, or a man who is angry at the system, as one might expect from someone who has been jailed for participating in civil rights demonstrations.

> My Dear Fellow Clergymen:
>
> While confined here in the Birmingham city jail, I came across your recent statement calling my present activities "unwise and untimely." . . . Since I feel that you are men of genuine good will and that your criticisms are sincerely set forth, I want to try to answer your statement in what I hope will be patient and reasonable terms.
>
> I think I should indicate why I am here in Birmingham, since you have been influenced by the view which argues against "outsiders coming in." . . . I, along with several members of my staff, am here because I was invited here. I am here because I have organizational ties here.
>
> But more basically, I am in Birmingham because injustice is here. Just as the prophets of the eighth century B.C. left their villages and carried their "thus saith the Lord" far beyond the boundaries of their home towns, and just as the Apostle Paul left his village of Tarsus and carried the gospel of Jesus Christ to the far corners of the Greco-Roman world, so am I compelled to carry the gospel of freedom beyond my own home town. Like Paul, I must constantly respond to the Macedonian call for aid.
>
> Moreover, I am cognizant of the interrelatedness of all communities and states. I cannot sit idly by in Atlanta and not be concerned about what happens in Birmingham. Injustice anywhere is a threat to justice everywhere. We are caught in an inescapable network of mutuality, tied in a single garment of destiny.

Whatever affects one directly, affects all indirectly. Never again can we afford to live with the narrow, provincial "outside agitator" idea. Anyone who lives inside the United States can never be considered an outsider anywhere within its bounds.

Highlight the language in these passages that you think King used to establish good *ethos* with his audience of eight clergymen. Notice how King deliberately uses language to project sincerity and goodwill toward his audience. He also selects examples and appeals to values that are compatible with his audience's interests and values. King's letter is a classic example of argument that establishes effective *ethos* with a particular audience.

LANGUAGE THAT APPEALS TO EMOTION

References to values and motives evoke feelings about what people regard as good and bad and about what they want, and authors use the language associated with emotional style in a variety of ways to express and evoke feelings about these matters. The following paragraphs describe a few special techniques that are characteristic of emotional style. Examples are drawn from the essay by Sara Rimer, "Jobs Illuminate What Riots Hid: Young Ideals," which appears in full in Chapter 3.

Emotionally loaded language evokes connotative meaning and causes the audience to experience feelings and associations at a personal level that are not described in dictionaries. Highlight the emotional language in this passage.

America has been bombarded with television images of the youth of South-Central Los Angeles: throwing bricks, looting stores, beating up innocent motorists. The Disneyland staff who interviewed the job applicants, ages 17 to 22, found a different neighborhood.

"They were wonderful kinds, outstanding kids," said Greg Albrecht, a spokesman for Disneyland. "We didn't know they were there." Nor, Mr. Albrecht added, had they known that the young people of South-Central Los Angeles would be so eager to work at Disneyland.[7]

There are several examples of emotional language here. Did you, for example, highlight the words used to describe the two types of kids the author claims live in South-Central Los Angeles: *throwing, looting,* and *beating up* in contrast to *wonderful* and *outstanding?*

Emotional examples engage the emotions, as in this example: "One of the 600 who wanted to work at Disneyland was Olivia Miles, at 18 the youngest of seven children of a nurse's aide and a disabled roofer." Miss Miles has humble origins but achieves success. Success stories of this type usually result in positive emotional responses from the reader.

Vivid description of an emotional scene creates an emotional reader response, as in this example:

---

[7]Sara Rimer, "Jobs Illuminate What Riots Hid: Young Ideals," *New York Times,* June 18, 1992, pp. A1, A12.

Aubrey Miles, who is 45, says he has taken pains to tell his daughter that there are good white people. They saved his life, he told her. He was putting a roof on an office building seven years ago when a vat of hot tar exploded. He was severely burned.

"The guys on the job, who were white, helped me," he said. "I was on the ground, on fire. They put the fire out. One guy sat me up and put his back against my back. I could feel the connection. Then, afterward in the hospital, it was the same thing with the doctors."

Notice how this description brings you into the scene, causing you to share the physical sensations and emotions of the individuals described and then to share in the conclusion about the people who helped.

Narratives of emotional events draw readers into a scene just as vivid description does. Here is a story about Olivia Miles and her reaction to the looting during the riots in Los Angeles.

The riots presented Olivia Miles with the biggest ethical quandary of her life. "I saw people on television coming out with boxes of shoes and pretty furniture," she said. Her smile was embarrassed. "It was like Christmas. I wanted to get some. I was asking my sister if we could go. She said, 'No, you can't go out.' I thought: 'She's going to go to work. Should I get it, or shouldn't I get it? It's not fair that I can't. Everyone else is going to get stuff.'"

This, too, her father had foreseen. "I told her, 'There are going to be a lot of opportunities for you to get things, so just stay in the house,'" Mr. Miles said. "She knew automatically that stealing was a no-no. . . ."

That Sunday, Olivia was in her regular pew at the Mt. Sinai Baptist Church. "The pastor was saying, 'If you took something, shame on you. That's a sin,'" she said. She looked relieved all over again. "I was so happy."

By describing the emotions of the characters in a narrative, the author invites the reader to share them also.

Emotional tone, created by emotional language and examples, indicates that the author has a strong feeling about the subject and wants the audience to share that feeling. Also, irony and sarcasm should always be viewed as examples of emotional tone. They indicate strong feeling and a desire for change.

Figurative analogies contribute to emotion in an argument, particularly when two emotional subjects are compared and the resulting effect appeals more to emotion than to reason.

Emotional style is the easiest of all the styles to recognize because it is emotionally charged and is often close to our own experiences. Do not commit the common reading error of noticing only emotional style, ignoring logic and *ethos,* and even missing the main point of the entire text because you become distracted by emotional material. Remember, in argument, logic is the plot, and emotion and *ethos* add support. Box 7.1 provides a summary of the characteristics of language used to appeal to reason, to establish *ethos,* and to appeal to emotion.

ETHICS AND MORALITY IN ARGUMENT

A person's ability to argue persuasively has been recognized as a potentially powerful influence over other people for centuries. Thus the classical argument theorists, Aristotle, Cicero, and Quintilian, all recognized that an arguer should be a good person with moral principles who is arguing for good causes. These writers

BOX 7.1	A Summary of Language and Style in Argument.

HOW DO YOU MAKE APPEALS IN ARGUMENT?

TO APPEAL TO LOGIC	TO DEVELOP ETHOS	TO APPEAL TO EMOTION
STYLE		
Theoretical, abstract language	Language appropriate to audience and subject	Vivid, concrete language
Denotative meanings	Restrained, sincere, fair-minded presentation	Emotionally loaded language
Reasons	Appropriate level of vocabulary	Connotative meanings
Literal and historical analogies	Correct grammar	Emotional examples
Explanations		Vivid descriptions
Definitions		Narratives of emotional events
Factual data and statistics		Emotional tone
Quotations		Figurative analogies
Citations from experts and authorities		
Informed opinion		
EFFECT		
Evokes a cognitive, rational response	Demonstrates author's reliability, competence, and respect for audience's ideas and values through reliable and appropriate use of support and general accuracy	Evokes an emotional response

criticized arguers who used their persuasive powers to manipulate people in order to achieve their own selfish ends. They stressed that an ethical arguer must have the courage and willingness to argue logically and honestly from a strong sense of personal integrity and values. Also, emotional and motivational appeals should be consistent with positive value systems that will benefit not just one individual but all of society. Using emotions to cloud judgment or to persuade individuals to accept ideas that the arguer does not really believe in is clearly unethical. Basic standards of good judgment and common honesty have always been critical to ethical argument both in classical times and in the present.

People were struck by some letters discovered in Germany a few years ago that were perfect examples of excellent argument but whose subject matter was totally immoral. These letters were the written orders for exterminating the Jews during World War II. Although Hitler was a convincing arguer, his values and his claims were immoral. In more recent years a political consultant working for the president of the United States was exposed as a person who had no core system of values and who was more interested in manipulating public opinion than in determining what was the best political course for the country. This individual was accused by the analysts at the time of believing in nothing.

Unethical individuals who argue mainly to manipulate public opinion often use unethical tactics to influence and gain adherence to their points of view. Such tactics include opinion polls that push for particular points of view, exaggerated or manipulated statistics, manufactured evidence, and deliberate fallacious reasoning. All of these techniques can be very effective in changing audience opinion even though they are based on false values and motives.

It is important that you learn to recognize the difference between ethical and unethical argument. You can begin by asking the two bottom-line questions: (1) *Am I convinced?* Does this argument change the way I think? Are the values honorable? Is the writer just and fair-minded? Is the support fair, accurate, and convincing? Can I accept the warrants? Should the claim be qualified if it isn't already? If you answer yes, that you are convinced, then you should also ask, (2) *Is this argument moral or immoral according to my values and standards of behavior?* You will need to judge the final moral worth of an argument by testing it against your own system of values.

VALUE OF THE PROOFS FOR READING AND WRITING ARGUMENT

Readers of argument find that analyzing the proofs in an argument makes it easier to answer the bottom-line questions: "Am I convinced?" and "Is this argument moral or immoral?" Analyzing the proofs in an argument focuses a reader's attention on the author's reasoning, use of supporting detail, and warrants. These are the elements in an argument that convince an audience. Applying the tests of validity to the proofs can also help a reader recognize faulty reasoning, which can reveal a manipulative or immoral purpose in the argument. Faulty reasoning, as you have learned, is not convincing once you figure out how it works.

Writers of argument can use the proofs to help them think of ways to develop a claim. By running through the list of proofs and asking relevant questions— What do I need to define? Should I use statistics? Can I generalize from some examples? What caused this? What can I compare this to? Whom should I quote? What audience values and motives can I appeal to?—authors invent ideas and locate material that can be used at a specific level in a paper. The specific material is what makes a paper convincing. Also, thinking about the proofs makes authors more consciously aware of their own warrants and helps them decide whether to make them explicit in the argument or whether to leave them implicit so that the audience has to supply them. Finally, an awareness of proofs can help writers avoid inadequate or irrelevant proof and faulty reasoning in their writing.

The exercises and activities for this chapter will provide you with practice in using the proofs to invent support and warrants for a position paper. The proofs and the tests for validity are summarized for both readers and writers in the Summary Charts on pages 443–448.

REVIEW QUESTIONS

1. Describe logical proofs. Name the seven types of logical proof. Use the mnemonic SICDADS to help you remember them.
2. Describe proofs that build *ethos,* or credibility. Name one type of proof that builds *ethos.*
3. Describe emotional proofs. Name two types of emotional support and explain why they appeal to the emotions.
4. Describe some of the features of the language and style associated with the three types of proof.
5. What is the difference between *ethos* in argument and ethics in argument?

EXERCISES AND ACTIVITIES

A. CLASS DISCUSSION: ANALYZING *LOGOS, PATHOS,* AND *ETHOS* IN AN ADVERTISEMENT

Study the advertisement on the next page, and identify the logical proofs, the emotional proofs, and the proofs that establish *ethos.* Use the mnemonics SICDADS and VAM to help you remember the proofs. Which type of proof is strongest in this ad, in your opinion? How effective is the ad? Why do you think so?

B. CLASS DISCUSSION: ANALYZING THE PROOFS IN AN ESSAY

Review the five essays in Chapter 6 (pages 162–174) that have the proofs labeled in the margin. Next, read the essay "Censorship or Common Sense?" (pages 221–222) and jot similar labels of the proofs in the margin. Then answer the following questions.

1. What is this author's claim? What does she want to prove?
2. What logical proofs does she use to prove her claim? Which are most effective, and why?
3. What emotional proofs does she use to prove her claim? What values and motives are present in this argument? Do you share them?
4. How does she use *ethos* to prove her claim? What authorities does she mention to strengthen her position?
5. Is this essay convincing? Why? Is it moral or immoral by your standards? Why?

Meet the Philip Morris Generation

A **record** to be **ashamed** of.

Philip Morris claims it doesn't want kids to smoke. But a major study shows that Marlboro, the Philip Morris flagship brand, is by far the best-selling cigarette among young smokers. On average, 60 percent of 8th, 10th and 12th graders — boys and girls — prefer Marlboro. Among white high school seniors it's even higher, at 70 percent.

This means that of the 3,000 kids who become regular smokers every day, about 1,800 head for Marlboro Country. A third of these kids will die early from tobacco-caused disease.

Once again, Philip Morris says one thing but does another.

Tobacco vs. Kids. Where America draws the line.®

American Cancer Society • American Medical Association • American Academy of Child & Adolescent Psychiatry • American Academy of Pediatrics • American Association for Respiratory Care • American College of Preventive Medicine • American Medical Women's Association • American Public Health Association • Association of Schools of Public Health • Girls Incorporated • INFACT • Interreligious Coalition on Smoking or Health • Latino Council on Alcohol and Tobacco • National Association of School Nurses • National Association of Secondary School Principals • National Hispanic Medical Association • Summit Health Coalition

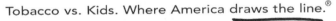

CAMPAIGN for TOBACCO-FREE Kids®

To learn more, call 800-284-KIDS or visit our web site at www.tobaccofreekids.org.
The National Center for Tobacco-Free Kids, 1707 L Street NW, Suite 800, Washington, DC 20036

SOURCE: Courtesy of the National Center for Tobacco-Free Kids.

CENSORSHIP OR COMMON SENSE?*

Roxana Robinson

Roxana Robinson is the author of the novel *This Is My Daughter.*

1   A 5-year-old is not ready to confront the world. This should be obvious, but it doesn't seem that way to many free-speech advocates, who are angry that some libraries around the country have installed software on their computers to block out Internet material that's unsuitable for children.

2   The objections are coming from some usual sources: the American Civil Liberties Union, for example, and Web publishers. But even the American Library Association has opposed the use of filtering software.

3   Traditionally, the library has been a safe place for children. And librarians have long been the guardians of public virtue. While they have been firm supporters of the First Amendment, they haven't generally interpreted it to mean that they should acquire large holdings of published pornography and make such materials available to children.

4   Librarians have always acquired books according to their own discrimination and their sense of what is appropriate to their neighborhoods. They generally refuse to buy, among other things, pornography. This isn't censorship; it's common sense.

5   If a library were to have a section of pornographic books, would we want these to be printed in large, colorfully illustrated, lightweight volumes, shelved near the floor where they were easily available to children? Probably not. But we have gone to a great deal of trouble to insure that computers are user friendly, with brightly colored graphics and easily accessible information.

6   Material on the Internet is not only uncensored but also unedited. Adults can be expected to make their own evaluations of what they find. Children, who lack experience and knowledge, cannot.

7   The debate over the filtering of the Internet is a bit like the debate over grants given out by the National Endowment for the Arts. It's all tangled up in false cries of censorship. Censorship is a legal term; it refers to government action prohibiting material from being circulated. This is very different from a situation in which a museum or an arts panel decides not to use public money to finance an exhibition or an artist.

8   Commendably, our society defends freedom of speech with great vigor. But there is a difference between allowing everything to be said and allowing everyone to hear it. We should know this by now, having seen the effects that exposure to television and movie violence has on children.

9   The A.C.L.U. and the American Library Association say that the use of filtering software in computers is censorship because it blocks access to constitutionally protected speech. But these cries are baffling and unfounded. The only control libraries are asserting is over a small portion of the audience, not over

New York Times, October 19, 1998, p. A21.

the material itself. Moreover, this control has a powerful historical precedent: parental guidance is even older than the Constitution.

10   The protection of children should be instinctive. A man may have the right to stand on the street and spew obscenities at passers-by, but he would be ordered to leave a kindergarten classroom.

11   It is absurd to pretend that adults and children are the same audience, and it is shameful to protect the child pornographer instead of the child.

FOR DISCUSSION: How would you resolve the issue in this essay? Free speech is guaranteed because of the First Amendment; should that include making objectionable material on the Internet available to everyone?

◆◆◆

C.   GROUP WORK AND DISCUSSION: ANALYZING MOTIVATIONAL AND VALUE PROOFS AND STYLE

Read the following article, "The Future Is Ours to Lose." Focus on the emotional proofs and style in the essay. Then answer the following questions and report your answers to the class.

1. What is the author's claim?
2. What are the motivational proofs in the essay? (Review the description on page 211.) What does the author fear some modern women want? What does she claim women should want?
3. What are the value proofs in the essay? (Review the description on pages 211–212.) What values does the author claim some modern women may have? What values does she claim they should have? What does she claim will be the result if women neglect to protect what they should value?
4. Do you share the author's values? Do you accept her claims? Elaborate.
5. Review the description of style in Box 7.1. What type of style predominates in this essay? What evidence from the essay leads you to think so?

THE FUTURE IS OURS TO LOSE*

Naomi Wolf

Naomi Wolf is the author of *The Beauty Myth* and *Promiscuities*. She writes frequently about women's issues.

1   Standing at the turn of the millennium, how odd it seems that women, the majority of the human species, have not, over the course of so many centuries,

---

New York Times Magazine, May 16, 1999, p. 134.

intervened successfully once and for all on their own behalf. That is, until you consider that women have been trained to see themselves as having no relationship to history, and no claim upon it. Feminism can be defined as women's ability to think about their subjugated role in history, and then to do something about it. The 21st century will see the End of Inequality—but only if women absorb the habit of historical self-awareness, becoming a mass of people who, rather than do it all, decide at last to change it all. The future is ours to lose.

2   Since there has always been some scattered awareness that women's low status was unfair, you could say that there has always been a women's movement. And just as you could say that there has always been a women's movement, you could also say that there has always been a backlash. It is truly striking how often Western humanity has taken the leap forward into more egalitarian, rational and democratic models of society and government, and made the decision—for a decision it had to be—to leave women out. At every turn, with a heroic effort of the will to ignore the obvious path of justice, men were granted, and granted themselves, more and more equality, and women of all races were left in history's tidewater.

3   Once again, we are at a turning point. This decade has seen one new landmark after another: the Family and Medical Leave Act; a feminist sitting on the Supreme Court; a woman in charge of American foreign policies that now include opposition to clitoridectomy. Indeed, feminism has become mainstream: Betty Friedan has met Betsy Ross; Barbie's ads now read "Dream With Your Eyes Wide Open" and "Be Your Own Hero." Oprah is talking about how to walk out of an abusive marriage, and Tori Amos and Fran Drescher speak out in the celebrity press about sexual assault. This flood tide could either crest further to change the landscape forever, or it could recede once again. This is what historians call an "open moment," and women have blown such moments in the past. What determines the outcome is the level of historical awareness we reach before the tide inevitably turns.

4   There are four ways that our culture militates against historical consciousness in women. One is the steady omission of women from history's first draft, the news. Women, Men and Media, a national watchdog project, reports that women are featured in only 15 percent of the front-page news—and then usually as victims or perpetrators of crime or misconduct. It is not because no one is interested in what women are doing that this ceiling of visibility is kept so low; nor is it a conscious conspiracy. But if tomorrow the editors in chief and publishers of national news media were to see front sections dominated by 53 percent female newsmakers, they would not shout, Stop the presses! Too many women! Rather, there would be the impression that somehow these publications had, by featuring newsmakers who are part of a majority, marginalized themselves. So women's advances take place with little day-by-day, let alone month-by-month, popular analysis.

5   The second pressure, which complements the omission of women from historical culture, is the omission of history from women's culture. One example:

under its previous editor, Ruth Whitney, *Glamour* magazine ran a political column. Bonnie Fuller, a new editor fresh from *Cosmopolitan*, has deleted this monthly column and added a horoscope. It's a shift from real-time—historical-political time—back into that dependent, dreamy, timeless state of Women's Time. In Women's Time, your fate is not in your own hands as an agent of historical change. Rather—Hey, are you a Pisces? Why bother running down your Manolo Blahniks to do something as *mousy* as voting? Your fate is in your cleavage, and in the stars.

6   Emerging naturally from this is the third pressure: the recurrent ideological theme that if women take themselves seriously they will lose femininity and, therefore, social status. If what they do, think, worry about and long for doesn't matter, surely it's not important that history pays them attention.

7   The fourth pressure is forgetfulness. Young women I have met on real college campuses think sex discrimination is a thing of the past. Or that the struggle for the vote lasted maybe 10 years, not more than 70. Or that women got the vote when African-Americans did. Or that it has always been legal to get an abortion in America. They are stunned to discover that in their mothers' lifetimes women could not get credit on their own. They are amazed to learn that it was African-American middle-class women's clubs that led the movement against lynching. They didn't know that women chained themselves to the gates of Congress, or went on hunger strikes and were force-fed—so that young women far into the future could take their rights for granted. These young women are shocked, in other words, to find that they have a history.

8   As a result, women remain dependent on other models of "revolution" for their own. They must catch the taste and techniques of activism like a hit song of the month wafting through the air. So one sees women slumbering and then "waking up" every 30 years or so; periods of feminism always follow periods of agitation by women on behalf of other, more respectable causes.

9   This past century shows how fragile conscious feminism has been. The 1910's, with their wave of populist reform, saw the crescendo of women's push for the vote. But the year before it was granted, in 1919, the term "post-feminist" had already expediently been coined. By the 20's pop culture was once again ridiculing the suffragists' generations as being man-hating old battle-axes, irrelevant and out of touch with "today's women."

10   A long sleep followed, with fitful waking. After Betty Friedan's 1963 book helped middle-class white women identify the causes of their deeper malaise, the magical 15 years, from 1965 to 1980, began, representing a high point of historical self-awareness for Western women. Again, other movements had to set the stage: the anti-war movement, the free-speech movement and the hippie movement all contributed to the idea that it was all right to break free of social roles. The civil rights movement trained a generation of African-American activists. The 70's were astonishing: the statutes against sex discrimination labeled Title VII and Title IX; Shirley Chisholm's 1972 race for the Democratic Presidential nomination. That era, personified by Steinem and Jong, NOW and the National Women's Political Caucus, showed what could happen for women when, as an energized mass in a democracy, they wanted change badly enough to make noise about it.

11   The predictable backlash came, as it always does; the evil 80's were a time of shoulder pads, silicone and retrenchment. Again—so quickly, so thoroughly—women "forgot." A *Time*/CNN poll found that only 33 percent of women called themselves feminists—and only 16 percent of college-age women. "Guilt" and "the Mommy Track" were the catchwords of the day. Once again, feminists were represented as hairy-legged man-hating shrews.

12   The heartbreak of those times was in seeing newly clueless young women come of age. Once, when I visited Yale as a speaker, a brilliant young Asian-American student joined her male debating society peers in loudly ridiculing feminism. Later, when we were alone for a moment, she confided that she didn't really believe what she said—but the guys were in charge of the club and she just wanted to get along with them. "Besides," she had said, as if parroting some women's magazine, "women my age just have to accept that we can't have it all." It was as if all those words—flextime, family leave, egalitarian marriage—had vanished, taking with them the ways in which that young woman could have reconsidered her life.

13   Enter the explosive 90's. Women are now the most important voting mass in America. "Women's Issues" dominate the agenda. The word "feminism" is as taboo as ever, but does it matter if you call yourself a feminist if you are living feminism? And American women are doing that, considering the number of their new businesses, and their new judgeships, new elected officials and new spending power. Feminism today is not a label; it's a way of life.

14   But here's the catch: if we remain indifferent to history, we risk losing it all. The bad old days are always ready to knock at your door, sisters: while you're packing your briefcase or getting into your truck, feeling confident, having thrown out the mailing from that advocacy group, you could just find that you can't get a legal abortion anymore; or that your boss knows that those sexual harassment statutes can be managed with a wink and a nod.

15   Women who are ignorant of their own history forget the main lessons, like: Here's how you mobilize; being nice is never as good as getting leverage; the nature-nurture debate has been going on forever, and neither side is going to win; your representatives pay attention when you use your money, your voice and your will. And voting millions can provide the will.

16   Maybe we will learn at last. Maybe we will create institutions that are willing to share influence with younger women coming up, rather than hoarding power for one generation. Maybe we will learn to honor our heroines and role models while they are still alive: maybe Gloria Steinem and Shirley Chisholm will get their commemorative stamps and parades in their own lifetimes, so our daughters will grow up with someone to turn to more powerful in their imaginations than Kate Moss and Calista Flockhart. Maybe we will learn at last that dissent and disagreement among women across the political spectrum is a sign of our diversity and strength. Maybe we will turn from the horoscope page to the *Congressional Quarterly*, and understand at last that our salvation lies not in our stars, but in ourselves.

◆◆◆

D. CLASS DISCUSSION AND WRITING ASSIGNMENT: PROOFS AND STYLE IN THE DECLARATION OF INDEPENDENCE

The Declaration of Independence, a classic argument, was written by Thomas Jefferson in 1776 to explain why the American colonies wanted to separate from Great Britain. It established America as independent states, and thus it is a revolutionary document with a revolutionary purpose.

1. Read the Declaration of Independence, and to understand it better, divide it into its three major component parts. Draw a line at the end of part 1, which explains the general principles behind the revolutionary action. Then draw a line at the end of part 2, which lists the reasons for the action. Finally, identify the purpose of the third and last brief part of the document.
2. The document presents an argument with the value warrants stated in part 1, the support in part 2, and the conclusion in part 3. Summarize the ideas in each part of the argument.
3. Test the argument by questioning the warrants and the support. Do you agree with them? If you accept them, you accept the conclusion.
4. Identify some of the proofs in the document, and comment on their effectiveness.
5. Describe the predominant style in the document, and give examples that support your answer.
6. Write a 250-word paper in which you explain the insights you now have about the structure, proofs, and style of the Declaration of Independence.

THE DECLARATION OF INDEPENDENCE

Thomas Jefferson

The Declaration of Independence was approved by Congress on July 2, 1776, and published two days later.

1   When in the course of human events, it becomes necessary for one people to dissolve the political bands which have connected them with another, and to assume among the Powers of the earth, the separate and equal station to which the Laws of Nature and of Nature's God entitle them, a decent respect to the opinions of mankind requires that they should declare the causes which impel them to the separation.

2   We hold these truths to be self-evident, that all men are created equal, that they are endowed by their Creator with certain unalienable Rights, that among these are Life, Liberty and the pursuit of Happiness.

3   That to secure these rights, Governments are instituted among Men, deriving their just powers from the consent of the governed.

4   That whenever any Form of Government becomes destructive of these ends, it is the Right of the People to alter or to abolish it, and to institute a new Government, laying its foundation on such principles and organizing its powers in such form, as to them shall seem most likely to effect their Safety and Happiness. Prudence, indeed, will dictate that Governments long established should not be changed for light and transient causes; and accordingly all experience hath shown that mankind are more disposed to suffer, while evils are sufferable, than to right themselves by abolishing the forms to which they are accustomed. But when a long train of abuses and usurpations pursuing invariably the same Object evinces a design to reduce them under absolute Despotism, it is their right, it is their duty, to throw off such government, and to provide new Guards for their future security.

5   Such has been the patient sufferance of these Colonies, and such is now the necessity which constrains them to alter their former Systems of Government. The history of the present King of Great Britain is a history of repeated injuries and usurpations, all having in direct object the establishment of an absolute Tyranny over these States. To prove this, let Facts be submitted to a candid world.

6   He has refused his Assent to Laws, the most wholesome and necessary for the public good.

7   He has forbidden his Governors to pass Laws of immediate and pressing importance, unless suspended in their operation till his Assent should be obtained; and when so suspended, he has utterly neglected to attend to them.

8   He has refused to pass over Laws for the accommodation of large districts of people, unless those people would relinquish the right of Representation in the Legislature, a right inestimable to them and formidable to tyrants only.

9   He has called together legislative bodies at places unusual, uncomfortable, and distant from the depository of their Public Records, for the sole purpose of fatiguing them into compliance with his measures.

10   He has dissolved Representative Houses repeatedly, for opposing with manly firmness his invasions on the rights of the people.

11   He has refused for a long time, after such dissolutions, to cause others to be elected; whereby the Legislative Powers, incapable of Annihilation, have returned to the People at large for their exercise; the State remaining in the meantime exposed to all the dangers of invasion from without, and convulsions within.

12   He has endeavored to prevent the population of these States; for that purpose obstructing the Laws for Naturalization of Foreigners; refusing to pass others to encourage their migration hither, and raising the conditions of new Appropriations of Lands.

13   He has obstructed the Administration of Justice, by refusing his Assent to Laws for establishing Judiciary Powers.

14   He has made Judges dependent on his Will alone, for the tenure of their offices, and the amount and payment of their salaries.

15   He has erected a multitude of New Offices, and sent hither swarms of Officers to harass our People, and eat out their substance.

16   He has kept among us, in time of peace, Standing Armies without the consent of our legislatures.

17   He has affected to render the Military independent of and superior to the Civil Power.

18   He has combined with others to subject us to jurisdictions foreign to our constitution, and unacknowledged by our laws; giving his Assent to their acts of pretended Legislation:

19   For quartering large bodies of armed troops among us:

20   For protecting them, by a mock Trial, from Punishment for any Murders which they should commit on the inhabitants of these States:

21   For cutting off our Trade with all parts of the world:

22   For imposing Taxes on us without our Consent:

23   For depriving us in many cases of the benefits of Trial by Jury:

24   For transporting us beyond Seas to be tried for pretended offenses:

25   For abolishing the free System of English Laws in a neighboring Province, establishing therein an Arbitrary government, and enlarging its Boundaries so as to render it at once an example and fit instrument for introducing the same absolute rule into these Colonies:

26   For taking away our Charters, abolishing our most valuable Laws, and altering fundamentally the Forms of our Governments:

27   For suspending our own Legislatures, and declaring themselves invested with Power to legislate for us in all cases whatsoever.

28   He has abdicated Government here, by declaring us out of his Protection and waging War against us.

29   He has plundered our seas, ravaged our Coasts, burnt our towns, and destroyed the Lives of our people.

30   He is at this time transporting large Armies of foreign Mercenaries to compleat the works of death, desolation and tyranny, already begun with circumstances of Cruelty & perfidy scarcely paralleled in the most barbarous ages, and totally unworthy the Head of a civilized nation.

31   He has constrained our fellow Citizens taken Captive on the high Seas to bear Arms against their Country, to become the executioners of their friends and Brethren, or to fall themselves by their Hands.

32   He has excited domestic insurrections amongst us, and has endeavored to bring on the inhabitants of our frontiers, the merciless Indian Savages, whose known rule of warfare, is an undistinguished destruction of all ages, sexes and conditions.

33   In every stage of these Oppressions We have Petitioned for Redress in the most humble terms: Our repeated Petitions have been answered only by repeated injury. A Prince, whose character is thus marked by every act which may define a Tyrant, is unfit to be the ruler of a free people.

34   Nor have We been wanting in attention to our British brethren. We have warned them from time to time of attempts by their legislature to extend an unwarrantable jurisdiction over us. We have reminded them of the circumstances of our emigration and settlement here. We have appealed to their native justice and magnanimity, and we have conjured them by the ties of our common kindred to disavow these usurpations, which would inevitably interrupt our connections and correspondence. They too have been deaf to the voice of justice and of

consanguinity. We must, therefore, acquiesce in the necessity, which denounces our Separation, and hold them, as we hold the rest of mankind, Enemies in War, in Peace Friends.

35   We, therefore, the Representatives of the *United States of America,* in General Congress, Assembled, appealing to the Supreme Judge of the world for the rectitude of our intentions, do, in the Name, and by authority of the good People of these Colonies, solemnly publish and declare, That these United Colonies are, and of Right ought to be Free and Independent States; that they are Absolved from all Allegiance to the British Crown, and that all political connection between them and the State of Great Britain, is and ought to be totally dissolved; and that as Free and Independent States, they have full power to levy War, conclude Peace, contract Alliances, establish Commerce, and to do all other Acts and Things which independent States may of right do. And for the support of this Declaration, with a firm reliance on the protection of Divine Providence, we mutually pledge to each other our Lives, our Fortunes and our sacred Honor.

FOR DISCUSSION: Describe the rhetorical situation for the Declaration of Independence. Why is it usually described as a "revolutionary document"? What are the four "self-evident" truths or human rights mentioned in this document? Do all people have equal claim to these rights, or can you think of constraining circumstances when certain individuals might be denied these rights? Do individuals pursue these rights, or do governments guarantee them? What is the difference? Discuss.

E. PREWRITING: USING THE PROOFS TO GET IDEAS FOR A POSITION PAPER

You have analyzed other authors' use of proofs in the preceding exercises. Now think about how you can use the proofs in your own writing. If you are working on a "Position Paper Based on 'The Reader'" (Exercise D in Chapter 8), you will already have a claim, and you may have already used the Toulmin model (pages 151–152) and the claim questions (pages 195–196) to help you develop the structure and some of the ideas for your paper. Use the mnemonics SICDADS and VAM to help you consider the proofs. Ask the following questions, and write out answers for those that are most promising.

1. *Signs:* What symptoms or signs will demonstrate that this is so?
2. *Induction:* What examples can I use and what conclusions can I draw from them? Are they convincing enough to help the reader make the "inductive leap"?
3. *Cause:* What has caused this? Why is this happening? Think of explanations and examples of both cause and effect.
4. *Deduction:* What concluding statements do I want to make? What general principles and examples (or cases) are they based on?

5. *Analogies:* How can I show that what happened in one case will probably happen again in another case? Can I use a literal analogy to compare items in the same general category? Can I use a figurative analogy to compare items from different categories? Can I demonstrate that history repeats itself by citing a historical analogy?

6. *Definition:* What words or concepts will I need to define?

7. *Statistics:* What statistics can I use? Would they be more convincing in graph form?

8. *Values:* What values can I appeal to? Should I spell them out or leave them implicit? Will narratives and emotional language make my appeals to values stronger?

9. *Authority:* Whom should I quote? What can I use from my own background and experience to establish my own expertise? How can I use language to create common ground and establish *ethos?*

10. *Motives:* What does my audience need and want in regard to this topic? How can I appeal to those needs? Will emotional language help?

Chapter 8 ❖

The Fallacies or Pseudoproofs

In an advertisement for a health club, an attractive, muscular man is embracing a beautiful, slim woman. Both are dressed in exercise clothing. The caption reads, "Studies show diets don't work. This picture shows exercise does." No further evidence is provided. You do not have to be an expert in argument theory to sense that something is wrong with this proof.

Responsible and honest proof relies on skillful use of support and acceptable warrants to prove a claim. Since argument deals with probability instead of certainty, an argument may be perceived as very convincing, somewhat convincing, or not convincing at all. The success of the argument depends on the proofs. Weak support or a faulty or unacceptable warrant weakens an argument, but it is still an argument. The reader must ask the test of validity questions identified in the preceding chapter in order to evaluate the reliability and strength of the proofs and ultimately of the entire argument itself to decide whether it is well developed or underdeveloped, acceptable or unacceptable, moral or immoral.

Sometimes, as in the case of the advertisement just described, a reader will encounter material that may appear at first to be a proof but really isn't a proof at all. It is a *pseudoproof,* which is commonly called a *fallacy.* Fallacies lead an audience astray, they distort and distract, they represent inadequate reasoning or non-reasoning, and they oversimplify a claim instead of proving it.

The author of the advertisement in the opening example expects the reader to accept a number of unstated warrants that most people would reject if they were explicitly stated: (1) The studies about dieting are a reasonable sample to show that dieting does not change the shape of your body; (2) the best way to get effective exercise and a well-shaped body is to join an exercise club; and (3) if you improve the shape of your body, you will find romance on the floor of the exercise club. The visual support is the picture of the two attractive people who are embracing in their exercise clothes. The final claim based on those warrants and that support, of course, is that you should join the exercise club.

Suppose you encounter the exercise club advertisement at a time when you feel overweight, out of shape, and unloved. You might be tempted to believe the argument because the warrants and the support reflect what you would like to believe. Fallacies can seem convincing when they appear to support what an audience already believes or wants to believe. Warrants that few people would find convincing can create the common ground necessary for successful argument if they hold an emotional appeal to someone's deep prejudices, unreasonable biases, or irrational beliefs or wishes. You may have encountered Web sites on the Internet, like those supported by hate groups, for example, that present support and warrants that you would never find acceptable. As you analyze the reasoning on these sites, you discover that much of it is extremist and that it supports only one narrow view. The support is often distorted, insufficient, unreliable, exaggerated, or oversimplified. Furthermore, the warrants are untrue, and emotional material is used to stir up excessive feelings rather than to prove a rational point. You can also often identify a number of specific fallacies on such sites. When you are tempted to believe an argument that does not seem logical to you or seems to have something wrong with it, consider why you are tempted to believe it. If fallacies and unacceptable reasoning are weakening the claim or proving the argument false, analyze it and expose these problems. This will be comparatively easy to do if you already strongly disagree with the ideas and harder to do if, for some reason, you are tempted to accept them.

You will encounter fallacies in advertisements, letters to the editor, and other argumentative writing that you find both in print and online. Avoid quoting sources that contain fallacies, and avoid fallacies in your own writing. Fallacies in your writing, whether created by you or by the authors you choose to quote, weaken your argument and damage your *ethos*. Recognize fallacies by asking, "Is this material even relevant? Is it adequate? Do I agree? Does it support the claim?" Learning some of the common types of fallacies will also help you recognize them. Here are some of the most common, organized under the same categories we have used for genuine proofs: logic, character (*ethos*), and emotion.

FALLACIES IN LOGIC

Fallacies pose as logical proof, but you will see that they are really pseudoproofs that prove nothing at all. You may have trouble remembering all of their names; many people do. Concentrate instead on the fallacious thinking characterized by each of them, such as introducing irrelevant material; providing wrong, unfair, inadequate, or even no support; harboring unacceptable warrants; drawing inappropriate conclusions; and oversimplifying the choices.

▲ *Begging the Question.* No support is provided by the arguer who begs the question, and the claim is simply restated, over and over again, in one form or another. For example, "Capital punishment deters crime because it keeps criminals from committing murder" simply restates the same idea in other words. Here are other familiar examples: "Why is this true? It's true because I know it's true." "Everyone knows that the president of the United States has done his best for the environment because he said so." You can remember the name of this fallacy, begging the question, by recalling that the arguer, when asked for support, begs off and simply restates the claim in the same or different words.

▲ *RED HERRING.* A red herring provides irrelevant and misleading support that pulls the audience away from the real argument. For example, "I don't believe we should elect this candidate because she would have to put her kids in day care" is a red herring; qualifications to hold office have nothing to do with household arrangements. Whether or not the police were racist in the O. J. Simpson trial was a red herring in the sense that even though their alleged racism might have provided a motive for planting evidence, their racism was unrelated to whether Simpson was innocent or guilty of murder. Another red herring in the O. J. Simpson case that influenced some people was the idea that the accused was a great sports hero and we should not degrade great sports heroes by trying them for murder. Authors of detective fiction sometimes use red herrings in their plots as false clues to divert the reader's attention from the real murderer. Remember the red herring fallacy by recalling that the fish, the red herring, was at one time used to train hunting dogs to follow a scent. It was not a true scent, however. The herring scent was irrelevant to the real smells of the real hunt, and the fallacy, the red herring, is irrelevant to an argument when it introduces such support as a person's parental responsibilities as a factor in the person's qualifications for a job or whether sports heroes should be treated differently from other people.

▲ *NON SEQUITUR.* *Non sequitur* is Latin for "it does not follow." In this type of fallacy, the conclusion does not follow from the evidence and the warrant. Here are some examples: the professor in the Hawaiian shirt and gold chains must be an easy grader; the self-consciously beautiful woman who has applied for a job as a secretary would not do the job well; that man with the powerful new computer must be highly skilled in the use of computer technology. The warrants for these three examples are that the professor's clothes indicate how he will grade, beautiful women cannot be good secretaries, and owning powerful equipment implies the ability to use it. You can probably sense the problems with these warrants. They are so difficult for most people to accept that none of these examples come across as convincing arguments. Here is another example of a *non sequitur:* Women should not be placed in executive positions because they cannot drive cars as well as men.

▲ *STRAW MAN.* A straw man involves attributing an argument to an opponent that the opponent never made and then refuting it in a devastating way. The arguer sets up an idea, refutes it, and appears to win, even though the idea may be unrelated to the issue being discussed. For example, a political candidate might set up a straw man by claiming that his opponent has said he is too old to do the job, when in fact the opponent has never mentioned age as an issue. Then the candidate refutes the age issue by detailing the advantages of age and appears to win the argument even though this is not an issue at all. In fact, by refuting this false issue, the candidate may give the impression that he could refute any other arguments put forth by the opposition as well. The use of a straw man suggests competence where it might not actually exist.

▲ *Stacked Evidence.* Stacking evidence to represent only one side of an issue that clearly has two sides gives a distorted impression of the issue. For example, to prove that television is an inspiring and uplifting medium, the only evidence given is that PBS nature shows are educational, *Friends* promotes personal bonds, and news programs and documentaries keep audiences informed. The sex and violence programming and the commercials are never mentioned.

▲ *Either-Or.* Some arguments are oversimplified by the arguer and presented as black-or-white, either-or choices when there are actually other alternatives. Some examples are "This country can either have a strong defense program or a strong social welfare program," "We can develop either a strong space program or an urban development program," "A woman can either be a mother or have a career," and "A man can either go to graduate school or become a company man." No alternative, middle-ground, or compromise positions are acknowledged.

▲ *Post Hoc.* This is short for *post hoc, ergo propter hoc,* a Latin phrase that translates as "after this, therefore because of this." To put it more simply, *post hoc* is the fallacy of faulty cause. For example, it is fallacious to claim in an advertisement that people will be more attractive and more popular if they drink a certain brand of cola. Look at other advertisements on television or in magazines, and you will easily find other examples of *post hoc,* the claim that one thing causes another when there is actually no causal relationship between them. Think about the outdoor healthy virility of the Marlboro man, for example, and the suggestion that he got that way by smoking cigarettes. Another example is the person who finds romance by serving a particular spaghetti sauce or using a specific cologne.

▲ *Hasty Generalization.* Sometimes arguers "jump to conclusions" by basing a conclusion on too few examples. For example, someone may conclude that the justice system is hopelessly flawed because a man is sent to jail by mistake or that since some students in urban schools belong to gangs, most students in those schools belong to gangs. Look back at the essay "Jobs Illuminate What Riots Hid: Young Ideals" (pages 80–83). This author attempts to counter the stereotypical idea that young people in South-Central Los Angeles are rioters and hoodlums. The example of the young woman who was industrious and got a job at Disneyland can encourage an opposite type of hasty generalization and suggests that most of these young people are instead "wonderful kids, outstanding kids." Hasty generalizations often contribute to stereotyping.

FALLACIES THAT AFFECT CHARACTER OR *ETHOS*

Fallacies that are aimed at attacking character or at using character instead of evidence for proof are misleading and can damage *ethos.*

▲ *Ad Hominem. Ad hominem* means "to the man" in Latin. An *ad hominem* argument attacks a person's character rather than a person's ideas. The press is notorious for such attacks during political campaigns, and so are some of the candidates themselves. The "character issue," for example, may receive more attention than more serious, substantive issues. Thus negative information is provided about the candidates' personal lives rather than about their ideas and the issues that concern them. The purpose of *ad hominem* arguments is to discredit these individuals with the public. Here is another example of an *ad hominem* attack: Piety is said to have no validity because of the careless personal and financial habits of some television evangelists. An *ad hominem* argument directs attention away from the issues and toward the person. Thus we become prejudiced and biased against an individual personally instead of evaluating that person's ideas.

▲ *GUILT BY ASSOCIATION.* The fallacy of guilt by association suggests that people's character can be judged by examining the character of their associates. For example, an employee in a company that defrauds the government is declared dishonest because of his association with the company, even though he may have known nothing of the fraud. Or an observer is thrown into jail along with some political protesters simply because she was in the wrong place at the wrong time. Political figures are often judged as morally defective if they associate with people with questionable values and reputations. It is assumed that these individuals are members of these groups and guilty by association.

▲ *USING AUTHORITY INSTEAD OF EVIDENCE.* This is a variation of begging the question. The arguer relies on personal authority to prove a point rather than on evidence. For example, a salesman tells you to buy the used car because he is honest and trustworthy and he knows your neighbor.

EMOTIONAL FALLACIES

Irrelevant, unrelated, and distracting emotional materials are often introduced into argument to try to convince the audience. Here are some examples.

▲ *BANDWAGON APPEAL.* The argument is that everyone is doing something, so you should too. For example, everyone is watching reality TV, so you should jump on the bandwagon and watch it also. Political and other public opinion polls are sometimes used to promote the bandwagon appeal. The suggestion is that since a majority of the people polled hold a certain opinion, you should adopt it also.

▲ *SLIPPERY SLOPE.* The slippery-slope fallacy is a scare tactic that suggests that if we allow one thing to happen, we will immediately be sliding down the slippery slope to disaster. This fallacy is sometimes introduced into environmental and abortion issues. If we allow loggers to cut a few trees, we will soon lose all the forests. Or if a woman is required to wait twenty-four hours to reconsider her decision to have an abortion, soon there will be so many restrictions that no one will be able to have an abortion. This fallacy is similar to the saying about the camel that gets its nose into the tent. If we permit the nose today, we have the whole camel to deal with tomorrow. It is better not to start because disaster may result.

▲ *Creating False Needs.* Emotional proofs, as you have learned, appeal to what people value and think they need. Sometimes an arguer will create a false sense of need where none exists or will unrealistically heighten an existing need. The intent is to make the argument more convincing. Advertising provides excellent examples. The housewife is told she needs a shining kitchen floor with a high gloss that only a certain wax can provide. Parents are reminded that they want smart, successful children, so they should buy a set of encyclopedias.

These examples of fallacies provide you with a good sense of what constitutes fallacious reasoning. Armed with this list and with the tests of validity for genuine proofs listed under "Tests of Validity" in the Summary Charts (pages 443–448), you now have what you need to evaluate the strength and validity of the proofs in an argument. This information will help you make evaluations, form rebuttals to challenge weak arguments, and create arguments of your own.

REVIEW QUESTIONS

1. What are fallacies? Why are they also described as pseudoproofs?
2. Under what circumstances might you be tempted to believe a fallacy?
3. What are some of the qualities that characterize fallacious thinking?
4. Name at least two of the fallacies in logic.
5. Name at least two fallacies that affect *ethos.*
6. Name at least two emotional fallacies.

EXERCISES AND ACTIVITIES

A. CLASS DISCUSSION: ANALYZING THE FALLACIES IN AN ADVERTISEMENT

1. Study the advertisement on the next page, and identify the most obvious fallacy in it.
2. Bring in an advertisement containing a fallacy and explain it to the class.

B. GROUP WORK AND DISCUSSION: ANALYZING FALLACIES IN WRITTEN ARGUMENT

The argument on pages 238–240 is written by an author who holds strong opinions about the subject. As you read the essay, focus on specific statements that you cannot agree with. Then figure out why you do not agree. Is the evidence weak or irrelevant? Or are there fallacies? Expose the weaknesses in this argument. Then discuss your findings with the class.

Looks like someone could use the right multivitamin.

Meetings, deadlines, and conference calls. And for a moment of peace, you head to the vending machine. Presenting Mega Men® from General Nutrition Centers. You see, it has thirty-nine premium vitamins, minerals, and herbs your body could really use. Including the things that are good for men, like saw palmetto, ginseng, and natural vitamin E. All of which must pass 150 quality checks before it gets to you. And, now is a great time to experience the benefits for yourself. Because when you pick up any GNC brand product, including Mega Men, we'll give you any other GNC brand product at half price.* It's just one more way we help you live your best life.

www.gnc.com

| 5,000 stores nationwide. | Nearly 70 years of expertise. | Backed by over 100 researchers & scientists. | A healthy 10 million customers each year. | GNC LiveWell. |

For the GNC location nearest you, call 1-800-477-4462. ©2002 General Nutrition Centers. May not be available outside the U.S. *See store for details.

SOURCE: *Prevention*, May 2002, p. 36.

THE LATEST FROM THE FEMINIST "FRONT"*

Rush Limbaugh

The following is excerpted from the book *See, I Told You So*. The author is well known for his widely aired radio show.

1   Few of my "Thirty-five Undeniable Truths of Life" have stirred as much controversy and outrage as Number Twenty-four: "Feminism was established so that unattractive women could have easier access to the mainstream of society."

2   Many have suggested that this statement is too rough, insensitive, cruel, and unnecessarily provocative. However, there is one absolute defense of this statement. It's called truth. Sometimes the truth hurts. Sometimes the truth is jarring. Sometimes the truth is the most provocative thing you can tell someone. But the truth is still the truth. And it needs to be heard.

3   Likewise, for years I've been telling you that the feminist leadership is basically anti-male. I've said this in many different ways on many different occasions. But no matter how many times I have said it and no matter how cleverly I have rephrased this message, skeptics abound.

4   "Oh, Rush," people say, "aren't you going a little too far? Aren't you overstating your case?"

5   Well, folks, once again, I have to say it. The evidence that I was right all along about feminism—as with so many other things—is now overwhelming. . . .

6   The people who define modern feminism are saying that normal male deportment is harassment, near rape, abuse, and disrespect. These extremists, who make up the intellectual leadership of the modern feminist movement, are attempting to make the case that any expression of interest by a man in a woman is harassment. Inevitably, this is going to lead to several serious problems.

7   First among those is that men will become fearful about making any advances. This attitude will confuse men about what is right and what kind of behavior is acceptable. If no approach is welcome, then women will, by necessity, have to become the aggressors. Men will be afraid of crossing the line.

8   The second major problem with this trend is that it trivializes real sexual harassment, real rape. When people are labeling everyday, normal, male-female conduct as sexual harassment, we not only obliterate relations between the sexes, but we greatly trivialize true sexual harassment. Harassment is now being so broadly defined by some that it entails behavior that offends or annoys or interrupts your life.

9   The fact of the matter is that women have far more power than most of them realize. It's a biological fact that males are the aggressors. We all know this is true. That means that the ultimate power—the power to say yes or no—lies with women.

---

*Rush H. Limbaugh III, *See, I Told You So* (New York: Simon & Schuster, 1993), pp. 221–223, 225–227.

10   If consent is denied and the aggressive male physically forces himself on the woman to the point of penetration, then you have rape—real rape. But this is the exception. Most men are not rapists. But militant feminists seek to blur the distinctions. Let's look at date rape, for example. I have a problem with feminists seeking to expand the concept of rape by adding such adjectives as *date* and *acquaintance*. Words mean things. . . . Especially in these times of hypersensitivity, it is very important that we are clear in our word usage. This is even more the case when the word in question represents criminal behavior, in some cases punishable by life imprisonment. This is dead-serious, folks. Rape means rape. It either is, or it isn't. It matters not whether it occurs on a date or on Mars. It is my belief that the date-rape concept has been promoted by those whose agenda it is to blur these distinctions. By calling it "date rape," the intent is to expand the scope of the very serious crime of rape, and to include within the category of "rape" behavior that certainly is not rape. Please don't misinterpret my meaning. As a firm believer that words have meaning, I'm very careful to use mine precisely. I condemn the act of rape as much as any other human being would. It is inexcusable. Confusing its definition by trying to expand its scope deceitfully will only redound to the detriment of real rape victims. That is unconscionable.

11   Some militant feminists apparently harbor such animosity for the opposite sex that they want to criminalize the process of courtship—the old-fashioned "chase." I have news for these people: It's normal for boys to pursue girls. It's natural for men to pursue women. This normal and natural process, once called the fine art of seduction, is being confused with harassment. What was once considered an important part of the process of finding a mate is being mischaracterized as rape.

12   How should you channel normal masculinity and the aggressive nature of the male? Would these women prefer men as husbands, or leaders of marauding gangs? That is basically the choice. Because women can be—and need to be—a great civilizing influence over men.

13   Do you realize that in some cities today men can be arrested for making a wolf whistle at a comely women? Now, I'm not suggesting that this is the kind of behavior we should encourage, but should it be criminalized? And what are the consequences of this sort of overreaction? The consequences are manifold. It's no wonder so many men and women have problems interacting. Rules and regulations like these are presumably meant to foster improved relations between men and women, but their effect is just the opposite. What is being fostered is an adversarial relationship between the sexes.

14   Take, for instance, the young star of "The Wonder Years," Fred Savage. The then sixteen-year-old was hit with a sexual-harassment suit by a former staffer of the show, Monique Long, who claimed that Savage repeatedly asked her to have an affair with him and—egads!—touched her by holding her hand. The lawsuit also charged that Jason Hervey, another actor on the show, harassed Long during her two years on the show as a costume designer, at one point touching her "in a sexual way." Long, thirty-two, claimed she was asked not to return to the show because of her complaints about the actors.

15   Have things gotten to the point where a man, or boy, can't ask a woman out? Can't flirt? Is it a crime to hold somebody's hand? Wouldn't a more appropriate response to questionable behavior have been for this thirty-two-year-old woman to call the teenager's parents? Or even slap him in the face? Is our society so confused now about relations between men and women that a mature adult doesn't know how to deal with a flirtatious sixteen-year-old?

◆◆◆

C. PREWRITING: QUESTIONS TO EVALUATE SUPPORT AND ELIMINATE FALLACIES

If you are working on a "Position Paper Based on 'The Reader'" (Exercise D in this chapter), you have already applied the Toulmin model to get a sense of the shape of your paper (page 146), and you have answered the claim questions (pages 195–196) and the proof questions (pages 229–230) to generate subclaims and support for your paper. Go back and evaluate your prewriting. Look at the subclaims and support to make certain all are complete and reliable, and look for fallacies. Correct or eliminate any items that might weaken your argument. Answer the following questions.

1. Do I have enough support to be convincing? What can I add?
2. Is my support reliable and convincing? How can I make it more so?
3. Is anything exaggerated or oversimplified? How can I be more accurate?
4. Do I rely too much on my own authority ("This is true because I say so") instead of giving support? Can I add support and the opinions of other authorities to be more convincing?
5. Am I weakening this argument with too much emotional appeal? Should any of it be eliminated?
6. Have I used any fallacies as proof? (Check especially for hasty generalizations and *post hoc* or faulty cause, probably the two most common fallacies. Look for other fallacies as well. If you find any, either rewrite so that they are acceptable, or eliminate them.)

D. WRITING ASSIGNMENT: A POSITION PAPER BASED ON "THE READER"

For this assignment, you will write a position paper in which you make a claim and prove it. Your claim should be related to a topic you have selected from "The Reader." Your paper should be about 1,000 words long, typed, and double-spaced.

Your purpose in this assignment is to use the argument theory you have learned in Chapters 5–8 to help you invent ideas and write. You will also draw on your own reasoning and information from the essays to help you argue.

PREWRITING

If you have not already done so, complete some or all of the following prewriting activities, explained on the pages cited, so that you will have plenty of material to draw on when you draft your paper.

1. Read the issue questions in "The Reader," select the one that interests you the most, read the related essays, and write an issue proposal (pages 27–28).
2. Write summary-response papers for each of the related essays (page 88).
3. Write an exploratory essay to help you understand your topic, and write a tentative claim at the end of it (pages 120–123).
4. Use the Toulmin model (pages 151–152) to help you find the elements for your paper, use the claim questions to refine and focus your claim and get further ideas for subclaims (pages 195–196), use the proof questions to develop convincing proofs for your claims (pages 229–230), and use the evaluation questions to improve your support and eliminate fallacies (page 240).

WRITING A LIST OR AN OUTLINE

Follow the instructions in Chapter 4 on page 102 for making an extended list or outline. Refer also to information about possible organizational patterns you might use to organize your ideas (pages 347–352). Or consider using one of the following patterns to organize your ideas and develop your claim.

- If you are writing a fact paper that answers the questions "What happened?" consider using a chronological pattern. Use transitions like *first, then,* and *next.* You may begin your paper with present events and use flashbacks to explain what occurred in the past, or you may simply explain things in the order in which they occurred.
- If you are writing a definition paper that answers the question "What is it?" consider using comparison to help establish meaning by showing what the item you are defining is like and what it is not like. Or you may want to present examples of several meanings for the item and finally settle on the best of these meanings for your conclusion.
- If you are writing a cause paper that answers the question "What caused it?" consider using a cause-and-effect or effect-and-cause pattern of organization. Cause and effect explains how certain causes result in certain effects, and effect and cause describes the effects first and then explains what caused them.
- If you are writing a value paper that answers the question "Is it good or bad?" consider a claim-plus-reasons pattern. Complete the sentence "It is (good or bad) because . . . ," and add reasons and evidence.
- If you are writing a policy paper that answers the question "What should we do?" consider using the problem-solution pattern of organization. Describe the problem first, and then describe one or more solutions.

DRAFTING, REVISING, AND FINAL EDITING

Use your extended list or outline to help you write a draft, revise the draft, and prepare the final copy. Follow the suggestions for drafting, revising, and editing in Chapter 4 (pages 102–109). Work quoted material into your draft as you write. Follow explanations and examples for integrating quoted material into your paper that appear in Chapter 4 (pages 115–116) and the Appendix to Chapter 12 (pages 367–370). Use MLA documentation to cite in-text references and to create a Works Cited page, unless you are advised otherwise.

Follow the instructions and examples for MLA documentation in Chapter 4 and the Appendix to Chapter 12.

Read the following example of a position paper based on an issue question in "The Reader." The question is "What should be done with young offenders?" This paper was written by Kelly Dickerson, a student in an argument class. The type of claim, the elements of the Toulmin model, and the proofs are identified in the margin.

Notice also how Kelly worked quoted material into her paper for ease of reading. Quotations flow with the rest of the text, and they are clear. Furthermore, introductions for the quotations, along with the in-text citations, show you where you could find the originals if you wanted to. Use this paper as a model to help you integrate your quotations into your paper and prepare a Works Cited page.*

Kelly Dickerson
Position Paper Based on "The Reader"
Professor Leston
English 1302
25 September 2003

Minor Problems?

1   Every time Americans tune in to local news broadcasts or read daily papers, they are likely to be shocked at the increasing number of serious crimes committed by youths who are only sixteen years old or even younger. It is sometimes difficult to imagine these youngsters behaving like hardened criminals, but statistics continually prove that their crimes are often just as brutal as those committed by their adult counterparts. Inevitably, people begin questioning how successful the juvenile justice system is in reforming these youths. Increasingly, violent juveniles are being tried and sentenced as adults in our legal system. Ron Powers, quoting Margaret Talbot, reports that between 1990 and 2000, forty-five states either passed new laws or strengthened old ones in order to bring harsher judgments to young offenders. As a result, the number of youths in adult prisons has doubled in ten years, reaching 7,400 in 1997 (549). After reading about this topic, I believe there is no question that juveniles convicted of serious crimes--including murder, rape, robbery, physical assault, and drug involvement--should face the same consequences as adults. We are on the right track in seeking harsher penalties.

Definition

Policy claim

*See the Appendix to Chapter 12 for the actual MLA format guidelines for student papers.

Subclaim: Problem

2   Yet in spite of these efforts, violent crimes committed by juveniles continue to increase. In Vermont, a state with one of the lowest overall crime rates in the nation, the number of juvenile inmates, aged sixteen to twenty-one, recently jumped 77 percent over a three-year period (Powers 543). Examples of teen crime are vivid and terrifying. Gerard Jones tells the story of Barry Loukaitis of Moses Lake, Washington, who didn't get along with his parents or classmates, became obsessed with violent video games, and ended up as the first school shooter (552). Others have followed in his footsteps. Shooting classmates seems to be a more and more common occurrence.

Support: Statistics

Induction

Warrant: The statistics and examples prove there is a problem.

Subclaim: The punishment does not always fit the crime.

3   Despite the staggering increase in serious crimes committed by young offenders, the punishment which juveniles receive has traditionally almost never fit the severity of the crimes. Because the system has historically viewed children as not being fully developed, physically or mentally, it has prevented them from being held accountable for their wrongdoing. Daniel Weinberger explains in "A Brain Too Young for Good Judgment" that the fifteen-year-old student who shot his fellow students at Santana High School has, because of his age, an immature brain. The part of the brain that is used for judgment and suppressing impulsive behavior is not fully formed at that age (556). Yet not all fifteen-year-olds commit such deadly crimes. Those who do should be held accountable.

Authority

Warrant: The punishment should fit the crime.

4   Many of the "children" who commit horribly vicious crimes have been routinely treated as victims of society who are too delicate to receive the punishments they deserve. Until very recently, lenient sentences and court proceedings have been the norm. The message they sent to serious juvenile criminals is that crime "pays" because there are no serious consequences for their actions. When the system lacks an element of fear, there is nothing to deter youthful offenders from committing future crimes. I agree with John Ashcroft, who has campaigned for tougher laws for young criminals and has developed a system that, in his words, no longer "hugs the juvenile terrorist" (Powers 548). Assigning adult sentences to youths who commit serious crimes is absolutely just if the punishment is to fit the crime.

Support: Cause and effect

Warrant: Adult sentences are a deterrent to crime.

Appeal to value of justice

Rebuttal: Cost to society is the same, so young offenders should get same treatment as adults.

5   Most pro-rehabilitation advocates argue that juvenile criminals are completely different from their adult counterparts and should therefore be treated differently in the justice system. However, the cost to society is the same regardless of the age of the criminal. What comfort does it give to the family of a slain or injured victim that the person who killed or maimed their loved one was a minor? Parents of children shot and killed at school by teenage killers suffer no less because their child was shot by a young offender. Instead of treating the loser who shot a fellow

Support: Cause and effect

Warrant: Cost to society should determine punishment.

student like a victim of society, the justice system should treat this person like any other criminal who victimizes society and causes pain to individuals and communities.

Subclaim: Use tougher measures

6   Even tougher measures must be taken to combat this growing problem of juvenile crime. In today's society, too many juveniles count on lenient sentences allotted by the juvenile justice system. Powers cautions that children "crave a sense of self-worth" and want to be included "in the intimate circles of

Support: Sign

family and community life" (549). The young offenders he describes seem to create their own community in prison where, unhindered, they enjoy planning future crimes together (545).

Warrant: Juveniles can still get off.

When there are no harsh consequences of being caught, committing crimes can be perceived as having positive benefits. As a result, juveniles are continuing to become more violent and less concerned with the value of human life.

7   Richard Rothstein advocates reading children's stories to young inmates as one method for rehabilitation. I agree that such efforts may be helpful in decreasing the amount of juvenile crime, particularly repeat crime. However, I believe that these measures

Qualifier

should be directed toward youths who have committed minor offenses. I believe that juveniles like the ones who shoot their classmates, those who are convicted of serious crimes--including

Restatement of claim and summary

murder, rape, robbery, physical assault, and drug involvement--should be tried as adults. Their actions are obviously more serious than misdemeanor offenses, almost always resulting in greater direct harm to society. A message has to be sent that we will no longer tolerate brutal crimes simply because of the age of the criminal. These youths must be held completely accountable for their crimes, suffering harsh consequences and ultimately realizing that they are no longer insulated from the law because of their age.

Works Cited

Jones, Gerard. "Not So Alone." <u>Killing Monsters: Why Children Need Fantasy, Super Heroes, and Make-Believe Violence</u>. New York: Perseus, 2002. Rpt. in Wood 550-55.

Powers, Ron. "The Apocalypse of Adolescents." <u>Atlantic Monthly</u> Mar. 2002: 62-74. Rpt. in Wood 542-49.

Rothstein, Richard. "Fairy Tales as a Learning Tool for Young Offenders." <u>New York Times</u> 24 July 2002: A16. Rpt. in Wood 557-58.

Weinberger, Daniel R. "A Brain Too Young for Good Judgment." <u>New York Times</u> 10 Mar. 2001: A27. Rpt. in Wood 555-57.

Wood, Nancy V. <u>Perspectives on Argument</u>. 4th ed. Upper Saddle River: Prentice, 2004.

❧ ❖ Chapter 9 ❖ ❧

Rogerian Argument and Common Ground

To this point, you have been studying traditional argument that has its origin in classical sources. It is the type of argument that predominates in American culture, and it is what you are used to when you listen to people argue on television or when you read arguments in many current periodicals or books. In traditional argument, the arguer states a claim and proves it by drawing on various types of proofs, including reasoning and evidence. The object is to convince an audience that the claim is valid and that the arguer is right. In this model of argument, the arguer uses the rebuttal to demonstrate how the opposition is wrong and to state why the audience should reject that position. The emphasis in traditional argument is on winning the argument. Debate, with participants on both sides trying to win by convincing a third-party judge, is one form of traditional argument, as is courtroom argument and all other single-perspective argument in which one person argues to convince one or more people of a particular point of view.

As you know from your own experience and from reading about argument in this book, traditional argument does not always achieve its aims with the audience. In fact, in certain situations when strongly held opinions or entire value systems are challenged, traditional argument may not be effective at all. The audience may in fact simply stop listening or walk away. When that happens, it is useful to have another argumentative strategy to turn to, one that might work better in cases where there seems to be a standoff or a lack of common ground among the arguing parties.

Rogerian argument, so called because it evolved from techniques originally applied by psychotherapist Carl Rogers, is a technique that is particularly useful for reducing conflict and establishing common ground between people who hold divergent positions and may even at times express hostility toward each other. Common ground may seem impossible to achieve in such situations, but two opposing parties can almost always find something to agree on if they try hard enough. Here is an anecdote that shows two hostile individuals establishing common ground. This comes from a column titled "In Politics, It Does Help to Be Smart" by Molly Ivins. Ivins claims that this is a true story.

> This is the perfect political story and also true, but the names have been changed to protect the players.
>
> Many years ago in the Texas Lege lurked two senators who loathed one another with livid passion. One was conservative, the other liberal; one from a rural area, the other urban; one a mean old bull and the other a witty cosmopolite. We'll call them Bubba and Cary.
>
> One afternoon, Bubba is drinking with a friend in a local dive when in walks Cary. Bubba looks at him and snarls, "You're a sorry ———!"
>
> Cary continues to the bar without comment. But after he gets a drink, he passes Bubba's table again, stops and says: "You think I'm a sorry ———, right?"
>
> "Right," says Bubba.
>
> "Well, I think you're a sorry ———."
>
> Bubba rears back, ready to rise and fight. Cary continues. "But we both *know* Senator Doakes is a sorry ———."
>
> Bubba laughs and says, "I'll drink to that."
>
> They were both smart politicians. And that's what smart politicians do: concentrate on the areas where they can agree, even if there's only one. That's how deals get done, the ball is moved forward, the system works and the people's interest is more or less served.[1]

Establishing common ground in Rogerian argument, as in this example, also involves discovering what two parties have in common. But Rogerian argument does more than that. Instead of using rebuttal to show how the opposition is wrong, as in traditional argument, Rogerian argument requires the arguer to spend at least some time at the beginning of the argument not only explaining how the opposition's position is right but also identifying situations where it might be valid. The arguer cannot do that very successfully without finding some common ground with the opposition. It is almost impossible to show how any part of another individual's opposing position is valid if you disagree with it totally.

Look back at the example in Chapter 1 (page 11) about the two individuals who are seeking common ground on methods for stopping random shooters. One of these individuals advocates that private citizens arm themselves with handguns as a deterrent to shooters. Another believes that the availability of handguns is the problem and advocates that private gun ownership be abolished. Common ground exists between the two parties because of their common concern for personal safety. To use Rogerian argument in this situation, the anti-handgun party would restate the pro-handgun party's position, and would emphasize the common concern they both have for protecting their safety, before they search together for a solution they can agree on.[2]

Additional descriptions and examples of Rogerian argument in this chapter and in the Exercises and Activities at the end of this chapter will demonstrate how various people achieve common ground through restatement and validation of their opponents' positions in Rogerian argument.

---

[1] Molly Ivins, "In Politics, It Does Help to Be Smart," *Fort Worth Star-Telegram*, October 28, 1999, p. 9B.
[2] I am indebted to Jenny Edbauer for this example.

You may find Rogerian argument frustrating at first, especially if you favor contention and agonistic debate in situations where your ideas and values seem to be under threat. Because Rogerian argument emphasizes making connections with the opposition and reducing hostility in such situations, you will need to curb your instincts to launch your argument by letting the opposition know how wrong you think they are. You can learn to use Rogerian argument, even if it is not your preferred or most natural style of arguing, in situations where traditional argument is no longer effective. It is a useful strategy when other strategies are failing. Let us look at a couple of examples.

ACHIEVING COMMON GROUND IN ROGERIAN ARGUMENT

"Where Are Men and Women Today?" was the title of a public performance staged in New York City by Deborah Tannen, author of *You Just Don't Understand*, linguistics professor, and expert in male-female communication, and Robert Bly, author of *Iron John: A Book about Men*. The press publicized this exchange as a "face-to-face, word-to-word confrontation." An all-out "battle of the sexes" was predicted. The sellout audience consisted of one thousand people, half men and half women.

The expectations of open conflict between the presenters were not realized, however. Instead, Bly and Tannen began the program by showing first what they agreed on. To establish a harmonious context for their exchange, Tannen began by reading a poem by Emily Dickenson, and while she read, Bly played a stringed instrument. Then Bly showed his appreciation of Tannen by reading aloud from her book. Tannen in turn showed her appreciation of Bly by reading aloud from his book. Then the dialogue began with Bly saying:

> The first time I came in contact with your book, my wife and I were having dinner up in northern Minnesota, and someone started to read out of it. We both fell off our chairs laughing, because it illuminated every mistake we had made, including every misunderstanding. . . .

He continued by explaining how Tannen's book had helped him and his wife gain insight and communicate better. Bly explained how he had learned from Tannen to build rapport with his wife. He had learned to use a style that Tannen identified as a "woman's style."

Tannen then replied:

> There's another side to this. You're assuming that it's good for men to learn to talk this way. And I always stop short of saying that because it's very important for me as a woman to say that men's styles are okay too.[3]

These two individuals, meeting for the first time at this special program, were determined not to fulfill the predictions of the press by providing a traditional

---

[3]Robert Bly and Deborah Tannen, "Where Are Men and Women Today?" transcript printed in *New Age Journal*, January–February 1992, pp. 28–33, 92–97.

war-between-the-sexes debate complete with the audience functioning as judge and trying to declare winners. Instead, they resorted to Rogerian argument, a special strategy that can be used at any time in argument to cool emotions, reduce conflict, and create sympathetic understanding. In their case, their strategy involved demonstrating at the outset that they both understood and valued one another's ideas by reading from one another's books and then commenting on how they had valued them.

Let us look at another real-life example of building common ground between disagreeing parties with each side demonstrating an understanding of the other's point of view. Environmentalists, who typically want to protect the environment at all costs, often find themselves in opposition to individuals who make their living by exploiting the environment. Loggers, ranchers, mill owners, and other industrialists, for example, can fall into this second category. Individuals from both groups, stereotyped as "nature haters" and "eco-freaks" by the press, met in Idaho to discuss efforts for protecting endangered wildlife in the area. The environmentalists went to the meeting with some trepidation, but "as they joked and sparred over steak and beer, they discovered that neither side lived up to its stereotype. 'We found that we didn't hate each other,' said Alex Irby, a manager at the Konkolville sawmill. 'Turns out, we all like to do a lot of the same things. We love the outdoors'." "Loggers in the back country sitting down with environmentalists is an astonishing change," reports Timothy Egan, who wrote about the details of the meeting.[4] One can infer that the common ground established in this meeting was brought about by each side's describing the value it placed on the environment and on outdoor activity in general. In such an exchange, both parties perceived that they had been heard, and further dialogue was then possible.

As you can see, understanding the rhetorical situation in general and the audience in particular by analyzing what the people involved think and value is of critical importance in Rogerian argument. In the two examples just cited, Tannen and Bly studied ahead of time and then demonstrated to the audience their understanding of each other's positions. The environmentalists, loggers, and mill workers discovered in conversation their shared values concerning the environment. In Chapter 10 you will learn how to analyze an audience yourself when you plan your researched position paper. As you read the rest of this chapter, including the examples of Rogerian argument, pay particular attention to how Rogerian arguers analyze their audiences' dissenting opinions and values and then respond to those as part of their overall strategy.

ROGERIAN ARGUMENT AS STRATEGY

Carl Rogers was a psychotherapist who was well known for the empathetic listening techniques he used in psychological counseling. He later became interested in how these same techniques could be used to improve communication in

---

[4]Timothy Egan, "Look Who's Hugging Trees Now," *New York Times Magazine*, July 7, 1996, p. 28.

other difficult, emotionally charged situations. Richard Young and his colleagues Alton Becker and Kenneth Pike built on Rogers's ideas to formulate Rogerian argument, a method for helping people in difficult situations make connections, create common ground, and understand one another. The object was to avoid undue conflict or, even worse, a mutual standoff.[5]

According to Young, Becker, and Pike, written Rogerian argument reduces the reader's sense of threat and conflict with the writer so that alternatives can be considered. Three things are accomplished by this strategy.

1. *Writers let readers know they have been understood.* To accomplish this purpose, the writer restates the opponent's position in summary form by using dispassionate, neutral language. The writer demonstrates that the reader has been heard and that the writer understands the issue exactly as the reader does. Thus Tannen and Bly begin their special presentation by reading from one another's works to demonstrate that they are hearing one another.

2. *Writers show how readers' positions are valid in certain contexts and under certain conditions.* The writer demonstrates to the reader that at least part of the reader's position is acceptable and thereby makes it easier for the reader to reciprocate and accept part of the writer's position. Notice how Bly says at the outset that Tannen's observations are valid and can be applied to conversations he has actually had with his wife. Tannen then points out that males' preferences in communicating are also OK. Thus they validate one another's positions.

3. *Writers get readers to believe that both of them share the same values, types of experience, attitudes, and perceptions and are thus similar in significant ways.* Tannen and Bly accomplish this end by borrowing one another's theories and applying them to their own personal experiences. They make it clear that they both share the same values and types of experience.

The most important feature of Rogerian argument is listening empathetically and nonjudgmentally. Rogers says that people usually listen judgmentally and evaluatively. They are eager to jump in, point out what is right or wrong, and make corrections or refutations. Rogerian listening puts the writer in the reader's place by requiring the writer to provide neutral summaries of the reader's position that show sympathetic understanding. Thus the writer encourages a continued and open exchange of ideas with the reader. In Rogers's words, the writer "listens with" as opposed to "evaluating about."

Beyond empathetic understanding, writers should also show congruence, or genuine agreement, and an unconditional positive regard for the opposition. In communicating these attitudes, Rogerian argument takes the heat of difficult argument that might otherwise result in a stalemate. Rogerian strategy cools the emotions and makes consensus more likely. The aim of the final reconciliation at the close of Rogerian argument attempts to show that the best solution to the issue may be a combination of what both parties want.

In real life, Rogerian argument is used frequently, particularly in business and politics, where agreement is indispensable. Some people in business claim they

---

[5]Richard Young, Alton Becker, and Kenneth Pike, *Rhetoric: Discovery and Change* (New York: Harcourt, Brace, and World, 1970), pp. 7–8, 274–290.

could not get anything done if they did not use Rogerian strategies on a daily basis. William L. Ury, one of the founders of the Program on Negotiation at Harvard Law School, claims that in business now, the best way to compete is to be able to cooperate. Cooperation is necessary because of the numerous mergers and cooperative ventures between companies. Many companies now work with the same markets and the same customers, and they cannot compete, as in former times, without weakening themselves as much as their competitors.[6] Some politicians have also resorted to Rogerian strategies to resolve difficult issues like health care and Social Security. Allowing tentative solutions to problems like these to split along party lines and stay that way is not always productive. Reaching across the lines to harness the best ideas from both political parties can be much more productive and usually leads to better solutions.

Box 9.1 contrasts Rogerian argument, as explained by Young, Becker, and Pike, with the traditional pro-and-con model of argument associated with debate.

In Chapter 5 you learned about the Toulmin model for argument. The Toulmin model and Rogerian argument have one extremely important feature in common. Even though the Toulmin model includes rebuttal, it also provides for the creation of common ground in the shared warrants between arguer and audience. Rogerian argument provides for common ground as well, but this is accomplished through the shared values and assumptions established through the summary and restatement of the opponent's position.

WRITING ROGERIAN ARGUMENT

To write Rogerian argument, according to Young, Becker, and Pike, the writer proceeds in phases rather than following set organizational patterns or argumentative strategies. These phases are as follows:

1. The writer introduces the issue and shows that the opponent's position is understood by restating it.
2. The writer shows in which contexts and under what conditions the opponent's position may be valid. Note that the opponent is never made to feel completely wrong.
3. The writer then states his or her own position, including the contexts in which it is valid.
4. The writer states how the opponent's position would benefit if the opponent were to adopt elements of the writer's position. An attempt is finally made to show that the two positions complement each other and that each supplies what the other lacks.

---

[6]William L. Ury, "Getting Past No . . . to Yes! The Art of Negotiation." Workshop, Dallas, October 12, 1999.

| BOX 9.1 | Traditional and Rogerian Argument Compared. | |

WHAT IS ROGERIAN ARGUMENT?

	TRADITIONAL ARGUMENT	ROGERIAN ARGUMENT
Basic strategy	Writer states the claim and gives reasons to prove it. Writer refutes the opponent by showing what is wrong or invalid.	Writer states the opponent's claim to demonstrate understanding and shows how it is valid.
Ethos	Writer establishes own character by demonstrating competence, fair-mindedness, and goodwill.	Writer builds opponent's and enhances own character through empathy.
Logos	Writer appeals to reason to establish a claim and refute the opponent's claim.	Writer proceeds in an explanatory fashion to analyze the conditions under which the position of either side is valid.
Pathos	Writer arouses emotions with evocative language to strengthen the claim.	Writer uses descriptive, dispassionate language to cool emotions on both sides.
Goal	Writer seeks to change opponent's mind and thereby win the argument.	Writer creates cooperation, the possibility that both sides might change, and a mutually advantageous outcome.
Use of argumentative techniques	Writer draws on the conventional structures and techniques taught in Chapters 5–8 of this book.	Writer throws out conventional structures and techniques because they may be threatening and focuses instead on connecting empathetically.

VARIATIONS OF ROGERIAN ARGUMENT

Rogerian argument as described by Young, Becker, and Pike is rarely if ever written exactly according to their format. You can learn more about Rogerian argument by practicing according to their format, however, and the Exercises and

Activities section of this chapter provides four examples of Rogerian argument papers written by students who followed this format. You also will be invited to write a Rogerian argument paper by using this format.

As you read professionally written argument, however, you are much more likely to find elements or variations of Rogerian argument rather than arguments that include all of the parts of the Young, Becker, and Pike model. Here are some variations of Rogerian argument that you may encounter in your academic reading.

1. *Report on past research at the beginning of an academic argument.* Authors of academic argument, as a matter of convention, often begin with a review of what previous writers have contributed to the subject. They identify the writers by name and summarize their contributions before identifying and developing their own contribution to the subject. Thus an ongoing chain of conversation is established that acknowledges what has gone before the new material that is the actual subject of the article.

2. *Research proposal.* Research proposals that request funds and resources from granting agencies typically begin with a positive summary of the contributions of past researchers. Only after this former work has been acknowledged does the researcher explain how the new proposed research will build on what has gone before.[7]

3. *Rogerian response paper.* This paper is written in response to an essay written by another person with whom the author disagrees. The author of a response paper typically rejects the position that the author of the other essay presents but hopes to create common ground and understanding with that person to keep a dialogue on the issue going. The goal is to make a connection with the author of the other essay and thus create a context of understanding so that both authors can continue exploring the issue. Such papers usually begin with a restatement of the other author's position along with an acknowledgment of what is valuable about that position before the author goes on to present a different view of the matter. You will be invited to try writing a Rogerian response paper yourself in Exercise C.

As you read arguments written by other authors, look for elements of Rogerian argument. The three examples just cited by no means exhaust the possibilities.

THE ADVANTAGES AND DISADVANTAGES OF ROGERIAN ARGUMENT

The advantages of Rogerian argument are clear. Such an approach helps release tension and disagreement and encourages negotiation and cooperation when values and aims are in conflict. Also, Rogerian argument has the potential of leveling

---

[7] I am indebted to Mary Stanley for alerting me to this use of Rogerian argument.

or at least controlling uneven power relationships that may interfere with the peaceful resolution of conflicting issues.

There are also perceived disadvantages of Rogerian argument. It is sometimes difficult for the writer to understand and restate the reader's position, particularly when the opponent is not present and no written material is available to explain the opposing position. Also, connecting with the opponent by restating the opposing position may be extremely difficult if the writer is emotionally involved and strongly dislikes the opposing ideas. It takes courage, Rogers says, to listen to and restate ideas that are strongly antithetical to your own. You have to want to make connections to succeed. You also have to be willing to risk change. After totally committing yourself to understanding a different viewpoint, your own ideas will almost inevitably shift and change somewhat.[8]

Rogerian argument has also been criticized as annoying to women. Some researchers claim that women have always been expected to understand others, sometimes even at the expense of understanding themselves. As one female critic puts it, Rogerian argument "feels too much like giving in."[9] Another critic finds the advice that the writer should always use unemotional, dispassionate language to restate the opponent's argument unrealistic and constraining. Avoiding rude or insulting language is necessary, a matter of common sense. But to avoid all emotionally connotative language may be impossible.[10]

Rogerian argument persists as a viable model in spite of some of its shortcomings. Its central notion, that it is important to understand and see some validity in other people's opposing positions, is sometimes the only way to create common ground in difficult situations.

REVIEW QUESTIONS

1. What are some of the special characteristics of Rogerian argument, and how does it differ from traditional argument?
2. In what types of argumentative situations do you think you might find Rogerian argument more productive than traditional argument? Give examples of at least two issues for which you might profitably resort to Rogerian argument.
3. What are some of the advantages and some of the disadvantages of Rogerian argument?
4. What difficulties, if any, do you contemplate in using Rogerian argument?

---

[8]I am indebted to Paul Parmeley for this insight.

[9]See Catherine Lamb, "Beyond Argument in Feminist Composition," *College Composition and Communication*, February 1991, pp. 11–24. See also Phyllis Lassner, "Feminist Response to Rogerian Rhetoric," *Rhetoric Review* 8 (1990): 220–232.

[10]Doug Brent, "Young, Becker, and Pike's 'Rogerian' Rhetoric: A Twenty-Year Reassessment," *College English* 53 (April 1991): 446–452.

EXERCISES AND ACTIVITIES

A. CLASS DISCUSSION: UNDERSTANDING ROGERIAN ARGUMENT AS A STRATEGY

The advertisement on the next page describes an effort to reduce hostility between environmentalists and an oil company. Analyze the Rogerian strategy in this selection, and answer the following questions.

1. Why do these parties feel hostile? What are their differences?
2. Which party is the author of this ad? What interest does this party have in resolving the issue? How do both parties reduce hostility and create common ground? What common ground do they share?
3. How is Rogerian strategy employed? Summarize the major parts of the argument, and show how they conform to Rogerian strategy.
4. How effective do you think Rogerian argument will be in resolving the issues between these two parties?

B. WRITING ASSIGNMENT: ROGERIAN ARGUMENT

You are now going to write a Rogerian argument of around 1,000 words on an issue of your choice. There are several ways to set up this assignment. Read through the following options, select one that appeals to you, and proceed with the rest of the instructions for the assignment. The basic instructions in option 1 apply to all four options. Examples for options 1, 2, and 3 are provided at the end of this exercise.

1. If you wrote an exploratory paper or a position paper, write a Rogerian argument in response to the position you discovered that is most unlike the position you defended. You may have already articulated this opposing position in your exploratory paper or in a rebuttal in your position paper. Move this position to the beginning of your Rogerian argument paper, and rewrite it until you believe you have fairly and dispassionately represented that other point of view. People who hold that view need to be able to agree that you have heard and understood them. Look for common ground with that other view. Use that common ground to describe contexts and conditions in which the opponent's position might be valid. Do not show what is wrong with this other position. Now write a transition that changes the subject to your position. Describe your position, and show the contexts in which is it valid. Finally, reconcile the two positions. Show how they can complement each other, how one supplies what the other lacks, and how everyone would benefit if elements of both were finally accepted. (See Example 1.)

2. Select any issue that you understand from at least two opposing points of view. It should be an issue that you feel strongly about, and you should also have strong negative feelings about the opposing viewpoint. Write a Rogerian argument in response to the opposing viewpoint. (See Example 2.)

<u>*Crossing the Environmental Divide; 1*</u>

When special care is called for

It can happen. An environmental organization and an oil company can overcome their traditional wariness and work together in an ecologically sensitive area. Here's a story of how progress can be made when people realize they share a common goal.

Scientists often compare the interdependence of life on earth with finely woven silk. Each species is a thread, and together we form a delicate fabric. Human development has, of course, altered the fabric, so there are few places left where native plants and animals are relatively untouched.

The Washington, D.C.-based environmental organization Conservation International (CI) is a leader in the effort to protect biodiversity "hotspots," regions rich in species that could be greatly affected by additional colonization, agriculture or industrialization. CI has compiled a list of 25 global hotspots that represent less than two percent of the planet's land surface but encompass more than half of the world's species. It has had much success with conservation efforts in these hotspots.

At the top of CI's list is the tropical Andes region, a narrow strip following the South American mountain range through Colombia, Ecuador, Peru and Bolivia. Within this region, which harbors over 20,000 plant species found nowhere else, lies the Tambopata River Valley. In an area as sensitive as Peru's Tambopata rain forest, even advances in farming can alter nature's fabric. Mining and oil exploration, if not properly carried out, can create tears that are difficult, if not impossible, to repair. CI has worked since 1990 with governments and local peoples to conserve and protect Tambopata's biodiversity.

So, when Mobil signed a contract in 1996 for petroleum exploration in part of the valley, CI's reaction was one of alarm. "Frankly, we didn't want to see oil development in Tambopata, but once the government granted the rights to exploration, we realized that we needed to view Mobil as another stakeholder," says Jorgen Thomsen, Vice President of CI's Conservation Biology Department. "We initiated a dialogue with the company."

Mobil was also concerned, because the company is committed to conducting exploration activities in an environmentally and socially responsible manner. We recognized that we needed to work openly and cooperatively with CI and other groups to achieve minimal environmental and social impact.

In the first phase of exploration, Mobil would obtain seismic data by setting off small energy charges and recording the resulting sound waves. We filed environmental plans with the Peruvian government showing that we would carve only yard-wide footpaths and small helicopter pads in the rain forest—best practices that are common for Mobil's seismic work. Before that work started, however, Mobil and CI held a five-day joint workshop to assess how they might work together. The participants learned a lot from each other. Perhaps the most valuable lesson was defining a common ground of shared interest.

What ultimately emerged was a unique collaborative effort that could lead to a demonstration of the coexistence of petroleum exploration and production with conservation efforts in sensitive ecosystems.

So far, we've taken just the first steps, but what we've accomplished is encouraging. In the next message, we'll discuss where the collaboration has taken both parties.

Mobil The energy to make a difference.

SOURCE: Courtesy of Exxon Mobil Corporation.

3. Recall the last time you were in an argument in which you were angry and no one seemed to win. Write a letter to the individual you were arguing with. Use Rogerian strategy. (See Example 3.)

4. Team up with a classmate who disagrees with you on an issue. Take turns, articulating your partner's position until that person feels "heard" and understood. Then write a Rogerian argument in response to that position.

PREWRITING

To help you prepare to write this paper, in addition to the instructions provided, write a one-paragraph summary of the opposing position and a one-paragraph summary of your position. Refer to these summaries when you write your paper.

WRITING

Write your paper, making sure you do all of the following:

1. Introduce the issue, and restate the opposing position to show you understand it.

2. Show in which contexts and under what conditions the opposing position may be valid. State it so that it is acceptable to the opposition.

3. Write a clear transition that moves the reader from the position you have just explained to the position that you favor and will now defend.

4. State your own position, and describe the context in which it is valid.

5. Show how the opposing position would be strengthened if it added elements of your position, and try to reconcile the two positions.

EXAMPLES

Here are three examples of Rogerian argument written by students.

Example 1 (Writing Assignment 1) "Human Cloning: Is It a Viable Option?" was written by a student in an argument class who had also written an exploratory paper and a position paper on this subject. This student conducted research for this paper. Her annotated bibliography appears on pages 338–343. (More information on writing research papers appears in Chapters 10–12.) In writing this paper, she began with the position she had discovered that was most unlike her own and rewrote it until she thought it would satisfy the individuals who hold this position. Notice that she was able to use the research for her other papers to add support for this paper as well. The marginal annotations make it easier for you to distinguish the parts of her paper. Following her paper is a Rogerian argument evaluation sheet that has been filled out to show how this argument conforms to the recommended parts of the Rogerian argument. The requirements for the Rogerian argument paper are described in the left column, and the right column shows how well this paper met those requirements. When you have finished reading the papers in Examples 2 and 3, see if you can identify and describe the parts of those papers well enough to complete evaluation sheets like the sample. This analysis will help you understand how to write your own Rogerian argument.*

---

*For all the student papers in Chapter 9, see the Appendix to Chapter 12 for the actual MLA format guidelines.

Angela A. Boatwright
Rogerian Argument
Professor Thorne
English 1302
3 October 2003

Human Cloning: Is It a Viable Option?

1

Introduction to issue
and summary of
rhetorical situation

Well, hello Dolly! Although research in animal or human cloning is not new, the technology has never had as much potential as it does today. Interest in what is and is not considered ethical in cloning research has surfaced since the historic announcement in Scotland of the existence of a cloned sheep named Dolly. Scientists were able to create a cloned sheep by taking the genes from a six-year-old sheep and putting them into an enucleated egg from another sheep. This egg was then implanted in the womb of yet another sheep, resulting in the birth of an identical twin that is six years younger than its sister (Bailey). This is the first known asexual reproduction of a mammal. It seems a reasonable assumption that a human clone is the next logical step down this technological pathway.

2

Explanation of
opposing position
to create common
ground

Those who support unregulated human cloning experimentation justify their position by citing the medical gains and potential benefits the technology has to offer. These people believe that the possible benefits of this technology far outweigh the risks and, furthermore, that it is an ethical practice because of its potential benefits. Some of these benefits include the generation of skin grafts for burn victims and bone marrow for patients undergoing cancer chemotherapy (Butler and Wadman 8). Cloning also shows promise for treating infertility and could become an option either for infertile couples or for people who have genetic defects and fear passing these defects on to their offspring.

3

Supporters of cloning believe that the arguments against cloning are vague and speculative and that they simply do not justify a ban. It is not the technology that frightens people so much as it is a lack of understanding. When people picture the result of an attempt at human cloning, they see images of Frankenstein or an army of Hitlers. Researchers believe that given time to digest the information, the public will one day regard cloning with the same openness and sense of normalcy that it now regards blood transfusions and organ transplants. They also reason that a ban on cloning could drive the technology underground, leading to a greater potential for unsafe, unregulated, and exploitative misuse.

4

Description of
context in which
opposing position
is valid

Everyone would probably agree that technological advances have changed our lives in positive ways, and cloning research is not likely to be an exception. The fear held by cloning supporters, that the sensationalism created by this issue has clouded the judgment of the public and lawmakers who support a ban on cloning, is certainly a valid concern. Although it is not clear that human cloning will offer any great benefits to humanity, no one has yet made a persuasive case that it would do any real harm either (Macklin 64). It would be an injustice to completely abandon the possibilities that could enhance the lives of so many people based solely on hypothetical applications of a technology that may never be realized. Each disease we are able to eradicate is another huge step for humankind.

Transition to author's view

Explanation of author's view

5   I agree that we should do everything in our power to improve the longevity and quality of life of all people, but I do not believe it should be at the expense of the dignity of human life. Many people who oppose cloning view it as an "invasion of personality." Even Dr. Ian Wilmut and his colleagues, the creators of Dolly, hold the position that cloning of humans would be unethical (64). He points out that it took 277 attempts to produce one live lamb. Of the 277 "reconstructed" embryos, 29 were implanted into recipient ewes, and 3 out of 5 lambs showed developmental abnormalities and died soon after birth. He believes similar tests with humans would not be acceptable.

6   Those of us who advocate anticloning measures believe that the potential abuse of such power could have disastrous consequences. The fear of the creation of human clones for the sole purpose of harvesting them for "spare parts" is too great to ignore. Another concern is that cloning will lead to efforts to breed individuals with perceived exceptional genetic qualities, eliminating the diversity that makes the human race what it is. There is a widespread belief that parents might create unrealistic expectations for cloned children, believing they no longer have the potential limitations of their genetic ancestors (Pence 135). Cloning is really a major step toward regarding our children as acceptable only if they conform to the choices of our will (Carey).

7   Many of us are also bound by the religious ideas we have been brought up with, telling us that only God has the right to create life. It is sinful to think of removing that sovereign right from an omnipotent God and placing it in the hands of mere mortals. Like the majority of Americans, I believe that human cloning experimentation should be banned before it can become an out-of-control reality.

Personal example to introduce idea of reconciliation of the two opposing positions

8   I am fortunate to be the mother of a wonderful and beautiful baby girl. If I had been given the opportunity to choose her characteristics, would I have elected to change my child? I absolutely would not. I would not trade any of her personal traits for something "better." I love her just as God gave her to me. Yet with absolute certainty, I can admit that if she developed a life-threatening ailment, I would not hesitate for a second to utilize any cloning technology available to cure her. This is not to say I

would sacrifice another life for hers, only that I would employ any and all resources available short of that alternative.

9

Reconciliation of positions

If we can agree that human life should always be held in the highest esteem, we have the basis for reconciling our positions. Cloning should not be used to pick and choose the type of people who are allowed to exist, but we should explore the potential medical benefits of cloning technology research. Many of the medical procedures we take for granted every day were once as controversial as cloning is at this very moment. Most of these procedures became successful at the cost of testing on live beings, but with their consent. We must never allow human beings to be the subjects of experimentation without their knowledge or permission. We may not impose conditions on human beings that they might not have consented to if allowed to make the decision for themselves.

10

A moratorium might be a better solution than an outright ban. A moratorium would authorize a temporary delay of human cloning research and allow us the time to sort out the details and ensure that an educated decision is made. It is easier to make an intelligent decision when there is not a feeling of impending doom hanging over our heads. "In a democratic society we don't usually pass laws outlawing something before there is actual or probable evidence of harm" (Macklin 64). This statement can serve as a guide for future policy on human cloning.

Works Cited

Bailey, Ronald. "The Twin Paradox: What Exactly Is Wrong with Cloning People?" Reasononline. 5 Sept. 1998. 13 Sept. 2003 <http://www.reason.com/9705/col.bailey.html>.

Butler, Declan, and Meredith Wadman. "Calls for Cloning Ban Sell Science Short." Nature 6 Mar. 1997: 8-9.

Carey, John. "Human Clones: It's Decision Time." Business Week 10 Aug. 1998: 32.

Macklin, Ruth. "Human Cloning? Don't Just Say No." US News and World Report 10 Mar. 1997: 64+.

Pence, Gregory E. Who's Afraid of Human Cloning? Lanham: Rowman, 1998.

Wilmut, Ian. "Roslin Institute Experiments: Creation of Dolly the Sheep." Congressional Digest Feb. 1998: 41+.

FOR DISCUSSION: Describe a rhetorical situation in which it would be better to write this paper in this form, using Rogerian strategy, than it would be to write it as a position paper, using traditional strategy. Describe the readers, constraints, and exigencies in particular as you imagine the rhetorical situation for this paper.

◆◆◆

EVALUATION SHEET FOR ROGERIAN ARGUMENT PAPER ➤

REQUIREMENTS OF ROGERIAN ARGUMENT	WHAT THE AUTHOR DID
1. Introduce the issue and state the opposing position to show you understand it.	1. Introduced the issue in paragraph 1 and presented the opposing view accompanied by good reasons in paragraphs 2 and 3.
2. Show how the opposition might be right.	2. Showed the contexts in which the opposition might be valid in paragraph 4.
3. Write a clear transition from the opposing position to your position.	3. Wrote a transition in the first sentence of paragraph 5 to move from opposing to own position.
4. Give your position and show how you might be right.	4. Presented own position in paragraphs 5, 6, and 7.
5. Reconcile the two positions.	5. Reconciled the two views in paragraphs 8, 9, and 10.

Example 2 (Writing Assignment 2) "Special Education's Best Intentions" was written by a student who had returned to school after several years and whose handicapped child required special education. The issue of how handicapped children are educated in the public schools was, understandably, a particularly compelling issue for her. She had often been frustrated by school officials who seemed more interested in procedures than in her child. Even though she felt hostility for some of these individuals, she still managed to state their point of view in a way that should be acceptable to them before she introduced her own. When she finished writing this paper, she commented that she usually feels powerless when talking with school officials. The approach taken here, she thought, would probably achieve better results than a confrontational argument that accused her audience of wrongdoing and neglect.

Lois Agnew
Rogerian Argument
Professor Dickerman
English 1302
13 October 2003

Special Education's Best Intentions

1   The American public's growing recognition of the educational rights of handicapped children culminated in the 1975 enactment of the Education for All Handicapped Children Act, Public Law 94-142. Once the need to provide quality education for all students was clearly established as a matter of public record,

it also became a need that would demand immediate action on the part of parents and educators; the issue at hand shifted from a question of whether it should be done to how it could be done.

2   It is natural in the midst of such change to turn to experts for guidance about how to face the challenges that lie ahead. In the years following the passage of PL 94-142, educators attempted to develop methods for identifying the needs of handicapped students in a way which would allow for the development of educational programs designed to serve their individual needs. As time went on, the methods for addressing students' goals became more carefully prescribed and were implemented primarily through the agency of designated professionals who were specially trained for dealing with such matters.

3   Of course, developing a system for helping students whose needs are out of the ordinary had been a necessary step in assimilating those students into the world of public education. Hurling handicapped students into a regular education classroom without careful assessment of their needs would unquestionably lead to frustration on all sides. The need to determine the level of each student's skills clearly indicates the need for some type of testing program and demands the presence of individuals trained to administer and interpret those tests. The entire process is obviously a crucial element in meeting the educational needs of handicapped children.

4   However, the challenge of efficiently offering help to massive numbers of students has inevitably resulted in the evolution of a bureaucratic network with all of the disadvantages inherent in such a system. State education agencies and local school districts alike have carefully allocated tremendous resources to carrying out the mandate of PL 94-142; the assurance they have provided anxious parents lies in their promise to find appropriate educational placement in the least restrictive environment possible for each child. The means for attempting such a mammoth task involves the use of a standard process of evaluation and diagnosis that will enable the experts assigned to the task to assess not only each child's present levels of performance educationally but also ultimately to make judgments about the child's potential for classroom performance in the future.

5   It is in this respect that the bureaucratic nature of the individual education program falters in meeting the needs of the individual child. As necessary as such a system may be to guarantee the efficient handling of large volumes of work, it becomes difficult in practice to maintain a focus on evaluation as the necessary means to the worthwhile end of providing children with new educational opportunities; too often it becomes an end in itself, a source of a convenient label that in turn is used to predict where a child's limits will lie. It is a tragedy of our educational system that in spite of the good intentions that have led us to emphasize test results and diagnosis for children with special needs, the machinelike efficiency of our program has achieved most of its goals without acknowledging what is most important, addressing the needs of students as individuals. The idea of trained diagnosticians administering objective tests to students to determine their educational placement must be

appealing to a society that values scientific method to the degree ours does; however, few real live children fall neatly into the categories that represent the conclusion of the process. Once their futures have been charted by the system, it becomes increasingly difficult for them to prove that they have potential beyond that predicted by the experts.

6   I am the parent of such a child and have on many occasions experienced the frustration of watching well-meaning educators become so absorbed with finding an appropriate label for my son that they have apparently lost sight of the goal of educating him. Although I share the interest they have in finding an appropriate educational placement for him, I have in the meantime grown weary of the process. I have seen my child through the ordeal of psychological, neurological, language, and educational evaluations, all conducted by authorities in their fields with an impressive assortment of credentials, and can state with certainty that the ability to help him is unrelated to the specialized training the system values most. Those who have made a significant difference in my son's life have been those rare people who have encountered him as an individual and have devoted their energies to bringing out his potential without reservation and have been willing in the process to stop worrying about how he should be labeled. My contact with other parents of children with special needs tells me that my reaction to the process is quite common.

7   There is no question about the fact that the special education bureaucracy serves a useful purpose in helping students find the classrooms and programs most suited to their needs. At the same time, it often appears to be a tendency for any bureaucratic system to become so absorbed with its own structure, so convinced of the infallibility of the experts it employs, that it fails to devote adequate attention to each person it attempts to serve. Because special education involves so many thousands of unique students, it seems almost impossible to find a balance between the efficiency that benefits everyone and the personal attention that is a crucial part of the process. Yet with children's lives at stake, it is critical that we never give up the effort to do so.

FOR DISCUSSION: Provide some examples from your own experiences in school when you were treated as a member of the group and when you were treated as an individual. What are some measures that administrators and teachers could take to provide more individual attention for students?

◆◆◆

Example 3 (Writing Assignment 3) "Dear Mom" was written by a student whose parents wanted her to move out of her apartment and either come home, find a cheaper apartment, or move back into the dormitories. This student wrote her Rogerian argument as a letter addressed to her mother. She began by stating her mother's view and even read this part to her mother to make certain she was stating it accurately. She then acknowledged the advantages of her mother's view but went on to show why her own views were also advantageous and valid. At the end, she reconciles her parents' views with her own and shows how her position benefits both of them. She finally gave this letter to both of her parents to read. The result was that her parents agreed to allow her to stay in her apartment.

Taryn Barnett
Rogerian Argument
Professor Berthiaume
English 1302
23 October 2003

Dear Mom

Dear Mom,

1   I wanted to write you a letter regarding the conversation we had yesterday. You said that you wanted me to do one of three things: move home, transfer to a cheaper complex, or move into the dorms. I understand that you believe these options would allow me to work less and save more money in order to concentrate on my studies. You think that this would be financially simpler for you and for me and much less stressful for me.

2   I understand the logic behind your position in that the whole financial situation would be easier if I were living at home. First of all, we would not have as many expenses. Living at home would eliminate rent payments, cable bills, and electricity bills, but it would not eliminate phone bills, insurance bills, gas bills, or personal items. This would allow me to take some of the money that I am earning now and save it to give myself a strong financial foundation as I become more independent in the future. If I did not have a job and were under a lot of stress, I could see how it would make sense to move back home. If safety were not an issue, I could see how it would save me money to move to a cheaper apartment complex. Also, moving into a cheaper apartment complex could eliminate the worries and the need for a roommate. For example, I have a roommate now, and I have to worry about whether or not she will pay her share of the bills on time or whether I will have to cover for her until she has the money. Now, if I were going away to school, I could see the advantages of living in the dorms. This would include not having to worry about the bills, meeting more people from school, and entering all of the social aspects of living on campus. It is also safer to live in a well-monitored environment. I see the ways your points are valid, so let us discuss those points and work together to find a good solution for both of us.

3   I believe that staying in school while working part-time in order to live in this complex is showing responsibility on my part. A big part of this for me is pride. I want to be able to prove to you and Dad that I can do it on my own with as minimal help from you as possible. Not only is having this independence important to me, but it also helps me learn about life through experience. To me, independence is learning to handle being responsible for myself and my actions, in which I figure out how to decide what to do, when to do it, and when

to buckle down. Taking things into my hands and making sure everything that needs to get done does get done is a responsibility that I have learned how to prioritize. Now, in having this independence and showing my responsibility by keeping up with paying the bills on time (cable, phone, rent, and electricity) and getting my schoolwork done for all four of my classes (Music Appreciation, Political Science, Psychology, and English), I am building up my credit and learning self-discipline. By self-discipline I mean teaching myself what is important to me and making sure I keep up with the work and reading in my classes. I pay $430 per month for rent in my apartment complex, and in comparison to some that are $395 per month all bills paid, I may not be in a cheap complex, but I am in a safe complex. When a young woman lives alone, that is essential. It is a well-known fact that the cheaper the area of the apartment complex, the more prevalent is crime.

4   Since I am a full-time student and I get financial assistance from you and Dad, I can work part-time and afford my apartment. If I were to move back home, I would not get the financial support from you and Dad. So I would still have to work the same number of hours in order to have any money because the only thing I would not have to worry about financially would be rent. Although this offers less financial stress for you, it increases personal and operational stress between us. So if we can keep our minds open, we can see how our points complement each other.

5   Our points of view are very similar because any way you go, I am saving the same amount of money. With your plan I have less income with less bills and work part-time to get by. With my plan I work the same number of hours and I get financial help from you and Dad to help pay for the living expenses, but I have more expenses. So you can see that either way I go to school, work, and save the same amount of money. Only if I stay in my apartment complex, I have all of the benefits, and I learn how to live independently. You also say you worry about my stress levels. It is true that living in an apartment is sometimes stressful. But it would be more stressful for both of us if I took the easy way and moved home. I would no longer be learning independence. To reassure you, I can call and visit you more often, and I can report on the progress I am making in my classes. I think, however, that both of our needs will best be met if I stay in my apartment, learn to manage my time to keep up with school and work, learn to manage my money and pay the bills, and learn to live independently. Both of us share that final goal for me. So unless I prove myself to be irresponsible, please do not ask me to give up my independence and move home.

Love,
Taryn

For Discussion: The student who wrote this letter was at a standoff with her parents on this issue. Why do you think the Rogerian approach helped her change her parents' minds? Describe what is effective in this letter. Could you write a Rogerian letter on a personal matter? What topics would you consider appropriate for a letter that employs this particular argument strategy?

◆◆◆

C. WRITING ASIGNMENT: THE ROGERIAN RESPONSE PAPER

A Rogerian response paper is somewhat different from the examples of Rogerian argument presented in Exercise B in that it is written in direct response to a particular essay. The process involves reading and understanding an essay with which you disagree and responding to it using Rogerian strategy.[11] Here are some possible articles to respond to.

1. Write a response to one of these articles. You will surely find yourself in disagreement with one of them: "Pay Your Own Way! (Then Thank Mom)" (pages 22–24), "What's Happened to Disney Films?" (pages 148–149), "The Future Is Ours to Lose" (pages 222–225), "The Latest from the Feminist 'Front'" (pages 238–240), "A Modest Proposal" (pages 430–436).
2. Find a letter to the editor in your local or school newspaper that you disagree with, and write a Rogerian response to it.

Your paper should be 500 to 750 words long.

PREWRITING

Write a brief summary of the opposing position and a brief summary of your position to make certain you understand them both clearly.

WRITING

Do all of the following in your paper.

1. State the opposition's position as presented in the article, and describe in what instances this position might work or be acceptable. As you write, imagine that the author of the article will be reading your response. Write so that that person will feel "heard."
2. Write a clear transition to your position on the issue.
3. State how your position would also work or be acceptable.
4. Try to reconcile the two positions.

The following Rogerian response paper was written by Jeff Burkholder, a student in an argument class, in response to an essay by Nate Stulman (pages 267–268). Stulman was a sophomore at Swarthmore College when he wrote "The Great Campus Goof-Off Machine." Read Stulman's essay either before or after Burkholder's. You may find that you have an entirely different perspective on computer use at college, in which case you may want to write a response to one of these essays yourself.

---

[11]I am indebted to Barbara Chiarello for the general concept of this assignment.

Jeff Burkholder
Rogerian Response
Professor Wood
English 1302
3 November 2003

The Great Campus Goof-Off Machine? Not for All Students

1   Most students who go to college in the United States understand the importance of computers in their lives. Where would education be without computers? Nate Stulman, however, a student himself, takes a different position. He describes the negative aspects of computers and their use in college in his essay "The Great Campus Goof-Off Machine." He believes that students spend much more time on their computers surfing the Web for new downloads and playing new PC games like Quake, Diablo, and Starcraft than on actual schoolwork or research for their classes. Stulman says the use of chat and instant messages has even caused students on campus to talk to their friends online instead of walking down the hall or street to have a real conversation which would take half of the time. In fact, he claims to have friends who may spend six, eight, or even ten hours in front of their computers at night in these types of activities. When I come to think of it, I know a lot of people like that too, people who aimlessly search the Internet for some totally useless information or even for a new screen saver. Stulman thinks the colleges themselves have helped create the problem, and he wonders what can be done.

2   I have to agree with Nate Stulman because I also believe that the average student wastes time on computers, up to ten hours a day. Students may also use their computers to play games all day and only occasionally use them for basic word processing. That is what I did in my first year of college, living in the dorms at California State University, San Diego. I played on my PC an average of four hours a night, and I wrote only five papers on it, the only papers that I had due that semester. I was a new kid living in a new city. I had no job my first year and had no car. The dorm was my home, and my computer was one of the few choices for entertainment on weekday nights.

3   Now here is where Stulman and I are in disagreement. He observed only students living on campus or in residence halls, who are usually new students who have gone away to college, like I did. Many students who live on campus do not own a car or even have a job, so they are confined to a small dorm room with little else to do but surf the Web or play a cool game on their PC.

4   I believe that average college students make good use of their computer time as long as they live somewhere other than the dorms. Stulman was using a very small sample of people (first-year or new students living in the dorms and a few students in the library) to collect data on the computer use of the average college student throughout the day. Had he followed some older off-campus students who drive to school every day, he would have noticed a different trend. Living off campus and having a job mean that students have less time to waste on the computer playing useless games. The older students get, and the more college courses they pass, the more time they will spend

using their computers productively. Students will have less time to waste on the computer because they spend time working, studying for harder classes, driving everywhere they have to go (I drive almost four hundred miles a week), and keeping up with the additional responsibilities they take on after the first year. The amount of work on my computer that I presently do as a junior at the University of Texas at Arlington is amazing. I have written more than thirty papers this semester and have spent at least two hundred productive hours on my computer compared to about fifty to seventy useless hours. So yes, I do agree with Stulman that computers with Internet access in the dorms are not the best thing for new students as far as academics are concerned. But he also makes it clear that the computer can be a good tool for students if used correctly. I have experienced both productive and nonproductive computer time myself. I believe that the majority of college students, especially those students taking upper-division courses, make good use of their computers. In fact, we are the students who make good use of all of our time.

FOR DISCUSSION: Do you think that Nate Stulman would feel "heard" and understood if he read this essay? Do you think Stulman's views might change as a result of reading this essay? If this essay were published in a magazine or newspaper as an answer to Stulman's essay, what do you think the effect would be on the people who happened to read it? What would they think about Nate Stulman? What would they think about Jeff Burkholder? Which of these authors is more convincing to you? To answer that question, take a look at Stulman's essay, if you have not already done so.

◆◆◆

THE GREAT CAMPUS GOOF-OFF MACHINE*

Nate Stulman

The author, a student himself, takes a position in this essay on the use of computers by college students. This essay prompted Jeff Burkholder to write the Rogerian response paper on pages 266–267. If you were to write a Rogerian response to this essay, what would you write?

1   Conventional wisdom says that computers are a necessary tool for higher education. Many colleges and universities these days require students to have personal computers, and some factor the cost of one into tuition. A number of

*New York Times, March 15, 1999, p. A25.

colleges have put high-speed Internet connections in every dorm room. But there are good reasons to question the wisdom of this preoccupation with computers and the Internet.

2 Take a walk through the residence halls of any college in the country and you'll find students seated at their desks, eyes transfixed on their computer monitors. What are they doing with their top-of-the-line PC's and high-speed T-1 Internet connections?

3 They are playing Tomb Raider instead of going to chemistry class, tweaking the configurations of their machines instead of writing the paper due tomorrow, collecting mostly useless information from the World Wide Web instead of doing a math problem set—and a host of other activity that has little or nothing to do with traditional academic work.

4 I have friends who have spent whole weekends doing nothing but playing Quake or Warcraft or other interactive computer games. One friend sometimes spends entire evenings—six to eight hours—scouring the Web for images and modifying them just to have a new background on his computer desktop.

5 And many others I know have amassed overwhelming collections of music on their computers. It's the searching and finding that they seem to enjoy: some of them have more music files on their computers than they could play in months.

6 Several people who live in my hall routinely stay awake all night chatting with dormmates on-line. Why walk 10 feet down the hall to have a conversation when you can chat on the computer—even if it takes three times as long?

7 You might expect that personal computers in dorm rooms would be used for nonacademic purposes, but the problem is not confined to residence halls. The other day I walked into the library's reference department, and five or six students were grouped around a computer—not conducting research, but playing Tetris. Every time I walk past the library's so-called research computers, it seems that at least half are being used to play games, chat or surf the Internet aimlessly.

8 Colleges and universities should be wary of placing such an emphasis on the use of computers and the Internet. The Web may be useful for finding simple facts, but serious research still means a trip to the library.

9 For most students, having a computer in the dorm is more of a distraction than a learning tool. Other than computer science or mathematics majors, few students need more than a word processing program and access to E-mail in their rooms.

10 It is true, of course, that students have always procrastinated and wasted time. But when students spend four, five, even ten hours a day on computers and the Internet, a more troubling picture emerges—a picture all the more disturbing because colleges themselves have helped create the problem.

◆◆◆

D. CLASS PROJECT: A CLASS DEBATE WITH ATTEMPTS TO RECONCILE THE OPPOSING POSITIONS

This activity will provide you with the opportunity to combine elements of traditional and Rogerian argument theory that you have learned in Chapters 5–9.

Debate is a traditional forum for argument, and your class can set up a debate in which everyone participates. A common model for debate is to have two people on each side of the issue present their views, and a judge then declares who wins. For this class debate, however, we will use a somewhat different strategy that involves not only stating the opposing viewpoints but also working to find some common ground between the two opposing positions to achieve more productive argument and to avoid a standoff with no agreement and no resolution of the issue.

We draw on social judgment theory to help organize the debate. Social judgment theorists, who study the positions that individuals take on issues, plot positions on a continuum that ranges from extremely positive to extremely negative. They then describe these positions in terms of latitudes of acceptance. Individuals at the extremes of the continuum have narrow latitudes of acceptance and can usually tolerate only positions that are very close to their own. Somewhere in the middle is a latitude of noncommitment. People in this area, who are not strongly involved with the issue, have comparatively wide latitudes of acceptance and can tolerate a wide range of positions. The object of this debate is to increase everyone's latitudes of acceptance so that productive argument can take place.

PREPARING FOR THE DEBATES

1. Select an Issue

The class may nominate possible issues from the following list of topics and articles in this book or make recommendations on their own and then vote on one of them as a topic for debate. The issue should be written in statement form, as in the list, so that individuals can either agree or disagree with it.

Resolved: Traditional families are best, with a mother and father happily raising children. See the articles by Cain (pages 455–458), Adler (pages 458–463), and Glaser (pages 463–465).

Resolved: Women should take the major responsibility for household chores. See the articles by Hewlett (pages 487–488), Brady (pages 58–60), and Adler (pages 458–463).

Resolved: Colleges should teach religion. See the articles by Rhodes (pages 496–503) and Sollod (pages 503–506).

Resolved: Capital punishment should be abolished. See the articles by Kozinski (pages 532–539) and Moore (pages 539–542).

Resolved: Racial profiling should be abolished. See the articles by Goldberg (pages 617–621), Clemetson and Naughton (pages 622–623), and Zakaria (pages 623–626).

Resolved: Wars are inevitable. See the articles by James (pages 671–675), Mead (pages 675–680), and Hanson (pages 680–684).

Or: Brainstorm campus or current events issues, and vote on one to debate.

2. Create Three Groups

The class will divide into three groups. Two groups are encouraged to take strong affirmative and negative positions and to argue from those points of view, presenting pro and con arguments, with presumably narrow latitudes of acceptance. A third, middle group with a wider latitude of acceptance will present suggestions for resolving some of the conflict. This group will look for common ground in the extreme positions, try to resolve conflict, and work to achieve better understanding and perhaps even a change of views in the opposing groups.

Group 1 is the affirmative group that is in favor of the subject for debate. Group 2 is the negative group that is against it. Group 3 is the moderate group that will attempt to resolve the conflict. The groups should be equal in size. To achieve this equality, some students may have to argue for positions that they do not in fact actually hold.

3. Do Background Reading and Writing

All three groups should do some background reading on the subject for debate. The negative and affirmative teams will read to get ideas for their arguments and to develop ideas for refutation. The moderates should read to understand the opposing positions. Students in groups 1 and 2 will write 250-word papers outside of class that present some arguments to support their positions. After they have listened to the debate, the moderates will write 250-word papers that make an effort to resolve the conflict.

CONDUCTING THE DEBATE

Day One

1. *Begin with the opening papers* (10 minutes). Two students from the affirmative group and two from the negative group agree to start the debate by reading their papers. The first affirmative, first negative, second affirmative, and second negative read papers in that order.

2. *Others join in* (20 minutes). Students may now raise their hands to be recognized by the instructor to give additional arguments from their papers. Each person should stand to speak. The speakers should represent each side in turn. The class should decide whether everyone should first be allowed to speak before anyone is permitted to speak a second time. The instructor should cut off speakers who are going on too long.

3. *Caucus and closing remarks* (15 minutes). The affirmative and negative groups caucus for 5 minutes to prepare their closing arguments. Each group selects a spokesperson who then presents the group's final, strongest arguments in a 2-minute closing presentation.

4. *Moderates prepare responses.* The moderates write 250-word responses outside of class that answer the following question: Now that you have heard both sides, how would you resolve the conflict?

Day Two

1. *Moderates read* (20 minutes). All moderates read their papers. Each paper should take about 2 minutes to read.
2. *Analyze outcomes* (30 minutes). The class should now discuss the outcomes of the debate by addressing the following questions.
   a. What, in general, were some of the outcomes?
   b. Who changed their opinions? Which opinions? Why?
   c. Who did not change? Why?
   d. What are some of the outcomes of the attempts to reduce conflict and establish common ground?
   e. What strategies have you learned from participating in this debate that can help you in real-life arguments?
   f. Did you detect any fallacies that weakened the arguments?

Appendix to Chapter 9

Review and Synthesis of the Strategies for Reading and Writing Argument

The purpose of this Appendix is to provide you with the opportunity to review and synthesize what you have learned about reading and writing argument in the first nine chapters of this book. You will apply argument theory as you read and understand a famous classic argument, Martin Luther King Jr.'s "Letter from Birmingham Jail."

When you finish, you will write a paper that answers the question "Why is King's letter considered a classic argument?" In answering this question, you will draw on what you know about traditional argument and Rogerian argument. Begin by reading about the rhetorical situation for the letter.

RHETORICAL SITUATION FOR MARTIN LUTHER KING JR.'S "LETTER FROM BIRMINGHAM JAIL"

Birmingham, Alabama, was a very strange place in 1963. Black people were allowed to sit only in certain parts of buses and restaurants, they were required to drink out of separate water fountains, and they were not allowed in white churches, schools, or various other public places. The Reverend Martin Luther King Jr. was a black Baptist minister who was a leader in the civil rights movement at that time. The purpose of the movement was to end segregation and discrimination and to obtain equal rights and access for black people.

King and others carefully prepared for demonstrations that would take place in Birmingham in the spring of 1963. The demonstrators began by "sitting in" at lunch counters that had never served blacks before and by picketing stores. Twenty people were arrested the first day on charges of trespassing. Next, the civil rights leaders applied for permits to picket and hold parades against the injustices of discrimination and segregation. They were refused permission, but they demonstrated and picketed anyway. King was served an injunction by a circuit

Photograph by Don Uhrbrock

Dr. Martin Luther King Jr. was jailed more than once during the civil rights movement. In this 1960 photo police in Atlanta, Georgia, are taking him to court in handcuffs for participating in a sit-in at a segregated lunch counter in a department store. He was sentenced in this instance to four months of hard labor and was released on bail pending appeal only after Bobby Kennedy phoned the judge.

SOURCE: From *Life in the '60s,* ed. Doris C. O'Neil (New York: Little, Brown & Co., 1989), p. 3. Copyright © 1989 by The Time Inc. Magazine Company.

judge that said civil rights leaders could not protest, demonstrate, boycott, or sit in. King and others decided that this was an unfair and unjust application of the law, and they decided to break it.

King himself decided to march on Good Friday, and he expected to go to jail. Indeed, before he had walked half a mile, he was arrested and jailed, along with fifty other people. King stayed in jail for eight days. During that time he wrote his famous letter. It was written in response to a letter signed by eight white clergymen that had been published in a local newspaper.

After King left jail, there were further protests and some violence. Thousands of people demonstrated, and thousands were jailed. Finally, black and white leaders began to negotiate, and some final terms were announced on May 10, 1963. All lunch counters, restrooms, fitting rooms, and drinking fountains in downtown stores were to be desegregated within ninety days; blacks were to be hired in clerical and sales jobs in stores within sixty days; the many people arrested during the demonstrations were to be released on low bail; and permanent lines of communication were to be established between black and white leaders. The demonstrations ended then, and the city settled down and began to implement the agreements.[1]

READING THE LETTERS AND REPORTING TO THE CLASS

Divide the class into seven groups, and assign one of the following focus topics to each group. To prepare for the group work, all students will read the two letters outside of class and make individual notes on the focus topics assigned to their groups. The brief questions in the margin will facilitate this reading and note taking. In class the groups will meet briefly to consolidate their views on the topic. Each group will then make a brief oral report, and other class members will discuss the results and take some notes. These notes will be used as prewriting materials for the paper described on page 272, paragraph 2.

Focus Topics

Group 1: Rhetorical situation and Rogerian elements. Answer these questions.

   a. What is the *exigence* for these two letters? What caused the authors to write them? What was the problem? Was it a new or recurring problem?
   b. Who is the *audience* for the clergymen's letter? For King's letter? What is the nature of these audiences? Can they be convinced? What are the expected outcomes?
   c. What are the *constraints?* Speculate about the beliefs, attitudes, habits, and traditions that were in place that limited or constrained both the clergymen and King. How did these constraining circumstances influence the audience at that time?
   d. Think about the *authors* of both letters. Who are they? Speculate about their background, experience, affiliations, and values. What motivated them to write?
   e. What kind of *text* is this? What effect do its special qualities and features have on the audience?

---

[1]This account is drawn from Lee E. Bains Jr., "Birmingham, 1963: Confrontation over Civil Rights," in *Birmingham, Alabama, 1956–1963: The Black Struggle for Civil Rights*, ed. David J. Garrow (Brooklyn: Carlson, 1989), pp. 175–183.

f. Think about *yourself as the reader.* What is your position on the issue? Do you experience constraints as you read? Do you perceive common ground with either the clergymen or King or both? Describe it. Are you influenced by these letters? How?

g. Are there any efforts to use *Rogerian argument strategies* and thereby build common ground by establishing that the opposition may at times be correct? If yes, provide some examples and analyze their effect.

Group 2: Organization and claims. Divide each letter into its main parts. What is the subject of each part? Why have the parts been placed in this particular order? What is the relationship between them? What is the main claim in each letter? What types of claims are they? What are some of the subclaims? What types of claims are they?

Group 3: Logical proofs and style. Analyze the use of logical proof in each of the letters. Provide examples. Describe their effect on the audience. Provide an example of the language of rational style in one of the letters.

Group 4: Emotional proofs and style. Analyze the use of emotional proof in each of the letters. Provide examples. Describe their effect on the audience. Provide an example of the language of emotional style in one of the letters.

Group 5: Proofs and style that establish *ethos*. Analyze the use of proofs that establish *ethos* or credibility in the letters. Provide examples. Describe their effect on the audience. Provide an example of language that establishes *ethos* in one of the letters.

Group 6: Warrants. Identify the warrants in each of the letters. How much common ground do you think exists between the authors of the letters? How much common ground do you share with the authors? As a result, which letter do you find more convincing? Why?

Group 7: Fallacious thinking and rebuttals. Provide examples of reasoning that is considered fallacious or wrongheaded by the opposing parties in each of the letters. What rebuttals are made in response to these? How effective are they?

A CALL FOR UNITY: A LETTER FROM EIGHT WHITE CLERGYMEN

April 12, 1963

1   We the undersigned clergymen are among those who, in January, issued "An Appeal for Law and Order and Common Sense," in dealing with racial problems in Alabama. We expressed understanding that honest convictions in racial matters could properly be pursued in the courts, but urged that decisions of those courts should in the meantime be peacefully obeyed.

2   Since that time there had been some evidence of increased forebearance and a willingness to face facts. Responsible citizens have undertaken to work on various problems which cause racial friction

What is the issue?

What is the clergymen's position?

What is the claim?

What type of claim is it?

and unrest. In Birmingham, recent public events have given indication that we all have opportunity for a new constructive and realistic approach to racial problems.

3

What are the rebuttals?

However, we are now confronted by a series of demonstrations by some of our Negro citizens, directed and led in part by outsiders. We recognize the natural impatience of people who feel that their hopes are slow in being realized. But we are convinced that these demonstrations are unwise and untimely.

How do the authors build *ethos*?

4

We agree rather with certain local Negro leadership which has called for honest and open negotiation of racial issues in our area. And we believe this kind of facing of issues can best be accomplished by citizens of our own metropolitan area, white and Negro, meeting with their knowledge and experience of the local situation. All of us need to face that responsibility and find proper channels for its accomplishment.

How do they appeal to logic?

5

Just as we formerly pointed out that "hatred and violence have no sanction in our religious and political traditions," we also point out that such actions as incite to hatred and violence, however technically peaceful those actions may be, have not contributed to the resolution of our local problems. We do not believe that these days of new hope are days when extreme measures are justified in Birmingham.

6

How do they appeal to emotion?

What are the warrants?

We commend the community as a whole, and the local news media and law enforcement officials in particular, on the calm manner in which these demonstrations have been handled. We urge the public to continue to show restraint should the demonstrations continue, and the law enforcement officials to remain calm and continue to protect our city from violence.

7

Describe the predominant style.

We further strongly urge our own Negro community to withdraw support from these demonstrations, and to unite locally in working peacefully for a better Birmingham. When rights are consistently denied, a cause should be pressed in the courts and in negotiations among local leaders, and not in the streets. We appeal to both our white and Negro citizenry to observe the principles of law and order and common sense.

(Signed)
C.C.J. Carpenter, D.D., L.L.D., Bishop of Alabama; Joseph A. Durick, D.D., Auxiliary Bishop, Diocese of Mobile-Birmingham; Rabbi Milton L. Grafman, Temple Emanu-El, Birmingham, Alabama; Bishop Paul Hardin, Bishop of the Alabama–West Florida Conference of the Methodist Church; Bishop Nolan B. Harmon, Bishop of the North Alabama Conference of the Methodist Church; George M. Murray, D.D., L.L.D., Bishop Coadjutor, Episcopal Diocese of Alabama; Edward V. Ramage, Moderator, Synod of the Alabama Presbyterian Church in the United States; Earl Stallings, Pastor, First Baptist Church, Birmingham

ESSAY
2

LETTER FROM BIRMINGHAM JAIL*

Martin Luther King Jr.

April 16, 1963

My Dear Fellow Clergymen:

1

What is the issue? What is King's position?

    While confined here in the Birmingham city jail, I came across your recent statement calling my present activities "unwise and untimely." Seldom do I pause to answer criticism of my work and ideas. If I sought to answer all the criticisms that cross my desk, my secretaries would have little time for anything other than such correspondence in the course of the day, and I would have no time for constructive work. But since I feel that you are men of genuine good will and that your criticisms are sincerely set forth, I want to try to answer your statement in what I hope will be patient and reasonable terms.

Identify and describe the Rogerian elements and efforts to establish common ground throughout this letter.

2

    I think I should indicate why I am here in Birmingham, since you have been influenced by the view which argues against "outsiders coming in." I have the honor of serving as president of the Southern Christian Leadership Conference, an organization operating in every southern state, with headquarters in Atlanta, Georgia. We have some eighty-five affiliated organizations across the South, and one of them is the Alabama Christian Movement for Human Rights. Frequently we share staff, educational and financial resources with our affiliates. Several months ago the affiliate here in Birmingham asked us to be on call to engage in a nonviolent direct-action program if such were deemed necessary. We readily consented, and when the hour came we lived up to our promise. So I, along with several members of my staff, am here because I was invited here. I am here because I have organizational ties here.

3

How does King build ethos?

What is the effect of the comparison with Paul?

    But more basically, I am in Birmingham because injustice is here. Just as the prophets of the eighth century B.C. left their villages and carried their "thus saith the Lord" far beyond the boundaries of their home towns, and just as the Apostle Paul left his village of Tarsus and carried the gospel of Jesus Christ to the far corners of the Greco-Roman world, so am I compelled to carry the

---

*Author's Note: This response to a published statement by eight fellow clergymen from Alabama (Bishop C.C.J. Carpenter, Bishop Joseph A. Durick, Rabbi Milton L. Grafman, Bishop Paul Hardin, Bishop Nolan B. Harmon, the Reverend George M. Murray, the Reverend Edward V. Ramage, and the Reverend Earl Stallings) was composed under somewhat constricting circumstances. Begun on the margins of the newspaper in which the statement appeared while I was in jail, the letter was continued on scraps of writing paper supplied by a friendly Negro trusty, and concluded on a pad my attorneys were eventually permitted to leave me. Although the text remains in substance unaltered, I have indulged in the author's prerogative of polishing it for publication.

Draw a line at the
end of the
introduction.

4

Draw a line at the
end of each of the
other major sections
of material. Label the
subject of each
section in the margin.

What is the subject
of this first
section?

5

What is the claim?

What type of claim
is it?

Is it qualified?

6

Identify and analyze
the effect of the
emotional appeals.

7

8

What are some of
the values expressed
in this argument?

gospel of freedom beyond my own home town. Like Paul, I must constantly respond to the Macedonian call for aid.

Moreover, I am cognizant of the interrelatedness of all communities and states. I cannot sit idly by in Atlanta and not be concerned about what happens in Birmingham. Injustice anywhere is a threat to justice everywhere. We are caught in an inescapable network of mutuality, tied in a single garment of destiny. Whatever affects one directly, affects all indirectly. Never again can we afford to live with the narrow, provincial "outside agitator" idea. Anyone who lives inside the United States can never be considered an outsider anywhere within its bounds.

You deplore the demonstrations taking place in Birmingham. But your statement, I am sorry to say, fails to express a similar concern for the conditions that brought about the demonstrations. I am sure that none of you would want to rest content with the superficial kind of social analysis that deals merely with effects and does not grapple with underlying causes. It is unfortunate that demonstrations are taking place in Birmingham, but it is even more unfortunate that the city's white power structure left the Negro community with no alternative.

In any nonviolent campaign there are four basic steps: collection of the facts to determine whether injustices exist; negotiation; self-purification; and direct action. We have gone through all these steps in Birmingham. There can be no gain-saying the fact that racial injustice engulfs this community. Birmingham is probably the most thoroughly segregated city in the United States. Its ugly record of brutality is widely known. Negroes have experienced grossly unjust treatment in the courts. There have been more unsolved bombings of Negro homes and churches in Birmingham than in any other city in the nation. These are the hard, brutal facts of the case. On the basis of these conditions, Negro leaders sought to negotiate with the city fathers. But the latter consistently refused to engage in good-faith negotiation.

Then, last September, came the opportunity to talk with leaders of Birmingham's economic community. In the course of the negotiations, certain promises were made by the merchants—for example, to remove the stores' humiliating racial signs. On the basis of these promises, the Reverend Fred Shuttlesworth and the leaders of the Alabama Christian Movement for Human Rights agreed to a moratorium on all demonstrations. As the weeks and months went by, we realized that we were the victims of a broken promise. A few signs, briefly removed, returned; the others remained.

As in so many past experiences, our hopes had been blasted, and the shadow of deep disappointment settled upon us. We had no alternative except to prepare for direct action, whereby we would present our very bodies as a means of laying our case before the conscience of the local and the national community. Mindful of the difficulties involved, we decided to undertake a process of self-purification. We began a series of workshops on nonviolence, and we repeatedly asked ourselves: "Are you able to accept blows without retaliating?" "Are you able to endure the ordeal of jail?" We decided to schedule our direct-action program for the Easter season, realizing that except for Christmas, this is the main shopping period of the year. Knowing that a strong economic-withdrawal program would be the by-product of direct action, we felt that this would be the best time to bring pressure to bear on the merchants for the needed change.

9   Then it occurred to us that Birmingham's mayoral election was coming up in March, and we speedily decided to postpone action until after election day. When we discovered that the Commissioner of Public Safety, Eugene "Bull" Connor, had piled up enough votes to be in the runoff, we decided again to postpone action until the day after the runoff so that the demonstrations could not be used to cloud the issues. Like many others, we waited to see Mr. Connor defeated, and to this end we endured postponement after postponement. Having aided in this community need, we felt that our direct-action program could be delayed no longer.

10   **Identify and describe the rebuttals.**

You may well ask: "Why direct action? Why sit-ins, marches and so forth? Isn't negotiation a better path?" You are quite right in calling for negotiation. Indeed, this is the very purpose of direct action. Nonviolent direct action seeks to create such a crisis and foster such a tension that a community which has constantly refused to negotiate is forced to confront the issue. It seeks so to dramatize the issue that it can no longer be ignored. My citing the creation of tension as part of the work of the nonviolent-resister may sound rather shocking. But I must confess that I am not afraid of the word "tension." I have earnestly opposed violent tension, but there is a type of constructive, nonviolent tension which is necessary for growth. Just as Socrates felt that it was necessary to create a tension in the mind so that individuals could rise from the bondage of myths and half-truths to the unfettered realm of creative analysis and objective appraisal, so must we see the need for nonviolent gadflies to create the kind of tension in society that will help men rise from the dark depths of prejudice and racism to the majestic heights of understanding and brotherhood.

What is the effect of the comparison with Socrates?

11   **What is King's planned argumentative strategy?**

The purpose of our direct-action program is to create a situation so crisis-packed that it will inevitably open the door to negotiation. I therefore concur with you in your call for negotiation. Too long has our beloved Southland been bogged down in a tragic effort to live in monologue rather than dialogue.

12   One of the basic points in your statement is that the action that I and my associates have taken in Birmingham is untimely. Some

have asked: "Why didn't you give the new city administration time to act?" The only answer that I can give to this query is that the new Birmingham administration must be prodded about as much as the outgoing one, before it will act. We are sadly mistaken if we feel that the election of Albert Boutwell as mayor will bring the millennium to Birmingham. While Mr. Boutwell is a much more gentle person than Mr. Connor, they are both segregationists, dedicated to the maintenance of the status quo. I have hope that Mr. Boutwell will be reasonable enough to see the futility of massive resistance to desegregation. But he will not see this without pressure from devotees of civil rights. My friends, I must say to you that we have not made a single gain in civil rights without determined legal and nonviolent pressure. Lamentably, it is a historical fact that privileged groups seldom give up their privileges voluntarily. Individuals may see the moral light and voluntarily give up their unjust posture; but, as Reinhold Niebuhr has reminded us, groups tend to be more immoral than individuals.

Why does King refer to history?

Why does he refer to Niebuhr?

13   We know through painful experience that freedom is never voluntarily given up by the oppressor; it must be demanded by the oppressed. Frankly, I have yet to engage in a direct-action campaign that was "well-timed" in the view of those who have not suffered unduly from the disease of segregation. For years now I have heard the word "Wait!" It rings in the ear of every Negro with piercing familiarity. This "Wait" has almost always meant "Never." We must come to see, with one of our distinguished jurists, that "justice too long delayed is justice denied."

Identify and analyze the emotional proof.

What human motives and values does King appeal to?

14   We have waited for more than 340 years for our constitutional and God-given rights. The nations of Asia and Africa are moving with jetlike speed toward gaining political independence, but we still creep at horse-and-buggy pace toward gaining a cup of coffee at a lunch counter. Perhaps it is easy for those who have never felt the stinging darts of segregation to say, "Wait." But when you have seen vicious mobs lynch your mothers and fathers at will and drown your sisters and brothers at whim; when you have seen hate-filled policemen curse, kick and even kill your black brothers and sisters; when you see the vast majority of your twenty million Negro brothers smothering in an airtight cage of poverty in the midst of an affluent society; when you suddenly find your tongue twisted and your speech stammering as you seek to explain to your six-year-old daughter why she can't go to the public amusement park that has just been advertised on television, and see tears welling up in her eyes when she is told that Fun-town is closed to colored children, and see ominous clouds of inferiority beginning to form in her little mental sky, and see her beginning to distort her personality by developing an unconscious bitterness toward white people; when you have to concoct an answer for a five-year-old son who is asking,

Identify emotional language, examples, and vivid description.

What is the effect of the emotional proof?

"Daddy, why do white people treat colored people so mean?"; when you take a cross-country drive and find it necessary to sleep night after night in the uncomfortable corners of your automobile because no motel will accept you; when you are humiliated day in and day out by nagging signs reading "white" and "colored"; when your first name becomes "nigger," your middle name becomes "boy" (however old you are) and your last name becomes "John," and your wife and mother are never given the respected title "Mrs."; when you are harried by day and haunted by night by the fact that you are a Negro, living constantly at tiptoe stance, never quite knowing what to expect next, and are plagued with inner fears and outer resentments; when you are forever fighting a degenerating sense of "nobodiness"—then you will understand why we find it difficult to wait. There comes a time when the cup of endurance runs over, and men are no longer willing to be plunged into the abyss of despair. I hope, sirs, you can understand our legitimate and unavoidable impatience.

What is the predominant type of proof in the first section of the letter?

15   You express a great deal of anxiety over our willingness to break laws. This is certainly a legitimate concern. Since we so diligently urge people to obey the Supreme Court's decision of 1954 outlawing segregation in the public schools, at first glance it may seem rather paradoxical for us consciously to break laws. One may well ask: "How can you advocate breaking some laws and obeying others?" The answer lies in the fact that there are two types of laws: just and unjust. I would be the first to advocate obeying just laws. Conversely, one has a moral responsibility to disobey unjust laws. I would agree with St. Augustine that "an unjust law is no law at all."

Draw a line where the subject changes. What is the subject of the second section?

16   Now, what is the difference between the two? How does one determine whether a law is just or unjust? A just law is a man-made code that squares with the moral law or the law of God. An unjust law is a code that is out of harmony with the moral law. To put it in the terms of St. Thomas Aquinas: An unjust law is a human law that is not rooted in eternal law and natural law. Any law that uplifts human personality is just. Any law that degrades human personality is unjust. All segregation statutes are unjust because segregation distorts the soul and damages the personality. It gives the segregator a false sense of superiority and the segregated a false sense of inferiority. Segregation, to use the terminology of the Jewish philosopher Martin Buber, substitutes an "I-it" relationship for an "I-thou" relationship and ends up relegating persons to the status of things. Hence segregation is not only politically, economically, and sociologically unsound, it is morally wrong and sinful. Paul Tillich has said that sin is separation. Is not segregation an existential expression of man's tragic separation, his awful estrangement, his terrible sinfulness? Thus it is that I can urge men to obey the 1954 decision of the Supreme Court, for it is morally right; and I can

How and why does King use definition?

How does he support the definition?

What is the effect of the support?

urge them to disobey segregation ordinances, for they are morally wrong.

17

Explain the example of just and unjust laws.

Let us consider a more concrete example of just and unjust laws. An unjust law is a code that a numerical or power majority group compels a minority group to obey but does not make binding on itself. This is *difference* made legal. By the same token, a just law is a code that a majority compels a minority to follow and that it is willing to follow itself. This is *sameness* made legal.

18

How does King further elaborate on this idea?

Let me give another explanation. A law is unjust if it is inflicted on a minority that, as a result of being denied the right to vote, had no part in enacting or devising the law. Who can say that the legislature of Alabama which set up the state's segregation laws was democratically elected? Throughout Alabama all sorts of devious methods are used to prevent Negroes from becoming registered voters, and there are some counties in which, even though Negroes constitute a majority of the population, not a single Negro is registered. Can any law enactment under such circumstances be considered democratically structured?

19

Sometimes a law is just on its face and unjust in its application. For instance, I have been arrested on a charge of parading without a permit. Now, there is nothing wrong in having an ordinance which requires a permit for a parade. But such an ordinance becomes unjust when it is used to maintain segregation and to deny citizens the First-Amendment privilege of peaceful assembly and protest.

20

Analyze the deductive reasoning in this paragraph.

I hope you are able to see the distinction I am trying to point out. In no sense do I advocate evading or defying the law, as would the rabid segregationist. That would lead to anarchy. One who breaks an unjust law must do so openly, lovingly, and with a willingness to accept the penalty. I submit that an individual who breaks a law that conscience tells him is unjust, and who willingly accepts the penalty of imprisonment in order to arouse the conscience of the community over its injustice, is in reality expressing the highest respect for law.

21

Identify and describe the effect of the historical analogies.

Of course, there is nothing new about this kind of civil disobedience. It was evidenced sublimely in the refusal of Shadrach, Meshach and Abednego to obey the laws of Nebuchadnezzar, on the ground that a higher moral law was at stake. It was practiced superbly by the early Christians, who were willing to face hungry lions and the excruciating pain of chopping blocks rather than submit to certain unjust laws of the Roman Empire. To a degree, academic freedom is a reality today because Socrates practiced civil disobedience. In our own nation, the Boston Tea Party represented a massive act of civil disobedience.

What type of   22
proof predominates
in the second part of
the letter?

We should never forget that everything Adolf Hitler did in Germany was "legal" and everything the Hungarian freedom fighters did in Hungary was "illegal." It was "illegal" to aid and comfort a

Jew in Hitler's Germany. Even so, I am sure that, had I lived in Germany at the time, I would have aided and comforted my Jewish brothers. If today I lived in a Communist country where certain principles dear to the Christian faith are suppressed, I would openly advocate disobeying that country's antireligious laws.

Draw a line where the subject changes. What is the subject of the third section?

23

What are King's warrants in this passage?

I must make two honest confessions to you, my Christian and Jewish brothers. First, I must confess that over the past few years I have been gravely disappointed with the white moderate. I have almost reached the regrettable conclusion that the Negro's great stumbling block in his stride toward freedom is not the White Citizen's Counciler or the Ku Klux Klanner, but the white moderate, who is more devoted to "order" than to justice; who prefers a negative peace which is the absence of tension to a positive peace which is the presence of justice; who constantly says: "I agree with you in the goal you seek, but I cannot agree with your methods of direct action"; who paternalistically believes he can set the timetable for another man's freedom; who lives by a mythical concept of time and who constantly advises the Negro to wait for a "more convenient season." Shallow understanding from people of good will is more frustrating than absolute misunderstanding from people of ill will. Lukewarm acceptance is much more bewildering than outright rejection.

24

How do King's warrants differ from the clergymen's?

How and why does King use definition here?

I had hoped that the white moderate would understand that law and order exist for the purpose of establishing justice and that when they fail in this purpose they become the dangerously structured dams that block the flow of social progress. I had hoped that the white moderate would understand that the present tension in the South is a necessary phase of the transition from an obnoxious negative peace, in which the Negro passively accepted his unjust plight, to a substantive and positive peace, in which all men will respect the dignity and worth of human personality. Actually, we who engage in nonviolent direct action are not the creators of tension. We merely bring to the surface the hidden tension that is already alive. We bring it out in the open, where it can be seen and dealt with. Like a boil that can never be cured so long as it is covered up but must be opened with all its ugliness to the natural medicines of air and light, injustice must be exposed, with all the tension its exposure creates, to the light of human conscience and the air of national opinion before it can be cured.

25

Identify and describe the effects of the analogies in these paragraphs.

In your statements you assert that our actions, even though peaceful, must be condemned because they precipitate violence. But is this a logical assertion? Isn't this like condemning a robbed man because his possession of money precipitated the evil act of robbery? Isn't this like condemning Socrates because his unswerving commitment to truth and his philosophical inquiries precipitated the act by the misguided populace in which they made him drink hemlock? Isn't this like condemning Jesus because his unique God-consciousness and never-ceasing devotion to God's will precipitated the evil act of crucifixion? We must come to see that, as the federal courts have consistently affirmed, it is wrong to urge an individual to cease his efforts to gain his basic constitutional rights because the quest may precipitate violence. Society must protect the robbed and punish the robber.

What is the fallacious thinking King complains of?

26   I had also hoped that the white moderate would reject the myth concerning time in relation to the struggle for freedom. I have just received a letter from a white brother in Texas. He writes: "All Christians know that the colored people will receive equal rights eventually, but it is possible that you are in too great a religious hurry. It has taken Christianity almost two thousand years to accomplish what it has. The teachings of Christ take time to come to earth." Such an attitude stems from a tragic misconception of time, from the strangely irrational notion that there is something in the very flow of time that will inevitably cure all ills. Actually, time itself is neutral; it can be used either destructively or constructively. More and more I feel that the people of ill will have used time much more effectively than have the people of good will. We will have to repent in this generation not merely for the hateful words and actions of the bad people but for the appalling silence of the good people. Human progress never rolls in on wheels of inevitability; it comes through the tireless efforts of men willing to be coworkers with God, and without this hard work, time itself becomes an ally of the forces of social stagnation. We must use time creatively, in the knowledge that the time is always right to do right. Now is the time to make real the promise of democracy and transform our pending national elegy into a creative psalm of brotherhood. Now is the time to lift our national policy from the quicksand of racial injustice to the solid rock of human dignity.

Summarize King's reasoning about time.

27   You speak of our activity in Birmingham as extreme. At first I was rather disappointed that fellow clergymen would see my non-violent efforts as those of an extremist. I began thinking about the fact that I stand in the middle of two opposing forces in the Negro community. One is a force of complacency, made up in part of Negroes who, as a result of long years of oppression, are so drained of self-respect and a sense of "somebodiness" that they have adjusted to segregation; and in part of a few middle-class Negroes who, because of a degree of academic and economic security and because in some ways they profit by segregation, have become insensitive to the problems of the masses. The other force is one of bitterness and hatred, and it comes perilously close to advocating violence. It is expressed in the various black nationalist groups that are springing up across the nation, the largest and best-known being Elijah Muhammad's Muslim movement. Nourished by the Negro's frustration

Describe the two opposing forces.

over the continued existence of racial discrimination, this movement is made up of people who have lost faith in America, who have absolutely repudiated Christianity, and who have concluded that the white man is an incorrigible "devil."

28

How and why does King attempt to reconcile the opposing forces?

I have tried to stand between these two forces, saying that we need emulate neither the "do-nothingism" of the complacent nor the hatred and despair of the black nationalist. For there is the more excellent way of love and nonviolent protest. I am grateful to God that, through the influence of the Negro church, the way of nonviolence became an integral part of our struggle.

29

Identify and describe the causal proof.

If this philosophy had not emerged, by now many streets of the South would, I am convinced, be flowing with blood. And I am further convinced that if our white brothers dismiss as "rabble-rousers" and "outside agitators" those of us who employ nonviolent direct action, and if they refuse to support our nonviolent efforts, millions of Negroes will, out of frustration and despair, seek solace and security in black-nationalist ideologies—a development that would inevitably lead to a frightening racial nightmare.

30

Summarize King's reasoning about the effects of oppression.

Oppressed people cannot remain oppressed forever. The yearning for freedom eventually manifests itself, and that is what has happened to the American Negro. Something within has reminded him of his birthright of freedom, and something without has reminded him that it can be gained. Consciously or unconsciously, he has been caught up by the *Zeitgeist,* and with his black brothers of Africa and his brown and yellow brothers of Asia, South America and the Caribbean, the United States Negro is moving with a sense of great urgency toward the promised land of racial justice. If one recognizes this vital urge that has engulfed the Negro community, one should readily understand why public demonstrations are taking place. The Negro has many pent-up resentments and latent frustrations, and he must release them. So let him march; let him make prayer pilgrimages to the city hall; let him go on freedom rides—and try to understand why he must do so. If his repressed emotions are not released in nonviolent ways, they will seek expression through violence; this is not a threat but a fact of history. So I have not said to my people: "Get rid of your discontent." Rather, I have tried to say that this normal and healthy discontent can be channeled into the creative outlet of nonviolent direct action. And now this approach is being termed extremist.

31

What is the effect of these comparisons?

But though I was initially disappointed at being categorized as an extremist, as I continued to think about the matter I gradually gained a measure of satisfaction from the label. Was not Jesus an extremist for love: "Love your enemies, bless them that curse you, do good to them that hate you, and pray for them which despitefully use you, and persecute you." Was not Amos an extremist for justice: "Let justice roll down like waters and righteousness like an everflowing stream." Was not Paul an extremist for the Christian gospel: "I bear in my body the marks of the Lord Jesus." Was not Martin Luther an extremist: "Here I stand; I cannot do otherwise, so help me God." And John Bunyan: "I will stay in jail to the end of my days before I make a butchery of my conscience." And Abraham Lincoln: "This nation cannot survive half slave and half free." And Thomas Jefferson: "We hold these truths to be self-evident, that all men are created equal. . . ." So the question is not whether we will be extremists, but what kind of extremists we will be. Will we be extremists for hate or for love? Will we be extremists for the preservation of injustice or for the extension of justice? In that dramatic scene on Calvary's hill three men were crucified. We must never forget that all three were crucified for the same crime—the crime of extremism. Two were extremists for immorality, and thus fell below their environment. The other, Jesus Christ, was an extremist for love, truth and goodness, and thereby rose above his environment. Perhaps the South, the nation and the world are in dire need of creative extremists.

32

Summarize King's description of the oppressor race.

I had hoped that the white moderate would see this need. Perhaps I was too optimistic; perhaps I expected too much. I suppose I should have realized that few members of the oppressor race can understand the deep groans and passionate yearnings of the oppressed race, and still fewer have the vision to see that injustice must be rooted out by strong, persistent and determined action. I am thankful, however, that some of our white brothers in the South have grasped the meaning of this social revolution and committed themselves to it. They are still all too few in quantity, but they are big in quality. Some—such as Ralph McGill, Lillian Smith, Harry Golden, James McBride Dabbs, Ann Braden and Sarah Patton Boyle—have written about our struggle in eloquent and prophetic terms. Others have marched with us down nameless streets of the South. They have languished in filthy, roach-infested jails, suffering the abuse and brutality of policemen who view them as "dirty nigger-lovers." Unlike so many of their moderate brothers and sisters, they have recognized the urgency of the moment and sensed the need for powerful "action" antidotes to combat the disease of segregation.

What types of proof are used in this third section?

33

Draw a line where the subject changes. What is the subject of the fourth section?

Reconsider the rhetorical situation: What went before? What will come later?

Let me take note of my other major disappointment. I have been so greatly disappointed with the white church and its leadership. Of course, there are some notable exceptions. I am not unmindful of the fact that each of you has taken some significant stands on this issue. I commend you, Reverend Stallings, for your Christian stand on this past Sunday, in welcoming Negroes to your worship service on a non-segregated basis. I commend the Catholic leaders of this state for integrating Spring Hill College several years ago.

34   But despite these notable exceptions, I must honestly reiterate that I have been disappointed with the church. I do not say this as one of those negative critics who can always find something wrong with the church. I say this as a minister of the gospel, who loves the church; who was nurtured in its bosom; who has been sustained by its spiritual blessings and who will remain true to it as long as the cord of life shall lengthen.

35   When I was suddenly catapulted into the leadership of the bus protest in Montgomery, Alabama, a few years ago, I felt we would be supported by the white church. I felt that the white ministers, priests and rabbis of the South would be among our strongest allies. Instead, some have been outright opponents, refusing to understand the freedom movement and misrepresenting its leaders; all too many others have been more cautious than courageous and have remained silent behind the anesthetizing security of stained-glass windows.

How does King build ethos in this fourth section?

36   In spite of my shattered dreams, I came to Birmingham with the hope that the white religious leadership of this community would see the justice of our cause and, with deep moral concern, would serve as the channel through which our just grievances could reach the power structure. I had hoped that each of you would understand. But again I have been disappointed.

What common ground did King hope for? How was he disappointed?

37   I have heard numerous southern religious leaders admonish their worshipers to comply with a desegregation decision because it is the law, but I have longed to hear white ministers declare: "Follow this decree because integration is morally right and because the Negro is your brother." In the midst of blatant injustices inflicted upon the Negro, I have watched white churchmen stand on the sideline and mouth pious irrelevancies and sanctimonious trivialities. In the midst of a mighty struggle to rid our nation of racial and economic injustice, I have heard many ministers say: "Those are social issues, with which the gospel has no real concern." And I have watched many churches commit themselves to a completely other-worldly religion which makes a strange, un-Biblical distinction between body and soul, between the sacred and the secular.

How and why does King use vivid description?

38   I have traveled the length and breadth of Alabama, Mississippi and all the other southern states. On sweltering summer days and crisp autumn mornings I have looked at the South's beautiful churches with their lofty spires pointing heavenward. I have beheld the impressive outlines of her massive religious-education buildings. Over and over I have found myself asking: "What kind of people worship here? Who is their God? Where were their voices when the lips of Governor Barnett dripped with words of interposition and nullification? Where were they when Governor Wallace gave a clarion call for defiance and hatred? Where were their voices of

support when bruised and weary Negro men and women decided to rise from the dark dungeons of complacency to the bright hills of creative protest?"

39

Yes, these questions are still in my mind. In deep disappointment I have wept over the laxity of the church. But be assured that my tears have been tears of love. There can be no deep disappointment where there is not deep love. Yes, I love the church. How could I do otherwise? I am in the rather unique position of being the son, the grandson and the great-grandson of preachers. Yes, I see the church as the body of Christ. But, oh! How we have blemished and scarred that body through social neglect and through fear of being nonconformists.

40

What is the effect of the historical analogy?

There was a time when the church was very powerful—in the time when the early Christians rejoiced at being deemed worthy to suffer for what they believed. In those days the church was not merely a thermometer that recorded the ideas and principles of popular opinion; it was a thermostat that transformed the mores of society. Whenever the early Christians entered a town, the people in power became disturbed and immediately sought to convict the Christians for being "disturbers of the peace" and "outside agitators." But the Christians pressed on, in the conviction that they were "a colony of heaven," called to obey God rather than man. Small in number, they were big in commitment. They were too God-intoxicated to be "astronomically intimidated." By their effort and example they brought an end to such ancient evils as infanticide and gladiatorial contests.

41

Things are different now. So often the contemporary church is a weak, ineffectual voice with an uncertain sound. So often it is an arch-defender of the status quo. Far from being disturbed by the presence of the church, the power structure of the average community is consoled by the church's silent—and often even vocal—sanction of things as they are.

42

But the judgment of God is upon the church as never before. If today's church does not recapture the sacrificial spirit of the early church, it will lose its authenticity, forfeit the loyalty of millions, and be dismissed as an irrelevant social club with no meaning for the twentieth century. Every day I meet young people whose disappointment with the church has turned into outright disgust.

43

How does King contrast organized religion and the inner church? What is the effect?

Perhaps I have once again been too optimistic. Is organized religion too inextricably bound to the status quo to save our nation and the world? Perhaps I must turn my faith to the inner spiritual church, the church within the church, as the true *ekklesia* and the hope of the world. But again I am thankful to God that some noble souls from the ranks of organized religion have broken loose from the paralyzing chains of conformity and joined us as active partners in the struggle for freedom. They have left their secure congregations and walked the streets of Albany, Georgia, with us. They have gone down the highways of the South on tortuous rides for freedom. Yes, they have gone to jail with us. Some have been dismissed from their churches, have lost the support of their bishops and fellow ministers. But they have acted in the faith that right defeated is stronger than evil triumphant. Their witness has been the spiritual salt that has preserved the true meaning of the gospel in these troubled times. They have carved a tunnel of hope through the dark mountain of disappointment.

44   I hope the church as a whole will meet the challenge of this decisive hour. But even if the church does not come to the aid of justice, I have no despair about the future. I have no fear about the outcome of our struggle in Birmingham, even if our motives are at present misunderstood. We will reach the goal of freedom in Birmingham and all over the nation, because the goal of America is freedom. Abused and scorned though we may be, our destiny is tied up with America's destiny. Before the pilgrims landed at Plymouth, we were here. Before the pen of Jefferson etched the majestic words of the Declaration of Independence across the pages of history, we were here. For more than two centuries our forebears labored in this country without wages; they made cotton king; they built the homes of their masters while suffering gross injustice and shameful humiliation—and yet out of a bottomless vitality they continued to thrive and develop. If the inexpressible cruelties of slavery could not stop us, the opposition we now face will surely fail. We will win our freedom because the sacred heritage of our nation and the eternal will of God are embodied in our echoing demands.

45   Before closing I feel impelled to mention one other point in your statement that has troubled me profoundly. You warmly commended the Birmingham police force for keeping "order" and "preventing violence." I doubt that you would have so warmly commended the police force if you had seen its dogs sinking their teeth into unarmed, nonviolent Negroes. I doubt that you would so quickly commend the policemen if you were to observe their ugly and inhumane treatment of Negroes here in the city jail; if you were to watch them push and curse old Negro women and young Negro girls; if you were to see them slap and kick old Negro men and young boys; if you were to observe them, as they did on two occasions, refuse to give us food because we wanted to sing our grace together. I cannot join you in your praise of the Birmingham police department.

46   It is true that the police have exercised a degree of discipline in handling the demonstrators. In this sense they have conducted themselves rather "nonviolently" in public. But for what purpose? To preserve the evil system of segregation. Over the past few years I have consistently preached that nonviolence demands that the

Why does King use historical analogies here?

What types of proof are used in the fourth section?

Draw a line where the subject changes. What is the subject of the fifth section?

What is the predominant type of proof in this fifth section?

Provide some examples.

Describe the effect.

means we use must be as pure as the ends we seek. I have tried to make clear that it is wrong to use immoral means to attain moral ends. But now I must affirm that it is just as wrong, or perhaps even more so, to use moral means to preserve immoral ends. Perhaps Mr. Connor and his policemen have been rather nonviolent in public, as was Chief Pritchett in Albany, Georgia, but they have used the moral means of nonviolence to maintain the immoral end of racial injustice. As T. S. Eliot has said: "The last temptation is the greatest treason: To do the right deed for the wrong reason."

47   I wish you had commended the Negro sit-inners and the demonstrators of Birmingham for their sublime courage, their willingness to suffer and their amazing discipline in the midst of great provocation. One day the South will recognize its real heroes. They will be the James Merediths, with the noble sense of purpose that enables them to face jeering and hostile mobs, and with the agonizing loneliness that characterizes the life of the pioneer. They will be old, oppressed, battered Negro women, symbolized in a seventy-two-year-old woman in Montgomery, Alabama, who rose up with a sense of dignity and with her people decided not to ride segregated buses, and who responded with ungrammatical profundity to one who inquired about her weariness: "My feets is tired, but my soul is at rest." They will be the young high school and college students, the young ministers of the gospel and a host of their elders, courageously and nonviolently sitting in at lunch counters and willingly going to jail for conscience' sake. One day the South will know that when these disinherited children of God sat down at lunch counters, they were in reality standing up for what is best in the American dream and for the most sacred values in our Judaeo-Christian heritage, thereby bringing our nation back to those great wells of democracy which were dug deep by the founding fathers in their formulation of the Constitution and the Declaration of Independence.

48   Never before have I written so long a letter. I'm afraid it is much too long to take your precious time. I can assure you that it would have been much shorter if I had been writing from a comfortable desk, but what else can one do when he is alone in a narrow jail cell, other than write long letters, think long thoughts and pray long prayers?

Draw a line to set off the conclusion. What is the concluding idea?

What is King's purpose in this conclusion?

49   If I have said anything in this letter that overstates the truth and indicates an unreasonable impatience, I beg you to forgive me. If I have said anything that understates the truth and indicates my having a patience that allows me to settle for anything less than brotherhood, I beg God to forgive me.

Do you find the two letters convincing? Why or why not?

50   I hope this letter finds you strong in the faith. I also hope that circumstances will soon make it possible for me to meet each of

you, not as an integrationist or a civil-rights leader but as a fellow clergyman and a Christian brother. Let us all hope that the dark clouds of racial prejudice will soon pass away and the deep fog of misunderstanding will be lifted from our fear-drenched communities, and in some not too distant tomorrow the radiant stars of love and brotherhood will shine over our great nation with all their scintillating beauty.

> Are the clergymen's and King's arguments moral or immoral according to your values and standards?

Yours for the cause of Peace and Brotherhood,
Martin Luther King, Jr.

Part Three

WRITING A RESEARCH PAPER THAT PRESENTS AN ARGUMENT

THE PURPOSE OF THE NEXT THREE CHAPTERS IS TO TEACH YOU TO WRITE AN ARGUMENT PAPER FROM YOUR OWN PERSPECTIVE THAT INCORPORATES RESEARCH MATERIALS FROM OUTSIDE SOURCES. SINCE OTHER PROFESSORS OR EVEN EMPLOYERS MAY ALSO ASK YOU TO PRODUCE SUCH PAPERS, THIS INSTRUCTION SHOULD BE USEFUL TO YOU NOT ONLY NOW BUT IN THE FUTURE AS WELL. CHAPTER 10 TEACHES YOU TO WRITE A CLAIM, CLARIFY THE PURPOSE FOR YOUR PAPER, AND ANALYZE YOUR AUDIENCE. CHAPTER 11 TEACHES YOU VARIOUS CREATIVE STRATEGIES FOR INVENTING AND GATHERING RESEARCH MATERIAL FOR YOUR PAPER. CHAPTER 12 AND ITS APPENDIX TEACH WAYS TO ORGANIZE THIS MATERIAL, WRITE AND REVISE THE PAPER, AND PREPARE THE FINAL COPY. METHODS FOR LOCATING, EVALUATING, AND USING RESOURCE MATERIALS FROM THE LIBRARY AND THE INTERNET ARE INCLUDED. WHEN YOU FINISH READING PART THREE:

◆ You will know how to write your claim and determine the main argumentative purpose of your research paper.

◆ You will know how to analyze your audience and predict how it might change.

◆ You will know how to think about your claim and gather material from your own background and experience to support it.

◆ You will know how to organize and conduct library and online research to support your claim further.

◆ You will know a variety of possible ways to organize the ideas for your paper.

◆ You will know how to incorporate research materials into your paper and prepare the final copy.

Chapter 10 ❧

The Research Paper: Clarifying Purpose and Understanding the Audience

This chapter and the two that follow form a self-contained unit. You may think of them as one long assignment. They present the information you will need to help you plan, research, and write a researched position paper. You will be familiar with some of the information in these chapters because you have encountered it in earlier chapters. The basic process for writing a researched position paper is much like the process for writing the position paper based on "The Reader" explained in Chapters 1–8. Some of the procedures for the researched position paper, however, are more elaborate than those you have encountered before in this book because a research paper is more complicated than the other papers you have written. As you read Chapters 10, 11, and 12, you can expect to encounter some familiar information along with some new material and ideas. All of this information, including the assignments in the Exercises and Activities at the end of each chapter, is included for one purpose: to help you plan and write a successful researched argumentative paper. Stay on top of these assignments, and you will be pleased with the final results.

The definition of argument quoted in Chapter 1 will help you focus on your final objective in writing this paper: you will seek "to create or increase the adherence of minds to the theses presented for [the audience's] assent."[1] In other words, you will try to get your reading audience to agree, at least to some extent, with your claim and the ideas you use to support it.

---

[1]Chaim Perelman and Lucie Olbrechts-Tyteca, *The New Rhetoric: A Treatise on Argumentation* (Notre Dame, Ind.: University of Notre Dame Press, 1969), p. 45.

UNDERSTANDING THE ASSIGNMENT
AND GETTING STARTED

You may want to turn to page 366 now to read the assignment for preparing the final copy of the researched position paper so that you will know from the outset what this paper should finally look like. Then, to get you started on this paper, consider following some of the suggestions made in earlier chapters. They will ease you into your paper, help you think, and make you feel knowledgeable and confident.

1. *Decide on an issue, and write an issue proposal.* An issue may be assigned by the instructor, it can be inspired by "The Reader" or a set of readings provided by your instructor, or it can be left entirely up to you. There is often a stronger personal exigence for writing if you select the issue yourself. You may have made lists of issues as subjects for future papers when you finished reading Chapter 1. Look back at them now. Or think about the unresolved issues in your other classes or in current newspapers and television newscasts. Work to find an issue that captures your attention and interest. Submit it to the twelve tests of an arguable issue in Box 1.3. These tests will help you ascertain whether or not your issue is potentially arguable. Then write an issue proposal to help you focus your issue and think about what more you need to learn. Follow the assignment and model on pages 27–28.

2. *Do some initial reading.* If you are not very familiar with your issue, locate one or more sources about it, and do some background reading. Read enough material to form an idea of the various positions that people are likely to take on this issue. If you need advice to help you locate some initial sources, read pages 323–328, which will provide you with the information you need to locate material in the library and on the Internet.

3. *Write an exploratory paper.* Either list and explain three or more perspectives on your issue, or write an exploratory paper in which you explain multiple perspectives. The exploratory paper is described on pages 114–116. This process of exploring the different views or approaches to your issue will help you find an original and interesting perspective of your own, and it will also help you understand some of the other perspectives people take so that you can better refute them when you write your research paper. Remember that the exploratory paper calls for a tentative claim at the end of the paper.

WRITING A CLAIM AND CLARIFYING YOUR PURPOSE

Whether you write an issue proposal and an exploratory paper or not, you will want to write your claim for your position paper as early in the process as possible. Your claim is important because it provides purpose, control, and direction for everything else that you include in your paper. Mapping your issue (see Chapter 3) or freewriting about it (Chapter 4) can help you narrow and focus an issue and write a claim. The five claim questions from Chapter 6 can also help you write a claim and establish the fundamental purpose of your paper. Write your issue as a question, and then freewrite in response to each of the claim questions to get a sense of the best purpose and claim for your paper. Here is an example of how the claim questions can be answered in response to an issue that came out of a specific rhetorical situation.

THE RHETORICAL SITUATION

A teenage white supremacist murdered a black middle-class family man. This crime was committed in Texas, where juries are impaneled both to decide guilt and to sentence the criminal. The jury decided the white supremacist was guilty and, in ignorance, sentenced him both to probation and a jail term. The law does not permit both sentences, and so the murderer ended up with probation. As you can imagine, there was public concern, and issues regarding the sentence surfaced. Here are the claim questions used to focus purpose and a claim.

QUESTIONS TO PLAN CLAIM AND PURPOSE

The issue question is, *How should I think about this sentence for murder?*

1. *To establish a claim of fact,* ask: What happened? Does it exist? Is it a fact? Is it true?

> *Example:* Something seems very wrong. I could analyze what is wrong, especially since some people are satisfied and others are dissatisfied with the sentence. My claim could be a claim of fact, *The murderer escaped an appropriate sentence.* I could organize the paper chronologically, giving a history of what has happened and quoting both facts and expert opinion to prove my claim.

2. *To establish a claim of definition,* ask: What is it? What is it like? How should we interpret it? How does its usual meaning change in this context?

> *Example:* There may be a definition problem in the sentencing procedure. The jury was supposed to assign an appropriate sentence for a murder. The audience needs a definition of an appropriate sentence for a murder. My claim could be, *Probation is not an appropriate sentence for murder.* I would rely on expert opinion and the citation of similar cases to illustrate what an appropriate sentence for murder should be.

3. *To establish a claim of cause,* ask: What caused it? Where did it come from? Why did it happen? What are the effects? What will the short-term and long-term results be?

> *Example:* Personal conversations and media reports indicate considerable confusion over the cause of the sentence. Some people think the jury was racially prejudiced, others think the murderer was assigned probation because he is young, and others are baffled. I think the cause was the jury's lack of information, and my claim could be, *The jury did not know and did not receive information about how to sentence murderers, and as a result it recommended an inappropriate sentence.* To prove this claim, I will examine the training provided to jurors. I will interview people who have served on juries. I will learn what training was available for this particular jury.

4. *To establish a claim of value,* ask: Is it good or bad? How bad? How good? Of what worth is it? Is it moral or immoral? Who thinks so? What criteria should I use to decide goodness or badness? Are these the same criteria the audience would apply?

Example: There seems to be some disagreement about whether this sentence was good or bad, but I think it is a bad sentence. My claim could be, *It was wrong of the jury to assign the murderer probation and no jail sentence.* To prove this, I will appeal to the standard needs and values I assume my audience holds, including a desire for physical safety, a sense of fairness and justness, and a respect for the jury system, which, I argue, has failed in this case.

5. *To establish a claim of policy,* ask: What should we do about it? What should be our future course of action? How can we solve the problem?

Example: Almost everyone thinks that the jury made a mistake. In fact, the criminal is back in jail on another charge waiting for a new trial. I could write a policy paper in which I recommend jury training so that this same problem will not recur. My claim would be, *Juries need pretrial training in order to make competent judgments.*

An example of a student's policy paper organized around this last policy claim and written in response to this actual rhetorical situation appears at the end of the Appendix to Chapter 12. Try writing in response to the claim questions in this way yourself. Then read what you have written, and decide which of the potential claims seems most promising to develop in a paper. Decide on your main purpose, and write your claim. Now you can begin to think about ways to develop your claim.

SOME PRELIMINARY QUESTIONS TO HELP YOU DEVELOP YOUR CLAIM

Ask the following questions to clarify and develop your claim. Some tentative answers to these questions now can help you stay on track and avoid problems with the development of your paper later.

▲ *Is the Claim Narrow and Focused?* You may have started with a broad issue area, such as technology or education, that suggests many specific related issues. You may have participated in mapping sessions in class to discover some of the specific issues related to an issue area, and this work may have helped you narrow your issue. You may now need to narrow your issue even further by focusing on one prong or aspect of it. Here is an example.

Issue area: The environment

    Specific related issue:
    What problems are associated with nuclear energy?

Aspects of that issue:
What should be done with nuclear waste?
How hazardous is nuclear energy, and how can we control the hazards?
What are the alternatives to nuclear energy?

In selecting a narrowed issue to write about, you may want to focus on only one of the three aspects of the nuclear energy problem. You might, for instance, decide to make this claim: *Solar power is better than nuclear energy.* Later, as you write, you may need to narrow this topic even further and revise your claim: *Solar power is better than nuclear energy for certain specified purposes.* Any topic can turn out to be too broad or complicated when you begin to write about it.

You may also need to change your focus or perspective to narrow your claim. You may, for example, begin to research the claim you have made in response to your issue but discover along the way that the real issue is something else. As a result, you decide to change your claim. For example, suppose you decide to write a policy paper about freedom of speech. Your claim is, *Freedom of speech should be protected in all situations.* As you read and research, however, you discover that an issue for many people is a narrower one related to freedom of speech, specifically as it relates to violence on television and children's behavior. In fact, you encounter an article that claims that television violence should be censored even if doing so violates free speech rights. You decide to refocus your paper and write a value paper that claims, *Television violence is harmful and not subject to the protection of free speech rights.*

▲ **WHICH CONTROVERSIAL WORDS IN YOUR CLAIM WILL YOU NEED TO DEFINE?** Identify the words in your claim that may need defining. In the example just used, you would need to be clear about what you mean by *television violence, censorship,* and *free speech rights.*

▲ **CAN YOU LEARN ENOUGH TO COVER THE CLAIM FULLY?** If the information for an effective paper is unavailable or too complicated, write another claim, one that you know more about and can research more successfully. Or narrow the claim further to an aspect that you can understand and develop.

▲ **WHAT ARE THE VARIOUS PERSPECTIVES ON YOUR ISSUE?** Make certain that your issue invites two or more perspectives. If you have written an exploratory paper on your issue, you already know what several views are. If you have not written such a paper, explore your issue by writing several claims that represent several points of view, and then select the one you want to prove. For example:

Solar power is better than nuclear energy.
Solar power is worse than nuclear energy.
Solar power has some advantages and some disadvantages when compared to nuclear energy.
Solar power is better than nuclear energy for certain specified purposes.

As you identify the perspectives on your issue, you can also begin to plan some refutation that will not alienate your audience. An angry or insulted audience is not likely to change.

▲ *How Can You Make Your Claim Both Interesting and Compelling to Yourself and Your Audience?* Develop a fresh perspective on your issue when writing your claim. Suppose you are writing a policy paper that claims public education should be changed. You get bored with it. You keep running into old reasons that everyone already knows. Then you discover a couple of new aspects of the issue that you could cover with more original ideas and material. You learn that some people think parents should be able to choose their children's school, and you learn that competition among schools might lead to improvement. You also learn that contractors can take over schools and manage them in order to improve them. You refocus your issue and your perspective. Your new fact claim is, *Competition among schools, like competition in business, leads to improvement.* The issue and your claim now have new interest for you and your audience because you are looking at them in a whole new way.

▲ *At What Point Are You and the Audience Entering the Conversation on the Issue?* Consider your audience's background and initial views on the issue to decide how to write a claim about it. If both you and your audience are new to the issue, you may decide to stick with claims of fact and definition. If your audience understands it to some extent but needs more analysis, you may decide on claims of cause or value. If both you and your audience have adequate background on the issue, you may want to write a policy claim and try to solve the problems associated with it. Keep in mind also that issues and audiences are dynamic. As soon as audiences engage with issues, both begin to change. So you need to be constantly aware of the current status of the issue and the audience's current stand on it.

▲ *What Secondary Purpose Do You Want to Address in Your Paper?* Even though you establish your predominant purpose as fact, for example, you may still want to answer the other claim questions, particularly if you think your audience needs that information. You may also need to speculate about cause. You may need to provide definitions for the key words. You may want to address value questions to engage your audience's motives and values. Finally, you may want to suggest policy even though your paper has another predominant purpose.

PRELIMINARY PLAN

A preliminary plan will guide your future thinking and research and help you maintain the focus and direction you have already established. Even though you may not know very much about your issue or your claim at this point, writing out what you know and what you want to learn can be valuable. Add some ideas to your plan for beginning research and getting started on a first draft. Box 10.1 (page 300) provides an example.

You now have the beginning of an argument paper: a claim, some reasons, and some ideas to explore further. Your claim may change, and your reasons will probably change as you think, read, and do research. Before you go further, however, you need to think more about the audience. The nature of your audience can have a major influence on how you will finally write your argument paper.

BOX 10.1   **A Preliminary Plan Helps You Get Started.**

A PRELIMINARY PLAN

VALUE CLAIM PLUS REASONS

Television violence is harmful and should not be subject to the protection of free speech rights because . . .

> violence on television and violence in life seem to be related.
>
> children do not always differentiate between television and reality.
>
> parents do not supervise their children's television viewing.
>
> even though free speech is a constitutional right, it should not be invoked to protect what is harmful to society.

RESEARCH NEEDS

I need to find out how free speech is usually defined. Does it include all freedom of expression, including violence on television? Also, I will need to find the latest studies on television violence and violent behavior, particularly in children. Will there be a cause–effect relationship? Even though I want to focus mainly on value and show that violent television is bad, I will also need to include definition and cause in this paper.

PLAN FOR FIRST DRAFT

I will define television violence and free speech. I need to do some background reading on censorship and freedom of speech and summarize some of this information for my readers. My strongest material will probably be on the relationship between violence on television and violence in real life. I think now I'll begin with that and end with the idea that the Constitution should not be invoked to protect harmful elements like television violence. I'm going to write for an audience that either has children or values children. I will use examples from an article I clipped about how children imitate what they see on television.

UNDERSTANDING THE AUDIENCE

Why is it important to understand your audience? Why not just argue for what you think is important? Some definitions and descriptions of effective argument emphasize the techniques of argument rather than the outcomes. They encourage the arguer to focus on what he or she thinks is important. For example, an argument with a clear claim, clear logic and reasoning, and good evidence will be described by some theorists as a good argument. The position in this book, however, has been different. If the argument does not reach the audience and create some common ground in order to convince or change it in some way, the argument, no matter how skillfully crafted, is not productive. Productive argument, according to the definitions we used in Chapter 1, must create common ground and achieve some definable audience outcomes.

In order for the writer of argument to reach the audience, create common ground, and bring about change, two essential requirements need to be met. First, the audience must be willing to listen and perhaps also be willing to change. Second, the author must be willing to study, understand, and appeal to the audience. Such analysis will enable the author to relate to the audience's present opinions, values, and motives and to show as often as possible that the author shares them to achieve the common ground essential for effective argument. Thus both audience and author need to cooperate to a certain degree for argument to achieve any outcomes at all.

Four strategies will help you begin the process of understanding and appealing to your audience: assess the audience's size and familiarity to you, determine how much you have in common with your audience, determine the audience's initial position and what changes in views or actions might occur as a result of your argument, and identify the audience's discourse community. Let us examine each in turn.

▲ *Assess the Audience's Size and Familiarity.* Audiences come in all sizes and may or may not include people you know. The smallest and most familiar audience is always yourself; you must convince yourself in internal argument. The next smallest audience is one other person. Larger audiences may include specific, known groups such as family members, classmates, work associates, or members of an organization you belong to. You may also at times write for a large unfamiliar audience composed of either local, national, or international members. And of course some audiences are mixed, including people you know and people you do not know. Your techniques will vary for building common ground with large and small, familiar and unfamiliar audiences, but your argumentative aim will not change.

▲ *Determine What You and the Audience Have in Common.* You may or may not consider yourself a member of your audience, depending on how closely you identify with it and share its views. For example, if you are a member of a union, you will probably identify and agree with its official position, particularly on work-related issues. If you work with management, you will hold other views about work-related issues. Your methods of achieving common ground with either of these audiences will be somewhat different, depending on whether you consider yourself a member of the group or not.

▲ *Determine the Audience's Initial Position and How It Might Change.* As part of your planning, project what you would regard as acceptable audience outcomes for your argument. Think about the degree of common ground you initially share with your audience, because it is then easier to imagine audience change. There are several possibilities of initial audience positions and possible changes or outcomes.

You may be writing for a *friendly* audience that is in near or total agreement with you from the outset. The planned outcome is to *confirm this audience's beliefs and strengthen its commitment.* You can be straightforward with this audience, addressing it directly and openly with the claim at the beginning, supported with evidence and warrants that it can accept. Political rallies, religious sermons, and public demonstrations by special-interest groups, such as civil rights or pro-life groups, all serve to make members more strongly committed to their original beliefs. When you write for a friendly audience, you will achieve the same effect.

Another type of audience either *mildly agrees* with you or *mildly opposes* you. This audience may possess no clear reasons for its tendencies or beliefs. Possible outcomes in this case usually include (1) *final agreement* with you, (2) a *new interest* in the issue and a commitment to work out a position on it, or (3) a *tentative decision* to accept what seems to be true for now. To establish common ground with this type of audience, get to the point quickly, and use support and warrants that will establish connections.

Other audiences may be *neutral* on your issue, uncommitted and uninterested in how it is resolved. Your aim will be to *change the level of their indifference* and encourage them to take a position. You may only be able to get their attention or raise their level of consciousness. As with other audiences, you will establish common ground with a neutral audience by analyzing its needs and by appealing to those needs.

A *hostile* audience that disagrees with you may be closed to the idea of change, at least at first. Anticipated outcomes for such audiences might include *avoiding more hostility* and *getting people to listen and consider possible alternative views*. Rogerian argument (see Chapter 9) or a delayed claim may be necessary to get such an audience to listen at all. It is always possible that a hostile audience might *change its mind* or at least *compromise*. If all else fails, sometimes you can get a hostile audience to *agree to disagree*, which is much better than increasing the hostility.

Think of your relationship with your audience as if it were plotted on a sliding scale. At one end are the people who agree with you, and at the other end are those who disagree. In the middle is the neutral audience. Other mildly hostile or mildly favorable audiences are positioned at various points in between. Your knowledge of human nature and argument theory will help you plan strategies of argument that will address all these audience types.

▲ *IDENTIFY THE AUDIENCE'S DISCOURSE COMMUNITY.* An audience's affiliations can help define its nature. Specialized groups that share subject matter, background, experience, values, and a common language (including specialized and technical vocabulary, jargon, or slang) are known as *discourse communities.* Common ground automatically exists among members of a discourse community because they understand one another easily.

Consider discourse communities composed of all scientists, all engineers, or all mathematicians. Their common background, training, language, and knowledge make it easier for them to connect, achieve common ground, and work toward conclusions. The discourse community itself, in fact, creates some of the common ground necessary for successful academic inquiry or for other types of argument.

You are a member of the university or college discourse community where you attend classes. This community is characterized by reasonable and educated people who share common background and interests that enable them to inquire into matters that are still at issue. You are also a member of the discourse community in your argument class, which has a common vocabulary and common tasks and assignments. Outsiders visiting your class would not be members of this community in the same way that you and your classmates are.

What other discourse communities do you belong to? How do the discourse communities in your home, among your friends, and at work differ from your university and argument class discourse communities? For some students, the differences are considerable. The strategies for connecting with others, building common ground, and arguing within the context of each of your discourse communities can vary considerably. With some reflection, you will be able to think of examples of the ways you have analyzed and adapted to each of them already. You can improve your natural ability to work with audiences by learning some conscious strategies for analyzing and adapting to both familiar and unfamiliar audiences.

ANALYZING A FAMILIAR AUDIENCE

At an early stage in the writing process, you need to answer certain key questions about your audience. To get this information, you may simply ask members of your audience some questions. Asking questions isn't always possible or advisable, however. More often, you will have to obtain your own answers by studying the audience and doing research.

The following list presents thirteen questions to ask about a familiar audience. You do not have to answer every question about every audience. You may need to add a question or two, depending on your audience. Answer questions that are suggested by the particular rhetorical situation for your argument. For example, the age range of the audience might be a factor to consider if you are writing about how to live a successful life; the diversity of the class might be important if you are writing about racial issues; or class member interests, particularly outdoor interests, might be useful to know if you are writing about the environment.

As you read through the audience analysis questions, imagine that you are continuing to work on the argument paper on the topic of jury trials. Recall that your claim is, *Juries need pretrial training in order to make competent judgments.* The information that you uncover about your audience follows each question.

1. Describe the audience in general. Who are its members? What do you have in common with them?

Example: My audience is my argument class. We have common educational goals, language, assignments, campus interests, and experiences.

2. What are some of the demographics of the group? Consider size, age, gender, nationality, education, and professional status.

Example: Two-thirds of the twenty-four students are eighteen to twenty years old, and one-third are over thirty. Fifty-eight percent are female, and 42 percent are male. Slightly less than half are white; about a third are black, Hispanic, and Asian; and the rest are international students. About three-fourths are freshmen and sophomores, and the rest are upper-division students. More than half of the class works at part-time outside jobs. Two have full-time professions in insurance and sales.

3. What are some of their organizational affiliations? Consider political parties, religion, social and living groups, and economic status.

Example: Roughly half say they are Democrats and half Republicans. Three say they are Libertarians. Fifty percent say they attend Christian churches, 20 percent are Jewish, and the rest either are Muslim or Hindu or say they are not religious. Four belong to fraternities or sororities, a few live in the dorms, and the rest live at home or in apartments. Most are in the middle or lower-middle class with aspirations to graduate, get better jobs, and move up.

4. What are their interests? Include outside interests, reading material, and perhaps majors.

Example: The group lists the following interests and activities: sports, movies, television, exercise and fitness, camping and hiking, attending lectures, repairing and driving cars, listening to music, reading local newspapers, and reading newsmagazines. They are all college students. Five are in engineering, six are in business, one is in nursing, and the rest are in humanities and social sciences.

5. What is their present position on your issue? What audience outcomes can you anticipate?

Example: My issue is jury trials, and my claim is, *Juries need pretrial training in order to make competent judgments.* Most members of the class have not thought about this issue and either are neutral or mildly agree. A show of hands reveals that five think juries need more training, fifteen don't know, and four favor the status quo. I can expect the neutral and status quo members to become interested and perhaps even agree. I can expect the others to agree more strongly than they do now.

6. Will they interpret the issue in the same way you have?

Example: This issue comes from a local event, and some class members may see a double-jeopardy issue or some other issue emerging from it. I will have to focus their attention on my issue and make it important to them.

7. How significant is your issue to the audience? Will it touch their lives or remain theoretical for them?

Example: This is a personally significant issue for the people planning to be lawyers. It has some personal significance for most of the others also because everyone who votes is a potential jury member. The international students will have interest in it, depending on their background and experience. I need to find out what their experiences have been.

8. Are there any obstacles that will prevent your audience from accepting your claim as soon as you state it?

Example: Part of this audience believes that juries are always effective and need no improvement. I will have to challenge that idea.

9. How involved are audience members in the ongoing conversation about the issue? Will they require background and definitions? Are they knowledgeable enough to contemplate policy change?

Example: Ninety percent know about the recent local case in which the jury made a poor judgment because of ignorance of procedures. Half of the class members have been called for jury duty, and two have served. Three intend to go to law school and have considerable background and interest in juries. This audience knows enough to think about policy changes.

10. What is the attitude of your audience toward you?

Example: I think I have a friendly audience, and I am an insider, a part of it. We have established an open atmosphere in this class, and there are no personal hostilities that I can see. We share the same discourse community.

11. What beliefs and values do you and your audience share?

Example: In regard to my issue, we all value trial by jury, a job well done, and education.

12. What motivates your audience? What are its members' goals and aims?

Example: The people in my audience would be motivated to do a good job if they were on a jury.

13. What argument style will work best with your audience?

Example: I don't want to debate this issue. I would like to get consensus and a sense of cooperation instead. In fact, I picked this issue because it is one that people will probably not fight about. I want to use examples that will appeal to my audience's experiences. I am willing to negotiate or qualify my conclusion if the class members who critique my paper have trouble with it.

Go through these questions, and try to answer them for your potential audience at an early stage of the writing process. To help you answer questions 11 and 12 about values and motives, refer to Box 10.2 (page 306).[2]

CONSTRUCTING AN UNFAMILIAR AUDIENCE

Sometimes you will not be able to gather direct information about your audience because it will be unfamiliar to you and unavailable for study. In this case, you will need to draw on your past experience for audience analysis. To do so you will have to imagine a particular kind of audience, a *universal audience*, and write for it when you cannot get direct audience information.

Chaim Perelman, who has written extensively about the difficulty of identifying the qualities of audiences with certainty, has developed the concept of the universal audience.[3] He suggests planning an argument for a composite audience that has individual differences but also important common qualities. This universal audience is educated, reasonable, normal, adult, and willing to listen. Every arguer constructs the universal audience from his or her own past experience,

---

[2]The list in Box 10.2 is based on Abraham Maslow's hierarchy of needs and motives from his book *Motion and Personality*, expanded by James A. Wood in *Speaking Effectively* (New York: Random House, 1988), pp. 203–204. Used with permission.

[3]See Perelman and Olbrechts-Tyteca, *The New Rhetoric*, for additional details on the universal audience.

| BOX 10.2 | **Needs and Values That Motivate Most Audiences.** |

WHAT MOTIVATES AN AUDIENCE?

1. **Survival needs:** food, warmth, and shelter; physical safety
2. **Health:** physical well-being, strength, endurance, energy; mental stability, optimism
3. **Financial well-being:** accumulation of wealth; increased earning capacity; lower costs and expenses; financial security
4. **Affection and friendship:** identification in a group; being accepted, liked, loved; being attractive to others; having others as friends or objects of affection
5. **Respect and esteem of others:** having the approval of others; having status in a group; being admired; having fame
6. **Self-esteem:** meeting one's own standards in such virtues as courage, fairness, honesty, generosity, good judgment, and compassion; meeting self-accepted obligations of one's role as employee, child or parent, citizen, member of an organization
7. **New experience:** travel; change in employment or location; new hobbies or leisure activities; new food or consumer products; variety in friends and acquaintances
8. **Self-actualization:** developing one's potential in skills and abilities; achieving ambitions; being creative; gaining the power to influence events and other people
9. **Convenience:** conserving time or energy; the ease with which the other motives can be satisfied

and consequently the concept of the universal audience varies somewhat from individual to individual and culture to culture.

The construct of the universal audience can be useful when you write argument and other papers for your other college classes. It is especially useful when the audience is largely unknown and you cannot obtain much information about it. Imagine writing for a universal audience on those occasions. Your professors and classmates as a group possess the general qualities of this audience.

It is also useful to try to construct an unfamiliar audience's possible initial position on your issue. When you do not know your audience's position, it is best to imagine it as neutral to mildly opposed to your views and direct your argument with that in mind. Imagining an unfamiliar audience as either hostile or friendly can lead to extreme positions that may cause the argument to fail. Imagining the audience as neutral or mildly opposed ensures an even tone to the argument that promotes audience interest and receptivity. The following excerpt from a speech report illustrates some of the problems that were created when the speaker assumed total agreement from the audience. Notice that the author, who describes himself as an audience member, is obviously different from the audience members imagined by the speaker. How is he different? What is the effect? What changes could this speaker make to create better common ground with all of her audience members? Consider what this speaker might have done differently if she had imagined a neutral or mildly opposed audience instead of a strongly friendly audience.

> I am listening to a lecture by Helen Caldicott, the environmental activist. Dr. Caldicott is in top form, holding forth with her usual bracing mixture of caustic wit and prophetical urgency. All around me, an audience of the faithful is responding with camp-meeting fervor, cheering her on as she itemizes a familiar checklist of impending calamities: acid rain, global warming, endangered species.
>
> She has even come up with a fresh wrinkle on one of the standard environmental horrors: nuclear energy. Did we know, she asks, that nuclear energy is producing scores of anencephalic births in the industrial shantytowns along the Mexican border? "Every time you turn on an electric light," she admonishes us, "you are making another brainless baby."
>
> Dr. Caldicott's presentation is meant to instill unease. In my case, she is succeeding, though not in the way she intends. She is making me worry, as so many of my fellow environmentalists have begun to make me worry—not simply for the fate of the Earth, but for the fate of this movement on which so much depends. As much as I want to endorse what I hear, Dr. Caldicott's effort to shock and shame just isn't taking. I am as sympathetic a listener as she can expect to find, yet rather than collapsing into self-castigation, as I once might have, I find myself going numb.
>
> Is it possible that green guilt, the mainstay of the movement, has lost its ethical sting?
>
> Despite my reservations, I do my best to go along with what Dr. Caldicott has to say—even though I suspect (as I think most of her audience does) that there is no connection between light bulbs and brainless babies.[4]

USING INFORMATION ABOUT YOUR AUDIENCE

When you complete your analysis of your audience, you need to go back through the information you have gathered and consciously decide which audience characteristics to appeal to in your paper. As an example, look back through the audience analysis of the argument class that was done for you. Suppose that you are the student who is planning to write the paper about jury training. You decide that the general questions about the makeup of the group suggest that you have a fairly typical college audience. Its members are varied enough in their background and experience so that you know they will not all share common opinions on all matters. They do have in common, however, their status as college students. Furthermore, all of you belong to the same group, so you can assume some common values and goals. All of them, you assume, want to be successful, to graduate, and to improve themselves and society; you can appeal to these common motives. All or most of them read local newspapers or watch local news programs, so they will have common background on the rhetorical situation for your issue. You have asked about their present views on jury training, and you know that many are neutral. Your strategy will be to break through this neutrality and get commitment for change.

---

[4]Theodore Roszak, "Green Guilt and Ecological Overload," *New York Times*, June 9, 1992, p. A27.

"I'll tell you what this election is about. It's about homework, and pitiful allowances, and having to clean your room. It's also about candy, and ice cream, and staying up late."

The Results of a Careful Audience Analysis.

SOURCE: *New Yorker,* May 27, 1996, p. 115. Copyright © 1996 by The New Yorker Collection. Robert Weber from <cartoonbank.com>. All rights reserved.

You decide, furthermore, that you may have to focus the issue for them because they are not likely to see it your way without help. They should also, you decide, know enough to contemplate policy change. You can appeal to their potential common experience as jurors and their need for physical safety, fairness, and good judgment in dealing with criminals. You can further assume that your audience values competence, expertise, and reasonableness, all important outcomes of the training system you intend to advocate. Your argument style will work with the group members because you have already analyzed styles, and yours is familiar to them. They either share your style or are flexible enough to adapt to it. You are now in a position to gather materials for your paper that will be convincing to this particular audience. You will develop reasoning, including support and warrants, that audience members can link to their personal values, motives, beliefs, knowledge, and experience.

You need to show the same care in adapting to the needs of a universal audience. Since this audience is reasonable, educated, and adult, support and warrants must be on its level and should also have broad applicability and acceptance. Odd or extreme perspectives or support will usually not be acceptable. An example is the electric light causing brainless babies in "Green Guilt and Ecological Overload." This example does not have universal appeal. Notice also that the universal audience, reasonable and well educated, should inspire a high level of argumentative writing. Careful research, intelligent reasoning, and clear style are requirements for this audience.

REVIEW QUESTIONS

1. What are the claim questions, and how can they be used to establish major and minor purposes in your position paper?
2. What are some additional preliminary questions that you can ask to help you develop your claim?
3. What is the purpose of the preliminary plan? What three main types of information are included on it?
4. What would you need to consider about an audience to discover how much common ground you share?
5. What is a discourse community? How does it help establish common ground?
6. What are a few items described in this chapter that you consider particularly important in conducting an audience analysis?
7. What is the universal audience? What are its special qualities? Why is it a useful idea?

EXERCISES AND ACTIVITIES

A. THE RESEARCHED POSITION PAPER: WRITING A CLAIM AND CLARIFYING YOUR PURPOSE

Complete the following worksheet by writing answers to the questions. They will help you focus on your claim and ways to develop it. Discuss your answers with the other members in your writing group, or discuss some of your answers with the whole class.

CLAIM DEVELOPMENT WORKSHEET

1. Write an issue question to focus your issue.
2. Freewrite in response to the claim questions. They are as follows:

   Fact: Did it happen? Does it exist?
   Definition: What is it? How can I define it?
   Cause: What caused it? What are the effects?
   Value: Is it good or bad? What criteria will help us decide?
   Policy: What should we do about it? What should be our future course of action?

(continued)

(continued)

3. Read what you have written, and decide on a purpose. Write your claim as a complete sentence.
4. Which will be your predominant argumentative purpose in developing the claim: fact, definition, cause, value, or policy?
5. What is your original slant on the issue, and is it evident in the claim?
6. Is the claim too broad, too narrow, or manageable for now? Elaborate.
7. How will you define the controversial words in your claim?
8. Do you predict at this point that you may have to qualify your claim to make it acceptable to the audience? How?

B. THE RESEARCHED POSITION PAPER: PRELIMINARY PLAN

Use the following worksheet to help you construct a preliminary plan and a guide for thinking and research.

PRELIMINARY PLAN WORKSHEET

TYPE OF CLAIM PLUS REASONS

Write your claim, write the word *because* after the claim, and list three to five possible reasons or subclaims that you might develop in your paper.

RESEARCH NEEDS

Anticipate your research needs. What parts of your paper can you develop with your present knowledge and information? What parts will you need to think about and research further? Can you learn enough to develop the claim, or should you simplify it? What types of research materials will you seek, and where will you seek them?

How much preliminary background reading do you need to do, and where should you do it? Would any of the reference books in the library help you? Or should you ask your professor or a librarian for a better source?

PLAN FOR FIRST DRAFT

How much background will you need to provide your readers? What terms will you need to define?

What are your strongest opinions? Your best reasons?

What is a tentative way to begin your paper? What is a tentative way to end it?

What original examples, descriptions, or comparisons occur to you now?

C. THE RESEARCHED POSITION PAPER: AUDIENCE ANALYSIS OF YOUR WRITING GROUP

Do an analysis of the small group of four or five individuals in your class who will serve as readers and critics of your paper from now until you hand it in. Your aim is to get an idea of how your audience regards your issue before you write. Your aim is to help your audience members become interested in reading your paper and perhaps even change their minds. Do this as a group project, with each group member in turn interviewing the others and jotting down answers to the questions in the following worksheet.

AUDIENCE ANALYSIS WORKSHEET

1. Describe your issue. What is your audience's present position on your issue? Describe some other perspectives on your issue, and ask for reactions to those ideas. State your claim and ask if there is anyone who cannot accept it as stated. If there is, ask why.
2. How significant is your issue to the audience? If it is not considered significant, describe why it is significant to you, and talk about ways you can make it more significant to the audience.
3. How involved are audience members in the ongoing conversation about the issue? What do they already know about it?
4. How will you build common ground? What beliefs and values do you and your audience share about your issue? What motivates audience members in regard to your issue?
5. What argument style will work best with them? A direct adversarial style? A consensual style? Why?
6. Write what you have learned from this analysis to help you plan your appeal to this audience. Include values and motives in your discussion.

Chapter 11

The Research Paper:
Invention and Research

The writing process requires both creative thinking and critical thinking. For example, invention and research are creative, and rewriting and revision are critical. This chapter is about creativity. It encourages you to think about what you already know and believe before you seek the opinions of others. As a result, your voice will become the major voice in your paper, and your ideas will predominate over those of others. Information and ideas from other sources will be brought in later to back up what you ultimately say.

The invention strategies presented here are appropriate for helping you think about and develop your ideas for your researched position paper. Use them along with the prewriting invention strategies that appear in Chapter 4. All of the invention strategies from both chapters are summarized on the invention worksheet on page 336.

The first two strategies described here are logical thinking methods to help you expand on your topic. These are followed by a review of argument theory from earlier chapters to help you invent ideas and identify the parts of your paper. The last sections of the chapter will help you do library and online research, other creative sources of information and opinion for your paper.

USING BURKE'S PENTAD TO ESTABLISH CAUSE

Asking *why* will help you establish cause for controversial incidents and human motives. So will a systematic application of Kenneth Burke's pentad as he describes it in his book *A Grammar of Motives*.[1] In his first sentence, Burke poses the question "What is involved, when we say what people are doing and why they

---

[1]Kenneth Burke, *A Grammar of Motives* (New York: Prentice Hall, 1945), p. xv. James Wood pointed out to me the value of Burke's pentad in attributing cause in argument.

are doing it?" Burke identified five terms and associated questions that can be used to examine possible causes for human action and events. Since establishing cause is an important part of many arguments, and especially of fact, cause, and policy arguments, the pentad is potentially very useful to the writer of argument. Here are Burke's terms and questions along with an example to demonstrate an application of the pentad. The example describes a controversial art exhibit that political leaders tried to shut down by withholding public funds from the art museum. Controversies about public funding of art occur from time to time. This specific example took place in Brooklyn, New York. When you have read the example, apply Burke's questions to your own issue to help you think about possible ways to describe its cause. The questions force a close analysis of an issue, and they will help you gain additional insight into the controversy associated with your issue. Burke's pentad, by the way, is similar to the journalist's questions *who, what, where, when, why,* and *how* except that it yields even more information than they do.

1. *Act: What was done?* What took place in thought or deed?

Example: An exhibit of works by modern British artists opened at the Brooklyn Museum of Art. It was controversial because it included some objects that are not usually considered art, including animal parts and an unusual presentation of the Virgin Mary. Some people objected.

2. *Scene: When or where was it done?* What is the background or scene in which it occurred?

Example: The primary scene was the art museum and the exhibit. The scene also extended beyond the museum to include the art scene, made up of art lovers, museum directors, and art connoisseurs who saw the exhibit as a bold and interesting experiment in modern art; the political and religious scene, made up of political and religious leaders who saw the exhibit as outrageous and blasphemous and tried to shut it down as a result; and the judicial scene, made up of the judge and the court that ruled against withholding funds and declared that act a form of censorship, contrary to the First Amendment guarantee of freedom of speech. Thus the long tradition of constitutional law is also part of the scene.

3. *Agent: Who did it?* What person or kind of person performed the act?

Example: The British artists who created the exhibit, and their sponsors who hoped to make money on it, are agents, as are the museum directors and art lovers, the mayor and the religious leaders, and the judge. Other agents include the individuals who visited the art exhibit and either liked it or did not and the other individuals who only read or heard about the exhibit but formed opinions about it anyway.

4. *Agency: How was it done?* What means or instruments were used?

Example: The unusual materials used in the art exhibit are part of the agency: elephant dung adorned with sequins, flies and rotting meat, obscene body parts glued to the Virgin Mary's gown, mattresses, buckets, and so on. The mass media were also part of the agency: numerous articles in newspapers and magazines either praised or condemned the exhibit. The availability of the museum, the funding for the exhibit provided by outside individuals as well as by the city, and the desire to profit from the exhibit are part of the agency, as are the power of the mayor's office to withhold money and the power of the law to declare the mayor's actions unconstitutional.

5. *Purpose: Why did it happen?* What was the main motivation?

Example: The artists' purpose was to extend the definition of art by creating new forms, to create more tolerance for contemporary art by creating extreme examples, and to stimulate critical thinking and debate about art. The artists and their sponsors also wanted to exhibit the art, improve their own artistic reputations, and make money. The mayor and the religious leaders wanted to shut down the exhibit because they regarded it as offensive and irreligious and believed that the public would not want to support it. The judge's purpose was to uphold constitutional law.

Notice that you can focus on a part of an answer to any one of the five questions and argue that it is the main cause of the controversy. Notice also that each of the five questions provides a different perspective on the cause. Furthermore, the answers to these questions stir controversy. You may in fact have found yourself disagreeing with the answers in the examples. As Burke puts it, "Men may violently disagree about the purposes behind a given act, or about the character of the person who did it, or how he did it, or in what kind of situation he acted; or they may even insist upon totally different words to name the act itself."[2] Still, he goes on to say, one can begin with some kinds of answers to these questions, which then provide a starting point for inquiry and argument. Apply Burke's pentad to every issue you write about to provide you with a deeper perspective on the causes or motives behind it. When you have done that, apply some of the additional invention strategies in this chapter to help you develop ideas for your paper.

USING CHAINS OF REASONS TO DEVELOP GREATER DEPTH OF ANALYSIS AND DETAIL

Another method of developing a claim or subclaim in your paper is to use chains of reasons to help you get a line of thinking going. You use this method quite naturally in verbal argument when you make a claim, someone asks you questions like *why* or *what for,* and you give additional reasons and evidence as support. For example:

You claim:	The university should be more student-friendly.
Someone asks:	Why do you think so? I think it's OK.
You answer:	Because students are its customers, and without us it would not exist.
Someone asks:	Why wouldn't it?
You answer:	Because we pay the money to keep it going.
Someone asks:	Why do students keep it going? There are other sources of income.
You answer:	Because our tuition is much more than the income of all of the other sources combined.

---

[2]Ibid., p. xv.

You get the idea. Imagining that you are in a dialogue with another person who keeps asking *why* enables you to create quantities of additional support and detailed development for your claim. Also, by laying out your argument in this way, you can see where you need more support. In the preceding example, you need to provide support to show what portion of the operating budget is funded by student tuition. You might also give examples of insensitive treatment of students and explain what students have in common with customers.

To chain an argument, repeat the *why . . . because* sequence three or four times, both for your main claim and for each of your subclaims. Add evidence in all the places where your argument is sketchy. You will end up with a detailed analysis and support for your claim that will make it much less vulnerable to attack.

USING ARGUMENT THEORY TO THINK SYSTEMATICALLY ABOUT YOUR ISSUE

Let us review what you have learned about argument in earlier chapters to help you think about your claim and some ways to develop it.

ANALYZE THE RHETORICAL SITUATION

Focus your attention on the total context for your argument, including the motivation for the issue, how you will write about it, and how your reader-audience will react to it. Use the rhetorical situation questions (TRACE), and apply them to your paper.

1. What will be the purpose and strategies of the *text* I produce?
2. Who is the *reader/audience?* That is, who besides me thinks the issue is a problem? How do these people view it?
3. What is motivating *me*, the *author*, to write about this issue? What makes me qualified?
4. What are the *constraints* (other people, events, affiliations, organizations, values, beliefs, or traditions) that influence the audience's perceptions of this issue, and will they bring us together or drive us apart?
5. What is the *exigence* (context, dramatic real-life situation) that makes me and others perceive this issue as controversial?

USE THE TOULMIN MODEL

By the time you have answered the following questions, you will have the essential parts of your paper.

1. *What is my claim?* Your claim tells your readers what you are trying to prove. Decide whether it would be stronger to place it at the beginning, in the middle, or at the end of your paper.
2. *What support should I use?* Consider how to include *facts, opinions,* and *examples. Facts* include descriptions of events you or others have observed, specific

examples or accounts of real happenings, narratives of both historical and recent events, and accurate and reliable statistical reports. To be convincing, facts must be vivid, real, and verifiable. *Opinions* include reasons, interpretations, explanations, and ideas about the issue and the factual information used to support it. Whereas facts by themselves are comparatively lifeless and boring, they become interesting and convincing when they are presented along with explanations about their significance and relevance. Besides your own opinions, you may want to include expert opinion that can be summarized, paraphrased, or quoted directly in your paper. *Examples* clarify points, make them interesting and easier to remember, and in argument help prove the claim. Remember that examples can be real or made up, long or short, and that real examples are more convincing than hypothetical examples.

3. *What are my warrants?* Remember that support and warrants, taken together, constitute the proofs or lines of argument for your paper. Every time you use a particular piece of support, a warrant, usually implicit, will cause your audience either to accept or reject it as appropriate support for the claim. Write down the warrants that are working in your paper, and answer three questions about them: (a) Do they link the evidence and the claim and make it convincing? (b) Do you believe your own warrants? If you do not, make some changes. Argument from personal conviction is the most convincing argument. (c) Will your audience share your warrants or reject them? If you think it will reject them, consider the possibility of stating them and providing some backing for them.

4. *What backing might I provide to make my warrants more acceptable and convincing?* You may use additional support, including facts, expert opinion, reports, studies, and polls, to back up your warrants. You can do the same to back up evidence when necessary. Add material, in other words, to make your paper more convincing whenever you think your audience requires it.

5. *How should I handle rebuttal?* Not all argument papers include rebuttal. You will usually strengthen your own position, however, if you decide to include rebuttal. It is particularly important to identify the arguments on the other side and point out what is wrong with them when the issue is familiar and obviously controversial. Your audience will be familiar with the other views and will expect your opinion on them in your paper.

When you plan rebuttal, here are some specific strategies to consider. Use your exploratory paper or do some background research to get a sense of the different perspectives on your issue. Then write your own claim and state reasons in favor of it; next, write one or more opposing claims and some reasons to support them. Next, study the claims and reasons that are different from your own, and attack their weakest features. What is most vulnerable—the support, the warrants, or the claims themselves? Name some of the weakest features of these other perspectives, and point out the problems associated with them in your paper.

Another strategy for rebuttal is to build a strong case of your own that undercuts an opposing position but does not specifically acknowledge it. State and demonstrate that yours is the strongest position available. Or you can always examine the opposition's major proofs and apply the tests of validity explained in

Chapter 7. In your paper, point out all problems with these proofs. Remember that rebuttal should not offend the audience. Angry people won't pay serious attention or change their minds. Watch members of the U.S. Congress on C-SPAN television for examples of cordial rebuttal. They constantly engage in rebuttal, but they are polite and usually compliment the opposition while disagreeing. This courtesy reduces hostility both in the opposition and in the audience.

6. *Will I need to qualify my claim?* If you believe strongly in your claim, you may want to state it as absolutely true. You must realize, however, that absolute positions will be acceptable only to people who already agree with you. To gain the adherence of more members of your audience, you may need to qualify your claim by using such words as *usually, often, probably, sometimes,* or *almost always.*

PLAN YOUR PROOFS

Here is a review of the types of proof. They represent distinct ways to think about and develop an argument. A variety of types in your paper will make it more interesting and convincing.

LOGICAL PROOFS. Logical proofs (SICDADS) are convincing because they are real and drawn from experience. Answer all of the proof questions that apply to your issue.

- *Signs:* What signs show that this might be true?
- *Induction:* What examples can I use? What conclusion can I draw from the examples? Can my readers make the "inductive leap" from the examples to an acceptance of the conclusion?
- *Cause:* What is the main cause of the controversy? What are the effects?
- *Deduction:* What conclusions will I draw? What general principles, warrants, and examples are they based on?
- *Analogies:* What comparisons can I make? Can I show that what happened in the past might happen again or that what happened in one case might happen in another?
- *Definition:* What do I need to define?
- *Statistics:* What statistics can I use? How should I present them?

PROOFS THAT AFFECT ETHOS. Proofs that affect *ethos* are convincing because they establish the authority of the quoted individuals. Answer these questions to establish your own *ethos* and that of the experts you quote.

- *Authority:* Whom should I quote? What background information should I supply both for myself and for those I quote to establish our expertise?

EMOTIONAL PROOFS. Emotional proofs are convincing because emotion can strengthen logical conviction. Ask the following questions to include emotional proofs in your paper.

- *Values:* What values can I appeal to? Should I spell them out or leave them unstated? Will emotional narratives, examples, descriptions, and language make my appeals to values stronger?

◆ *Motives:* What do my readers need and want in regard to my issue? How can I appeal to those needs? Will emotional materials help?

PRESENTING STATISTICS IN GRAPHS AND CHARTS

As you gather your proofs for your paper, you may want to think about presenting any data or statistics you intend to use in the form of graphs and charts, particularly since computer software now makes this relatively easy to do. Graphs and charts can be especially useful when the statistical information is too cumbersome to include in the written body of your paper. There are many different kinds of graphs, but the most commonly used are line, bar, and circle (or pie) graphs. These three kinds of graphs can be easily generated through common word processing packages such as Microsoft Word or WordPerfect. The examples that follow present graphs of data from *The World Almanac,* an excellent source for up-to-date statistics on many subjects. *Bar graphs* are usually used when you want to compare measurements of some kind. The numbers used in the measurements are often large, and the bar graph offers a picture that makes the numbers easily understood. *Line graphs* are most often used to show a change in a measurement over time. Some of the different measurements associated with line graphs are temperature, height and weight, test scores, population changes, and profits. *Circle graphs* are ordinarily used to show how something is divided. For instance, a circle graph would be an effective way to show where the government spent its money over a specific period of time. Whatever kind of graph you use, however, you must be sure that it is correctly and clearly titled and labeled, that the units of measurement are noted, and that you report the source of the statistical information used in the graph.

If you are writing a paper arguing the ineffectiveness of AIDS education in America (including North and South America and the Caribbean) and Africa, and you want to give your audience some background concerning the number of AIDS cases reported in these parts of the world over several years, a bar graph might be the best way to present this information. Figure 11.1 provides an example.

A line graph is most effective when showing change over a period of time. If you are writing a paper arguing that the United States needs to take care of its debt, you might want to show the change in the deficit over a number of years to let your reader better understand the growth pattern of the debt. The line graph in Figure 11.2 (page 320) shows this information.

A circle or pie graph can quickly show how something is divided up. If you are writing a paper arguing that people are largely ignoring the depletion of the ozone caused by automobile emissions, you might want to sum the percentage of the different sizes of cars sold in the United States during a recent year. A circle graph would be an effective way to present this information. An example is provided in Figure 11.3 (page 320).

Sometimes the statistical information you need to include in your paper is very detailed and too lengthy for a graph. In this case, a chart or a table is usually

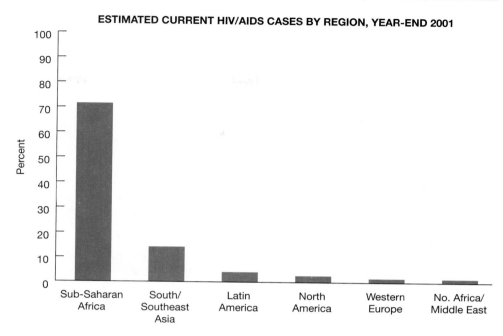

FIGURE 11.1 **Bar Graph Comparing Large Numbers.**

SOURCE: UNAIDS/Joint United Nations Program on HIV/AIDS.

recommended. For instance, if you wanted to argue for zero population growth, you might want to give some of the projected figures for populations of major countries. A table would probably be the most effective way of presenting this material. See the example in Figure 11.4 (page 321).

As a final check on the validity of your graphs and tables, make sure that nothing significant has been omitted and that the charts and graphs are accurately labeled.

USING PROOFS AND SUPPORT APPROPRIATE FOR THE PURPOSE OR TYPE OF CLAIM

Some proofs and support work better than others to establish different types of claims.[3] The following are not rules, just suggestions for you to consider.

FACT AND CAUSE. Fact and cause papers call for factual support, including data and statistics. Consider also naming specific *causes* and *effects*, naming and describing *symptoms* and *signs*, using *induction* to prove a claim based on examples, using

---

[3] I am indebted to Wayne E. Brockriede and Douglas Ehninger for some of the suggestions in this section. They identify some types of proof as appropriate for different sorts of claims in their article "Toulmin on Argument: An Interpretation and Application," *Quarterly Journal of Speech* 46 (1960): 44–53.

PUBLIC DEBT OF THE UNITED STATES

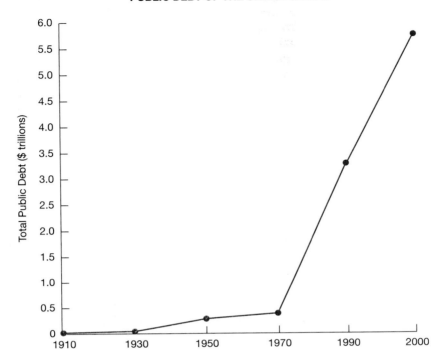

FIGURE 11.2   Line Graph Showing Change over Time.

SOURCE: Bureau of Public Debt, U.S. Department of the Treasury.

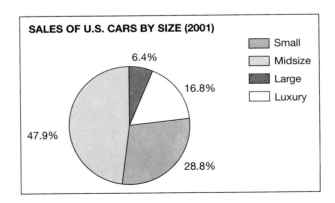

**FIGURE 11.3   Circle Graph Showing How
a Population or Market Is Divided Up.**

SOURCE: Ward's Communications.

POPULATION PROJECTIONS FOR SELECTED COUNTRIES:
2002, 2025, AND 2050 (in thousands)

Country	2002	2025	2050
Bangladesh	133,377	179,129	211,020
Brazil	176,030	209,587	228,145
China	1,284,304	1,407,739	1,322,435
India	1,045,845	1,415,274	1,706,951
Japan	126,975	119,865	101,334
Mexico	103,400	141,593	167,479
Nigeria	129,935	203,423	337,591
Russia	144,979	138,842	121,777
Saudi Arabia	23,513	50,374	97,120
United States of America	280,562	335,360	394,241

FIGURE 11.4   **Table Presenting Comparison Data.**

SOURCE: Bureau of the Census, U.S. Department of Commerce.

analogies to suggest that items coexist and share qualities and outcomes, and using *definitions* that place items in classes or categories. Also consider quoting an *authority* to verify that something is a fact. Emotional proofs are less valuable than the other types for establishing fact or cause.

DEFINITION. Definition papers can be developed with *literal analogies* that invite comparisons of similar items; with *historical analogies* that suggest that if one thing happens, another thing will also; and with *classification,* or putting the item in a category with known characteristics. *Authorities* can be used to define the subject or support a particular view or interpretation of it. *Emotional proofs* are relevant only if the subject is emotional and you want the audience to accept an emotional definition—for example, "Modern art is rubbish."

VALUE ARGUMENT. Value arguments require *motivational proofs* and *value proofs,* and they must be connected to the needs and values of the audience. *Authorities* may be used to establish the value of something. *Definition* can be used to put an item in a good or bad category or class. *Analogies* that compare good or bad items or outcomes may be used. Value arguments also require criteria for making value judgments. You will need to establish these criteria and describe where they came from. They may be your own, society's, a particular group's, or those of the universal audience.

POLICY. Policy papers can be developed with *literal analogies* showing that what worked in one case will also work in another. *Authorities* can be used to establish either the severity of the problem or the efficacy of the solution. *Motivational proofs* may be used to demonstrate how certain solutions or policies

TABLE 11.1 **Proofs and Support That Are Particularly Appropriate for Developing Specific Types of Claims.**

CLAIMS OF FACT	CLAIMS OF DEFINITION	CLAIMS OF CAUSE	CLAIMS OF VALUE	CLAIMS OF POLICY
Facts	Reliable authorities	Facts	Value proofs	Data
Statistics	Accepted sources	Statistics	Motivational proofs	Motivational proofs
Real examples	Analogies with the familiar	Historical analogies	Literal analogies	Value proofs
Quotations from reliable authorities	Examples (real or made up)	Literal analogies	Figurative analogies	Literal analogies
Induction	Signs	Signs	Quotations from reliable authorities	Reliable authorities
Literal and historical analogies		Induction	Induction	Deduction
Signs		Deduction	Signs	Definition
Informed opinion		Quotations from reliable authorities	Definition	Statistics
			Cause	Cause

meet the needs of the audience. Table 11.1 summarizes the proofs that are appropriate for developing specific types of claims.

USING ORGANIZATIONAL PATTERNS TO HELP YOU THINK

Organizational patterns represent established ways of thinking about, developing, and organizing ideas. Chapter 12 will teach you to use organizational patterns to help you shape your paper when you are ready to write it. Now, however, during the early stages of your paper, organizational patterns can also be used to help you discover material for your paper and to help you think about it. Here are some of the most commonly used organizational patterns for argumentative writing.

◆ *Claim with reasons.* Write your claim, and think of some reasons that will support it. Add various types of examples and other evidence.

- *Problem-solution.* This is a pattern commonly used for policy papers. If you find yourself thinking of your topic in policy terms—that is, what should be done—consider describing the problem first and then proposing a solution that should solve it.
- *Cause and effect.* If you are trying to establish cause in your paper, you will find it useful to think in terms of both causes and their effects.
- *Chronology or narrative.* You may find it useful to consider your topic as it evolves over a period of time. This is a useful pattern to use for fact arguments, especially when you are trying to establish what happened.
- *Comparison and contrast.* If you are thinking about definition, it is useful to show what your subject is like and also what it is not like.

When you have worked through a few of the invention strategies described so far, you will be ready to do some research and get additional information from outside sources for your paper. Research is much easier to perform when you are fairly certain about your own thoughts and feelings on your particular issue. However, continue to interweave inventional strategies with library or online research as you go along. All of the strategies in this chapter, though described separately, should be integrated to maintain a high level of creativity through the information-gathering phase.

SUGGESTIONS TO HELP YOU WITH LIBRARY AND ONLINE RESEARCH

Searching for research materials in the library and online is a creative process that allows you to expand your ideas. Here are some suggestions to streamline your research.

GET ORGANIZED FOR RESEARCH

First, to help you find print materials, get acquainted with the library itself. Locate the card or computer catalogs and indexes to books and articles, the books and articles themselves (including those on microfilm), and the government documents and reference books. In addition, find out where the copy center or copy machines are located in your library. Finally, find the reference desk and the reference librarians who will answer your questions when you get stuck. Now, get prepared to write. Bring pens, sheets of paper, and 3-by-5 cards. If you are going to take notes on cards, think about buying three different colors of cards to color-code the three types of information you will write on them: white for bibliography, yellow for all material you will cite in your paper, and blue for your own ideas. Also, bring money for the copy machine. If you make copies of some of your research materials, you will be able to mark what you want to use right on the copies themselves and thus save the time it takes to copy the same information onto cards. Acquire a yellow highlighter to mark this information.

To help you find electronic sources, locate your library's computers. If you are unfamiliar with accessing the Internet, see if your library offers free classes or printed material to help you get started. If you are connected to the Internet at home, you can also ask the librarians how to gain access to the library's online databases from your home computer so that you can conduct some of your research at home. You will be able to print copies of some of the articles that you find on the Internet and highlight the information you want to quote or paraphrase on the printouts themselves.

LEARN TO USE THE CARD CATALOG OR THE COMPUTER INDEX

Locate the books and journals that contain the articles you want to find in the library by consulting either the card catalog or the computer index. If your library still maintains a card catalog, you will find that each book is represented in it with three different cards: the first, with the author's name printed at the top, is filed in the *author section* of the catalog; the second, with the title of the book printed at the top, is filed in the *title section;* and the third, with the subject of the book printed at the top, is filed in the *subject section* of the catalog. The subject section will be particularly useful to you in the early stages of research because all of the library's books on your subject will be cataloged there in one place. You can often read the titles and decide which books might be useful.

Most libraries have eliminated the card catalog and now store the same information in a computer index. You use a computer terminal to call up the information you would find in the card catalog. Thus you may search for a book by author, title, or subject and look for a journal by title or subject. Computer indexes also permit you to search by "key word." Enter a key word that represents your topic, such as *clear-cutting,* and the computer will display all titles of the books and articles in the library that contain that word. Key word searches are the quickest way to find relevant sources for your paper. The key word search is a powerful and effective research tool. Read the titles of the books and articles as they appear on the screen to identify those that might be useful. When you have found a book title that looks promising, move to the screen that gives complete information about that book. There you will find all of the other subject headings under which that book is listed in the index. Use those subject headings, or key words extracted from them, to expand your search. For instance, you might move from the original key word, *clear-cutting,* to a new key word, *erosion,* in order to access more varied material. Computer indexes are user-friendly and will tell you on the screen how to use them. Follow the directions exactly, and ask for help if you get frustrated.

USE YOUR PRELIMINARY PLAN TO GUIDE YOUR RESEARCH

Be specific about the material you seek in the library and online so that you do not get off course and waste time reading aimlessly. Use your preliminary plan (see pages 299–300), with its brief outline and description of your research needs, to keep you on track. Once you begin research, you may change some of your ideas about your topic. When you incorporate new ideas, change your brief outline so that it continues to focus and guide your research. Except when you are reading creatively to get ideas, every piece of research material that you copy on a card or highlight on a printed source should be related to an item on your outline.

SEARCH FOR INFORMATION IN THE LIBRARY

You may want to find books, articles, material on microform (which includes newspapers and some magazines), reference books, and government documents in your library. Here is some advice on how to accomplish that.

To find books, you will need first to obtain the *call number*. You will find it listed with the book title in the computer index or the card catalog. Copy it exactly; find out where the book is located by consulting a directory, which is usually in plain sight in the lobby of the library; and go to the shelf where it belongs. If you cannot find it, look at the other books in the area. They will be on the same subject, and one of them may serve you just as well as the one you cannot find.

To find articles in the library, you will need to consult indexes to periodical literature, such as *Reader's Guide to Periodical Literature, Social Sciences Index, Humanities Index, Education Index,* and *Engineering Index.* There are quite a few of these indexes, representing a variety of subject areas. They are usually shelved together in one area of the library. Take some time to read their titles and browse in them. Browsing will help you discover the ones that will be most useful for directing you to articles on your topic. When you have located an article, copy information about the journal and the issue in which it appears, look up the call number of the journal in the computer index or card catalog, and look for the journal in the same way you would look for a book. Be forewarned—some of the older issues of a periodical may be in bound volumes in the book stacks, some of the newer ones may be on microfilm, and the newest issues may be stacked on shelves in the current periodicals section of the library. You may have to look for a while to find what you want.

Newspapers, such as the *New York Times,* the *Wall Street Journal,* the *Christian Science Monitor,* and the *London Times,* along with newsmagazines like *Time* and *Newsweek,* are kept on microfilm in a special section of the library. Some books and many other journals are kept in this form also. When you encounter the abbreviations *mic, mf, mc,* or *mfc* as part of the catalog information for a book or magazine, you will need to look in the microfilm section. Machines are available there that enlarge the tiny images so that you can read them. Other machines enable you to print copies of microfilm material.

Indexes to newspapers and some magazines are available in the microfilm section as well. *Newsbank* is a particularly useful index for authors of argument papers. Check if your library has it. It collects newspaper articles from 150 urban newspapers starting from 1970 on almost any contemporary issue you can think of. Look up your topic in the *Newsbank* index, and it will lead you to a microfiche card that may contain 15 to 20 relevant articles. Indexes to large daily newspapers and newsmagazines are also available in the microfilm section. Look up your subject in one of them, and then find the articles they identify in the microfilm files.

You may also want to do research in other areas of the library, such as the reference room or the government documents area. The reference room contains a variety of volumes that provide biographical information. If you need to establish the credibility of one of your authorities, you can get biographical information from *Biography Index, Current Biography,* or the various editions of *Who's Who.*

Government documents contain data and other factual information useful for argument. Indexes to consult to help you locate material in government documents include the *Public Affairs Information Bulletin,* the *Monthly Catalog,* and the *Index to U.S. Government Periodicals.* Look up your topic in each of them. Your librarian will help you locate the actual materials among the government documents.

SEARCH FOR INFORMATION ONLINE

Online research can be fast, it can take you to material that is unavailable in your library, and it can retrieve a large volume of resources to help you develop background and understand the controversy and perspectives associated with your issue. To search for information online, you need to know how to use search engines and library databases. You will also need to know some key words associated with your topic to help you search. You may want to consult a thesaurus to find a list of relevant key words.

SEARCH ENGINES. Use Netscape Navigator or Microsoft Internet Explorer to gain access to the World Wide Web. You can then use either of these programs to begin your search for information on your issue. Netscape, for example, offers a text line in which you may type an Internet address (known as a URL, or "uniform research locator") or a key word. Once you have typed in the information, simply use the mouse to click on the Search button to find the particular site of the URL or sites related to the key word.

No search engine can search all of the Web pages on the Internet. Most engines, in fact, find only a small percentage of the information that is available. When you have searched with Netscape or Explorer, you may then type on the text line the addresses of several additional search engines and metasearch engines to help you find still more information. These search engines take the search terms (key words) that you enter, comb the Net, and give you a search report, which is a list of titles and descriptions along with hypertext links that take you directly to the documents. The results that the engine judges most relevant will be at the top of the list. Different engines rank the results differently. Many simply count the number of times your search terms appear in the title or in the document.

Some engines allow you to use operators like *and, or,* and *not* to combine your key words in a more specific way so that the search results can be more relevant for you. By using specific key words and their grammatical variations and synonyms along with these operators, you can find more particular information. Some of the search engines take you directly to your subject, and others first present a directory of categories that are generated by the authors of the Web sites. They include subject guides (lists of categories like *science* and *education*) that can lead you to good general information about your issue as well as sites that serve as good starting points by offering lots of links.

Here are a few of the most powerful search engines along with their addresses.

- *AltaVista* <www.altavista.com> is large and fast, allowing advanced searches. It is case-sensitive, so avoid using capital letters.
- *Lycos* <www.lycos.com> also acts as a directory. Examine the subject guide that comes up on your search screen to see if any of the categories match what you are looking for.
- *Google* <www.google.com> does thorough searches, and it is highly recommended if you are looking for serious sources. It does not offer a subject guide.
- *Infoseek* <infoseek.go.com> will also search newsgroups and e-mail addresses. This engine may ask you to pay for further information once it has given you a certain amount.
- *Yahoo* <www.yahoo.com> is closely organized, making use of specific document summaries.
- *Magellan* <magellan.excite.com> reviews and rates many of the sites in its lists.
- *MetaCrawler* <www.go2net.com/search> is a metasearch engine that uses several search engines at a time. Try this if you are desperate to find a particular kind of information or a specific source that you were unable to find otherwise.

Some of the other top search engines include *Excite* <www.excite.com>, *HotBot* <www.hotbot.com>, *LookSmart* <www.LookSmart.com>, *Snap* <www.snap.com>, and *Webcrawler* <www.webcrawler.com>.

DATABASES. Your library will also help you gain access to periodical indexes that are available on the computer. They are called databases. Two of the most common are *Infotrac* and *Firstsearch*. You can use these databases by typing in subjects or key words and executing a search. A list of associated articles in periodicals and scholarly journals will be displayed on the screen, with the most current appearing first. Many of the entries include an annotation or a brief explanation of what the article contains. By reading the annotations, you can save time and be more certain which articles will be important for you to locate and read.

Chances are your library subscribes to online services that allow you to search multiple databases at the same time. Each database specializes in an area of research and lists journals, magazines, newspapers, books, and other media relating to that area. Many online databases can do more than merely list a title and provide an abstract of the material; often they can provide the full text of an article. It is worth learning to use library online services such as *ProQuest Direct, Lexis-Nexis,* and *EBSCOhost.*

You can surf the Internet in other ways to help you get information for your paper. For example, the Internet offers a forum for you to discuss your issue with other interested people: you can send e-mail to addresses made available on Web sites, and you can take part in "live" chats in discussion rooms. If you are taking an English class in a computer classroom, your instructor might be able to give you the opportunity to discuss your issue anonymously on the computer with your classmates. Remember that e-mail and chatting are potential sources for your paper, so always generate a print copy of any exchanges you think are particularly interesting or pertinent. Your instructor may in fact want you to submit print copies of all electronic material you quote or paraphrase in your final paper, so it is best to keep print copies of everything you use from the Internet.[4]

CREATE A BIBLIOGRAPHY

The bibliography is the list of sources you finally decide you will want to locate and read to add information to your paper. Make a bibliography card for each item of information you are likely to use, or you may write bibliography information right on the pages you have photocopied or printed from the Internet. For online material, make a note of the author's name (if known), the title of the article (in quotation marks), the title of the journal or book (underlined), the date of publication, volume and number, plus pages or paragraph numbers for articles (if available), the date you visited the site, and the full address (URL). You will need this information later when you assemble the bibliography for your paper, so write it all out accurately. You will not want to go back and try to find it again later. Add an annotation that includes a brief summary of the site's content and a note on how you intend to use it in your paper. Figure 11.5 offers an example.

Also, you should make a separate bibliography card (or note) for every book, article, or pamphlet that looks useful and that you want to locate. A bibliography card for a book must include the author, title, place of publication, publisher, date of publication, and call number so that you can find it later in the library. Add a summary and an explanation of how you will use the source in your paper. Figure 11.6 provides an example.

Wright, Kendra E., and Paul M. Lewin. "Drug War Facts." Common Sense for Drug Policy. November 1999. 21 Apr. 2000 <http://www.csdp.org/factbook>.

Use for statistics to support more treatment and less imprisonment.

1. "Treatment is 10 times more cost effective than interdiction in reducing the use of cocaine in the United States."

2. "Over 80% of the increase in the federal prison population from 1985-1995 was due to drug convictions."

FIGURE 11.5 Bibliography Card for an Article from the Internet.

---

[4]I am indebted to Samantha Masterton, Christine Flynn Cavanaugh, and Robert Leston for providing information about online research. Christine Flynn Cavanaugh and Robert Leston also contributed ideas for evaluating online sources.

> Gray, Mike. <u>Drug Crazy: How We Got into This Mess and How We Can Get Out</u>. New York: Random, 1998.
>
> Cite text to show historical failures and drawbacks of the current laws and systems in place to fight the drug war. Author has produced award-winning documentaries and written three books, all of which deal with investigative reporting.
>
> Fairly objective. The author consulted various agencies, including the DEA, U.S. Border Patrol, and U.S. Customs.
>
> Wide audience appeal.
>
> Call number:
> HV
> 5825
> .G6955

FIGURE 11.6   Bibliography Card for a Book.

A bibliography card for an article must include the author's name (if there is one), the title of the article, name of the publication, volume (if there is one), the date of publication, the page numbers, and the call number or other description of location in the library. Add a summary to each card and a note about how you will use the source in your paper. Figure 11.7 provides an example.

When you complete your bibliography search, you will have a card or a note for each item you want to find along with its location in the library or on the Internet. You will also have written how you now think you will use each source in your paper. You can add author information and a general evaluation to this annotation later when you get your hands on the source itself.[5]

> Massing, Michael. "It's Time for Realism." <u>The Nation</u>. 20 Sept. 1999: 11+.
>
> Use for arguments against harsh drug laws and for better rehabilitation programs. Also use for statistics on drug crimes. Author has researched historical and current drug war information for his article. He's written a text on which this article is based.
>
> Very objective source--written by a journalist/journalism professor. Wide appeal.

FIGURE 11.7   Bibliography Card for an Article in a Magazine.

---

[5]I am indebted to Peggy Kulesz for the idea of adding annotations.

Your instructor may want you to create an annotated bibliography to help you organize the research for your paper. An annotated bibliography is an alphabetical listing of all of the sources you might use in your paper. Each listing is accompanied by a summary and a description of how you could use the source. Include more items than you are likely to use on an annotated bibliography, or in a stack of bibliography cards, so that if you cannot find all of the sources, you will still find some of them. An example of an annotated bibliography appears on pages 338–343.

SURVEY AND SKIM

When you have located your research material, do not try to read all of it. You will never finish. It is important, however, to understand the context of the material you quote and to learn something about the author. Survey rather than read books and articles (see Chapter 3). Use this technique to locate information quickly. It is especially important to read the preface to a book to learn the author's position on the issue. Then use the table of contents and index to find specific information. After you have surveyed, you can skim relevant parts to find the specific information you need. To skim, read every fourth or fifth line quickly, or sweep your eyes across the page. If you know what you are looking for and you are concentrating on finding it, you will be able to use these means to locate information quickly and successfully.

READ CREATIVELY TO GENERATE IDEAS

Surveying and skimming may not always yield the understanding that you require, particularly if the material is difficult or dense or if you do not know exactly what information you are looking for. In these situations, switch from surveying or skimming to creative reading to help you think about and get additional ideas for your paper.

Creative reading is different from some of the other types of reading that you do. For example, *leisure reading* is done for relaxation and pleasure. *Study reading* requires you to understand, learn, and remember material so that you can pass a test. *Critical reading*, which you learned to do in Parts One and Two of this book, has you identify and analyze the parts of an argument within an overall context. *Creative reading* enables you to form original ideas and think critically. Here are some questions that you can keep in mind to guide creative reading.

- What strikes me in this text? What interests me? Why?
- What new ideas and answers are occurring to me as I read?
- How does this new material fit with what I already know?
- Do these new ideas challenge any of my existing ideas? How? Can I reconcile the differences?
- What are the implications of these new ideas?
- How can I use these new ideas in my paper?

Using the Toulmin model to read will also help you find information quickly. You will focus on the important parts of a written argument: the claim, the support, and the warrants. The model will also call your attention to the different ways that other authors handle rebuttal. You may want to follow someone's example when you write your own.

TAKE NOTES AND FILL IN YOUR OUTLINE

Keep the most current version of your preliminary plan handy as you read and take notes. Then take notes to fill in your outline, and revise it as needed.

Either write notes on cards, or photocopy or print the material you intend to use in your paper. Whichever system you use, you must differentiate among the material you quote, the material you write in your own words (paraphrase), the material you summarize, and your own ideas. Code the different types of information by using different colors of cards, by writing with different colors of pens, or by labeling each type of information. When you intersperse your own insights with material quoted from others, place your ideas in brackets [ ] to set them off. Always indicate directly quoted material by placing it in quotation marks.

If you decide to use copied or printed material, instead of writing on note cards, be sure to copy the entire article or entire section of a book and write brief source information on it. You only need brief source information on your note cards or printed sources because complete information is available on your bibliography cards or on your annotated bibliography. The author's name is usually enough to write on a note card, unless you are using more than one book by the same author. Then write the author's name and a short version of the title at the top of each note. Copy or mark quoted material exactly, and place it in quotation marks, so that it will go into your paper that way. You may omit words to make a quotation shorter and more to the point; indicate where words have been omitted with three spaced periods, known as an *ellipsis*. If the omitted material occurs at the end of a sentence, add a period immediately after the last remaining word, followed by the three spaced periods. Add the page number after the closing quotation mark. See Figure 11.8 (page 332) for an example of a note card with a direct quotation using ellipses and a page number.

Indicate at the top of the card, in the margin of copied material, or on your annotated bibliography where you intend to use the source in your paper. Use a brief heading on your preliminary outline for this cross-referencing. The example in Figure 11.8 shows one way to do this.

Paraphrased or summarized material should also be recorded carefully and accurately with the page number at the end. Since you are condensing or changing the wording of this material, do not place it in quotation marks. You will still have to let your reader know where you got it when you write your paper, so include on the card the author's name and page number. Also indicate where you will use it in your paper. Figure 11.9 (page 332) provides an example. Figure 11.10 (page 333) provides an example of a note card with the student essayist's original idea on it.

Arrange these cards as you go along according to the categories that are written at the top. Then place the categories in the sequence you think you will follow in your paper. The cards are now ready to work into your paper when you write the first draft.

Problems--current system

Gray

"Not only has America nothing to show . . . , but the failed attempt has clearly made everything worse. After blowing hundreds of billions of dollars and tens of thousands of lives, the drugs on the street today are stronger, cheaper, more pure and more widely available. . . ." p. 189

FIGURE 11.8   Note Card with Quoted Material.

Introduction--statistics

Massing

He quotes figures indicating there are more than 1.5 million drug arrests per year. Laws are discriminatory in that a large percentage of drug arrests are of black and Latino men. p. 11

U.S. spends $18 billion annually to fight the war on drugs. p. 14

FIGURE 11.9   Paraphrased Note Card.

EVALUATING PRINT AND ONLINE SOURCES

Good, reliable sources add to your credibility as an author, making your argument more convincing. In the same way, bad sources reflect poorly on your judgment and detract from your credibility. You will need to evaluate every source that you use in your paper, whether it is a printed source you found in the library or an online source. Printed sources that are also to be found online should be evaluated as print sources.

You can evaluate each source by comparing it with other sources on the same subject, by analyzing the warrants, by applying the tests for the validity of the proofs, by determining whether or not the source in which you found it is biased, by noticing the nationality and date of publication, by looking up reviews or a

---

Need for change

Mine

If harsh laws for minor drug possession were reformed and if more money were spent on treatment of hard-core drug users, our jails would have more room for dangerous criminals.

FIGURE 11.10   Note Card with an Original Idea or Reaction on It.

biography of the author, and by asking your professor or librarian for an opinion about it.

Be especially wary of the material you find on the Internet. Not much of it goes through a publisher or editor; in fact, anyone familiar with computers can set up a Web site and put articles or other documents on it. You cannot always be certain of a writer's authority or credibility, so you must be careful. Not all of the information on the Internet is reliable. To maintain your credibility, a good rule of thumb is that no source from the Internet should be used unless it has gone through a submission process and has been selected for publication by an editor of a reputable publication. While finding sources from well-known professional organizations is generally safe, selecting sources from second-rate publications or from individuals lacking credentials reflects negatively on your own credibility. Consequently, it is wise to use online articles and information sparingly unless directed otherwise by your instructor. Your paper will benefit from your using a variety of sources.

To help you determine the credibility of online sources, ask the following questions.

1. *Is the source associated with an organization that is recognized in the field?* For example, an American Civil Liberties Union Web site on capital punishment is credible because the ACLU is a nationally known organization that deals with issues of civil rights.
2. *Is the source listed under a reputable domain?* Look at what comes after "www" in the URL. For example, information found at <www.stanford.edu> has some credibility because it is associated with a university. Universities are considered reliable sources of information. Of course, any Stanford student, faculty member, or staff member could publish material online. The material would not necessarily be credible, so you have to review it carefully.

3. *Is the source published in an online journal that is peer-reviewed?* The journal will usually advertise this on its front page. For example, *Modern Language Notes*, published by Johns Hopkins University Press, is credible because everything written in it has been reviewed by a panel of experts to ensure that it meets a high standard of scholarship.

4. *Is the online source duplicated in print?* For example, material appearing on <www.nytimes.com> is credible because the *New York Times*, a nationally respected newspaper, sponsors it.

5. *Is the source accessed by a large number of people?* For example, a daily-updated news site, <www.drudgereport.com>, is read and talked about across the country.

6. *Is the source directed mainly to extremist, biased true believers?* You will recognize such sources by their emotional language, extreme examples, and implicit value systems that are associated with extremist rather than mainstream groups. Learn what you can about such groups, and try to determine whether or not they have a wide appeal. Your goal should be to find information with sufficiently wide appeal so that it might be acceptable to a universal audience.

7. *Is the evidence in the source stacked to represent one point of view?* Again, an unusual amount of emotional language, carefully selected or stacked evidence, and quotations from biased sources and authorities characterize this material. You can attack the obvious bias in this material if you want to refute it.

8. *Is the source sloppily edited, undocumented, or unreasonable?* Material that is poorly edited, infrequently updated, or old may be untrustworthy. Other red flags are inflammatory language and no identified author. Sweeping generalizations made without evidence, undocumented statistics, or unreasonable arguments indicate questionable sources for research.

9. *Is the source moral or immoral, ethical or unethical according to your values?* This is the bottom-line question that will help you differentiate credible from noncredible sources for research.

REVIEW QUESTIONS

1. What three invention strategies discussed in this chapter particularly appeal to you? Describe them and explain how you might use them.

2. What are the five elements of Burke's pentad? How is the pentad useful in argument? What in particular does it help establish?

3. What method is suggested in this chapter to help you create a chain of reasons about your issue?

4. Several argument theories and models were reviewed in this chapter to help you review your ideas and think about them. Choose two that will be particularly useful to you. Why are they useful?

5. What is the value of making a bibliography, writing annotations, and writing how you might use the source? In what ways can these activities help you as you research and write your paper?

6. What three types of information might you write on note cards?
7. What should you take into consideration when you evaluate your research sources? Discuss both print and online sources in your answer.

EXERCISES AND ACTIVITIES

A. THE RESEARCHED POSITION PAPER: USING BURKE'S PENTAD TO FORM IDEAS

Use Burke's pentad to analyze the whole context and particularly the cause for your issue. Write out your issue so that you will focus on it, and then answer the following questions. Use the information generated by these questions in your paper.

1. *Act:* What was done?
2. *Scene:* When or where was it done?
3. *Agent:* Who did it?
4. *Agency:* How was it done?
5. *Purpose:* Why did it happen?

B. THE RESEARCHED POSITION PAPER: USING BURKE'S PENTAD AND CHAINS OF REASONS

1. On your own, answer each of the five questions in Burke's pentad as it applies to your issue: What was done? When or where was it done? Who did it? How was it done? And why did it happen? Write a paragraph of at least 100 words in which you synthesize your responses.
2. Exchange your synthesis with a classmate. Read each other's syntheses, and write a thought-provoking question that asks for additional information about the topic or about the author's point of view. Return the paper to its author. Each author should read the question and write a reasoned response of two or three sentences. Exchange papers again, read the responses, and ask another question. Continue this questioning and answering until time is called.
3. When the time is up, read over the chain of reasons you have developed for your issue. What surprised you? What do you need to research more? Where do you think your answers were the strongest? Once you have examined this particular chain of reasons closely, add to your outline or draft plan to indicate how this additional information might apply when you write your paper.[6]

C. THE RESEARCHED POSITION PAPER: INVENTING IDEAS

Read through the list of invention strategies on the following worksheet. They represent a composite of those described in this chapter and in Chapter 4. Some of them will be "hot spots" for you. That is, they will immediately suggest profitable activity for developing your paper. Check those that you want to use at this point, and complete them. There may be only two or three. Include the Toulmin model, however. It is one of the best invention strategies for argument.

---

[6]I am indebted to Corri Wells for this class exercise.

INVENTION WORKSHEET

Your claim: _____

Begin to develop your claim by using some of the following invention strategies. If you cannot generate information and ideas, do some background reading, and then come back to these.

1. Freewrite for five minutes.
2. Brainstorm additional ideas and details in brief phrases for another five minutes.
3. Make a list or map that shows the parts of your paper.
4. Explain to someone in your class or group what you expect to accomplish in your paper, or talk into a tape recorder about it.
5. Write your insights in a journal or on sheets of paper filed in a folder.
6. Mentally visualize and write a description of a scene related to your claim.
7. Make a preliminary plan. Write your claim plus three to five reasons. Add ideas for research and a draft plan.
8. Think about possible organizational patterns to shape your paper. What might work best—a claim with reasons, problem-solution, cause and effect, chronology or narrative, comparison and contrast, or a combination of two or more patterns?
9. Think through the rhetorical situation. Remember TRACE: text, reader, author, constraints, exigence.
10. Use the Toulmin model to come up with the key parts of your paper. Consider the claim, support, warrants, backing for the warrants, rebuttal, and qualifiers.
11. Ask the claim questions: Did it happen? What is it? What caused it? Is it good or bad? What should we do about it?
12. Decide on some proofs that are appropriate for your type of claim. Remember SICDADS—sign, induction, cause, deduction, analogies (literal, figurative, historical), definition, and sign—and VAM—value, authoritative, and motivational proofs.
13. Apply critical thinking prompts. Start with your claim, but then make these recursive; that is, apply them at any point and more than once during the process.

Associate it.	Think about it as it is now.	Evaluate it.
Describe it.	Think about it over time.	Elaborate on it.
Compare it.	Decide what it is a part of.	Project and predict.
Apply it.	Analyze its parts.	Ask why.
Divide it.	Synthesize it.	

14. Use Burke's pentad to establish cause: act, scene, agent, agency, purpose.
15. Use chains of reasons to develop your claim through five repetitions of *claim, why, because*. Describe where you need to add evidence.
16. Make a more complete outline, set of notes, or list to guide your writing.
17. Write chunks or bits of your paper as they begin to form in your mind.

D. PAIRS OF STUDENTS: BECOMING FAMILIAR WITH THE LIBRARY

Visit your library with a partner, and begin to do research. This exercise will take roughly one class period if the two of you work quickly.

You and your partner should explore the issues you have selected to write about in your position papers. Use the library to practice finding sources. To find your sources, work through the six library stations until you have completed the assignment. If you need help locating a source, ask a librarian for assistance.

LIBRARY STATIONS

1. *Online catalog or card catalog and periodical indexes.* At this station, locate books and articles about your subject by using the computer to do a key word or subject search; or use the card catalog to find books about your subject and one of the periodical indexes to find articles. Determine also how to find the call numbers for the periodicals if they are not listed in the computer. You will need to find a variety of sources that focus on your topic. Write down the call numbers of *a book about your subject, a current periodical* (one that has not yet been bound), *a bound periodical,* and *an article that has been preserved on microfilm or microfiche,* such as one from a weekly newsmagazine.

2. *The stacks.* Next, go to the stacks, and use the call number to locate the book about your subject. When you find it, use a copy machine to make a copy of the title page or of the title page and the pages you will quote, paraphrase, or summarize in your paper.

3. *Bound periodicals.* Locate the bound periodicals in your library, and find the magazine article you selected. Make a copy of the entire article if you intend to draw information from it for your paper.

4. *Current periodicals.* Locate the current periodicals, and find the article you selected. Make a copy of the entire article if you intend to use it.

5. *Microfilm or microfiche.* Next, go to the part of your library that houses the microforms. Using the viewer, find your article, and write down one interesting quote from the article, along with the name of the source, the date, and the number of the page where you found your quote.

6. *Reference desk.* Find the reference desk at your library. Now you will know where to go to get assistance from reference librarians.[7]

E. THE RESEARCHED POSITION PAPER: CONDUCTING RESEARCH

Follow the steps delineated in the research worksheet on page 338.

F. THE RESEARCHED POSITION PAPER: WRITING AN ANNOTATED BIBLIOGRAPHY

Find ten quality sources that you think will be valuable for your researched position paper. Copy all the information you will need to cite your sources in MLA or APA format (see the Appendix to Chapter 12 for information on how

---

[7]This exercise was prepared by Leslie Snow.

RESEARCH WORKSHEET

1. Get organized for research: gather cards, pencils, money for the copy machine, paper, and a big envelope or folder. Review your preliminary outline and research plan.
2. Create a bibliography of ten to twelve sources. Plan to locate and use at least four to six for your paper. Include both books and articles, and write pertinent information on cards or on an annotated bibliography (see Exercise F). Add annotations that summarize and indicate possible use.
3. Survey and skim for specific information. Take notes.
4. Read creatively for original ideas. Take notes.
5. Make evaluative judgments about each source.

to do this). Survey, skim, and read selected parts of each source so that you can summarize them, and write brief statements of how you might use them in your paper. Alphabetize the ten sources, and type them up. The following is an example of an annotated bibliography.*

Angela A. Boatwright
Annotated Bibliography
Professor Thorne
English 1302
20 September 2003

Human Cloning: An Annotated Bibliography

On-line journal

Bailey, Ronald. "The Twin Paradox: What Exactly Is Wrong with Cloning People?" Reasononline. 5 Sept. 1998. 13 Sept. 2003 <http://www.reason.com/9705/col.bailey.html>.

This article explains simply, in nonscientific terms, exactly what was done to clone Dolly the sheep. The author briefly explains the legislation that has resulted from the first asexual reproduction of a mammal. Bailey explains what a clone would be and discusses the reasons why human clones could in no way be exact copies of their predecessors. Clones would have different personalities and would be as different as identical twins. He doesn't feel it is unethical to clone humans because they would be treated with the same moral status as any identical twins or triplets. He states that as long as we treat cloned individuals as

---

*See the Appendix to Chapter 12 for the actual MLA format guidelines for student papers.

we would treat any other human being, all other ethical problems we have concerning cloning would essentially disappear.

This article answers the questions I had regarding exactly what a clone would be like in relation to the "original model." It reinforces the belief I had that clones would be different people because of different social influences and environmental factors that have so much to do with the personality of an individual.

Article from weekly journal

Butler, Declan, and Meredith Wadman. "Calls for Cloning Ban Sell Science Short." <u>Nature</u> 6 Mar. 1997: 8-9.

This article acknowledges the need for ethical debate but states that many scientists argue that politicians and the media are focusing on applications of cloning technology that are not even realistically possible. These authors believe that human cloning is not for tomorrow and may never be a practical proposition. There is also a belief that medical ethics is unlikely to deter wealthy or powerful individuals from conducting experimentation out of the public eye. This article further stresses that a ban on all research on human cloning could prevent the development of lifesaving medical treatments. Cloning techniques could be used to generate skin grafts for burn victims and bone marrow for patients undergoing cancer chemotherapy.

I liked this article because it made the point that the public is not frightened of all progress, just rapid progress. While I believe this is true, I had not thought of it in this way. This article will support the views of cloning proponents.

Magazine article

Carey, John. "Human Clones: It's Decision Time." <u>Business Week</u> 10 Aug. 1998: 32.

This article states that with the news that scientists had cloned fifty mice from adult mouse cells, we now know that the procedure that produced Dolly might be reduced to an almost humdrum process. The author indicates that cloning itself is only the beginning of potential genetic manipulations. The article mentions how cloning technology might lead to manipulation that could produce superior humans. One scientist claims this is a major step toward regarding our children as acceptable only if they conform to the choices of our will. The article implies that cloning would be similar to manufacturing, with physical traits preplanned. Although many researchers claim there would probably be no public interest in human cloning, a business in the Bahamas had over a hundred people interested in paying a fee of $200,000 or more for the chance to have a clone produced.

I will use this article to support my view of limits on cloning, based on the possible abuses the technology could allow.

Magazine article Gibbs, Nancy. "Abducting the Cloning Debate." Time 13 Jan. 2003: 46-49.

This article is about a recent announcement by the Raelians that they have succeeded in cloning two human babies. The Raelians are a religious cult that believes humans were originally cloned from aliens, and they support a group called Clonaid. This group has not proved that they have cloned humans successfully, and scientists and politicians are skeptical about the truth of their claims. Still, the potential effects of this announcement are troubling. For instance, some members of Congress want to ban all cloning activities, including related research that uses some cloning techniques and may in time be used to cure diseases like Parkinson's and Alzheimer's. Many scientists fear the Raelian claims could result in legislation that not only bans human cloning but also bans all related activities. The article provides an excellent description with pictures of the standard procedure for cloning, but makes it clear that it has been impossible so far for the best scientists to clone human beings successfully.

This article made me think about how dangerous it can be when scientific procedures are taken over and used by groups whose values are radically different from those of the mainline culture. The results can be so negative that good procedures as well as bad ones can be jeopardized.

Magazine article Macklin, Ruth. "Human Cloning? Don't Just Say No." US News and World Report 10 Mar. 1997: 64+.

This author believes that to justify human cloning, instead of looking for the benefits to humanity that cloning can offer, we should consider that no one has yet made a persuasive case that it would do any real harm either. She thinks efforts in cloning to breed individuals with genetic qualities that someone might deem exceptional is really no different from the "selective breeding" already practiced in democratic societies where, for example, lawyers are free to choose to marry and have children with other lawyers. She uses sperm banks as another example of selective breeding. She believes that as a democratic society, we should not pass laws outlawing something before there is actual evidence of harm.

I liked this article because it also discussed the fear we have of cloning being used to create spare parts. While the author does not believe cloning is a threat to human rights, she actually made several points that caused me to consider just that. I think some of her ideas are not credible.

Magazine article

Mann, Charles C. "The First Cloning Superpower." <u>Wired</u> Jan. 2003: 116+.

The author has interviewed a number of scientists in China who are working on therapeutic cloning techniques that employ stem cell research with the ultimate end of growing human replacement organs and tissues. China does not have as many regulations against experimenting with human stem cells as do the United States and some other Western countries. China allows almost complete freedom to scientists in this field, disallowing only human reproductive cloning experiments. This means that scientists can experiment with embryonic stem cells to clone spare human parts, to regenerate damaged nerve and other tissue, and to find cures for diseases that have had no cures in the past. The author gives several examples of Chinese scientists who received their education in the United States but could not conduct stem cell research there because of bans on such research, and who have now returned to China where they have the freedom and access to funding and materials to conduct such research. The Chinese government hopes to win a Nobel Prize for China's work with therapeutic cloning.

While the United States debates the morality of this technology, China, with a different set of values, pursues it. Stem cell research and therapeutic cloning will be carried on in other parts of the world even while being banned in the United States. This is probably a good thing, since this science is not likely to go away, and it is potentially extremely valuable to humans.

Book

Pence, Gregory E. <u>Who's Afraid of Human Cloning?</u> Lanham: Rowman, 1998.

This book is a comprehensive source of information on cloning. It provides a complete overview, including discussions on the misconceptions, ethics, regulation, and arguments for and against human cloning. This author is most definitely an advocate of human cloning technology. He feels the discussion concerning the issue has been horribly one-sided. He states that never in the history of modern science had the world seen such an instant, overwhelming condemnation of the application to humanity of a scientific breakthrough. His aim is to correct this problem of a one-sided debate over the issue.

I will probably cite this book because of the wealth of information it contains. Although the author advocates human cloning, his book is a fairly good source of material for arguing against human cloning.

Magazine article

Tuma, Rabiya S. "Biologists Discover Why Most Clones Die." <u>Discover</u> Jan. 2003: 35.

> Only four percent of the eggs that receive a transplanted nucleus in cloning experiments actually survive. This author explains research that identifies a gene called *Oct4* as the culprit. This gene helps embryonic cells develop, and any change in the activity of *Oct4* genes can misdirect the growth of the cell. In natural embryos this problem does not occur. Scientists predict that it will probably be too difficult to get this gene to behave appropriately for cloning people, but for basic stem cell research, it should be easier to control it.

> This article shows that continuing research may, over a period of time, make cloning technology easier. How and when to use this technology will have to be determined soon, in order to keep up with the growing technology.

Journal article

Wilmut, Ian. "Roslin Institute Experiments: Creation of Dolly the Sheep." <u>Congressional Digest</u> Feb. 1998: 41+.

> The man responsible for the experiments that led to the creation of Dolly, the first cloned sheep, wrote this article. The creation of Dolly was the exigence for this article. Dr. Wilmut briefly summarizes the experiments that he and his colleagues at Roslin Institute and PPL Therapeutics reported. He then discusses the practical uses of cloning technology in animal breeding. He explains some of the difficulties encountered during the experiments leading to the successful creation of Dolly. He gives some specific statistics concerning his experiments. Finally, he explains his stance on the issue of human cloning. He and his colleagues believe that cloning of humans would be unethical. He also believes that it may not even be technically possible.

> This article is one of my favorite references because I was surprised by Dr. Wilmut's position on human cloning. For no other reason than my own ignorance, I fully expected Dr. Wilmut to support human cloning. His statement that cloning of humans would be unethical held a great deal of importance to me. He states that similar experiments with humans would be totally unacceptable.

Article in print and online

Wilson, Jim. "Cloning Humans." <u>Popular Mechanics</u> June 2002: 42-44. <u>Academic Search Premier</u>. EBSCO. UTA Lib., Arlington, TX. 12 Sept. 2003 <http://www.epnet.com>.

> This article discusses the technological progress of cloning and the "inevitability" that humans will soon be cloned. Wilson begins by showing that cloning humans is not much different from the procedure used for in vitro fertilization (IVF). For IVF, a child is

conceived in a glass lab dish, grows into an embryo, and is then implanted in a human uterus. Human clones will go through the same process, Wilson tells us. The difference between IVF and cloned embryos is that the genetic blueprint for IVF cases comes from two parents whereas clones require only one. Wilson traces the potential for human cloning back to 1997 and shows that while the world marveled at the cloning of Dolly the sheep, the scientific community marveled that researchers from Duke University Medical Center had learned that cloning humans would be simpler than cloning sheep. Once this discovery was made, Italian researcher Severino Antinori argued that the genetic pattern of sterile males could be passed on via clones. Antinori, who successfully performed IVF for a woman 62 years of age, presented his findings at the International Cloning Consortium in Rome in 2001. His case was taken quite seriously by the scientific community, and since then, a number of cloning projects have emerged. The formation of the first human-cloning company, Clonaid, was announced recently by founder Claude Vorilhon. Clonaid's chief scientist is Brigitte Boisselier, a chemist who perfected the process of forcing DNA-inoculated cells to divide successfully. Thanks to Boisselier, this cloning process is no less successful than that of standard fertility techniques. The market for this process is fertility clinics.

This article shows how the technology for cloning may be used in a way that is more insidious than many may have previously thought. Combining cloning with fertility treatment to allow couples and individuals to pass along their genetic traits may be a way for cloning to become silently mainstreamed.

◆◆◆

Chapter 12

The Research Paper: Organizing, Writing, and Revising

This chapter will provide you with the information you need to create some order in the material you have gathered so that you can now write your researched position paper. Specifically, you will be taught some ways to organize and outline, to incorporate research into your first draft, and to revise and prepare the final copy. Organization, or deciding on a framework of ideas for your paper, will be dealt with first.

USING ORGANIZATION TO HELP YOUR READER UNDERSTAND

Everyone has a natural tendency to associate or group ideas and to place them in an order so that they make sense and are easier to remember. You have probably already begun to do this with the materials for your paper. You may have made a preliminary plan, labeled note cards, and written some lists. Eventually, these activities will help your reader, who will understand organized ideas far more easily than disorganized ones. To illustrate this fact, here are two examples.

Example 1
The ideas and information presented here are a brainstormed list of ideas for a value paper that have not yet been organized. Brainstorming is one of the recommended ways to collect ideas for a paper.

> *Claim: Women have more opportunities for variety in their lives now than they had fifty years ago.*
> Women's movement.
> Several causes for changes in women's opportunities.
> Desire to satisfy personal ambition.

Comparison between women at mid-twentieth century and at start of twenty-first century.

Some women are dysfunctional.

Examples of three satisfied contemporary women: professional, military, homemaker.

Not all changes are good—signs of stress in women, men, children.

Women are now self-actualized.

Statistical data suggesting the variety of positions occupied by women in the 1950s and in the late 1990s and early 2000s.

Labor-saving devices, education, economy, and women's ambitions contribute to change.

A review of human needs and motivation and how they relate to women.

Improved opportunities for women.

The effects of the changes on men and children.

Analysis of the causes for the changes in opportunities for women.

Donna Reed and Ally McBeal.

How can this jumble of ideas and information be organized for an effective argument paper? Thinking about organization requires that you identify the *parts,* place them in an *order,* and establish some *relationships* among them. In other words, you must establish reasons for discussing one idea before another.

Example 2

Here the parts have been rearranged. The same items appear here as in Example 1, but they have been organized according to the following rationale.

1. The issue is introduced as a fact, that women have more opportunity now. This fact is illustrated with examples and statistics to focus the issue and get attention and interest.
2. Burke's pentad is used to explore causes for the changes: agency (labor-saving devices), scene (education and economy), agent (women and women's movement), and purpose (to satisfy personal ambition) are cited as causes.
3. The effects of the changes are explained and illustrated with examples.
4. The opposition is refuted, and negative perceptions are changed to positive values.
5. The value claim, that the changes are good, is stated and made more convincing with a quotation.

Title: Improved Opportunities for Women

I. **Introduction:** *Women now have a wide range of opportunities.*

- A comparison between women at mid-twentieth century and start of twenty-first century. Example, two television characters who reflect social mores: Donna Reed (1950s) and Ally McBeal (2000s).
- Statistical data suggesting the variety of roles occupied by women in the 1950s and in the late 1990s and early 2000s.

II. **Analysis of the causes for the changes in women's opportunities.**
   - Labor-saving devices—freed-up time.
   - Education—improved competencies.
   - Economy—requires two incomes.
   - Women's movement—made women more aware of human needs and motivation and how they relate to women.
   - Desire to satisfy personal ambition.

III. **Effects of the changes.**
   - Women now able to meet needs for self-actualization in a variety of ways, some of which were formerly reserved for men.
   - Examples of three contemporary women who are satisfied with their lives: professional, military, homemaker.

IV. **Rebuttal: Some people argue that not all changes have been good and that there are signs of stress in women, men, and children. Actually, the effects they perceive as bad are good.**
   - The stress for women is good stress because they now choose what they want to do.
   - Men are closer to their children because fathers share responsibility for child care.
   - Children learn to take more initiative and shoulder more responsibility.
   - People made dysfunctional by the changes would probably have problems in any setting.

V. **Conclusion:** *Claim: Women have more opportunities for variety in their lives now than they had fifty years ago.*
   - The benefits outweigh the problems.
   - Quotation from an authority about women's current satisfaction.
   - No one would want to go back.

This is not the only organizational strategy that could have been used for this paper. The rebuttal, for example, could have been placed first. The effects could have been described before the causes. The value claim could have been placed at the beginning instead of at the end. Any one of these alternatives might have worked as well as another, provided they made sense to the author and were convincing to the audience.

Read the materials you have gathered for your own paper and think about (1) how they can be divided into *parts*, (2) how these parts can be placed in an *order*, and (3) what the logical *relationships* are among them. List the parts, tentatively number them to reflect order, and clarify the rationale for your decisions.

To help you plan the *parts*, keep the Toulmin model in mind. Your parts should include a claim, support, and warrants and possibly also backing for the warrants, a rebuttal, and a qualifier for the claim. Think also about the subclaims that represent the major sections of the paper and the facts, examples, and opinions that support them. Tentatively plan the introduction and conclusion and what to include in them. The usual functions of the introduction are to focus and introduce the topic, provide some background, and get the attention of the audience. The conclusion usually refocuses the claim through restatement and final, compelling reasons.

To help you think about *order,* keep in mind that the beginning of your paper is a strong position for arguments, but the end is even stronger. Put your strongest material at or near the end, other strong material at the beginning, and the less impressive material in the middle. Also, think about your audience when determining order. For instance, for a hostile audience, you might argue about women's roles by admitting that the 1950s were a good time for women but adding that times have changed and finally showing how the 1950s way of life is now impractical. For a neutral audience, you might want to present strong and interesting examples at the beginning to get attention and create interest. For a friendly audience, you can show how things are better right away and thus confirm an already favorable opinion.

To focus on *relationships,* use words that name the relationships you have worked out. As in Example 2, write the words *causes, effects,* and *rebuttal* into your plan to clarify the main sections and suggest the relationships among them.

USING ORGANIZATIONAL PATTERNS TO HELP YOU THINK AND ORGANIZE

For centuries, authors have used certain established patterns of thought to help them think about, develop, and organize ideas. This practice benefits not only authors but also readers, who are consequently able to follow and understand the material more easily. Some of these patterns of thought are particularly helpful for organizing the ideas in argument. The following list describes those most commonly used. These patterns, by the way, can shape your paper as the dominant pattern or can combine as minor patterns within the dominant pattern to organize some of the sections.

CLAIM WITH REASONS (OR REASONS FOLLOWED BY CLAIM)

This pattern takes the following form.

> Statement of claim
> Reason 1
> Reason 2
> Reason 3, and so forth

Set this pattern up by writing the claim, following it with the word *because,* and listing some reasons. Or list some reasons, follow them with the word *therefore,* and write the claim. For example, you may present the claim that we need a national health care program, which is followed by reasons: the unemployed have no insurance, the elderly cannot afford medicine, many children do not receive adequate health care. The reasons may be distinct and different from one another and set up like separate topics in your paper. Or you may have created a chain of related reasons by asking *why* and answering *because* five or six times. Also, some of your reasons may be used to refute, others to prove, and still others to show how your claim will meet the needs and values of the audience. Support all reasons with facts, examples, and opinions. You may use transitional phrases such as *one reason, another reason, a related reason,* and *a final reason* to emphasize your reasons and make them stand out in your paper.

CAUSE AND EFFECT (OR EFFECT AND CAUSE)

The cause-and-effect pattern may be used to identify one or more causes followed by one or more effects or results. Or you may reverse this sequence and describe effects first and then the cause or causes. For example, the causes of water pollution might be followed by its effects on both humans and animals. You may use obvious transitions to clarify cause and effect, such as "What are the results? Here are some of them," or simply the words *cause, effect,* and *result.*

APPLIED CRITERIA

This pattern establishes criteria or standards for evaluation and judgment and then shows how the claim meets them. For example, in an argument about children in day care, you might set out physical safety, psychological security, sociability, and creativity as criteria for measuring the success of day care. Then you might claim that day-care centers meet those criteria as well as or even better than home care, and provide support. The applied criteria pattern is obviously useful for value arguments. It is also useful in policy arguments to establish a way of evaluating a proposed solution. You may want to use the words and phrases *criteria, standards, needs,* and *meets those criteria or needs* to clarify the parts of your paper.

PROBLEM–SOLUTION

The problem-solution pattern is commonly used in policy papers. There are at least three ways to organize these papers. The problem is described, followed by the solution. In this case, the claim is the solution, and it may be stated at the beginning of the solution section or at the end of the paper. An alternative is to propose the solution first and then describe the problems that motivated it. Or a problem may be followed by several solutions, one of which is selected as the best. When the solution or claim is stated at the end of the paper, the pattern is sometimes called the *delayed proposal.* For a hostile audience, it may be effective to describe the problem, show why other solutions do not work, and finally suggest the favored solution. For example, you may want to claim that labor unions are the best solution for reducing unemployment. First you describe the unemployment problem in vivid detail so that the audience really wants a solution. Then you show that government mandates and individual company initiatives have not worked. Finally, you show how labor unions protect employment for workers. You may use the words *problem* and *solution* to signal the main sections of your paper for your reader.

CHRONOLOGY OR NARRATIVE

Material arranged chronologically is explained as it occurs in time. This pattern may be used to establish what happened for an argument of fact. For example, you may want to give a history of childhood traumas to account for an individual's current criminal behavior. Or you may want to tell a story to develop one or more points in your argument. Use transitional words like *then, next,* and *finally* to make the parts of the chronology clear.

DEDUCTION

Recall that deductive reasoning involves reasoning from a generalization, applying it to cases or examples, and drawing a conclusion. For instance, you may generalize that the open land in the West is becoming overgrazed; follow this assertion with examples of erosion, threatened wildlife, and other environmental harms; and conclude that the government must restrict grazing to designated areas. The conclusion is the claim. You may use such transitional phrases as *for instance, for example,* and *to clarify* to set your examples off from the rest of the argument and *therefore, thus, consequently,* or *in conclusion* to lead into your claim.

INDUCTION

The inductive pattern involves citing one or more examples and then making the "inductive leap" to the conclusion. For instance, five or six examples of boatloads of illegal immigrants landing in the United States who require expensive social services lead some people to conclude that they should be sent home. Other people may conclude that the immigrants should be allowed to stay. No matter which claim or conclusion is chosen, it can be stated at the beginning or at the end of the paper. The only requirement is that it be based on the examples. The same transitional words used for the deductive pattern are also useful for the inductive: *for instance, for example,* or *some examples* to emphasize the examples; *therefore, thus,* or *consequently* to lead in to the claim.

COMPARISON AND CONTRAST

This pattern is particularly useful in definition arguments and in other arguments that show how a subject is like or unlike similar subjects. It is also often used to demonstrate a variety of similarities or differences. For examples, the claim is made that drug abuse is a medical problem instead of a criminal justice problem. The proof consists of literal analogies that compare drug abuse to AIDS, cancer, and heart disease in a number of areas to redefine it as a medical problem. The transitional words *by contrast, in comparison, while, some,* and *others* are sometimes used to clarify the ideas in this pattern.

ROGERIAN ARGUMENT

You were introduced to Rogerian argument in Chapter 9, where the recommended organizational strategy for this pattern of argument was explained. You first introduce the issue and state the opponent's position on it. Then you show that you understand the opponent's position, that you value it, and that you consider it valid in certain contexts or under certain conditions. Next, you state your own position and show the contexts in which it is valid. Finally, you show how the opponent's position would be improved by adopting all or at least some elements of your position. In other words, you finally reconcile the two positions and show how they complement one another.

For example, the issue of homosexuals in the military, each time it surfaces, results in particularly adamant positions on either side. Some military leaders fear people with a gay identity may exhibit openly gay behavior while they are on military duty, which would be just as wrong as straight people exhibiting openly straight behavior in this same situation. Thus these leaders oppose homosexuals in the military because they worry about how they might behave. Gay activists, by contrast, do not seek to exhibit openly gay behavior so much as not to be penalized for acknowledging a gay orientation. Rogerian strategy aimed at convincing military leaders to change their minds requires an opening statement that explains their position and gives reasons and evidence to show that it is understood and considered valid in certain circumstances. Next, the counterposition that homosexuals should be allowed to acknowledge their orientation is offered along with reminders that gay military personnel have served well in the past and that their behavior has not been objectionable. Finally, the claim is made that the military is improved by allowing gays and lesbians to serve openly because they are happier and better-adjusted employees.

You may rewrite your Rogerian paper as a position paper by moving your own position on the issue to the beginning of the paper and then refuting the opponent's position. Or you may rearrange a position paper you have written and present it according to Rogerian strategy by moving the position least like your own to the beginning and proceeding from there. These changes are comparatively easy to make if you have saved these papers in a computer file.

MOTIVATED SEQUENCE

A common distinction between argument and persuasion is that argument results in agreement or conviction and persuasion results in action or changed behavior. The motivated sequence is a persuasive pattern that is used to motivate an audience to do something. You may find it useful when you want to persuade your audience to act. There are five steps. We will use, as an example, the campus issue that is a problem at some schools: insufficient numbers of classes for all the students who want to enroll.

1. *Attention.* First, create some interest and desire.

Example: How often have you tried to register for a class only to be told that it is closed and you must try again next semester?

2. *Need.* Heighten the audience's need to do something about this situation.

Example: A problem arises because you, like many other students, had planned to graduate at the end of this semester. If you cannot get into the classes you need to graduate, you must put your life on hold for another half year. And what guarantee exists that the needed classes will be available to you next semester? The frustration may continue.

3. *Satisfaction.* Next, show that your proposed plan of action will solve the problem and satisfy the audience's needs.

Example: There is a way of dealing with this problem. Enroll in a nearby college, take the course there, and transfer the credit back here to be counted toward your graduation. You will complete your coursework on schedule, learn just as much, and be ready to take that job you lined up at the time you agreed to start. You may have to drive more and complete some extra paperwork, but the effort will ultimately be worthwhile.

4. *Visualization.* Describe how things will be if the plan is put into action. Be positive.

Example: Imagine yourself six months from now with your diploma in hand, ready to tackle the real world, take on an interesting job, and make some money for a change. You'll be able to make car payments, move into a nice apartment, and put aside the pressures of school, including trying to get into closed classes.

5. *Action.* Finally, tell the audience what it needs to do to satisfy its needs and create the desired outcomes.

Example: It's easy to enroll at the other college. Call the registrar and start the necessary paperwork today.

Note that the motivated sequence includes the introduction and conclusion in its total structure. The other organizational patterns do not.[1]

EXPLORATION

The pattern you used to write your exploratory paper can be expanded for a researched position paper. Recall that you explained the positions of those in favor of the issue, those against it, and those with various views in between. Your objective was to explain the range of different perspectives on the issue. Having stated these positions, you can now expand your exploratory paper by refuting some of them and by stating and supporting your own. You may want to use another pattern, such as the claim with reasons, to organize your own position on the issue.

As an alternative, you can explain the various positions from your exploratory paper at the beginning of your position paper and show the advantages of each of them, then identify one position as probably best, and finally spend the rest of your paper developing that idea. This strategy impresses readers as fair-minded and convincing because each major perspective is acknowledged. To write such a position paper, go to your exploratory paper file in your computer and build parts of it into your position paper.

---

[1] The motivated sequence pattern is popularized by Alan Monroe in his public speaking textbooks.

HOW TO MATCH PATTERNS TO CLAIMS

Some of these organizational patterns are particularly appropriate for specific types of claims. Table 12.1 suggests patterns you might want to consider as promising for particular argumentative purposes. You may of course combine more than one pattern to develop a paper. For example, you may begin with a narrative of what happened, then describe its causes and effects, and finally propose a solution for dealing with the problems created by the effects.

Use organizational patterns to help you think and organize your ideas. The patterns may be too constraining if you start with one and try to fill it in with your own material. You may prefer to work with your ideas first, without the conscious constraints of a pattern to guide you. At some point, however, when you are finished or nearly finished organizing your ideas, move out of the creative mode and into the critical mode to analyze what you have done. You may find that you have arranged your ideas according to one or more of the patterns without being consciously aware of it. This is a common discovery. Now use what you know about the patterns to improve and sharpen the divisions among your ideas and to clarify these ideas with transitions. You will ultimately improve the readability of your paper by making it conform more closely to one or more specific patterns of organization.

TABLE 12.1   Appropriate Patterns for Developing Types of Claims (in descending order of suitability).

CLAIMS OF FACT	CLAIMS OF DEFINITION	CLAIMS OF CAUSE	CLAIMS OF VALUE	CLAIMS OF POLICY
Claim with reasons	Deduction	Cause and effect	Applied criteria	Problem-solution
Induction	Claim with reasons	Claim with reasons	Cause and effect	Applied criteria
Chronology or narrative	Comparison and contrast	Rogerian argument	Claim with reasons	Motivated sequence
Cause and effect	Rogerian argument	Deduction	Chronology or narrative	Cause and effect
Rogerian argument	Exploration	Exploration	Rogerian argument	Claim with reasons
Exploration	Induction		Induction	Rogerian argument
			Deduction	Exploration
			Comparison and contrast	
			Exploration	

OUTLINING YOUR PAPER AND CROSS-REFERENCING YOUR NOTES

You have already been provided with a rationale and some ideas for outlining in Chapter 4. Some people find they can draft simple papers that require little or no research without an outline or list. They can later rearrange material on the computer until it is in a logical order. Most people, however, need some sort of outline or list to guide their writing when they are working with their own ideas or with material from outside sources.

Try making an outline or list for your research paper, and make one that works best for you. Think of your outline as a guide that will help you write later. At the very least, indicate on your outline the major ideas, in the order you intend to write about them, and add the ideas and research you will use for support and development. Read your invention and research notes, and check to make certain that all are cross-referenced in some way to the outline. Identify the places where you need more information and research. If you have gathered research material on cards, paper-clip the cards to the places on the outline where they will be used later. If you have photocopied or printed material, use numbers to cross-reference to your outline the highlighted passages you intend to quote. Work with your outline until it flows logically and makes sense. Pay attention to the parts, the order of the parts, and the relationships among the parts.

If you have the opportunity, discuss your outline or plan with your instructor, a peer editing group, or a friend. Someone else can often tell you if the organization is clear and logical, point out places where you will need more support and evidence, and also tell you whether or not the warrants will be generally acceptable.

Here is an example. The following outline is more complete than a preliminary plan to guide research. It would be complete enough to guide writing for some people. Other people might want to add more detail to it before attempting the first draft. It is the sort of outline one might take to a peer editing group to discuss and get suggestions for the actual writing of the paper.

WORKING TITLE: **IS TECHNOLOGY GOOD OR BAD? THE TECHNOPHOBIC PERSPECTIVE**

INTRODUCTION

Value claim: Even though most people claim to be technophiles, many are really closet technophobes, and that may represent a desirable state of affairs. (Define *technophobia* as a fundamental distrust of modern technology, and give some examples, like getting the answering machine when you need to talk with a human, the constant updating and planned obsolescence of modern computers, and automated teller machines and credit cards that cause some people to lose control over their financial resources.)

(continued)

(continued)

REASONS

I. Technology is advancing too rapidly, which causes some people to lag behind and resent it.
  - It's hard to learn the new ways and give up the old ones.
  - It's hard to adjust to constant change.

II. Technology is perceived as dehumanizing by many people.
  - Technology reduces human initiative.
  - New machines sometimes have a higher profile than individual people.
  - People forget how to relate to other people.

III. Technology changes the way many of us use our time, and we resent it.
  - We spend less time thinking and reflecting and more time engaged with machines. (Example: People who spend hours a day on the Internet)
  - We spend less time outdoors communing with nature and more time inside watching movies and television.
  - We are losing our sense of what is "real."

IV. Many people become nostalgic for the way things were.

CONCLUSION

It is time for technophobes to declare themselves, and they should not be ashamed of their technophobia. It may lead to a healthy skepticism about technology that will help humans maintain their humanity while they objectively evaluate what technology can and cannot contribute to their lives.

Note that this outline is worked out in detail in some areas but not in others. The ideas in it so far, however, belong to the author. The peer group that critiques it at this stage would be able to identify the areas in which this paper is likely to need more development and would suggest areas for research. The author goes to the library and finds three relevant articles—about (1) students who spend too much time on the Internet, (2) a writer who likes word processing but does not like the Internet, and (3) a teacher who likes her old bicycle.

Figures 12.1 to 12.5 illustrate notes that this author has taken on cards to use in the rough draft of the paper. The notes are based on the essay that follows. The first card is the bibliography card, which presents full information about the source and a brief statement about how it might be used in the paper. The other four cards are note cards. They represent examples of the four types of notes authors take as they do research for a paper: the direct quotation, the paraphrase, the summary, and the author's own ideas. You can begin to see the advantage of cards. They can be alphabetized, labeled, laid out to read more easily, and physically rearranged to fit into the parts of the paper. Cards are best for big projects. Highlighting with cross-referenced numbering on photocopied or printed research material works best for simpler, shorter projects.

Mednick, Johanne. "The Highs of Low Technology."
Toronto Globe and Mail. 23 July 1993: 16.

Use as an example of IV, nostalgia.

FIGURE 12.1 Bibliography Card for the Article by Mednick, with Annotation.

IV. Nostalgia

Mednick

"Perhaps my bike is representative of a world gone
by. . . . My bike is certainly not built for speed. . . .
It's built for taking time. It makes people feel relaxed."
p. 16

FIGURE 12.2 Direct Quotation (with ellipses) from Paragraph 6 of Mednick's Article.

II. Dehumanizing

Mednick

She says that her microwave and her computer make
her feel that life is getting too complicated and out
of control. p. 16

FIGURE 12.3 Paraphrase of the Ideas in Paragraph 7 of Mednick's Article.

IV. Nostalgia

Mednick

She claims that people still long for the older, simpler machines like her old bicycle and the simpler way of life they represented. p. 16

FIGURE 12.4 Summary of Mednick's Article.

IV. Nostalgia

Mine

Examples of nostalgia for the old, besides Mednick's bicycle: wood stoves, old typewriters, old cash registers. People save these because of the ways of life they represent – they are still attractive to them.

FIGURE 12.5 Card with the Author's Original Insight.

THE HIGHS OF LOW TECHNOLOGY*

Johanne Mednick

Johanne Mednick is a teacher who lives in Canada.

1   I have a wonderful bicycle. Most people refer to it as "the old clunker," an ancient piece of metal the likes of which can be found in the dump or, if you're lucky, at garage sales.

Toronto Globe and Mail, July 23, 1993, p. 16.

2 In other words, people trashed these things a long time ago. Mine is a souped-up version of the basic "no-speeder," vintage 1930 or '40—two large wheels, seat, handle bars, basket, bell and the simple mechanism that allows me to pedal my way to wherever I'm going. I go uphill and downhill, easily gliding past all the riders on racers and mountain bikes intent on engaging the right gear for the occasion.

3 It's not that I'm an Amazon bike rider or anything. In fact, I won't make it up those hills if I don't get the necessary run at the start. But I have confidence in my bike. It gives me power, and I cherish its simplicity.

4 What intrigues me, in this age of technological innovation (which is nowhere more apparent than in the bicycle world), is the number of people who stop me and comment on my bike. It's a regular conversation piece. "Where did you get that thing?" "I haven't seen one of those in ages." "What a great bike." I get all kinds of comments—the best one being from a motorcycle gang who cornered me while I was locking it up. They politely suggested to me that I wear gloves while riding to protect my hands. Maybe I should also don a leather jacket.

5 But really, what is it that people are admiring? Are they admiring me for resisting the lure toward mass bicycle consumerism? I must look like an eyesore pedalling behind my family, who all ride the latest model of designer-coloured mountain bike. (To them, I'm some sort of anomaly, an embarrassment not fit to be on the road.) On the other hand, maybe people are just genuinely curious, as they would be if confronted with a dinosaur bone. I never get the feeling that they think I'm crazy for riding something archaic when I could be fiddling with gears and having a presumably easier time of things. I believe that this curiosity runs deeper. My bike seems to touch a sensitive chord in people, and I'm not quite sure what or why that is.

6 Perhaps my bike is representative of a world gone by, the world before gimmicks and gadgets, accessories and attachments, a time when people thought in terms of settling into a cushioned seat, stopping the movement with their heel and travelling a bit slower than we are travelling now. My bike is certainly not built for speed, but who needs speed when I can coast along the streets, hold my head high and deliciously feel the wind on my face? It's built for taking time. It makes people feel relaxed.

7 When I'm riding my bike, I feel as though I have control. And I don't feel that way about most things these days. I don't deny that my computer or my microwave make my life a lot easier. I use these things, but they also make me feel rather small and, in a strange way, inadequate. What if I press the wrong button? What if something goes wrong? Maybe if I learned to understand these appliances I'd feel better, more secure about my relationship with technology. But frankly, I'm not comforted by manuals and how-to courses. Of course there are always "experts" I could go to who seem to know everything about anything. Relative, friend or salesperson, these people seem to breathe the latest invention and revel in ingenuity.

8 I just don't get excited over yet another thing I could do if I pulled the right lever or set the right program. Nervous and unsure in the beginning, I eventually adapt to these so-called conveniences and accept them as a part of life, but I'm

not entirely convinced of their merit. I crave simplicity and I have a sneaking suspicion that many people feel the same way. That's why they admire my bike. It comforts them and gives them a sense of something manageable, not too complicated.

9   I'm not suggesting that we go back to a pioneer-village mentality. But I do think it's important to respect that which is simple and manageable—no doubt difficult in a time when more is better and new is best. I'm proud that my clunker makes me and others feel good. It allows me the opportunity to relax and, at best when I'm heading down the road, escape what I don't understand.

◆◆◇

Now look back at the note cards in Figures 12.1 to 12.5 and the outline on pages 353–354. Note that at the top of each card, the number and a short title of the relevant subidea on the outline are recorded. Thus "IV. Nostalgia" refers to point IV on the outline. Note also that the quoted material from paragraph 6 is placed in quotation marks to remind the author that these are the essayist's exact words. The paraphrase, or rephrasing of the ideas in paragraph 7, is written in the author's words and thus is without quotation marks. The summary, also in the author's words and without quotation marks, states the main point of the article. When all of the notes have been taken on all of the articles, they can be stacked in the order in which they will be used in the paper and placed next to the outline. The author is now ready to begin the draft. Most of the material in the paper will be the insights, observations, ideas, and examples of the author. Outside research material will be incorporated into the paper to add interest and improve the clarity and credibility of the final paper.

INCORPORATING RESEARCH INTO YOUR FIRST DRAFT

Use common sense in working your research materials into your draft. Your objective is to create a smooth document that can be easily read while at the same time demonstrating to your readers exactly which materials are yours and which are drawn from outside sources. Here are some suggestions to help you accomplish this.

1. *Use quoted material sparingly.* You want to have the controlling voice in your paper. No more than 20 percent of your paper should be made up of direct quotations of other people's words. When you do quote, select material that is interesting, vivid, and best stated in the quoted words.

2. *Paraphrase or summarize when you do not know enough to use your own explanations.* Use your own words to rephrase or summarize other people's explanations and ideas so that your voice is the dominant voice in your paper.

3. *Begin and end your paper with your own words instead of a quotation, paraphrase, or summary of other people's ideas.* The beginning and end are emphatic places in a paper. Put *your* best ideas there, not someone else's.

4. *Introduce each quotation, paraphrase, or summary in your paper so that your readers will know who wrote it originally.* Make it clear where your words and ideas leave off and where someone else's begin. Introduce each quotation, paraphrase, or summary with the name of the person who wrote it. Consider also adding a description of that person's credentials to establish his or her *ethos* and authority.

> *Example:* According to Johanne Mednick, a teacher in Canada, an old bicycle is better than newer models (16).

5. *Integrate every quotation into your paper so that it flows with the rest of the text and makes sense to the reader.* Avoid sticking in quoted sentences that do not make much sense in the context you have created. Instead, work in the quotations so that they make sense in context.

> *Example:* People have various reasons for preferring the old to the new. Mednick's reasons for preferring her old bicycle are clear in her concluding statement. In describing her bicycle, she says, "It allows me the opportunity to relax and, at best when I'm heading down the road, escape what I don't understand"(16).

6. *If your author quotes someone else and you want to use that quote in your own paper, introduce the quotation by indicating who originated it.* Make clear that the quotation is not your source's but someone your source quoted.

> *Example:* Mednick declares that other people show a great deal of interest in her old bicycle. Strangers come up to her regularly and make such comments as "Where did you get that thing?" and "I haven't seen one of those in ages" (16).

7. *Cite the source of the quotation, paraphrase, or summary in parentheses at the end of it.* Further instructions for writing in-text parenthetical citations are given in the Appendix to this chapter.

Write all quotations, paraphrases, and summaries into your first draft so that your entire paper will be in place for smooth reading. The following three paragraphs show the quoted, paraphrased, and summarized material from the Mednick article worked into the first draft so that it is absolutely clear as to what is the author's and what is Mednick's.

Many people become nostalgic for the ways things were. Some people keep old cash registers at their businesses to remind customers of days gone by. Other people fire up wood stoves to help them remember earlier times. Johanne Mednick, a teacher in Canada, claims that many people still long for older, simpler machines and also for the way of life they represent (16).

Mednick uses her old bicycle as an example. "Perhaps my bike is representative of a world gone by," she says. "My bike is certainly not built for speed. . . . It's built for taking time. It makes people feel relaxed" (16).

New computers and microwave ovens, by contrast, make people feel that life is getting too complicated and out of control (Mednick 16).

Notice that in the first paragraph, Johanne Mednick's entire name is used to introduce her material, and in subsequent references she is referred to as Mednick. Notice also that in the first two paragraphs, Mednick's name is used to introduce the material that is attributed to her. Since it is clear from the context where her material begins and where it leaves off, it is only necessary to insert the page number of her article at the end of the borrowed material. In the third paragraph, Mednick's name is not included in the text, and it is less clear whose idea this is. To make it absolutely clear to the reader that this is another idea of Mednick's, her last name along with the page number is placed at the end of the borrowed idea. The full information about this source and where it was first located will be placed on bibliography pages at the end of the paper. The reader who wants to know when and where Mednick published her article can refer to those pages.

Clearly Identify Words and Ideas from Outside Sources

Sometimes students mix their words in with the words of the author they are quoting and neglect to put the author's quoted words in quotation marks. The result is a strange mix of styles and voices that creates a problem for the reader who cannot easily sort out the students' words from those of the person being quoted. First look at an example of this error.

Low technology can be a high for many people. A wonderful bicycle that most people would refer to as an old clunker might bring its owner considerable pleasure. Its two large wheels, seat, handle bars, basket, bell, and pedals help its owner glide past all of the riders on racers and mountain bikes who are intent on engaging the right gear for the occasion. People admire her bike because it gives them a sense of something manageable, not too complicated (Mednick 16).

The problem with that paragraph is that the author has copied Mednick's original language from paragraphs 1, 2, and 8 without putting any of it in quotation marks. Even though the citation at the end of the paragraph indicates that the ideas are Mednick's, the reader does not know which words came directly from Mednick's essay and which have been supplied by the author.

Now let's examine two better ways to incorporate research. One is to *paraphrase the ideas in your own words.*

Not everyone likes new bicycles. Johanne Mednick describes her old bicycle and the pleasure it brings her. She never envies people who pass her by on new bikes. She prefers the familiar comfort of her old bicycle (16).

An alternative is to *combine your words with the author's, but place the author's words in quotations marks.*

Johanne Mednick claims in her essay "The Highs of Low Technology" that she prefers her old bicycle to new racing bikes or mountain bikes. She describes her old bicycle in admiring terms. It has, she says, "two large wheels, seat, handle bars, basket, bell and the simple mechanism that allows me to pedal my way to wherever I'm going" (16). She is often able to pass people on newer bikes because they have to slow down to shift gears (16).

AVOID PLAGIARISM

As just noted, whenever you use quoted, paraphrased, and summarized material from other sources in your paper, you must indicate where your words leave off and someone else's begin, and you must identify the original source for all borrowed material.

Using other people's ideas or words in your paper without acknowledging where they came from or with whom they originated is a form of academic theft called *plagiarism.* It is regarded as an extremely serious violation in educational circles because it negates the whole purpose of education, which is to encourage original and analytical thinking. The writer of our first example was guilty of plagiarism by using a considerable amount of Mednick's language verbatim without indicating that it is hers. The source credit at the end of the paragraph does not justify using her words but presenting them as the writer's own.

You were cautioned against plagiarism in Chapter 4. The late Stephen E. Ambrose, an author of popular history books, was accused of plagiarism when his book *The Wild Blue* was published in 2001.[2] Both professional historians and the media criticized him publicly, and he suffered considerable embarrassment. Illustrations of the plagiarized passages along with the original passages were published in the *New York Times* and are presented in Figure 12.6 (page 362). Ambrose added footnotes in his book to show in general where the material came from, but he did not place quotation marks around the material that he copied directly. The *New York Times* critic reflects the opinions of several professional historians when he explains, "Mr. Ambrose should have marked direct quotations in the text, or at the very least noted the closeness of his paraphrase in his footnotes, historians say. College students caught employing the same practices would be in trouble."[3] When criticized, Ambrose admitted his mistake, and he was quoted as saying, "I wish I had put the quotation marks in, but I didn't."[4] He said he would do things differently in future books: "I am sure going to put quotes around anything that comes out of a secondary work, always."[5] Compare the passages in Figure 12.6 until you understand why those in the right-hand column present a problem. This will help you avoid making the same mistake yourself.

Online research seems to have increased the incidence of plagiarism in student work. Some students find it tempting to copy and paste information from Internet articles into their own papers without showing where it came from. Professors can usually detect paragraphs that belong to other writers, and they can easily go to the Internet themselves and find the material that has been copied. In other words, you are not likely to get away with this practice. The best approach, now that you understand plagiarism, is to differentiate between your ideas and those of others at all stages of the paper-writing process. This is why you were advised to enclose all direct quotations in quotation marks in your notes and to

---

[2]David D. Kirkpatrick, "As Historian's Fame Grows, So Do Questions on Methods," *New York Times,* January 11, 2002, pp. A1, A19.
[3]Ibid., p. A19.
[4]Ibid., p. A1.
[5]Ibid., p. A19.

EXCERPTS

ECHOES IN PRINT

Stephen E. Ambrose, the author of historic best-sellers, appears to have reused the words and phrases from other works, though passages are attributed in footnotes to original authors. Here are four examples:

From *The Army Air Forces in World War II*, 1949, edited by Wesley F. Craven and J. L. Cate.

From *The Wild Blue*, 2001, Mr. Ambrose's current best-seller.

ON B-17 AND B-24 BOMBERS

"The heavy bomber offensive was an impersonal sort of war and monotonous in its own peculiar way. Day after day, as weather and equipment permitted, B-17's and B-24's went out, dropped their deadly load, and turned homeward. The immediate results of their strikes could be photographed and assessed by intelligence officers in categories reminiscent of high school "grades"–bombing was excellent, good, fair or poor. But rarely was a single mission or series of missions decisive."

"The Eighth Air Force's heavy bomber offensive was an impersonal sort of war, monotonous in its own peculiar way. Day after day, as weather and the available force permitted, B-17's and B-24's went out, dropped their bombs, and returned to England. The immediate results of their missions could be photographed and assessed by intelligence officers. The bombers were scored in categories that sound like high school grades—excellent, good, fair, poor. But missions, or a series of them, were rarely if ever decisive."

ON THE GERMAN ECONOMY DURING THE WAR

"Actually, Germany had been almost paralyzed economically by January 1945, and she was ruined by April."

"By January 1945, Germany had been almost paralyzed economically, and by April she was ruined."

From *The Rise of American Air Power*, 1987, by Michael S. Sherry.

From *The Wild Blue*.

ON JOHN STEINBECK'S WORK WRITING PROPAGANDA ABOUT AIRMEN

"Crewmen supposedly sprang from the frontier tradition of the 'Kentucky hunter and the Western Indian fighter.' . . . Like Lindbergh 15 years earlier, the airman was presented as both individualist and joiner, relic of the past and harbinger of the new era, free spirit and disciplined technician, democrat and superman, 'Dan'l Boone and Henry Ford.'"

"Steinbeck wrote that the men of the AAF sprang from the frontier tradition of the 'Kentucky hunter and the Western Indian fighter.' He presented the airman as both individualist and a joiner, a relic of the past and a harbinger of a new era, a free spirit and a disciplined technician, a democrat and a superman, 'Dan'l Boone and Henry Ford.'"

ON THE DANGERS OF ANOXIA (DEPRIVATION OF OXYGEN)

"Anoxia from shortages of oxygen both compounded the perils of frostbite and posed a serious danger in and of itself."

"Anoxia from shortages of oxygen compounded the threat of frostbite and posed a serious danger in and of itself."

FIGURE 12.6 Examples of Plagiarism.

SOURCE: David D. Kirkpatrick, "As Historian's Fame Grows, So Do Questions on Methods," *New York Times*, January 11, 2002, p. A19.

color-code your note cards to keep your ideas separate from the direct quotes, paraphrases, and summaries drawn from other people's works. Use other people's ideas and words in your paper, but acknowledge that they are theirs. Penalties for plagiarism can be severe, ranging from a failing grade to probation or suspension from college.

DOCUMENT YOUR SOURCES

Some of the main features of source acknowledgment are explained in the Appendix to this chapter. Use the Appendix as a reference guide when you are working borrowed material into your paper and also when you are preparing the final list of the works you have used. These methods will inform your reader as to exactly what material in your paper is yours, what belongs to other people, and where you found the material in the first place. You will first be shown examples of ways to incorporate borrowed material into the text of your paper and to use in-text citations (page numbers in parentheses) to indicate succinctly where it originally appeared. You will then be shown how to prepare entries for the list of sources that you have used. This list will appear at the end of your paper. The list of sources in the Appendix may suggest resources for your paper that you have not thought of.

As you incorporate borrowed material from other sources, you will need to follow a system and a set of conventions that has been prescribed for this purpose. There are several such systems. The two that are taught in the Appendix are MLA style, which is recommended by the Modern Language Association for papers written in the humanities, and APA style, recommended by the American Psychological Association for papers written in the social sciences. Both give advice on how to acknowledge the work of other individuals in your paper and also how to give full information about these sources in a list of "Works Cited" (MLA) or "References" (APA) at the end of the paper. The Council of Science Editors publishes the *CSE Manual,* which shows how to document sources in scientific papers in such areas as the natural sciences, chemistry, geography, and geology. Other styles of documentation are detailed in the *Chicago Manual,* the style manual of the University of Chicago Press.[6] *Chicago* style is followed in this book. No matter which system you use, be consistent throughout your paper.

Additional examples of incorporating quoted, paraphrased, and summarized material along with lists of works cited and references appear in the two student argument papers at the end of the Appendix to this chapter. Study the annotations in the margins of these papers. They demonstrate how quoted and summarized material can be incorporated into papers and acknowledged according to MLA style in the first paper and APA style in the second.

---

[6]Documentation styles are explained in detail in various handbooks for writers. One handbook that provides information on all four of the styles mentioned here is Lynn Quitman Troyka, *Simon & Schuster Handbook for Writers,* 6th ed. (Upper Saddle River, N.J.: Prentice Hall, 2002).

MAKING REVISIONS AND PREPARING THE FINAL COPY

Review Chapter 4 for additional information to help you write and rewrite your paper. It may take several tries, but you will eventually get a version of your paper that you are content to show to other readers. Seek the help of your peer editing group, a tutor, your instructor, or other readers once again, when you have improved your paper as much as possible on your own. When you get to this point, you will think your paper is pretty good. However, a new reader will always find ways to improve your paper. So this is the time to put aside your pride and let others take a final look at what you have written. During this final revision process, you and your readers can use the Toulmin model to help you identify and revise the major elements in your paper.

1. Find your claim. Is it clear? Is it well positioned?
2. Check the quantity and quality of your support. Is there enough? Is it relevant? Is it authoritative and accurate?
3. Check your warrants. Are they likely to be acceptable to your audience?
4. Think about backing for your warrants. Would backing make your warrants stronger and more acceptable to your audience?
5. Focus on your rebuttal, if you have one. Does it effectively address the opposing arguments?
6. Consider a qualifier. Would a qualified claim make your argument stronger?

As you go through your paper these final times, make all the remaining changes, large and small. If you haven't done so already, write a meaningful title that reflects the content of your paper. Rewrite parts by using more evocative words, cut out anything that doesn't contribute to the meaning, add text where necessary, rearrange things if you have a good reason to do so, read your paper aloud to catch additional problems, and make all final corrections. You will finally reach a point where you are satisfied. Now it is time to prepare the final copy.

Type your paper on standard $8\frac{1}{2}$-by-11-inch paper, and double-space all of it, including the "Works Cited" (MLA) or "References" (APA). See pages 379–392 for further instructions. If you are following MLA style, leave 1-inch margins all around. Type your last name and the page number 1/2 inch from the top in the right-hand corner. Repeat this on all subsequent pages. One inch from the top of the first page, by the left-hand margin, type and double-space your name, your instructor's name, the course name and number, and the date. (Your instructor may ask you to add the type of assignment.) Double-space again, and type the title, centered. Double-space once more, and begin typing your paper. Attach the list of "Works Cited" at the end.

If you are following APA style, prepare a title page (if your professor requires it) on which you type a short version of your title and the page number in the top right-hand corner as on all subsequent pages. Drop down to midpage and type the title, centered. Then double-space and type your name; double-space again and type the name of your school. Begin your paper on the next page with the short title and page number in the top right-hand corner. Then double-space and type the title. Double-space again and begin your paper. Attach the list of "References" at the end, starting on a new page, numbered sequentially.

Spell-check your paper if you are using a computer, and proofread it one last time. Correct all of the errors that you can find. Errors in a research paper damage your *ethos* with your readers. Careless errors communicate that you do not really value your own work or your audience. When your paper is as error-free as you can make it, it is ready for submission.

REVIEW QUESTIONS

1. Why is it important to organize the ideas in a paper? How does organization help the reader? How does it help the writer?
2. What advice was given in the chapter to help you organize the ideas in your paper?
3. What are some examples of organizational patterns that you might use in a position paper? Name five and describe their main features or rationale.
4. How might making an outline or fairly complete list of ideas help you write the first draft of your paper?
5. What are some of the potential values of a peer editing session?
6. Describe the first draft. What should you probably include in it?
7. What are some of the things you should keep in mind when you revise your paper?
8. What is the purpose of in-text citations and the final list of sources?

EXERCISES AND ACTIVITIES

A. THE RESEARCHED POSITION PAPER: PEER CRITIQUE OF OUTLINE

Write an outline or a partial manuscript that will serve as a plan for your paper, and bring it to class. Organize peer editing groups of three or four students. Explain to the group what your paper is about and how you plan to organize and develop it. Get suggestions from the others to help with ideas and organization and also with adding research.

B. THE RESEARCHED POSITION PAPER: PEER CRITIQUE SHEET

The peer critique sheet is a worksheet that provides a guide for critique and revision. Make a list on the board of all of the special requirements for a good researched position paper: a clear claim, adequate support, accurate documentation, and so on. Select five to ten items from this list that you believe are essential elements to consider during revision. Organize them on a peer critique sheet. The peer editing groups can now use these sheets to critique individual student papers and make recommendations for revision.

C. THE RESEARCHED POSITION PAPER: PEER CRITIQUE OF DRAFT

Finish drafting your paper, and then revise it. Bring it to class again to be reviewed by your peer editing group. The group should first read all of the papers either silently or aloud, and reviewers should make a few notes on the peer critique sheets created in Exercise B. Then each paper should be discussed, and members of the group should offer observations and recommendations for improvement to each author. As the discussion progresses, the peer critics may continue to add suggestions to the peer critique sheets, which should finally be given to the authors at the end of the session.

D. THE RESEARCHED POSITION PAPER: ASSIGNMENT FOR PREPARING FINAL COPY

Make final revisions, and prepare the final copy. Your paper should be 1,500 to 1,800 words in length. It should be double-spaced and should use four to six outside sources. Use MLA format throughout unless advised to use APA or some other format. The two student papers in the Appendix to this chapter can be used as examples. The first demonstrates general format, in-text citations, and "Works Cited" requirements for MLA style. The second demonstrates similar requirements for APA style. Notice also that in both papers, the ideas that control the papers are the authors' original ideas and opinions and that the quoted and paraphrased material is used to provide support.

E. THE RESEARCHED POSITION PAPER: TOULMIN ANALYSIS

Write a one-page Toulmin analysis of your paper, and submit it with your paper.

F. THE RESEARCHED POSITION PAPER: SUBMISSION LETTER

Write a letter to your instructor, and submit it with your final paper. Describe what you like about your paper and what still dissatisfies you. Identify problems or passages on which you would like some feedback.

G. CLASS PROJECT: CONDUCTING A SYMPOSIUM AND PRESENTING YOUR RESEARCH

Present your researched position paper to the class as part of a symposium.

1. Write a 250-word abstract of your paper. State the claim, the main points made about it, some of the evidence, and your conclusion. Your abstract will take two to three minutes to read or to explain to the class.
2. Organize groups around the same or related topics. The best group size is five to seven students with a moderator. The moderator calls on the students in the group to present the abstracts of their research papers.
3. Each set of papers is followed by a five- to ten-minute question-and-answer period. Two sets of papers can usually be presented in a class period. Thus most classes can complete the symposium activity in two class periods.

Appendix to Chapter 12

How to Document Sources Using MLA and APA Styles

The following material will demonstrate how to use in-text citations to show your readers exactly what material you have included in your paper from outside sources. It will then show how to prepare a final list of sources with publication details at the end of your paper, called either "Works Cited" if you are following MLA style or "References" if you are following APA style. For additional detail on how to use MLA style, consult the *MLA Handbook for Writers of Research Papers* (6th ed., 2003), published by the Modern Language Association; for APA style, consult the *Publication Manual of the American Psychological Association* (5th ed., 2001), published by the American Psychological Association.

HOW TO WRITE IN-TEXT PARENTHETICAL CITATIONS

Both the MLA and APA systems of documentation ask that you show where you originally found a direct quotation, a paraphrase, or a summary by inserting a brief parenthetical citation at the end of the borrowed material in your written text. The MLA system requires that you provide the author's name and the page number: (Jones 5). The APA system requires that you provide the author's name, the date of publication, and the page numbers, which are introduced by *p.* or *pp.* for books and newspapers *only:* (Jones, 1983, p. 5). If, however, you mention the name of the author in the text, you do not need to repeat the author's name in the parenthetical material for either style. The following are examples.

1. Direct quotation with the author mentioned in the text

MLA: As Howard Rheingold describes his first trip into virtual reality, "My body wasn't in the computer world" (15-16).

APA: As Howard Rheingold (1991) describes his first trip into virtual reality, "My body wasn't in the computer world" (pp. 15-16).

2. Direct quotation with the author not mentioned in the text

MLA: Virtual reality changes perceptions radically. As one participant explains it, "My body wasn't in the computer world. I could see around me, but one of my hands had accompanied my point of view onto the vast electronic plain that seemed to surround me" (Rheingold 15-16).

APA: As one participant explains it, "My body wasn't in the computer world. I could see around me" (Rheingold, 1991, pp. 15-16).

3. Paraphrase or summary with the author mentioned in the text

MLA: Howard Rheingold describes his first trip into virtual reality as one that involved his hand and arm but not his whole body (15-16).

APA: Howard Rheingold (1991) describes his first trip into virtual reality as one that involved his hand and arm but not his whole body (pp. 15-16).

4. Paraphrase or summary with the author not mentioned in the text

MLA: One's whole body is not always a part of the virtual reality experience. Sometimes only a hand and arm enters that reality (Rheingold 15-16).

APA: One's whole body is not always a part of the virtual reality experience. Sometimes only a hand and arm enters that reality (Rheingold, 1991, pp. 15-16).

5. Two or more authors. If two or three authors have written the material you have borrowed, include all of their names in either the introductory material or the citation.

MLA: "Virtual reality is all about illusion" (Pimentel and Teixeira 7).

APA: Pimental and Teixeira (1993) remind us, "Virtual reality is all about illusion" (p. 7).

For more than three authors, use only the first author's name and add *et al.* to the citation for MLA. For APA, list all of the authors' names (up to five) for the first reference, then use the first name and *et al.* for subsequent references. For six or more authors, use the first author's name followed by *et al.* in all citations. (See item 3 on page 372.)

6. Two books by the same author. To indicate which book you are citing, either include the name of the book in the introductory material or add a short title to the parenthetical information to differentiate between the books for MLA. For APA, use the publication dates to distinguish between the books. For example, if you are using *The Second Self: Computers and the Human Spirit* (1984) and *Life on the Screen: Identity in the Age of the Internet* (1995), both by Sherry Turkle, document as follows:

MLA: Sherry Turkle says the computer is like a mirror that has a strong psychological hold over her (Second Self 306). She explains further that "the computer tantalizes me with its holding power" (Life 30).

APA: The computer can have a strong psychological hold over some individuals (Turkle, 1984, p. 306). In fact, the computer can tantalize "with its holding power--in my case, the promise that if I do it right, <u>it</u> will do it right, and right away" (Turkle, 1995, p. 30).

7. *Corporate author or organization.* Sometimes written materials are attributed to a corporate or group author rather than to an individual author. In this case, use the name of the corporation or group, preferably in the material that precedes the quotation.

MLA: According to the <u>Notebook</u> published by the Network Project, "The results show . . ." (7).

Or you can mention the corporate author at the end.

APA: "The results show . . ." (Network Project, 1992, p. 7).

8. *Unknown author/title only.* When no author is listed for either a book or an article, use the title or the first words of an abbreviated title in your citation.

MLA: *Article:* ("Creativity and Television" 14).
       Book: (<u>Nielsen Television</u> 17).

APA: *Article:* ("Creativity and Television," 1973, p. 14).
       Book: (*Nielsen Television*, 1975, p. 17).

9. *Article in a book.* If you quote an article that is reprinted or excerpted in a book such as this one, use the name of the author of the article in your citation, not the author or editor of the book. Thus a quotation from the first page of the essay by Naomi Wolf on pages 222–225 of this book would be cited as (Wolf 222) according to MLA or (Wolf, 2001, p. 222) according to APA.

10. *Electronic source.* Cite electronic sources just as you would print sources. For MLA, introduce the quotation with the author's name in the text, or place the author's name (or the title if there is no author) with a page or paragraph number (if there is one) in parentheses at the end. If no page or paragraph numbers are available for the electronic source, place the author's name only in parentheses. For APA, include the author's name, the date, and the page or paragraph numbers (if available) in parentheses, just as you would for a print source.

11. *Quotations.* Follow special MLA and APA instructions for including short and long quotations. Type short quotations (four lines or less for MLA or forty words or less for APA) like any other sentences in your paper, enclosing them in quotation marks.

Short quotations

MLA: According to Nate Stulman, many college students in his dormitory "routinely stay awake all night chatting with dormmates on-line. Why walk 10 feet down the hall to have a conversation when you can chat on the computer--even if it takes three times as long?" (268).

(*Note:* When you quote a question, put the question mark inside the quotation marks and a period after the closing parenthesis.)

APA: Author Benjamin Cheever (1999) says he uses his computer to "write and read letters, and if it did not involve the elimination of envelopes and a certain parallel loosening of style, the process would be similar to the one that once involved lambskins and sharpened feathers" (p. 7).

Long quotations

Longer quotations should be indented ten spaces from the left-hand margin for MLA and five spaces for APA. For both styles double-space to introduce and end a quotation, and double-space the quotation itself. Do not use quotation marks. The parenthetical citations for both MLA and APA appear right after the final period for long quotations.

MLA: Nate Stulman describes the various uses of computers by the students at his school:

> Several people who live in my hall routinely stay awake all night chatting with dormmates on-line. Why walk 10 feet down the hall to have a conversation when you can chat on the computer--even if it takes three times as long?
>
> You might expect that personal computers in dorm rooms would be used for nonacademic purposes, but the problem is not confined to residence halls. The other day I walked into the library's reference department, and five or six students were grouped around a computer--not conducting research, but playing Tetris. Every time I walk past the library's so-called research computers, it seems that at least half are being used to play games, chat, or surf the Internet aimlessly. (268)[1]

These experiences may be typical of students' computer use at other colleges as well.

APA: Author Benjamin Cheever (1999) contrasts his use of the computer with individuals who spend a lot of time on the Internet:

> The news bulges with stories about dispensing therapy on the Net, doing business on the Net, trolling for unsuspecting sexual prey on the Net. Not on this computer. Most of what I do on the electronic superhighway is write and read letters, and if it did not involve the elimination of envelopes and a certain parallel loosening of style, the process would be similar to the one that once involved lambskins and sharpened feathers. (p. 7)[2]

Cheever has essentially substituted computers and their word processing programs for his old typewriter.

---

[1] This article appears on pages 267–268.
[2] The full citation for this article appears in item 14 on page 374.

HOW TO WRITE THE LIST OF "WORKS CITED" (MLA)
OR "REFERENCES" (APA)

Attach to your draft an alphabetized list of all the works you have quoted or paraphrased in your paper along with full publication information for each of them. This list is titled either "Works Cited" (MLA) or "References" (APA). *All the information on these lists should be double-spaced, just like the rest of your final paper.*

Look at the student papers appearing at the end of this Appendix. The first follows MLA format, and the second follows APA. Include on your list only the works you have actually cited in your paper. The easiest way to prepare this list is to alphabetize your bibliography cards according to the authors' last names or, if no author is listed, by the title of the work. (Ignore the words *A, An,* and *The* when alphabetizing.) If you have prepared an annotated bibliography, simply eliminate the annotations to create these pages.

For both the MLA "Works Cited" and the APA "References," start each citation at the left margin and indent each successive line five spaces.

Basic Format for Books and Articles

Books

MLA: Author. <u>Title of Book</u>. City: Publisher Name in Shortened Form, date.

APA: Author. (Date). *Title of book.* City: Publisher Name in Full.

Articles in newspapers

MLA: Author. "Title of Article." <u>Name of Newspaper</u> date of publication: page numbers.

APA: Author. (Date). Title of article. *The Name of Newspaper,* pp. page numbers.

Articles in magazines or journals

MLA: Author. "Title of Article." <u>Name of Magazine or Journal</u> volume number (year): page numbers.

APA: Author. (Date). Title of article. *The Name of Magazine or Journal, volume number,* page numbers.

Note that in book and article titles, MLA capitalizes all important words, headline style, and APA capitalizes only the first word of the title and any subtitle and all proper nouns, sentence style. Also note that for article titles, MLA uses quotation marks and APA does not. The titles of periodicals are written headline style for both MLA and APA. In APA the words *A, An,* and *The* are included in titles of journals, magazines, and newspapers. Titles of books, newspapers, and journals or magazines are underlined in MLA style and italicized in APA style.

Here are some examples of the types of sources that are most commonly cited for argument papers. Examples of both MLA and APA styles are provided.

How to List Books

1. Book by one author

MLA: Rheingold, Howard. <u>Virtual Reality</u>. New York: Simon, 1991.

APA: Rheingold, H. (1991). *Virtual reality.* New York: Simon & Schuster.

2. Book by two or three authors

MLA: Pimentel, Ken, and Kevin Teixeira. <u>Virtual Reality: Through the New Looking Glass</u>. New York: McGraw, 1993.

APA: Pimentel, K., & Teixeira, K. (1993). *Virtual reality: Through the new looking glass.* New York: McGraw-Hill.

Follow the same format to add a third author, using *and* (MLA) or an ampersand (APA) before the final name.

3. Book by more than three authors

MLA: Comstock, George, et al. <u>Television and Human Behavior</u>. New York: Columbia UP, 1978.

APA: Comstock, G., Chaffee, S., Katzman N., McCombs, M., & Roberts, D. (1978). *Television and human behavior.* New York: Columbia University Press.

4. Two or more books by the same author

MLA: Rheingold, Howard. <u>Tools for Thought</u>. New York: Simon, 1985.

        ---. <u>Virtual Reality</u>. New York: Simon, 1991.

APA: Rheingold, H. (1985). *Tools for thought.* New York: Simon & Schuster.

        Rheingold, H. (1991). *Virtual reality.* New York: Simon & Schuster.

For MLA, arrange the works in alphabetical order by titles. For APA, arrange the works in chronological order, earliest year first.

5. Book by a corporate author

MLA: VPL Research. <u>Virtual Reality at Texpo '89</u>. Redwood City: VPL Research, 1989.

APA: VPL Research, Inc. (1989). *Virtual reality at Texpo '89.* Redwood City, CA: Author.

6. Book with no author named

MLA: <u>Virtual Reality Marketplace</u>. Westport: Meckler, 1992.

APA: *Virtual reality marketplace.* (1992). Westport, CT: Meckler.

7. Book reprinted in a later edition

MLA: Malthus, Thomas R. <u>An Essay on the Principle of Population</u>. 1798. London: Pickering, 1986.

APA: Malthus, T. R. (1986). *An essay on the principle of population*. London: Pickering. (Original work published 1798)

8. Translation

MLA: Rousseau, Jean-Jacques. <u>La Nouvelle Héloïse</u>. 1761. Trans. Judith H. McDowell. University Park: Pennsylvania State UP, 1968.

APA: Rousseau, J.-J. (1968). *La nouvelle Héloïse*. (J. H. McDowell, Trans.). University Park: Pennsylvania State University Press. (Original work published 1761)

9. Subsequent editions

MLA: Thompson, Warren S. <u>Population Problems</u>. 4th ed. New York: McGraw, 1953.

APA: Thompson, W. S. (1953). *Population problems* (4th ed.) New York: McGraw-Hill.

10. Proceedings from a conference or symposium

MLA: McKerrow, Raymie E., ed. <u>Argument and the Postmodern Challenge: Proceedings of the Eighth SCA/AFA Conference on Argumentation</u>. 5-8 Aug. 1993. Annandale: Speech Communication Assn., 1993.

APA: McKerrow, R. E. (Ed.). (1993). *Argument and the postmodern challenge: Proceedings of the eighth SCA/AFA conference on argumentation*. Annandale, VA: Speech Communication Association.

11. Introduction, preface, foreword, or afterword

MLA: Schneiderman, Ben. Foreword. <u>Interacting with Virtual Environments</u>. Ed. Lindsay MacDonald and John Vince. Chichester, Eng.: Wiley, 1994. x-xi.

APA: Schneiderman, B. (1994). Foreword. In L. MacDonald & J. Vince (Eds.), *Interacting with virtual environments* (pp. x-xi). Chichester, England: Wiley.

12. Government documents

MLA: United States. FBI. Dept. of Justice. <u>Uniform Crime Reports for the United States</u>. Washington: GPO, 1990.

APA: Federal Bureau of Investigation. U.S. Department of Justice. (1990). *Uniform crime reports for the United States*. Washington, DC: U.S. Government Printing Office.

How to List Articles

13. Article from a periodical

MLA: Monastersky, Richard. "The Deforestation Debate." <u>Science News</u> 10 July
                1993: 26-27.

APA: Monastersky, R. (1993, July 10). The deforestation debate. *Science News*,
                26-27.

14. Article from a newspaper

MLA: Cheever, Benjamin. "He'll Take His Web Pages Straight, with No Java
                Jive." <u>New York Times</u> 4 Feb. 1999: D7.

APA: Cheever, B. (1999, February 4). He'll take his Web pages straight, with no
                java jive. *The New York Times*, p. D7.

15. Article in a periodical with no author listed

MLA: "A Democratic Army." <u>New Yorker</u> 28 June 1993: 4+.

APA: A democratic army. (1993, June 28). *The New Yorker*, 4, 6.

For MLA, use a plus sign when the pages are not successive. For APA, list all pages
on which the article is printed.

16. Article in a journal with continuous pagination in each volume

MLA: Jasinski, James. "Rhetoric and Judgment in the Constitutional
                Ratification Debate of 1787-1788: An Exploration of the
                Relationship between Theory and Critical Practice."
                <u>Quarterly Journal of Speech</u> 78 (1992): 197-218.

APA: Jasinski, J. (1992). Rhetoric and judgment in the constitutional ratification
                debate of 1787-1788: An exploration of the relationship between
                theory and critical practice. *The Quarterly Journal of Speech, 78,*
                197-218.

17. Article in a journal that pages each issue separately

MLA: Rosenbloom, Nancy J. "In Defense of the Moving Pictures: The People's
                Institute, the National Board of Censorship, and the Problem of
                Leisure in Urban America." <u>American Studies</u> 33.2 (1992): 41-60.

APA: Rosenbloom, N. J. (1992). In defense of the moving pictures: The People's
                Institute, the National Board of Censorship, and the problem of
                leisure in urban America. *American Studies, 33*(2), 41-60.

18. Edited collection of articles or an anthology

MLA: Forester, Tom, ed. <u>The Information Technology Revolution</u>. Cambridge:
                MIT P, 1985.

APA: Forester, T. (Ed.). (1985). *The information technology revolution.*
                Cambridge, MA: MIT Press.

19. Article in an edited collection or an anthology

MLA: Boden, Margaret A. "The Social Impact of Thinking Machines." The Information Technology Revolution. Ed. Tom Foster. Cambridge: MIT P, 1985. 95-103.

APA: Boden, M. A. (1985). The social impact of thinking machines. In T. Foster (Ed.), *The information technology revolution* (pp. 95-103). Cambridge, MA: MIT Press.

20. Reprinted article in an edited volume or collection (like an essay in "The Reader" in this book)

MLA: Fox, Lyla. "Hold Your Horsepower." Newsweek 25 Mar. 1996: 16. Rpt. in Perspectives on Argument. By Nancy V. Wood. 4th ed. Upper Saddle River: Prentice, 2004. 193-94.

APA: Fox, L. (2004). Hold your horsepower. In N. V. Wood, *Perspectives on argument* (4th ed., pp. 193-194). Upper Saddle River, NJ: Prentice Hall.

21. Signed article in a reference work

MLA: Davidson, W. S., II. "Crime." Encyclopedia of Psychology. Ed. Raymond J. Corsini. 4 vols. New York: Wiley, 1984. 310-12.

APA: Davidson, W. S. II. (1984). Crime. In R. J. Corsini (Ed.), *Encyclopedia of psychology* (Vol. 1, pp. 310-312). New York: Wiley.

22. Unsigned article in a reference work

MLA: "Quindlen, Anna." Current Biography Yearbook. Ed. Judith Graham. New York: Wilson, 1993. 477-81.

APA: Quindlen, Anna. (1993). In J. Graham, *Current biography yearbook* (pp. 477-481). New York: Wilson.

23. Review

MLA: Watts, Steven. "Sinners in the Hands of an Angry Critic: Christopher Lasch's Struggle with Progressive America." Rev. of The True and Only Heaven: Progress and Its Critics, by Christopher Lasch. American Studies 33.2 (1992): 113-20.

APA: Watts, S. (1992). Sinners in the hands of an angry critic: Christopher Lasch's struggle with progressive America. [Review of the book *The true and only heaven: Progress and its critics*]. *American Studies, 33*(2), 113-120.

24. Letter to the editor

MLA: McCaffrey, Mark. Letter. Utne Reader July-Aug. 1993: 10.

APA: McCaffrey, M. (1993, July-August). [Letter to the editor]. *Utne Reader,* 10.

25. Editorial

MLA: "A Touch of Class for the Court." Editorial. <u>New York Times</u> 25 July 1993: E16.

APA: A touch of class for the court. (1993, July 25). [Editorial]. *The New York Times*, p. E16.

How to List Electronic Sources

The basic elements of an MLA "Works Cited" entry are author, title, editor, publication specifics including date of publication or update by an organization and the name of the organization that sponsors the information, editor of the site (if applicable), date you accessed the information, and the URL (online address) placed in angle brackets and followed by a period.

The basic elements of an APA "References" entry are author, publication date in parentheses, title of the article, title of the periodical or electronic text, volume number and/or pages (if any), date retrieved from the World Wide Web, and the URL with no brackets and no period at the end.

26. Professional or personal Web site

MLA: Herman, Peter. "Milton Assignments." <u>Milton List Home Page</u>. Ed. Kevin Creamer. 15 Jan. 2003 <http://www.richmond.edu/~creamer/milton/>.

APA: Herman, P. (n.d.). Milton assignments. *Milton List Home Page*. Retrieved January 15, 2003, from http://www.richmond.edu/~creamer/milton/

27. Book

MLA: Nettleship, Richard Lewis. <u>The Theory of Education in the Republic of Plato</u>. 1968. Classics in Education Series. 15 Jan. 2003 <http://www.ilt.columbia.edu/academic/CESdigital/CESdigital.html>.

APA: Nettleship, R. L. (1968). *The theory of education in the Republic of Plato*. Classics in Education Series [Online book]. Retrieved January 15, 2003, from http://www.ilt.columbia.edu/academic/CESdigital/CESdigital.html

28. Article in an electronic journal

MLA: Rolls, Mitchell. "Why I Don't Want to Be an 'Ethical' Researcher." <u>Australian Humanities Review</u> Jan.-Mar. 2003. 15 Jan. 2003 <http://www.lib.latrobe.edu.au/AHR/>.

APA: Rolls, M. (2003, January-March). Why I don't want to be an "ethical" researcher. *Australian Humanities Review*. Retrieved January 15, 2003, from http://www.lib.latrobe.edu.au/AHR/

29. Article in print and online. For MLA, include all the information listed for the print journal followed by the access date and the Web address. For APA, simply add "Electronic version" in brackets after the title as in the following example.

MLA: Chace, James. "Imperial America and the Common Interest." World Policy Journal, 29.1 (2002): 1-9. 2 June 2002 <http://www.worldpolicy.org/journal/wpj02-1html>.

APA: Chace, J. (2002). Imperial America and the common interest [Electronic version]. *World Policy Journal, 29*(1), 1-9.

30. Article accessed through a library online database or service. For MLA, include all the information for the print version of the article followed by the underlined name of the database (if known), the name of the service (not underlined), the library and location, and the date of access. Add a URL address for the service home page if you know it. For APA, include the information for the print version, followed by the retrieval date and the name of the database.

MLA: Menand, Louis. "Is College Too Late to Learn to Write?" New Yorker 11 Sept. 2002: 92. Academic Universe. Lexis-Nexis. U of Texas at Arlington Lib., Arlington. 17 Nov. 2002 <http://www.lexis-nexis.com/>.

APA: Menand, L. (2002, September 11). Is college too late to learn how to write? *The New Yorker.* Retrieved November 17, 2002, from Academic Universe database.

31. Article in a newspaper

MLA: Safire, William. "Free Pills for Geezers?" New York Times on the Web 28 June 1999. 15 Jan. 2003 <http://www.nytimes.com/library/opinion/safire/062899safi.html>.

APA: Safire, W. (1999, June 28). Free pills for geezers? *The New York Times on the Web* [Online newspaper]. Retrieved January 15, 2003, from http://www.nytimes.com/library/opinion/safire/062899safi.html

32. CD-ROM

MLA: The Oxford English Dictionary. 2nd ed. CD-ROM. Oxford: Oxford UP, 1992.

APA: *The Oxford English dictionary.* (1992). [CD-ROM]. Oxford, England: Oxford University Press.

33. Electronic mail (e-mail)

MLA: Rieder, David. "Re: Jobs." E-mail to Debi Reese. 4 Oct. 2003.

In APA style, you would not cite this in the "References." Cite in the text as

D. Rieder (personal communication, October 4, 2003).

34. FTP site

MLA: Freenet Directory. 28 June 1999 <ftp://ftp.cwru.edu/pub/freenet/freedomshrine/timelines>.

APA: Freenet Directory. Retrieved June 28, 1999, from ftp://ftp.cwru.edu/pub/freenet/freedomshrine/timelines

How to List Media: Microforms, Videotape, Radio/Television, Film

35. *ERIC Information Service (microform)*

MLA: Bernhardt, Victoria L. <u>The School Portfolio: A Comprehensive Framework for School Improvement</u>. 2nd ed. Larchmont, NY: Eye on Education, 1999. ERIC ED 431 783.

APA: Bernhardt, V. L. (1999). *The school portfolio: A comprehensive framework for school improvement* (2nd ed.). Larchmont, NY: Eye on Education. (ERIC Document Reproduction Service No. ED431783)

36. *Videotape*

MLA: <u>Composition</u>. Prod. ABC/Prentice Hall Video Library. Videocassette. Prentice, 1993.

APA: ABC/Prentice Hall Video Library (Producer). (1993). *Composition* [Videotape]. Englewood Cliffs, NJ: Prentice Hall.

37. *Radio or television program*

MLA: "Resolved: Political Correctness Is a Menace and a Bore." Prod. and dir. Warren Steibel. Mod. William F. Buckley Jr. <u>Firing Line</u>. PBS. KDTN, Dallas. 2 Dec. 1993.

APA: Steibel, W. (Producer and Director). (1993, December 2). Resolved: Political correctness is a menace and a bore. *Firing Line* [Television broadcast]. New York: Public Broadcasting Service.

38. *Film*

MLA: <u>JFK</u>. Dir. Oliver Stone. Warner, 1991.

APA: Stone, O. (Director). (1991). *JFK* [Motion picture]. Los Angeles: Warner Bros.

How to List Interviews and Speeches

39. *Published interview*

MLA: Hardin, Garrett. Interview with Cathy Spencer. <u>Omni</u> June 1992: 55-63.

APA: Hardin, G. (1992, June). [Interview with C. Spencer]. *Omni*, 55-63.

40. *Personal interview*

MLA: Wick, Audrey. Personal interview. 27 May 2003.

In APA style, you would not cite this in the "References." Cite in the text as

A. Wick (personal communication, May 27, 2003).

41. *Lectures, speeches, addresses*

MLA: Yeltsin, Boris. Address. US Congress, Washington. 18 June 1992.

APA: Yeltsin, B. (1992, June 18). Address to the U.S. Congress, Washington, DC.

PAPER IN MLA STYLE

The audience analysis and exigence that motivated this student paper is explained on pages 303–305.

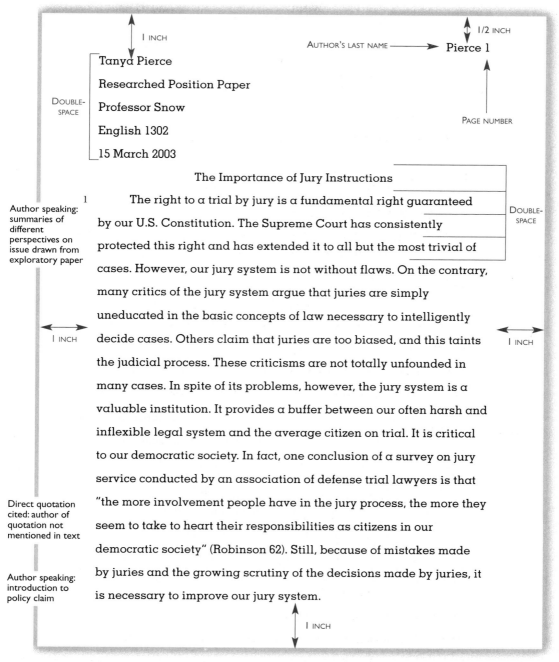

1 INCH

AUTHOR'S LAST NAME ⟶ Pierce 1

1/2 INCH

PAGE NUMBER

Tanya Pierce

Researched Position Paper

Professor Snow

English 1302

15 March 2003

DOUBLE-SPACE

The Importance of Jury Instructions

The right to a trial by jury is a fundamental right guaranteed by our U.S. Constitution. The Supreme Court has consistently protected this right and has extended it to all but the most trivial of cases. However, our jury system is not without flaws. On the contrary, many critics of the jury system argue that juries are simply uneducated in the basic concepts of law necessary to intelligently decide cases. Others claim that juries are too biased, and this taints the judicial process. These criticisms are not totally unfounded in many cases. In spite of its problems, however, the jury system is a valuable institution. It provides a buffer between our often harsh and inflexible legal system and the average citizen on trial. It is critical to our democratic society. In fact, one conclusion of a survey on jury service conducted by an association of defense trial lawyers is that "the more involvement people have in the jury process, the more they seem to take to heart their responsibilities as citizens in our democratic society" (Robinson 62). Still, because of mistakes made by juries and the growing scrutiny of the decisions made by juries, it is necessary to improve our jury system.

DOUBLE-SPACE

1 INCH

1 INCH

1 INCH

Author speaking: summaries of different perspectives on issue drawn from exploratory paper

Direct quotation cited: author of quotation not mentioned in text

Author speaking: introduction to policy claim

(continued)

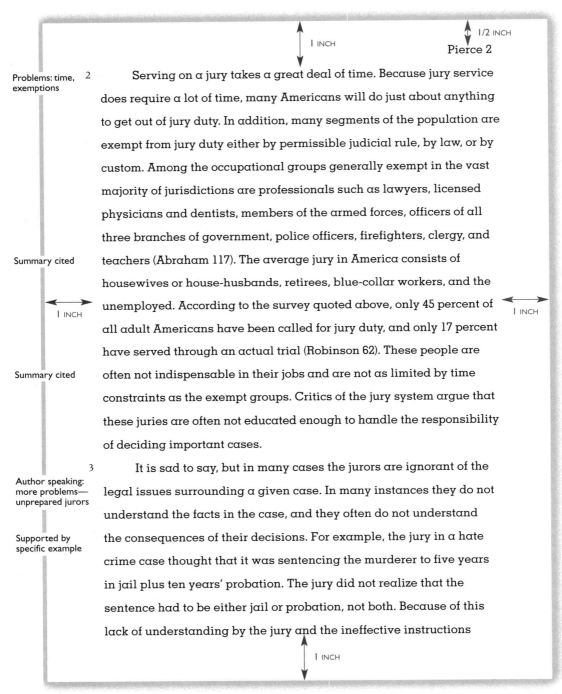

1/2 INCH

Pierce 2

1 INCH

Problems: time, exemptions

2　　　　Serving on a jury takes a great deal of time. Because jury service does require a lot of time, many Americans will do just about anything to get out of jury duty. In addition, many segments of the population are exempt from jury duty either by permissible judicial rule, by law, or by custom. Among the occupational groups generally exempt in the vast majority of jurisdictions are professionals such as lawyers, licensed physicians and dentists, members of the armed forces, officers of all three branches of government, police officers, firefighters, clergy, and

Summary cited

teachers (Abraham 117). The average jury in America consists of housewives or house-husbands, retirees, blue-collar workers, and the

1 INCH

unemployed. According to the survey quoted above, only 45 percent of all adult Americans have been called for jury duty, and only 17 percent have served through an actual trial (Robinson 62). These people are

1 INCH

Summary cited

often not indispensable in their jobs and are not as limited by time constraints as the exempt groups. Critics of the jury system argue that these juries are often not educated enough to handle the responsibility of deciding important cases.

Author speaking: more problems— unprepared jurors

3　　　　It is sad to say, but in many cases the jurors are ignorant of the legal issues surrounding a given case. In many instances they do not understand the facts in the case, and they often do not understand

Supported by specific example

the consequences of their decisions. For example, the jury in a hate crime case thought that it was sentencing the murderer to five years in jail plus ten years' probation. The jury did not realize that the sentence had to be either jail or probation, not both. Because of this lack of understanding by the jury and the ineffective instructions

1 INCH

(continued)

1/2 INCH

1 INCH

Pierce 3

given by the judge and attorneys involved in the case, a grave and irreversible injustice was done. The murderer was given only ten years' probation for killing another human being (Korosec 1A). This is just one of numerous cases in which the jury's lack of knowledge has led to disastrous decisions.

Transition: current solutions and their problems

Something clearly needs to be done to educate jurors. Current practice requires the judge to give instructions, called a charge, to the jury before it begins deliberations. Henry Abraham, who has written extensively on the judicial process, says, "Much thought

Direct quotation cited: author in text

goes--or should go--into this charge, which is intended as an exposition of the law and is delivered orally in most, although not all, cases" (131).

1 INCH

1 INCH

One of the problems with the judge's charge, however, is that most states do not permit the jurors to take either a copy or a tape recording of it with them when they leave the courtroom to make

Summary cited: author in text

their deliberations. Seymour Wishman, a criminal lawyer who has tried hundreds of cases before juries, quotes one judge who supports the idea of allowing jurors to take written or audiotaped instructions with them. According to this judge, we expect people to listen to instructions once and remember them well enough to make "monumental decisions" (224).

Transition

The judge's instructions are not only difficult to remember; they are also sometimes difficult for the jury to understand. Wishman

Direct quotations cited: authors in text

goes on to claim, "Jury instructions are often incomprehensible because they are drafted by lawyers and judges who do not realize

1 INCH

(continued)

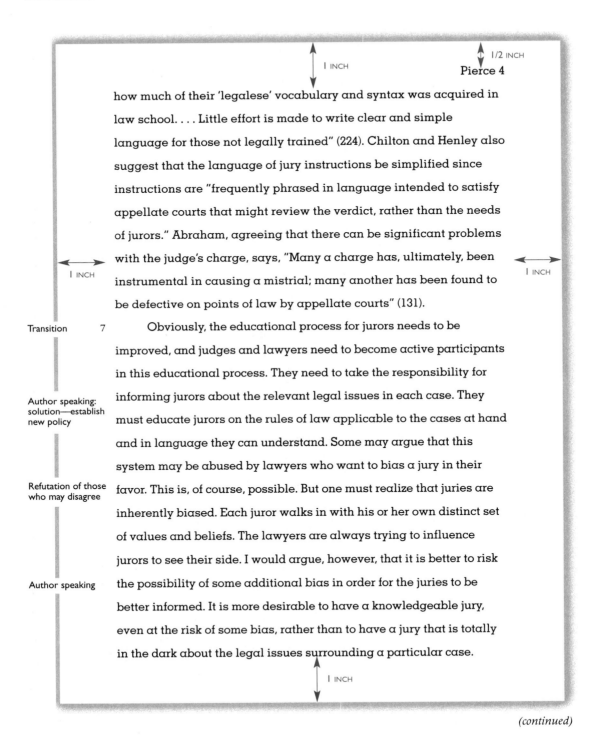

Pierce 4

how much of their 'legalese' vocabulary and syntax was acquired in law school. . . . Little effort is made to write clear and simple language for those not legally trained" (224). Chilton and Henley also suggest that the language of jury instructions be simplified since instructions are "frequently phrased in language intended to satisfy appellate courts that might review the verdict, rather than the needs of jurors." Abraham, agreeing that there can be significant problems with the judge's charge, says, "Many a charge has, ultimately, been instrumental in causing a mistrial; many another has been found to be defective on points of law by appellate courts" (131).

Transition 7   Obviously, the educational process for jurors needs to be improved, and judges and lawyers need to become active participants in this educational process. They need to take the responsibility for informing jurors about the relevant legal issues in each case. They **[Author speaking: solution—establish new policy]** must educate jurors on the rules of law applicable to the cases at hand and in language they can understand. Some may argue that this system may be abused by lawyers who want to bias a jury in their **[Refutation of those who may disagree]** favor. This is, of course, possible. But one must realize that juries are inherently biased. Each juror walks in with his or her own distinct set of values and beliefs. The lawyers are always trying to influence jurors to see their side. I would argue, however, that it is better to risk **[Author speaking]** the possibility of some additional bias in order for the juries to be better informed. It is more desirable to have a knowledgeable jury, even at the risk of some bias, rather than to have a jury that is totally in the dark about the legal issues surrounding a particular case.

1 INCH

(continued)

Pierce 5

1/2 INCH

1 INCH

Support for
solution

8   Some research suggests that juries should be given lessons in the law before the trial begins and also at various points during the trial. Chilton and Henley agree. They urge that instructions be given at the beginning of the trial to give jurors "a framework in which to fit the evidence they are hearing and help them decide the case more quickly and more accurately." Psychological studies have consistently shown that early exposure and frequent exposure to legal principles correlate with juries that are more likely to presume

1 INCH

1 INCH

Summary cited

innocence in a case until sufficient evidence is provided to decide otherwise. Experimental mock juries questioned midway through testimony showed a significantly higher indecision rate when they had been informed about the legal issues involved before the start of testimony than those who had not been instructed earlier (Heuer and Penrod 429). This suggests that juries instructed prior to the presentation of evidence are more likely to consider all of the evidence of a case before arriving at a decision of guilt or innocence.

Author speaking:
more refutation
and benefits of
solution

9   Although some may interpret these psychological data as suggesting that informing juries early and frequently would delay the judicial process, I believe the opposite is true. Instructing juries on the basic legal concepts will help them be more open-minded. They will have more intelligent discussions during deliberations because they will know what issues to concentrate on. Psychological tests have also demonstrated that when jurors are informed on legal

Summary cited

concepts, trials are less likely to result in a hung jury (Goldberg 456). This latter finding is especially valuable since so much government

1 INCH

(continued)

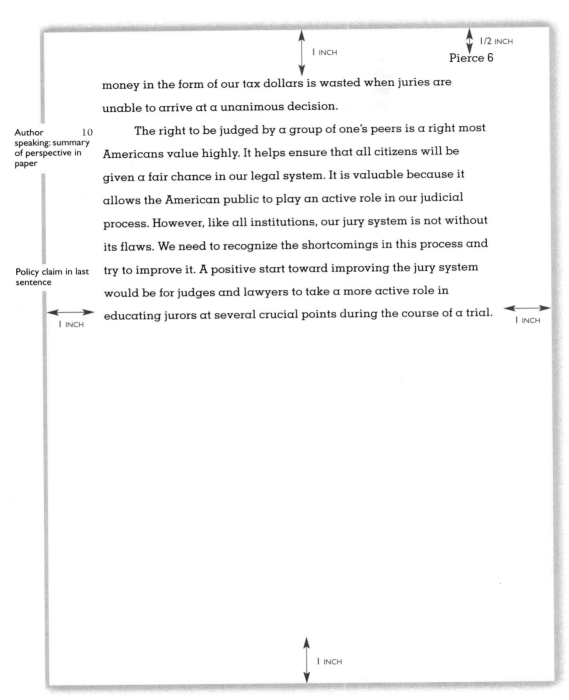

1/2 INCH

Pierce 6

1 INCH

money in the form of our tax dollars is wasted when juries are

unable to arrive at a unanimous decision.

Author 10 speaking: summary of perspective in paper

       The right to be judged by a group of one's peers is a right most

Americans value highly. It helps ensure that all citizens will be

given a fair chance in our legal system. It is valuable because it

allows the American public to play an active role in our judicial

process. However, like all institutions, our jury system is not without

its flaws. We need to recognize the shortcomings in this process and

Policy claim in last sentence

try to improve it. A positive start toward improving the jury system

would be for judges and lawyers to take a more active role in

educating jurors at several crucial points during the course of a trial.

1 INCH

1 INCH

1 INCH

(continued)

Pierce 7

Works Cited

Abraham, Henry J. <u>The Judicial Process: An Introductory Analysis of</u>

5 SPACES <u>the Courts of the United States, England, and France</u>. 5th ed.

New York: Oxford UP, 1986.

Chilton, Ellen, and Patricia Henley. "Jury Instructions: Helping Jurors

Understand the Evidence and the Law." <u>Improving the Jury</u>

<u>System</u>. 2001. Public Law Research Institute, UC Hastings

College of the Law. 15 Jan. 2003 <http://www.uchastings.edu/

plri/spr96t>.

Goldberg, Janice G. "Memory, Magic, and Myth: The Timing of Jury

Instructions." <u>Oregon Law Review</u> 59 (1981): 451-75.

Heuer, Larry, and Steven Penrod. "A Field Experiment with Written

and Preliminary Instructions." <u>Law and Human Behavior</u>

13 (1989): 409-30.

Korosec, Thomas. "Brosky Probation Stirs More Protests." <u>Fort Worth</u>

<u>Star-Telegram</u> 26 Mar. 1993, Tarrant ed.: 1A+.

Robinson, Archie S. "We the Jury: Who Serves, Who Doesn't." <u>USA</u>

<u>Today: The Magazine of the American Scene</u> 120 (Jan. 1992):

62-63.

Wishman, Seymour. <u>Anatomy of a Jury: The System on Trial</u>. New

York: Times, 1986.

PAPER IN APA STYLE

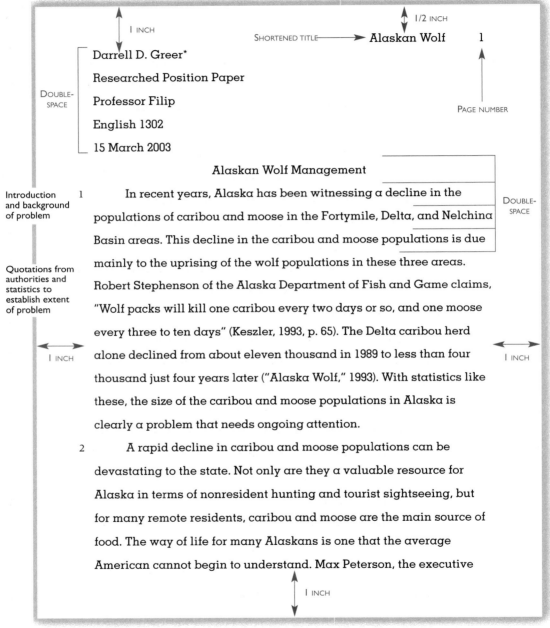

(continued)

---

*APA guidelines call for a separate title page, which includes a running head for publication, the full title, and the author's name and institutional affiliation (see the *Publication Manual of the American Psychological Association,* 5th ed., 2001). Your professor, however, may ask you to present your identifying information as shown here.

1/2 INCH

1 INCH

Alaskan Wolf   2

Quotations worked into text that suggest the unique character of the problem in Alaska

director of the International Association of Wildlife Agencies, says that in Alaska, "people interact as another predator in the ecosystem," and as a result, "the interest in Alaska by people outside Alaska certainly is greater than their knowledge of Alaska" (Keszler, 1993, p. 67). Ted Williams (1993) clarifies the lifestyle that many rural Alaskans lead:

A long quotation of more than forty words is indented and written in block from. No quotation marks are necessary for indented quotations. The page number of the source is indicated at the end. Note that the author is mentioned in the text.

> Genuine subsistence is the most environmentally benign of all possible lifestyles. Subsisters do not--indeed cannot--deplete fish and wildlife because if they do, they will subsist no more. But even in the remotest native villages, Alaska as trackless wilderness where people blend with nature is just an old dream. Many villagers are now on social welfare programs and are therefore cash dependent. (p. 49)

1 INCH

Failing to protect existing caribou and moose populations could lower the subsistence level for some Alaskans, even more than it is at present.

1 INCH

Statistics and quotations from authorities to strengthen the solution preferred by this author

3

The biologists of the state of Alaska commonly believe that wolf populations are nowhere close to being endangered. In 1993 they estimated the total wolf population in Alaska to be between 5,900 and 7,200. In the three areas up for wildlife management (about 3.5 percent of the state), Rodney Boertje, an Alaska Department of Fish and Game wildlife biologist, reported, "Wolf populations can sustain harvest rates of twenty-five to forty percent. So sixty to eighty-five percent of wolves must be removed for control efforts to be effective" (Keszler, 1993, p. 66). This amount totals between three hundred and four hundred wolves in these three areas. Wildlife management

1 INCH

(continued)

1/2 INCH

1 INCH

Alaskan Wolf　　　3

experts believe the most humane and efficient way of accomplishing this task is through aerial shootings of wolves.

Refutation of
the animal rights
groups and their
solutions to the
problem

4

With the announcement of the wolf management plan proposed by Alaska Governor Walter Hickel and the Alaska Department of Fish and Game in 1993 that involved aerial shootings of wolves, the animal rights groups started an all-out war with the state. They organized widespread mailings to the governor and threatened massive boycotts of tourism in Alaska if the plan was not repealed (Keszler, 1993, p. 65). The animal rights groups believed that other methods of management could increase caribou and moose populations. One such method involved reducing bag limits, shortening hunting seasons, or totally eliminating hunting in these three areas. This type of management was not effective, however, since hunters were not the real cause of the problem. Pete Buist, a Fairbanks, Alaska, resident, pointed out at the time, "In control areas, hunters are taking less than five percent of the annual production of meat animals. Predators are taking more than seventy-five percent" (1993). Animal rights groups commonly point to hunters as the culprits in animal conservation efforts. According to Arms (1994), however, "nowadays in developed countries, groups representing hunting and fishing interests are the most active conservationists. They understand that their sport and, sometimes, their livelihood depend on sustained or increasing populations of the organisms they hunt or fish" (p. 347). As mentioned earlier, rural Alaskans who depend on caribou and moose for subsistence are some of these hunters who

1 INCH

1 INCH

1 INCH

(continued)

1 INCH   1/2 INCH

Alaskan Wolf   4

continue to take these animals but not in dangerously large numbers.

5   Another alternative management method that has been brought up by the animal rights groups is tranquilizing and capturing the wolves and chemically sterilizing them or using some other sort of contraception. This method has not been scientifically proved to work. Even if it did work, this method would take entirely too long to be effective for this situation. Contraception only deals with the wolf numbers down the road, not with existing numbers, which would remain the same for now. Existing wolves in the immediate future may devastate the caribou and moose populations so that they will not be able to recover.

1 INCH

Evaluation and
refutation of other
solutions

6   In the U.S. Constitution, the management of fish and wildlife is left up to the individual states. When Alaska made the professional decision that the best way to control its wolf population was by aerial shootings, the animal rights groups picked only that part of a larger plan to attack. In media reports, activists "portrayed the plan simply as a mass extermination of wolves designed to increase game numbers for out-of-state hunters and wildlife watchers" (Keszler, 1993, p. 39). They showed through commercials "visions of helicopter gunships slaughtering wolves by the hundreds" (p. 39) when in fact the aerial shooting of wolves is just one small part of the plan. The animal rights groups did not focus on the parts of the plan that dealt with the restrictions to help the wolves in other areas. In Denali National Park and Preserve, Alaskan conservationists plan to do away with all

1 INCH

(continued)

1 INCH

1/2 INCH

Alaskan Wolf   5

hunting and trapping to give the wolves a sanctuary with no outside pressure (p. 65). Other laws and bans on hunting and trapping to protect wolves would take place in areas around Anchorage and Fairbanks. The practice of land-and-shoot hunting (used by many trappers to locate game by helicopter, land the helicopter, and start hunting) would be banned statewide (p. 65). But none of these efforts to protect the wolf population were even discussed by the animal rights activists.

Establishment of the *ethos* of conservationists in Alaska to make their plan acceptable

7   The professional wildlife biologists at the Alaska Department of Fish and Game have taken a lot of heat from the animal rights media reports on their decision to go ahead with the original plan to manage wolf populations through aerial shooting and other methods not mentioned by the media. The biologists of the state of Alaska have devoted their lives to the preservation of wildlife. They know Alaska and Alaska's wildlife better than anyone else. After researching and trying other methods, they believe the best solution to their problem is aerial shooting. Their main concern is to protect the wildlife population as a whole, not just to wage a "war on wolves." While the animal rightists are sitting around in their offices wondering which animals to save, the biologists at Alaska's Department of Fish and Game are in the field researching the range conditions and overall population conditions to manage the wildlife community as a whole.

1 INCH

1 INCH

Author has identified a problem, evaluated several solutions, and arrived at this solution as the best possible. This is a value argument because it claims one of several considered solutions is the best.

Problem-solution and policy are also strong features in this argument.

8   In more recent years, under Governor Tony Knowles, new legislation has supported animal rights groups with bills in 1996 and 2000 that banned the aerial shooting of wolves in Alaska (*Wolves*). In

1 INCH

(continued)

Alaskan Wolf 6

a presentation to the Alaska Board of Game in March 2002, however, Wayne Regelin, the director of the Division of Wildlife Conservation, Alaska Department of Fish and Game, reported:

> The department and the board have tried to develop a policy that recognizes the importance of the wolf to Alaska, recognizes the widely divergent values people have about wolves, and allows wolf populations to be regulated when necessary to maintain the ability of people to harvest moose and caribou. (Management Plan section, para. 4)

He further points out that since this issue is still "as controversial as ever," many efforts to establish policy have either "failed or been inconclusive" (para. 4). The resolution of the Alaskan wolf management issue needs to be left to the experts. As inhumane and immoral as it might seem to many citizens, the aerial shooting of wolves is sometimes the best solution for game management in Alaska.

Online source with no page numbers: heading in report and paragraph number provided to help reader locate information

Claim in last sentence

1 INCH 1/2 INCH 1 INCH 1 INCH 1 INCH

(continued)

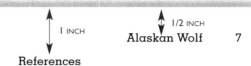

I INCH   1/2 INCH

Alaskan Wolf   7

References

Alaska wolf update. (1993, August). *American Hunter,* 6.

Arms, K. (1994). *Environmental science* (2nd ed.). Fort Worth, TX:

Harcourt Brace.

Buist, P. (1993, September). [Letter to the editor]. *American Hunter,* 12.

Keszler, E. (1993, May). Wolves and big game: Searching for balance in

Alaska. *American Hunter,* 38-39, 65-67.

Regelin, W. L. (2002). *Wolf management in Alaska with an historic*

perspective. Retrieved January 16, 2003, from Alaska Department

of Fish and Game Wildlife Conservation Web site:

http://www.state.ak.us/adfg/wildlife/geninfo/game/wolf-mgt.htm

I INCH   I INCH

Williams, T. (1993, May-June). Alaska's war on the wolves. *Audubon,*

44-47, 49-50.

Wolves. (n.d.). Retrieved January 16, 2003, from Defenders of Wildlife

Web site: http://www.defenders.org/akwfact.html

I INCH

Part Four

FURTHER APPLICATIONS: VISUAL AND ORAL ARGUMENT/ ARGUMENT AND LITERATURE

CHAPTER 13 ALERTS YOU TO SOME SPECIAL FEATURES THAT CAN MAKE VISUAL AND ORAL ARGUMENT PARTICULARLY CONVINCING. VISUAL ARGUMENT INCLUDES PICTURES, BOTH STILL AND MOVING, THAT ARE USED IN ARGUMENTATIVE CONTEXTS EITHER TO MAKE OR TO SUPPORT A CLAIM. EXAMPLES RANGE FROM ADVERTISEMENTS TO TEXTBOOKS TO MOTION PICTURES. ORAL ARGUMENT INCLUDES SPEECHES, LECTURES, SONGS, AND ALL OTHER TYPES OF ARGUMENT THAT YOU LISTEN TO. YOU ENCOUNTER THESE FORMS OF ARGUMENT DAILY, BUT YOU MAY NOT ALWAYS THINK OF THEM OR ANALYZE THEM AS ARGUMENTS. CHAPTER 14 SUGGESTS SOME WAYS TO APPLY ARGUMENT THEORY TO READING AND WRITING ABOUT LITERATURE. WHEN YOU FINISH READING PART FOUR:

◆ You will understand how and why visual argument is used to convince.

◆ You will understand how and why oral argument is used to convince.

◆ You will have some ideas about how to use visual and oral argument yourself.

◆ You will know how to analyze arguments in literature and how to write your own arguments about literature.

Chapter 13

Visual and Oral Argument

You may discover that you spend more time seeing and listening to argument than you do reading and writing it. In his article "Rise of the Visual Puts Words on the Defensive," David Carr claims, "In most magazines on today's newsstands, words are increasingly beside the point, mere graphic elements that are generally used to frame pictures."[1] Many of these pictures are used to express perspectives on argument. The same can be said of most advertisements you encounter in both magazines and newspapers. They usually contain pictures with comparatively few words of explanation. Textbooks also now have more pictures than they did in the past. Add the Internet, movies, and television, and you will discover that much of the material you take in is visual and that it is often used to make or support an argument.

Now, consider the amount of time you spend listening to lectures, radio programs, television shows, and movies, along with the time you spend speaking, conversing, and discussing issues and ideas with other people. As you reflect on all that is communicated through speech, consider how often that material can be classified as argumentative. The idea introduced in Chapter 1 that argument is everywhere will take on expanded meaning if you begin to apply what you now know about argument to the various types of visual and oral argument you encounter. This chapter will teach you to recognize and analyze these types of argument. You will be given suggestions to help you use them effectively yourself in the Exercises and Activities section at the end of the chapter.

---

[1] *New York Times*, April 1, 2002, p. C8.

RECOGNIZING VISUAL AND ORAL ARGUMENT

You will need to discover, first, whether you are looking at or listening to an argument. Discover this by asking, *Is the visual or spoken material about an issue that has not been resolved or settled?* and *Does this issue potentially inspire two or more different views?* If your answer to both of these questions is yes, then attempt to describe the issue and the perspective being developed. Next, use two types of information for further analysis. First, analyze the special features of the visual or oral argument that are explained later in this chapter to get a sense of how the argument works and how powerful it is. Second, apply argument theory to understand the material better as an argument. You already gained some experience with visual argument when you analyzed the advertisements on pages 147 and 220. You can extend that experience to analyze oral argument as well.

Reviewing the section "Recognizing Written Argument" on pages 63–64 will also help you recognize and classify types of visual and oral argument. Just like written argument, visual and oral argument can be straightforward, with an obvious purpose and claim; covert, with a hidden claim that you may need to infer; or even unconscious, with the artist or speaker advocating a point of view without being fully aware of it. Furthermore, argument expressed through pictures and speech can represent either commonly held or extreme points of view and can present one or several different views on an issue.

You will encounter visual argument in a variety of forms, including advertisements, photographs, drawings, illustrations, paintings, sculptures, cartoons, diagrams, flowcharts, various types of graphs, visual demonstrations, tables of numbers, or even maps. All these types of visual material, whether in still or moving picture form, are often employed to further an argument and convince you of a particular point of view.

You will encounter oral argument in a variety of forms as well, including lectures, formal and informal discussions, dialogue in movies and plays, music lyrics, commentary in television advertisements and programs, and various types of public speeches, whether you hear them in person, on television, or on the Internet.

Now let us look at some of the special features of visual and oral argument that make them particularly effective for advancing arguments.

WHY IS VISUAL ARGUMENT CONVINCING?

The following special features of visual argument will demonstrate how it works and why it is convincing. Not all visual argument demonstrates all of the special features described below, and sometimes these features combine or overlap with one another. They are separated and described here for purposes of instruction. Becoming aware of them will help you look at visuals as potential argument and also understand how they achieve their persuasive effect with an audience. Most of the examples of visual argument in this chapter are classic photographs drawn from dramatic periods in U.S. history: World War II, the civil rights movement, and the Vietnam War. The photographs in the color portfolio in this book are additional examples of visual argument.

1. *Visual argument is immediate and tangible and pulls you into the picture.* Visual argument works on a different level of perception than written argument. It communicates fast and evokes a rich, dense, and immediate response from a viewer. For example, if you are watching a moving picture, you may have the experience of either sharing or even taking part in the action yourself. At the least, you will react in some immediate way to what you are seeing. If the picture is still, you may experience its immediacy and timelessness. A moment has been captured and preserved forever on film.

Look at the photograph in Figure 13.1. It has been characterized as the most famous picture from the Vietnam War. An officer in the South Vietnamese army is shooting a suspected member of the Vietcong, and the photographer has captured the moment when the bullet enters this man's head and kills him. This picture provoked strong antiwar arguments in its time, and it continues to invite responses to issues associated with war. What issue does it raise for you? What position do you take on the issue?

FIGURE 13.1   Street Execution of a Vietcong Prisoner, 1968.

SOURCE: *The Photography Book* (London: Phaidon Press Limited, 2000).

2. *Visual argument often establishes common ground and invites viewer identification.* You learned in Chapter 1 that common ground is a necessary ingredient of productive argument. Visual argument usually establishes common ground, including a sense of personal identification with the characters, the action, or the scene, and it does so more quickly than print. All viewers, however, may not experience the same degree of common ground or the same type of identification.

Look at the photograph in Figure 13.2. This is a picture of Dorothy Courts, an African American girl who enrolled in a newly desegregated high school in Little Rock, Arkansas, during the civil rights movement. Escorted by the individuals on either side of her, she makes her way to her first day of school. Dorothy is being taunted by white students in the background who wanted to keep their school segregated. With whom do you identify and experience the greatest amount of common ground in this picture? Do you identify with Dorothy as she moves toward her first experiences in her new school? Do you identify with either of the individuals escorting her? Do you have anything in common with the white

Photograph by Douglas Martin

FIGURE 13.2   Dorothy Courts Entering a Newly Desegregated School, 1957.

SOURCE: *The Photography Book* (London: Phaidon Press Limited, 2000).

students in the background? What issue does the picture raise for you, and what position would you take on it?

3. *Visual argument often evokes an emotional response.* Visual argument operates more directly on the emotions than written argument because images communicate more directly than words. Visual argument is also less subject to conscious critical awareness and monitoring since most people think less critically about a picture than they do print. You can test this yourself. Imagine reading an unillustrated account of a new car in the automotive section of the newspaper. Compare that with watching a hyped-up television advertisement about the same car that includes pictures of interesting people driving to exotic locations. You will probably be more likely to think critically and rationally about the written account and more likely to respond emotionally to the pictures in the advertisement.

Look again at the photograph in Figure 13.1. Would you characterize your response to this picture as primarily rational or emotional? What in the picture prompts your response?

4. *Visual argument often relies on the juxtaposition of materials from radically different categories, inviting the viewer to make new links and associations.* Use what you learned about figurative analogies in Chapter 7 (pages 205–207) to help you understand the strategy of juxtaposition in visual argument. In placing objects, people, or actions that are not usually associated with each other in a common context, a photographer invites the viewer to establish new associations and even to reach new conclusions.

Figure 13.3 is a well-known photograph of an anti–Vietnam War demonstrator at a march on the Pentagon in 1967. He is placing flowers that symbolize peace in the gun barrels of the troops that have been called in to protect the area. The juxtaposition of flowers and guns in this context invites the viewer to think of them and the ideas associated with them in new ways. What associations do you have with guns and flowers? Think of them separately and then together. How would you state the claim in this picture? Would you accept or argue against this claim?

5. *Visual argument often employs icons to prompt an immediate response from a viewer.* Icons are images that people have seen so often that they respond to them immediately and in predictable ways—or at least, that is what people who include them as part of visual argument rely on. The American eagle, for example, is more than a bird to most U.S. citizens. It symbolizes America and the values associated with a democratic form of government. Icons appear on computer screens and on the cash registers at McDonald's to prompt quicker responses than the words or numbers they replace. Examples of icons that might appear in visual argument include the villain and the good guy in western movies, the pert housewife and the cute baby in television commercials, the cross or the Star of David in religious pictures, or a picture of a starving child in an appeal for money.

The photograph in Figure 13.4 (page 400) of Marines raising the U.S. flag on Iwo Jima toward the end of World War II has been printed so many times, including on postage stamps, that it has become a national icon. What does this photograph communicate to you? How might someone use it in an argument about war or peace?

FIGURE 13.3 **A Vietnam War Protestor Placing Flowers in the Rifle Barrels of Troops Guarding the Pentagon during an Antiwar Demonstration, 1967.**

SOURCE: John Mack Faragher et al., *Out of Many: A History of the American People,* 2nd ed. (Upper Saddle River, N.J.: Prentice Hall, 1997), p. 938.

6. *Visual argument often employs symbols.* You have just seen how icons invite viewers to add the commonly held, established meanings and feelings that are usually associated with them. Icons are symbolic since most people look beyond their literal meaning and add the extra meaning they have come to represent. Not all symbols that are used in argument, however, are so familiar that they can be classified as icons.

Look at the color photograph of the split tree in Plate 8 of the color portfolio. This tree is located near the U.S.-Mexican border in El Paso, Texas, and appears in a book called *The Border* by Douglas Kent Hall. Consider the location of this tree and that it was included in a book describing life on the border. What symbolic meaning would you assign to it as it appears in the border context? If you have trouble answering that question, turn to the essay "Documented/Undocumented" by Guillermo Gómez-Peña (pages 573–576 in "The Reader"), in which he describes his life on the border. How would you describe the symbolism of the tree now?

7. *Visual argument is selective.* Whenever you look at a visual argument, you need to think not only about what is included in the picture but also about what is omitted from it. If you could stand back and see more of the entire scene, of which the picture itself is only a small part, your perception of the picture itself might change a great deal. Instead of this, however, you are allowed to see just

Photograph by Joe Rosenthal

FIGURE 13.4   Marines Raising the Flag on Iwo Jima, 1945.

SOURCE: *The Photography Book* (London: Phaidon Press Limited, 2000).

what the photographer wants you to see. You can only infer or imagine what else is going on outside the frame of the picture.

Look at the well-known photograph in Figure 13.5, showing African Americans being pelted with water from a fire hose during the civil rights movement of the 1960s. Notice that the person who holds the hose is outside the photo and thus does not possess an individual identity. The focus in the picture, instead, is on the victims and the stream of water as it forcefully strikes the man on the right and frightens the people in front of him, who appear to be trapped against a building. The photographer thus creates more attention and sympathy for the victims than if he had stood back and photographed the larger scene. Can you articulate a claim for this picture? Besides the picture itself, what additional evidence might you use to support your claim?

8. *Visual argument invites unique interpretations from viewers.* Usually no two people looking at a visual argument will interpret it in exactly the same way since individual viewers bring information and associations from their own past experience and use it to fill in some of the meaning suggested by the picture. Readers do that too, of course, particularly when they infer a claim or supply the warrants

(1)

CONTEXT: This advertisement for State Farm Insurance appeared in *Time* magazine.

FOR DISCUSSION: How does the author of the ad create common ground between the company and the family? With whom do you identify in the picture? Why? How is juxtaposition used in the picture, and what is the result? How is selectivity used in the picture: What is included, what is left out, and why? State the claim for the overall ad and for the picture alone. Are they different? How are *ethos*, *logos*, and *pathos* used in this ad?

FOR WRITING: What is the purpose of this ad? What other picture might State Farm have used to communicate the claim in the ad and accomplish the same purpose? How would you compare the effectiveness of another picture with that of the woman and her children?

(2)

CONTEXT: This photograph of astronaut Buzz Aldrin was taken on July 20, 1969, by his fellow astronaut Neil Armstrong. It records the first successful moon landing. The photograph is titled *Buzz Aldrin on the Moon*.

FOR DISCUSSION: What is the effect of the juxtaposition of the man, the space suit, and the lunar landscape in this photograph? What new links and associations are created as a result? How would people in 1969 have stated the claim implied by this picture? How would you state its claim today? What is the evidence? What are the warrants? To what extent do you identify with Buzz Aldrin in this photo, and how does this identification influence the way you state your claim? What effect does the reflection of Armstrong and the moon-landing craft in Aldrin's visor have on the argument?

FOR WRITING: Consider this photograph as an American icon. What does it accomplish, as an argument, when it is considered in this way?

(3)

CONTEXT: This photograph accompanies an article from *Newsweek* magazine titled *Bringing Up Adultlescents*. Its aim is to establish the fact that "millions of Americans in their 20s and 30s are still supported by their parents."

FOR DISCUSSION: Do you identify with anyone in this picture? With whom, and why? Identify the icons that elicit immediate responses in this picture, and comment on their effects. What is the claim? What details in the picture support the claim? How would you state the warrants?

FOR WRITING: Comment on the quotation from the essay that accompanies this photograph: "It's hard to feel like a Master of the Universe when you're sleeping in your old twin bed."

Michelangelo, Creation of Adam. Detail of the Sistine Chapel. Superstock.

(4)

CONTEXT: The work of art above, depicting the creation of Adam, was painted on the ceiling of the Sistine Chapel in Rome by Michelangelo in 1511. The postcard collage below, titled *Play Ball*, adds a baseball to the hands of Adam and God.

FOR DISCUSSION: What associations form in your mind with the juxtaposition of the hands in the painting and in the postcard? What additional associations are created by the presence of the baseball?

FOR WRITING: Write a Toulmin analysis of the argument in each of the two pictures: State the claim, the evidence, and the warrants. How are the pictures alike? How are they different? Comment on the effectiveness of these pictures as arguments.

Michael Langensten, "Play Ball" 1982, Collection of Mr. and Mrs. Samuel A. Ramirez/Photographer Robert Rubic.

(5)

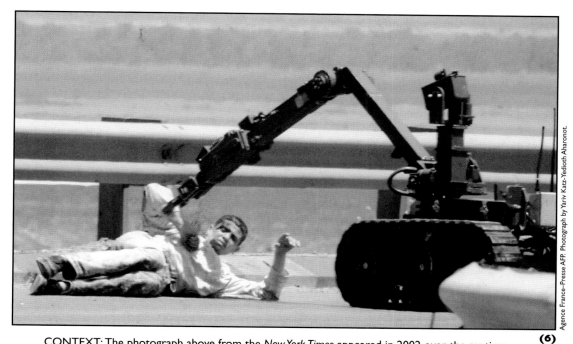

Agence France-Presse AFP. Photograph by Yariv Katz-Yedioth Aharonot.

(6)

CONTEXT: The photograph above from the *New York Times* appeared in 2002 over the caption: "A robot with a grappler holding a wounded Palestinian yesterday on a highway in Megiddo, Israel, 12 miles southeast of Haifa. Israeli Radio said the man was a suicide bomber whose explosives detonated prematurely." The 1980 photograph below, titled *Hands*, shows the hands of a Ugandan child and a missionary.

FOR DISCUSSION: How is juxtaposition used in each photograph, and what is the result? What associations are created by each? What is included, what is left out, and what is the effect?

FOR WRITING: Compare the pairs of hands in each of the photographs. How are the hands similar? How are they different? Comment on the effectiveness of these photographs as arguments.

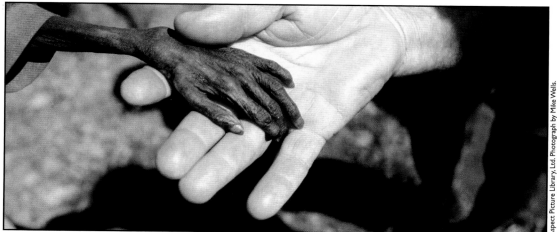

Aspect Picture Library, Ltd. Photograph by Mike Wells.

(7)

(8)

CONTEXT: This photograph appears in *The Border: Life on the Line* by Douglas Kent Hall.
The caption under the picture is "Near El Paso, Texas." El Paso is located on the Texas-Mexico border.

FOR DISCUSSION: Considering the context in which it appears, might this photograph have symbolic significance? How would you describe it? What claim do you infer from looking at this picture? How might someone refute that claim? What type of proof is the tree in this context?

FOR WRITING: This quotation by Graham Greene appears in the front of the book in which this picture appears: "How can life on the border be other than reckless? You are pulled by different ties of love and hate." Consider the picture and this quotation together and write your response.

SIPA Press. Photograph by Ahmet Sel.

(9)

CONTEXT: This photograph appeared by itself in *Wired* magazine with this comment: "The Human Element: Boy swims in heavily polluted lake near copper foundry in Russian town of Karabash." The editors apparently thought the photograph would speak for itself.

FOR DISCUSSION: What important elements are placed in juxtaposition in this photograph, and what claim do you think the photographer is making? What is the main focus of the photograph, and how does that influence the power of its message? What is your emotional response to this photograph? Why do you respond as you do? What values are implied?

FOR WRITING: What comments are made by objects in the background? How effective are they? Elaborate.

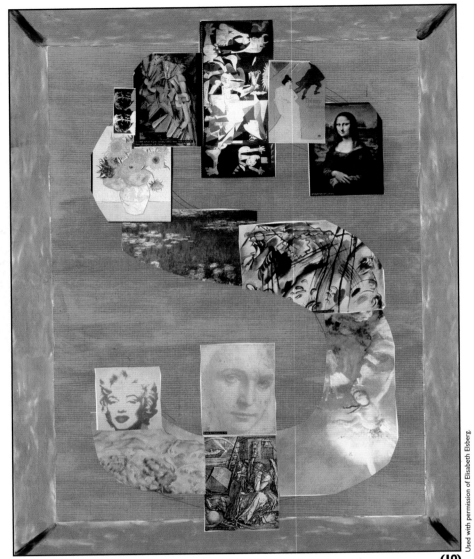

(10)

CONTEXT: This is a visual argument made by a student. By cutting out images from famous works of art and configuring them as a dollar sign, the student makes the claim that art is very expensive. The implication is that few people can own professional artwork.

FOR DISCUSSION: How could you create a visual argument that makes a claim drawn from one of the papers you have written? If not, what other claim would lend itself to visual presentation? What types of visual materials could you use in your argument? How might you configure them? How would you include some of the special features of visual argument: Visual argument pulls the viewer in, creates common ground, evokes an emotional response, uses juxtaposition, employs icons, uses symbols, is selective, and sometimes invites unique interpretations.

FOR WRITING: Write a Toulmin analysis of your visual argument and submit it with your work to show that you have created an argument.

Photograph by Charles Moore

FIGURE 13.5   African Americans Being Pelted with Water from a Fire Hose during a Civil Rights Confrontation in Birmingham, Alabama, 1963.

SOURCE: *The Photography Book* (London: Phaidon Press Limited, 2000).

in a written argument. When viewers, like readers, draw on their backgrounds to fill out the meaning of a visual argument, they become vested in its message since some of the meaning now belongs to them. As a result, these viewers are more likely to accept the argument.

Look, for example, at Plate 4 in the color portfolio. It shows a detail from Michelangelo's scene of the Creation, which appears on the ceiling of the Sistine Chapel in Rome. Here God is passing life to human beings by stretching out His life-giving finger to the lifeless, limp finger of Adam. Now look at the close-up of the hands in Plate 5 on the same page. In this postcard picture, God is passing a baseball along with the first impulses of human life. One viewer, looking at this picture, says the artist is claiming, "We have had baseball from the beginning of time." Another puts the claim this way: "God is giving baseball to the entire universe." A third viewer has a different idea: "God is playing games with human beings." How would you interpret the meaning of this picture? How would you argue in favor of your interpretation? Your answer, at least in part, will probably depend on your views about baseball.

So far the examples of the special features of visual argument have been applied mostly to still photography. All of these features can be applied to motion pictures as well. Many documentaries and mainstream entertainment films take positions on controversial issues and argue for particular points of view. Examples of films that present arguments appear in the introductory material to each of the seven issue areas in "The Reader."

Motion picture directors and editors can create powerfully persuasive effects through the selection and juxtaposition of shots that lead the audience to see links and make associations that would not otherwise occur to them. Motion pictures also draw in the audience, engage their emotions, establish common ground, invite multiple interpretations, and rely on icons and symbols to create some of their meaning.

Let us turn now to an examination of some of the features of oral argument that make it particularly effective in changing minds and achieving an argumentative purpose.

WHY IS ORAL ARGUMENT CONVINCING?

Like visual argument, oral argument possesses special features that make it uniquely effective for presenting arguments. Oral argument has been around much longer than written argument. In Chapter 5 you read about Aristotle's *Rhetoric*, which was written twenty-five hundred years ago to train public speakers to be convincing to audiences. Then, as now, people recognized that speakers have certain advantages over writers in presenting effective argument. Here are a few of these advantages.

1. *Oral argument is immediate.* When the speaker and the audience are together in the same physical location, face to face, the potential for effective argument is greatly enhanced. This is true of all forms of oral argument, whether spoken, chanted, or sung. The physical presence of an effective speaker intensifies what is said, and the audience is thus more likely to pay attention and be influenced. Furthermore, a good speaker is always aware of the audience and can adapt both words and delivery to keep listeners' attention and influence them in desired ways. Oral argument delivered through the media, such as television, the Internet, print, radio, or film, usually lacks some of the sense of immediacy and consequent power that the actual presence of the speaker provides, but it can still be very effective.

2. *Oral argument employs physical as well as verbal strategies.* Speakers are able to influence perception in ways that writers cannot. For example, speakers can use physical gestures, vocal inflections, facial expressions, eye contact, physical setting, dress, and physical appearance in effective and dramatic ways to strengthen delivery and make their words more powerfully convincing. Combine these physical attributes with a strong message and a sincere motivation to persuade the audience through direct speech, and the potential for successful and productive argument is usually stronger than in a written essay.

3. *Oral argument is a continuous stream of fleeting content that is sometimes difficult to monitor and evaluate.* A reader of written argument can always stop to reread or

turn back to find a previous passage that could illuminate a confusing passage. Listeners do not have this advantage. They have only one chance to understand the speaker. Sometimes, of course, listeners have the opportunity to interrupt and ask the speaker to repeat or clarify what has just been said. This is often not the case, however. As a result, the listener does not have the same opportunity that the reader has to do a close evaluation of the speaker's content. Instead, a listener is usually left with a powerful impression of the main argument that the speaker wants to get across, along with some of the ideas and examples that support that argument. This fact can be an advantage to a speaker who wants to overwhelm and convince the audience. The listener, always hearing the next words, has a diminished opportunity to consciously monitor and critique everything that is said during the speech. Think of evangelists and politicians you have heard who rely on physical setting, their voice, gestures, and appearance, and a stream of content that often includes emotionally loaded language and examples that are crafted to convince you. In many cases such speakers can be more powerfully convincing than writers.

4. *Oral argument usually employs a less formal style than written argument and can be easier to understand and respond to.* When compared with written argument, oral argument usually has fewer main points, more support of all kinds, and more obvious transitions to help the listener move from one idea to another. Oral argument is usually also more repetitious, contains more personal pronouns (*I, you, we, us*), includes direct questions that engage the audience, and contains less perfect sentence structure than written argument. Such informality results in an enhanced rapport and the establishment of more common ground between the speaker and the audience. The informality of spoken argument, when compared with written argument, is often more inviting to an audience and makes it easier for listeners to pay attention, believe the speaker, and become convinced.

Watch for some of these special features that make oral argument convincing by attending public speeches, observing speakers on television, or listening to the lectures in some of your classes. You may also study oral argument by visiting a Web site that preserves the texts of a hundred important American speeches made since 1900; see Exercise E at the end of this chapter.

USING ARGUMENT THEORY TO CRITIQUE VISUAL AND ORAL ARGUMENT

The Summary Charts on pages 438–448 provide a quick review of the argument theory you can use to analyze all types of visual and oral argument in the same way as you would analyze written argument.

Consider the rhetorical situation to gain insight into the context for the argument, including the type of visual or oral argument you are examining, the intended listeners or viewers, the artist's or speaker's background and motivation, the possible constraints of all parties, and the exigence or outside motivation for the argument. Apply the Toulmin model to discover the claim, support, and warrants and, if present, backing for the warrants, a rebuttal, or a qualifier.

Learn more about the claim and purpose for the argument by asking the claim questions. Establish which type of claim tends to predominate: a fact claim establishes what happened; a definition claim defines and clarifies what it is; a cause claim looks for causes and sometimes shows effects; a value claim looks at whether it is good or bad; and a policy claim establishes what we should do about it.

Then analyze the proofs. Which are present, *logos, ethos,* and/or *pathos,* and which type of proof predominates in the argument? What is the effect of the proofs? Then look at specific types of proof, including signs, induction, cause, deduction, analogies, definition, statistics, values, authority, and motives. How do those that are present further the argument? Refer to the tests of validity for each of the proofs you identify to judge their effectiveness. Also look for fallacies and consider the effect they have on the overall argument. Finally, ask the two bottom-line questions: Am I convinced? Is the argument moral or immoral according to my values and standards of behavior?

SAMPLE ANALYSIS OF A VISUAL ARGUMENT

The following analysis of the political cartoon in Figure 13.6 draws on both the special features of visual argument and argument theory.[2]

SPECIAL FEATURES OF VISUAL ARGUMENT EMPLOYED IN THE CARTOON. Visual argument pulls the viewer in, creates common ground, evokes an emotional response, uses juxtaposition, employs icons, uses symbols, is selective, and invites a unique interpretation from the viewer.

1. I am pulled into this picture by the date on the large stocking and by the Christmas setting. Furthermore, common ground is established through the Christmas tree and hearth, which I associate with goodwill toward others and also with giving.
2. The word *Charities,* the date September 11, and the Christmas tree and stockings evoke an emotional response. Also, the juxtaposition of these items causes me to associate Christmas with giving to the victims of September 11 and reminds me of other needy groups, including needy people who live in my area, whom I should remember at Christmastime.
3. The Christmas tree, the stockings, and the date September 11 have been seen so often that they can be considered icons. Thus they communicate quickly and forcefully.
4. The cartoonist has selected what he wants to feature in this picture: the large and the small stockings, the date September 11, and the words

---

[2]I am indebted to Sandi Hubnik for the cartoon and some of the analysis in this example.

FIGURE 13.6   A Political Cartoon Making a Visual Argument.

SOURCE: Tribune Media Services, 2001.

Charities and *Others*. The fireplace and Christmas tree are only partially depicted, and no presents or people are included. As a result, the focus is on generous giving, like at Christmas, but to people outside our immediate families.

5. I interpret this picture by remembering all the people in New York who needed help after September 11, 2001, and I wonder which other charities were neglected as a result of funneling so much charitable giving to the 9/11 cause. I also remember the Salvation Army volunteers who solicit money for charity at Christmas. To me this picture means I should give more generously, like I would at Christmas, to all groups outside my family that I consider needy and worthwhile.

ARGUMENT THEORY USED FOR ANALYSIS OF THE CARTOON. Useful theory includes applying the rhetorical situation (TRACE), the Toulmin model, the claim questions, and the types of proof; identifying fallacies; and determining whether or not the argument is convincing and ethical.

Rhetorical Situation:
   Text: Political cartoon with an argumentative intent.
   Reader/viewer: People who are able to give to charities.
   Author/artist: Doug Marlette, a political cartoonist for Tribune Media Services.

Constraints: Some viewers may be wary of giving to charities because they are not sure the money gets to the people who need it; the artist is in favor of giving and thus makes us associate charitable giving with Christmas.
Exigence: The destruction of the Twin Towers by terrorists in New York on September 11, 2001.

Toulmin Model:
  Claim: We should give to all charities, not just 9/11 charities.
  Support: The big 9/11 stocking and the small "Other" stockings.
  Warrant: The "Other" charities are as important and deserving as the 9/11 charities.

Type of Claim: This is a policy claim. It suggests what we should do in the future.

Types of Proof:
  Cause: The problem of uneven giving has been caused by 9/11.
  Analogies: Stockings are like charities; giving to charities should be like stuffing stockings at Christmas.
  Value: We value Christmas and giving to others. We value fairness.
  Motivation: Christmas stockings should be equal in size because we all want the same amount of rewards.

Fallacies: We could test the validity of the analogy between Christmas stockings and charities. In this case the analogy works because a logical link can be made between Christmas giving and charitable giving, so there is no fallacy.

Bottom-Line Questions:
  Convincing? Yes, because giving to 9/11 and other charities is positive and necessary.
  Ethical? Yes, because charitable giving is an ethical activity.

You can follow these procedures in analyzing an oral argument. If you have heard a speaker in person, consider the effects of physical presence along with the use of physical and verbal strategies like gestures and vocal inflection. Consider the final effect of the total message, even if you cannot reproduce every idea you have heard. Notice, also, the person's speaking style and think about its effect on the argumentative message. You can analyze these same features for a speech on television or in the movies. Then use argument theory to continue your analysis.

Practice applying argument theory to visual and oral arguments as you work with the Exercises and Activities that follow.

REVIEW QUESTIONS

  1. What are the eight special features of visual argument that make it convincing?
  2. What are four special features of oral argument that make it different from written argument and also convincing?

3. What information about argument theory from earlier chapters in this book might you employ to help you analyze visual and oral argument?
4. What might be the benefits of combining argument theory and the special features of visual or oral argument to analyze a particular argument?

EXERCISES AND ACTIVITIES

VISUAL ARGUMENT

A. GROUP WORK AND CLASS DISCUSSION: ANALYZING AN ADVERTISEMENT

The advertisement for Sharp computers on page 408 relies mainly on a picture to make its point, but it also employs some written text. Use the following methods to analyze the purpose and effectiveness of the advertisement.

1. Consider the eight features of visual argument that make it convincing. Here is the list again.
   a. Visual argument pulls the viewer into the picture.
   b. Visual argument creates common ground with the viewer.
   c. Visual argument evokes an emotional response from the viewer.
   d. Visual argument uses juxtaposition to create fresh associations.
   e. Visual argument employs icons for immediate understanding.
   f. Visual argument employs symbols to suggest additional meanings.
   g. Visual argument is selective regarding what is included in the frame of the picture.
   h. Visual argument invites a unique interpretation from each individual viewer.

   Apply the special features to this picture. Discover which are used here and how they are used. Read the text below the picture. How does this text contribute to the argument in the ad?
2. Consider the rhetorical situation for the advertisement. Answer these questions in particular: Who is the audience? What are the constraints? What is the exigence for this advertisement?
3. Apply the Toulmin model to the advertisement. What is the claim? What is the support? What are the warrants?
4. How effective is this advertisement for you? Are you an appropriate audience? Do you share the warrants? How convincing do you think this advertisement is for readers of *Wired* magazine, where it appeared?

B. INDIVIDUAL WORK AND CLASS DISCUSSION: ANALYZING COVERS ON MUSIC CDS

Look at the covers of some music CDs. Do any of them make arguments about issues? Bring a CD to class. Identify the issue. Then point out how the picture on the cover employs special features of visual argument to make it more

convincing. Identify the claim, even if you have to infer it, along with the support and the warrants in the picture. Do you find the argument convincing? Why or why not?

C. GROUP WORK AND CLASS DISCUSSION: ANALYZING A VISUAL ARGUMENT

In a small group analyze one of the pictures that appear in the color portfolio in this book.

1. Read the context for the picture that appears below it. What issues are raised by the picture? What position does the photographer seem to take? Who is the audience the photographer may have imagined? What are some of the constraints of both the photographer and the potential audience? What is the exigence that motivated the photographer to take the picture?
2. Identify and analyze the special features of visuals that are employed in this picture. How and why are they used? Which seem to be particularly effective?
3. Employ the Toulmin model. What is the claim? What is the support? What are the warrants?
4. Analyze the proofs. Which predominates? *Pathos? Ethos? Logos?* Which types of proof can you identify in the picture?
5. What is your final assessment of the picture as an argument? Do you find it convincing? Why or why not?

D. INDIVIDUAL WORK: CREATING A VISUAL ARGUMENT

1. Identify an issue that you can make an argument about by using visual material. Consider using an issue from one of the argument papers you have already written.
2. Make a claim about the issue.
3. Decide what kinds of visual materials you want to use to make and support your claim. Consider cutting and pasting visual material from magazines and newspapers, drawing, using photographs you have taken yourself, or experimenting with other ways to visually present your argument to the class. Review the special features of visual argument, and think about how you can employ some of them. You may also use short explanations written in large letters that are easy to read and help get your message across. Test your work with the Toulmin model to make certain you have created an argument.
4. Share your visual argument with the class. A student-made visual argument appears as Plate 10 in the color portfolio. Here is a possible Toulmin analysis of this argument.

> *Issue:* Has art become too expensive?
> *Claim:* Art is too expensive.
> *Support:* The examples of art pasted on the dollar sign are expensive.
> *Warrant:* I can't afford those artworks.
> *Inferred rebuttal:* I have money to buy less expensive artworks, and I think they are just as enjoyable to own.

ORAL ARGUMENT

E. INDIVIDUAL WORK AND CLASS DISCUSSION: ANALYZING A SPEECH

1. If you have access to the Internet, visit the Web site of top American speeches at <http://www.americanrhetoric.com/newtop100speeches.htm> and listen to Martin Luther King Jr.'s speech "I Have a Dream." It is listed there as the number 1 speech of the twentieth century. If you do not have access to the Internet, read the text (pages 411–414).

   "I Have a Dream" was delivered at the Lincoln Memorial in Washington, D.C., on August 28, 1963, to more than a quarter of a million people, the largest audience to gather for a political speech in American history. Most members of the audience were African Americans, but fifty thousand white Americans were also present. The purpose of the gathering was to demonstrate for better jobs and more freedom for African Americans. People sang freedom songs and listened to speeches all day. At the end of the day, Martin Luther King Jr., standing in front of the Lincoln Memorial, gave his "I Have a Dream" speech.

2. Answer the following questions.

   a. Which of the features of oral argument described in this chapter are present in King's speech? You will have to imagine some of them from the description above. What do you think their effect might have been on the people present that day?

   b. How is the style of the speech different from King's written style (see King's "Letter from Birmingham Jail" on pages 277–291)?

   c. What is the claim in this speech? What is the support? What are the warrants?

   d. Why is this speech listed as the most famous speech of the twentieth century on the "Top 100 American Speeches" Web site? What makes it powerful and convincing?

F. INDIVIDUAL WORK AND CLASS DISCUSSION: ANALYZING SONG LYRICS

Select a song that is about an issue and that makes an argument. Bring the lyrics to class and be prepared to identify the issue, the claim, the support, and the warrants. Describe how the musicians emphasize the ideas in their musical argument and how they use musical effects and oral style to make their argument more powerful. Is the argument convincing? Why or why not?

G. INDIVIDUAL WORK: CREATING AN ORAL ARGUMENT

Adapt one of the papers you have written this semester so that you can make an oral presentation that is 5 to 10 minutes long. Follow these instructions.

1. Work with your written manuscript to change it into an oral report. Underline and number the most important ideas. Since oral argument usually has fewer main ideas than written argument, limit yourself to three to five main ideas so that you can explain them in the time you have.

2. Think about your audience. How much background information about your topic will you have to present or possibly add at the beginning of your speech to help your audience understand it?

3. Remember, also, that your listeners have only one chance to understand the ideas. Add examples, informal comments, and other details to clarify the main ideas. Add some obvious transitions to clarify your main ideas and make them stand out. These might include, for example, explaining your main points in your introduction, numbering them as you explain them, and restating and summarizing them at the end of your speech.

4. You will not read your speech. You may want to make a speech outline that you can glance at occasionally to help you keep on track. Write out in sentences the key parts of this outline—like the introduction, main points, and summary. List the examples in words or phrases.

5. Practice your speech and time it. If anything in the speech seems to be unclear or awkward, make revisions. Work with the speech until it fits the time frame.

6. Create a visual aid if it will improve your speech. Remember the rules: (a) make it large enough for your audience to read easily, and (b) do not put it in front of your audience until you are ready to discuss it.

7. Practice your speech several times until you can give it fluently.

8. When you give your speech, use eye contact and experiment with some gestures. Above all, concentrate on communicating with your audience.

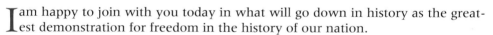

I HAVE A DREAM*

Martin Luther King Jr.

1   I am happy to join with you today in what will go down in history as the greatest demonstration for freedom in the history of our nation.

2   Five score years ago, a great American, in whose symbolic shadow we stand today, signed the Emancipation Proclamation. This momentous decree came as a great beacon light of hope to millions of Negro slaves, who had been seared in the flames of withering injustice. It came as a joyous daybreak to end the long night of their captivity.

3   But one hundred years later, the Negro still is not free. One hundred years later, the life of the Negro is still sadly crippled by the manacles of segregation and the chains of discrimination. One hundred years later, the Negro lives on a lonely island of poverty in the midst of a vast ocean of material prosperity. One hundred years later, the Negro is still languished in the corners of American society and finds himself an exile in his own land. And so we've come here today to dramatize a shameful condition.

4   In a sense we have come to our nation's capital to cash a check. When the architects of our republic wrote the magnificent words of the Constitution and the

---

*The text of this speech comes from the Web site listed in Exercise E (page 410).

Declaration of Independence, they were signing a promissory note to which every American was to fall heir. This note was a promise that all men, yes, black men as well as white men, would be guaranteed the inalienable rights of life, liberty, and the pursuit of happiness. It is obvious today that America has defaulted on this promissory note, insofar as her citizens of color are concerned. Instead of honoring this sacred obligation, America has given the Negro people a bad check, a check which has come back marked "insufficient funds."

5   But we refuse to believe that the bank of justice is bankrupt. We refuse to believe that there are insufficient funds in the great vaults of opportunity of this nation. And so we have come to cash this check, a check that will give us upon demand the riches of freedom and the security of justice.

6   We have also come to this hallowed spot to remind America of the fierce urgency of Now. This is no time to engage in the luxury of cooling off or to take the tranquilizing drug of gradualism. Now is the time to make real the promises of democracy. Now is the time to rise from the dark and desolate valley of segregation to the sunlit path of racial justice. Now is the time to lift our nation from the quicksands of racial injustice to the solid rock of brotherhood. Now is the time to make justice a reality for all of God's children.

7   It would be fatal for the nation to overlook the urgency of the moment. This sweltering summer of the Negro's legitimate discontent will not pass until there is an invigorating autumn of freedom and equality. Nineteen sixty-three is not an end but a beginning. Those who hope that the Negro needed to blow off steam and will now be content will have a rude awakening if the nation returns to business as usual. There will be neither rest nor tranquility in America until the Negro is granted his citizenship rights. The whirlwinds of revolt will continue to shake the foundations of our nation until the bright day of justice emerges.

8   But there is something that I must say to my people who stand on the warm threshold which leads into the palace of justice. In the process of gaining our rightful place we must not be guilty of wrongful deeds. Let us not seek to satisfy our thirst for freedom by drinking from the cup of bitterness and hatred. We must ever conduct our struggle on the high plane of dignity and discipline. We must not allow our creative protest to degenerate into physical violence. Again and again we must rise to the majestic heights of meeting physical force with soul force.

9   The marvelous new militancy which has engulfed the Negro community must not lead us to a distrust of all white people, for many of our white brothers, as evidenced by their presence here today, have come to realize that their destiny is tied up with our destiny. And they have come to realize that their freedom is inextricably bound to our freedom. We cannot walk alone.

10   And as we walk, we must make the pledge that we shall always march ahead. We cannot turn back. There are those who are asking the devotees of civil rights, "When will you be satisfied?" We can never be satisfied as long as the Negro is the victim of the unspeakable horrors of police brutality. We can never be satisfied as long as our bodies, heavy with the fatigue of travel, cannot gain lodging in the motels of the highways and the hotels of the cities. We cannot be satisfied as long as a Negro in Mississippi cannot vote and a Negro in New York believes he has

nothing for which to vote. No, no, we are not satisfied and we will not be satisfied until justice rolls down like waters and righteousness like a mighty stream.

11   I am not unmindful that some of you have come here out of great trials and tribulations. Some of you have come fresh from narrow jail cells. Some of you have come from areas where your quest for freedom left you battered by the storms of persecutions and staggered by the winds of police brutality. You have been the veterans of creative suffering. Continue to work with the faith that un-earned suffering is redemptive. Go back to Mississippi, go back to Alabama, go back to South Carolina, go back to Georgia, go back to Louisiana, go back to the slums and ghettos of our northern cities, knowing that somehow this situation can and will be changed. Let us not wallow in the valley of despair, I say to you today, my friends. And so even though we face the difficulties of today and to-morrow, I still have a dream. It is a dream deeply rooted in the American dream.

12   I have a dream that one day this nation will rise up and live out the true meaning of its creed: We hold these truths to be self-evident that all men are created equal.

13   I have a dream that one day on the red hills of Georgia the sons of former slaves and the sons of former slave owners will be able to sit down together at the table of brotherhood.

14   I have a dream that one day even the state of Mississippi, a state sweltering with the heat of injustice, sweltering with the heat of oppression, will be trans-formed into an oasis of freedom and justice.

15   I have a dream that my four little children will one day live in a nation where they will not be judged by the color of their skin but by the content of their char-acter. I have a dream today!

16   I have a dream that one day, down in Alabama, with its vicious racists, with its governor having his lips dripping with the words of interposition and nullifica-tion; one day right down in Alabama little black boys and black girls will be able to join hands with little white boys and white girls as sisters and brothers. I have a dream today!

17   I have a dream that one day every valley shall be exalted, and every hill and mountain shall be made low, the rough places will be made plain, and the crooked places will be made straight, and the glory of the Lord shall be revealed and all flesh shall see it together.

18   This is our hope. This is the faith that I will go back to the South with. With this faith we will be able to hew out of the mountain of despair a stone of hope. With this faith we will be able to transform the jangling discords of our nation into a beautiful symphony of brotherhood. With this faith we will be able to work together, to pray together, to struggle together, to go to jail together, to stand up for freedom together, knowing that we will be free one day. And this will be the day, this will be the day when all of God's children will be able to sing with new meaning, "My country 'tis of thee, sweet land of liberty, of thee I sing. Land where my fathers died, land of the Pilgrim's pride, from every mountainside, let freedom ring!" And if America is to be a great nation, this must become true.

19   And so let freedom ring—from the prodigious hilltops of New Hampshire.

20   Let freedom ring—from the mighty mountains of New York.

21   Let freedom ring—from the heightening Alleghenies of Pennsylvania.

22   Let freedom ring—from the snow-capped Rockies of Colorado.

23   Let freedom ring—from the curvaceous slopes of California.

24   But not only that.

25   Let freedom ring—from Stone Mountain of Georgia.

26   Let freedom ring—from Lookout Mountain of Tennessee.

27   Let freedom ring—from every hill and molehill of Mississippi, from every mountainside, let freedom ring!

28   And when this happens, when we allow freedom to ring, when we let it ring from every village and every hamlet, from every state and every city, we will be able to speed up that day when all of God's children, black men and white men, Jews and Gentiles, Protestants and Catholics, will be able to join hands and sing in the words of the old Negro spiritual,

29   Free at last, free at last.

30   Thank God Almighty, we are free at last.

◆◆◆

Chapter 14

Argument and Literature

The purpose of this chapter is to extend the applications of argument theory and to suggest that you apply this theory, as one of many possible theories, both when you read imaginative literature and when you write papers about literature, including poetry, short stories, plays, and novels. Any theory that is applied to literature can help you look at it in whole new ways. Argument theory works this way also. Argument theory is useful for speculating about the ideas and themes in literature, especially when there is no general agreement about what these ideas are exactly, and it can also provide insight into literary characters, particularly into how they argue and interact with one another. Finally, argument theory can help you write papers about literature and argue in favor of your own understandings and insights.

A basic idea in this book has been that argument can be found everywhere—particularly where people are. Creative writers, along with the imaginative characters they create, are as argumentative as any other people. It should not surprise you that argument is as pervasive in literature as it is in real life. In fact, literature often raises issues, takes positions on them, and even changes people's views about them. Literature can be convincing because it invites readers to identify with its characters, which creates common ground, and because it almost always employs effective emotional appeal. Literature has high interest appeal as well. Argument achieved through literary narrative can be one of the most convincing forms of argument.

This chapter will provide you with examples and focus questions to help you apply argument theory to literature. The exercises and activities will furnish you with sufficient practice to get you started. Note also that in the introductory material to each of the seven issues in "The Reader," the suggestion is made to expand your perspective on the issues through literature and film. Specific examples of relevant literature and film are provided. Film, like literature, raises issues, makes claims, and changes people's views about controversial subjects. You can analyze arguments in film and write arguments about film just as you would a piece of literature.

FINDING AND ANALYZING ARGUMENTS IN LITERATURE

When you apply argument theory to the reading of literature, you will be "inside the text," so to speak, analyzing what is there and working to understand it. Your focus may be on the main argument made by the text, or it may be on one or more of the characters and the arguments they make. Let's consider first how to analyze the main argument.

WHAT IS AT ISSUE? WHAT IS THE CLAIM?

To use argument theory to read a literary text and analyze the main argument, focus on the issues raised in the work, the perspectives that are expressed, and the claims that are made. The claims may be explicit, overt and openly expressed, or they may be implicit, covert and merely suggested, so that you will need to infer them yourself. There may also be conflicting claims in a single work that seem at times to contradict each other. The Toulmin model is useful for analyzing and understanding the main line of argument in a literary work.

For example, here is a poem by Robert Herrick (1591–1674) that makes an explicit argument.

To the Virgins to Make Much of Time

Gather ye rosebuds while ye may:
  Old Time is still a-flying;
And this same flower that smiles today,
  Tomorrow will be dying.

The glorious lamp of heaven, the sun,
  The higher he's a-getting,
The sooner will his race be run,
  And nearer he's to setting.

That age is best which is the first,
  When youth and blood are warmer;
But being spent, the worse, and worst
  Times still succeed the former.

Then be not coy, but use your time;
  And while ye may, go marry:
For having lost but once your prime,
  You may for ever tarry.

In applying the Toulmin model to this poem, most readers would agree that a policy claim is stated in the first line and restated in different language in the last stanza. There would not be much disagreement, furthermore, about that claim: "Young women should marry in their prime and not later" would be one way of putting it. Or the poet's first line, "Gather ye rosebuds while ye may," taken metaphorically to mean that one should take advantage of good things when they are available, serves as well to express the claim of this poem. The support is supplied in the form of reasons: time is flying, and it is better to marry when one is young than when one is old. The warrant that connects the support to the claim is that women will want to marry in the first place. Women who accept this warrant may be persuaded that they should, indeed, seize the day and wait no longer.

The claims in imaginative literature are not always this easy to identify. Sometimes it is necessary to ask some questions to identify what is at issue and to formulate the claim. Here are some questions to help you make these determinations.

1. *What is most of this work about?* The answer will help you identify the subject of the work.
2. *Can the subject be regarded as controversial?* That is, would it invite more than one perspective? This question will help you discover the issues.
3. *What positions are taken on the issue, and who takes them?* This question will help you discover both explicit and implicit claims along with who is making them: the author, a narrator, or various characters in the text.
4. *If the claim is not stated, what evidence can I use from the text to help me state it myself?* Draw on such evidence to help you make the claim explicit.
5. *Will everyone agree that this is a viable claim, or will I need to make a case for it?* Paper topics often come from disagreements over how to state the main argument in a literary work.

In her poem "The Mother," Gwendolyn Brooks begins, "Abortions will not let you forget." She continues by saying that she has never forgotten her "killed children," and she ends the poem:

> oh, what shall I say, how is the truth to be said?
> You were born, you had body, you died.
> It is just that you never giggled or planned or cried.
>
> Believe me, I loved you all.
> Believe me, I knew you, though faintly, and I loved,
>   I loved you all.

One could argue that the claim of the poem is in the first sentence, "Abortions will not let you forget," a claim of fact. However, by the time one has read the entire poem, one can also infer and make a case for a value claim, that abortions cause the mothers who seek them considerable psychological pain and are difficult for them to endure as time goes on. There is sufficient evidence in the poem to make an argument for that second claim as well.

Still other literary texts may express conflicting claims about an issue. In poet Robert Frost's "Mending Wall," two claims are made about the issue concerning the value of fences. The two claims are "Something there is that doesn't love a wall" and "Good fences make good neighbors." These claims contradict each other. Furthermore, careful readers have pointed out that convincing arguments are made for both of these positions in the poem. In the case of "Mending Wall," the poem tends to start an argument rather than deliver one.[1] Once again, paper topics come out of such disagreements and can provide you with material to write papers about. You can always take a position yourself on any argument started by a literary work.

In other literary texts, arguments are made entirely through metaphor, as in Frost's poem "Birches," where swinging on birch trees becomes a way of escaping from the cares of life, or in another Frost poem, "The Road Not Taken," where the two roads in the poem become metaphors for two possible life choices. Metaphors are comparisons of items from two different categories. They work like figurative analogies since they invite readers to make unique mental connections and to expand their perspective on a subject in new and original ways. The meanings of metaphors in a literary work are often difficult to pin down exactly. Thus they become the subject of controversy and are often open to a variety of interpretations. The disputed meaning of a key metaphor in a literary work can become a fruitful paper topic.

CHARACTERS MAKING ARGUMENTS

The second way to employ argument theory to analyze literature is to apply it to specific arguments that are made by characters in the context of a literary text. Also enlightening is to consider how these individual characters' arguments contribute to the main argument of the text. Focusing on the rhetorical situation and the modes of appeal, identifying fallacies, and applying the Toulmin model all help with this type of analysis.

It is further useful to identify the form that the argument takes in the work (see Chapter 1, pages 6–8). For example, a character may argue internally with himself as Hamlet does when he asks, "To be or not to be, that is the question" in Shakespeare's *Hamlet*. A character may also argue with an imaginary audience, like the woman who constructs an imaginary argument with her child's counselor in the short story "I Stand Here Ironing" by Tillie Olsen. Two individuals may argue one on one, both trying to convince the other, as in the poem "Myth" by Muriel Rukeyser; or the character may make a single-perspective argument to convince a mass audience as Marc Antony does in his speech that begins "Friends, Romans, Countrymen, lend me your ears" in Shakespeare's *Julius Caesar*. The characters may argue in front of a third-party judge as they do in the play *Inherit the Wind*. Identifying the form of the argument will help you understand the rhetorical situation in which it takes place. It will focus your attention on who is arguing, with whom these characters are arguing, and to what end.

A famous literary argument is Satan's persuasion of Eve in John Milton's seventeenth-century epic *Paradise Lost*. The story is familiar. Adam and Eve have been placed in the garden of Eden by God and have been told they may eat

---

[1]Tim Morris provided me with some of the examples and insights in this chapter, such as this one, as well as with some of the literary examples in "The Reader."

anything in the garden except the fruit from the tree of knowledge. The rhetorical situation goes like this: Satan is the arguer. He sneaks into the garden, inhab-
its the serpent, and in that guise tempts Eve, his audience, to eat the forbidden
fruit. This is a one-on-one argument with Satan trying to convince Eve. The exigence of Satan's argument is that he needs to get a foothold on earth so that he
can spend more time there and less time in Hell, a very unpleasant place in this
poem. Satan's constraints are that he must get Eve alone because he's afraid he
cannot persuade Adam, Eve is a bit vain as he has discovered, and there are good
angels around who could frustrate his plan. Thus he decides to hide in the serpent. Satan's persuasive argument, full of fallacies as it is, is successful with Eve.
She eats the fruit, she gets Adam to eat it also, and as a result, they are expelled
from the garden forever.

In the poem we witness the entire persuasive process that involves Satan
and Eve, from the audience analysis carried on by Satan as he hides in the garden, watching Eve and analyzing her weaknesses, to the final changes in Eve's
thought and action brought about by Satan's argumentative speeches. As part of
this process, we overhear Satan's initial planning of his argument, and as he
schemes and plans, we observe that there is a vast difference between his private
feelings and beliefs and the roles he adopts to establish *ethos* with Eve. Satan is not
an ethical arguer; he is an immoral manipulator. We also watch Satan deliberately
plant a highly emotional version of the temptation in Eve's mind in the form of a
dream. The remembered pleasure and emotional appeal of this dream will help
make the later logical argument even more readily acceptable to Eve.

When Satan in the serpent delivers the speeches in book 9 of the poem that
finally convince Eve that she should eat the apple, he employs *ethos, pathos,* and
logos to strengthen his argument. He flatters Eve, he appeals to her desire to
be more powerful, he refutes what God has told her with fallacious reasoning, he
uses induction to show that he ate the fruit and did not die so Eve will not die
either, he points to himself as a sign of the intelligence and power that can come
from eating the fruit, and he uses a deductive argument that can be summarized
as follows:

> Eve should know evil in order to recognize good.
> Eating the fruit will help Eve know evil.
> Therefore, Eve should eat the fruit in order to recognize good.

There are other examples of logical and emotional appeal in this argument that
are not detailed here. Furthermore, if the Toulmin model is also employed to analyze Satan's argument, his purpose and strategy become even clearer, particularly as we examine some of his warrants. One of these, for example, is that
humans want to become gods. Satan himself envies God and assumes that humans will also.

Another unique feature of the argument in *Paradise Lost* is that we are allowed to witness the argument outcomes. Not only do we observe Eve's outward
actions, but we are also a party to her inner thoughts following Satan's speech.
We see her eat the fruit. We also learn from her private musings how her reasoning, her emotional state, and the credibility she places in the serpent have been

changed by Satan's speeches. We have a full explanation of what has convinced Eve to disobey God and why the argument has been successful.

If you become interested in analyzing the argument in *Paradise Lost,* you might also like to know that Satan makes no fewer than twenty public addresses in the poem and that his audiences range in size from the single Eve to the multitudes of the fallen angels. Furthermore, Adam, Eve, God, the Son, and some of the angels in the poem make arguments of their own that can be profitably analyzed with argument theory.

Here is a list of questions that you can use to help you analyze the arguments of fictional characters in literature. Any one of these questions could help you discover a claim for a paper on a literary work. You would develop your claim by drawing examples from the literary work itself to illustrate your argument.

1. What is at issue in the literary work?
2. Who is the character taking a position on this issue, and what is the character's position on the issue?
3. What is the rhetorical situation for the argument?
4. What is the claim made by the character? Is it stated overtly? Is it implied? Write it yourself as a statement, and identify its type.
5. How does the character establish credibility? What logical and emotional proofs does the character use?
6. What type of language predominates: language that appeals to reason, language that appeals to emotion, or language that establishes credibility? Describe the language.
7. What are the warrants?
8. How does the character establish common ground? Through warrants? Through Rogerian argument? What else?
9. Are rebuttals used? How effective are they?
10. Are there fallacies? How do they distort the argument?
11. What are the outcomes of the argument? Is it convincing? To whom? What happens as a result?
12. Is the argument moral or immoral according to the standards established in the text itself? How would you evaluate the argument according to your own standards and values?
13. How does the argument made by the character contribute to the main argument of the text?

WRITING ARGUMENTS ABOUT LITERATURE

Argument theory can also be used to help you formulate your own argument about your insights and understanding of a literary text. At this point you will move "outside the text," and you will begin by identifying an issue about the text on which there is no general agreement. You will then take a position on that issue, state your position in a claim, and present evidence from the text to prove it. Argument theory can be extremely beneficial in writing scholarly argument of this type. The Toulmin model will help you the most. It can help you identify an issue to write about in the first place, and it can also help you set up the elements of your argument.

Your first challenge will be to move from reading literature to writing about it. First, you will need to find an issue to write about. To help you find an issue, ask, *What is unclear about this text that I think I can explain?* or *What is left out by the author that I think I can explain?* Focus on the main argument of the text, on the characters themselves, on what the narrator says about the characters, or on the meaning of metaphors to help you discover possible issues to write about. Controversy often resides in those locations. Also, issues may emerge in class discussion, or issues may come from the questions in your literature anthology. If all else fails, write a summary of a literary text along with your reaction to it. Then read your reaction and circle the most promising idea in it. It should be an idea that you think you can make a claim about and defend with evidence from the text.

Here are some examples of issues that appear in literary texts. In Henry James's novel *The Turn of the Screw,* there is an unresolved question about whether the ghosts are real or not. One student actually went through the novel and highlighted in one color all of the evidence that suggests they are real and then highlighted in another color all of the evidence that suggests they are imaginary. According to this student, the quantity of evidence for both explanations was roughly comparable in the novel. If you decided to write about that issue, you could argue for either position and find plenty of people who would agree with you. Your instructor would evaluate your paper on the quality of its argument rather than on whether you had resolved the controversy or not. Some literary controversies cannot be finally resolved any more than many issues in life can be finally resolved. Here is another example of a literary issue. At the end of Ernest Hemingway's short story "The Short Happy Life of Francis Macomber," a wounded and enraged buffalo charges the main character, who is on an African safari. His wife shoots, but the bullet kills her husband instead of the buffalo. The "great white hunter" who is leading this expedition assumes the wife meant to kill her husband instead of the buffalo, and there is plenty of evidence in the story to suggest that this might have been her intent. But it is equally possible to argue that she was really shooting at the buffalo and hit her husband by mistake. You could write a paper in which you argue for either position just so long as you provide plenty of evidence from the story to support your position. In other words, you could make either position convincing. One student wrote a paper about a poem by William Butler Yeats in which she argued in favor of one interpretation, and she got an A. The next year, in another class, she argued in favor of a completely different interpretation of the same poem, and she got another A. In both cases she provided plenty of evidence from the poem itself to support the claims she made. Both of her arguments were convincing.

Here are some questions to help you make a claim about a literary work and write a convincing argument to support it.

1. What is an issue raised by this text that needs clarification?
2. What are the different perspectives that can be taken on this issue?
3. Which perspective will I take?

4. What support from the text will I use to defend my position?
5. What warrants are implicit in my argument, and will they be acceptable to the person who will evaluate this paper? Should I use backing for any of these warrants?
6. Would my paper be more convincing if I included a rebuttal of the opposing positions?
7. Will my claim be more acceptable to my audience if I qualify it?

Once you have read and thought about a literary text and you have answered these questions, you will write your paper just like you would write any other position paper in which your aim is to state what you think and provide evidence to support it. You can use suggestions from the other chapters in this book to help you meet this aim.

REVIEW QUESTIONS

1. How can argument theory be used in the study of literature? Name and describe the three approaches described in this chapter.
2. What are some of the questions the reader can ask to arrive at a claim in a work of literature? What are some of the ways in which claims are expressed in literature?
3. Describe the argument theory you would employ to help you analyze an argument that a character makes in a literary work.
4. What are some of the suggestions made in this chapter to help you find a topic for a position paper you might write about an issue in literature?
5. What is your main responsibility as a writer when you argue on one side or the other of a literary issue?

EXERCISES AND ACTIVITIES

A. WRITING ASSIGNMENT: ANALYZING THE ARGUMENT IN A POEM

The poem on the next page was written by Langston Hughes in 1926 while he was a student at Columbia University in New York City.

1. Read the poem; then freewrite for five minutes to capture your original thoughts and reactions.
2. As a class, discuss the answers to the following questions.
   a. What is the rhetorical situation? Use TRACE to think it through.
   b. What are the issues in the poem?
   c. What is the claim? Try to get consensus. What are some subclaims?
   d. What supports the claim? Give examples.
   e. How does the author create common ground?
   f. What are the warrants?
3. Write a 300- to 400-word paper about the main argument in this poem and how it is developed.

THEME FOR ENGLISH B*

Langston Hughes

The instructor said,

    Go home and write
      a page tonight,
    And let that page come out of you—
5   Then, it will be true.

I wonder if it's that simple?

I am twenty-two, colored, born in Winston-Salem.
    I went to school there, then Durham, then here
to this college on the hill above Harlem.
10   I am the only colored student in my class.

The steps from the hill lead down to Harlem,
    through a park, then I cross St. Nicholas,
Eighth Avenue, Seventh, and I come to the Y,
    the Harlem Branch Y, where I take the elevator
15 up to my room, sit down, and write this page:
    It's not easy to know what is true for you or me
at twenty-two, my age. But I guess I'm what

I feel and see and hear. Harlem, I hear you:
    hear you, hear me—we two—you, me talk on this page.
20 (I hear New York, too.) Me—who?

Well, I like to eat, sleep, drink, and be in love.
    I like to work, read, learn, and understand life.
I like a pipe for a Christmas present,
    or records—Bessie, bop, or Bach.

25 I guess being colored doesn't make me not like
    the same things other folks like who are other races.
So will my page be colored that I write?
    Being me, it will not be white.
But it will be
30   a part of you, instructor.
You are white—
    yet a part of me, as I am a part of you.
That's American.

Sometimes perhaps you don't want to be a part of me.
35 Nor do I often want to be a part of you.
    But we are, that's true!

---

*Used with permission of Alfred A. Knopf, Inc.

> As I learn from you,
>   I guess you learn from me—
> although you're older—and white—
>   and somewhat more free.
>
> This is my page for English B.

40

For Discussion: What is the relationship established between the teacher and the student in this poem? Think about similarities, differences, and common ground between them. How does the student in the poem interpret the writing assignment? How does he respond to it? What do you think of his version of this assignment?

◆◆◆

B. WRITING ASSIGNMENT: AN ARGUMENT ABOUT A LITERARY WORK

The purpose of this assignment is to discover an issue, make a claim, and write about your interpretation of a story. The author of the following story has said that she was prompted to write the story by a remark she came across in William James's story "The Moral Philosopher and the Moral Life." In it, James suggests that if multitudes of people could be "kept permanently happy on the one simple condition that a certain lost soul on the far-off edge of things should lead a life of lonely torment," our moral sense would make us immediately reject that bargain. The story is written as a parable—that is, it is written to illustrate a principle. Think about these things as you read the story.

1. When you have finished reading the story, freewrite for five minutes to capture your original thoughts and reactions.
2. As a class, discuss the answers to the following questions.
    a. What is this story about? What issues are raised by this story?
    b. What are some of the perspectives in the story? Who takes them? Which do you identify with?
    c. Write a claim made by this story, and put a few of these claims on the board. Which of these claims could be supported with evidence from the text? Which would you like to write about? Write your claim. Read some of these claims to the class.
3. Answer the next three questions to plan your paper.
    a. What evidence from the text can you use to support your claim (examples, quotations, etc.)? Underline it.
    b. What warrants are implicit in your argument? Will they be acceptable to the person who reads your paper, or should you provide backing?
    c. Would your paper be more convincing if you included a rebuttal? What would it be?

d. Will your claim be more acceptable if you qualify it? How would you do that?

4. Write a 500-word position paper defending the claim you have made about this story.

THE ONES WHO WALK AWAY FROM OMELAS*

Ursula K. Le Guin

1   With a clamor of bells that set the swallows soaring, the Festival of Summer came to the city Omelas, bright-towered by the sea. The rigging of the boats in harbor sparkled with flags. In the streets between houses with red roofs and painted walls, between old moss-gardens and under avenues of trees, past great parks and public buildings, processions moved. Some were decorous: old people in long stiff robes of mauve and gray, grave master workmen, quiet, merry women carrying their babies and chatting as they walked. In other streets the music beat faster, a shimmering of gong and tambourine, and the people went dancing, the procession was a dance. Children dodged in and out, their high calls rising like the swallows' crossing flights over the music and the singing. All the processions wound towards the north side of the city, where on the great water-meadow called the Green Fields boys and girls, naked in the bright air, with mud-stained feet and ankles and long, lithe arms, exercised their restive horses before the race. The horses wore no gear at all but a halter without bit. Their manes were braided with streamers of silver, gold, and green. They flared their nostrils and pranced and boasted to one another; they were vastly excited, the horse being the only animal who has adopted our ceremonies as his own. Far off to the north and west the mountains stood up half encircling Omelas on her bay. The air of morning was so clear that the snow still crowning the Eighteen Peaks burned with white-gold fire across the miles of sunlit air, under the dark blue of the sky. There was just enough wind to make the banners that marked the racecourse snap and flutter now and then. In the silence of the broad green meadows one could hear the music winding through the city streets, farther and nearer and ever approaching, a cheerful faint sweetness of the air that from time to time trembled and gathered together and broke out into the great joyous clanging of the bells.

2   Joyous! How is one to tell about joy? How describe the citizens of Omelas?

3   They were not simple folk, you see, though they were happy. But we do not say the words of cheer much any more. All smiles have become archaic. Given a description such as this one tends to make certain assumptions. Given a description such as this one tends to look next for the King, mounted on a splendid stallion and surrounded by his noble knights, or perhaps in a golden litter borne by

---

*Used with permission of the author.

great-muscled slaves. But there was no king. They did not use swords, or keep slaves. They were not barbarians. I do not know the rules and laws of their society, but I suspect that they were singularly few. As they did without monarchy and slavery, so they also got on without the stock exchange, the advertisement, the secret police, and the bomb. Yet I repeat that these were not simple folk, not dulcet shepherds, noble savages, bland utopians. They were not less complex than us. The trouble is that we have a bad habit, encouraged by pedants and sophisticates, of considering happiness as something rather stupid. Only pain is intellectual, only evil interesting. This is the treason of the artist: a refusal to admit the banality of evil and the terrible boredom of pain. If you can't lick 'em, join 'em. If it hurts, repeat it. But to praise despair is to condemn delight, to embrace violence is to lose hold of everything else. We have almost lost hold, we can no longer describe a happy man, nor make any celebration of joy. How can I tell you about the people of Omelas? They were not naïve and happy children—though their children were, in fact, happy. They were mature, intelligent, passionate adults whose lives were not wretched. O miracle! but I wish I could describe it better. I wish I could convince you. Omelas sounds in my words like a city in a fairy tale, long ago and far away, once upon a time. Perhaps it would be best if you imagined it as your own fancy bids, assuming it will rise to the occasion, for certainly I cannot suit you all. For instance, how about technology? I think that there would be no cars or helicopters in and above the streets; this follows from the fact that the people of Omelas are happy people. Happiness is based on a just discrimination of what is necessary, what is neither necessary nor destructive, and what is destructive. In the middle category, however—that of the unnecessary but undestructive, that of comfort, luxury, exuberance, etc.—they could perfectly well have central heating, subway trains, washing machines, and all kinds of marvelous devices not yet invented here, floating light-sources, fuelless power, a cure for the common cold. Or they could have none of that: it doesn't matter. As you like it. I incline to think that people from towns up and down the coast have been coming in to Omelas during the last days before the Festival on very fast little trains and double-decked trams, and that the train station of Omelas is actually the handsomest building in town, though plainer than the magnificent Farmer's Market. But even granted trains, I fear that Omelas so far strikes some of you as goody-goody. Smiles, bells, parades, horses, bleh. If So, please add an orgy. If an orgy would help, don't hesitate. Let us not, however, have temples from which issue beautiful nude priests and priestesses already half in ecstasy and ready to copulate with any man or woman, lover or stranger, who desires union with the deep godhead of the blood, although that was my first idea. But really it would be better not to have any temples in Omelas—at least, not manned temples. Religion yes, clergy no. Surely the beautiful nudes can just wander about, offering themselves like divine soufflés to the hunger of the needy and the rapture of the flesh. Let them join the processions. Let tambourines be struck above the copulations, and the glory of desire be proclaimed upon the gongs, and (a not unimportant point) let the offspring of these delightful rituals be beloved and looked after by all. One thing I know there is none of in Omelas is guilt. But what else should there be? I thought that first there were no drugs, but that is puritanical. For those who like it, the faint insistent sweetness of *drooz* may perfume the ways of the city, *drooz* which first brings a great lightness and brilliance to the mind and limbs, and then after some hours a dreamy languor, and wonderful visions at last of the very arcana and inmost secrets of the Universe, as well as exciting the pleasure of sex beyond all belief; and it is not habit-forming. For more modest tastes I think there ought to be beer. What else, what else belongs in the joyous city? The sense of victory, surely, the celebration of courage. But as we did without clergy, let us do without soldiers. The joy built upon successful slaughter is not the right kind of joy; it will not do; it is fearful and it is trivial. A boundless and generous contentment, a magnanimous triumph felt not against some outer enemy but in communion with the finest and fairest in the souls of all men everywhere and the splendor of the world's summer: this is what swells the hearts of the people of Omelas, and the victory they celebrate is that of life. I really don't think many of them need to take *drooz*.

4   Most of the processions have reached the Green Fields by now. A marvelous smell of cooking goes forth from the red and blue tents of the provisioners. The faces of small children are amiably sticky; in the benign grey beard of a man a couple of crumbs of rich pastry are entangled. The youths and girls have mounted their horses and are beginning to group around the starting line of the course. An old woman, small, fat, and laughing, is passing out flowers from a basket, and tall young men wear her flowers in their shining hair. A child of nine or ten sits at the edge of the crowd, alone, playing on a wooden flute. People pause to listen, and they smile, but they do not speak to him, for he never ceases playing and never sees them, his dark eyes wholly rapt in the sweet, thin magic of the tune.

5   He finishes, and slowly lowers his hands holding the wooden flute.

6   As if that little private silence were the signal, all at once a trumpet sounds from the pavilion near the starting line: imperious, melancholy, piercing. The horses rear on their slender legs, and some of them neigh in answer. Sober-faced, the young riders stroke the horses' necks and soothe them, whispering, "Quiet, quiet, there my beauty, my hope. . . ." They begin to form in rank along the straight line. The crowds along the racecourse are like a field of grass and flowers in the wind. The Festival of Summer has begun.

7   Do you believe? Do you accept the festival, the city, the joy? No? Then let me describe one more thing.

8   In a basement under one of the beautiful public buildings of Omelas, or perhaps in the cellar of one of its spacious private homes, there is a room. It has one locked door, and no window. A little light seeps in dustily between cracks in the boards, secondhand from a cobwebbed window somewhere across the cellar. In one corner of the little room a couple of mops, with stiff, clotted, foul-smelling heads, stand near a rusty bucket. The floor is dirt, a little damp to the touch, as cellar dirt usually is. The room is about three paces long and two wide: a mere broom closet or disused tool room. In the room a child is sitting. It could be a boy or a girl. It looks about six, but actually is nearly ten. It is feeble-minded. Perhaps it was born defective, or perhaps it has become imbecile through fear, malnutrition, and neglect. It picks its nose and occasionally fumbles vaguely with its toes or genitals, as it sits hunched in the corner farthest from the bucket and the two

mops. It is afraid of the mops. It finds them horrible. It shuts its eyes, but it knows the mops are still standing there; and the door is locked; and nobody will come. The door is always locked; and nobody ever comes, except that sometimes—the child has no understanding of time or interval—sometimes the door rattles terribly and opens, and a person, or several people, are there. One of them may come in and kick the child to make it stand up. The others never come close, but peer in at it with frightened, disgusted eyes. The food bowl and the water jug are hastily filled, the door is locked, the eyes disappear. The people at the door never say anything, but the child, who has not always lived in the tool room, and can remember sunlight and its mother's voice, sometimes speaks. "I will be good," it says. "Please let me out. I will be good!" They never answer. The child used to scream for help at night, and cry a good deal, but now it only makes a kind of whining, "eh-haa, eh-haa," and it speaks less and less often. It is so thin there are no calves to its legs; its belly protrudes; it lives on a half-bowl of corn meal and grease a day. It is naked. Its buttocks and thighs are a mass of festered sores, as it sits in its own excrement continually.

9   They all know it is there, all the people of Omelas. Some of them have come to see it, others are content merely to know it is there. They all know that it has to be there. Some of them understand why, and some do not, but they all understand that their happiness, the beauty of their city, the tenderness of their friendships, the health of their children, the wisdom of their scholars, the skill of their makers, even the abundance of their harvest and the kindly weathers of their skies, depend wholly on this child's abominable misery.

10   This is usually explained to children when they are between eight and twelve, whenever they seem capable of understanding; and most of those who come to see the child are young people, though often enough an adult comes, or comes back, to see the child. No matter how well the matter has been explained to them, these young spectators are always shocked and sickened at the sight. They feel disgust, which they had thought themselves superior to. They feel anger, outrage, impotence, despite all the explanations. They would like to do something for the child. But there is nothing they can do. If the child were brought up into the sunlight out of that vile place, if it were cleaned and fed and comforted, that would be a good thing, indeed; but if it were done, in that day and hour all the prosperity and beauty and delight of Omelas would wither and be destroyed. Those are the terms. To exchange all the goodness and grace of every life in Omelas for that single, small improvement: to throw away the happiness of thousands for the chance of the happiness of one: that would be to let guilt within the walls indeed.

11   The terms are strict and absolute; there may not even be a kind word spoken to the child.

12   Often the young people go home in tears, or in a tearless rage, when they have seen the child and faced this terrible paradox. They may brood over it for weeks or years. But as time goes on they begin to realize that even if the child could be released, it would not get much good of its freedom: a little vague pleasure of warmth and food, no doubt, but little more. It is too degraded and imbecile to know any real joy. It has been afraid too long ever to be free of fear. Its

habits are too uncouth for it to respond to humane treatment. Indeed, after so long it would probably be wretched without walls about it to protect it, and darkness for its eyes, and its own excrement to sit in. Their tears at the bitter injustice dry when they begin to perceive the terrible justice of reality, and to accept it. Yet it is their tears and anger, the trying of their generosity and the acceptance of their helplessness, which are perhaps the true source of the splendor of their lives. Theirs is no vapid, irresponsible happiness. They know that they, like the child, are not free. They know compassion. It is the existence of the child, and their knowledge of its existence, that makes possible the nobility of their architecture, the poignancy of their music, the profundity of their science. It is because of the child that they are so gentle with children. They know that if the wretched one were not there sniveling in the dark, the other one, the flute-player, could make no joyful music as the young riders line up in their beauty for the race in the sunlight of the first morning of summer.

13   Now do you believe in them? Are they not more credible? But there is one more thing to tell, and this is quite incredible.

14   At times one of the adolescent girls or boys who go to see the child does not go home to weep or rage, does not, in fact, go home at all. Sometimes also a man or woman much older falls silent for a day or two, and then leaves home. These people go out into the street, and walk down the street alone. They keep walking, and walk straight out of the city of Omelas, through the beautiful gates. They keep walking across the farmlands of Omelas. Each one goes alone, youth or girl, man or woman. Night falls; the traveler must pass down village streets, between the houses with yellow-lit windows, and on out into the darkness of the fields. Each alone, they go west or north, towards the mountains. They go on. They leave Omelas, they walk ahead into the darkness, and they do not come back. The place they go towards is a place even less imaginable to most of us than the city of happiness. I cannot describe it at all. It is possible that it does not exist. But they seem to know where they are going, the ones who walk away from Omelas.

FOR DISCUSSION: How is happiness defined in this story? Who gets to define it? Why? Why do some walk away? Make some connections: What actual societies or organized groups of people existing either now or in history might be suggested by this parable? Why do you think so?

◆◆◇

C. WRITING ASSIGNMENT: ANALYZING THE ARGUMENT IN A LITERARY ESSAY

The following essay was written by Jonathan Swift in 1729, when England was exploiting Ireland to the point of debilitation. Its complete title when it first appeared in pamphlet form was "A Modest Proposal for Preventing the Children of Poor People in Ireland from Being a Burden to Their Parents or Country, and for Making Them Beneficial to the Public." You will see, as you read this essay, that Swift has problems with both the Irish, who encouraged high birthrates for religious reasons and lived in terrible poverty, and the English landlords, who were stripping Ireland of the resources it needed for economic survival.

1. Break the class into five groups. Each group will take one of the following questions, work for ten minutes, and then report back to the class.

   a. Apply the Toulmin model. What is the stated claim (proposal) in this essay? What is the implied claim? What reasons and evidence does the narrator give? What are the warrants? Are there any rebuttals or qualifiers?

   b. How does the narrator use emotional appeal and incite *pathos* in the audience? Cite examples in the essay that cause the audience to feel emotion.

   c. What are some examples of logical appeal that the narrator uses to convince the audience?

   d. How does the narrator destroy the *ethos* of the wealthy English? How does he develop a positive *ethos* for himself?

   e. Would you say that the narrator is a moral or immoral person in the context of the essay?

2. Write a 500- to 750-word paper in which you draw on the answers to the questions above to explain Swift's argumentative strategy in his essay. Include your evaluation of the effectiveness of the argumentative strategy as a response to the particular rhetorical situation.

A MODEST PROPOSAL FOR PREVENTING THE CHILDREN OF IRELAND FROM BEING A BURDEN TO THEIR PARENTS OR COUNTRY*

Jonathan Swift

1   It is a melancholly Object to those, who walk through this great Town or travel in the Country, when they see the Streets, the Roads and Cabbin-doors crowded with Beggers of the Female Sex, followed by three, four, or six Children, all in Rags, and importuning every Passenger for an Alms. These Mothers instead of being able to work for their honest livelyhood, are forced to employ all their time in Stroling to beg Sustenance for their helpless Infants, who, as they grow up, either turn Thieves for want of Work, or leave their dear Native Country, to fight for the Pretender in Spain, or sell themselves to the Barbadoes.

2   I think it is agreed by all Parties, that this prodigious number of Children in the Arms, or on the Backs, or at the Heels of their Mothers, and frequently of their Fathers, is in the present deplorable state of the Kingdom, a very great

*From Jonathan Swift, *Satires and Personal Writings,* edited by William Alfred Eddy (London: Oxford University Press, 1932), pp. 21–31.

additional grievance; and therefore whoever could find out a fair, cheap and easy method of making these Children sound and useful Members of the Commonwealth, would deserve so well of the publick, as to have his Statue set up for a Preserver of the Nation.

3   But my Intention is very far from being confined to provide only for the Children of professed Beggers, it is of a much greater Extent, and shall take in the whole Number of Infants at a certain Age, who are born of Parents in effect as little able to support them, as those who demand our Charity in the Streets.

4   As to my own part, having turned my Thoughts, for many Years, upon this important Subject, and maturely weighed the several Schemes of other Projectors, I have always found them grossly mistaken in their computation. It is true, a Child just dropt from its Dam, may be supported by her Milk, for a Solar Year with little other Nourishment, at most not above the Value of two Shillings, which the Mother may certainly get, or the Value in Scraps, by her lawful Occupation of Begging; and it is exactly at one Year Old that I propose to provide for them in such a manner, as, instead of being a Charge upon their Parents, or the Parish, or wanting Food and Raiment for the rest of their Lives, they shall, on the Contrary, contribute to the Feeding and partly to the Cloathing of many Thousands.

5   There is likewise another great Advantage in my Scheme, that it will prevent those voluntary Abortions, and that horrid practice of Women murdering their Bastard Children, alas! too frequent among us, Sacrificing the poor innocent Babes, I doubt, more to avoid the Expence than the Shame, which would move Tears and Pity in the most Savage and inhuman breast.

6   The number of Souls in this Kingdom being usually reckoned one Million and a half, Of these I calculate there may be about two hundred thousand Couples whose Wives are Breeders; from which number I substract thirty Thousand Couples, who are able to maintain their own Children, although I apprehend there cannot be so many, under the present Distresses of the Kingdom; but this being granted, there will remain an hundred and seventy thousand Breeders. I again Substract fifty thousand, for those Women who miscarry, or whose Children die by accident, or disease within the Year. There only remain an hundred and twenty thousand Children of poor Parents annually born: The question therefore is, How this number shall be reared, and provided for? which, as I have already said, under the present Situation of Affairs, is utterly impossible by all the Methods hitherto proposed; for we can neither employ them in Handicraft or Agriculture; we neither build Houses, (I mean in the Country) nor cultivate Land: They can very seldom pick up a Livelihood by Stealing till they arrive at six years Old; except where they are of towardly parts; although, I confess, they learn the Rudiments much earlier; during which time they can however be properly looked upon only as Probationers; as I have been informed by a principal Gentleman in the Country of Cavan, who protested to me, that he never knew above one or two Instances under the Age of six, even in a part of the Kingdom so renowned for the quickest proficiency in that Art.

7   I am assured by our Merchants, that a Boy or a Girl before twelve years Old, is no saleable Commodity, and even when they come to this Age, they will not

yield above three Pounds, or three Pounds and half a Crown at most, on the Exchange; which cannot turn to Account either to the Parents or Kingdom, the Charge of Nutriment and Rags having been at least four times that Value.

8   I shall now therefore humbly propose my own Thoughts, which I hope will not be liable to the least Objection.

9   I have been assured by a very knowing American of my acquaintance in London, that a young healthy Child well Nursed is at a year Old a most delicious nourishing and wholesome Food, whether Stewed, Roasted, Baked, or Boiled; and I make no doubt that it will equally serve in a Fricasie, or a Ragoust.

10   I do therefore humbly offer it to publick consideration, that of the Hundred and twenty thousand Children, already computed, twenty thousand may be reserved for Breed, whereof only one fourth part to be Males; which is more than we allow to Sheep, black Cattle, or Swine, and my Reason is, that these Children are seldom the Fruits of Marriage, a Circumstance not much regarded by our Savages, therefore, one Male will be sufficient to serve four Females. That the remaining Hundred thousand may at a year Old be offered in Sale to the Persons of Quality and Fortune, through the Kingdom, always advising the Mother to let them Suck plentifully in the last Month, so as to render them Plump, and Fat for a good Table. A Child will make two Dishes at an Entertainment for Friends, and when the Family dines alone, the fore or hind Quarter will make a reasonable Dish, and seasoned with a little Pepper or Salt will be very good Boiled on the fourth Day, especially in Winter.

11   I have reckoned upon a Medium, that a Child just born will weigh 12 pounds, and in a solar Year, if tolerably nursed, encreaseth to 28 pounds.

12   I grant this food will be somewhat dear, and therefore very proper for Landlords, who, as they have already devoured most of the Parents seem to have the best Title to the Children.

13   Infant's flesh will be in Season throughout the Year, but more plentiful in March, and a little before and after; for we are told by a grave Author an eminent French Physician, that Fish being a prolifick Dyet, there are more Children born in Roman Catholick Countries about nine Months after Lent, than at any other Season; therefore reckoning a Year after Lent, the Markets will be more glutted than usual, because the Number of Popish Infants, is at least three to one in this Kingdom, and therefore it will have one other Collateral advantage, by lessening the Number of Papists among us.

14   I have already computed the Charge of nursing a Begger's Child (in which List I reckon all Cottagers, Labourers and four fifths of the Farmers) to be about two Shillings per Annum, Rags included; and I believe no Gentleman would repine to give Ten Shillings for the Carcass of a good fat Child, which, as I have said will make four Dishes of excellent Nutritive Meat, when he hath only some particular Friend, or his own Family to dine with him. Thus the Squire will learn to be a good Landlord, and grow popular among his Tenants, the Mother will have Eight Shillings neat Profit, and be fit for Work till she produces another Child.

15   Those who are more thrifty (as I must confess the Times require) may flay the Carcass; the Skin of which, Artificially dressed, will make admirable Gloves for Ladies, and Summer Boots for fine Gentlemen.

16   As to our City of Dublin, Shambles may be appointed for this purpose, in the most convenient parts of it, and Butchers we may be assured will not be wanting; although I rather recommend buying the Children alive, and dressing them hot from the Knife, as we do roasting Pigs.

17   A very worthy Person, a true Lover of his Country, and whose Virtues I highly esteem, was lately pleased, in discoursing on this matter, to offer a refinement upon my Scheme. He said, that many Gentlemen of this Kingdom, having of late destroyed their Deer, he conceived that the Want of Venison might be well sup-ply'd by the Bodies of young Lads and Maidens, not exceeding fourteen Years of Age, nor under twelve; so great a Number of both Sexes in every Country being now ready to Starve, for want of Work and Service: And these to be disposed of by their Parents if alive, or otherwise by their nearest Relations. But with due defer-ence to so excellent a Friend, and so deserving a Patriot, I cannot be altogether in his Sentiments; for as to the Males, my American acquaintance assured me from frequent Experience, that their Flesh was generally Tough and Lean, like that of our Schoolboys, by continual exercise, and their Taste disagreeable, and to fatten them would not answer the Charge. Then as to the Females, it would, I think with humble Submission, be a Loss to the Publick, because they soon would be-come Breeders themselves: And besides it is not improbable that some scrupulous People might be apt to Censure such a Practice, (although indeed very unjustly) as a little bordering upon Cruelty, which, I confess, hath always been with me the strongest Objection against any Project, how well soever intended.

18   But in order to justify my Friend, he confessed, that this expedient was put into his Head by the famous Sallmanaazor, a Native of the Island Formosa, who came from thence to London, above twenty Years ago, and in Conversation told my Friend, that in his Country when any young Person happened to be put to Death, the Executioner sold the Carcass to Persons of Quality, as a prime Dainty, and that, in his Time, the Body of a plump Girl of fifteen, who was crucified for an attempt to poison the Emperor, was sold to his Imperial Majesty's prime Minister of State, and other great Mandarins of the Court, in Joints from the Gibbet, at four hundred Crowns. Neither indeed can I deny, that if the same Use were made of several plump young Girls in this Town, who, without one single Groat to their Fortunes, cannot stir abroad without a Chair, and appear at a Play-house, and As-semblies in Foreign fineries, which they never will pay for; the Kingdom would not be the worse.

19   Some Persons of a desponding Spirit are in great concern about that vast Number of poor People, who are Aged, Diseased, or Maimed, and I have been de-sired to imploy my Thoughts what Course may be taken, to ease the Nation of so grievous an Incumbrance. But I am not in the least Pain upon that matter, be-cause it is very well known, that they are every Day dying, and rotting, by cold and famine, and filth, and vermin, as fast as can be reasonably expected. And as to the younger Labourers, they are now in almost as hopeful a Condition. They cannot get Work, and consequently pine away for want of Nourishment, to a degree, that if at any Time they are accidentally hired to common Labour, they have not Strength to perform it, and thus the Country and themselves are happily delivered from the Evils to come.

20   I have too long digressed, and therefore shall return to my Subject. I think the Advantages by the Proposal which I have made are obvious and many, as well as of the highest Importance.

21   For *First,* as I have already observed, it would greatly lessen the Number of Papists, with whom we are Yearly over-run, being the principal Breeders of the Nation, as well as our most dangerous Enemies, and who stay at home on purpose with a Design to deliver the Kingdom to the Pretender, hoping to take their Advantage by the Absence of so many good Protestants, who have chosen rather to leave their Country, than stay at home, and pay Tithes against their Conscience, to an Episcopal Curate.

22   *Secondly,* The poorer Tenants will have something valuable of their own which by Law may be made lyable to Distress, and help to pay their Landlord's Rent, their Corn and Cattle being already seized, and Money a Thing unknown.

23   *Thirdly,* Whereas the Maintenance of an hundred thousand Children, from two Years old, and upwards, cannot be computed at less than Ten Shillings a Piece per Annum, the Nation's Stock will be thereby increased fifty thousand Pounds per Annum, besides the Profit of a new Dish, introduced to the Tables of all Gentlemen of Fortune in the Kingdom, who have any Refinement in Taste, and the Money will circulate among our Selves, the Goods being entirely of our own Growth and Manufacture.

24   *Fourthly,* The constant Breeders, besides the gain of eight Shillings Sterling per Annum, by the Sale of their Children, will be rid of the Charge of maintaining them after the first Year.

25   *Fifthly,* This Food would likewise bring great Custom to Taverns, where the Vintners will certainly be so prudent as to procure the best Receipts for dressing it to Perfection; and consequently have their Houses frequented by all the fine Gentlemen, who justly value themselves upon their Knowledge in good Eating; and a skilful Cook, who understands how to oblige his Guests, will contrive to make it as expensive as they please.

26   *Sixthly,* This would be a great Inducement to Marriage, which all wise Nations have either encouraged by Rewards, or enforced by Laws and Penalties. It would encrease the Care and Tenderness of Mothers towards their Children, when they were sure of a Settlement for Life, to the poor Babes, provided in some Sort by the Publick, to their annual Profit instead of Expence; we should soon see an honest Emulation among the married Women, which of them could bring the fattest Child to the Market. Men would become as fond of their Wives, during the Time of their Pregnancy, as they are now of their Mares in Foal, their Cows in Calf, or Sows when they are ready to farrow, nor offer to beat or kick them (as is too frequent a Practice) for fear of a Miscarriage.

27   Many other Advantages might be enumerated. For Instance, the Addition of some thousand Carcasses in our Exportation of Barrel'd Beef: The Propagation of Swine's Flesh, and Improvement in the Art of making good Bacon, so much wanted among us by the great Destruction of Pigs, too frequent at our Tables, which are no way comparable in Taste, or Magnificence to a well grown, fat yearling Child, which roasted whole will make a considerable Figure at a Lord

Mayor's Feast, or any other Publick Entertainment. But this, and many others, I omit, being studious of Brevity.

28   Supposing that one thousand Families in this City, would be constant Customers for Infant's Flesh, besides others who might have it at merry Meetings, particularly at Weddings and Christenings, I compute that Dublin would take off Annually about twenty thousand Carcasses, and the rest of the Kingdom (where probably they will be sold somewhat cheaper) the remaining eighty Thousand.

29   I can think of no one Objection, that will possibly be raised against this Proposal, unless it should be urged, that the Number of People will be thereby much lessened in the Kingdom. This I freely own, and 'twas indeed one principal Design in offering it to the World. I desire the Reader will observe, that I calculate my Remedy for this one individual Kingdom of Ireland, and for no Other that ever was, is, or, I think, ever can be upon Earth. Therefore let no man talk to me of other Expedients: Of taxing our Absentees at five Shillings a Pound: Of using neither Cloaths, nor Household Furniture, except what is of our own Growth and Manufacture: Of utterly rejecting the Materials and Instruments that promote Foreign Luxury: Of curing the Expensiveness of Pride, Vanity, Idleness, and Gaming in our Women: Of introducing a Vein of Parcimony, Prudence and Temperance: Of learning to love our Country, wherein we differ even from Laplanders, and the Inhabitants of Topinamboo: Of quitting our Animosities, and Factions, nor act any longer like the Jews, who were murdering one another at the very Moment their City was taken: Of being a little cautious not to sell our Country and Consciences for nothing: Of teaching Landlords to have at least one Degree of Mercy towards their Tenants. Lastly, Of putting a Spirit of Honesty, Industry, and Skill into our Shop-keepers, who, if a Resolution could now be taken to buy only our Native Goods, would immediately unite to cheat and exact upon us in the Price, the Measure, and the Goodness, nor could ever yet be brought to make one fair Proposal of just Dealing, though often and earnestly invited to it.

30   Therefore I repeat, let no Man talk to me of these and the like Expedients, till he hath at least some Glimpse of Hope, that there will ever be some hearty and sincere Attempt to put them in Practice.

31   But as to my self, having been wearied out for many Years with offering vain, idle, visionary Thoughts, and at length utterly despairing of Success, I fortunately fell upon this Proposal, which as it is wholly new, so it hath something Solid and Real, of no Expence and little Trouble, full in our own Power, and whereby we can incur no Danger in disobliging England. For this kind of Commodity will not bear Exportation, the Flesh being of too tender a Consistence, to admit a long Continuance in Salt, although perhaps I cou'd name a Country, which wou'd be glad to eat up our whole Nation without it.

32   After all, I am not violently bent upon my own Opinion, as to reject any Offer, proposed by wise Men, which shall be found equally Innocent, Cheap, Easy, and Effectual. But before something of that Kind shall be advanced in Contradiction to my Scheme, and offering a better, I desire the Author or Authors, will be pleased maturely to consider two Points. *First,* As Things now stand, how they will be able to find Food and Raiment for a hundred Thousand useless

Mouths and Backs. And *Secondly,* There being a round Million of Creatures in Human Figure, throughout this Kingdom, whose whole Subsistence put into a common Stock, would leave them in Debt two Millions of Pounds Sterling, adding those, who are Beggers by Profession, to the Bulk of Farmers, Cottagers and Labourers, with their Wives and Children, who are Beggers in Effect; I desire those Politicians, who dislike my Overture, and may perhaps be so bold to attempt an Answer, that they will first ask the Parents of these Mortals, Whether they would not at this Day think it a great Happiness to have been sold for Food at a Year Old, in the manner I prescribe, and thereby have avoided such a perpetual Scene of Misfortunes, as they have since gone through, by the Oppression of Landlords, the Impossibility of paying Rent without Money or Trade, the Want of common Sustenance, with neither House nor Cloaths to cover them from the Inclemencies of the Weather, and the most inevitable Prospect of intailing the like, or greater Miseries, upon their Breed for ever.

33   I profess in the Sincerity of my Heart, that I have not the least Personal Interest in endeavouring to promote this necessary Work, having no other Motive than the Publick Good of my Country, by advancing our Trade, providing for Infants, relieving the Poor, and giving some Pleasure to the Rich. I have no Children, by which I can propose to get a single Penny; the youngest being nine Years Old, and my Wife past Child-bearing.

FOR DISCUSSION: Irony entails saying one thing while actually meaning something directly opposite. How does "A Modest Proposal" exemplify irony? Swift creates a first-person narrator to present the proposal. Describe this narrator and his general effectiveness. Why do you think Swift chose to use irony in writing this essay instead of writing it in a straightforward style?

◆◆◆

SYNTHESIS OF CHAPTERS 1–14
Summary Charts

THE RHETORICAL SITUATION

For You as the Reader	For the Targeted Reader at the Time the Text Was Written	For You as the Writer
Text. What kind of text is it? What are its special qualities and features? What is it about?	**Text.** What kind of text is it? Is it unique to its time?	**Text.** What is the assignment? What should your completed paper look like?
Reader. Are you one of the readers the writer anticipated? Do you share common ground with the author and other audience members? Are you open to change?	**Reader.** What was the nature of the targeted readers? Were they convinced? How are they different from other or modern readers?	**Reader.** Who are your readers? Where do they stand on the issue? How can you establish common ground? Can they change?
Author. Who is the author? How is the author influenced by background, experience, education, affiliations, values? What is the author's motivation to write?	**Author.** Who is the author? What influenced the author? Why was the author motivated to write?	**Author.** What is your argumentative strategy? What is your purpose and perspective? How will you make your paper convincing?
Constraints.* What beliefs, attitudes, habits, affiliations, or traditions will influence the way you and the author view the argument?	**Constraints.*** What beliefs, attitudes, habits, affiliations, or traditions influenced the author's and the readers' views in this argument?	**Constraints.*** How are your training, background, affiliations, and values either in harmony or in conflict with your audience? Will they drive you apart or help build common ground?
Exigence. What caused the argument, and do you perceive it as a defect or problem?	**Exigence.** What happened to cause the argument? Why was it a problem? Has it recurred?	**Exigence.** What happened? What is motivating you to write on this issue? Why is it compelling to you?

*Do not confuse constraints with warrants. Constraints are a broader concept. See page 137.

THE PROCESS

Be selective and flexible in using the strategies, and remember there is no best order. You will backtrack and repeat.

When You Are the Reader

Prereading Strategies

- **Read the title and first paragraph; consult your background.** Identify the issue. Free-associate, and write words and phrases that the issue brings to mind.
- **Evaluate and improve your background.** Do you know enough? If not, read or discuss to get background. Look up a key word or two.
- **Survey the material.** Locate the claim (the main assertion) and some of the subclaims (the ideas that support it); notice how they are organized. Do not slow down and read.
- **Write out your present position on the issue.**
- **Make some predictions, and write one big question.** Jot down two or three ideas that you think the author may discuss, and write one question you would like to have answered.

Reading Strategies

- **Pick up a pencil, underline, and annotate** the ideas that seem important.
- **Identify** and **read** the information in the **introduction, body,** and **conclusion.**
- **Look for the claim, subclaims, and support.** Box the **transitions** to highlight relationships between ideas and changes of subject.
- **Find the key words** that represent major concepts, and jot down meanings if necessary.
- **Analyze the rhetorical situation.** Remember TRACE: Text, Reader, Author, Constraints, Exigence.
- **Read with an open mind, and analyze the common ground** between you and the author.

Strategies for Reading Difficult Material

- **Read all the way through once** without stopping.
- **Write a list** of what you understand and what you do not understand.
- **Identify words and concepts** you do not understand, look them up, and analyze how they are used in context.

When You Are the Writer

Prewriting Strategies

- **Get organized to write.** Set up a place with materials. Get motivated.
- **Understand the writing assignment, and schedule time.** Break a complicated writing task into manageable parts, and set aside time to write.
- **Identify an issue, and do some initial reading.** Use the Twelve Tests (Box 1.3) to make certain you have an arguable issue.
- **Analyze the rhetorical situation,** particularly the exigence, the audience, and the constraints.
- **Focus** on your issue, and **freewrite.**
- **Brainstorm, make lists, and map ideas.**
- **Talk it through** with a friend, your instructor, or members of a peer editing group.
- **Keep a journal, notebook, or folder of ideas.**
- **Mentally visualize** the major concepts.
- Do some directed **reading and thinking.**
- **Use argument strategies.**
- **Use reading strategies.**
- **Use critical thinking prompts.**
- Plan and conduct **library research.**
- Make an **expanded list or outline** to guide your writing.
- **Talk it through again.**

Writing Strategies

- **Write the first draft.** Get your ideas on paper so that you can work with them. Use your outline and notes to help you. Either write and rewrite as you go, or write the draft quickly with the knowledge that you can reread or rewrite later.

Strategies to Use When You Get Stuck

- **Read more,** and **take more notes**.
- **Read your outline, rearrange parts, and add information to it.**
- **Freewrite** on the issue, **read some more**, and then **freewrite** some more.
- **Talk about your ideas** with someone else.

(continued)

THE PROCESS *(continued)*

When You Are the Reader

- **Reread the material,** and add to your list of what you can and cannot understand.
- **Reread again** if you need to.
- **Discuss the material** with someone who has also read the material to get further clarification and understanding.

Postreading Strategies

- **Monitor your comprehension.** Insist on understanding. Check the accuracy of your **predictions,** and answer your **question.**
- **Analyze the organization,** and write either a **simplified outline** or a **summary** to help you understand and remember. Or make a map.
- **Write a response** to help you think.
- **Compare your present position** with your position before you began to read.
- **Evaluate the argument,** and decide whether it is convincing or not.

When You Are the Writer

- **Lower your expectations for your first draft.** It does not have to be perfect at this point.

Postwriting Strategies

- **Read your draft critically,** and also **have someone else read it.** Put it aside for 24 hours, if you can, to develop a better perspective for reading and improving.
- **Rewrite and revise.** Make changes and additions until you think your paper is ready for other people to read. Move sections, cross out material, add other material, and rephrase, as necessary.
- **Check your paper** for final mechanical and spelling errors, **write the final title,** and **type or print the paper.**

THE TOULMIN MODEL

When You Are the Reader

1. *What is the claim?* What is this author trying to prove? Look for the claim at the beginning or at the end, or infer it.
2. *What is the support?* What information does the author use to convince you of the claim? Look for reasons, explanations, facts, opinions, personal narratives, and examples.
3. *What are the warrants?* What assumptions, general principles, values, beliefs, and appeals to human motives are implicit in the argument? Do you share the author's values? Does the support develop the claim? Are the warrants stated, or must they be inferred?
4. *Is backing supplied for the warrants?* See if additional support is provided to make the warrants more acceptable to the reader.
5. *Is there a rebuttal?* Are other perspectives on the issue stated in the argument? Are they refuted? Are counterarguments given?
6. *Has the claim been qualified?* Look for qualifying words like *sometimes, most, probably,* and *possibly.* Decide what is probably the best position to take on the issue, for now.

When You Are the Writer

1. *What is my claim?* Decide on the type of claim and the subclaims. Decide where to put the claim in your paper.
2. *What support will I use?* Invent reasons, opinions, and examples. Research and quote authorities and facts. Consider using personal narratives.
3. *What are my warrants?* Write out the warrants. Do they strengthen the argument by linking the support to the claim? Do you believe them yourself? Will the audience share them or reject them?
4. *What backing for the warrants should I provide?* Add polls, studies, reports, expert opinion, or facts to make your warrants convincing.
5. *How should I handle rebuttal?* Include other perspectives and point out what is wrong with them. Make counterarguments.
6. *Will I need to qualify my claim?* Decide if you can strengthen your claim by adding qualifying words like *usually, often,* or *probably.*

TYPES OF CLAIMS

CLAIMS OF FACT

What happened? Is it true? Does it exist? Is it a fact?

Examples:

Increasing population threatens the environment.
Television content promotes violence.
Women are not as effective as men in combat.

Readers

- Look for claims that state facts.
- Look for facts, statistics, real examples, and quotations from reliable authorities.
- Anticipate induction, analogies, and signs.
- Look for chronological or topical organization or a claim plus reasons.

Writers

- State the claim as a fact even though it is controversial.
- Use factual evidence and expert opinion.
- Use induction, historical and literal analogies, and signs.
- Consider arranging your material as a claim with reasons.

CLAIMS OF DEFINITION

What is it? What is it like? How should it be classified? How should it be interpreted?
How does its usual meaning change in a particular context?

Examples:

We need to define what constitutes a family before we discuss family values.
A definition will demonstrate that the riots were an instance of civil disobedience.

Readers

- Look for a claim that contains or is followed by a definition.
- Look for reliable authorities and sources for definitions.
- Look for comparisons and examples.
- Look for comparison-and-contrast, topical, or deductive organization.

Writers

- State your claim, and define the key terms.
- Quote authorities, or go to dictionaries, encyclopedias, or other reliable sources for definitions.
- If you are comparing to help define, use comparison-and-contrast organization.
- Use deductive organization.

CLAIMS OF CAUSE

What caused it? Where did it come from? Why did it happen? What are the effects?
What probably will be the results on both a short-term and a long-term basis?

Examples:

Clear-cutting is the main cause of the destruction of ancient forests.
Censorship can result in limits on freedom of speech.
The American people's current mood has been caused by the state of the economy.

Readers

- Look for a claim that states or implies cause or effect.

Writers

- Make a claim that states or implies cause or effect.

(continued)

TYPES OF CLAIMS *(continued)*

Readers	Writers
• Look for facts and statistics, comparisons such as historical analogies, signs, induction, deduction, and causal arguments. • Look for cause-and-effect or effect-and-cause organization.	• Use facts and statistics. • Apply Burke's pentad to focus the main cause. • Use historical analogies, signs, induction, and deduction. • Consider using cause-and-effect or effect-and-cause organization.

CLAIMS OF VALUE

Is it good or bad? How good? How bad? Of what worth is it? Is it moral or immoral? Who thinks so?
What do those people value? What values or criteria should I use to determine its goodness or badness?
Are my values different from other people's or the author's?

Examples:
Computers are a valuable addition to modern education.
School prayer has a moral function in the public schools.
Animal rights are as important as human rights.

Readers   **Writers**

Readers	Writers
• Look for claims that make a value statement. • Look for value proofs, motivational proofs, literal and figurative analogies, quotations from authorities, signs, and definitions. • Expect emotional language. • Look for applied criteria, topical, and narrative patterns of organization.	• State your claim as a judgment or value statement. • Analyze your audience's needs and values, and appeal to them. • Use literal and figurative analogies, quotations from authorities, signs, and definitions. • Use emotional language appropriately. • Consider the applied criteria, claim with reasons, or narrative organizational patterns.

CLAIMS OF POLICY

What should we do? How should we act? What should future policy be? How can we solve this problem?
What course of action should we pursue?

Examples:
The criminal should be sent to prison rather than to a mental hospital.
Sex education should be part of the public school curriculum.
Battered women who take revenge should not be placed in jail.

Readers   **Writers**

Readers	Writers
• Look for claims that state that something should be done. • Look for statistical data, motivational appeals, literal analogies, and argument from authority. • Anticipate the problem-solution pattern of organization.	• State the claim as something that should be done. • Use statistical data, motivational appeals, analogies, and authorities as proof. • Use emotional language appropriately. • Consider the problem-solution pattern of organization.

TYPES OF PROOF AND TESTS OF VALIDITY

LOGICAL PROOFS

Don't confuse proofs with support. A proof represents a complete line of argument that includes a claim, support, and warrant. A proof demonstrates a particular way of thinking about and developing the main claim of the argument. The logical proofs have been arranged according to the mnemonic SICDADS: Sign, Induction, Cause, Deduction, Analogies, Definition, Statistics.

When You Are the Reader		When You Are the Writer

SIGN

Look for clues, symptoms, and occurrences that are explained as signs or symptoms that something is so.

Pointing out the symptoms or signs that something is so.

Example:

Claim: The child has chickenpox.
Support: The child has spots.
Warrant: Those spots are a sign of chickenpox.

Test of Validity: Ask if this is really a sign of what the author claims, or if there is another explanation.

Think of symptoms or signs that you can use to demonstrate that something is so.

INDUCTION

Look for a conclusion or claim based on examples or cases.

Drawing a conclusion (claim) from a number of representative cases or examples.

Example:

Claim: Everyone liked that movie.
Support: I know three people who liked it.
Warrant: Three examples are enough.

Tests of Validity: Ask if there are enough examples, or if this is a "hasty" conclusion or claim. Try to think of an exception that would change the conclusion or claim. See if you can make the "inductive leap" from the examples to the conclusion or claim and accept it as probably true.

Give some examples and draw a conclusion/claim based on them; *or* make the claim and back it up with a series of examples.

(continued)

TYPES OF PROOF AND TESTS OF VALIDITY *(continued)*

LOGICAL PROOFS

When You Are the Reader		When You Are the Writer

CAUSE

When You Are the Reader	LOGICAL PROOFS	When You Are the Writer
Look for examples, trends, people, or events that are cited as causes for the claim. Look for effects of the claim.	Placing the claim in a cause-and-effect relationship to show that it is either the cause of an effect or an effect of a cause. *Example:* *Warrant:* Depression in a group of people has increased. *Support:* This group of people has also increased its use of the Internet. *Claim/conclusion:* The Internet may be causing depression. **Tests of Validity:** Ask if these causes alone are sufficient to create these effects or if these effects could result from other causes. Try to think of exceptions to the cause-and-effect outcome.	Make a claim, and ask what caused it. Apply Burke's pentad to focus the main cause. What was done? Where was it done? Who did it? How was it done? Why did it happen?

DEDUCTION

When You Are the Reader	LOGICAL PROOFS	When You Are the Writer
Locate or infer the general principle (warrant). Apply it to the example or case. Draw a conclusion or claim.	Applying a general principle (warrant) to an example or a case and drawing a conclusion. *Example:* *Warrant:* Most uneven footprints are left by people who limp. *Support:* These footprints are uneven. *Claim:* The person who left these footprints walks with a limp. **Test of Validity:** Ask if the general principle (warrant) and the support are probably true, because then the claim is also probably true.	Make a general statement. Apply it to an example or a case. Draw a conclusion. Decide whether to make the general statement (warrant) explicit or implicit.

(continued)

When You Are the Reader	LOGICAL PROOFS	When You Are the Writer
	ANALOGIES: LITERAL, HISTORICAL, AND FIGURATIVE	

Literal and historical analogy:
Look for items, events, people, or periods of time that are being compared.

Interpreting what we do not understand by comparing it with something we do. Literal and historical analogies compare similar items, and figurative analogies compare items from radically different categories.

Example of historical analogy:
Claim: Many people will die of AIDS.
Support: Many people died of the Black Death.
Warrant: AIDS and the Black Death are similar.

Example of literal analogy:
Claim: The state should spend more money on education.
Support: Another state spent more money with good results.
Warrant: The two states are similar, and the results of one will be the results of the other.

Example of figurative analogy:
Claim: Reading a difficult book should take time.
Support: Digesting a large meal takes time.
Warrant: Reading and eating are sufficiently alike that they can be compared.

Tests of Validity: For literal analogies, ask if the cases are so similar that the results of one will be the results of the other. For historical analogies, ask if history will repeat itself. For figurative analogies, ask if the qualities of the items being compared are real enough to provide logical support or if they are so dissimilar that they do not prove anything.

Literal and historical analogy:
Think of items in the same category that can be compared. Show that what happened in one case will also happen in the other. Or demonstrate that history repeats itself.

Figurative analogy:
Look for extended metaphors or items being compared that are from totally different categories.

Figurative analogy:
Think of comparisons with items from other categories. Try to compare items that have similar qualities, characteristics, or outcomes.

(continued)

445

TYPES OF PROOF AND TESTS OF VALIDITY *(continued)*

When You Are the Reader	LOGICAL PROOFS	When You Are the Writer
	DEFINITION	
Look for definitions of key words or concepts. Definitions can be short, a word or sentence, or long, several paragraphs or an entire essay. Notice if the reader is supposed to accept the claim "by definition" because it has been placed in an established category.	Describing the fundamental properties and qualities of a term or placing an item in a category and proving it "by definition." *Example:* *Warrant:* Family values characterize the good citizen. *Support:* Radical feminists lack family values. *Claim:* Radical feminists are not good citizens. **Tests of Validity:** Ask if the definition is accurate and reliable or if there are exceptions or other definitions that would make it less reliable. Ask if the item belongs in the category in which it has been placed.	Define the key terms and concepts in your claim. Define all other terms that you and your reader must agree on for the argument to work. Place some ideas or items in established categories and argue that they are so "by definition."
	STATISTICS	
Look for numbers, data, and tables of figures along with interpretations of them.	Using figures or data to prove a claim. *Example:* *Claim:* We should end draft registration. *Support:* It costs $27.5 million per year. *Warrant:* This is too much; it proves we should end it. **Tests of Validity:** Ask where the statistics came from, to what dates they apply, and if they are fair and accurate. Ask if they have been exaggerated or skewed. Ask if they prove what they are supposed to prove.	Find data, statistics, and tables of figures to use as evidence to back up your claim. Make clear where you get the statistics, and add your interpretations and those of experts.

(continued)

When You Are the Reader	PROOF TO ESTABLISH *ETHOS*	When You Are the Writer
	AUTHORITY	
Look for references to the author's credentials, background, and training. Look for credential statements about quoted authorities.	Quoting established authorities or experts or establishing one's own authority and credibility. *Example:* *Claim:* California will have an earthquake. *Support:* Professors and scientists say so. *Warrant:* These experts are reliable. **Test of Validity:** Ask if the experts, including both outside authorities and the author, are really experts. Remember that argument from authority is only as good as the authorities themselves.	Refer to your own experience and background to establish expertise. Quote the best and most reliable authorities. Establish common ground and respect by using appropriate language and tone.
	EMOTIONAL PROOFS	
	MOTIVES	
Look for references to items or qualities you might need or want and advice on how to get them. Look for emotional language, description, and tone.	Appealing to what all audiences are supposed to need, such as food, drink, warmth, shelter, sex, security, belonging, self-esteem, creativity, and self-expression. Urging audiences to take steps to meet their needs. *Example:* *Claim:* You should support this candidate. *Support:* The candidate can help you get job security and safe neighborhoods. *Warrant:* You want job security and safe neighborhoods. **Tests of Validity:** Ask if you really need what the author assumes you need. Ask if doing what is recommended will satisfy the need as described.	Think about what the members of your audience need, and show how your ideas will help them meet these needs. Use emotional language and tone where appropriate.

(continued)

TYPES OF PROOF AND TESTS OF VALIDITY *(continued)*

When You Are the Reader

Look for examples or narratives that display values.

Infer values (warrants) that are not explicitly stated.

Look for emotional language and tone.

EMOTIONAL PROOFS

VALUES

Appealing to what all audiences are supposed to value, such as reliability, honesty, loyalty, industry, patriotism, courage, conviction, faithfulness, dependability, creativity, integrity, freedom, equality, devotion to duty, and acceptance by others.

Example:

Claim: The curriculum should be multicultural.

Support: A multicultural curriculum will contribute to equality and acceptance.

Warrant: You value equality and acceptance.

Tests of Validity: Ask if you share the author's values. Ask about the effect that differences in values will have on the argument.

When You Are the Writer

Appeal to your audience's values through warrants, explicit value statements, and narratives that illustrate values.

Use emotional language and tone where appropriate.

Part Five

THE READER

INTRODUCTION TO "THE READER": READING AND WRITING ABOUT ISSUE AREAS

"**T**he Reader" contains seven sections that introduce you to broad issue areas that engage modern society: families, marriages, and relationships; education; crime and the treatment of criminals; race, culture, and identity; freedom; the future; and war and peace. Essays are then organized under specific related issues in each broad category. "The Reader" contains essays that explore some of the individual perspectives and positions people have taken in regard to these issues both now and in the past. You may expand your information and understanding of these issues by doing additional research and reading in other sources on the Internet, in the library, or elsewhere.

Internet sources for further online research appear in the introduction to each issue area of "The Reader." You may also expand your perspective on each of these issues through film and literature; a list of related films and literary works that treat these issues in interesting ways is provided in the introduction to each issue area. The films are available on videotape, and the literature is available in anthologies and in the library.

PURPOSE OF "THE READER"

"The Reader" serves three main purposes.

1. It introduces you to big issue areas and a few of their specific related issues. It also helps you build background and provides you with information to quote in your papers.
2. It provides you with models of different types of arguments and thus gives you a better idea of how argument works in general. It provides you with examples and strategies for improving your own written arguments.
3. It helps you think and invent arguments and ideas of your own by providing you with essays that function as springboards for your own thoughts and reactions.

HOW TO USE "THE READER"

Refer to the chapters indicated for details or review.

1. Select an issue area that is compelling for you. Understand why it is compelling. Consult your background on it. Anticipate ways to build common ground with those who oppose you. (Chapters 1 and 9)
2. Survey it: read the titles and summaries of the articles in the table of contents, read the introductory material and "The Rhetorical Situation" at the beginning of the issue area, and read the introductions to the articles. (Chapter 3)
3. Select the specific related issue that interests you the most. (Chapters 1 and 3)
4. Read the articles about the related issue, and jot down the claim and some of the major support and warrants for each article. (Chapters 3 and 5)
5. Make a map or write a list of all of the smaller related issues that you can think of that are related to the issue you have read about. Discover the aspect of the issue that interests you the most. This will be your issue. (Chapter 3)
6. Understand the perspectives presented by the articles in "The Reader" on your issue. You may also want to do outside research. Write an exploratory paper in which you explain at least three perspectives on your issue. (Chapter 4)
7. Take a position on your issue, and phrase it as a question. Apply the Twelve Tests in Box 1.3 to make certain you have an arguable issue. (Chapter 1)
8. State your claim, clarify your purpose, and plan and write an argument paper that presents your position on the issue. (Chapters 8 and 10–12)

QUESTIONS TO HELP YOU READ CRITICALLY AND ANALYTICALLY

1. What is at issue?
2. What is the claim? What type of claim is it?
3. What is the support?
4. What are the warrants?
5. What are the weaknesses in the argument, and how can I refute them?
6. What are some other perspectives on the issue?
7. Where do I stand now in regard to this issue?

QUESTIONS TO HELP YOU READ CREATIVELY AND MOVE FROM READING TO WRITING

1. What is my exigence for writing about this topic?
2. What is my general position compared to the author's?
3. With which specific ideas do I agree or disagree?
4. Do the essays confirm what I think, or do they cause me to change my mind?
5. What original or related ideas are occurring to me as I read?
6. What original perspective can I take?
7. What type of claim do I want to make?
8. What can I quote, paraphrase, or summarize in my paper?

⇒ Section I ⇐

Issues Concerning Families, Marriages, and Relationships

THE ISSUES

A. WHAT IS THE STATUS OF THE TRADITIONAL AMERICAN FAMILY? HOW FAR ARE WE WILLING TO GO TO FIND ALTERNATIVES?

The traditional family is usually thought of as composed of two members of the opposite sex, the man acting as the breadwinner and the woman as the caretaker for the home and the children. The articles in this section offer a variety of ways to consider the traditional family, the institution of marriage supporting it, and the roles of mothers and fathers. All the authors agree that the family unit described above has changed considerably over time, and each advocates a different way of trying to make sense of the family unit in an increasingly complex society. As you read, you will need to think about the criteria that are necessary for a family to be effective. See also "Culture by the Campfire" (page 581) and "Bringing Up Adultolescents" (page 189).

B. WHAT ARE THE BENEFITS AND PITFALLS OF BEING MARRIED?

The three articles in this section consider the institution of marriage in terms of research that has taken place over the past forty years. Although it is generally agreed that couples benefit more from happy marriages than they do from remaining single, experts generally disagree on the value of divorce. You might want to consider the social implications of "no-fault" divorce laws as you read. James Q. Wilson opens this section by discussing the rise of the modern marriage along with the rise of modern divorce. Stephanie Coontz looks at some alternatives to traditional marriages, and Sylvia Ann Hewlett examines the modern marriage in the context of modern women's liberation. See also "Paying the Price of Female Neglect" (page 167) and "Why I Want a Wife" (page 58).

C. WHAT CREATES SUCCESSFUL RELATIONSHIPS? WHAT CAUSES THEM TO FAIL?

This section takes a close look at why relationships are successful and why they fail. Harville Hendrix discusses various psychological theories that explain why men and women are attracted to each other and suggests that once we understand why we are attracted to a certain person, we can set about having a healthy, productive relationship. Hewlett shows that while things have changed for women in the workplace, they have not necessarily changed at home. E. Mavis Hetherington offers an in-depth analysis of the complexity of marriage and divorce and warns policy makers that they need to understand the complexity of the issue before getting too involved with the business of marriage.

D. WEB SITES FOR FURTHER EXPLORATION AND RESEARCH

All Family Resources	http://www.familymanagement.com
American Psychological Association	http://helping.apa.org/family/index.html
Children and Family Research Center	http://cfrcwww.social.uiuc.edu
Focus on Family	http://www.family.org
Harvard Family Research Project	http://www.gse.harvard.edu/~hfrp/index.htm
The National Marriage Project	http://marriage.rutgers.edu/
The National Center for Fathering	http://www.fathers.com
The National Fatherhood Initiative	http://www.fatherhood.org
National Association of Mothers' Centers	http://www.motherscenter.org
Parent Stages	http://www.parentstages.com
Relationshipweb	http://www.relationshipweb.com

E. FILMS AND LITERATURE RELATED TO FAMILIES, MARRIAGES, AND RELATIONSHIPS

Films: *Disclosure*, 1996; *Annie Hall*, 1977; *The Birdcage*, 1996; *Guess Who's Coming to Dinner*, 1967; *When Harry Met Sally*, 1989; *Kramer vs. Kramer*, 1979; *The Champ*, 1979; *Mr. Mom*, 1983; *Mrs. Doubtfire*, 1993.

Literature: poem: "Myth" by Muriel Rukeyser; short story: "The Chrysanthemums" by John Steinbeck; plays: *A Doll's House* by Henrik Ibsen; *M. Butterfly* by David Henry Hwang; novel: *Persuasion* by Jane Austen; memoirs: *The Color of Water: A Black Man's Tribute to His White Mother* by James McBride.

THE RHETORICAL SITUATION

Marriage, the organization of families, and the nature and quality of the human relationships within them have always been a source of controversy. The world's religions, along with social customs and traditions, provide both the constraints and many of the warrants for the positions individuals take on issues associated with these topics. In this section, contemporary authors provide their perspectives not only on modern families but also on the institution of marriage itself and on the subject of relationships. They raise issues about the organization of families, including both traditional and alternative forms, and examine their relative effectiveness. They also look at the advantages and disadvantages of both marriage and divorce, including who is benefited or burdened by each. The final set of articles provides some perspectives on both successful and unsuccessful relationships.

Some people think that the women's movement in the second half of the twentieth century changed what women and men expect from each other in relationships, marriages, and families. Many women now choose to work first and have children later or not at all. Working women also expect men to do their share of the housework. The women's movement has provided new opportunities for women, but it has also been blamed for the high rates of divorce and troubled children.

Whatever the reason for the change in the modern family, one thing is certain—the institution of marriage is not what it used to be. According to figures from the 2000 census, only 52 percent of all householders in the United States are married, compared with 78 percent in 1950. The percentage of children living in two-parent households has also declined. In 1970, 90 percent of white children, 58 percent of black children, and 78 percent of Hispanic children lived in two-parent households. By 2000, those figures had declined to 74, 36, and 64 percent, respectively.

These figures and increasing divorce rates have had an impact on policy makers concerned about the dissolution of the family and the decline of social stability. Politicians on the left and the right are trying to cut the divorce rate and offer incentives for people to stay married. Should the government get involved with marriage promotion? The articles in this section will help you think of different ways of considering this question.

Marriage, family, and relationship issues touch everyone's life, so there is a constant exigency for these issues. Look at the best-seller list, or browse in the magazine section of a bookstore. What are some of the related issues on this subject? Which of them affect you? These issues are intensely personal, and you will probably want to consult your own experience as you read and write about them.

A. WHAT IS THE STATUS OF THE TRADITIONAL AMERICAN FAMILY? HOW FAR ARE WE WILLING TO GO TO FIND ALTERNATIVES?

QUESTIONS TO CONSIDER BEFORE YOU READ

Were your own family experiences mostly positive or mostly negative? Characterize them. Are you from, or do you know anyone who came from, a nontraditional family? What would you consider to be the difference between a nontraditional family and a dysfunctional family? Why is the difference important?

THE CHILDLESS REVOLUTION*

Madelyn Cain

Madelyn Cain teaches English at Mission College in Southern California. The following article is an excerpt from her book The Childless Revolution: What It Means to Be Childless Today. *In this piece, Cain argues against the negative stereotypes associated with an ever increasing number of women who choose to be childless.*

Utne Reader, July–August 2002, pp. 71–72.

1   When Katharine Hepburn chose childlessness in the 1940s, she claimed that "I was ambitious and knew I would not have children. I wanted total freedom." Her views were thought to be scandalous. But when Oprah Winfrey admitted in 1994 to *People* magazine that "what it takes one on one [to parent], I don't have," she was not pilloried but praised for understanding her own needs.

2   For a variety of reasons—including greater education for women, effective birth control, and later marriage—there has been a dramatic increase in the number of childless women over the past 30 years. According to the U.S. Census Bureau, in 1993 there were 34.9 million American families that were childless and only 33.3 million families with a child under the age of 18. Childlessness is about to come bursting out of the closet.

3   In interviewing more than a hundred childless women for my book *The Childless Revolution*, my goal was simply to put a face on childless women, not to make a major discovery about them. What I was not prepared for was uncovering a revolution in the making.

4   Childless women today are on the precipice of redefining womanhood in the most fundamental way ever. Entering the workforce was merely the initial step toward redefining women—and possibly the first toward childlessness. The advent of the pill, the legalization of abortion, and advanced education for women were essential adjuncts to this change. The move toward remaining childless, however, is more profound. For a society based on "family values," this shift is historic. At its most fundamental level, the emergence of childlessness means that women are seizing the opportunity to be fully realized, self-determined individuals—regardless of what society at large thinks of them.

5   Not all women without children actively choose the childless life, of course, but among those who have chosen it, I found three distinct groups: those who are positively childfree, those who are religiously childfree, and those who are environmentally childfree.

6   Women who are positively childfree rarely express even a flicker of doubt about their decision. They range from those who love other people's children to those who admit to actively disliking kids. The religiously childfree are those who have made a decision to follow a spiritual path that requires them to remain childless. Women who are environmentally childfree have made a conscious decision to forgo having children for the good of the planet.

7   Although 43 percent of the adult female population is childless, these women—and the option—are still treated as though they do not exist. Childless women permeate our world. They are our neighbors, our co-workers, our sisters, and our best friends. But because these women do not conform to traditional roles, their existence is denied. What little knowledge we do have of childless women is based on negative stereotypes, such as the child-hating workaholic.

8   We maintain this negative view of childlessness, I believe, because we know nothing about the positive side. It has never been extolled. It is considered "un-womanly" to admit to feeling happy and whole without children. Yet the childless women I interviewed spoke of many benefits: the latitude to develop their careers fully; the intimacy they share with their mates; the lack of financial, emotional,

and time pressures; the freedom from fear of being a bad mother or having a difficult child; the spiritual growth that takes place thanks to the availability of unfettered time; the relief of not having to raise a loved one in a world some view as too violent or selfish.

9   Childless women are often told they are selfish and destined for a dire future. Even perfect strangers may feel free to warn them about a lonely old age. It takes gargantuan strength to defend against this kind of pessimism, particularly since few of us are ever 100 percent certain about any decision we make in life. I was happy to pass along some good news to the women I interviewed. The inevitability of a lonely old age for the childless is refuted by every study ever done. In other words, as noted in a study published in the *Journal of Gerontology* (1998), there are "no significant differences in loneliness and depression between parents and childless adults."

10   There appears to be a generational gap with regard to women's feelings about their childlessness. Women in their 50s acknowledged a strong societal imperative toward having children, which in turn left them feeling inadequate because they had not. Women in their 40s had mixed reactions: Some felt that a societal expectation was placed on them, whereas others did not. Women under 35 did not feel this sense of obligation, having grown up in a society more open to allowing individuals to make their own choices. That has allowed younger, more liberated women to be comfortable with childlessness. The next generation could well be childless without reservations.

11   Childlessness is not just an American phenomenon. According to the United Nations, fertility rates in the following countries are currently below replacement level: the United States, Ireland, Norway, China, Australia, Denmark, the United Kingdom, France, Sweden, Belgium, Canada, Switzerland, Japan, Germany, Italy, and Spain.

12   While some commentators worry about the impact of childlessness on societies where a higher percentage of the population will be older, David Pearce Snyder, a renowned futurist and a contributing editor of *The Futurist* magazine, sees a positive side to the movement. Our reasons for having children have changed over time, he notes. Whereas in earlier days children were needed to support a family, social safety nets (such as Medicare and Social Security) have taken care of those needs. Therefore, we now have children out of desire, not necessity. Conversely, he says that those who do not want children should not have them: "People who do not have children because they are wise enough to say they will not be good parents are an indication of the maturing of our society." He feels certain that the entire society will benefit from this fundamental change. Snyder claims that the family is the most adaptive institution in society. He goes on to say that this new development toward childlessness gives us the opportunity to expand the extended family.

13   I too see the move toward thoughtful parenting and conscientious childlessness as positive. For years, couples who enjoyed parenthood were on the defensive if they produced more than the approved two children. Conversely, women who were childless were derided for not producing. How much healthier society would be if only those who really wanted children had them.

14   Our reluctance to approve of childlessness stems from ignorance, a case of not trusting, even fearing, what we've never experienced.

15   Doomsayers predicted terrible consequences when women entered the workforce, when divorce became more acceptable, when birth control became available. But for the most part, the consequences of liberation have been positive. More women than ever are choosing a life that does not conform to the old standard. The time has come to absorb into our consciousness a new version of femaleness, one that is predicated on the measure of a woman's character, not on the issue of her body. ◆◆

BUILDING A BETTER DAD*

Jerry Adler

Jerry Adler is a frequent writer for Newsweek *magazine.*

1   How do we assess a man's life? The late William S. Paley, founder and longtime chairman of CBS, devoted his life to the pursuit of wealth, power, fame and worldly pleasure—just like me, come to think of it, except he was very much luckier at it. But what I remember best about him is a telling remark in one of his many fulsome obituaries. Paley, said a friend, wasn't the kind of guy to attend his kids' Little League games, but when they needed him, he was there for them. And I thought, gee, how could one of the great visionaries of American industry be such a putz? Little League games are precisely when your kids need you the most. I accept that I will never own a Cézanne or sleep with a starlet, but nobody will say anything so dumb about me when I die, because *I've been to more goddam ball games in the past eight years than Cal Ripken Jr.*

2   Ha-ha. Just kidding, guys. I love Little League games, the earlier on Saturday morning the better. They remind me that it's always been hard to be a man. That was true even for my father, in the heyday of American malehood, the 1950s, when he would haul his weary suitbound hide off the bus every day at 6 P.M. and, responding to the invariable question, mutter, "Every day is hard when you're trying to make a living." By the standards then in effect, he was a model father, without once taking his kids backpacking, helping them sew costumes for their Kwanzaa pageant or making marinara sauce from scratch for their dinners. These are just a few of the ways in which men of my generation have redefined their roles beyond the business of making a living. Of course, most men still have to make a living, too, so in a single generation, fatherhood (like motherhood) has gotten twice as hard. I don't want to take anything away from Paley's achievements, but as far as I'm concerned, creating CBS would have been a more impressive feat if he'd done it while lugging his kids to the office in a Snugli.

*Newsweek, June 17, 1996, pp. 58–64.

3   Which he might actually do, if he were alive today. Men today "have permission to care for their children that they didn't have a generation ago," says Betty Thomson of the Center for Demography and Ecology at the University of Wisconsin. It's no coincidence that society gave men this permission just when they were needed to watch the kids so their wives could go to law school. By 1991, 20 percent of American fathers were taking care of young children in the home. (Two years later, as the economy improved, that proportion dropped to 16 percent.) But this cultural shift goes deeper than home economics. Baby boomers have transformed paternity, as they have every other institution they have touched, into an all-consuming vocation and never-ending quest for improvement and self-fulfillment. An outpouring of books, tapes, magazines and seminars—especially notable in the weeks leading up to Father's Day—both celebrates the pleasures of fatherhood and exhorts men to improve their performance in it.

◆◆◆◆

4   Executives [now] quit lucrative jobs to spend more time with their families, a phrase that used to mean "he couldn't find his way out of the men's room." Jeffrey E. Stiefler, the 49-year-old president of American Express, resigned last year to become a consultant and "watch his sons grow up." "How many presidents of Fortune 500 companies get to do that?" his former wife remarked in *The Wall Street Journal*. Bill Galston, President Clinton's domestic-policy adviser, quit to return to teaching after his 10-year-old son told him "baseball's not fun when there's no one there to applaud you." I say go for it, Bill—*and don't even think of bringing that laptop to the game Saturday.*

5   Just kidding, Bill; you wouldn't do that. You know that fathering today demands far more concentration and effort than it did when you were growing up in the 1950s, that discredited era of emotionally distant, conformist, workaholic dads. To an astonishing extent, today's fathers define themselves in opposition to the generation that raised them. There is "a substantial gulf between the boomer generation and their fathers," says Don Eberley of the National Fatherhood Initiative. "There is disappointment, a sense of loss, regret bordering on anger."

6   This, of course, was the seminal kvetch of the men's movement: the alienation of fathers from their families, dating from the Industrial Revolution, which separated the worlds of work and home. A son who feels let down by his father carries a lifelong grievance. How could he have been so blind, so indifferent to my needs, so absorbed in the stupid newspaper? At the age of 49, Robert Blumenfeld, a San Francisco businessman, recalls exactly how many times his father played ball with him (once) and what his father said when he graduated from high school *cum laude:* that some other 18-year-old had just signed with a baseball team for $100,000. Dan Koenigshofer, a 46-year-old engineer in Chapel Hill, N.C., "can't ever recall that my dad said he loved me" (although he's sure that he did love him, in his taciturn 1950s way). David Weinstein, a Harvard economist, even knows where his father was when he was born, 32 years ago. He was in his office. Back then, the next day was soon enough for a new father to visit his son; Weinstein's dad was presumably in no hurry to learn how to change a diaper, since most men in those years didn't expect they would ever need to know.

7   Something changed in the culture when these men grew up, and sociologists are still trying to figure out exactly what it was. Somehow, out of the poignancy

of memories such as these, men forged a determination to do better. There was new research: around 1980 psychologists discovered that attachment to the father—previously assumed to commence around the time a child began drawing a weekly allowance—actually forms at the same time as the maternal bond, six to eight months. Weinstein, taking no chances, made sure that he was the very first thing his son, Jeremy, saw when he poked his head into the world almost two years ago. But the most profound changes didn't grow out of a laboratory. Koenigshofer tells his kids—ages 4 and 1—he loves them "a dozen times a day." "You no longer see families where the dad says, upon finding that a kid has a dirty diaper, 'Go find your mother,'" says Michael Lamb, a psychologist at the National Institutes of Health and a leading authority on American family structure. "But it was universal 20 years ago." A *Newsweek* poll found that seven out of 10 American fathers spend more time with their children than their own fathers did; nearly half think they are doing a better job and only 3 percent think they're worse. What other area of American life has shown such improvement in just a generation?

8   Of course, *Newsweek* didn't poll the kids. Their wives, for what it's worth, tended to agree with them. But proving that men are actually being better fathers—as opposed to talking and writing books about it—is one of the great unsolved problems of contemporary sociology. "We all think there's been a change," says Thomson, "but I haven't seen any data that convinces me it's true." Part of the problem is that the same quest for self-realization that has led men to seek fulfillment in nurturing and sacrifice has also led them in increasing numbers to pursue their destiny with a sexy divorcée from their aerobics class. More than half of all American children born in the 1970s and 1980s are expected to spend part of their childhoods with just their mothers. A Census Bureau study found that 16.3 million American children were living with just a mother in 1994—and 40 percent of those hadn't seen their father in at least a year. It would take an awful lot of millionaire executives quitting the rat race to offset that statistic. "Men today are better fathers when they're around—and worse when they're not," says Andrew Cherlin, a Johns Hopkins sociologist who studies American families.

9   True, some studies have shown that fathers today are more involved with their children. But even those researchers admit that the demonstrable changes are small compared with what you'd expect from watching Donahue over the years. Studies of different nations show that American fathers are about average in parental involvement, spending on average 45 minutes a day caring for their children by themselves; American mothers, by the way, spend the most among women of any nation studied, more than 10 hours daily. (The least-involved fathers: Japanese, averaging three minutes a day.) "Women are still doing twice as much [child care] as men, although 20 years ago they were doing three times as much," says James A. Levine, director of the Fatherhood Project of the Families and Work Institute. "Progress has been slow, and it will continue to be slow."

10   Levine's assumption, clearly, is that it is desirable—for children, for society and for fathers themselves—for men to spend more time with their children. This seems obvious at first glance, although advocacy groups for fatherhood can also summon up reams of statistics to demonstrate it. "What reduces crime, child

poverty, teen pregnancy AND requires no new taxes?" asks a handout from the National Fatherhood Initiative. The answer, of course, is responsible fatherhood (although like many panaceas, this one is vulnerable to the counterexample: if fathers can prevent all these social ills, how has Japan escaped them?). This organization was founded in 1994 to "reinstate fatherhood as a national priority," and it focuses mostly on public-policy issues related to divorce, abandonment and unwed motherhood. Its materials are thick with sound-bite-size statistics asserting, for instance, that "Fatherless children are twice as likely to drop out of school" or that "Seventy percent of the juveniles in state reform institutions grew up in single- or no-parent institutions." The National Center for Fathering, by contrast, has a more evangelical approach, exhorting individual fathers to greater "commitment" and to enhancement of their fathering "skills." Levine's organization promotes the compatibility of family life and work for men who may still feel guilty about sneaking out on, say, a half-written magazine story on the remote chance that this will be the day someone hits a ball right to where their kids are standing in right field.

11   Most married parents would agree that one grown-up is not enough to raise a child, although if pressed they would probably admit that two grown-ups are not nearly enough either. But when sociologists began studying the long-term effects of fathers' involvement, they didn't find what they'd expected. A few studies, mostly with highly educated and motivated fathers who displayed a superhuman threshold of boredom, did indeed show a correspondence between the time fathers spent with their children and such desirable traits as "increased cognitive competence" and "a more internal locus of control." But in an influential review of the research Lamb concluded dolefully that in general "there is little evidence and no coherent reason to expect that increased paternal involvement in itself has any clear-cut or direct effects." *So tell your coach Daddy had to work really, really hard this week and he's too tired to pitch batting practice Saturday, OK?*

12   Just kidding. This is so counterintuitive, so potentially dangerous and subversive, that not even the experts want to believe it. Instead, they're trying to prove that what counts is the quality of the father's involvement. To do this requires a statistically useful standard for judging fathers. Lamb's collaborator, Joseph Pleck of the University of Illinois, describes "positive paternal involvement" as being "high in interaction, accessibility and responsibility, and within the engagement component, performing positive activities and possessing positive stylistic characteristics." Before you get too worked up about this discovery, though, Pleck cautions that "to date, no research has directly tested this perhaps obvious prediction."

13   There is, however, one undisputed benefit to "paternal involvement," according to psychologists: it's better for the fathers. The effects of taking care of one's children include enhanced self-esteem, increased marital happiness and the quality psychoanalyst Erik Erikson called "generativity," referring to the ability to sacrifice and take responsibility for others. There are other ways to achieve this, such as devoting one's life to the betterment of humanity. But fatherhood is by far the most common test of selflessness, and in some ways the most exacting.

14   That's right: all those high-powered executives who are dropping out so they never have to miss another Little League game are in for a shock: their new career requires just as much intensity, focus and mastery of technique as business or war. That is the message of Ken Canfield, an educator who founded the National Center for Fathering in 1990. "There are rising expectations for fathers," warns Canfield, whose column in *Today's Father* magazine is ominously titled "In the Trenches." In the 1950s, good fathers paid the bills and handed out discipline. Now, he says, "you have to be sensitive, you have to be emotionally involved, you have to forgo job advancement to be a good dad." Books like Canfield's *Seven Secrets of Effective Fathers* or *The Five Key Habits of Smart Dads,* by Paul Lewis, bring to bear on fatherhood the same management-by-objective insight that has inspired 10,000 business best sellers. ("Effective fathers have a task orientation toward fathering" . . . "Without some simple guidelines to help them win at being dads, most men lack the confidence that breeds success.") Other books focus on developing specific skills, like making a popping sound with your finger in your mouth. ("Keep your cheek taut and your forefinger stiff and hooked," advise John Boswell and Ron Barrett in *How to Dad.*) "Men want things summarized," says Canfield. "They want orientation. They want to know: 'What should I be doing?'"

15   And dads are doing it! Dads like Blumenfeld, who gets up every morning at 6:30 to make breakfast for his 13-year-old son, Bryan. Blumenfeld craftily sets the sports section next to Bryan's cereal bowl, and in that way, he says, "I guess I trick him into doing 20 more minutes of reading before school." How's that for task orientation? Or Robert Jones, a Birmingham, Ala., lawyer, who came into four tickets to a baseball game, and told his then 10-year-old son to invite two friends. When Jones got home, there were three friends instead of two, so Jones taught his son a lesson; he left him home and took the other boys to the game. That's how you win at being a dad—especially if, like Jones, you then demonstrate your sensitivity by getting all teary at the game and bringing everyone home after the first inning.

16   The analogy between fathering and managing a corporation breaks down, though, at one critical point. The return on investment is outside your control. The limits of possible success are set, more or less arbitrarily, at the moment of conception. You can do everything the books say and your kid still won't develop enough "increased cognitive competence" to get into Harvard.

17   And, naturally, you don't get paid for being a father—quite the contrary, as everyone knows—which explains the persistence of the myth that it's actually tremendous fun. There is a whole literature of fathers' lush, almost sensuous tributes to their own kids, the smell of their scalps after their baths, the secret pleasure of tiptoeing into their rooms to watch them sleep. People who have experienced only romantic love may find it hard to believe that the parental kind can turn one's brain to mush just as readily.

18   Boston TV producer Michael Greene likes to put some Aretha Franklin on the stereo, crank it up real high, and dance with his 5-year-old daughter, an experience that moves him to unparsable rhapsodies about "getting connected back to some basic essence of my life." Sitting quietly late at night with his infant son

dreamily gumming a bottle was "like falling in love again," says Weinstein. In "Father's Day: Notes from a New Dad in the Real World," Bill McCoy, an editor of *Parents* magazine, describes how during softball games his mind would wander to "the way my daughter pushes me over when I'm sitting cross-legged on the carpet, then tumbles into my arms as I fall." His solution was to give up softball. Art Perlman, a writer and lyricist who works from his New York apartment, looks after 6-year-old Jason while his wife puts in long days in her law office. Father and son fill their afternoons discussing topics Perlman lists as "colonial history, U.S. presidents, dinosaurs, space and science and animals in general." I don't think I'd given dinosaurs more than five minutes' thought in the year before my first son was born—and then, suddenly, my life opened up to a menagerie of fascinating, exotic creatures *that I wish had stayed buried for another 200 million years.*

19   Just kidding. I love dinosaurs, Barney especially. I don't want to sound like my own father, who frankly disdained them—a typical attitude of 1950s-era dads. Yet I detect a paradox in this frantic rejection of the values of the Eisenhower era. At the time, the postwar years in America were actually regarded as a remarkable experiment in family togetherness. Much of the iconography of American domestic life—the Saturday Little League games, the Sunday barbecues, the backyard birthday parties—dates from just that despised era. Parents, after all, moved to the suburbs for their children, not in order to work late at the office or eat out more often. And, as David Blankenhorn pointedly observes in *Fatherless America*, fathers of the 1950s overwhelmingly stayed married and supported their families with their paychecks—an example that seems lost on all too many of their offspring.

20   And for me, Lord, if I can do no more, at least help me do no less: to come home to my family each night, to take care of them to the best of my ability, to raise my children with the certainty that no matter how much they screw up the rest of their lives, one person loved them unconditionally. Like millions of other men, I have made my choice. We will never know what greatness might have lain within our reach, not to mention starlets. And we will find satisfaction in knowing we did what was right, *without expecting any gratitude for it.*

21   Just kidding. ◆◆

MARRIAGE AS WE SEE IT*

Chris Glaser

Chris Glaser is the author of Uncommon Calling: A Gay Christian's Struggle to Serve the Church. *He describes how exchanging vows with his partner in a church ceremony made him feel transformed.*

---

*Newsweek, September 16, 1996, p. 19.

1 Between my own Presbyterian church's vote rejecting ordination of gays and lesbians and the House vote against same-sex marriages, I feel beaten up. The one-two punch came early in July. Had I been the victim of a street gay-bashing, I would be able to seek comfort from my church and legal redress from the government. When the gay-bashers are my own church and government, I'm bewildered, wondering where to turn.

2 The two most sacred commitments in my life—my calling to the ministry and my same-gender marriage—are under attack because they are deemed threatening to a church and a society troubled by the lack of family cohesion, so-called "traditional family values." Our culture fails to see this as a largely heterosexual problem but instead scapegoats homosexuals, just as we who are gay and lesbian attempt to maintain relationships within our biological families and establish our own family units. Our birth families often come under attack for supporting us; our chosen families are refused recognition. Our families of faith treat us as society once treated illegitimate children. In the body politic, rights taken for granted by heterosexuals are called "special" when applied to us.

3 I've lived long enough in the gay movement to witness those who oppose us come full circle in their reasons that we should be outcasts from church and society. Twenty years ago, gay love was opposed because it supposedly didn't lead to long-term relationships and the rearing of children. Today gay love is attacked because gay people in committed relationships and gay couples with children are coming out. In the past, gays were denounced because we supposedly were "selfish" and "irresponsible." Now we're denounced if our selfless service—from the ministry to the military—is revealed. This damned-if-we-don't-and-damned-if-we-do syndrome should offer a clue to our opponents that their basis for being anti-gay is not reason.

4 From 1976 to 1978 I served on a national Presbyterian task force whose mandate was to lead our denomination in a study of homosexuality, particularly as it related to ordination. During one regional hearing, a minister testified that homosexuals shouldn't be ordained because we didn't form lasting relationships. Another pastor spoke proudly of leading a female couple in his church to see the "error" of their ways, thus breaking up their 20-year relationship. During these hearings, when anyone mentioned the possibility of sanctioning gay marriages, audible gasps came from the crowd. We could talk about gay ordination, but marriage was more sacrosanct!

5 In 1991 a Presbyterian committee on human sexuality endorsed a sexual ethic of "justice-love" for sexual relationships, including heterosexual marriage and homosexual unions. Fellow churchgoers went ballistic. To suggest that heterosexual marriage was not the bastion of all that is good and sacred about sexuality was too radical a concept for most of the church. The committee's report pointed out that heterosexual marriage as a holy paradigm had clay feet, mentioning the subjugation of women in most marriages, the problems of marital rape and parent-child incest, as well as adultery. The study also clearly affirmed gays and lesbians and our relationships. During the assembly that rejected the report, some opponents seemed to be saying to gay people, "We'll give you ordination—just give us back marriage."

6   Resistance to calling same-sex unions marriages is beyond my understanding. In no way does it lessen the sacred or civil nature of marriage. Indeed, its value is bolstered by the recognition that both homosexuals and heterosexuals wish to enter into such a covenant. Commonly, both procreation and companionship are viewed as independent satisfactory goals of marriage. Gay and lesbian couples enjoy companionship; some lesbians bear children; many lesbian and gay couples rear them.

7   It's true that the most ancient biblical sexual ethic is procreation-obsessed. That's why the Bible accepts practices we now find unacceptable, such as polygamy, concubinage and required sexual intercourse with the childless wife of a dead brother. It is also true that Jesus, the source of Christianity, saw fidelity, not gender, as the central issue in marriage and redefined family as fellow believers rather than blood relatives. Until a few centuries ago in Western culture, marriage was primarily an economic institution that ensured inheritance rights, protected political arrangements and produced offspring. Only relatively recently did the ideal of romantic love supplant these reasons. That change redefined marriage far more dramatically than will the inclusion of same-gender couples under the rubric.

8   When my partner's and my relationship was blessed two years ago by our Presbyterian church in Atlanta, I felt transformed by our exchange of vows before God and a supportive community of family, friends and church members. I felt even more tenderly toward my partner and I understood more profoundly the sacred nature of our commitment. But when the local newspaper ran a notice of our ceremony, other Presbyterians demanded that our pastor be reprimanded and our blessing "undone."

9   Another male couple attending the ceremony expressed regret that they had never had such a ceremony. Less than two weeks later, one was killed in a traffic accident. Because most members of their congregation were unaware of the significance of their relationship, the surviving partner did not receive the support that might have otherwise been offered by fellow churchgoers.

10   Even as the position on anti-gay ordination goes to presbyteries for ratification and the marriage bill is taken up by the Senate, I'm grateful to know that if something were to happen to me or my partner, our congregation, family and neighborhood would be there for us, caring for us in trouble, challenging us to keep faith in God and one another. I grieve that the same cannot be said of all congregations, families and communities throughout this land. ◆◆

B. WHAT ARE THE BENEFITS AND PITFALLS OF BEING MARRIED?

QUESTIONS TO CONSIDER BEFORE YOU READ

Do you know anyone who comes from a divorced family or has been divorced? How do you think men and women are usually affected after getting divorced? Who seems to be affected more, men or women? Why? Do you think men or women benefit more from being married? Why?

THE MARRIAGE PROBLEM:
HOW OUR CULTURE HAS WEAKENED FAMILIES*

James Q. Wilson

James Q. Wilson is a professor of government at Harvard University and the author of several books, including The Moral Sense. *The following essay is excerpted from chapter 4 of* The Marriage Problem, *titled "The Rise of the Modern Marriage." In this chapter Wilson argues that the strength and endurance of marriage in the United States has decreased because American culture values the individual more than it values social cohesion and stability.*

1   A common view of families is that once upon a time marriages were arranged by parents who decided what boy should marry what girl. Though the contemporary mind usually finds such arrangements distasteful, at least they produced large, extended families in which many grandparents, aunts, and uncles lived under one roof with the married couple so that every person could help care for everyone else. Romance and love were less important then, but those days are now gone. Now men and women marry out of romantic attachment and, for better or worse, live in small, nuclear families. Such families are nice, but some of us miss the old days of extended families and the social support they provided.

2   Unfortunately, every one of these views is either wrong or seriously misleading. In the West, and especially in England and the lands settled by English people, marriages, except among the aristocrats, were usually not arranged since at least the thirteenth century. Men and women have for hundreds of years chosen for themselves whom to marry or at least with whom to live, since a formal marriage was sometimes ignored. In much of medieval England, no public ceremony was required to make a marriage valid, and so a lot of these unions were conducted privately, at home, before few or even no witnesses, and sometimes done in bed, a garden, a tavern, or a field. Many of these unions were later solemnized in a church, but many were not.[1] And these families—the ones that first settled this country—were nuclear from the beginning. Occasionally, of course, several generations of relatives might live with the husband and wife, but scholars have learned that for many centuries the average size of a household changed only slightly, if at all. In family size and personal consent, Western families today are pretty much what they have been for centuries.

3   It is remarkable that this family system should be so old. Considering how much is often at stake, letting people decide for themselves whom to marry needs to be explained. How can property be managed and the elderly cared for if we let a couple of young people decide for themselves, and sometimes only after the girl has gotten pregnant, that they would live together in their own home? The farm might be neglected, the children badly raised, and their parents ignored when they needed help.

---

*James Q. Wilson, *The Marriage Problem: How Our Culture Has Weakened Families* (New York: HarperCollins, 2002), pp. 65–67, 69, 99–100, 101–102, 103–105.

4   Since the beginning of history, a marriage has always meant more than merely a lasting sexual union confirmed by some social custom or religious liturgy. Marriages involved more than sex; they involved the identity and custody of children, the management and often the ownership of property, and the history of one or more families that extended through the generations, an enduring legacy of social identity and personal history that implied status, obligations, and expectations. The family is not only a universal practice, it is the fundamental social unit of any society, and on its foundation there is erected the essential structure of social order—who can be preferred to whom, who must care for whom, who can exchange what with whom. The family not only created the basis for this vast array of social habits, it has also been the arena in which children learn how to act in the larger world. Surely one would expect that creating a family, with so vast an array of social roles, would rarely, if ever, be left merely to the romantic passions of two young people.

5   The Chinese have long thought that filial piety requires that no one acting alone can arrange his or her marriage. Instead, the family must do this. Edward Westermarck has summarized this and countless other examples of parent-arranged marriages.[2] Among the ancient Hebrews the father had the absolute right to give his daughters in marriage and to choose wives for his sons, a right that forms an important part of the motion picture *Fiddler on the Roof.* The ancient Romans made the wife as well as all the children the personal property of the husband, and his consent was essential to his children's marriage. Few other civilizations gave to the father the absolute authority conferred by Roman law, but ancient Greek fathers could give their daughters in marriage to a man she might not know, and the authority of Hindu fathers has always been very strong. In contemporary India, though the opinions of the man and woman are sometimes consulted, most marriages are arranged. These unions usually lead to affection between husband and wife, but many Indians assume that this fondness will be the result and not the precondition of marriage.[3] For many centuries in Eastern Europe and elsewhere, land was owned by clans—that is, by extended families—and it was hard for marriage to occur except by the consent of the elders.

6   In addition to these European and Asian examples, there have been very different kinds of family life found in much of Africa. In Europe monogamy was almost always the ideal, a new family required property, brides were accompanied by dowries paid to their husbands, and concubines were common. By contrast, in much of Africa polygyny was frequent, a new family might require cattle but rarely property, husbands paid bridewealth to their brides' families, and concubines were rare.

◆◆◆◆

PROPERTY AND MARRIAGE

7   When a man and a woman acting alone can choose to marry, we have a modern marriage market. This market seems to have arisen in England and parts of northern Europe many centuries ago for reasons that are not altogether clear. To understand marriages today, we must first understand the long history that has produced them. If we think that today's marriage problems are merely the result

of that all-powerful secular deity, "the sixties," we will not understand why so many nations do not have these problems even though youthful emancipation and the rise of individual self-expression have affected people everywhere.

8   For most of its history, marriage has not been simply about sex or reproduction, it has been about property. People live on land; they inherit land; they buy, sell, and bequeath land; and they have a stake in trades, licenses, economic activities, and other forms of personal property. In many cultures, valuable land is in short supply, and so rules must be designed to manage access to it. The best account of how property rules affect marriage has been given by Alan Macfarlane.[4]

9   There are chiefly two ways of managing land. The first is for a group—a clan, tribe, or a family—to own it and decide who would use it. The second is for an individual—a person or a married couple—to own and work it. I shall call the first method group control and the second individual control. Group control is characteristic of peasant societies. A plot of land has no individual owner; it is managed by a group, usually consisting of an extended family. One man might take the lead in this management, but he would not own the property or be able to sell it. Only the household, and through it a larger clan, could do this.

◆◆◆◆

10   In the fifteen years that began in 1965, family life and the laws that govern it underwent a remarkable transformation. For a billion or so people in the industrialized nations, divorces and the birth of out-of-wedlock children rose sharply. These changes, as one scholar pointed out, are unique in family history: they were sharp, immediate, and affected virtually every industrialized nation all at once.[5]

11   Sweeping new divorce laws were passed in England in 1969, Sweden in 1973, France in 1975, West Germany in 1976, and by almost all American states between 1969 and 1985. As Mary Ann Glendon at Harvard has pointed out, not long before these laws were passed, a marriage could only be ended for one of a few serious causes; after they were passed, marriage was more or less terminable at will.[6] The laws of these and other industrialized nations differed in details and implementation, but a fair generalization is that today any married couple that agrees it wishes a divorce can get one. Under no-fault laws, divorce has been essentially deregulated. Even in England, where there has been some effort to maintain a theory of blame, an uncontested divorce is granted, and most divorces are uncontested. It is often not even necessary to confront a judge. In one study, uncontested divorces took an average of less than five minutes.[7] In France there are several constraints, including a waiting period, so that the system, though it makes divorce easily available, does not quite grant it simply on demand. West Germany adopted a more liberal approach so that uncontested divorces are quickly granted. Sweden, needless to say, went the furthest. It replaced its old view that divorce should only be allowed after adultery or desertion with one that eliminates all reference to fault or reasons; divorce is granted on request. In adopting its new procedures, Swedish officials made it clear that in their view all laws bearing on couples should be written so as not to give marriage any advantage over cohabitation. As one said, a legal marriage should simply be "a form of voluntary cohabitation between independent persons."[8] By 1987 eighteen

American states had adopted no-fault as the sole basis for divorce; by 1996 almost every other state had added no-fault to existing grievances.[9] Given these changes, it is today the case that for any adult couple, both marriage and divorce are readily available. Easy in, easy out.

◆◆◆◆

12   In Carl Schneider's view, family law in the West has pretty much abandoned the moral basis on which it once rested. That basis was powerfully reinforced in the nineteenth century, when English and American statutes were written that regularized how families were to be formed and on what terms they could be ended. Laws were written governing how marriages were arranged and divorces obtained, what alimony would be owed to whom and for how long, how property was to be divided and who was to have custody of children, the bans on adultery and cohabitation, how adoptions could be arranged, and the circumstances, if any, when contraception and abortions might occur.[10] These laws rested on the moral argument that the family was vital, a decisive determinant of the character and social status of the spouses and their children, and an essential element of any organized society.[11]

13   Leading figures in England and America at the end of the nineteenth century spoke of marriage as a "state of existence ordained by the Creator," a "consummation of the Divine command to multiply and replenish the earth," "the highest state of existence," and "the only stable substructure of social, civil, and religious institutions." Each marriage, many said, affects not only the spouses, but all other persons. The Supreme Court described marriage as more than a "mere contract"; it was instead "a sacred obligation," "a holy estate," and "the foundation of the family and society, without which there would be neither civilization nor progress."[12]

14   And in the family the father was the leader. One might quarrel with some of these views, especially the patriarchal one, but what is most important is not whether the views were in each case correct but that they rested on a claim that the family, and marriage in particular, were not simply negotiable contracts but were moral statements about how a good life would be lived.

15   A century later, virtually every one of these laws has been changed, some for the better, some for the worse, but everywhere in ways that denied that marriage and the family had any moral status. Cohabitation and fornication are no longer crimes, divorce can be arranged without anyone proving that the partner was at fault, child custody shall be decided without regard to "the conduct of a proposed custodian that does not affect his relationship to the child,"[13] contraception and abortion are both legal, and (in many places) an "implied contract" discerned by a court will govern the allocation of property at the end of cohabitation. The Supreme Court put the matter bluntly in a decision upholding the right of people to buy contraceptive devices: "The marital couple is not an independent entity . . . but an association of two individuals each with a separate intellectual and emotional makeup. If the right of privacy means anything, it is the right of the *individual,* married or single, to be free from unwanted government intrusion. . . ."[14]

16   These changes in family law are fully in accord with the rise of a modern, secular, individualistic state. No one should be surprised that a freely choosing individual should be the centerpiece of family law any more than we would be surprised that such a person is the centerpiece of civil rights or contract law. The rise of the modern marriage market was part of a broad transformation in Western culture from one of ascribed status to one of personal choice. At one time, an individual belonged to a family; today, the family belongs to the individual.[15] At one time, the law was concerned about how families were formed and how long they lasted but little concerned with what happened inside the family. Today the law is much less concerned with how a family is formed or how long it lasts but greatly concerned with what happens inside it. That new concern, expressed by legal inquiries into the possibility of marital rape or the abuse of a spouse or a child, takes with utmost seriousness the experiences of an individual while giving much less attention to the strength of the union.

◆◆◆◆

17   What is striking is not that there are so many divorces and so many cohabiting couples, but that there are any marriages at all. How can one explain marriage, which taken literally is a solemn and public promise to live together forever, forsaking all others, and to do so in sickness and in health? Simply living together provides the immediate benefits without any legal formalities. Why promise to live together forever instead of promising to live together so long as I find it pleasurable? Why forsake all others instead of forsaking others until someone richer or more beautiful comes along? Why get married if with abortion and the birth-control pill one can avoid having children? Why not just live together for as long as it is enjoyable? Of course cohabitation provides *only* the immediate benefits; it rarely provides what so many men and women in time discover they need—care and companionship over the long term, a term that is getting longer with every improvement in medicine but one that for any cohabiting couple can quickly be interrupted when one partner decides to walk away and find what they imagine is true happiness with someone else.

18   It is in a way astonishing that people get married at all. How can we explain it? (In Sweden no explanation is necessary, since marriage is rapidly being replaced by cohabitation.) The answer seems to be some combination of love, a desire for children, a hope for long-term companionship, and the expectations of family and friends. But since love is universal, all that can explain differences over time or across cultures is a desire for children, companionship, and cultural expectations. And everywhere cultural expectations are vulnerable to the new individualistic ethos, as we can see with rising levels of cohabitation. Which leaves a desire for children and companionship. And that, I suspect, is where matters now stand. Some people can see far enough into the future to recognize that marriage offers long-term benefits. For them marriage will be preferable. But many people do not see very far into the future, and for them cultural pressures are important. And those pressures are declining.

19   But marriage lingers on. Some 90 percent of the American people get married by the time they die. Among women who married between 1940 and 1959, nearly two-thirds were still living in that first marriage.[16] Among men and

women who are fifty-five years of age or older, fewer than 5 percent have never been married. The majority of children are raised by two parents. Marriage survives despite the absence of many sexual or economic reasons for it. Men and women will make public pledges of loyalty to one another even when both the man and the woman can buy sex on the marketplace and when women can use birth control or abortion to eliminate the chances of unwanted children and take advantage of educational opportunities and an open job market to make their own careers. Despite the apparent advantages of the single life, the desire for children and companionship is not a weak force among humans. This desire is found in most people, perhaps because human experience over the millennia have made such feelings a deep part of human emotions. Evolution has selected for sentiments that encourage marriage but not for those that require it.

20   Evolution does not make marriage universal. Its existence depends in part on a changing culture. The argument of this chapter implies that the greatest familial problems would exist in countries where the culture has most fully embraced the Enlightenment ideal. The cultural expectation of an enduring marriage would be weakest where the emancipation of the individual has been the strongest. This suggests that high levels of cohabitation, divorce, and children born out of wedlock would be most common in England, the countries founded by England, and much of northwestern Europe, and that, I think, is pretty much what we find. These circumstances exist most dramatically in the United States, the United Kingdom, Canada, Australia, New Zealand, Denmark, and Sweden but are much less true in China, Indonesia, Italy, Japan, Spain, and Taiwan and least of all in countries where clan power remains strong, as in much of the Middle East.[17]

21   People everywhere enter families, but the strength and endurance of what they have entered depends crucially on culture. In the West, that culture has changed, slowly at some times (as in the eighteenth and nineteenth centuries), rapidly at others (as in the 1920s and the 1960s). Those who are dismayed by what has happened must wonder whether those changes can be altered. We shall see. ◆◆

NOTES

1. R. H. Helmholz, *Marriage Litigation in Medieval England* (Cambridge: Cambridge University Press, 1974), 27–31.
2. Edward Westermarck, *Marriage* (New York: Jonathan Cape, 1929), 48–54.
3. Giri Raj Gupta, "Love, Arranged Marriage and the Indian Social Structure," in *Cross-Cultural Perspectives of Mate-Selection and Marriage,* ed. George Kurian (Westport, Conn.: Greenwood Press, 1979).
4. Alan Macfarlane, *The Origins of English Individualism* (New York: Cambridge University Press, 1978); and Macfarlane, *Marriage and Love in England* (London: Basil Blackwell, 1986).
5. Louis Roussel, quoted in Mary Ann Glendon, *The Transformation of Family Law* (Chicago: University of Chicago Press, 1989), 144.
6. Glendon, 149.
7. Ibid., 156.

8. Ibid., 274.
9. Linda D. Elrod and Robert G. Spector, "A Review of the Year in Family Law," *Family Law Quarterly* 29 (1996): 773.
10. Carl E. Schneider, "Moral Discourse and the Transformation of American Family Law," *Michigan Law Review* 83 (1985): 1805, 1820.
11. Glendon, 291–92.
12. These phrases are quoted in Witte, 194.
13. Schneider, 1811, quoting the Uniform Marriage and Divorce Act.
14. *Eisenstadt* v. *Baird* 405 U.S. 438 (1972).
15. Glendon, 292, quoting Alain Benabent.
16. Bureau of the Census, *Current Population Survey of Fertility and Marital History Supplement, 1995*. The data were compiled for me from this source by Melissa Knauer.
17. On divorce, see the tables in William J. Goode, *World Changes in Divorce Patterns* (New Haven: Yale University Press, 1993).

THE FUTURE OF MARRIAGE*

Stephanie Coontz

Stephanie Coontz is a historian and writer. She has appeared on several television panels to discuss family issues.

1   Most Americans support the emergence of alternative ways of organizing parenthood and marriage. They don't want to reestablish the supremacy of the male breadwinner model or to define masculine and feminine roles in any monolithic way. Many people worry, however, about the growth of alternatives to marriage itself. They fear that in some of today's new families parents may not be devoting enough time and resources to their children. The rise of divorce and unwed motherhood is particularly worrisome, because people correctly recognize that children need more than one adult involved in their lives.

2   As a result, many people who object to the "modified male breadwinner" program of the "new consensus" crusaders are still willing to sign on to the other general goals of that movement: "to increase the proportion of children who grow up with two married parents," to "reclaim the ideal of marital permanence," to keep men "involved in family life," and to establish the principle "that every child deserves a father."[1]

3   Who could disagree? When we appear on panels together, leaders of "traditional values" groups often ask me if I accept the notion that, on the whole, two parents are better than one. If they would add an adjective such as two *good*

*Stephanie Coontz, *The Way We Really Are: Coming to Terms with America's Changing Families* (New York: Basic Books, 1997), pp. 77–80, 93–95, 196–197, 201.

parents, or even two *adequate* ones, I'd certainly agree. And of course it's better to try to make a marriage work than to walk away at the first sign of trouble.

4   As a historian, however, I've learned that when truisms are touted as stunning new research, when aphorisms everyone agrees with are presented as a courageous political program, and when exceptions or complications are ignored for the sake of establishing the basic principles, it's worth taking a close look for a hidden agenda behind the clichés. And, in fact, the new consensus crowd's program for supporting the two-parent family turns out to be far more radical than the feel-good slogans might lead you to believe.

5   Members of groups such as the Council on Families in America claim they are simply expressing a new consensus when they talk about "reinstitutionalizing enduring marriage," but in the very next breath they declare that it "is time to raise the stakes." They want nothing less than to make lifelong marriage the "primary institutional expression of commitment and obligation to others," the main mechanism for regulating sexuality, male-female relations, economic redistribution, and child rearing. Charles Murray says that the goal is "restoration of marriage as an utterly distinct, legal relationship." Since marriage must be "privileged," other family forms or child-rearing arrangements should not receive tax breaks, insurance benefits, or access to public housing and federal programs. Any reform that would make it easier for divorced parents, singles, unmarried partners, or stepfamilies to function is suspect because it removes "incentives" for people to get and stay married. Thus, these groups argue, adoption and foster care policies should "reinforce marriage as the child-rearing norm." Married couples, and only married couples, should be given special tax relief to raise their children. Some leaders of the Institute for American Values propose that we encourage both private parties and government bodies "to distinguish between married and unmarried *couples* in housing, credit, zoning, and other areas." Divorce and illegitimacy should be stigmatized.[2]

6   We've come quite a way from the original innocuous statements about the value of two-parent families and the importance of fathers to children. Now we find out that we must make marriage the only socially sanctioned method for organizing male-female roles and fulfilling adult obligations to the young. "There is no realistic alternative to the one we propose," claims the Council on Families in America. To assess this claim, we need to take a close look at what the consensus crusaders mean when they talk about the need to reverse the "deinstitutionalizing" of marriage.[3]

7   Normally, social scientists have something very specific in mind when they say that a custom or behavior is "institutionalized." They mean it comes "with a well-understood set of obligations and rights," all of which are backed up by law, customs, rituals, and social expectations. In this sense, marriage is still one of America's most important and valued institutions.[4]

8   But it is true that marriage has lost its former monopoly over the organization of people's major life transitions. Alongside a continuing commitment to marriage, other arrangements for regulating sexual behavior, channeling relations between men and women, and raising children now exist. Marriage was once the primary way of organizing work along lines of age and sex. It determined the

roles that men and women played at home and in public. It was the main vehicle for redistributing resources to old and young, and it served as the most important marker of adulthood and respectable status.

9   All this is no longer the case. Marriage has become an option rather than a necessity for men and women, even during the child-raising years. Today only half of American children live in nuclear families with both biological parents present. One child in five lives in a stepfamily and one in four lives in a "single-parent" home. The number of single parents increased from 3.8 million in 1970 to 6.9 million in 1980, a rate that averages out to a truly unprecedented 6 percent increase each year. In the 1980s, the rate of increase slowed and from 1990 to 1995 it leveled off, but the total numbers have continued to mount, reaching 12.2 million by 1996.[5]

10   These figures understate how many children actually have two parents in the home, because they confuse marital status with living arrangements. Approximately a quarter of all births to unmarried mothers occur in households where the father is present, so those children have two parents at home in fact if not in law. Focusing solely on the marriage license distorts our understanding of trends in children's living arrangements. For example, the rise in cohabitation between 1970 and 1984 led to more children being classified as living in single-parent families. But when researchers counted unmarried couples living together as two-parent families, they found that children were spending *more* time, not less, with both parents in 1984 than in 1970. Still, this simply confirms the fact that formal marriage no longer organizes as many life decisions and transitions as it did in the past.[6]

11   Divorce, cohabitation, remarriage, and single motherhood are not the only factors responsible for the eclipse of marriage as the primary institution for organizing sex roles and interpersonal obligations in America today. More people are living on their own before marriage, so that more young adults live outside a family environment than in earlier times. And the dramatic extension of life spans means that more people live alone after the death of a spouse.[7]

12   The growing number of people living on their own ensures that there are proportionately fewer families of *any* kind than there used to be. The Census Bureau defines families as residences with more than one householder related by blood, marriage, or adoption. In 1940, under this definition, families accounted for 90 percent of all households in the country. By 1970, they represented just 81 percent of all households, and by 1990 they represented 71 percent. The relative weight of marriage in society has decreased. Social institutions and values have adapted to the needs, buying decisions, and lifestyle choices of singles. Arrangements other than nuclear family transactions have developed to meet people's economic and interpersonal needs. Elders, for example, increasingly depend on Social Security and private pension plans, rather than the family, for their care.[8]

13   Part of the deinstitutionalization of marriage, then, comes from factors that few people would want to change even if they could. Who wants to shorten the life spans of the elderly, even though that means many more people are living outside the institution of marriage than formerly? Should we lower the age of

marriage, even though marrying young makes people more likely to divorce?[9] Or should young people be forced to live at home until they do marry? Do we really want to try to make marriage, once again, the only path for living a productive and fulfilling adult life?

◆◆◆◆

REALITY BITES

14 It makes little sense to whip up hysteria about an issue if you don't have any concrete solutions. Yet for people who believe we're on the verge of "cultural suicide," the measures proposed by the family values crusaders are curiously halfhearted. Amitai Etzioni urges individuals to make "supervows," voluntary premarriage contracts indicating "that they take their marriage more seriously than the law requires." One of the few concrete reforms David Blankenhorn proposes to ensure "a father for every child" is that we forbid unmarried women access to sperm banks and artificial insemination. In addition, he asks men to take pledges that "marriage is the pathway to effective fatherhood," wants the president to issue an annual report on the "state of fatherhood," and thinks Congress should designate "Safe Zones" for male responsibility. Can anyone who looks at the historical trends in divorce, unwed motherhood, and reproductive technology seriously think such measures will bring back the married-couple–biological-parent monopoly over child rearing?[10]

15 Barbara Dafoe Whitehead of the Institute for American Values advocates "restigmatization" of divorce and unwed motherhood; "stigmatization," she argues, "is a powerful means of regulating behavior, as any smoker or overeater will testify." But while overeaters may now feel "a stronger sense of shame than in the past," this has hardly wiped out the problem of obesity. Indeed, the proportion of overweight Americans has increased steadily since the 1950s. As for curbing smoking, the progress here has come from stringent public regulations against smoking, combined with intensive (and expensive) interventions to help people quit. The pretended "consensus" of the new family values crusaders would quickly evaporate if they attempted to institute an equally severe campaign against single parents. After all, 90 percent of the people in a 1995 Harris poll believe society "should value all types of families."[11]

16 Besides, stigmatization is a blunt instrument that does not distinguish between the innocent and the guilty any better than no-fault divorce. Dan Quayle's latest book, for example, includes a divorced family among five examples he gives of the "strong" families that still exist in America. He puts a divorced single mother into a book intended to prove that "intact" families are ideal because, "Though Kathy experienced divorce, she did not foresee or want it." It was not this woman's intent, Quayle explains, to pursue "a fast-track career." She "expected to play the traditional role, to raise her children and create a home for a husband of whom she was proud." Such distinctions put the consensus brokers in the tricky business of examining people's motives to decide which divorced or single parents had good intentions and therefore should be exempt from stigmatization.[12]

17   It would be easy to dismiss the flimsy reforms proposed by the "new consensus" proponents as fuzzy-headed wishful thinking were it not for the fact that their approach opens such a dangerous gap between practice and theory. At best, affirming lifelong marriage as a principle while issuing exceptions for people whose *intentions* were good encourages a hypocrisy that is already far too common in today's political and cultural debates. Consider Congressman Newt Gingrich, who was born into a single-parent family, made his ex-wife a single mom by divorcing her, and has a half-sister who is gay. "I'm not sitting here as someone who is unfamiliar with the late twentieth century," he has said. "I know life can be complicated." Yet that didn't stop him from blaming Susan Smith's murder of her two children in 1994 on lack of family values—though he considered it irrelevant that the stepfather who abused her was a member of the Christian Coalition.[13]

18   At worst, this approach offers right-wing extremists moderate-sounding cover for attempts to penalize or coerce families and individuals that such groups find offensive. Insisting that everyone give lip service to lifelong marriage as an ideal while recognizing in practice that life is complicated is like having a law on the books that *everyone* breaks at one time or another. Authorities can use it selectively to discipline the poor, the powerless, or the unpopular, while letting everyone else off the hook.

19   The family values crusade may sound appealing in the abstract. But it offers families no constructive way to resolve the new dilemmas of family life. Forbidding unmarried women access to sperm banks, for instance, is hardly going to put the package of child rearing and marriage back together. It would take a lot more repression than that to reinstitutionalize lifelong marriage in today's society.

20   As Katha Pollitt argues, "we'd have to bring back the whole nineteenth century: Restore the cult of virginity and the double standard, ban birth control, restrict divorce, kick women out of decent jobs, force unwed pregnant women to put their babies up for adoption on pain of social death, make out-of-wedlock children legal nonpersons. That's not going to happen."[14] If it did happen, American families would be worse off, not better, than they are right now. ◆◆

NOTES

1. "Marriage in America: A Report to the Nation," Council on Families in America, New York, N.Y., March 1995, pp. 10–11, 13.
2. David Popenoe, "Modern Marriage: Revising the Cultural Script," in David Popenoe, Jean Bethke Elshtain, and David Blankenhorn, eds., *Promises to Keep: Decline and Renewal of Marriage in America* (Lanham, Md.: Rowman and Littlefield, 1996), p. 254; "Marriage in America," p. 4; David Popenoe, *Life Without Father: Compelling New Evidence That Fatherhood and Marriage Are Indispensable for the Good of Children and Society* (New York: The Free Press, 1996), p. 222; David Blankenhorn, *Fatherless America: Confronting Our Most Urgent Social Problem* (New York: Basic Books, 1995), p. 229; Charles Murray, "Keep It in the Family," *Times of London,*

November 14, 1993; Maggie Gallagher, *The Abolition of Marriage: How We Destroy Lasting Love* (Washington, D.C.: Regnery Publishing, 1996), pp. 250–257; Barbara Dafoe Whitehead, "Dan Quayle Was Right," *Atlantic Monthly* 271 (April 1993), p. 49.

3. "Marriage in America," p. 4. The "deinstitutionalizing" phrase comes from Blankenhorn, *Fatherless America,* p. 224.

4. William Goode, *World Changes in Divorce Patterns* (New Haven, Conn.: Yale University Press, 1993), p. 330.

5. On the leveling off of family change, see Peter Kilborn, "Shifts in Families Reach a Plateau," *New York Times,* November 27, 1996. Other information in this and the following three paragraphs, unless otherwise noted, come from Steven Rawlings and Arlene Saluter, *Household and Family Characteristics: March 1994,* Current Population Reports Series P20–483 (Washington, D.C.: Bureau of the Census, U.S. Department of Commerce, September 1995), pp. xvii–ix; Michael Haines, "Long-Term Marriage Patterns in the United States from Colonial Times to the Present," *History of the Family* 1 (1996); Arthur Norton and Louisa Miller, *Marriage, Divorce, and Remarriage in the 1990s*, Current Population Reports Series P23–180 (Washington, D.C.: Bureau of the Census, October 1992); Richard Gelles, *Contemporary Families: A Sociological View* (Thousand Oaks, Calif.: Sage, 1995), pp. 116–120, 176; Shirley Zimmerman, "Family Trends: What Implications for Family Policy?" *Family Relations* 41 (1992), p. 424; Margaret Usdansky, "Single Motherhood: Stereotypes vs. Statistics," *New York Times,* February 11, 1996, p. 4; *New York Times,* August 30, 1994, p. A9; *New York Times,* March 10, 1996, p. A11, and March 17, 1996, p. A8; U.S. Bureau of the Census, *Statistical Abstracts of the United States* (Washington, D.C., 1992); McLanahan and Casper, "Growing Diversity and Inequality in the American Family," in Reynolds Farley, ed., *State of the Union: America in the 1990s,* vol. 1 (New York: Russell Sage, 1995).

6. Larry Bumpass, "Patterns, Causes, and Consequences of Out-of-Wedlock Childbearing; What Can Government Do?" *Focus* 17 (University of Wisconsin–Madison Institute for Research on Poverty, 1995), p. 42; Larry Bumpass and R. Kelly Raley, "Redefining Single-Parent Families: Cohabitation and Changing Family Reality," *Demography* 32 (1995); p. 98.

7. *Olympian,* February 26, 1996, p. D6.

8. Susan Watkins, Jane Menken, and John Bongaarts, "Demographic Foundations of Family Change," *American Sociological Review* 52 (1987), pp. 346–358.

9. Barbara Wilson and Sally Clarke, "Remarriages: A Demographic Profile," *Journal of Family Issues* 13 (1992).

10. Ruth Shalit, "Family Mongers," *New Republic,* August 16, 1993, p. 13; Popenoe, *Life Without Father,* p. 194; David Popenoe, "American Family Decline, 1960–1990," *Journal of Marriage and the Family* 55 (1993), p. 539; Blankenhorn, *Fatherless America,* pp. 220–233; and quoted in *Newsweek,* February 6, 1995, p. 43; "Marriage in America," p. 4.

11. Whitehead, "Dan Quayle Was Right," p. 49; Carole Sugarman, "Jack Sprat Should Eat Some Fat," *Washington Post National Weekly Edition,* May 2–8, 1994; *Olympian,* February 5, 1996, p. A8; Janet Giele, "Decline of the Family: Conservative, Liberal, and Feminist Views," in Popenoe, Elshtain, and Blankenhorn, *Promises to Keep,* p. 104.

12. Dan Quayle and Diane Medved, *The American Family: Discovering the Values That Make Us Strong* (New York: HarperCollins, 1996), pp. 2, 87, 114.

13. Katharine Seelye, "The Complications and Ideals," *New York Times,* November 24, 1994.

14. Katha Pollitt, "Bothered and Bewildered," *New York Times,* July 22, 1993.

PREDATORS AND NURTURERS*

Sylvia Ann Hewlett

Sylvia Ann Hewlett is a well-known author of several books, including When the Bough Breaks *and* The War Against Parents. *The following piece is excerpted from chapter 4 of her book* Creating a Life: Professional Women and the Quest for Children. *This is a good piece to read along with the article by E. Mavis Hetherington (page 489). Using recent research to support her findings, Hewlett argues against the established notion among the college-educated that marriage is good for men and bad for women.*

1   Over the last 30 years the idea that marriage is good for men and bad for women has become an established fact for educated American women. Back in the early seventies, sociologist Jessie Bernard planted the seed for this now widely accepted notion in her acclaimed book, *The Future of Marriage.* In it, she argued that "in every marital union there are really two marriages, his and hers," and his is a whole lot better than hers.[1] For husbands, marriage brings health and happiness; for wives, marriage brings depression and lower self-esteem. According to Bernard, marriage affects women like a low-grade fever, gradually debilitating her emotional and mental state. Indeed Bernard believed that marriage was so fundamentally bad for women that any housewife claiming to be happy must be out of her mind. In her words, "we do not clip wings or bind feet, but we do . . . 'deform' the minds of girls, as traditional Chinese used to deform their feet, in order to shape them for happiness in marriage."[2]

2   Her study fell on fertile ground. In the early 1970s, cultural attitudes were changing and people were prepared to believe that marriage threatened an individual's ability to realize his or her capabilities. An emerging human potential movement contended that autonomy, growth, and creativity were the highest forms of human development and marriage was something that interfered. At the same time, new-wave feminists were beginning to stress ways in which the patriarchal institution of marriage severely limited a woman's ability to pursue any type of self-development. Radical feminists talked about the ways in which marriage constituted "slavery" and "legalized rape," while more mainstream types talked about the ways in which marriage circumscribed a woman's intellectual horizons and caused her to suppress her sense of self.

3   There was more than a grain of truth in these attacks on marriage. As Betty Friedan described so convincingly in *The Feminine Mystique,* marriage, fifties-style, could be suffocating, particularly for college-educated women. They had a hard time seeing how "clearing up after three meals a day, getting at the fuzz behind the radiators with the hard rubber appliance of the vacuum cleaner, emptying wastebaskets, and washing bathroom floors day after day, week after week, year after year, added up to a sum total of anything except minutiae that, laid end to

---

*Sylvia Ann Hewlett, *Creating a Life: Professional Women and the Quest for Children* (New York: Talk Miramax, 2002), pp. 186–193.

end, reach nowhere."[3] After a steady diet of housework that could be "capably handled by an eight-year-old"[4]— to use Friedan's words—these women were ready to leave the doll's house and spark a women's revolution.

4   Forty years have now rolled by and women have won a great many new freedoms both inside and outside the home. For today's young women, the relevant question is: what does marriage 2001-style do to a woman's life? Does it help her achieve health, wealth, and happiness? Or does it trigger depression and expose her to other serious risks? Over the last ten years research has been trickling out to suggest either that Bernard's pessimism was unfounded, or that marriage is actually becoming healthier for women.[5]

5   Let's start with mental health. Thirty years ago Bernard contended that marriage caused women to be unhappy and depressed. Recent research shows quite the opposite. A 1996 Rutgers University study that followed the mental health of 1,400 young men and women over a seven-year period found that marriage boosted the happiness or well-being of both sexes and that young adults who got and stayed married had higher levels of well-being than those who remained single.[6] Similarly, a recent study by David Blanchflower and Andrew Oswald, which examined life satisfaction among 100,000 randomly sampled Americans and Britons from the early 1970s to the 1990s, found that the well-being of women fell over this time period mainly due to a fall-off in the number of women who were married. In both countries, this twenty-year time span saw a large increase in the number of women who either never married, or divorced.[7]

6   Money, health, and sex are also areas where the new research is unequivocal: women are better off when married. Blanchflower and Oswald demonstrate that in both the United States and Britain, a lasting marriage is worth approximately $100,000 over a lifetime when compared to being widowed or divorced. While Linda Waite and Maggie Gallagher, in their book *The Case for Marriage,* show that while the marriage premium is particularly high for men, it is also significant for women. Married men seem to make better workers than single men: they have lower rates of absenteeism and work longer hours. As a result married men earn somewhere between 10 percent and 40 percent more than single men. For women, the relationship between marriage and money is more complicated. Married women without children receive a small marriage premium, ranging from 5 percent to 10 percent, but the big boost for married women comes in the form of security in old age. Married couples save a good deal more than single people.[8] Besides which, husbands and wives almost always leave their worldly goods—including pension benefits—to one another, creating the equivalent of an annuity for the surviving spouse. Given that wives tend to be younger than husbands, and women live an average of seven years longer than men, these annuities are most commonly enjoyed by women.[9]

7   Married people also tend to be healthier. According to a review article in the *Journal of Marriage and the Family,* "The nonmarried have higher rates of mortality than the married, about 50 percent higher among women and 250 percent higher among men." Unmarried people (divorced, widowed, and never married) it turns out, are far more likely to die from a whole variety of causes—heart disease,

pneumonia, cancer, car accidents, cirrhosis of the liver, and suicide. And this is true cross-culturally. In countries as different as Japan and the Netherlands, the unmarried die off much earlier than the married.

8   Single men tend to endanger their health by indulging in risky behavior—they drink and smoke too much, take drugs, drive dangerously, eat badly, and fail to get medical checkups. Single women are not nearly as careless or accident-prone, but they also are less healthy than their married peers because they miss out on the economic protection of marriage. Married women enjoy significantly higher household incomes than single women, and these higher incomes translate into better housing, safer neighborhoods, and improved access to private health insurance.

9   Finally we come to sex. Contrary to popular opinion—which tends to assume that swinging singles are the ones with the "hot" sex lives—married people have more and better sex than single people.[10] Over the last decade, several new studies, including The National Sex Survey—conducted at the University of Chicago and based on a sample of 3,500 adults—fill us in on what is happening. Fully 43 percent of married men report having sex at least twice a week, while only 26 percent of single men say they have sex this often. The picture is similar for women. Thirty-nine percent of married women have sex two or three times a week, compared to 20 percent of single women. In addition, both husbands and wives are more satisfied with sex than sexually active singles. The figures are particularly impressive for wives: 42 percent of married women say they find sex extremely emotionally and physically satisfying, compared to just 31 percent of single women.

10   The new research is quite startling in its clarity. Marriage can be an exceptionally good deal for both men and women. As might be expected, there are gender differences—men and women benefit in distinct and separate ways—but overall, married folks lead happier, healthier, and more prosperous lives than their single counterparts.

11   On the face of it this would seem like an extremely powerful set of findings, a treasure trove of important information for young people to sink their teeth into as they wrestle with challenging life decisions. The only problem is, very few people seem aware of this body of work on the benefits of marriage.

◆◆◆◆

12   Why hasn't this new research made more of a dent on our collective conscience? The answer to this question lies deep in our political culture.

13   There is enormous inertia around ideas, particularly ideas that help sustain a powerful ideology. Jessie Bernard's critique of marriage is a case in point. Once her analysis was accepted as "fact," it proved to be extremely useful in bolstering the feminist case against traditional marriage. And this, in turn, made her ideas exceedingly difficult to dislodge, even as times and circumstances have changed. So Bernard's analysis lives on, coloring if not distorting women's views on marriage. At least among the college-educated, it is the exceptional woman who does not have a lingering sense that marriage is bad for her, that it will pin her down and erode her potential. ◆◆

NOTES

1. Jessie Bernard, *The Future of Marriage*. New Haven, Conn.: Yale University Press, 1982, p. 14.
2. Ibid., p. 51.
3. Betty Friedan, *The Feminine Mystique*. New York: Dell Publishing, 1963, p. 256.
4. Ibid., p. 203.
5. Much of this new research is pulled together in a book by Waite and Gallagher. See Linda J. Waite and Maggie Gallagher, *The Case for Marriage: Why Married People Are Happier, Healthier and Better Off Financially*. New York: Doubleday, 2000.
6. Allan V. Horwitz, Helene Raskin White, and Sandra Howell-White, "Becoming Married and Mental Health: A Longitudinal Study of a Cohort of Young Adults," *Journal of Marriage and the Family*, vol. 58, 1996, pp. 895–907. It should be noted that this study controlled for premarital rates of mental health—to eliminate the possibility that a relationship between marital status and well-being exists only because healthier individuals tend to be the ones that get married.
7. David G. Blanchflower and Andrew J. Oswald, "Well-being over time in Britain and the USA," Working Paper 7487, National Bureau of Economic Research, Cambridge, Mass., January 2000.
8. Lupton and Smith found that over a five-year period, married couples saved $11,000–$14,000 more than nonmarried households. See Joseph Lupton and James P. Smith, "Marriage, Assets, and Savings," RAND, Labor and Population Program, Working Paper 99–12, November 1999, p. 20. See also Waite and Gallagher, *The Case for Marriage*, op. cit., pp. 97–124.
9. Laurence J. Kotlikoff and Avia Spivak, "The Family as an Incomplete Annuities Market," *Journal of Political Economy*, vol. 89, 1981, pp. 372–391.
10. All figures cited in this paragraph are taken from "The National Health and Social Life Survey," carried out in 1992 at the University of Chicago by Edward Laumann, John Gagnon, Robert Michael, and Stuart Michaels. This survey is popularly known as "The National Sex Survey."

C. WHAT CREATES SUCCESSFUL RELATIONSHIPS? WHAT CAUSES THEM TO FAIL?

QUESTIONS TO CONSIDER BEFORE YOU READ

What attracts you to another person? What criteria do you keep in mind when looking for a mate? How do you know when it is time to move on? What effect do the responsibilities for housework and other family chores have on a relationship? How do your own relationships measure up to those of others you know? What do you do to maintain a good relationship?

THE MYSTERY OF ATTRACTION*

Harville Hendrix

Harville Hendrix is a former professor at Southern Methodist University and the author of several books on relationships, including Giving the Love That Heals: A Guide for Parents

---

*Harville Hendrix, *Getting the Love You Want: A Guide for Couples* (New York: Harperperennial Library, 1990), pp. 3–8, 10, 14, 90–92, 281–282.

and Keeping the Love You Find: A Guide for Singles. *In the following excerpt from* Getting the Love You Want: A Guide for Couples, *Hendrix explains that more often than not, people looking for love search for a very particular set of negative and positive personality traits in their potential mates. Once this is realized, marriage participants can have successful relationships by consciously making themselves better partners rather than trying to change their mates.*

1   When couples come to me for marital therapy, I usually ask them how they met. Maggie and Victor, a couple in their mid-fifties who were contemplating divorce after twenty-nine years of marriage, told me this story:

2   "We met in graduate school," Maggie recalled. "We were renting rooms in a big house with a shared kitchen. I was cooking breakfast when I looked up and saw this man—Victor—walk into the room. I had the strangest reaction. My legs wanted to carry me to him, but my head was telling me to stay away. The feelings were so strong that I felt faint and had to sit down."

3   Once Maggie recovered from shock, she introduced herself to Victor, and the two of them spent half the morning talking. "That was it," said Victor. "We were together every possible moment for the next two months, and then we eloped."

4   "If those had been more sexually liberated times," added Maggie, "I'm sure we would have been lovers from that very first week. I've never felt so intensely about anyone in my entire life."

5   Not all first encounters produce seismic shock waves. Rayna and Mark, a couple ten years younger, had a more tepid and prolonged courtship. They met through a mutual friend. Rayna asked a friend if she knew any single men, and her friend said she knew an interesting man named Mark who had recently separated from his wife. She hesitated to introduce him to Rayna, however, because she didn't think that they would be a good match. "He's very tall and you're short," the friend explained; "he's Protestant and you're Jewish; he's very quiet and you talk all the time." But Rayna said none of that mattered. "Besides," she said, "how bad could it be for one date?"

6   Against her better judgment, the friend invited Rayna and Mark to an election-night party in 1972. "I liked Mark right away," Rayna recalled. "He was interesting in a quiet sort of way. We spent the whole evening talking in the kitchen." Rayna laughed and then added, "I suspect that I did most of the talking."

7   Rayna was certain that Mark was equally attracted to her, and she expected to hear from him the next day. But three weeks went by, and she didn't hear a word. Eventually she prompted her friend to find out if Mark was interested in her. With the friend's urging, Mark invited Rayna to the movies. That was the beginning of their courtship, but it was never a torrid romance. "We dated for a while, then we stopped for a while," said Mark. "Then we started dating again. Finally, in 1975, we got married."

8   "By the way," added Rayna, "Mark and I are still married, and the friend who didn't want to introduce us is now divorced."

9   These contrasting stories raise some interesting questions. Why do some people fall in love with such intensity, seemingly at first glance? Why do some couples ease into marriage with a levelheaded friendship? And why, as in the case of

Rayna and Mark, do so many couples seem to have opposite personality traits? When we have the answers to these questions, we will also have our first clues to the hidden psychological desires that underlie marriage.

UNRAVELING THE MYSTERY OF ROMANTIC ATTRACTION

10   In recent years, scientists from various disciplines have labored to deepen our understanding of romantic love, and valuable insights have come from each area of research. Some biologists contend that there is a certain "bio-logic" to courtship behavior. According to this broad, evolutionary view of love, we instinctively select mates who will enhance the survival of the species. Men are drawn to classically beautiful women—ones with clear skin, bright eyes, shiny hair, good bone structure, red lips, and rosy cheeks—not because of fad or fashion but because these qualities indicate youth and robust health, signs that a woman is in the peak of her childbearing years.

11   Women select mates for slightly different biological reasons. Because youth and physical health aren't essential to the male reproductive role, women instinctively favor mates with pronounced "alpha" qualities, the ability to dominate other males and bring home more than their share of the kill. The assumption is that male dominance ensures the survival of the family group more than youth or beauty. Thus a fifty-year-old chairman of the board—the human equivalent of the silver-backed male gorilla—is as attractive to women as a young, handsome, virile, but less successful male.

12   If we can put aside, for a moment, our indignity at having our attractiveness to the opposite sex reduced to our breeding and food/money-gathering potential, there is some validity to this theory. Whether we like it or not, a woman's youth and physical appearance and a man's power and social status *do* play a role in mate selection, as a quick scan of the personal messages in the classified ads will attest: "Successful forty-five-year-old S.W.M. with private jet desires attractive, slim, twenty-year-old S.W.F.," and so on. But even though biological factors play a key role in our amorous advances, there's got to be more to love than this.

13   Let's move on to another field of study, social psychology, and explore what is known as the "exchange" theory of mate selection.[1] The basic idea of the exchange theory is that we select mates who are more or less our equals. When we are on a search-and-find mission for a partner, we size each other up as coolly as business executives contemplating a merger, noting each other's physical appeal, financial status, and social rank, as well as various personality traits such as kindness, creativity, and a sense of humor. With computerlike speed, we tally up each other's scores, and if the numbers are roughly equivalent, the trading bell rings and the bidding begins.

14   The exchange theory gives us a more comprehensive view of mate selection than the simple biological model. It's not just youth, beauty, and social rank that interest us, say the social psychologists, but the whole person. For example, the fact that a woman is past her prime or that a man has a low-status job can be offset by the fact that he or she is a charming, intelligent, compassionate person.

15   A third idea, the "persona" theory, adds yet another dimension to the phenomenon of romantic attraction.[2] The persona theory maintains that an

important factor in mate selection is the way a potential suitor enhances our self-esteem. Each of us has a mask, a persona, which is the face that we show to other people. The persona theory suggests that we select a mate who will enhance this self-image. The operative question here is: "What will it do to my sense of self if I am seen with this person?" There appears to be some validity to this theory. We have all experienced some pride and perhaps some embarrassment because of the way we believe our mates are perceived by others; it does indeed matter to us what others think.

16   Although these three theories help explain some aspects of romantic love, we are still left with our original questions. What accounts for the intensity of romantic love—as in the case of Maggie and Victor—those feelings of ecstasy that can be so overpowering? And why—as in the case of Rayna and Mark—do so many couples have complementary traits?

17   In fact, the more deeply we look at the phenomenon of romantic attraction, the more incomplete these theories appear to be. For example, what accounts for the emotional devastation that frequently accompanies the breakup of a relationship, that deadly undertow of feelings that can drown us in anxiety and self-pity? One client said to me as his girlfriend was leaving him: "I can't sleep or eat. My chest feels like it's going to explode. I cry all the time, and I don't know what to do." The theories of attraction we've looked at so far suggest that a more appropriate response to a failed romance would be simply to plunge into another round of mate selection.

18   There is another puzzling aspect of romantic attraction: we seem to have much more discriminating tastes than any of these theories would indicate. To see what I mean, take a moment to reflect on your own dating history. In your lifetime you have met thousands of people; as a conservative estimate, let's suppose that several hundred of them were physically attractive enough or successful enough to catch your eye. When we narrow this field by applying the social-exchange theory, we might come up with fifty or a hundred people out of this select group who would have a combined "point value" equal to or greater than yours. Logically, you should have fallen in love with scores of people. Yet most people have been deeply attracted to only a few individuals. In fact, when I counsel single people, I hear again and again that "there just aren't any good men (or women) out there!" The world is littered with their rejects.

19   Furthermore—and this is a curious fact—those few individuals that people are attracted to tend to resemble one another quite closely. Take a moment and think about the personality traits of the people that you have seriously considered as mates. If you were to make a list of their predominant personality traits, you would discover a lot of similarities, including, surprisingly, their negative traits.

20   From my vantage point as a marriage therapist, I see the unmistakable pattern in my clients' choice of marriage partners. One night, in a group-therapy session, I was listening to a man who was three months into his second marriage. When his first marriage broke up, he had vowed to the group that he would never be involved with a woman like his first wife. He thought she was mean, grasping, and selfish. Yet he confessed during the session that the day before he

had "heard" the voice of his ex-wife coming from the lips of his new partner. With a sense of panic he realized that the two women had nearly identical personalities. *It appears that each one of us is compulsively searching for a mate with a very particular set of positive and negative personality traits.*

♦♦♦♦

THE NEW BRAIN AND THE OLD BRAIN*

21   . . . Your new brain is the part of you that is conscious, alert, and in contact with your daily surroundings. It's the part of you that makes decisions, thinks, observes, plans, anticipates, responds, organizes information, and creates ideas. The new brain is inherently logical and tries to find a cause for every effect and an effect for every cause. To a degree, it can moderate some of the instinctual reactions of your old brain.[3] By and large, this analytical, probing, questioning part of your mind is the part that you think of as being "you." . . .

22   In sharp contrast to the new brain, you are unaware of most of the functions of your old brain. Trying to comprehend this part of your being is a maddening task, because you have to turn your conscious mind around to examine its own underbelly. Scientists who have subjected the old brain to this kind of scrutiny tell us that its main concern is self-preservation. Ever on the alert, the old brain constantly asks the primeval question: "Is it safe?"

♦♦♦♦

23   What we are doing, I have discovered from years of theoretical research and clinical observation, is looking for someone who has the predominant character traits of the people who raised us. Our old brain, trapped in the eternal now and having only a dim awareness of the outside world, is trying to re-create the environment of childhood. And the reason the old brain is trying to resurrect the past is not a matter of habit or blind compulsion but of a compelling need to heal old childhood wounds.

24   The ultimate reason you fell in love with your mate, I am suggesting, is not that your mate was young and beautiful, had an impressive job, had a "point value" equal to yours, or had a kind disposition. You fell in love because your old brain had your partner confused with your parents! Your old brain believed that it had finally found the ideal candidate to make up for the psychological and emotional damage you experienced in childhood.

♦♦♦♦

TEN CHARACTERISTICS OF A CONSCIOUS MARRIAGE

25   *1. You realize that your love relationship has a hidden purpose—the healing of childhood wounds.* Instead of focusing entirely on surface needs and desires, you learn to recognize the unresolved childhood issues that underlie them. When you look at marriage with this X-ray vision, your daily interactions take on more meaning. Puzzling aspects of your relationship begin to make sense to you, and you have a greater sense of control.

---

*The conscious and unconscious minds.

26   *2. You create a more accurate image of your partner.* At the very moment of attraction, you began fusing your lover with your primary caretakers. Later you projected your negative traits onto your partner, further obscuring your partner's essential reality. As you move toward a conscious marriage, you gradually let go of these illusions and begin to see more of your partner's truth. You see your partner not as your savior but as another wounded human being, struggling to be healed.

27   *3. You take responsibility for communicating your needs and desires to your partner.* In an unconscious marriage, you cling to the childhood belief that your partner automatically intuits your needs. In a conscious marriage, you accept the fact that, in order to understand each other, you have to develop clear channels of communication.

28   *4. You become more intentional in your interactions.* In an unconscious marriage, you tend to react without thinking. You allow the primitive response of your old brain to control your behavior. In a conscious marriage, you train yourself to behave in a more constructive manner.

29   *5. You learn to value your partner's needs and wishes as highly as you value your own.* In an unconscious marriage, you assume that your partner's role in life is to take care of your needs magically. In a conscious marriage, you let go of this narcissistic view and divert more and more of your energy to meeting your partner's needs.

30   *6. You embrace the dark side of your personality.* In a conscious marriage, you openly acknowledge the fact that you, like everyone else, have negative traits. As you accept responsibility for this dark side of your nature, you lessen your tendency to project your negative traits onto your mate, which creates a less hostile environment.

31   *7. You learn new techniques to satisfy your basic needs and desires.* During the power struggle, you cajole, harangue, and blame in an attempt to coerce your partner to meet your needs. When you move beyond this stage, you realize that your partner *can indeed be a resource for you*—once you abandon your self-defeating tactics.

32   *8. You search within yourself for the strengths and abilities you are lacking.* One reason you were attracted to your partner is that your partner had strengths and abilities that you lacked. Therefore, being with your partner gave you an illusory sense of wholeness. In a conscious marriage, you learn that the only way you can truly recapture a sense of oneness is to develop the hidden traits within yourself.

33   *9. You become more aware of your drive to be loving and whole and united with the universe.* As a part of your God-given nature, you have the ability to love unconditionally and to experience unity with the world around you. Social conditioning and imperfect parenting made you lose touch with these qualities. In a conscious marriage, you begin to rediscover your original nature.

34   *10. You accept the difficulty of creating a good marriage.* In an unconscious marriage, you believe that the way to have a good marriage is to pick the right partner. In a conscious marriage, you realize you have to be the right partner. As you gain a more realistic view of love relationships, you realize that a good

marriage requires commitment, discipline, and the courage to grow and change; marriage is hard work. ◆◆

NOTES

1. This theory, that people tend to select mates who are more or less their equals, also attempts to explain the stability of some couples. In a study of 537 dating men and women reported in the July 22, 1986, edition of *The New York Times* by writer Daniel Goleman, the researchers found that people who perceived their partners to be superior to them felt guilty and insecure. People who perceived their partners to be inferior to them reported feelings of anger. When partners perceived themselves to be equals, their relationships were relatively conflict-free and stable.
2. C. G. Jung, *Two Essays in Analytical Psychology*, pp. 155–56. See also *The Archetypes and the Collective Unconscious*, vol. 9, pp. 122–23.
3. The question of freedom and determinism divides various disciplines into opposing camps. In philosophy and religion, the question has been debated for centuries with no resolution. Psychological schools are distinguished by their adherence to a mechanistic versus an organismic view of human beings. This question is crucial for marriages, because if we are destined to certain marital fates, then what is the value of therapies that offer hope and change? To my way of thinking, both sides of most polarities are valid. The old/new-brain metaphor offers a resolution to the dialogue—we are both determined and free. The old brain, with its built-in survival programs, determines our basic reactions, and the new brain can become aware of reactions that are not effective and devise new options. The survival directives of the old brain cannot be overridden, but the new brain can re-educate the old brain with regard to what is dangerous and what is not. We are free within limits, but our limits are not absolute.

THE SECOND SHIFT*

Sylvia Ann Hewlett

In this excerpt taken from Creating a Life: Professional Women and the Quest for Children, *Sylvia Ann Hewlett argues that even successful married women still do the lion's share of domestic housework.*

1   High-achieving women continue to carry the lion's share of domestic responsibilities. Fifty percent of married, high-achieving women assume prime responsibility for meal preparation—only 9 percent of their husbands/partners take prime responsibility for this task.[1] Fifty-six percent of these women take prime responsibility for doing the laundry; only 10 percent of husbands take care of this task. And 45 percent of women make sure the house is cleaned; only 5 percent of husbands take care of this task. Younger wives do slightly less than older wives, and younger husbands do slightly more than older husbands, indicating that the

---

*Sylvia Ann Hewlett, *Creating a Life: Professional Women and the Quest for Children* (New York: Talk Miramax, 2002), pp. 106–109.

division of labor has become slightly more equal over the years. However, these shifts have been quite small. To pick one example, 8 percent of older husbands take care of the laundry, compared to 13 percent of younger husbands.

2   At the end of the day, the division of labor on the home front boils down to one startling fact: *43 percent of older, high-achieving women, and 37 percent of younger, high-achieving women feel that their husbands create more work for them around the house than they contribute.* Thirty-nine percent of ultra-achieving women also feel this way, despite the fact that half the women in this group are married to men who earn less than they do. As might be expected, the unequal load at home can be the source of marital tension.

3   Deborah, 37, lives in St. Paul, Minnesota, and is president of a small publishing company. She talked about her feelings:

4   I loved the question about husbands creating more work than they contribute. Don't I have one of those! Dan's a wonderful man, but enormously difficult to live with. I know which room he has spent time in because he leaves behind a trail of discarded stuff—beer bottles, coffee mugs, wet towels, dental floss, junk mail, you name it. He tells me he doesn't really "see" disorder or mess, which is why he doesn't get around to picking any of it up.

5   If I ask him to do something specific, he'll do it, but so badly that I generally have to do it over. When he clears the table he is very likely to dump all the dishes in the sink rather than empty the dishwasher and put the dirty dishes where they need to be. When he does the grocery shopping he refuses to use a list—he thinks lists are annoying—so invariably I have to go back to the store and pick up the things he forgot. And it's not as though any of these problems are new. For thirteen years I've tried to find a way of changing his behavior—I've wheedled, I've cajoled, I've threatened, I've staged temper tantrums. But nothing works, it's like water on a duck's back.

6   Back in the days when he was under more work pressure than I was, I didn't mind so much—picking up after him, doing the lion's share of the housework. But now that I earn more than he does—and work longer hours—it drives me crazy. His latest excuse is, "You can't teach an old dog new tricks." Give me a break! Is that supposed to make me feel better?

7   When it comes to responsibility for children, husbands don't do much better. *High-Achieving Women, 2001** tells us that only 9 percent of husbands take time off from work when a child is sick, while the figure is 51 percent for their high-achieving wives. Nine percent of husbands take prime responsibility for helping children with homework, compared to 37 percent of wives. And 3 percent of these husbands organize activities such as play dates and summer camp, compared to 61 percent of their wives. ◆◆

NOTES

1. According to *High-Achieving Women, 2001,* when neither spouse takes prime responsibility for a house-related or child-related task, it is either shared between the spouses or not done at all.

---

*See the surveys in *High-Achieving Women, 2001* (New York: National Parenting Association, April 2002).

MARRIAGE AND DIVORCE AMERICAN STYLE*

E. Mavis Hetherington

E. Mavis Hetherington is a professor of psychology at the University of Virginia and is co-author of For Better or for Worse: Divorce Reconsidered. *In this article, Hetherington discusses his research from a project on marriage and divorce he directed at the Hetherington Laboratory at the university. He argues that marriage and divorce is too complex an issue for policy makers to adopt a "one-size-fits-all" approach.*

1   On average, recent studies show, parents and children in married families are happier, healthier, wealthier, and better adjusted than those in single-parent households. But these averages conceal wide variations. Before betting the farm on marriage with a host of new government programs aimed at promoting traditional two-parent families and discouraging divorce, policy makers should take another look at the research. It reveals that there are many kinds of marriage and not all are salutary. Nor are all divorces and single-parent experiences associated with lasting distress. It is not the inevitability of positive or negative responses to marriage or divorce that is striking, but the diversity of them.

2   Men do seem to benefit simply from the state of being married. Married men enjoy better health and longevity and fewer psychological and behavioral problems than single men. But women, studies repeatedly have found, are more sensitive to the emotional quality of the marriage. They benefit from being in a well-functioning marriage, but in troubled marriages they are likely to experience depression, immune-system breakdowns, and other health-related problems. We saw the same thing in the project I directed at the Hetherington Laboratory at the University of Virginia, which followed 1,400 divorced families, including 2,500 kids—some for as long as 30 years—interviewing them, testing them, and observing them at home, at school, and in the community. This was the most comprehensive study of divorce and remarriage ever undertaken; for policy makers, the complexity of the findings is perhaps its most important revelation.

GOOD MARRIAGES, BAD MARRIAGES

3   By statistical analysis, we identified five broad types of marriage—ranging from "pursuer-distancer" marriages (which we found were the most likely to end in divorce), to disengaged marriages, to operatic marriages, to "cohesive-individuated" marriages, and, finally, to traditional marriages (which had the least risk of instability).

4   To describe them briefly:

5   ◆ Pursuer-distancer marriages are those mismatches in which one spouse, usually the wife, wants to confront and discuss problems and feelings and the other, usually the husband, wants to avoid confrontations and either denies problems or withdraws.

*American Prospect, April 8, 2002, p. 62.

6 ◆ Disengaged marriages are ones where couples share few interests, activities, or friends. Conflict is low, but so is affection and sexual satisfaction.

7 ◆ Operatic marriages involve couples who like to function at a level of extreme emotional arousal. They are intensely attracted, attached, and volatile, given both to frequent fighting and to passionate lovemaking.

8 ◆ Cohesive-individuated marriages are the yuppie and feminist ideal, characterized by equity, respect, warmth, and mutual support, but also by both partners retaining the autonomy to pursue their own goals and to have their own friends.

9 ◆ Traditional marriages are those in which the husband is the main income producer and the wife's role is one of nurturance, support, and home and child care. These marriages work well as long as both partners continue to share a traditional view of gender roles.

10 We found that not just the risk of divorce but also the extent of women's psychological and health troubles varies according to marriage type—with wives in pursuer-distancer and disengaged marriages experiencing the most problems, those in operatic marriages significantly having fewer, and those in cohesive-individuated and traditional marriages the fewest. Like so many other studies, we found that men's responses are less nuanced; the only differentiation among them was that men in pursuer-distancer marriages have more problems than those in the other four types.

11 The issue is not simply the amount of disagreement in the marriage; disagreements, after all, are endemic in close personal relations. It is *how* people disagree and solve problems—how they interact—that turns out to be closely associated with both the duration of their marriages and the well-being of wives and, to a lesser extent, husbands. Contempt, hostile criticism, belligerence, denial, and withdrawal erode a marriage. Affection, respect, trust, support, and making the partner feel valued and worthwhile strengthen the relationship.

GOOD DIVORCES, BAD DIVORCES

12 Divorce experiences also are varied. Initially, especially in marriages involving children, divorce is miserable for most couples. In the early years, ex-spouses typically must cope with lingering attachments; with resentment and anger, self-doubts, guilt, depression, and loneliness; with the stress of separation from children or of raising them alone; and with the loss of social networks and, for women, of economic security. Nonetheless, we found that a gradual recovery usually begins by the end of the second year. And by six years after divorce, 80 percent of both men and women have moved on to build reasonably or exceptionally fulfilling lives.

13 Indeed, about 20 percent of the women we observed eventually emerged from divorce enhanced and exhibiting competencies they never would have developed in an unhappy or constraining marriage. They had gone back to school or work to ensure the economic stability of their families, they had built new social networks, and they had become involved and effective parents and socially

responsible citizens. Often they had happy second marriages. Divorce had offered them an opportunity to build new and more satisfying relationships and the freedom they needed for personal growth. This was especially true for women moving from a pursuer-distancer or disengaged marriage, or from one in which a contemptuous or belligerent husband undermined their self-esteem and child-rearing practices. Divorced men, we found, are less likely to undergo such remarkable personal growth; still, the vast majority of the men in our study did construct reasonably happy new lives for themselves.

14   As those pressing for government programs to promote marriage will no doubt note, we found that the single most important predictor of a divorced parent's subsequent adjustment is whether he or she has formed a new and mutually supportive intimate relationship. But what should also be noticed is that successful repartnering takes many forms. We found that about 75 percent of men and 60 percent of women eventually remarry, but an increasing number of adults are opting to cohabit instead—or to remain single and meet their need for intimacy with a dating arrangement, a friendship, or a network of friends or family.

◆◆◆◆

15   There is general agreement among researchers that parents' repartnering does not do as much for their children. Both young children and adolescents in divorced and remarried families have been found to have, on average, more social, emotional, academic, and behavioral problems than kids in two-parent, non-divorced families. My own research, and that of many other investigators, finds twice as many serious psychological disorders and behavioral problems—such as teenage pregnancy, dropping out of school, substance abuse, unemployment, and marital breakups—among the offspring of divorced parents as among the children of nondivorced families. This is a closer association than between smoking and cancer.

16   However, the troubled youngsters remain a relatively small proportion of the total. In our study, we found that after a period of initial disruption 75 percent to 80 percent of children and adolescents from divorced families are able to cope with the divorce and their new life situation and develop into reasonably or exceptionally well-adjusted individuals. In fact, as we saw with women, some girls eventually emerge from their parents' divorces remarkably competent and responsible. They also learn from the divorce experience how to handle later stresses in their lives.

17   Without ignoring the serious pain and distress experienced by many divorced parents and children, it is important to underscore that substantial research findings confirm the ability of the vast majority to move on successfully.

18   It is also important to recognize that many of the adjustment problems in parents and children and much of the inept parenting and destructive family relations that policy makers attribute to divorce actually are present *before* divorce. Being in a dysfunctional family has taken its toll before the breakup occurs.

19   Predicting the aftermath of divorce is complex, and the truth is obscured if one looks only at averages. Differences in experience or personality account for more variation than the averages would suggest. A number of studies have found, for instance, that adults and children who perceived their pre-divorce life as happy and satisfying tend to be more upset by a marital breakup than those who viewed the marriage as contentious, threatening, or unfulfilling. Other studies show that adults and children who are mature, stable, self-regulated, and adaptable are more likely able to cope with the challenges of divorce. Those who are neurotic, antisocial, and impulsive—and who lack a sense of their own efficacy—are likely to have these characteristics exacerbated by the breakup. In other words, the psychologically poor get poorer after a divorce while the rich often get richer.

◆◆◆◆

20   The diversity of American marriages makes it unlikely that any one-size-fits-all policy to promote marriage and prevent divorce will be beneficial. Policy makers are now talking about offering people very brief, untested education and counseling programs, but such approaches rarely have long-lasting effects. And they are generally least successful with the very groups that policy makers are most eager to marry off—single mothers and the poor.

21   In their recent definitive review of the research on family interventions, Phil Cowan, Douglas Powell, and Carolyn Pape Cowan find that the most effective approaches are the most comprehensive ones—those that deal with both parents and children, with family dynamics, and with a family's needs for jobs, education, day care, and health care. Beyond that, which interventions work best seems to vary, depending on people's stage of life, their ethnic group or the kind of family they are in, and the specific challenges before them.

22   Strengthening and promoting positive family relationships and improving the many settings in which children develop is a laudable goal. However, policies that constrain or encourage people to remain in destructive marriages—or that push uncommitted couples to marry—are likely to do more harm than good. The same is true of marriage incentives and rewards designed to create traditional families with the husband as the economic provider and the wife as homemaker. If our social policies do not recognize the diversity and varied needs of American families, we easily could end up undermining them. ◆◆

QUESTIONS TO HELP YOU THINK AND WRITE ABOUT FAMILY, MARRIAGE, AND RELATIONSHIP ISSUES

1. How have the opinions of Adler, Cain, and Glaser influenced your views of the traditional family? What were your views before you read these essays? What are your views now?

2. Consider the articles by Cain and Adler together and notice how each differs on what they say about raising children. What does Adler consider to be the

best arrangement? What about Cain? What are the convincing points of each? After reading these essays, what do you think is the optimal familial arrangement for raising children?

3. Coontz makes the statement, "Most Americans support the emergence of alternative ways of organizing parenthood and marriage." As a class, make a list of all of the ways you can think of to organize a family. Then take a vote to see how many members of your class wholeheartedly support, support with reservations, or do not support each of the options. Which are the most popular family models in your class? Why? Which are your favorite models? Which did you reject? Give reasons for your choices.

4. The issue of building a sense of community to take the place of the extended family is discussed by James Q. Wilson in "The Future of Marriage." Citing the research of historians, Wilson argues that in the West the size of the family has remained largely unchanged for centuries. Most people have lived in small nuclear families as opposed to extended families. How strong do you think communities are in America? Using Wilson to fuel your writing, write an essay exploring how marriage affects the social cohesion and stability that communities can provide.

5. In "Predators and Nurturers," Hewlett asks what effects marriage has on the modern woman and goes on to argue that it is a fallacy that women do not benefit from being married. But if read along with the essay by Coontz, the issue becomes more complicated. What are the indicators Hewlett uses to determine whether marriage is beneficial to women? What are the indicators Coontz uses? What do each of these writers mean by the term *beneficial*?

6. Hendrix's essay posits that men and women are attracted to others because we are searching "for someone who has the predominant characteristics of the people who raised us." Test Hendrix's hypothesis on yourself. Make a list of the predominant characteristics of your parent(s) and a second list of the predominant characteristics of people with whom you have had close relationships. Ask others to participate in the same comparison. After conducting your research, would you agree that people are searching for a mate in order to fill a void left by their parents? Give reasons for your explanation.

7. Contrary to Hewlett's position in "Predators and Nurturers," the research offered by Hetherington supports the notion that men benefit from marriage but women do not. How do you explain the reasons for these different findings?

8. Hetherington's essay leads one to believe that the issue of divorce and marriage is complex, with a sometimes daunting set of variables that determine whether or not a marriage can be successful. Taking the ten steps Hendrix offers for creating a successful relationship, how do you think applying these methods would affect the complexity of maintaining a successful relationship that Hetherington points out?

❧ Section II ❧

Issues in Education

THE ISSUES

A. WHAT SHOULD COLLEGES AND UNIVERSITIES TEACH? IS THERE ANYTHING THEY SHOULD NOT TEACH?

The four articles in this section address a variety of ways to consider the difficult task that universities face—what to teach. Linking academic instruction to particular vocations, for example, must be balanced with the responsibility for turning entering first-year students into dependable and informed citizens and problem solvers. The articles by Rhodes, Sollod, Gonshak, and Payne offer distinct ways of achieving the curricular goals of higher education. See also "Theme for English B" (page 423).

B. WHAT HELPS STUDENTS LEARN AND SUCCEED IN COLLEGE? WHAT HINDERS THEM?

The three essays in this section offer ways to help make students' experiences at college fulfilling and also pose challenges to traditional teaching methods. Light's essay shows the importance of ethnic diversity in learning; Zernicke's essay encourages students to be proactive in achieving a successful university experience; and Freire's essay advocates critical thinking and active approaches to teaching and learning that benefit both student and teacher. See also "Pay Your Own Way! (Then Thank Mom)" (page 22); "The Laptop Ate My Attention Span" (page 24); "One of Our Own: Training Native Teachers for the 21st Century" (page 56); "The Great Campus Goof-Off Machine" (page 267); and "The Great Campus Goof-Off Machine? Not for All Students" (page 266).

C. WEB SITES FOR FURTHER EXPLORATION AND RESEARCH

Education Week	http://www.edweek.org
Chronicle of Higher Education	http://chronicle.com
Collegiate Way	http://www.collegiateway.org
National Center for Education Studies	http://nces.ed.gov

D. FILMS AND LITERATURE RELATED TO EDUCATION

Films: *Mr. Holland's Opus*, 1996; *Dead Poets Society*, 1989; *Stand and Deliver*, 1987; *Back to School*, 1986; *Soul Man*, 1986.

Literature: poems: "The Student" by Marianne Moore; "Learning to Read" by Frances E. W. Harper; essay: "Education" by E. B. White; short story: "The Lesson" by Toni Cade Bambara; novels: *The Chosen* by Chaim Potok; *A Separate Peace* by John Knowles.

THE RHETORICAL SITUATION

In classical times, Plato argued that students should not be allowed to read poetry because it appealed to emotion and warped the perception of truth. In the seventeenth century, Milton made a strong case for introducing writing instruction late in students' careers, after they had read widely and deeply on many subjects. What students should learn, when and under what conditions they should learn it, who should teach it, and how learning should be evaluated are enduring issues that continue to receive lively attention.

What college students should know and be able to do when they leave school and take their places as workers and citizens is at the heart of higher education issues. Who decides what gets taught at universities and colleges? Should the decision-making process be handled at the local or the national level? What role should a community have in deciding what its local college should be allowed to teach? Should a university encourage open-mindedness and tolerance (imparting its own beliefs and values on its students) or should it reflect the values of the local community? These are some of the questions that decision makers and responsible citizens must ask themselves.

But higher education cannot be concerned only with what gets taught; it must consider how students are able to derive value from their educational experiences. Participating as a member of an ethnically diverse group of students, becoming proactive in acquiring one's own education, and learning to critically examine methods of teaching and learning are some ways students can gain the most from their educational careers. Successful education, in most people's minds, leads to successful lives and a successful society. Agreement on what constitutes a successful life and successful society provides some of the value warrants for this issue.

Because students who leave college are expected to have specialized skills in a specific discipline and also to be informed, conscientious decision makers and citizens, there is a constant exigency for a wide variety of higher education issues. Only a few of them are represented here. They include ideas about what is appropriate for schools to teach, the ways students learn best, the role of traditional versus collaborative teaching methods, how students can be proactive in making their educational careers successful, and how ethnic diversity contributes to learning. As a student yourself, you will undoubtedly be able to add your own related issues to this list.

A. WHAT SHOULD COLLEGES AND UNIVERSITIES TEACH? IS THERE ANYTHING THEY SHOULD NOT TEACH?

QUESTIONS TO CONSIDER BEFORE YOU READ

Think back on your own educational experiences. Aside from personal interest areas, have you ever been in a class in which you thought the content you were being taught was inappropriate or did not belong in the classroom? What do you consider appropriate and inappropriate content in college courses? In your opinion, what is the purpose of a college education? How do you feel about required courses that entering students must take? What do you think the rationale might be for requiring students to take certain courses?

A BATTLE PLAN FOR PROFESSORS TO RECAPTURE THE CURRICULUM*

Frank H. T. Rhodes

Frank H. T. Rhodes is a professor emeritus from Cornell University. The following essay is adapted from his book The Creation of the Future: The Role of the American University. *If you were president of a college or university, what would be some of your curricular goals and objectives? What roles would the arts, humanities, sciences, social sciences, and recreational and spiritual activities play in your school? How would you compare your curriculum design to Rhodes's proposal?*

1   As we enter the new century, society's agreement on what defines an educated person, what constitutes essential knowledge and common discourse, has essentially collapsed. As a result, universities in the United States have a problem in the area of curriculum that has been widely recognized. *Curriculum* means, literally, a running track, but, in recent years, it has been called "a cafeteria with little indication of which are the entrees and which the desserts" and "Dante's definition of hell, where nothing connects with nothing."

2   Today's students are offered hundreds and thousands of courses in catalogs more than an inch thick, but rarely receive any overarching, meaningful statement of educational goals and intellectual purpose within a larger, coherent framework. Because professors have been reluctant to suggest that one subject is more valuable or significant than another, they have replaced requirements with electives and substituted excessive numbers of undergraduate courses without any critical assessment of their relative merits.

3   Three major obstacles have thwarted curricular reform during the past decade. First, while some faculty members and administrators have proposed a return to a core curriculum, others have argued that it is biased to presume that the history of Western civilization reflects the history of all U.S. citizens—and have called for more diversification through a multicultural curriculum. The standoff between the two groups has resulted in little progress in either direction.

4   The second obstacle has been student demand. More students see college as the pathway to a job and tend to enroll in narrow vocational majors rather than pursue liberal-arts degrees. For example, students graduating with a B.A. in arts and sciences plummeted from 47 percent of all B.A. degrees in 1968 to 26 percent in 1986.

---

*Chronicle of Higher Education, September 14, 2001, p. B7.

5   Third, the fragmentation of the disciplines has slowed reform efforts. Lacking a commitment to common educational goals, faculty members have added courses that reflect their own, increasingly specialized, interests. The rapid spread in most universities of free-standing programs, centers, and even departments devoted to specialized studies as well as a host of cultural issues—poverty, peace, race, ethnicity, gender, and sexual preference—has also tended to compartmentalize knowledge.

6   The scholarly literature on the subject of the undergraduate curriculum has contributed little of practical value to the debate. Exquisitely footnoted but excessively cautious, exhaustingly inclusive but elegantly inconclusive, it seems to confirm the very lack of imaginative engagement of which its critics complain. It is learned but lifeless, knowledgeable but superficial, analytical but arid.

7   So what should universities do? Simply stated, faculty members must recapture the curriculum. They must collectively face difficult and divisive questions about goals, priorities, and requirements, and then design effective ways to achieve them. Unfortunately, little has changed in the century that has passed since Horace Mann declared that to disperse an angry mob, one just had to announce a lecture on education. Every dean knows that the way to guarantee the absence of a quorum in a faculty meeting is to announce that there is to be a discussion of the curriculum. Eyes glaze over; tempers shorten; people of generosity and good will become intolerant, and those of sound judgment and thoughtful balance become rigid, hard-line advocates. Changing the curriculum, it has been said, is like moving a graveyard; it is a solemn undertaking.

◆◆◆◆

8   But faculties must tackle the issue, like it or not, for unless they can agree on meaningful goals, universities can never fully succeed. The trouble with having no goals, it has been said, is that you may achieve them.

9   In fact, the greatest privilege a faculty member can have is to design and support a curriculum. All the riches of human experience are there. All the teeming problems and noisy issues of our society are there. All our capacity and hopes for the well-being of our planet and our people are there. How can the faculty shirk the challenge and the opportunity this presents?

10   No model curriculum exists for all institutions. A successful curriculum, like a successful life, is strictly a do-it-yourself job. Consultants may give advice; presidents, trustees, and provosts may exhort; students may demand. But in the end, it needs local agreement; it depends on local resources; it is conducted by local faculty members; and it benefits local students. It cannot be exported or imported; it has to be a homegrown product.

11   Yet to develop a new curriculum, one has to agree on a few essentials: Should all students share a common body of knowledge, skills, and values? If so, what should that be? How should universities best prepare graduates for a future in which the average American will change jobs, and even careers, six times; in which specialized knowledge has a half-life as short as five years; in which societal and ethical questions are deeply entwined with technical ones; and in which relentless learning over a lifetime is a prerequisite for professional and personal success?

12   Based on my experience over 50 years in five universities as a student, professor, dean, provost, and president, I believe that the best way to respond to such questions is to consider not what courses universities should require, but what qualities they should seek to nurture in their students.

13   My list of such qualities would probably look like the following:

14   **Openness to others and the ability to communicate with clarity and precision.** Openness is not achieved by courses on openness. It emerges as students live in a widening circle of individuals from other backgrounds and persuasions, as they begin to discover and compare the treasures of other traditions, and as they observe others—professors, fellow students, coaches, advisers, authors, artists—who are themselves open to others. Openness, then, should be a by-product of the classroom, the playing field, the library, the residence hall, and the generous and inquiring climate of the campus.

15   But openness alone is not enough. As we move further into the information age and the age of global competition, the ability to communicate effectively has never been more important.

16   The typical freshman writing program will take already competent students and develop their reading and writing skills with imaginative assignments. At Cornell, for example, most freshmen take two semester-long seminars, taught in discussion sections with no more than 17 other students. They select their seminar topics from a list of about 125, including subjects as varied as Greek tragedy, jazz, global warming, and economic competition.

17   The seminars help students learn to write good expository prose while also gaining a greater understanding of topics of interest to them. Continuing students can develop their writing skills further through the "Writing in the Majors" program, which incorporates a strong writing component into upper-level courses in specific fields.

18   The ability to read with comprehension and to write and speak with precision is crucial to success and fulfillment in any career, indeed in life itself. There is no opting out of that requirement.

19   **Self-confidence and curiosity, with the skills required to satisfy both.** Self-confidence and curiosity are also byproducts of a satisfying university career. But certain skills are also needed, and those most frequently lacking in our graduates seem to be proportional thinking, analytical comparison, and a quantitative approach and apprehension.

20   Why should a student who plans to major in English be required to study computer science or statistics? Why should a French major be obliged to appreciate physics or philosophy? Quite simply because university graduates must be more than skilled specialists or technicians in their fields. Students of the sciences must master quantitative and formal reasoning; it is a necessary step on the path to the discipline of science. But nonscience majors must also be able to reason in quantitative and formal terms, because it is a necessary step toward being an informed citizen.

21   More than half of the issues before the U.S. Supreme Court and the Congress in an average year are in some way science-related, as Edward O. Wilson, the two-time Pulitzer Prize–winning biologist from Harvard, has observed. To

understand such issues, even as a layperson, requires some understanding of the kind of thinking that underlies them—which, at some point, involves quantitative and formal reasoning.

22   But such thinking is not needed only for scientific issues. Consider how frequently opinion polls are presented and relied upon in this country, or how often businesses use surveys to bolster their claims. And then consider how easily numbers can be used to represent, or misrepresent, any alleged facts that one wishes. It is clear that even to be able to read critically what appears in the daily newspaper, to draw inferences from it, and to judge its implications calls upon specific analytical skills.

23   Each institution will determine how that understanding is to be achieved. But the goal itself—the cultivation of self-confidence and curiosity, along with the necessary analytical skills—is an essential part of the preparation required for a meaningful existence.

24   **A sense of proportion and context in the worlds of nature and society.** The responsible citizen, as well as the competent professional, needs increasingly to draw on an appreciation of the natural world if he or she is to make sense of the policy issues that are most important to us today. How can one responsibly decide whether the government should provide more support for the National Aeronautics and Space Administration, for example, without some understanding of the significance of its programs? And how can one even begin to consider environmental concerns such as the greenhouse effect without some grasp of physics and chemistry?

25   Universities need to create courses in the natural sciences that appeal to non-scientists as well as scientists if they are to prepare all students to be citizens of the world. I don't mean that universities should offer classes like "Physics for Poets" or "Chemistry for Composers." The goal is to provide an introduction to, and an appreciation of, the natural sciences within the context of human societies, rather than to study each in isolation. That can be achieved not by diluting the content of a course, but by incorporating aspects of the history of discovery and the work of individual scientists, the critical assumptions and underlying philosophy of science, the great debates and controversies, the false starts and discarded theories, the working methods, and the application and implications of such subjects. Such an appreciation of the natural world also can be gained through courses in such areas as astronomy, geology, and oceanography because of the larger issues they raise, their dependence on and linkages with other sciences, and the fascination of fieldwork and observational experience.

26   When I was a professor of geology, for instance, I used to take my students on one or two extended field trips a year. One excursion involved a group of about 30 beginning students who traveled to Britain for three weeks to explore its geology. Our focus was scientific, but each student was required to present two papers on the influence of geology and landscape upon some other major topic: the Roman invasion, the location of industry, the novels of Thomas Hardy, the poems of William Wordsworth, the paintings of J.M.W. Turner, the sculptures of Henry Moore, the pattern of agriculture, the location of breweries, the building stones and architecture of cathedrals, the changes in climate, the components of the

Industrial Revolution, the form of cities, and so on. Any course, anywhere, offers comparable possibilities for linkage and enrichment.

27   But the natural world is only one part of the context in which we live; we are also part of a social web of great complexity. National concerns like poverty, crime, and drug abuse are embedded in questions of ethics, economics, politics, and the law. We need to understand problems through the particular prism of the social sciences and within social contexts. Only equipped with such perspectives can anyone offer effective recommendations for reform or cast a vote with understanding.

28   At the same time, we must not assume that we are the first society to grapple with such problems, or the first to experience them with intensity. Some understanding of a time and culture other than our own is one of the components of any balanced view and sense of proportion. Language and literature courses, area studies, history, art, and anthropology can all provide ready insights. So can other means beyond traditional courses: exhibitions, movies, lectures, societies, and volunteer activities in the local community or elsewhere. The presence of international students benefits everyone, and the option of a junior year abroad, or a summer research or service project abroad, offers rich opportunities.

29   At some universities, noisy debates on the role of Western civilization have deflected attention from the more basic issue of the need for comparative understanding of other times and cultures. Exactly how such understanding is achieved will be each institution's decision, but it is a desirable expectation for all colleges and universities.

30   **Delight in the richness and variety of human experience and expression.** Literature, art, religion, music, dance, and drama are the records of personal experience and encounters. Although many institutions are becoming increasingly preoccupied with technology transfer, entrepreneurial centers, and new revenue-producing activities, universities must reassert that the humanities are central to the curriculum, and that the values they embody remain of vital concern to every discipline and profession. Whatever the critical methods of current fashion, universities must be unapologetic about the sweeping range of issues and concerns that the humanities embody, and about their implications for all human experience.

31   The university years offer golden opportunities to explore literature and the arts, but the challenge is to marshal the richness of university resources so that they are appealing rather than indigestible to busy undergraduates. We must excite and interest, whet the appetite, invite a lifelong intimacy. The aim should be not so much to develop a smattering of understanding of all the arts, but to develop a taste for and curiosity about some. Better an enthusiasm for Mozart and Monet than uninspired A's in forgotten courses on Baroque music and Impressionist art.

32   Plato insisted that art should provide the basis of all education. It is not now and never has been some frill added to the garment of human experience. It is, instead, a basic expression of human understanding. Art is ubiquitous and influential in every culture worth the name, from ancient Egypt and Greece to Renaissance Italy. It has been in the most literal sense the embodiment of insight, an

assertion of the human spirit. The most sophisticated skill—whether technical or academic—is barren without the insights that art provides. As in other attributes, so in this; the aim of education is to encourage the imaginative encounter, the reflective experience that can enrich every aspect of life.

33   **Intellectual mastery and passion in one chosen area.** The mark of an educated person is not the mere possession of knowledge but its comprehension, not its volume but its significance. If we neglect that greater comprehension, we shall become like Bette Davis's father: "Daddy, in his infinite wisdom, always saw the roots and not the flowers," she wrote. "He took the watches of the world apart and never knew what time it was."

34   Pursuing a major is often the crowning experience of the undergraduate years. But at its worst, it is a string of unrelated courses, each of interest in its own way, but all leaving unexamined the critical methodology and principles of the discipline.

35   The major should be the undergraduate's capstone experience, and the preparation and presentation of a thesis should be the introduction and bridge to a professional career. Thesis topics are of immense value because they require the assimilation and utilization of extensive information, whether obtained from books or from firsthand observation. This means, of course, that the thesis topic should not be overly restrictive, that it should require a broad approach, and that it should be related in some appropriate fashion to other areas of significance.

36   A student who maps the geology of an area of Nevada with silver deposits, for example, may be required to examine the balance among mining opportunities, economic trends, and market prices, or might alternatively be required, as part of a history project, to study the impact of silver mining on the economy and social structure of ancient Greece. A student working on the genetics of *Drosophila* might be required to demonstrate an understanding of the contemporary issues— scientific and ethical—of gene therapy or the macromutation-evolution debates of the early 20th century. A student writing a thesis on Mozart's early chamber music might be required to include a chapter on the technical development of 18th-century stringed instruments, or the physics of the cello, or the composition of court audiences, or the economics of ecclesiastical patronage.

37   What is needed is a faculty adviser who is attentive, creative, and committed to the joint discovery between teacher and student that a good thesis involves. What is also needed is a faculty adviser who knows the student as well as his or her own colleagues in other disciplines, someone who takes a lively interest in the larger community of learning.

38   **A commitment to responsible citizenship, including respect for and an ability to get along with others.** In the candid and noisy debate of cosmopolitan campuses is a national experiment in understanding. Ideally, disagreements can take place without those involved being disagreeable. A difference of opinion is not a misfortune but an opportunity for further understanding. It is where one interest or persuasion competes with another, and one skill or approach complements and enriches another, that freedom of inquiry flourishes.

39   Yet in practice, many higher-education institutions are defined in terms of groups or factions. Of course, groups will exist: geographic, disciplinary, ethnic,

service, scholarly, athletic, musical, residential, religious, political, and more. It is not group identification that is at issue, but group segregation. It is not association but separation that weakens the university and limits the exchange of ideas.

40   That is why any attempt by one group or discipline to impose its own restraints or methods on other areas restricts the freedom that is vital to the work of the university. Those in higher education have to learn to live together, not concealing their convictions, disguising their differences, or minimizing their concerns, but sharing them, step by step, forging a larger community that unites them in their humanity.

41   Perhaps the best way to mobilize a campus as a national demonstration in community-building is to deliberately tackle a selection of challenging issues in the neighborhood through student volunteer efforts, research studies, development models, business plans, and environmental proposals. There is a world of difference between the energizing, demanding climate of such a university and the sheltered passivity and intellectual timidity of a campus population that is fragmented. Higher-education institutions must remain places of openness, tolerance, inquiry, robust debate, generous spirit, and welcoming inclusiveness.

42   **A sense of direction, with the self-discipline, personal values, and moral conviction to pursue it.** Fifty years ago, President Harry S. Truman appointed the Zook Commission, giving it the basic charge of providing students with "the values, attitudes, knowledge and skills to live rightly and well in a free society." Few faculty members today would accept that charge as wholly appropriate for universities. There would be careful editing, selective deletion. I can almost hear the complaint: "'Knowledge and skills' sound right, but 'values and attitudes . . . to live rightly and well' gives me some problem. That seems inappropriate for a university. Too directive. Too paternalistic."

43   But universities have some responsibility for the moral well-being, as well as the intellectual development, of their students. That is, after all, why most universities were founded.

44   The rhetoric of college catalogs and university announcements gives expression to the issue. Consider Cornell's admissions brochure, which states that the university gives full consideration to those "intangible, but important factors that form good character and an effective personality."

◆◆◆◆

45   The problem is not lack of assent to the general proposition, but rather a lack of any agreement as to how to go about forming a good character and effective personality. The situation is aggravated by the extent to which analytical abstraction and critical techniques, which are the faculty's scholarly stocks-in-trade, shake the foundations and unsettle the convictions of students. If universities succeed only in questioning assumptions or destroying convictions, while not encouraging students in their attempts to rebuild or refine or replace them, they leave students deprived.

46   Some in higher education may contend that, while the student is free to absorb values by osmosis, values should not be openly recognized or discussed. But it is impossible to teach without imparting values. Faculty members will stand for something, whether deliberately or by neglect, and that stance will permeate

their teaching; whether we like it or not, the teacher is a role model for his or her students.

◆◆◆◆

47   Universities are committed to strive for rigorous objectivity, however unattainable it may be in practice. But one component of that objectivity is that we should acknowledge our assumptions, as well as accept a common responsibility for accuracy and integrity. Higher-education institutions exist neither to indoctrinate activists nor to create saints. They exist to educate students, but that has to involve more than the mere credentialing of narrow technical competence.

48   Yet universities must also insist that any exploration of values must clearly and deliberately leave the fundamental freedom and responsibility of choice to the individual student. Indeed, the integrity of the values themselves will be destroyed if universities attempt to indoctrinate or to moralize at every turn. Vacuous moral generalizations are as dangerous as empty neutralism. Moral development ought to be a result, rather than the purpose, of teaching.

49   In recognizing the need to grapple with questions of values, universities will align themselves with their past. "Knowledge is virtue and virtue knowledge," declared Socrates. If more-recent critics have been more skeptical, they still generally have recognized the link between knowledge and virtue; when Will Rogers observed, "A simple man may steal from a freight train, but give him a college degree and he will steal the whole railroad," he shared a common assumption with Socrates—even though he reached a rather different conclusion.

50   It will be claimed that the qualities that I've outlined are the fruits of a lifetime rather than of four years. So they are. It is true that higher-education institutions are not charged with certifying fully mature characters at age 22.

51   But universities can establish a climate in which these qualities can be nurtured. Because they are contagious, they influence the growth and development of the undergraduate and, through those individuals, are carried out into the larger society. That is why the curriculum is an important topic for public debate. It shapes the society we are and hope to become. ◆◆

THE HOLLOW CURRICULUM*

Robert N. Sollod

Robert N. Sollod teaches psychology at Cleveland State University.

1   The past decade in academe has seen widespread controversy over curriculum reform. We have explored many of the deeply rooted, core assumptions that have guided past decisions about which subjects should be emphasized in the curriculum and how they should be approached. Yet I have found myself repeatedly

Chronicle of Higher Education, March 18, 1992, p. A60.

disappointed by the lack of significant discussion concerning the place of religion and spirituality in colleges' curricula and in the lives of educated persons.

2   I do not mean to suggest that universities should indoctrinate students with specific viewpoints or approaches to life; that is not their proper function. But American universities now largely ignore religion and spirituality, rather than considering what aspects of religious and spiritual teachings should enter the curriculum and how those subjects should be taught. The curricula that most undergraduates study do little to rectify the fact that many Americans are ignorant of religious and spiritual teachings, of their significance in the history of this and other civilizations, and of their significance in contemporary society. Omitting this major facet of human experience and thought contributes to a continuing shallowness and imbalance in much of university life today.

3   Let us take the current discussions of multiculturalism as one example. It is hardly arguable that an educated person should approach life with knowledge of several cultures or patterns of experience. Appreciation and understanding of human diversity are worthy educational ideals. Should such an appreciation exclude the religious and spiritually based concepts of reality that are the backbone upon which entire cultures have been based?

4   Multiculturalism that does not include appreciation of the deepest visions of reality reminds me of the travelogues that I saw in the cinema as a child—full of details of quaint and somewhat mysterious behavior that evoked some superficial empathy but no real, in-depth understanding. Implicit in a multicultural approach that ignores spiritual factors is a kind of critical and patronizing attitude. It assumes that we can understand and evaluate the experiences of other cultures without comprehension of their deepest beliefs.

5   Incomprehensibly, traditionalists who oppose adding multicultural content to the curriculum also ignore the religious and theological bases of the Western civilization that they seek to defend. Today's advocates of Western traditionalism focus, for the most part, on conveying a type of rationalism that is only a single strain in Western thought. Their approach does not demonstrate sufficient awareness of the contributions of Western religions and spirituality to philosophy and literature, to moral and legal codes, to the development of governmental and political institutions, and to the mores of our society.

6   Nor is the lack of attention to religion and spirituality new. I recall taking undergraduate philosophy classes in the 1960's in which Plato and Socrates were taught without reference to the fact that they were contemplative mystics who believed in immortality and reincarnation. Everything that I learned in my formal undergraduate education about Christianity came through studying a little Thomas Aquinas in a philosophy course, and even there we focused more on the logical sequence of his arguments than on the fundamentals of the Christian doctrine that he espoused.

7   I recall that Dostoyevsky was presented as an existentialist, with hardly a nod given to the fervent Christian beliefs so clearly apparent in his writings. I even recall my professors referring to their Christian colleagues, somewhat disparagingly, as "Christers." I learned about mystical and spiritual interpretations of Shakespeare's sonnets and plays many years after taking college English courses.

8   We can see the significance of omitting teaching about religion and spirituality in the discipline of psychology and, in particular, in my own field of clinical psychology. I am a member of the Task Force on Religious Issues in Graduate Education and Training in Division 36 of the American Psychological Association, a panel chaired by Edward Shafranske of Pepperdine University. In this work, I have discovered that graduate programs generally do not require students to learn anything about the role of religion in people's lives.

9   Almost no courses are available to teach psychologists how to deal with the religious values or concerns expressed by their clients. Nor are such courses required or generally available at the undergraduate level for psychology majors. Allusions to religion and spirituality often are completely missing in textbooks on introductory psychology, personality theory, concepts of psychotherapy, and developmental psychology.

10   Recent attempts to add a multicultural perspective to clinical training almost completely ignore the role of religion and spirituality as core elements of many racial, ethnic, and national identities. Prayer is widely practiced, yet poorly understood and rarely studied by psychologists. When presented, religious ideas are usually found in case histories of patients manifesting severe psychopathology.

11   Yet spiritual and mystical experiences are not unusual in our culture. And research has shown that religion is an important factor in the lives of many Americans; some studies have suggested that a client's religious identification may affect the psychotherapeutic relationship, as well as the course and outcome of therapy. Some patterns of religious commitment have been found to be associated with high levels of mental health and ego strength. A small number of psychologists are beginning to actively challenge the field's inertia and indifference by researching and writing on topics related to religion and spirituality. Their efforts have not as yet, however, markedly affected the climate or curricula in most psychology departments.

12   Is it any wonder that religion for the typical psychotherapist is a mysterious and taboo topic? It should not be surprising that therapists are not equipped even to ask the appropriate questions regarding a person's religious or spiritual life—much less deal with psychological aspects of spiritual crises.

13   Or consider the field of political science. Our scholars and policy makers have been unable to predict or understand the major social and political movements that produced upheavals around the world during the last decade. That is at least partly because many significant events—the remarkable rise of Islamic fundamentalism, the victory of Afghanistan over the Soviet Union, the unanticipated velvet revolutions in Eastern Europe and in the Soviet Union, and the continuing conflicts in Cyprus, Israel, Lebanon, Northern Ireland, Pakistan, Sri Lanka, Tibet, and Yugoslavia—can hardly be appreciated without a deep understanding of the religious views of those involved. The tender wisdom of our contemporary political scientists cannot seem to comprehend the deep spirituality inherent in many of today's important social movements.

14   Far from being an anachronism, religious conviction has proved to be a more potent contemporary force than most, if not all, secular ideologies. Too often, however, people with strong religious sentiments are simply dismissed as "zealots" or "fanatics"—whether they be Jewish settlers on the West Bank,

Iranian demonstrators, Russian Baptists, Shiite leaders, anti-abortion activists, or evangelical Christians.

15   Most sadly, the continuing neglect of spirituality and religion by colleges and universities also results in a kind of segregation of the life of the spirit from the life of the mind in American culture. This situation is far from the ideals of Thoreau, Emerson, or William James. Spirituality in our society too often represents a retreat from the world of intellectual discourse, and spiritual pursuits are often cloaked in a reflexive anti-intellectualism, which mirrors the view in academe of spirituality as an irrational cultural residue. Students with spiritual interests and concerns learn that the university will not validate or feed their interests. They learn either to suppress their spiritual life or to split their spiritual life apart from their formal education.

16   Much has been written about the loss of ethics, a sense of decency, moderation, and fair play in American society. I would submit that much of this loss is a result of the increasing ignorance, in circles of presumably educated people, of religious and spiritual world views. It is difficult to imagine, for example, how ethical issues can be intelligently approached and discussed or how wise ethical decisions can be reached without either knowledge or reference to those religious and spiritual principles that underlie our legal system and moral codes.

17   Our colleges and universities should reclaim one of their earliest purposes—to educate and inform students concerning the spiritual and religious underpinnings of thought and society. To the extent that such education is lacking, our colleges and universities are presenting a narrow and fragmented view of human experience.

18   Both core curricula and more advanced courses in the humanities and social sciences should be evaluated for their coverage of religious topics. Active leadership at the university, college, and departmental levels is needed to encourage and carry out needed additions and changes in course content. Campus organizations should develop forums and committees to examine the issue, exchange information, and develop specific proposals.

19   National debate and discussion about the best way to educate students concerning religion and spirituality are long overdue. ◆◆

STARTING A GAY-STUDIES COURSE*

Henry Gonshak

Henry Gonshak teaches in the English department at Montana College of Mineral Science and Technology. This article appeared first in the Chronicle of Higher Education *and was later condensed for* Education Digest.

1   When I proposed a summer course in gay and lesbian studies at the Montana College of Mineral Science and Technology, where I teach English, a

---

Education Digest, January 1995, pp. 49–52.

fundamentalist Christian minister in our largely conservative, blue-collar community tried to have it canceled, and a furor erupted. In fighting to save my class, I made mistakes; my determination sometimes wavered. Still, I think my failures, as much as my successes, may prove instructive.

2   I'm sure my experience isn't unique, and I suspect, unfortunately, it will become more common. As our culture wars continue, the religious right is likely to expand its censorious crusades from public elementary and high schools to state-sponsored colleges and universities. And if any one subject proves most contentious, it's sure to be gay and lesbian studies.

3   My proposed class, approved by my department without dissent, would have covered several topics: differing attitudes toward homosexuality in the Judeo-Christian and Greco-Roman worlds; the history of the modern gay-rights movement; the impact of AIDS on the gay community and the significance of social perceptions of the epidemic as a "gay" disease; gay literature, theater, and film; scientific investigations into a "gay gene"; political battles over such issues as gays in the military and anti-gay legislation.

4   I suspect that a student in the pastor's congregation told him of the heresies afoot. The pastor's letter to the local newspaper, which sparked the community debate, encapsulated the gay-bashing tactics of the religious right.

5   After praising Montana Tech for its success in training engineers, he reproached it for offering a course in gay studies. While admitting he was "unclear" as to what the class would cover, he warned that "radical homosexuals have an agenda." He lamented the expenditure of tax money on gay studies during a time of cuts in education spending and thunderously concluded: "Our children are important!"

6   My reply, in the paper two days later, noted the unfairness of the pastor's insinuation that my course would promote a "radical homosexual agenda." I insisted the class would consider every point of view and pointed out how patronizing it was for him to call Tech students "children" who should let him decide what they should study. After inviting him to voice his objections to homosexuality in my class, I concluded: "To try to censor a course before it has even begun runs contrary to . . . every right a democratic society holds dear."

7   The pastor's challenge to academic freedom rallied many on campus to my course's defense. As one might expect at a technical college, most of my colleagues are hardly in the vanguard of gay liberation. However, everyone understood the ominous precedent if someone unaffiliated with the college could dictate what went on in our classrooms.

8   With both the pastor's and my positions publicly staked out, and several weeks to go before the course began, the battle was on. A local radio talk show was swamped with calls from listeners who vehemently debated the class's merits. The local paper ran a front-page story. However, the dispute was played out most fully in the paper's letters to the editor. A colleague noted that the course wouldn't "waste" taxpayers' money: Our summer classes are self-supporting.

9   Every letter writer who supported the course was sent, anonymously, a comic-book-style pamphlet titled "Doom Town: The Story of Sodom," issued by an evangelical Christian publisher. However, not all the local clergy echoed the homophobic venom expressed in "Doom Town" and in the pastor's letter.

10   In fact, two local Congregational ministers sharply challenged the notion that Christianity is irrefutably anti-gay. "The Bible has little to say about homosexuality," one wrote, while the second insisted that Jesus's core message of love, acceptance, and support for the downtrodden demanded that Christians accept all kinds of people, no matter how different.

11   With all the backing it received, my course might have withstood the pastor's campaign, had he not adopted a second, shrewd strategy—aggressively petitioning the Montana Tech Alumni Association. Mostly mining-industry bigwigs, the alumni soon began besieging Tech administrators with letters and telephone calls. They threatened to withdraw thousands of dollars in contributions unless the class was dropped.

12   Late on a Friday afternoon, only hours before the alumni association met to discuss my course, my division head asked me to cancel it. Having learned that a local television-news team was planning to cover the first day of class, he felt cancellation was in the best interests of the students, who risked getting caught in a "media circus." I suspect I complied less because I found his rationale defensible than because I was weary of being beleaguered by a controversy that seemed to be escalating out of control.

13   By that evening, I knew I'd made an awful mistake. To live with myself, I knew I had to do all I could to get the course reinstated. That weekend, I telephoned every departmental colleague I could reach and received their unanimous support—including that of the division head himself. A kind and decent man, he had had, I suspect, grave doubts about his decision all along. Monday morning, he and I met with the academic dean, who agreed to reauthorize the class, asking only that we give the more innocuous title, "Differing Views on Homosexuality."

14   Could the whole dispute have been avoided if I chose that title originally? One administrator told me that, while to him the word "homosexual" simply connoted someone with atypical sexual desires, when he heard "gay and lesbian," he pictured an activist chanting, "We're queer! We're here! Get used to it!" Perhaps it would have been more politic to have chosen this alternate title.

15   Still, as an English professor, I'm well aware that no language is ever purely neutral. "Homosexual" is the word preferred by straights, whereas "gay" is a term gay people have picked. Since the course would deal with current issues surrounding the gay culture, shouldn't it use the designation the culture itself uses?

16   Even with a new, less inflammatory title, however, reinstating the course was still unacceptable to the college president. He argued that re-authorizing it after the administration had officially announced its cancellation to the alumni would make the institution look indecisive.

17   Instead, he said I could "repackage" the class, somewhat shifting its focus while still retaining much of its original content, so it wouldn't appear that the college was reversing its initial decision. Since the alternative was losing the course entirely, it was an easy offer to accept.

18   The president, dean, division head, and I then concocted a "new course," insipidly titled "Differing Views on Alternative Lifestyles." While still addressing homosexuality, it would also cover a grab bag of other "nontraditional" lifestyles, including single parenting, living together, and "open" marriages.

19   And then the dispute faded away. I've no idea why the pastor chose not to protest the new class. Surely, from his perspective, a course that not only covered homosexuality but also lumped in study of a host of other "sins" could hardly be much of an improvement. Perhaps he gave up because he was just as worn out as I was.

20   I now view the whole affair ambivalently, seeing neither victory nor defeat. The best way to fight the Christian right, I've concluded, is to stress the theocratic nature of their politics, which clash directly with the democratic principles of individual rights and freedom of speech.

21   In a state college such as Montana Tech, the constitutional separation of church and state applies, just as it does in any other public institution. If church groups can have a gay-studies class dropped due to conflicts with Christian doctrine, why not also censor a course on evolution (as is already done in some public elementary and secondary schools) or comparative religion or existential philosophy—all subjects that question church teachings?

22   Moreover, my struggle taught me that no one battling fundamentalism should be silenced by the constant cry of the religious right that its opponents are intolerant of religion—a charge leveled against me frequently during the controversy. Critics of the Christian right should stress that they are not objecting to the fact that fundamentalist politics are rooted in faith (as legitimate a foundation for a political agenda as any other) but rather to the specific political positions espoused in the name of that faith.

23   In short, once a religious group enters the political arena, it has no right to call intolerant those who simply disagree with its politics.

24   Professors intent on introducing controversial courses should be ready for trouble—especially if the college is tax-supported and situated anywhere in the traditionalist American heartland. Had I anticipated the furor my class would inspire, I'd have met beforehand with the administration and my department colleagues to develop strategies to combat potential criticism. Such strategies should be assertive rather than defensive, based on staunch adherence to the principle that higher education has a mission to explore all areas of human experience, especially those that have been long suppressed.

25   Of course, upholding this principle amid closed-minded attacks demands considerable courage—a virtue seldom required in the sheltered groves of academe. But don't we discover the strength of our beliefs only when we are called upon to defend them? ◆◆

CAN OR SHOULD A COLLEGE TEACH VIRTUE?*

Harry C. Payne

Harry C. Payne is a professor of history and president of Williams College. In the following article, Payne considers the role of teaching virtue in higher education. Before one can teach

_____

Liberal Education 82.4 (1996): 18–26.

virtue, one must understand what is meant by the term. How would you define the term virtue? *Is there an appropriate place for it in the university or college curriculum?*

1 One cannot underestimate the deep moral importance of the intellectual and character virtues instilled when we do our centuries-old job right. Strengthening intellectual virtues—such as the willingness to explore widely, the ability to test one's ideas against those of others, the capacity to listen thoughtfully, the strength to adduce reasons for assertions—has a clear relationship to strengthening character virtues like honesty, humility, integrity, and independence.

2 So, too, when one works to create an effective residential community among a diverse group of students, one also works to nurture such virtues as mutual understanding, civility, and cooperation. Moral education is embedded in the definition of what we have always been committed to do. Initiatives like new ethics courses and additional emphasis on community service are welcome, but one should not assume that these are value-laden activities being added to a value-neutral endeavor.

DEFINING VIRTUE

3 The first task is deciding what we might mean by the word *virtue*. A simple word, but not as simple as might first appear. There are, once you look, many meanings to the word *virtue*.

4 I think we would all consider it as a term of praise, indicating some association with being good, helpful, uplifting. I suppose few would object to being called virtuous, though many might actually feel some discomfort, in that to be expected to be virtuous might be a slightly higher standard than desired.

5 I think that is the case because we often associate virtue with purity, some kind of willful or even heroic distance from the impure world of the body or of everyday activity. There is a long tradition in Western thought which sees the body as the regrettably impure and fallen seat of the spirit, and the world of everyday activity a lesser world from the spiritual escape from worldliness.

6 We do sometimes talk about liberal learning as "learning for its own sake," presumably opposed to learning for specific technical and professional purposes—and seem to imply that this posture makes liberal learning superior. I have always found such a position to be puzzling. Learning is hard work, and I am not at all sure it makes sense to learn for "its" sake. Somehow I think we can show that all learning is for the sake of something beyond the act of learning itself.

7 Still, those of us who live and teach in our colleges sometimes describe ourselves in quasi-monastic fashion as persons who have sacrificed worldly success for something unsullied by the passions and interests of the world of profit. We are not above implying that this gives us a certain holy aura. (Remember, we do wear monks' robes at our rituals!) Also, students often refer to the "real world" as something somehow beyond our boundaries, with a sense that ours is, if not a superior world, at least one that is more innocent, a kind of walled garden. Now, I do think ours is a noble calling, but whether it is noble in a way different from much other professional activity in our society is not entirely self-evident.

Participation in this noble enterprise certainly does not seem wholly to immunize us from the normal play of passions, interests, and politics.

8   If we are from time to time inclined to view our isolation as a mark of virtue, the "real world" does not always return the compliment. Think for a moment of how common language uses the word *academic*—as in the sentence, "It seems to me that this issue is merely academic." That is, trivial. And I might add, the word *trivial* is itself derived from the word *trivium,* which meant the curriculum of grammar, rhetoric, and logic taught in the original colleges and universities. In this instance, our divorce from everyday life is seen as a weakness, not a strength.

9   Let's turn to a potentially more fruitful path: the idea that virtue consists in adherence to certain universal rules of behavior. In this case, we assume that there are certain universal rules of decency and that a college would be engaged in teaching those. This seems attractive at first, but a trifle bland. I feel embarrassed to say that, since who could be against teaching universal rules of decency? The feeling of blandness arises, I think, not because the rules are unimportant but precisely because we tend to think of them as universal. It is our human nature to wish for something unique in what we do, a peculiar mission as individuals and institutions, and universals do not offer such a feeling. We should do our share for universal morality, I suppose, but this strikes me as a broad and ill-defined road.

10   Just to give this question a little edge, I have tried to measure Williams College by its role in teaching a widely recognized set of moral rules, the Ten Commandments. The result may be instructive. We have, first of all, the theological commandments declaring the unity and priority of the God of Israel, and the ban on graven images of that God, and the keeping of the Sabbath. Here we are absolutely at a loss, as a nonsectarian institution that teaches critical inquiry. It was not always so, but clearly we have devolved from religious roots and affiliations. This is not to say that there is not a place in the academy for the religiously rooted institution. But that is not what we in the academy do.

11   Then there are the non-theological social commands regarding veneration of parents, killing, adultery, stealing, coveting, and lying. Here we have a mixed bag. We recruit students with a clean record on the worst crimes—murder and stealing—but there is no cause for self-congratulation there and certainly not much teaching to be done, I expect. As for the other crimes and sins—disrespect for parents, sexual disloyalty, envy, and deceit—I expect we display the normal range of human strengths and weaknesses. With the exception of lying, which in the form of cheating and plagiarism violates our community norms and practices, I expect we academics are broadly tolerant of many human weaknesses justly condemned in more specifically moralistic enterprises.

ANOTHER MEANING OF VIRTUE

12   As an alternative, I would suggest that we are on the most solid ground when we expect a bit less of the term *virtue,* when we do not try to tie it to some stark notion of ascetic self-sacrifice or some universal notion of morality. For there is another use of the word which is common in parlance but not commonly addressed

in discussions of these kinds. In its original form the term has its roots in the Latin word *virtus,* which means strength or capacity. A virtue is, therefore, nothing in and of itself. It is always related to a task at hand. It is a well-formed capacity to accomplish something necessary and desirable.

13   In the most narrow sense, *virtus* originally meant manliness. But its meaning was generalized over the centuries to mean a power, strength, or excellence in the more general sense. These uses still vary. For instance, you may hope that this essay will have the virtue of being short. Or that a judge will show the virtue of impartiality. Or that the root of a plant will have the virtue of curing a certain disease. And so on. Though varied, all of these uses imply an excellence, a strength; they all use the term as a form of praise; and their meaning is largely contextual. Impartiality is a virtue for a judge but not for a sports fan. Brevity is often appreciated as a virtue in a speaker, but may be a grave mistake in a legal judgment. The root of the plant serves us well in some contexts, but in other ways is one root among many, and may be a poison in other instances or quantities.

ACADEMIC VIRTUES

14   The question, therefore, is whether there are virtues specific to our context, the academy, which represent the strengths to create the excellence of the enterprise. I think there are. We certainly have no monopoly on them, but they are a unique combination in a unique setting, making us strong and perhaps even noble when we exhibit them. I would suggest a short list of the central academic virtues:

- ◆ the capacity for determined inquiry and for accountability, whereby no statement is sufficient to itself but must be open to the work of critical reflection, sober cross-examination, and even humorous testing of its capacities;
- ◆ the capacity for argument, for stating reasons, hearing counterarguments, and patient response;
- ◆ the capacity for listening, for truly hearing others out and granting the perspectives of others a provisional grace and a full-hearted understanding;
- ◆ the capacity for pushing investigation beyond the obvious, to be exhaustive within the bounds of human energy;
- ◆ the capacity for crossing received boundaries and trying out new maps of learning, new roads to travel; and
- ◆ the capacity to find the right words, numbers, lines, and movements in whatever domain we choose, to recognize that the way we express ourselves ought to be the mirror of the best fruits of our thinking.

15   Certainly these virtues are often functional in the "real world," but not always. They presuppose a kind of total leisure, a divorce from the rough-and-tumble of everyday life, the luxury of pushing argument and inquiry to the ultimate. Our habits along these lines sometimes even look a bit strange and dysfunctional to those outside the academy. That is not, however, the point. No

one says that all people should always have the time to do these things at the most intensive levels, but that it is good for all people to have done so long enough at some point in their lives to have acquired good habits.

16   Habits. Now we are slipping into trickier territory. Is there more? To use an old distinction, do we have a role in promoting character as well as intellectual virtues? I would argue that one is not truly possible without the other, that there are powerful strengths of character embedded in the intellectual virtues.

17   The intellectual academic virtues presuppose and hence strengthen a noble view of each other. They do not work unless they are acted out against a backdrop of tolerance, empathy, patience, mutual respect, cooperation. These are neither purely intellectual nor purely social. In fact, they show that the distinction is incorrect to begin with. One cannot be a determined and effective inquirer without the character virtues of empathy and humility. One cannot be a successful intellectual explorer without the character virtue of courage. One cannot find the best expressions of one's thoughts without the character virtue of integrity. ◆◆

B. WHAT HELPS STUDENTS LEARN AND SUCCEED IN COLLEGE? WHAT HINDERS THEM?

QUESTIONS TO CONSIDER BEFORE YOU READ

Looking back on your previous educational experiences, what kind of advice could you offer a younger student to make his or her academic career more successful? What steps do you think entering college students can take to make their collegiate experience the best it can be?

THE HARVARD GUIDE TO HAPPINESS*

Kate Zernicke

Kate Zernicke reports on education matters for the New York Times.

1   Lost in the current obsession to get into The Best U is something most adults readily admit, at least in hindsight: It doesn't matter so much where you go to college, but what you make of the experience.

2   So how to make the most of it?

3   In 1986, Derek Bok, then the president of Harvard, summoned a professor at the Graduate School of Education and asked him to evaluate how well the university educated its students and ways it might improve. Why, Dr. Bok wanted to know, did some students have a great experience while others did not?

---

*New York Times: Education Life, April 8, 2001, pp. 18+.

4　　The professor, Richard J. Light, a statistician by training, gathered colleagues and deans from 24 other institutions to examine the question and come up with a scientific method to find the answer.

5　　Over 10 years researchers interviewed 1,600 Harvard students, asking a range of questions about everything from what they did in their spare time to the quality of teaching and advising. They looked for patterns—say, what made certain courses effective. They also correlated students' academic and personal choices with their grades and how happy and intellectually engaged they said they were. The goal was to determine which factors were more likely to improve learning and overall happiness. A factor always linked to success would be rated 1; one with a significant relationship to success would be 0.50; and one with no effect would be 0. (Not every factor got a rating because of inconsistencies in how questions were asked.)

6　　Fifteen years later, Harvard has made policy changes based on the study, like assigning students homework to do in groups and scheduling some classes later in the day so discussions can continue over dinner.

7　　"It turns out there are a whole range of concrete ways students can improve their experience," said Professor Light, who teaches at the John F. Kennedy School of Government as well as at the education school. Professor Light has gathered the best ideas in a book, *Making the Most of College* (Harvard University Press, 2001). The suggestions are often simple. Still, he said, "It's amazing how little thought people give to these decisions."

8　　***1. Meet the faculty.*** Professor Light now tells each of the students he advises the same thing at the beginning of each term: "Your job is to get to know one faculty member reasonably well and get that faculty member to know you reasonably well. If you do nothing else, do that." On the most opportunistic level, this means that at the end of four years—two semesters each—the student has eight professors to write recommendations for jobs or for graduate school. But more important, the relationship makes a student feel more connected to the institution.

9　　The most satisfied students in the Harvard interviews sought detailed feedback and asked specific questions of professors and advisers—not "Why didn't I get a better grade?" but "Point out the paragraphs in this essay where my argument faltered."

10　　And don't try to hide academic problems. The researchers working for Professor Light interviewed a sample of 40 students who stumbled academically in their first year. The 20 who asked for help improved their grades, the 20 who did not spiraled downward—isolated, failing and unhappy.

11　　***2. Take a mix of courses.*** Nearly without exception, the students in the study who were struggling were taking nothing but large introductory courses that were needed to complete their degree. Why? To get them out of the way. Advice from well-meaning parents often goes something like this: First year, take required courses. Second year, choose a major. Third year, take advanced classes required for your major. Save fun electives, like dessert, for last.

12　　The trouble is, introductory courses range across so much material they often fail to offer students anything to sink their teeth into. So when it comes time to choose a major, students don't know what really interests them. By senior year, when taking courses that stimulate them, they are wondering why they didn't take more courses in Japanese/medieval social history/statistics earlier. Those who treat the early years like a shopping excursion, taking not only required classes but also ones that pique their interest, feel more engaged and happier with their major.

13   "The less satisfied students were the ones who said, 'My tack was to get all the requirements out of the way,'" Professor Light said. "The successful students do the exact opposite."

14   The corollary to this recommendation: Take small classes, which encourages faculty interaction and a feeling of connectedness. Taking classes with 15 or fewer students had a 0.52 correlation with overall engagement and a 0.24 correlation with good grades—both considered significant.

15   **3. *Study in groups.*** Doing homework is important, but what really matters is doing it in a way that helps you understand the material. Students who studied on their own and then discussed the work in groups of four to six, even just once a week, understood material better and felt more engaged with their classes. This was especially true with science, which requires so much solitary work and has complicated concepts.

16   **4. *Write, write, write.*** Choose courses with many short papers instead of one or two long ones. This means additional work—more than 12 hours a week versus fewer then 9, or about 40 percent more time—but it also improves grades. In a class that requires only one 20-page paper at the end of the term, there is no chance of recovering from a poor showing. Courses with four five-page papers offer chances for a midcourse correction.

17   And the more writing, the better. In all of Professor Light's research, no factor was more important to engagement and good grades than the amount of writing a student did. Students in the study recommended taking courses with a lot of writing in the last two years, when you have adjusted to the challenges of being in college and are preparing to write a long senior thesis.

18   **5. *Speak another language.*** Foreign language courses are the best-kept secret on campus. Many students arrive with enough skills to test out of a college's language requirement. But language was the most commonly mentioned among "favorite classes." Sixty percent of students put them in the category of "hard work but pure pleasure"; 57 percent of those interviewed again after leaving college recommended not testing out. Why? Classes are small, instructors insist on participation, students work in groups, and assignments include lots of written work and frequent quizzes, allowing for repeated midcourse corrections. In short, foreign language courses combine all the elements that lead to more learning and more engagement.

19   **6. *Consider time.*** In the Harvard interviews, there was one striking difference between those who did well in their courses and those who did not. Those who did well mentioned the word "time"; those who did not never used the word. Students reported that they did not succeed when they studied the way they had in high school, squeezing in 25 minutes in a study hall, 35 minutes after sports practice and 45 minutes after dinner. Grades and understanding improved when they set aside an uninterrupted stretch of a few hours. Professor Light even suggests keeping a time log for a few weeks and showing it to an adviser, who can help figure out the best way to allocate time.

20   **7. Hold the drum.** Students often flounder in college because they do not have the same social or family support network they had at home. Those who get involved in outside activities, even ones not aimed at padding a résumé or a graduate school application, are happiest. Professor Light tells the story of one young woman arriving unhappy in her adviser's office. When the adviser encouraged her to do something beyond her studies, she demurred. She had no talent; she could not play on a team or sing in the choir. "How about band?" her adviser prodded. She replied that she did not play an instrument. "That's O.K.," he said. "Ask them if you can hold the drum." Years later, when asked to describe why her college experience had been so positive, she repeatedly referred to the band, which got her involved at pep rallies and football games and introduced her to a diverse range of students.

21   Students who have worked hard to get into college, Professor Light said, tend to arrive and say, "Academic work is my priority, and doing other things will hurt that." In fact, the Harvard research found otherwise.

22   "What goes on in situations outside of class is just as important, and in some situations, it turns out to be a bigger deal than what happens in class," he said. "Very often an experience outside of class can have a profound effect on the courses students choose and even what they want to do with their lives."

23   The study found that students who worked long hours at a job had the same grades as those who worked a few hours or not at all. Students who volunteered actually had higher grades and reported being happier. The only students whose outside activities hurt their grades were intercollegiate athletes. Still, Professor Light said, they are the happiest students on campus. ◆◆

GETTING IN STUDENTS' WAY*

Richard J. Light

Richard J. Light is a professor of education at Harvard University and has taught at the college level for over thirty years. The following excerpt from his book Making the Most of College: Students Speak Their Minds *describes effective learning in a multicultural environment. Would you expect a learning environment to be successful when the group reflects a multiethnic configuration?*

1   At the beginning of this book, I quoted a dean from another university who said the strategy at his college was to admit a talented group of students and then just "get out of their way." It seems clear to me from the dozens of anecdotes and examples in this book that campus leaders should indeed implement the first part of that plan—admit a talented group of students—and then do exactly the opposite of that dean's recommendation. They should make a thoughtful,

*Richard J. Light, *Making the Most of College*: *Students Speak Their Minds* (Cambridge: Harvard University Press, 2001), pp. 209–214.

evidence-based, purposeful effort to get *in* each student's way. In fact, shaping a certain kind of campus culture may be the biggest contribution campus leaders can make.

2   In our interviews, student after student has shared stories that cumulatively illustrate an overarching theme, and I want to stress it. That theme is the interplay, the complex interaction, among different parts of campus life. Learning in classes can be enhanced, sometimes dramatically, by activities outside of classes. Good advice on course selection can make the difference between a happy young scholar and a frustrated one. Students report that their most powerful memories come from incidents and experiences outside of classes, usually during interactions with fellow students. These experiences are heavily influenced by residential living choices, which in turn are influenced by campus policies concerning who gets to live where.

3   This key idea shines through many student anecdotes: life at college is a complex system, with interrelated parts. Choosing which classes to take when, figuring out how to get to know professors, relating activities outside of classes to learning in formal courses, and especially decisions about whom to live with at a time of dramatically changing demographics on campus—these are choices each student must make.

4   So a critical role for campus leaders is to "get in the way" of each student, to help that young adult evaluate and reevaluate his or her choices, always in the spirit of trying to do just a bit better next time. After ten years of research, we now have a substantial number of specific suggestions we can make to undergraduates. Students can and should do many things on their own. Yet adults, as campus leaders, should not hesitate to help.

5   I want to close with my favorite anecdote. It is so rich that I find it hard to tell whether it is politically tilted to the left or to the right—and perhaps that's why I find it so appealing. I asked a graduating senior whether he could go beyond platitudes about the changing demographics on campus and give a specific example of the complexity of modern campus life that he actually experienced. I also asked if he could offer future students any lessons from his experience. Here is his response:

6   You ask whether diversity had any impact on my learning here at college. In some ways it has been the single biggest factor that affected my experience here. I am very happy in Cabot House as a Senior. Looking back, much of it started because of sophomore tutorial. Seven of us at Cabot House are doing social studies. The department organized sophomore tutorial so that the seven of us met every week right at the House. The instructor was a young economist. He played an important role in unexpected ways.

7   First let me tell you about the seven of us. There were two white guys, two white women, a man from India, a black woman, and a Chinese-American man. We didn't all know each other yet, since we had just arrived at the House. This was our first course meeting. Everything was new. I think when everyone looked at the reading list we all felt pretty overwhelmed. Reading unending amounts of material from Weber, Durkheim, Burke, Adam Smith, Karl Marx, John Stuart Mill, Freud, and some other political philosophers had us all a little nervous.

8   Now here is where the diversity among the group began to matter. One of the women said she couldn't help noticing there was not exactly a heavy representation

of people like her on the reading list. The black woman agreed. The instructor seemed hesitant to give a speech about why this was a great reading list, which in my eyes it was. Then the other white woman said something like, yes the reading list consisted of a dozen dead white males. But they are the "great" political philosophers and so let's not argue about the reading list. What she would like to do, she suggested, is take a more current political controversy, and after the group has discussed each author's work, let's try to apply that author's ideas to the current controversy.

9   So the Asian guy suggested we take affirmative action as the current controversy. There was total silence for a moment. We all looked around the table to see everyone's reaction. Then our instructor spoke up. He said he thought the idea sounded great, as long as we didn't give short shrift to those reading assignments. He assured us some of those readings were hard going. Since it was our first session and there was no assignment for that day, we took a few minutes to share our views about affirmative action. No one was shy, and there was plenty of disagreement. To oversimplify a little, two of the whites were for affirmative action, and two, including me, were against. The Indian guy was against, the black woman was for, and the Asian guy was against. And of course there were shadings of these opinions. A lot of those differences were obviously shaped by the ethnic diversity in the room, and the different backgrounds we had growing up.

10 Well, that whole year's tutorial made my Harvard education. First, we were very respectful of one another's views, because we all understood those views had evolved from our very different backgrounds. After all, I have to be pretty tactful as a white guy when I tell a talented black woman I think she is hurting herself in the long run by supporting affirmative action. Some of this stuff can be pretty personal. Second, we had great discussions nearly every week, because none of us could possibly ever really know what Freud or Durkheim or Weber would have thought of affirmative action. And our instructor pushed us really hard to relate our arguments to each week's readings, so the discussions never became some sort of touchy-feely waste of time. If anything, our discussions helped to clarify the readings.

11 Your original question was about the educational effects of diversity. Well, the effects were strong. And lasting. Everyone read the assigned authors carefully. Partly because some are not so easy to understand. But partly because we knew we would be discussing how those writings would relate to modern debates about affirmative action. You think that is easy? It's not. Then, sometimes people got to bring their personal backgrounds into the conversation.

12 One time the Asian guy turned to the black woman who supports affirmative action and basically said, "I arrived here in America when I was six years old, and my parents had nothing. We were penniless refugees. You grew up in Scarsdale. How can you argue for affirmative action after reading John Stuart Mill and Edmund Burke? And if affirmative action exists, why are you a candidate for it? And when does it end? Your parents are well off. They are highly educated. You went to a great high school. You are now at Harvard. When you graduate, do you expect on top of all that to still get preferences in hiring? When should affirmative action end for you?"

13 I particularly remember that day because it was an electric moment. It was the first time I could see how our conversations were leading people around the table to change their minds. That day was also a test of our civility to one another, and our capacity to disagree with respect. We all passed that test with flying colors. No one was offended by these conversations. We all treated them as a special opportunity to discuss a topic that is sometimes awkward, and even to use that topic as

a wedge to help all of us understand the writings of those very distinguished dead white males, whom I happen to admire.

14   Now as a senior I can say that whole year was the best experience I had here. Five of the seven of us have remained close friends for three years. We all are still at Cabot House. And the difference between these friends and all my other friends is that a significant part of our friendship is based around substantive discussions about ideas. None of us feels hesitant about initiating a discussion or question about Freud or whomever. After all, we did it every week for a whole year together in a room here where we live, right down the hall. And we certainly learned a lot about each other, and from each other.

15   Mixing our different personal backgrounds, that came from growing up in different circumstances, with some back-breakingly dense readings was a new experience for me. For example, it made me rethink what a meritocracy really means. I hadn't thought of it before as so complicated. Now I do. I actually changed my mind about how a meritocracy might work because of these discussions. And I saw other students in the group gradually change their minds, or temper their views. Watching those changes was amazing. Isn't that what a college education is all about? And now, to answer your original question about the educational impact of diversity, can you ever imagine seven white guys, all just like me, sitting around a table and accomplishing the same thing? ◆◆

THE BANKING CONCEPT OF EDUCATION*

Paulo Freire

A revolutionary education theorist and one of the most prominent educators in the world, Paulo Freire died in 1997. The following essay is an excerpt from his best-known work, Pedagogy of the Oppressed. *Can you remember a time when you experienced the "banking" model of education? If you could speak to Freire, what would you tell him of your experiences?*

1   A careful analysis of the teacher-student relationship at any level, inside or outside the school, reveals its fundamentally *narrative* character. This relationship involves a narrating subject (the teacher) and patient, listening objects (the students). The contents, whether values or empirical dimensions of reality, tend in the process of being narrated to become lifeless and petrified. Education is suffering from narration sickness.

2   The teacher talks about reality as if it were motionless, static, compartmentalized, and predictable. Or else he expounds on a topic completely alien to the existential experience of the students. His task is to "fill" the students with the contents of his narration—contents which are detached from reality, disconnected from the totality that engendered them and could give them significance. Words are emptied of their concreteness and become a hollow, alienated, and alienating verbosity.

---

*Paulo Freire, *Pedagogy of the Oppressed* (New York: Continuum, 2001), pp. 71–81.

3   The outstanding characteristic of this narrative education, then, is the sonority of words, not their transforming power. "Four times four is sixteen; the capital of Pará is Belém." The student records, memorizes, and repeats these phrases without perceiving what four times four really means, or realizing the true significance of "capital" in the affirmation "the capital of Pará is Belém," that is, what Belém means for Pará and what Pará means for Brazil.

4   Narration (with the teacher as narrator) leads the students to memorize mechanically the narrated content. Worse yet, it turns them into "containers," into "receptacles" to be "filled" by the teacher. The more completely she fills the receptacles, the better a teacher she is. The more meekly the receptacles permit themselves to be filled, the better students they are.

5   Education thus becomes an act of depositing, in which the students are the depositories and the teacher is the depositor. Instead of communicating, the teacher issues communiqués and makes deposits which the students patiently receive, memorize, and repeat. This is the "banking" concept of education, in which the scope of action allowed to the students extends only as far as receiving, filing, and storing the deposits. They do, it is true, have the opportunity to become collectors or cataloguers of the things they store. But in the last analysis, it is the people themselves who are filed away through the lack of creativity, transformation, and knowledge in this (at best) misguided system. For apart from inquiry, apart from the praxis, individuals cannot be truly human. Knowledge emerges only through invention and re-invention, through the restless, impatient, continuing, hopeful inquiry human beings pursue in the world, with the world, and with each other.

6   In the banking concept of education, knowledge is a gift bestowed by those who consider themselves knowledgeable upon those whom they consider to know nothing. Projecting an absolute ignorance onto others, a characteristic of the ideology of oppression, negates education and knowledge as processes of inquiry. The teacher presents himself to his students as their necessary opposite; by considering their ignorance absolute, he justifies his own existence. The students, alienated like the slave in the Hegelian dialectic, accept their ignorance as justifying the teacher's existence—but, unlike the slave, they never discover that they educate the teacher.

7   The *raison d'être* of libertarian education, on the other hand, lies in its drive towards reconciliation. Education must begin with the solution of the teacher-student contradiction, by reconciling the poles of the contradiction so that both are simultaneously teachers *and* students.

8   This solution is not (nor can it be) found in the banking concept. On the contrary, banking education maintains and even stimulates the contradiction through the following attitudes and practices, which mirror oppressive society as a whole:

    a. the teacher teaches and the students are taught;
    b. the teacher knows everything and the students know nothing;
    c. the teacher thinks and the students are thought about;
    d. the teacher talks and the students listen—meekly;
    e. the teacher disciplines and the students are disciplined;

f. the teacher chooses and enforces his choice, and the students comply;

g. the teacher acts and the students have the illusion of acting through the action of the teacher;

h. the teacher chooses the program content, and the students (who were not consulted) adapt to it;

i. the teacher confuses the authority of knowledge with his or her own professional authority, which she or he sets in opposition to the freedom of the students;

j. the teacher is the Subject of the learning process, while the pupils are mere objects.

9   It is not surprising that the banking concept of education regards men as adaptable, manageable beings. The more students work at storing the deposits entrusted to them, the less they develop the critical consciousness which would result from their intervention in the world as transformers of that world. The more completely they accept the passive role imposed on them, the more they tend simply to adapt to the world as it is and to the fragmented view of reality deposited in them.

10   The capability of banking education to minimize or annul the students' creative power and to stimulate their credulity serves the interests of the oppressors, who care neither to have the world revealed nor to see it transformed. The oppressors use their "humanitarianism" to preserve a profitable situation. Thus they react almost instinctively against any experiment in education which stimulates the critical faculties and is not content with a partial view of reality but always seeks out the ties which link one point to another and one problem to another.

11   Indeed, the interests of the oppressors lie in "changing the consciousness of the oppressed, not the situation which oppresses them";[1] for the more the oppressed can be led to adapt to that situation, the more easily they can be dominated. To achieve this end, the oppressors use the banking concept of education in conjunction with a paternalistic social action apparatus, within which the oppressed receive the euphemistic title of "welfare recipients." They are treated as individual cases, as marginal persons who deviate from the general configuration of a "good, organized, and just" society. The oppressed are regarded as the pathology of the healthy society, which must therefore adjust these "incompetent and lazy" folk to its own patterns by changing their mentality. These marginals need to be "integrated," "incorporated" into the healthy society that they have "forsaken."

12   The truth is, however, that the oppressed are not "marginals," are not people living "outside" society. They have always been "inside"—inside the structure which made them "beings for others." The solution is not to "integrate" them into the structure of oppression, but to transform that structure so that they can become "beings for themselves." Such transformation, of course, would undermine the oppressors' purposes; hence their utilization of the banking concept of education to avoid the threat of student *conscientização*.

13   The banking approach to adult education, for example, will never propose to students that they critically consider reality. It will deal instead with such vital questions as whether Roger gave green grass to the goat, and insist upon the

importance of learning that, on the contrary, *Roger gave green grass to the rabbit.* The "humanism" of the banking approach masks the effort to turn women and men into automatons—the very negation of their ontological vocation to be more fully human.

14   Those who use the banking approach, knowingly or unknowingly (for there are innumerable well-intentioned bank-clerk teachers who do not realize that they are serving only to dehumanize), fail to perceive that the deposits themselves contain contradictions about reality. But, sooner or later, these contradictions may lead formerly passive students to turn against their domestication and the attempt to domesticate reality. They may discover through existential experience that their present way of life is irreconcilable with their vocation to become fully human. They may perceive through their relations with reality that reality is really a *process*, undergoing constant transformation. If men and women are searchers and their ontological vocation is humanization, sooner or later they may perceive the contradiction in which banking education seeks to maintain them, and then engage themselves in the struggle for their liberation.

15   But the humanist, revolutionary educator cannot wait for this possibility to materialize. From the outset, her efforts must coincide with those of the students to engage in critical thinking and the quest for mutual humanization. His efforts must be imbued with a profound trust in people and their creative power. To achieve this, they must be partners of the students in their relations with them.

16   The banking concept does not admit to such partnership—and necessarily so. To resolve the teacher-student contradiction, to exchange the role of depositor, prescriber, domesticator, for the role of student among students would be to undermine the power of oppression and serve the cause of liberation.

◆◆◆◆

17   Those truly committed to liberation must reject the banking concept in its entirety, adopting instead a concept of women and men as conscious beings, and consciousness as consciousness intent upon the world. They must abandon the educational goal of deposit-making and replace it with the posing of the problems of human beings in their relations with the world. "Problem-posing" education, responding to the essence of consciousness—*intentionality*—rejects communiqués and embodies communication. It epitomizes the special characteristic of consciousness: being *conscious of*, not only as intent on objects but as turned in upon itself in a Jasperian "split"—consciousness as consciousness *of* consciousness.

18   Liberating education consists in acts of cognition, not transferrals of information. It is a learning situation in which the cognizable object (far from being the end of the cognitive act) intermediates the cognitive actors—teacher on the one hand and students on the other. Accordingly, the practice of problem-posing education entails at the outset that the teacher-student contradiction be resolved. Dialogical relations—indispensable to the capacity of cognitive actors to cooperate in perceiving the same cognizable object—are otherwise impossible.

19   Indeed, problem-posing education, which breaks with the vertical patterns characteristic of banking education, can fulfill its function as the practice of freedom only if it can overcome the above contradiction. Through dialogue, the teacher-of-the-students and the students-of-the-teacher cease to exist and a new

term emerges: teacher-student with students-teachers. The teacher is no longer merely the-one-who-teaches, but one who is himself taught in dialogue with the students, who in turn while being taught also teach. They become jointly responsible for a process in which all grow. In this process, arguments based on "authority" are no longer valid; in order to function, authority must be *on the side of* freedom, not *against* it. Here, no one teaches another, nor is anyone self-taught. People teach each other, mediated by the world, by the cognizable objects which in banking education are "owned" by the teacher.

20   The banking concept (with its tendency to dichotomize everything) distinguishes two stages in the action of the educator. During the first, he cognizes a cognizable object while he prepares his lessons in his study or his laboratory; during the second, he expounds to his students about that object. The students are not called upon to know, but to memorize the contents narrated by the teacher. Nor do the students practice any act of cognition, since the object towards which that act should be directed is the property of the teacher rather than a medium evoking the critical reflection of both teacher and students. Hence in the name of the "preservation of culture and knowledge" we have a system which achieves neither true knowledge nor true culture.

21   The problem-posing method does not dichotomize the activity of the teacher-student: she is not "cognitive" at one point and "narrative" at another. She is always "cognitive," whether preparing a project or engaging in dialogue with the students. He does not regard cognizable objects as his private property, but as the object of reflection by himself and the students. In this way, the problem-posing educator constantly re-forms his reflections in the reflection of the students. The students—no longer docile listeners—are now critical co-investigators in dialogue with the teacher. The teacher presents the material to the students for their consideration, and re-considers her earlier considerations as the students express their own. The role of the problem-posing educator is to create, together with the students, the conditions under which knowledge at the level of the *doxa*[2] is superseded by true knowledge, at the level of the *logos*.[3] ◆◆

NOTES

1. Simone de Beauvoir, *La Pensée de Droite, Aujourd'hui* (Paris); ST, *El Pensamiento político de la Derecha* (Buenos Aires, 1963), p.34.
2. Conventional opinion.
3. Cosmic truth.

QUESTIONS TO HELP YOU THINK AND WRITE ABOUT EDUCATION ISSUES

1. In "A Battle Plan for Professors to Recapture the Curriculum," does Rhodes's proposal for giving the curriculum back to the faculty take into consideration the desire to teach religion (Sollod), gay studies (Gonshak), and virtue (Payne)? How can the essay by Rhodes be read or interpreted to be inclusive of these various voices?

2. Read the article by Sollod. Draw a line down the middle of a sheet of paper, and make lists of the advantages and disadvantages of teaching religion and

spirituality at college. What do you value? Why? What is consistent with your current educational experiences?

3. Read the essays by Sollod and Payne together. What does Sollod mean by arguing that universities ought to teach religion? Does his view conflict with the separation between church and state? Does Payne risk falling into the same quagmire? Do you think Payne and Sollod would agree with each other about what universities or colleges should teach?

4. Aside from training students to be experts in a particular field, Rhodes argues that "universities have some responsibility for the moral well-being, as well as the intellectual development, of their students." What, exactly, do you think Rhodes means by this sentence? How would he define "moral well-being"? How would you define it? Most importantly, how can a university effectively instruct in this way?

5. Read Zernicke's article about Professor Light's research and jot down on a piece of paper each of the seven recommendations for having a successful college career. Next to each one, give your ranking on a scale of one to five, with five being the best. Which ones scored highest? What recommendations would you add to the list?

6. The student responding to the questions at the end of the piece by Light says, "And now, to answer your original question about the educational impact of diversity, can you ever imagine seven white guys, all just like me, sitting around a table and accomplishing the same thing?" Would it be realistic to expect that a group having similar backgrounds could have a session as productive as the diverse group shown in the essay? How does the ethnic configuration of a group have an impact on productivity and learning?

7. Read Freire's and Light's essays together. After reading the piece by Freire, how would you describe the teaching method employed by the economics professor discussed in Light's article? What method of education was being used? What was the result?

8. After reading Freire's article, if you had the opportunity to design a class, how would you do it? How would you select the content materials? How would you conduct the class?

❧ Section III ❧

Issues Concerning Crime and the Treatment of Criminals

THE ISSUES

A. HOW SHOULD WE TREAT CONVICTED CRIMINALS?

Four authors provide different perspectives on the treatment of criminals and how to avoid the problems caused by repeat offenders. Gilligan and Will offer inventive approaches for dealing with criminals. Kozinski reflects on the difficulty of sentencing criminals to death, and Moore discusses the problems with capital punishment in the United States. As you read these selections, you will want to think about your definition of punishment and its purpose in our society. You will also want to think about our current prison system and its reputed effectiveness. Also see "Giving People a Second Chance" (page 54) and "The Color of Suspicion" (page 617).

B. WHAT SHOULD BE DONE WITH YOUNG OFFENDERS?

The focus here is on the escalating problem of children and teenagers who commit crimes and acts of violence. The arguments establish the nature of the problem, discuss its causes, evaluate how bad the problem is, and propose some ways of solving it. Powers discusses a new type of criminal, the mainstream kid. Jones argues that violence and fantasy are necessary to the well-being of children. Weinberger provides evidence that shows that the minds of adolescents are not mature enough to reason for themselves. Rothstein shows how fairy tales can help rehabilitate young offenders, and Feuer follows a young man from the Bronx ghetto who is released from prison on a drug charge, showing the vicious circle of poverty, drugs, and crime that young offenders contend with daily.

C. WEB SITES FOR FURTHER EXPLORATION AND RESEARCH

The Crime Library	http://www.crimelibrary.com
National Center for Victims of Crime	http://www.ncvc.org
Religious Tolerance	http://www.religioustolerance.org/execute.htm
ACLU Execution Watch	http://www.aclu.org/executionwatch.html
Amnesty International: Execution of Child Offenders	http://www.amnesty-usa.org/abolish/juvexec.html
Youth Violence: A Report of the Surgeon General (2001)	http://www.surgeongeneral.gov/library/youthviolence
Mothers Against Teen Violence (MATV)	http://www.matvinc.org/index.asp
The Electric Chair.Com	http://www.electricchair.com

D. FILMS AND LITERATURE RELATED TO CRIME

Films: *A Clockwork Orange,* 1971; *Dead Man Walking,* 1996; *Boyz N the Hood,* 1991; *The Green Mile,* 1996; *The Shawshank Redemption,* 1994; *Escape from Alcatraz,* 1979; *Dancer in the Dark,* 2000; *The Man Who Wasn't There,* 2002; *Road to Perdition,* 2002.

Literature: poem: "The Ballad of Reading Gaol" by Oscar Wilde; short story: "Billy Budd" by Herman Melville; autobiography: *Live from Death Row* by Mumia Abu-Jamal; novels: *Crime and Punishment* by Fyodor Dostoyevsky; *Of Mice and Men* by John Steinbeck; *A Clockwork Orange* by Anthony Burgess.

THE RHETORICAL SITUATION

Everyone seems to have opinions about the issues associated with crime and the treatment of criminals. Recent presidents of the United States have made it a major issue in their campaigns and administrations, yet the problems persist. According to the perceptions of many, the country is becoming increasingly lawless. Motivational warrants linked to the need for safety are implicit in many of the arguments about crime issues.

It has been said that a society is known by the prisoners it keeps. The issues related to crime that are included in this section deal with the treatment of convicted criminals, unconventional punishment for criminals, and the growing problem of young offenders. The fairly new problem of children and young teenagers breaking the law and committing particularly heinous crimes concerns many people. This problem has become so serious that some people believe severe punishments are as justified for young offenders as for adult offenders.

Capital punishment, though fairly widely practiced, is still controversial. The death penalty has had an interesting history. It was banned in this country in 1972 and ruled constitutional again in 1976. According to various polls, the majority of Americans favor the death penalty for particularly horrible crimes, but with the recent exoneration of some death row inmates after DNA testing, this trend may be turning. Other people argue for crime prevention, including various types of interventions, and for rehabilitation for all criminals, young or old. There is a strong exigency in the United States to understand and solve the problems associated with crime.

A.   HOW SHOULD WE TREAT CONVICTED CRIMINALS?

QUESTIONS TO CONSIDER BEFORE YOU READ

Have you or anyone you have ever known gotten into trouble with the police? Was justice administered fairly? What do you think the purpose of prisons ought to be? Do prisons exist to punish criminals or to rehabilitate criminals? What do you think the difficulties are with rehabilitation in our prison system? What is your current stance on capital punishment? How committed are you to your stance? Are there instances in which you can see yourself leaning in the other direction? When and why?

REFLECTIONS FROM A LIFE BEHIND BARS: BUILD COLLEGES, NOT PRISONS*

James Gilligan

James Gilligan is the former director of mental health for the Massachusetts prison system. He is also a clinical instructor in psychiatry at Harvard Medical School who has twenty-five years

---

Chronicle of Higher Education, October 16, 1998, pp. B7–B9.

of experience as a prison psychiatrist. He believes that education is the key to preventing recidivism.

1   Neither words nor pictures, no matter how vivid, can do more than give a faint suggestion of the horror, brutalization, and degradation of the prisons of this country. I speak from extensive personal knowledge of this subject, for I have spent 25 years of my professional life behind bars—not as an inmate, but as a prison psychiatrist.

2   I am a physician, and I see violence (whether it is legal or illegal, homicidal or suicidal, intentional or careless) as a public-health problem—indeed, the most important and dangerous threat to public health in our time. Because it affects mostly the young, violence kills more people under the age of 65 in this country than do cancer and heart disease, the two illnesses that are often (and mistakenly) thought to be the most significant causes of death.

3   So I cannot emphasize too strongly how seriously I take the problem of violence. Far from being tolerant or permissive toward it, I am far more strongly opposed to violence in all its forms and in all its legal statuses, and far less tolerant and permissive toward it than are those who believe that our salvation lies in building more and more punitive (i.e., violent) prisons.

4   There is a widespread misimpression that punishment deters violence—in other words, that punishment is one means of preventing violence. However, the overwhelming weight of empirical evidence suggests that exactly the opposite is true—namely, that punishment, far from inhibiting or preventing violence, is the most potent stimulus or cause of violence that we have yet discovered. Several different lines of evidence, from several different populations and stages of the life cycle, converge in supporting that conclusion.

5   For example, child-rearing is such an inherently and inescapably complicated subject that there are relatively few findings from the past several decades of research on it that are so clear, so unmistakable, and so consistently replicated that they are virtually universally agreed on. But among those few is this: The more severely punished children are, the more violent they become, both as children and as adults. This is especially true of violent punishments. For example, children who are subjected to corporal discipline are significantly more likely to subject other people to physical punishments (i.e., inflict violence on them), both while they are still children and after they have reached adulthood. That is hardly surprising, of course, for corporal discipline is simply another name for physical violence; it would be called assault and battery if committed against an adult.

6   In fact, even with respect to nonviolent behavior, such as bed-wetting or excessive dependency or passivity ("laziness"), punishment has a counterproductive effect; that is, the more severely children are punished for a given behavior, the more strongly they persist in repeating it. To put it the other way around: If we want to produce as violent a generation of children and adults as possible, the most effective thing we can do is to punish our children and adults as severely as possible.

7   While the research just referred to can be found in the literature on child development and child abuse, there is no reason to think that the psychology of adults differs in this respect from that of children, and every reason to think that

it is the same. In fact, I have been able to confirm those findings on children from my own clinical experience of over 25 years with violent adult criminals and the violent mentally ill. The degree of violent child abuse to which this population had been subjected was so extreme that the only way to summarize it is to say that the most violent people in our society—those who murder others—are disproportionately the survivors of attempted murder themselves, or of the completed murders of their closest relatives, siblings, or parents.

8   Thus, if punishment could prevent violence, these men would never have become violent in the first place, for they were already punished, even before they became violent, as severely as it is possible to punish a person without actually killing him. Many were beaten nearly to death as children, so when they became adults, they did beat someone else to death.

9   Fortunately, we not only know what stimulates violence (punishment, humiliation), we also know what prevents violence, both in society in general and in the criminal-justice and prison systems in particular. Unfortunately, we Americans have been dismantling the conditions that do prevent violence as rapidly as we could over the past 25 years, with the entirely predictable result that the levels of violent crimes, such as murder, have repeatedly reached the highest recorded levels in our history. For example, for the last quarter of a century our murder rates have been twice as high as they were 40 years ago, and five to ten times as high as they currently are in any other democracy and developed economy on earth.

10   What are the conditions that prevent violence? Among general social conditions, there are several, but space permits mentioning only the most powerful one: a relatively classless society, with an equitable social and economic system in which there are minimal discrepancies in wealth, income, and standard of living between the poorest and the wealthiest factions of the population (people are vulnerable to feelings of shame and inferiority if they are poor, or economically inferior, while other people are rich, or economically superior).

11   Around the world, the nations with the most equitable economic systems, such as Sweden and Japan, are significantly more likely to have the lowest murder rates. And those with the greatest economic discrepancies between the rich and the poor (of which the United States is the world leader among developed democracies) have the highest murder rates (a statistic in which the United States is also the world leader). Even within the United States, the most equitable or "classless" states have the lowest murder rates, and those with the most inequitable degrees of class stratification have the highest. Yet the last Congress dismantled one of the few programs we had that tended to equalize income in this country—the earned-income tax credit.

12   Among the conditions in the prison system that prevent violent behavior (both during imprisonment and after release to the community), the most powerful is education. In Massachusetts, for example, when I headed the prison mental-health service, we did a study to see what programs within the prison had been most effective in preventing recidivism among prison inmates after they had been released from prison and returned to the community. While several programs had worked, the most successful of all, and the only one that had been

100 percent effective in preventing recidivism, was the program that allowed inmates to receive a college degree while in prison. Several hundred prisoners in Massachusetts had completed at least a bachelor's degree while in prison over a 25-year period, and not one of them had been returned to prison for a new crime.

13   Immediately after I announced this finding in a public lecture at Harvard, and it made its way into the newspaper, our new governor, William Weld, who had not previously been aware that prison inmates could take college courses, gave a press conference on television in which he declared that Massachusetts should rescind that "privilege," or else the poor would start committing crimes in order to be sent to prison so they could get a free college education! And lest one think that that was merely the rather bizarre response of one particularly cynical demagogue, it is worth noting that the U.S. Congress responded the same way. The last Congress declared that inmates throughout the federal prison system would no longer be eligible to receive Pell grants.

14   It is too late now to even begin to attempt to "reform" prisons. The only thing that can be done with them is to tear them all down, for their architecture alone renders them unfit for human beings. Or even animals: No humane society permits animals in zoos to be housed in conditions as intolerable as those in which we cage humans. The reason for the difference, of course, is clear: Zoos are not intended for punishment; prisons are. That is why it would benefit every man, woman, and child in this country, and it would hurt no one, to demolish the prisons and replace them with much smaller, locked, secure residential schools and colleges in which the residents could acquire as much education as their intelligence and curiosity would permit.

15   Such institutions would of course be most effective in their only rational purpose, which would be to prevent crime and violence, if they were designed to be as humane and homelike as possible, and as near the prisoners' own homes as possible, so that their families could visit as freely as possible (including frequent conjugal visits), and so they could visit their families as freely as possible. (For conjugal and home visits have repeatedly been shown, in this country and around the world, to be associated with lowered rates of violence, both during incarceration and after release into the community—which is probably why both have been effectively abolished in this country.)

16   Since there is no reason to isolate anyone from the community against his will unless he poses a danger of physically harming others, these residential schools would need to be limited to those who have been, or have threatened or attempted to be, violent. (Very few, if any, nonviolent "criminals" need to be removed from the community at all. Nor should those who have committed only nonviolent crimes ever have to be housed with those who have been seriously violent; and there are many reasons why they should not be.)

17   Thus one of the most constructive responses I can think of . . . would be the designing of an "anti-prison"—not prison reform, but prison replacement; not prison construction, but prison deconstruction. If we replaced prisons with a boarding-school "home away from home" for many people who are literally homeless in the so-called community, and provided them with the tools they need in order to acquire knowledge and skill, self-esteem and self-respect, and

the esteem and respect of others, these new facilities could actually reduce the rates of crime and violence in our society, instead of feeding them, as our current prisons do.

18   Of course, before we could do that, we would need to overcome our own irrational need to inflict revenge (i.e., punishment) on those who are weaker than we. Nothing corrodes the soul of the vengeful person as thoroughly as his own vengeful impulses. Thus the main reason we need to abolish [prisons] is not only, or even primarily, for the sake of those who get imprisoned in them, but in order to heal our own souls—and indeed, our whole society, which is sick with an epidemic of violence, both legal and illegal. ◆◆

A JAILBREAK FOR GERIATRICS*

George F. Will

George F. Will offers another solution for reducing recidivism and government spending.

1   Federal and state governments can significantly reduce spending in a field of soaring costs, while radically reducing their rates of recidivism among criminals released from prison. All they need to do is put hundreds, perhaps thousands, of convicts where they belong, which is—really—back in society. This idea will probably be a hard sell to a crime-conscious public in a conservative era. But consider Quenton Brown, whose case gave rise to POPS (the Project for Older Prisoners). And consider the case of Noah Wade, who also illustrates the point of POPS.

2   In June 1973 Brown, then 50, with an IQ of 51, stole $117 and a 15-cent cherry pie from a Morgan City, La., store. He crossed the street, crawled under a house, ate the pie and docilely surrendered himself and his .38 pistol, which may not have been in working order, to police when they arrived. He was sentenced to 30 years without parole.

3   Seventeen years into that sentence, at age 67, he came to the attention of a young Tulane law professor, Jonathan Turley, who was struck by the anomaly of the graying prison population—aging men becoming more and more expensive to warehouse as they become less and less dangerous. By the time he had won a parole for Brown, Turley and more than 200 Tulane law students had become founders of POPS, an organization devoted to culling low-risk geriatrics from overcrowded prisons.

4   In 1944, Noah Wade, then probably 19, had consensual sex with a 15-year-old. Virginia charged him with statutory rape. Wade says the girl's father said Wade must marry her. Wade says he was already married to a 14-year-old. Sentenced to seven years, he got into a fight with an inmate. Both men wielded prison-made shanks, both were stabbed. The other man died. Wade was sentenced

---

*Newsweek, July 20, 1998, p. 70.

to life. In 1992, shortly before Virginia's prison system became so crowded that the state started paying other states to incarcerate some of its convicts, POPS got Wade paroled to a Richmond nursing home.

5   It costs about $20,000 a year to imprison a young, healthy, dangerous man. Because of the normal medical costs associated with aging, and the unhealthy nature of prison life, it costs two to three times that, and sometimes more, to imprison someone 55 or older. (Because they usually have led hard lives before prison, and because of the chronic stress, idleness and the rest of prison life, 55-year-old prisoners often are, physiologically, akin to people seven or eight years older than that.) Men 55 and older comprise one of the fastest-growing cohorts in the prison population. And because of society's turn toward long sentences and away from parole, by the end of this decade there may be 90,000 prisoners over the age of 50.

6   Which is not to say that there should be wholesale de-institutionalization of the elderly. Organizations advocating victim's rights insist, reasonably, that retribution should not be lightly abandoned for budgetary reasons. They denounce the notion of "senior-citizen discounts" for criminals. However, their sensible philosophy encounters a stubborn fact: no matter how fast billions are poured into increasing the supply of cells, the supply of truly dangerous convicts increases faster. This is partly because, Turley says, sheriffs read newspapers: "They know when a new prison is coming online and they start to execute warrants. And in state after state, we see a self-adjusting market." And, inevitably, courts get involved.

7   At any given time nowadays, upwards of 40 states' prison systems are under court orders to rectify overcrowding. Some states' prisons even have a "zero sum" status: the addition of a new inmate requires the release of an existing one—public safety at the mercy of arithmetic.

8   Therefore the practical question is not whether but which prisoners are going to be released before their full sentences have been served. And a salient fact is that age is the surest predictor of recidivism. These two variables vary inversely.

9   It is unclear what cocktail of biological and cultural factors determines this. But in any case, the rate of rearrest (for a felony or serious misdemeanor) for state prisoners within three years of release from prison is 68 percent among those ages 18 to 24; 65 percent among those 25–29; 63 percent among those 30–34; 57 percent among those 35–39; 49 percent among those 40–44; 40 percent among those over 45. The rate among the almost 200 prisoners paroled or pardoned because of POPS' efforts is zero.

10   This is partly because POPS is meticulous in selecting candidates for release. POPS never challenges an inmate's conviction, and to be eligible for POPS' help, inmates must acknowledge their guilt. Although predicting recidivism is not an exact science, extensive interviewing can establish each inmate's ranking on a recidivism risk scale.

11   States can also reap sizable savings by designating some prisoners for incarceration in minimum-security facilities for geriatrics—essentially, nursing homes—or assigning them to live at large but wearing electronic bracelets for monitoring. Turley, who is now at the George Washington University Law

School, says that prisons are designed for vigorous and violent young predators, but now increasingly valuable cells are being occupied by decreasingly dangerous individuals. These elderly are taxing the capacity of prison medical systems, which are already buckling under the burden of the AIDS epidemic.

12   Although prison medical care often is not optimum, courts have held that denial of adequate care violates the Eighth Amendment prohibition of cruel and unusual punishments. Which is how America may come to regard the tax burden of its correctional system (in what sense are prisoners "corrected"?) unless it moves in the direction POPS is pointing.

13   By the way, when Quenton Brown was paroled, POPS got him a job with a Tampa firm that made pies. The employers asked Turley if Brown had ever worked with pastries. "Oh, yeah," Turley replied. "He loves pastries." ◆◆

TINKERING WITH DEATH*

Alex Kozinski

This essay was first published in the New Yorker *magazine in February 1997. The author is a death penalty judge who reflects on the question "How does it feel to send another man to die?" What is your present opinion about the death penalty? If you were a judge responsible for sentencing people to death, how would you feel?*

1.

1   I woke with a start and sat upright in the darkness.

2   He must be dead by now.

3   The thought filled my head and gave me a weird sense of relief. But no, it couldn't be. The execution was set for Sunday morning at seven—long after daybreak. The display on the digital clock showed 1:23. I fell back on my pillow and tried to chase Thomas Baal from my mind.

4   I had first heard his name just three days earlier. My friend and mentor Supreme Court Justice Anthony M. Kennedy had mentioned during a telephone conversation that an execution was scheduled that night somewhere in my jurisdiction. As a judge on the United States Court of Appeals for the Ninth Circuit, I hear cases from nine states and two territories spread over the Western United States and Oceania.

5   "Must not be mine," I told him, "or I'd have heard about it by now." And left for lunch. When I returned, the fax was chattering away.

6   "The clerk's office called," my secretary said. "Guess who's been drawn for that execution?"

---

*New Yorker, February 10, 1997, pp. 48–53.

7   "How can it be? A man is scheduled to die tonight and this is the first I hear of it?"

8   "He doesn't want a stay," my law clerk interjected. "I've been reading the documents and it looks like he's ready to swallow the bitter pill. It's his mom and dad who are trying to stop the execution. They say he's not competent to waive his right to appeal. The district court is holding a hearing even as we speak."

9   "Oh, good," I muttered. "Maybe the district judge will enter a stay."

10   "Fat chance," my secretary and my law clerk said in unison. "Better read those papers."

2.

11   As I drifted back to sleep, I thought that Thomas Baal was not such a bad fellow compared with some of his neighbors on death row. On February 26, 1988, Baal had robbed thirty-four-year-old Frances Maves at knifepoint. Maves gave him twenty dollars, but Baal demanded more. She struggled. "You shouldn't have done that," Baal told her. "Now you pay. I sentence you to death." He stabbed Maves eight times.

12   I had seen my first death cases shortly after law school, when I clerked at the United States Supreme Court for former Chief Justice Warren E. Burger. That was almost two decades ago now, but I've never quite gotten over the experience. Whatever qualms I had about the efficacy or the morality of the death penalty were drowned out by the pitiful cries of the victims screaming from between the lines of dry legal prose:

13   On the afternoon of May 14, 1973, defendant and three others . . . drove to the residence of Jerry Alday. . . . The defendant and one of his companions entered the mobile home for the purpose of burglary. Shortly thereafter two members of the Alday family, Jerry and his father, Ned Alday, arrived in a jeep, were escorted at gunpoint into the trailer, and were shot to death at close range with handguns. . . .

14   Shortly thereafter a tractor driven by Jerry's brother, Jimmy Alday, arrived at the trailer. After being forced to empty his pockets, he was placed on the living room sofa and killed with a handgun fired at close range.

15   While one of the four was moving the tractor out of the driveway, Jerry's wife, Mary, arrived at her home by car. . . . Two other members of the Alday family, Aubrey and Chester, Jerry's uncle and brother, arrived in a pickup truck. Mary was forced into the bathroom while Aubrey and Chester were taken at gunpoint into the bedrooms and shot in a manner similar to the first two victims. . . .

16   Mary Alday was then raped by two or more of the men. . . . She was then taken, bound and blindfolded, in her car about six miles to a wooded area where she was raped by two of the men, beaten when she refused to commit oral sodomy, and her breasts mutilated. She was then killed with two shots. Her watch was then removed from her nude body. . . .

17   Brutal facts have immense power; they etched deep marks in my psyche. Those who commit such atrocities, I concluded, forfeit their own right to live. We tarnish the memory of the dead and heap needless misery on their surviving families by letting the perpetrators live.

18   Still, it's one thing to feel and another to do. It's one thing to give advice to a judge and quite another to *be* the judge signing the order that will lead to the death of another human being—even a very bad one. Baal was my first.

3.

19   Another start. The clock showed 3 A.M. Would this night never end? I knew I had done the right thing; I had no doubts. Still, I wished it were over.

20   The district court had made its decision around 6 P.M. Thursday. Yes, Baal was competent; he could—and did—waive his right to all appeals, state and federal. This finding was based on the affidavits of the psychiatrists who had examined Baal, and on Baal's courtroom responses:

21   THE COURT: Do you want us to stop [the execution], sir, to give you an opportunity to appeal . . . ?

22   THE DEFENDANT: No, I feel that I've gone through a lot of problems in there and I'm just—I feel that the death penalty is needed. And I don't feel that I have to stick around ten years and try to fight this thing out because it's just not in me.

23   THE COURT: You know that your act here in the Courtroom of saying, "Don't stop the execution," will result in your death. You're aware of that, are you not?

24   THE DEFENDANT: Yes. . . .

25   THE COURT: Now, you know that the choice that you're making here is either life or death. Do you understand that?

26   THE DEFENDANT: I understand. I choose death. . . .

27   THE COURT: Is there anything else?

28   THE DEFENDANT: Just bring me a hooker.

29   THE COURT: Obviously the court can't grant requests such as that. Any other requests?

30   THE DEFENDANT: Just my last meal and let's get the ball rolling.

31   In desperation, Baal's parents had submitted an affidavit from a psychiatrist who, without examining Baal, could say only that he *might* not be competent. The district judge didn't buy it. Stay denied.

32   The case officially landed in my lap just as I was leaving the office for dinner at a friend's house. I arranged with the two other judges who had been selected to hear the case for a telephone conference with the lawyers later that evening. Nothing stops the conversation at a dinner party quite like the half-whispered explanation "I have to take this call. It's a stay in a death case. Don't hold dessert."

33   Last-minute stay petitions in death cases are not unusual; they're a reflex. Except in rare cases where the prisoner decides to give up his appeal rights, death cases are meticulously litigated, first in state court and then in federal court—often bouncing between the two systems several times—literally until the prisoner's dying breath. Once the execution date is set, the process takes on a frantic pace. The death warrant is usually valid only for a limited time—in some states only for a single day—and the two sides battle furiously over that piece of legal territory.

34   If the condemned man . . . can delay the execution long enough for the death warrant to expire, he will have bought himself a substantial reprieve—at least a

few weeks, sometimes months or years. But, if the state can carry out the execution, the game ends in sudden death and the prisoner's arguments die with him.

35 The first time I had seen this battle was in 1977, when a platoon of American Civil Liberties Union lawyers descended on the United States Supreme Court in a vain effort to save Gary Gilmore's life. Gilmore's case was pivotal to death-penalty opponents, because he would be the first to be executed since the Supreme Court had emptied the nation's death rows in 1972 by declaring all existing death-penalty statutes unconstitutional. A number of states had quickly retooled their death statutes, but opponents hoped to use procedural delays to stave off all executions for many years. Gilmore upset this calculation by waiving his appeals after he was found guilty.

36 Gilmore was scheduled to face the firing squad on the morning of January 17, 1977. Efforts to obtain a stay from the lower federal courts during the night had proved unsuccessful, and the lawyers brought a stack of papers to the Supreme Court Clerk's office. The Court was due to hear cases at ten, which was also when the execution was scheduled. In the hour before the Justices took the bench, Michael Rodak, the Clerk of the Supreme Court, carried the petition to them in their chambers—first to one, then to another. The Justices entered the courtroom at the stroke of ten, and Rodak hurried back to his office. A few minutes after ten, he placed a call to the state prison in Draper, Utah, where Gilmore was being held. He first identified himself with a password: "This is Mickey from Wheeling, West Virginia." He continued, "I've presented the stay petition to the Justices, and it was denied. You may proceed with the execution."

37 Rodak then fell silent for a few seconds as he listened to the response from the other end of the line.

38 "Oh. . . . You mean he's already dead?"

4.

39 So as not to wake my wife with my tossing, I went to the kitchen and made myself a cup of tea. As I sipped the hot liquid, I thumbed through the small mountain of papers that had accumulated over the past seventy-two hours.

40 With the stakes in death cases so high, it's hard to escape the feeling of being manipulated, the suspicion that everything the lawyers say or do is designed to entice or intimidate you into giving them what they want. Professional distance—the detachment that is the lawyers' stock-in-trade in ordinary cases—is absent in death cases. It's the battle of the zealots.

41 And it's not just the lawyers. Death cases—particularly as the execution draws near—distort the deliberative process and turn judges into advocates. There are those of my colleagues who have never voted to uphold a death sentence and doubtless never will. The view that judges are morally justified in undermining the death penalty, even though it has been approved by the Supreme Court, was legitimized by the former Supreme Court Justices William J. Brennan, Jr., and Thurgood Marshall, who voted to vacate as cruel and unusual every single death sentence that came before the Court. Just before retiring, in 1994, Justice Harry A. Blackmun adopted a similar view, by pronouncing, "From this day forward, I shall no longer tinker with the machinery of death."

42   Refusing to enforce a valid law is a violation of the judges' oath—something that most judges consider a shameful breach of duty. But death is different, or so the thinking goes, and to slow down the pace of executions by finding fault with every death sentence is considered by some to be highly honorable. In the words of Justice Brennan, this practice "embod[ies] a community striving for human dignity for all, although perhaps not yet arrived."

43   Judges like me, who support the death penalty, are swept right along. Observing manipulation by the lawyers and complicity from liberal colleagues, conservative judges often see it as their duty to prevent death-row inmates from diminishing the severity of their sentence by endlessly postponing the day of reckoning. . . .

44   Families of murder victims are among the most fervent supporters of the death penalty. They often use the press and political channels to agitate for the hasty demise of the monster who shattered their lives. Yet no one seems to have given serious thought to whether families are helped or harmed by the process, especially when it is long delayed. Does watching the perpetrator die help the families reach closure, or does the frustrated hope of execution in the face of endless appeals keep the psychological wounds open, sometimes for decades?

5.

45   Another hour passed, but sleep eluded me. Events of the last three days kept knocking around in my head.

46   Over my friend's kitchen telephone, the lawyers spoke with great urgency and took predictable positions. Afterward, my colleagues and I conferred. One of them—who has never seen a death sentence he liked—quickly voted to issue a stay. Almost instinctively, I took the opposite view. After some discussion, the third judge voted for a stay, and the execution was halted.

47   We spent all day Friday and most of that night preparing the stay order and my dissent. My colleagues argued that Baal's parents made a strong showing that he was not competent to surrender his life: he had a long history of "behavioral and mental problems," had attempted suicide on several occasions, and had been found to suffer from a variety of psychiatric disorders. Twice in the past, he had waived his legal remedies but had later changed his mind.

48   My dissent emphasized the diagnosis of the psychiatrists who had examined him; the state court's finding—just a week earlier—that he was competent; and Baal's lucid and appropriate answers to questions posed from the bench. I ended by arguing that Baal's decision to forgo the protracted trauma of numerous death-row appeals was rational, and that my colleagues were denying his humanity by refusing to accept his decision:

49   It has been said that capital punishment is cruel and unusual because it is degrading to human dignity. . . . But the dignity of human life comes not from mere existence, but from that ability which separates us from the beasts—the ability to choose; freedom of will. *See* Immanuel Kant, "Critique of Pure Reason." When we say that a man—even a man who has committed a horrible crime—is not free to choose, we take away his dignity just as surely as we do when we kill him. Thomas Baal has made a decision to accept society's punishment and be done with it. By refusing to respect his decision we denigrate his status as a human being.

50   The idea that a long sojourn on death row is itself an excruciating punishment—and violates basic human rights—has gained some notable adherents. . . .

6.

51   Dawn broke as I drifted off into fitful sleep, but a part of me kept reaching out to the man I knew was living the last hour of his life. Awareness of death is intrinsic to the human condition, but what is it like to know precisely—to the minute—when your life is going to end? Does time stand still? Does it race? How can you swallow, much less digest, that last meal? Or even think of hookers?

52   Though I've now had a hand in a dozen or more executions, I have never witnessed one. The closest I came was a conversation with Bill Allen, a lawyer from my former law firm. I ran into him at a reception and his face was gray, his eyes—usually sharp and clear—seemed out of focus.

53   "Not well," Bill answered when I asked how he was doing. "I lost a client. His name was Linwood Briley. I saw him die in the electric chair a couple of days ago."

54   "Was it rough?"

55   "What do you think? It was awful."

56   "What was it like when they turned on the juice?"

57   "Oh, by the time they got done strapping him down, putting the goop on his head and the mask on his face, the thing sitting in that chair hardly looked human. But the really strange part was before: looking at him, talking to him, even joking with him, fully aware he'd be dead in half an hour."

58   "Why did you go?"

59   "I thought he should have a friend there with him in his final minutes."

60   The look on Bill's face stayed with me a long time. It was enough to persuade me that I'd never want to witness an execution. Yet I sometimes wonder whether those of us who make life-and-death decisions on a regular basis should not be required to watch as the machinery of death grinds up a human being. I ponder what it says about me that I can, with cool precision, cast votes and write opinions that seal another human being's fate but lack the courage to witness the consequences of my actions.

61   After filing my dissent, at 2:59 A.M. Saturday, I put Baal out of my mind, figuring that it would be quite some time before I'd have to think about him again. Much to my surprise, however, the Supreme Court issued an order that evening, lifting our stay. The execution was on. The Court had more or less adopted my reasoning—even cited me by name. I felt triumphant.

62   But, as Saturday turned to night, it began to sink in that Baal really *was* going to die, and that I would have played a part in ending his life. The thought took hold of my mind and would not let go. It filled me with a nagging sense of unease, something like motion sickness.

7.

63   I finally plunged into a deep sleep from which I awoke long after the execution was over. I was grateful not to have been awake to imagine in real time how Baal was strapped onto a gurney, how his vein was opened, how the deadly fluids were pumped into his body.

64   Lethal injection, which has overtaken the electric chair as the execution method of choice, is favored because it is sure, painless, and nonviolent. But I find it creepy that we pervert the instruments of healing—the needle, the pump, the catheter, F.D.A.-approved drugs—by putting them to such an antithetical use. It also bothers me that we mask the most violent act that society can inflict on one of its members with such an antiseptic veneer. Isn't death by firing squad, with mutilation and bloodshed, more honest?

8.

65   Some three hundred and sixty people have been executed since Gary Gilmore. The most we have dispatched in any one year was fifty-six, in 1995. There are thirty-one hundred or so awaiting their date with the executioner, and the number is growing. Impatient with the delays, Congress last year passed the Effective Death Penalty Act, which will probably hasten the pace of executions. Even then, it's doubtful we have the resources or the will even to keep up with the three hundred or so convicted murderers we add to our death rows every year.

66   With the pace of executions quickening and the total number of executions rising, I fear it's only a matter of time before we learn that we've executed the wrong man. There have already been cases where prisoners on death row were freed after evidence turned up proving them innocent. I dread the day we are confronted with a case in which the conclusive proof of innocence turns up too late.

67   And I sometimes wonder whether the death penalty is not an expensive and distracting sideshow to our battle against violent crime. Has our national fascination with capital punishment diverted talent and resources from mundane methods of preventing violent crime? Take William Bonin, the notorious Freeway Killer, who raped, tortured, and murdered fourteen teen-age boys, then dumped their bodies along Southern California's freeways. If anyone deserved execution, surely it was Bonin. And on February 23, 1996, after fourteen years on death row, he went to his death, even then mocking the families of his victims. Asked if he had any regrets, the confessed killer admitted that, indeed, he did: "Well, probably I went in the [military] service too soon, because I was peaking in my bowling career. I was carrying, like, a 186 to a 190 average. . . . I've always loved bowling."

68   Yet, looking at the record in his case, one can't help noting that Bonin had given us ample warning of his proclivities. While serving in Vietnam, he had sexually assaulted at gunpoint two soldiers under his command. After returning to civilian life, he had been convicted of molesting four boys between the ages of twelve and eighteen. He had served three years for those crimes and, upon his release, molested another boy. Again, he had served only three years and had then been set free to commence his killing spree.

69   Bonin is not unique. My concurring opinion in his case lists a number of other killers who gave us fair warning that they were dangerous but were nevertheless set free to prey on an unsuspecting and vulnerable population. Surely putting to death ten convicted killers isn't nearly as useful as stopping a single Bonin before he tastes blood.

9.

70 It's late Saturday night. Another execution is scheduled for next week, and the machinery of death is humming through my fax. And, despite the qualms, despite the queasiness I still feel every time an execution is carried out in my jurisdiction, I tinker away. I do it because I have taken an oath. But there's more. I do it because I believe that society is entitled to take the life of those who have shown utter contempt for the lives of others. And because I hear the tortured voices of the victims crying out to me for vindication. ◆◆

ONE BIG HAPPY PRISON*

Michael Moore

Michael Moore is a filmmaker, author, and political activist. His films include Roger and Me *(1989),* The Big One *(1997), and* Bowling for Columbine *(2002). His books include* Downsize This: Unarmed Threats from an Unarmed American *and* Adventures in a T.V. Nation. *The following excerpt is from* Stupid White Men: And Other Sorry Excuses for the State of the Nation. *This essay can help us critically reevaluate the death penalty in the United States. Should people under the age of eighteen be sentenced to die? How does this country's policies on capital punishment compare to those of other countries? These are the kinds of questions Michael Moore thinks Americans should be asking.*

1 Thirty-eight states have the death penalty. So [do] the federal government and the U.S. military. Twelve states, plus the District of Columbia (that little piece of swampland with a majority of African-Americans and those offensive license plates), do not.

2 Since 1976, there have been over seven hundred executions in the United States.

3 The top execution-happy states are:

Texas (248 executions—nearly one-third of all U.S. executions since 1976)
Virginia (82)
Florida (51)
Missouri (50)
Oklahoma (43)
Louisiana (26)
South Carolina (25)
Arkansas (24)
Alabama (23)
Arizona (22)
North Carolina (17)
Delaware (13)

---

*Michael Moore, *Stupid White Men: And Other Sorry Excuses for the State of the Nation* (New York: Harper-Collins, 2002), pp. 204–208.

Illinois (12)
California (9)
Nevada (9)
Indiana (8)
Utah (6)

4   A shocking recent death penalty study of 4,578 cases in a twenty-three-year period (1973–1995) concluded that the courts found serious, reversible error in nearly 7 of every 10 capital sentence cases that were fully reviewed during the period. It also found that death sentences were being overturned in 2 out of 3 appeals. The overall prejudicial review error rate was 68 percent.

5   Since 1973, some ninety-five death row inmates have been *fully exonerated* by the courts—that is, found innocent of the crimes for which they were sentenced to die. Ninety-six persons have been released as a result of DNA testing.

6   And what were the most common errors?

   1. Egregiously incompetent defense lawyers who didn't even look for, or missed important evidence that would have proved innocence or demonstrated that their client didn't deserve to die.
   2. Police or prosecutors who *did* discover that kind of evidence but *suppressed* it, actively derailing the judicial process.

7   In half the years studied, including the most recent one, the error rate was over 60 percent. High error rates exist across the country. In 85 percent of death penalty cases the error rates are 60 percent or higher. Three-fifths have error rates of 70 percent or higher.

8   Catching these errors takes time—a national average of nine years from death sentence to execution. In most cases, death row inmates wait years for the lengthy review procedures needed to uncover all these errors—whereupon their death sentences are very often reversed. This imposes a terrible cost on taxpayers, victims' families, the judicial system, and the wrongly condemned.

9   Among the inmates involved in the study who had their death verdicts overturned, nearly all were given a sentence less than death (82 percent), and many were found innocent on retrial (7 percent).

10   The number of errors has risen since 1996, when President Clinton made it tougher for death row inmates to prove their innocence by signing into law a one-year limit on the time inmates have to appeal to federal courts after exhausting their appeals in state courts. In light of the study that proved how many of these inmates are either innocent or not legally deserving of the death penalty, this attempt to curb their appeals was simply outrageous.

11   We are one of the few countries in the world that puts to death *both* the mentally retarded and juveniles offenders. The United States is among only six countries that impose the death penalty on juveniles. The others are Iran, Nigeria, Pakistan, Saudi Arabia, and Yemen.

12   The United States is also the only country besides Somalia that has not signed the United Nations Convention on the Rights of the Child. Why? Because it contains a provision prohibiting the execution of children under eighteen, and we want to remain free to execute our children.

13   *No other industrialized nation executes its children.*

14   Even China prohibits the death penalty for those under eighteen—this from a country that has shown an intolerable lack of respect for human rights.

15   Currently the total number of death row inmates in the United States tops 3,700. Seventy of those death row inmates are minors (or were when they committed their crime).

16   But our Supreme Court doesn't find it cruel and unusual punishment (in the terms of the Eighth Amendment to the U.S. Constitution) to execute those who were sixteen years old when they committed a capital crime. This despite the fact that same court has ruled that sixteen-year-olds do not have "the maturity or judgment" to sign *contracts.*

17   Odd, isn't it, that a child's diminished capacity for signing contracts is viewed as a legal barrier to enforcing a contract, but when it comes to the right to be executed, a child's capacity is equal to that of an adult?

18   Eighteen states allow juvenile offenders as young as sixteen to be executed. Five others allow the execution of those who were seventeen or older when they committed their crime. In 1999 Oklahoma executed Sean Sellers, who was sixteen at the time of the murders he was found guilty of committing. Sellers's multiple personality disorder wasn't revealed to the jury that convicted him. A federal appeals court found that Sellers might have been "factually innocent" because of his mental disorder, but that "innocence alone is not sufficient to grant federal relief." Unbelievable.

19   The American public is not stupid, and now that the truth has been coming out about the innocent people who have been sent to death row, they are at least responding with a sense of shame. Just a few years ago public opinion polls showed that upwards of 80 percent of the American people supported the death penalty. But now, with the truth out, a recent *Washington Post*/ABC News poll found that public approval of capital punishment has declined, while the proportion of Americans who favor replacing the death penalty with life in prison has increased. Fifty-one percent favored halting all executions until a commission is established to determine whether the death penalty is being administered fairly.

20   Sixty-eight percent said the death penalty is unfair because innocent people are sometimes executed. Recent Gallup Polls have shown that support for the death penalty is at a nineteen-year low. Sixty-five percent agreed that a poor person is more likely than a person of average or above-average income to receive the death penalty for the same crime. Fifty percent agreed that a black person is more likely than a white person to receive the death penalty for the same crime. Even in the killing machine known as the state of Texas, the *Houston Chronicle* reported that 59 percent of Texans surveyed believed that their state *has executed an innocent person!*, while 72 percent favor changing state law to include the sentencing option of life without parole, and 60 percent are now opposed to the state executing an inmate who is mentally retarded.

21   What we have done, in this great country, is to wage a war *not* on crime *but on the poor we feel comfortable blaming for it.* Somewhere along the way we forgot about people's rights, because we didn't want to spend the money.

22   We live in a society that rewards and honors corporate gangsters—corporate leaders who directly and indirectly plunder the earth's resources and look out for the shareholders' profits above all else—while subjecting the poor to a random and brutal system of "justice."

23   But the public is starting to realize this is wrong.

24   We need to reorder society so that every person within it is seen as precious, sacred, and valuable, and that NO man is above the law, no matter how many candidates he buys off. Until this changes, we can utter the words "with liberty and justice for all" only with shame. ◆◆

NOTES AND SOURCES

The study of error rates in death penalty cases is "A Broken System: Error Rates in Capital Cases, 1973–1995," James S. Liebman, Jeffrey Fagan, and Valerie West, June 12, 2000; and was reported in the *New York Times*, "Death Sentences Being Overturned in 2 of 3 Appeals," Fox Butterfield, June 12, 2000.

The Death Penalty Information Center compiled statistics and information on the United States use of the death penalty on juveniles and the mentally retarded.

Polls measuring public support of the death penalty are published in the *Washington Post,* "Support for Death Penalty Eases; McVeigh's Execution Approved, While Principle Splits Public," Richard Morin, Claudia Deane, May 3, 2001; and the *Houston Chronicle:* "Harris County Is a Pipeline to Death Row," Allan Turner, February 4, "Complication; DNA, Retardation Problems for Death Penalty," by the *Chronicle* staff, February 6, "A Deadly Distinction," Mike Tolson, February 7, 2001.

B. WHAT SHOULD BE DONE WITH YOUNG OFFENDERS?

QUESTIONS TO CONSIDER BEFORE YOU READ

Why do you think so many young people are incited to cause violence? Do you think films, music, and video games at times advocate violence? How do young people handle these influences? Do you think young people feel alienated by the adult world? How can adults help young people feel less emotionally alienated?

THE APOCALYPSE OF ADOLESCENCE*

Ron Powers

Ron Powers is a contributing writer to the Atlantic Monthly. *In this article, Powers discusses the rising problem of youthful offenders in Vermont and reflects on the new trend of young criminals and this country's inability to rehabilitate young offenders. As you consider this reading, you might ask yourself whether the purpose of the criminal system is to rehabilitate or punish offenders. Does punishment lead to the perpetuation of crime? Does rehabilitation work?*

---

*Atlantic Monthly, March 2002, pp. 62–74.

BEWILDERED CHILDREN

1   Bewildered, depraved children, behind bars, are a great deal more commonplace in Vermont than national surveys and tourist brochures would have us believe. The plight of children—or, as certain adult Vermonters demonstrably prefer to look at it, the *inconvenience* of children, the downright *menace* of children—has become a dominant theme of life in the state in the years I have lived there. Although Vermont enjoys one of the lowest crime rates in the nation, and although the region is recovering from a harsh economic slump that hit at the beginning of the 1990s, signs persist that the connections between children and their host culture here are unraveling. Kids are in trouble even here in Vermont. The reasons elude easy explanation.

2   That an explosion in serious juvenile crime has occurred in Vermont is undeniable. Data gathered by the Vermont Department of Corrections in 1999 revealed that the number of jail inmates aged sixteen to twenty-one had jumped by more than 77 percent in three years. (By that time overcrowding had obliged Vermont to start shipping some of its prisoners off to Virginia and other states.) Vermont's Department of Corrections reported that it supervised or housed one in ten Vermont males of high school age. The annual DOC budget more than doubled during the 1990s, from $27 million to more than $70 million. A report by the northern New England consortium Justiceworks, released in 2000, asserted that "while overall crime rates are down in northern New England, a greater proportion of those crimes are being committed by children under the age of 18."

3   Panic-inducing mischief has also become a fact of adolescent daily life. In the year following the April 1999 Columbine massacre Vermont experienced an epidemic of anonymous bomb threats that caused school evacuations up and down the state. The threats grew so routine that the administration at one sizable high school in the southeastern part of the state installed a voice message for people who telephoned the school during a crisis: "We're sorry, but we cannot take your call now, due to an evacuation." Police guards, uniformed and armed, became fixtures in many of Vermont's public schools. In February of last year a seventeen-year-old named Bradley Bell, from Milton, Vermont, was arrested for manufacturing pipe bombs in his house. County prosecutors said their information indicated that Bell might have intended to plant the bombs at the high school. As of this writing, this case has not come to trial.

4   The number of dropouts in the state's public schools showed an increase of nearly 50 percent in the 1990s—from 1,060 in 1992 to 1,585 in 1998. Meanwhile, admissions to Corrections Education, a program run for adolescent offenders by the state's Department of Corrections, grew in 1998 from 160 in June to 220 in November. The number of young people without a high school diploma in the "corrections" population increased from 87 percent to 93 percent from 1987 to 1998.

5   Heroin addiction was virtually unknown among Vermont children as recently as three years ago, but by 2000 heroin abuse was an established crisis throughout the state, and by early last year the volume of confiscated heroin had increased fourfold since 1999. Young addicts turned up in nearly every town of substantial

size. Newspapers began reporting deaths resulting from overdose. Last September the police in Winooski, which borders Burlington, arrested an eighteen-year-old and charged him with dealing heroin from an apartment next door to a school. The police said they had found 397 bags of the narcotic in his possession.

6   "Heroin is almost as easy to get in Burlington as a gallon of maple syrup," *The Burlington Free Press* reported in February of 2001. The same edition of the paper chronicled a horrifying heroin-related story about a sixteen-year-old Burlington girl, Christal Jones, who had been found murdered a month earlier in a Bronx apartment. A runaway and sometime ward of the state's social-services agencies, Christal had developed a heroin habit that led her into prostitution. She was one of several young Vermont women drawn into the prostitution ring of a Burlington hustler with connections in New York.

◆◆◆◆

THE LANGUAGE OF APOCALYPSE

7   Theo Padnos is a slightly clerkish-looking man of thirty-four, small and pale, whose horn-rimmed glasses and mop of curly, uncombed hair make it easy not to notice the wiry mountain-biker's sinews in his arms and legs. It's easy not to notice Padnos's presence at all, in fact, which is the way he likes it, especially when he is doing what he does best: paying acute attention.

8   Padnos is a former bicycle-shop salesman and telemarketer who often has had trouble finding a suitable job. He has a Ph.D. in comparative literature, which he earned in June of 2000 from the University of Massachusetts at Amherst, but this has not helped him much in his quest for employment. He can be impressive in ticking off the list of university teaching jobs throughout the United States and Canada for which he has applied without success.

9   A couple of years ago, desperate for an income and hungry to teach something to somebody, Padnos applied for a part-time job teaching literature to adolescents in the Community High School of Vermont, a program administered by the state's Department of Corrections. Its pupils are inmates in the prison system. Padnos was assigned to the regional correctional facility in Woodstock, on the state's southeastern border—just across the Connecticut River from Hanover. The facility, built in 1935 and scheduled for abandonment by the corrections system this spring, is wedged between an auto-parts outlet and a convenience store on the unfashionable eastern edge of a fashionable town. Its exterior, red brick and white-washed wooden trim, evokes a schoolhouse. Its interior, in the words of the state's commissioner of corrections, evokes "a James Cagney movie": it's an antiquated warren of locked metal doors, Plexiglas monitoring windows, and iron grillwork, with gray paint and a prevailing odor—diluted by disinfectant—of burned meat from the cafeteria. Its capacity is seventy-five inmates. Its superintendent says he "hates" to see the population rise above eighty. About half are convicted adult felons, the other half kids awaiting trial. The two populations mix indiscriminately. Padnos taught in a basement classroom there for thirteen months.

10   Teachers in the Vermont correctional system are offered several layers of protection from their charges: surveillance cameras in the classrooms, walkie-talkies they can clip to their belts, classroom doors left open to allow fast entry by guards

in case of trouble. Most teachers accept the full inventory, but Padnos rejected everything. His motives had less to do with bravado than with practical concerns, he told me when we spoke recently. "I got rid of the camera, I let the inmates close and lock the door, and I even allowed them to expel the jail snitches if they wanted to," he said. "I allowed this because, as a teacher in the liberal arts, I try to humanize my students. I was interested in staging an intimate, private encounter with literature, and I thought that a measure of privacy and separation from the inhuman jail would help."

11   Padnos found himself inside a compacted sampling of the sub-population from which the deliverers of sudden violence have lately been emerging: the young, the male, the white, the angry, the ignored, the overstimulated, the intelligent if not well educated. The dangerous dreamers. Most of his charges were in for mid-level crimes such as drug use, assault, and robbery. If they had lacked for attentive adult mentors in the outside world, they now lived at close quarters with plenty of them: adult rapists, gang members, and murderers. Although largely poor and from rural communities, these young inmates represented a range of social classes in Vermont, a rural state that is laced with pockets of poverty. With one eminent exception, they had not yet broken through to the level of crime that stops the larger world in its tracks. But as Padnos quickly came to perceive, such an achievement preoccupied most of them. It formed their imaginative agendas. "They're fascinated by the details of their crimes," he told me, "and by violence in general. Violent crime is the one topic to which they can devote sustained concentration. When my classes touched on this subject, as almost all jail classes eventually do, they became a kind of seminar. Everyone was well informed, everyone felt entitled to participate, and everyone was prepared to teach something. When I asked the students how often they read the police files they carried with them to class—all the witness statements, the blood and ballistics analyses the prosecution had turned over to the defense—they would say, 'All the time. Over and over. And over.'"

12   Arranging their future crimes was the long-term extracurricular project that kept them busy, Padnos learned, and they received constant guidance and reinforcement from the hardened jailbirds in their midst. "The parole and probation people may have thought they had these kids in their radar," he told me, "but the kids were already thinking way beyond rehabilitation. They weren't talking about getting jobs, going back to school, anything like that. It was through crime that they intended to reintroduce themselves to the world."

13   The facility's superintendent, William R. Anderson, backs up Padnos's observations. He told me that although instances of violent crime in Vermont had not increased in recent years, the severity of violence had intensified "significantly." "I'm seeing something in young people coming into jail today I've never seen before," he said. "The seventeen-, eighteen-, nineteen-year-old kids I see, they don't care about anything, including themselves. They have absolutely no respect for any kind of authority. They have no direction in their lives whatsoever. They're content to come back to jail time after time after time."

14   Into this context Padnos brought an ambitious syllabus: James Baldwin, Edgar Allan Poe, Cormac McCarthy, Flannery O'Connor, Mark Twain. "I wanted

to teach them to imagine themselves in the situations of others in similar predicaments," he said. "I wanted to show them that they are not the *isolatos* they take themselves for. What they are going through is not unique to them; these struggles have been experienced and written about all through history."

15   As he thinks back on it now, Padnos concedes that aside from a few scattered, near accidental moments when the literature, the students, and his instruction coalesced, his course was a failure. "They were too far gone by the time they arrived in prison," he said. "This was true of the middle-class, public high school, bomb-threatening kids; it was even true of the well-educated preppie kids. And their experience in prison pushed most of them even further away from any hope for involvement with a civil, productive life. Just once in a while I saw it happen: they'd relate to something I'd brought them to read or talk about, and for a few minutes they'd be transformed into children—wide-eyed, frightened, hopelessly lost. Then a jailer would give a knock, tell 'em time was up, and that moment would be over."

16   But something else began to happen in those jagged sessions, a transformation that Padnos had not anticipated. The jailed kids, gradually and roughly, came to accept him as one of themselves. The key to the process, he believes, was his jettisoning of the classroom safeguards. None of the other teachers had dared to let go of those, and their refusal amounted to a statement of irreducible fear, disgust, and membership in the target world. Padnos's students made him prove that he meant the gesture: they sized him up, shouted him down, mocked his questions, cursed and tried to intimidate him for a while. They demanded to know why anybody like him would spend time in jail if he didn't have to.

17   Padnos became a player under inmates' rules. He believes that his youthfulness helped, and also his unconcealed affinity for the outlaw point of view. "I have an attraction to people who don't mind causing offense," he told me. "People who are disappointments to themselves, and whose families don't know how to account for them." Whatever the reasons, when the layers of distrust had burned away, Padnos found himself privy to, and taking part in, conversations of the sort that usually unspool only among the dispossessed, and only in those moments when they feel they are free from interlopers, secure with their own kind.

18   What Padnos began hearing in these conversations, he says, was the language of apocalypse. "The goal for the bright ones is to truly mesmerize the middle class with violence," he told me. "They've been transfixed by disaster themselves—in their families, at the movies, in the company of their mentors in crime. They've come to feel that there's nothing out there for them. And so they know exactly the effect they're looking for. They keep up with the news. They read about their deeds in the papers. They've been ignored all their lives, and they're pleased to see that the public is finally giving them some of the attention they're due. The papers always describe their crimes as 'senseless,' and 'meaningless,' and 'unmotivated,' and these kids themselves always come off as 'cold' and 'distant' to the reporters. The details of their crimes are always covered with the tightest possible focus, as if meaning might be found there. The result is just what they'd been hoping for: terrifying, mesmerizing violence, and no context."

19   Padnos, who is writing a book about his experiences, hardly endorses this violence. His classroom goal, in fact, had been to transmute the violent impulse into

a quest for self-understanding through the medium of literature. He had hoped, in the best postgraduate fashion, that through a guided reading of "The Cask of Amontillado," or *Cities of the Plain*, he might awaken his young charges to the healing awareness that their torments are part of the human condition.

20   Instead Padnos found himself becoming a student in a different kind of seminar. Listening to the boys in his classroom, he began to comprehend that the deeds they had committed, and the language with which they described future deeds, amounted to a text that American society has so far stubbornly resisted decoding. The message Padnos found embedded in this text is that in a world otherwise stripped of meaning and self-identity, adolescents can come to understand violence itself as a morally grounded gesture, a kind of purifying attempt to intervene against the nothingness.

21   "They're a community of believers, in a way," he told me. "They come from all kinds of backgrounds. But what unites them are these apocalyptic suspicions that they have. They think and act as though it's an extremely late hour in the day, and nothing much matters anymore. A lot of them are suicidal. Most of them see themselves as frustrated travelers. Solitary wayfarers. They've done things that have broken them off from their past and set off on the open road. Eventually they got arrested. This may be hard for some people to swallow, I guess, but they talk about their crimes almost as if they were acts of faith. Maybe these kids themselves wouldn't use those words. But the things they've done, on some level, strike me as almost ecstatic attempts to vault over the shabby facts of their everyday lives. They haven't read much. But some of them, the more down-and-out ones especially, read the Book of Revelation a lot."

22   These kids also watch a lot of movies and TV. No surprise there. But it's what they extract from these sources that engrosses Padnos. "They're drawn to the myths built into these violent movies, not just the violence itself," he said. "Prison life, especially for kids—maybe life in general for kids—is soaked in myths about outlaws, self-reliance. People traveling a rough landscape that is their true home. People who mete out justice to anyone who impinges on their native liberties. Post-apocalyptic heroes, just like they want to be—violent, suicidal, the sort of people who are preparing themselves for what happens after everything ends.

23   "These kids half believe that their destination is the same as these screen heroes'. That it's something like the roadside shantytown in *Mad Max*. They devour *Taxi Driver*, especially the Travis Bickle speech in which he prophesies a great rain and promises that it will wash the streets of their scum. They relate to themes in *Terminator II* and *The Postman*, and *Reservoir Dogs*, and *Wild Things*. These were practically our class canon." Padnos thought for a minute. "I admire my students," he said. "Sometimes I wish that I had the courage they have. I just think of them as passionate, thoughtful, lucid, well-informed, literate, morally sophisticated, homicidal all-American kids."

THEY ARE US

24   To most people, the notion that an apocalyptic nihilism is taking root in this nation's children will seem alarmist. Much of the evidence can be seen as variations on age-old complaints, familiar generational impasses, and inevitable exceptions

to a reassuring general rule: that tranquillity still reigns. After all, are not most kids well-adjusted? Do not the vast majority of them pass through adolescence without episodes of addiction, pregnancy, criminal behavior, self-destruction? Have grown-ups not complained since time immemorial about "kids these days"? And have not kids forever groused that the adults in their lives don't understand them? Have there not always been instances of violent aggression among a few antisocial delinquents?

25   Parents who generalize from the apparent contentedness of their own children are indulging a dangerous fallacy. Children, like people in general, present different faces to different groups within their social universes, a state of affairs amply documented by Judith Rich Harris in her important book The *Nurture Assumption* (1998), which illustrated the multiple, often contradictory personas elicited variably by parents, peer groups, siblings, and prevailing societal influences. Equally treacherous is the view that the young have always been inscrutable to adults and have always complained about being misunderstood. Since the end of World War II adolescents have been chafing against an ever more impervious, unheeding social system. Their outrage has found expression, with increasing intensity, among the inchoate "juvenile delinquents" of the early postwar years, the Beats of the 1950s, the hippies and political radicals of the 1960s, the drug and gangland subcultures of more recent years. And now it's expressed by the kids who carry out school shootings and other acts of vicious and inexplicable violence. The questions we must ask ourselves today, therefore, are these: Why are so many children plotting to blow up their worlds and themselves? For each act of gratuitous violence that is actually carried out, how many unconsummated dark fantasies are transmuted into depression, resignation, or a benumbed withdrawal from participation in civic society?

26   What we are witnessing is clearly something new. A frightening momentum has been building, and the qualities of generational understanding and assurance that once earned America a worldwide reputation as child-centered are fading fast. And yet despite a growing awareness of this fact, the public policy that we are developing to cope with troubled kids is only exacerbating the situation. Let us leave aside considerations of withering support for public education and inadequate federal support for impoverished working mothers. Let us consider our present policy in its rawest and most adversarial form: in the state's growing arrogation of power to punish rather than to rehabilitate. This is a policy that expresses both fear of and contempt for children.

27   In the 1990s public figures such as John Ashcroft and William Bennett successfully campaigned to make certain that the juvenile justice system no longer "hugs the juvenile terrorist," in Ashcroft's words. As Margaret Talbot pointed out in *The New York Times Magazine* in September 2000, forty-five states in that decade passed new laws or enacted changes in old ones that toughened criminal justice and criminal penalties for the errant young. Fifteen states transferred to prosecutors from judges the power to choose adult prosecution in certain crimes. Twenty-eight states created statutory requirements for adult trials in some crimes of violence, theft and robbery, and drug use. In 1994

President Clinton's Violent Crime Control and Law Enforcement Act federalized many of the states' initiatives, authorizing adult prosecution of children thirteen and over who were charged with certain serious crimes, and expanding the death penalty to cover some sixty offenses. As Talbot wrote, "The number of youths under 18 held in adult prisons, and in many cases mixed in with adult criminals, has doubled in the last 10 years or so . . . to 7,400 in 1997. Of the juveniles incarcerated on any given day, one in 10 are in adult jails or prisons."

28   These draconian efforts seem to fly in the face of emerging scientific research demonstrating that the brains of children and adolescents are not yet fully formed—not yet equipped to make precisely the sort of emotional and rational decisions necessary to restrain impulses in certain situations that can lead to anti-social and criminal behavior. Adolescents, with directed and scrupulous supervision, can indeed change and grow emotionally and psychologically, but our public policy seems intent on denying this possibility. But if the government is in denial, the marketplace is not: with the help of exhaustive behavioral research, corporations have in recent decades spent hundreds of millions of dollars ransacking and exploiting the emotions and thought processes of adolescents and pre-adolescents. RoperASW (with its *Roper Youth Report*), Teenage Research Unlimited, and similar organizations, using methods derived from the behavioral sciences, advise merchandisers and advertising companies on the latest semiotics of "cool" and consumer-friendly subversion. "We understand how teens think, what they want, what they like, what they aspire to be, what excites them, and what concerns them," the Teenage Research Unlimited Web site brags. What this understanding translates into in the marketplace is hypersexuality, aggression, addiction, coldness, and irony-laced civic disaffection—the very seedbed of apocalyptic nihilism.

29   The national task of recentering ourselves and our children will be enormous, and will require painful shifts in our expectations of expediency, personal gratification, and the unfettered accumulation of wealth. But the goals are necessary and anything but obscure. Children crave a sense of self-worth. That craving is answered most readily through respectful inclusion: through a reintegration of our young into the intimate circles of family and community life. We must face the fact that having ceased to exploit children as laborers, we now exploit them as consumers. We must find ways to offer them useful functions, tailored to their evolving capacities. Closely allied to this goal is an expanded definition of "education"—one that ranges far beyond debates over public and private schools and how much to spend on them to embrace an ethic of sustained mentoring that extends from community to personal relationships.

30   The societal shift of consciousness necessary for such a recentering is—in a pre-apocalyptic context, at least—virtually unthinkable. But America is lately learning to rethink many assumptions it once comfortably took for granted, out of terrorist promptings eerily similar to the bloody messages being delivered by certain of our young. ◆◆

NOT SO ALONE*

Gerard Jones

A former comic-book writer and screenwriter, Gerard Jones has also written such books as Honey I'm Home: Sitcoms Selling the American Dream *and* The Comic Book Heroes. *The following essay is an excerpt from chapter 12 of* Killing Monsters: Why Children Need Fantasy, Super Heroes, and Make-Believe Violence. *Jones wonders why children and adolescents have so much rage and anger in their hearts that they feel the need to express it through violence. When was the last time you were angry? Were you ever angry with the "adult world"? Why? How can the world of adults be responsible for causing anger in children? How can anger be channeled into productive energy?*

1   "My concern about media's influence isn't so much for children in supportive families," said developmental psychologist Carla Seal-Wanner, "but for those who lack other mediating influences. For them, media can have a more powerful, even dominant socializing role."

2   There's a lot to inspire concern in the media that young people love, especially to those of us raised on less harsh, less confrontational styles. On top of the quantity and intensity of violence, a trend in some ways even more distressing is the rage that has been increasingly shaping youth entertainment over the past two decades. It's in the rappers, the rockers, the games, the movies, even the cartoons and comic books kids love. Action heroes don't step up stoically to fight the bad guy but snarl, "This time it's *personal!*" Video game martial artists stomp on their fallen foes and turn to the player with a sadistic sneer. Eminem acts as though he's conciliating his critics for his antigay slurs by performing at the Grammies with Elton John, and then concludes by giving the world the finger. A gay teenager in one of my workshops loved Eminem for blasting the hypocritical adult world with his anger, even when the anger seemed directed at young men like himself. Then he flung himself back into his funny but angry story about a prostitute setting up a hypocritical cop for a fall. When I asked another kid, a smart, academically successful kid who never got in trouble, why he adopted the gangster-imitating "whigga" style of clothing, he said, "because it scares people."

3   Even in the mild, dorky world of comic books, the 1980s and 1990s were marked by the rise of the snarling hero. The blithely grinning Superman, the hyperrational Batman, the tormented but mild Spider-Man, were nudged aside by the bestial Wolverine with his slashing metal claws. To keep the old heroes popular, writers and artists had to keep pace with their audience's growing taste for rampant passion. Stories and dialogue got meaner. The art grew more jagged, more "in your face," heavier with black ink. Superman, the first and corniest of superheroes, was killed and brought back as a snarling, sweating, fist-clenching, eye-blazing embodiment of righteous rage. Even the kids who

*Gerard Jones, *Killing Monsters: Why Children Need Fantasy, Super Heroes, and Make-Believe Violence* (New York: Perseus, 2002), pp. 205–217.

want the simplest dramas of good and evil also want their heroes to express a baseline of anger.

4   It's natural to respond to anger with a defensive anger of our own or a fear of where it will lead. We respond more effectively, however, when we first ask, why are kids so angry?

5   In her nationwide surveys of violent youth, Dr. Helen Smith said she found "a tremendous number of young people who compare school to *prison*." She read me quote after quote from kids who feel they're being held captive, controlled, not cared about, not protected from the bullying of other kids. Many feel that home is just a different cell in the prison, especially if they have performance-driven parents who keep them under constant scrutiny. They look ahead to adult society and the work world and can only imagine more of the same, and they conclude, "I don't see how real prison could be any worse than this."

6   Most of them feel that they can't change their circumstances because adults won't acknowledge that there's a problem. "They feel anger and alienation from what they perceive as the *hypocrisy* of the adult world," Smith said. Parents and teachers are preoccupied with violence but don't like to acknowledge young people's rage. Kids feel that complaining in school only gets *them* viewed as the problem, while their parents either don't care or side with the school in clamping down tighter on them. They feel that no one knows they're there, no one understands their feelings, no one cares. "Attacks on the school or the world as a whole," said Smith, "from vandalism to threats to actually bringing weapons are often presaged by specific complaints about being dismissed. Sometimes they just keep escalating their negative actions until they think they've finally been *noticed*."

7   Forensic psychologist James McGee, an authority on classroom violence, studied all the videotaped rants and Web postings left by the Columbine shooters and said one thread ran through nearly every minute and page of them: the demand to be seen. They drew attention to themselves with Gothic makeup and costumes, made offensively violent movies for class, posted to hate-mongering Web sites under their own names. They not only played the violent video game *Doom* but—much more importantly, in McGee's view—they proclaimed their love of the game and its violence loudly at a time when such games were drawing fire from parents, psychologists, and legislators for contributing to teen violence. When their parents and the authorities didn't respond as strongly as they wanted, their frustration increased. Their parents seemed unable or unwilling to notice even that they were filling their homes with guns and bombs. Finally, wanting attention more than life itself, the boys created a horrific scenario that would leave the world no choice but to notice them.

8   The late Dr. Rachel Lauer, chief psychologist of the New York City Schools, spoke of the adult world's inability, or unwillingness, to see the problem: "Doesn't the adult population cherish its young—do everything possible to turn kids into well behaved, attractive, skillful, productive citizens responsible for each other, for the fate of the world? Indeed we do. We cherish our young so much that when our determined ministrations are resisted we exercise a long repertoire of 'remedies.' We 'attack' the problem and 'handle' it by rewarding, punishing,

[handwritten margin notes: "School is prison" beside paragraph 5; "attention" beside paragraph 7]

requiring, mandating, directing, expecting, teasing, threatening, ridiculing, failing, jailing, beating, restricting, insulting, advising, ministering, assessing. ~~Our young are our favorite objects for our manipulative skills—all for their own good, of course.~~ As parents and educators we measure our own power and worth according to our success in producing youths who have learned what they're supposed to and how willing they are to learn it quickly, well, now, and better than someone else's kids."

9   Some fight back or drop out, but even kids who try to live by the rules may feel they're in a coercive society. "Like all hostages or slaves who comply with their oppressors, they build a rage inside," said Lauer. "Some identify with their oppressors and learn to act the same domineering way toward others. Sometimes they rage against themselves and become depressed. They constantly focus attention upon 'doing what you're supposed to do.' It means constantly attuning to external signals of what to do every moment of the day. Externally oriented, they live virtually in a state of, 'O.K. now I've done that, what do I have to do next?' By giving up so much authorship of their own lives, they lose the feeling of being alive or real."

10   They may feel that their lives are meaningless. Dr. William Damon of the Stanford Center on Adolescence has argued that everyone needs something to believe in, some greater cause to belong to in order to make our lives feel worthwhile, and that modern American society provides little of that for young people. We fear kids, we try to control them, we nervously track their scores on statistical tests, or we bring ourselves down to their level and try to win their favor, but we don't demand that they meet higher moral, social, and civic expectations. Damon has described the frustration and lonely anxiety of young people who aren't given a purpose—much like the feelings described by the "prisoners" of Helen Smith's survey, who feel that they are confined in adult institutions but never given a good reason to be there.

11   "If kids don't feel that society has anything meaningful to give them," Damon said, "then they'll find meaning wherever they can. That's likely to be the media. If they are particularly angry with society, they may come to identify with the media's most antisocial models. That's when they can be influenced by hate sites on the Web or a movie like *Natural Born Killers.*"

12   There have been young people like Barry Loukaitis of Moses Lake, Washington, rejected by his parents, picked on in high school, never very good at anything, who became obsessed with *Natural Born Killers* and a Pearl Jam video showing a teenager shooting classmates. Those quick-cut, Technicolor, grunge-rock revenge fantasies gave him the feeling of meaning he'd lacked. He started making pronouncements like, "Murder is pure—people make it impure." Then he took a gun to school and became America's first widely publicized school shooter.

13   There have been a lot of young people like Ruben Diaz, too. "I was the stereotype of the kid you're supposed to be afraid of," he said. He grew up in a public housing project in the South Bronx during the 1980s with no father and a working mother who couldn't be around much. Afraid at school and on the street, he spent his teen years in his apartment watching TV, listening to rap music, and reading comic books. He wasn't shown much by a negligent government, a

decimated educational establishment, or a crime-obsessed news media to make him think that society had much use for a nonwhite, low-income teenager. He found his most meaningful models in gangster rappers and superheroes. In their very different ways, both demonstrated how individual anger could be channeled into the power to confront corruption and change the world. And both, Diaz realized, were created by commercial storytellers in not-quite-respectable fields who were willing to say what kids were really thinking and fantasizing.

14   Diaz discovered comic book fandom, a social group that helped channel his interests into a life direction. He got a job as an editorial assistant at DC Comics, then worked his way up to full editorship. I worked with him on a few projects—we'd come from very different worlds to the same place through a form of entertainment that had been able to speak powerfully to both of us in adolescence. He believed in comics like *X-Men* that excited young readers with combat, rage, and melodrama but also made them think about the way the world worked. He enjoyed contact with his young readers, and he discovered that he had something to say to them. After a few years, he left the business, went back to college for a teaching credential, and took a job as an English teacher at a high school in his old neighborhood in the Bronx.

15   "It was entertainment media that told me there were stories in me worth telling," Diaz said, "and that the world could be different from what we'd been handed. So I don't have a lot of patience for people from sheltered backgrounds saying that poor kids and kids without parental supervision need to be protected from the media."

16   When young people feel that the official world is hostile, indifferent, or irrelevant, the feelings of recognition and belonging that entertainment brings them can be transformative. Music historian Ricky Vincent has argued that gangster rap helped inner-city youths during the gang wars of the 1980s make sense of a fragmented society and take more control of their lives. This is the power of mirroring again. We speak of rap "glamorizing" gang violence, but more importantly it tells its audience that their reality has been seen, and so it helps them feel important enough to make more of themselves. The quieting of the gang wars in the 1990s was no doubt due in part to intervention programs, new school policies, and other official remedies. But it owed at least as much to the efforts of the gang leaders who finally said, "enough," and to those of the rappers who used their positions as trusted spokesmen for the community to spread the message.

17   Ice-T recorded a rap in 1993 called "Gotta Lotta Love," in which he described as "the most beautiful thing I'd seen in years," two guys settling their differences in a public park with "just a straight-up fistfight, one on one, nobody jumping in, nobody pulling a gun." It wasn't a sentiment that any school district could fit into its conflict-resolution program, but to an angry kid in a violent world, that punched-out, sentimental valorization of keeping rage within conscious bounds was a meaningful affirmation of personal power.

18   Ice-T's words had power because he'd proven that he could speak for the most alienated young people. On the same album with "Gotta Lotta Love" was "That's How I'm Livin'," Ice-T's story of how he became a street criminal in his teens and how creating raps lifted him out of crime by giving him purpose and perspective. Both of those raps would have been fairly easy for a parent or

teacher to endorse—but the title track of the same album was "Home Invasion." That track opened with the sounds of a gang of armed thugs smashing their way into a house, threatening to kill the owners, screaming, "All we want are the motherfuckin' kids!" Ice-T then boasted to parents about his power to steal the minds of their children: "I might get 'em up under my fuckin' spell, they might start givin' you fuckin' hell . . . might start callin' you a fool, tellin' you why they hate school. . . ." It wasn't an easy rap for even the hippest adult to embrace as an ally in the work of socializing young people. But for many kids, who had been given so few symbols and so few outlets to express their rage at a controlling but uncomprehending adult world, it was powerfully liberating and emboldening—and not only for kids of Ice-T's social background.

19   I know a woman named Sarah who was fifteen when *Home Invasion* came out. Her parents were attorneys, she grew up in a luxury condo far from the ghetto, and she attended a top-ranked private school where she excelled academically. She was also alone a great deal while her parents worked, and when they were home they were often preoccupied with their own stresses and marital conflicts. Sarah felt they didn't spend much time trying to understand what she was going through, but they swooped down on her with anger and restrictions when she misbehaved. Ice-T, she said, "came through the door like my personal savior. From the first twenty seconds of 'Home Invasion' I felt like here was somebody who was going to fight for *me,* who wasn't afraid of parents and teachers, and wasn't going to tell the polite lies that we were always supposed to uphold." She clung to confrontational rap and rock music through a turbulent adolescence and bonded with other angry kids who shared her passions. She has credited the music with helping her channel her rage into politics and writing instead of the pointless, self-destructive rebellions that some of her peers fell into. In graduate school, she decided to become a schoolteacher and children's rights advocate.

◆◆◆◆

20   We've been taught to fear stories. Popular articles, teacher training programs, handouts from pediatricians often list "an interest in violent stories or entertainment" as one of the warning signs that a child has the potential for violent behavior. And violent kids *are* interested in such things. But so are many of the kids who are trying mightily to take control of their feelings of anger and powerlessness *without* violence. If kids bully other kids, hit or verbally abuse their girlfriends or boyfriends, or explode over small slights; if they show cruelty to animals or boast of cruel deeds or plans; if they nurse long grudges, destroy property, or talk or write about specific revenge fantasies against real people; if they cut themselves or talk about suicide, then their fascination for violent stories may be part of a pattern that will escalate to real violence or self-violence. But the stories themselves are more likely to be the ways they speak their feelings and hope for us to listen.

21   Young people often haven't learned how to see their anger from the outside even as they experience it. Powerful stories can lead them into their feelings but leave them spinning there. That's where the adult ability to put emotions and fantasy in perspective can serve them well. The simplest displays of adult empathy can open the door for kids to engage with us, and the simplest applications of

adult perspective can open doors within ourselves. In my workshops, I see kids' relief at being able to talk to an adult stranger about their games, movies, songs, or comics. I get e-mails from kids who are being told by their schools and their parents and every other adult in their lives that the video games or rap music they love are turning them into monsters. "The games make me feel stronger," wrote one. "I think me feeling stronger is what they don't want." I tell them that adults are afraid—of change and the future, and so of young people and new entertainment. And I tell them not to be afraid of themselves. Sometimes I point them toward Web sites or resources where intelligent people talk about these things in moderated forums, where they might get some modeling and mentoring. Mostly I just try to acknowledge what they're saying. It's like clutching your chest and falling down when you're shot, or just looking at a child and smiling. ◆◆

A BRAIN TOO YOUNG FOR GOOD JUDGMENT*

Daniel R. Weinberger

This article first appeared in the op-ed section of the New York Times. *The author is director of the Clinical Brain Disorders Laboratory at the National Institutes of Health. Do adolescents possess brains that are biologically mature enough for them to exhibit rational behavior? What do you think?*

1   This week's shootings at Santana High School in California led quickly to now-familiar attempts to explain the seemingly unexplainable in terms of culture and circumstance: violent entertainment, a lack of accountability for deviant behavior, broken homes. While each of these issues may play some role in the tragedies of school shootings, to understand what goes wrong in the teenagers who fire the guns, you have to understand something about the biology of the teenage brain.

2   Andy Williams, the boy held in the Santana shootings, is 15. Many other school shooters have been about the same age or even younger. And the brain of a 15-year-old is not mature—particularly in an area called the prefrontal cortex, which is critical to good judgment and the suppression of impulse.

3   The human brain has required many millennia and many evolutionary stages to reach its current complex status. It enables us to do all kinds of amazing and uniquely human things: to unravel the human genome, to imagine the future, to fall in love. As part of its capacity for achievement, it must also be able to exercise control that stops maladaptive behavior. Everyone gets angry; everybody has felt a desire for vengeance. The capacity to control impulses that arise from these feelings is a function of the prefrontal cortex.

4   This is the part that distinguishes our brain most decisively from those of all other animals, even our closest relatives. It allows us to act on the basis of reason.

New York Times, March 10, 2001, p. A27.

It can preclude an overwhelming tendency for action (e.g., to run from a fire in a crowded theater), because an abstract memory (e.g., "don't panic,") makes more sense. It knows that all that glitters is not gold. Without a prefrontal cortex, it would be impossible to have societies based on moral and legal codes.

5   Sometimes violent behavior may be adaptive (for example, in self-defense), in which case the prefrontal cortex will help plan an effective strategy. However, controlling violent impulses when they are maladaptive can be a very taxing duty for the prefrontal cortex, especially if the desire for action is great or if the brain is weakened in its capacity to exercise such control.

6   Many factors can impair the capacity of the prefrontal cortex to serve its full impulse-control function: for example, neurological diseases that kill cells in the prefrontal cortex, head injuries that damage these cells, alcohol and drugs that impair their function, and biological immaturity.

7   The inhibitory functions are not present at birth; it takes many years for the necessary biological processes to hone a prefrontal cortex into an effective, efficient executive. These processes are now being identified by scientific research. They involve how nerve cells communicate with each other, how they form interactive networks to handle complex computational tasks and how they respond to experience. It takes at least two decades to form a fully functional prefrontal cortex.

8   Scientists have shown that the pace of the biological refinements quickens considerably in late adolescence, as the brain makes a final maturational push to tackle the exigencies of independent adult life. But the evidence is unequivocal that the prefrontal cortex of a 15-year-old is biologically immature. The connections are not final, the networks are still being strengthened and the full capacity for inhibitory control is still years away.

9   The 15-year-old brain does not have the biological machinery to inhibit impulses in the service of long-range planning. This is why it is important for adults to help children make plans and set rules, and why institutions are created to impose limits on behavior that children are incapable of limiting. Parents provide their children with a lend-lease prefrontal cortex during all those years that it takes to grow one, particularly when the inner urges for impulsive action intensify.

◆◆◆◆

10   Adolescents have always had to deal with feeling hurt, ashamed and powerless. In the face of ridicule they may want revenge. Thirty years ago, a teenager in this position might have started a fight, maybe even pulled a knife. If he was afraid that he could not defend himself, he might have recruited a tough guy to help him out. One way or another, he would have tried to teach his tormentors a lesson. Very likely, however, no one would have died.

11   But times have changed, and now this angry teenager lives in a culture that romanticizes gunplay, and he may well have access to guns. I doubt that most school shooters intend to kill, in the adult sense of permanently ending a life and paying the price for the rest of their own lives. Such intention would require a fully developed prefrontal cortex, which could anticipate the future and

rationally appreciate cause and effect. The young school shooter probably does not think about the specifics of shooting at all. The often reported lack of apparent remorse illustrates how unreal the reality is to these teenagers.

12   This brief lesson in brain development is not meant to absolve criminal behavior or make the horrors any less unconscionable. But the shooter at Santana High, like other adolescents, needed people or institutions to prevent him from being in a potentially deadly situation where his immature brain was left to its own devices. No matter what the town or the school, if a gun is put in the control of the prefrontal cortex of a hurt and vengeful 15-year-old, and it is pointed at a human target, it will very likely go off. ◆◆

FAIRY TALES AS A LEARNING TOOL FOR YOUNG OFFENDERS*

Richard Rothstein

Richard Rothstein is the education columnist for the New York Times. *The author examines the impact storytelling can have on developing minds. After all that has been said about fantasy having a negative impact on young minds, can fantasy's influence also be positive? Can literature act as a deterrent to keep children from committing crimes?*

1   Most people recognize the importance of reading stories to toddlers, who can then learn how books work (for example, that a line of text proceeds from left to right), how letters form words and how narrative flows.

2   But literacy is only one benefit of storytelling. Another is the chance for children to identify with fanciful characters who try to work out conflicts with others and within themselves. If very young children can't do this in the safety of an adult's lap, the later costs to them and to society can be greater than poor reading skills.

3   Can any of this loss be made up later? A storybook program at a San Antonio juvenile prison suggests that it may never be too late.

4   Three people came together to create the program. Celeste Guzman works for Gemini Ink, a group that seeks opportunities for creative writers to give workshops in schools, seniors' centers, shelters for battered women and prisons. Glenn Faulk, a prison officer at the Cyndi Taylor Krier Juvenile Correctional Treatment Center, designs activities for violent youths while they serve their sentences. Grady Hillman, a poet, trains artists and writers to teach in community settings.

5   Their plan evolved slowly, with few of its possibilities apparent at first.

6   Youths at the Krier juvenile prison are expected to perform public service. Mr. Faulk proposed to several that rather than mow lawns at the courthouse or

*New York Times, July 24 2002, p. A16.

pick up trash on the highway, they write children's books that could be donated to a library at a battered-women's shelter. He thought the idea might be particularly attractive to youths who had themselves fathered children before being imprisoned. He also knew that in writing children's stories, the youths would be forced to abandon their tough-guy street language.

7   Ms. Guzman then recruited Mr. Hillman to run a writing workshop for seven juvenile offenders who volunteered. He began each session by reading a children's book aloud, expecting to teach story structure and character development. But it soon became apparent that the storytelling had another, unanticipated effect: the six young men and one young woman, none of whom had lived healthy childhoods that included adults' reading stories, were enjoying the tales themselves.

8   Their favorite, Mr. Hillman said, was "Millions of Cats," by Wanda Gag. It is an "ugly duckling" kind of story in which an old woman wants to pick a single cat as a pet, from millions of cats who hope to be selected. Her choice is unexpected, a cat who has been least aggressive in seeking her favor.

9   Mr. Hillman surmised that the story was popular because the youths had spent their adolescence driven toward arrogance and feigning toughness. The notion that humility might have a reward was surprisingly attractive to them.

10   Mr. Hillman's own favorite was "The Tale of Peter Rabbit," by Beatrix Potter. Because Peter disobeys his mother's rules, he is trapped in Mr. McGregor's garden. Peter's predicament becomes progressively worse, but he ultimately resolves it and escapes to the security of home. This, Mr. Hillman thought, might be a parable for the young offenders' own lives.

11   The workshop's explicit goal was the youths' contribution of their work to the community. Each of them wrote a story. Some were fanciful, like a tale about a wizard who can't spell and whose wishes are therefore fulfilled improperly: when he wants a bath, he spells "bat," and so instead of getting a bath, he gets a bat that chases him around his cave. Some stories were more realistic, like one about a girl who has to accept that she is shorter than others.

12   Ms. Guzman had the storybooks printed, and in May the youths read their stories aloud at a prison meeting to which their parents were invited. Now, as the young offenders earn behavior points that make them eligible for supervised trips away from the center, they will be permitted to perform readings for children on the outside.

13   Thirty years ago, literacy programs were more common in adult and juvenile prisons alike, because reading and writing skills were thought important for future employment. Some adult programs included "bibliotherapy," using literature to explore psychological problems as a step to rehabilitation.

14   But today, prisons give more emphasis to punishment, protection of the community and restitution. The San Antonio program is an exception to that trend, though not the only one. Mr. Hillman now hopes to train writers around the country to use storybooks with youthful offenders. If all children heard fairy tales when they were small enough to sit on laps, though, perhaps fewer would have to do so in prison. ◆◆

OUT OF JAIL, INTO TEMPTATION: A DAY IN A LIFE*

Alan Feuer

The following article appeared in the New York Times. *In it, journalist Alan Feuer reports on the day in the life of a New York City convict, Nando, on the day of his release from prison. Given the world that Nando was released back into, what are his chances for success?*

1 Nando came home from jail to a small apartment in the Bronx that stank like a backed-up toilet.

2 He had been gone eight months, behind bars for selling crack, and as he came through the door from Rikers Island, he wrinkled his nose at the smell. His spider plant was dead. Its blackened leaves crumpled under his touch. His telephone was dead. He blew in the receiver, but the line was out.

3 The bathroom faucet spewed brown water. A bag of chips in the kitchen was covered in dust.

4 "It's like a garbage dump," he said. "I've got a lot of work to do."

5 The work would not be easy. What lay ahead for Nando, a 20-year-old man who agreed to spend his first day out of jail with a reporter and photographer as long as his last name did not appear in print, would prove to be a veil of dark temptation, a toxic mix of the traps and troubles that sent him off to prison to begin with.

6 Each year, more than 20,000 inmates are released from the C-76 jail on Rikers Island, which houses those serving terms of a year or less. Unlike state prisoners, these city convicts have no probation or parole officers to report to once they are released. They are free to find jobs, or buy drugs, without the authorities watching.

7 Nando was released at 5 A.M. on Feb. 4. By 7 A.M. he had learned that his best friend had just been arrested on a crack charge. By 9 A.M., he was languishing in a welfare office. By 10, he had been offered a joint. By 10:15, he had been offered his old job back, selling crack and marijuana.

8 By the end of the day, he had watched an old friend try to hide her drug habit from her curious toddler son. He had stood at the hospital bed of his catatonic mother. He had sorted through the mail that had piled up for months. The electric company was threatening to shut his power off.

9 He chose to return to his fifth-floor walk-up in the Morrisania section of the Bronx. His girlfriend and his old pals were still in the neighborhood; so was his past as an addict and a dealer. Though home seemed the natural place to go, it was also where his problems had started. Nando knew that in advance. He knew it the moment he stepped off the Rikers Island bus in northern Queens at 5:16 A.M.

10 It was still dark and the other men ran for the subway. Nando sniffed the air and smiled. "It's good to be out," he said.

New York Times, February 28, 2002, pp. A1+.

11   Nando, short for Fernando, is a skinny man with scruff on his chin and Chinese characters tattooed along his neck. He started peddling drugs at 14, started using them at 15. He was jailed last June for selling 200 grams of crack to an undercover officer.

12   The city releases Rikers Island inmates on a squalid street corner in Queens Plaza every day between 3 and 5:30 A.M. Each one carries a $3 MetroCard provided by the prison and his jailhouse chattel in a paper bag. Nando got off the bus with a Hermann Hesse novel in his bag and an ambitious to-do list in his head: Reconnect with family. Stay off drugs. Enroll in college. Find a job.

13   His first stop was his father's apartment in Co-op City. He arrived about 6. His younger brother, David, hugged him in the kitchen, still wearing his pajamas. His father, Fernando Sr., handed him a winter coat, a videotape of the Super Bowl and a couple of $20 bills.

14   "I never expected any kid of mine to wind up where he wound up," the father said. "I ain't never going back, not even on a visit. Don't know about him, but I ain't never going back."

15   It was a brief reunion. Nando's father was due at the factory where he works and his brother was due at school. His father gave Nando keys to the apartment. Nando mused that he might just buy a dog.

16   It was a terrible idea, his father said. "No dogs," he ordered. "Right now, you can't afford to feed yourself."

17   East Tremont Avenue cuts through the Bronx like a swollen femoral artery. It is a wide urban boulevard of barber shops and Spanish greasy spoons. But to Nando, it might as well have been the only road in a tiny town.

18   He knew everyone. The woman walking by was the manager of a grocery store, he said. The crumpled man on the corner was a crackhead. An unmarked Chevrolet rolled by and, out of instinct, Nando ducked; it was a prowling team of undercover cops.

19   "I don't want to be here, but there's nowhere else to go," he muttered as the car drove by. "Lots of us end up right back in the same damn place. It makes me want to blow up the 'hood."

BAD NEWS ABOUT A FRIEND

20   He turned down Boston Road until he came to a dim apartment house on Crotona Park East. Nando put his hands to his mouth and hooted like an owl. "Hey yo, Chuckie!" he yelled. "Hey yo, where's Chuck?"

21   A woman appeared in a fourth-floor window and shouted for him to come inside. The lobby smelled like feces. Its ceiling light was smashed. The walls looked like a notebook, covered in graffiti. The scrawl praised murder and masturbation.

22   The woman in the window was Nando's former girlfriend, Jackie, who quickly gave him the news: Chuckie—her brother and Nando's friend—had been arrested the day before.

23   Nando was crushed. He had just left Rikers Island, and now Chuckie might be headed there himself.

24   Five minutes later, Nando left. "The ghetto of all ghettos," he said as he walked toward home.

25   At his old apartment, the stench got up to meet him. It smelled like a stadium men's room on a hot summer's day. Dirty dishes were piled in the sink; a box of Cheerios stood open on the table. He turned on the television, and the screen looked like a finger-painting. The picture tube was blown.

26   It was starting to dawn on him, he said: he was out of jail, responsible for himself, alone. He popped a compact disc in the player and sat down on his rocking chair. "I used to sit here for hours getting high," he said, rocking slowly, staring at his hands. "I can feel the whole thing pulling at me. What am I going to do?"

27   On the walk home from Jackie's, he had called his girlfriend, Mery, and set a date for 9 A.M. He needed to clean himself, but first he had to clean the shower. A thick layer of scum had settled in the tub.

28   He went to the bathroom with a toilet brush. There, on the sink, were his mother's false teeth.

A REMINDER OF HIS MOTHER

29   Six months ago, a guard woke him to say, "Your mother's had a heart attack. She's in the hospital in Brooklyn." The jail allowed him a visit. He went and stared at his mother. All she could do was twitch her head.

30   Nando ignored the teeth. He cleaned the tub and showered. Then he looked for clothes in the bedroom his mother had used before she had fallen ill. The bed was stripped of sheets and gave the impression of a vacant lot. Nando ignored that, too.

31   Three hours earlier, after getting off the prison bus, Nando had laughed at a movie billboard with the slogan, "Behind every good man, there is a woman kicking his butt." At 9 A.M., Mery was waiting for him on the corner of Suburban Place and Boston Road. Her smile lit up the sidewalk two full blocks away.

32   They hugged. They kissed. She touched his hair, grown long on Rikers Island. They kissed again and didn't care who watched.

33   Mery is going to college while living in a homeless shelter. She is Nando's one good thing, and Nando freely admits it. Still, he sometimes finds her loving attention hard to take.

34   They walked down Boston Road to the subway station so Mery could head to school. She scooted up the stairs, then turned around. "Yo, behave!" was all she said.

35   At the welfare office across the street, Nando filled out forms for Medicaid. It was 9:15, and the room was already packed. Telephones rang. Babies cried. Nando put his name on the list. He was 21st in line.

36   The form asked, "Do you have any of these problems?" Nando checked the boxes next to "Urgent Personal or Family Problems" and "No Food."

37   Thirty minutes later a clerk informed him that he had come to the wrong place. The office he needed was on 138th Street, 40 blocks away.

38   He was mad at the clerk. He was mad at himself. He stormed outside to a pay phone and punched in a number. "Yeah," he said. "What up? I'm on the block. I'm home."

39   Minutes later, a bony man in a baggy sweatshirt came walking down the block. His name was Rob, and he was a member of Nando's former drug crew. On

Boston Road, the two old friends bumped chests. Rob made fun of Nando's hair.

40   "What you up to, son?" Nando asked.

41   Rob did not waste time. "I'm smoking a blunt with you."

EVERYWHERE, TEMPTATION

42   Suddenly, a choice: Go to the welfare office or get high with Rob. The choice got harder when Rob's cellphone began to ring. The call was for Nando. It was his old crack boss, asking if he wanted to go back to work.

43   According to city officials, 80 percent of Rikers Island's inmates test positive for drug use, and drugs are why most end up on the island to begin with. In the past, Nando had taken drugs and sold drugs. Now, within 60 seconds, he'd had offers to do both again.

44   "No, I'm straight," he told the boss, "but I'll let you know." Then he turned down Rob's joint. But as he stood there talking, his old crack customers walked by. They waved and nodded. It was as if he'd never left.

45   With Rob in tow, Nando went back to Jackie's place. He wanted someplace quiet to use the phone. He wanted the address of his mother's hospital in Brooklyn. It had been six months; he wanted to see her face.

46   When Jackie opened the door, the marijuana smoke enveloped him like a blanket. He called information for the hospital's address, trying to ignore the smell. Jackie ran through the rooms, opening windows, spraying a can of air freshener. Her little boy, Aaron, came down the hallway. Aaron is 3. Jackie is 18.

47   Nando headed for the door and as he went out, Rob came in. He had bought a cheap cigar and stuffed it full of dope.

48   Nando unloaded on him on the street.

49   "Keep doing that and you'll wind up on Rikers Island," he said. Rob brushed him off. Nando let out a cold laugh at his buddy. "You best make sure you don't wind up in jail," he said.

50   The trip to the hospital took an hour. As Nando approached his mother's room, an orderly stopped him in the hall.

51   "Who are you?" she asked. She was baffled by the answer. "Her son?" the woman said. "Why don't you ever visit? Where have you been the last six months?"

52   His mother's limbs were frozen, her eyes so empty of emotion they looked like dirty glass. Her face twitched uncontrollably, and Nando stood there, wordless. The orderly told him if he pinched her fingers she would feel it. But other than that, she would not respond.

53   Nando stared at his mother for 30 minutes, trying to fight back tears. On the nightstand was the fake red rose he had bought on the way to see her.

54   "A day in my life," he said on the street again, his voice gone soft. "Anyone want it?" It was 2:15 P.M.

A REMINDER IN THE MAIL

55   Back at home, he planned his week. Hit the job center. Hit the right welfare office.

56   Then he went downstairs to get his mail.

57   On Rikers, he had taken a writing class, and his last assignment was to write

a letter to himself as a happy 70-year-old man. He was to describe that happy life, writing from the future, to himself as he was now, at 20. He had to describe the choices he had made.

58   The letter was in his mailbox.

Dear Nando,

I remember those days we spent on Rikers Island. Pretty rough, huhh! Well, as for me, I made the best of it. I chose to change a couple of things about myself in order to get where I'm at now. Let's just say I'm at a place where it's always sunny and hot and when it rains, it really rains. I got a few kids now and a beautiful wife with a handful of grandchildren. What I chose to do was leave all the drugs and negative things alone. It was really rough at first, but I never gave up. I always knew I could do more.

Sincerely,
Nando

59   He sat on the rocking chair and read the letter, twice. Then he lay down on his mother's bed.

60   It was 4 P.M. and he wasn't sleepy. Tomorrow was only eight hours away. ◆◆

QUESTIONS TO HELP YOU THINK AND WRITE ABOUT CRIME ISSUES

1. Gilligan calls for a complete renovation of the current prison system. He claims prisons should focus on educating the criminals they hold. Do you agree or disagree with Gilligan's claim? Identify the reasons for your answer. What are the benefits of adopting Gilligan's plan? What are the drawbacks? In your opinion, what should the purpose of prison be?

2. What is your response to Will's ideas about shortening the prison sentences of older prisoners, even if they have been sentenced to life in prison? Would this practice achieve what society hopes to achieve by punishing criminals? How do you react to this variation in the usual practice?

3. How does Kozinski intellectually justify sentencing other people to death? How do you respond to his justification? If read along with the statistics Moore offers for the high number of innocent people sentenced to death, how do you think Judge Kozinski would react to his own conclusion?

4. After reading the essays by Kozinski and Moore, what do you think about the death penalty? Did your opinions change as a result of reading? That is, (a) did reading make your original convictions stronger; (b) did reading change your beginning opinion; or (c) did reading awaken a new interest in the subject? Describe how these readings affected you.

5. Weinberger states that the brain of a fifteen-year-old is not developed enough for long-term planning. Do you agree or disagree with this statement? Why?

6. Compare Powers's and Jones's essays. How can Jones's essay shed light on the problems Powers discusses? Jones states that many young people are angry and respond to the countercultures of various types of music. Do you think Powers would agree that many young people are angry? How can adults take a more active role in relieving the frustration of young people?

7. How do you react to Rothstein's account that young offenders who read fairy tales respond in a way that helps them cope with their own histories? What role do you think literature can play in forming the characters of children? What role do you think character formation at a young age has on the potential to prevent a person from committing crimes later in life?

8. Feuer's article about Nando paints a bleak picture. How long do you think a person like Nando can last after being released from prison with nothing but a transportation pass good for one day? Do you think Nando will turn back to drugs? What policies could be changed to stop the hopeless circle described in Feuer's article?

❖ Section IV ❖

Issues Concerning Race, Culture, and Identity

THE ISSUES

A. HOW DO RACE AND CULTURE CONTRIBUTE TO AN INDIVIDUAL'S SENSE OF IDENTITY?

Five articles explore the issues associated with racial and cultural identity. Black and white relationships and how they are represented in film and television is the subject of bell hooks's article. Dyer claims that whites are represented in the media as existing outside of racial and ethnic categories and suggests the concept of "whiteness" be racialized. Gómez-Peña writes about the various cultural identities he experiences from living on the Mexican-American border, and Kondo writes about the confusion in identity that can result from trying to retain one's culture while being pressured by others to change it. Finally, Pan and Keene-Osborn describe a venture to address mixed cultural issues. See also "A View from Berkeley" (page 51), "A Simple 'Hai' Won't Do" (page 60), and "We Knew What Glory Was" (page 49).

B. TO WHAT EXTENT SHOULD INDIVIDUALS ALLOW THEIR CULTURAL HERITAGE TO BE ASSIMILATED?

Three authors examine the degree to which people from other cultures perceive themselves to be mainly separate or mainly a part of the dominant American culture. Yahlin Chang gives examples of Asians in America who have kept their ethnic identities and compares them with other Asians who have not. Anouar Majid claims that education can help Muslims live in the United States while they maintain their distinct religion and culture. Edward S. Shapiro gives the history of the identity problems Jews have had in discovering what it means to be Jewish in a country in which they are a minority. See also "Letter from Birmingham Jail" (page 277) and "Jobs Illuminate What Riot Hid: Young Ideals" (page 80).

C. WEB SITES FOR FURTHER EXPLORATION AND RESEARCH

Interracial Voice	http://www.webcom.com/intvoice
Jewish Encyclopedia.com	http://www.jewishencyclopedia.com/index.jsp
Jews for Morality	http://www.jewsformorality.org/essays.htm
The Muslim News	http://www.muslimnews.co.uk
Muslim Answers	http://www.muslim-answers.org
Le Monde Diplomatique	http://mondediplo.com
National Foundation for Jewish Culture	http://www.jewishculture.org/index.htm
Race and Ethnic Diversity in the United States (U.S. Department of State)	http://usinfo.state.gov/usa/race
Asian American Resources	http://www.ai.mit.edu/people/irie/aar
The New American Studies Web	http://cfdev.georgetown.edu/cndls/asw
The Center for Latin American Studies	http://www.brown.edu/Departments/ Watson_ Institute/CLAS/CLAS_index.html

D. FILMS AND LITERATURE RELATED TO RACE, CULTURE, AND IDENTITY

Films: Mississippi Burning, 1988; *Lone Star,* 1996; *Ghosts of Mississippi,* 1996; *American History X,* 1998; *Gentlemen's Agreement,* 1948; *Monster's Ball,* 2002; *Do the Right Thing,* 1989; *The Joy Luck Club,* 1993; *Zebrahead,* 1992.

Literature: poems: "Incident" by Countee Cullen; "Poem for the Young White Man" by Lorna Dee Cervantes; autobiography: *Borderlands* by Gloria Anzaldua; "How It Feels to Be Colored Me" by Zora Neale Hurston; *I Know Why the Caged Bird Sings* by Maya Angelou; play: *A Raisin in the Sun* by Lorraine Hansberry; novels: *Beloved* by Toni Morrison; *To Kill a Mockingbird* by Harper Lee; *Flight to Canada* by Ishmael Reed; *The Woman Warrior* by Maxine Hong Kingston; *The Joy Luck Club* by Amy Tan.

THE RHETORICAL SITUATION

Dorinne K. Kondo, one of the authors in this section, makes the statement that "race, language, and culture are intertwined." Furthermore, certain combinations of race, language, and culture create expectations in many people's minds. We often expect individuals who possess particular combinations of these qualities to think, speak, or behave in certain ways. To understand these statements, you may want to think about how your race, culture, and language intertwine to contribute to your own sense of personal identity and also how they cause other people to regard you in particular ways. How would you characterize yourself in terms of your race, your culture, and your language? What group of people do you primarily identify with? How would you characterize the knowledge, beliefs, and behavior of this group, and how does the group itself influence your values and behavior? What language are you most comfortable speaking? In summary, how do your race, culture, and language help explain who you are?

One of the issues associated with racial and cultural identity is whether or not the special characteristics of races and cultures should be preserved. Some people think that races and cultures may eventually become so similar that differences among them will cease to exist, and complete assimilation and equality will result. They see this as a desirable result because it would reduce friction among groups. Other people think that differences in race and culture are valuable and that individuals should appreciate and strive to preserve the unique characteristics of their own race and culture. Certainly people experience confusion and dissonance when they leave their own culture for another. It is difficult to decide which parts of the former culture to retain and which parts to give up in order to fit more smoothly with the new one while still maintaining a cultural identity and sense of one's own ethnic pride. This is often an issue for people who live in countries like the United States that are home to many diverse cultures, as well as for people who study or live in another country for a significant period of time.

For some individuals, cultural and racial issues and the identity problems associated with them are the most important issues in their lives, and for others, these issues barely exist. How do you regard these issues, and what provides the exigency for your interest or lack of interest?

A. HOW DO RACE AND CULTURE CONTRIBUTE TO AN INDIVIDUAL'S SENSE OF IDENTITY?

QUESTIONS TO CONSIDER BEFORE YOU READ

Consider your own cultural and racial heritage. How has your ethnicity or cultural heritage shaped the person that you are? Has your race played a significant part in forming the way in which you think about yourself? How has race or racism been a factor in your life?

TEACHING RESISTANCE: THE RACIAL POLITICS OF MASS MEDIA*

bell hooks

bell hooks is Distinguished Professor of English at the City College of New York. This excerpt is from her book Killing Rage: Ending Racism, *which was published in 1995.*

1   For the most part television and movies depict a world where blacks and whites coexist in harmony although the subtext is clear; this harmony is maintained because no one really moves from the location white supremacy allocates to them

---

*bell hooks, *Killing Rage: Ending Racism* (New York: Holt, 1995), pp. 113–115.

on the race-sex hierarchy. Denzel Washington and Julia Roberts may play opposite one another in *The Pelican Brief* but there will not be a romance. True love in television and movies is almost always an occurrence between those who share the same race. When love happens across boundaries as in *The Bodyguard, Zebrahead,* or *A Bronx Tale*, it is doomed for no apparent reason and/or has tragic consequences. White and black people learning lessons from mass media about racial bonding are taught that curiosity about those who are racially different can be expressed as long as boundaries are not actually crossed and no genuine intimacy emerges. Many television viewers of all races and ethnicities were enchanted by a series called *I'll Fly Away,* which highlighted a liberal white family's struggle in the South and the perspective of the black woman who works as a servant in their home. Even though the series is often centered on the maid, her status is never changed or challenged. Indeed she is one of the "stars" of the show. It does not disturb most viewers that at this moment in history black women continue to be represented in movies and on television as the servants of whites. The fact that a black woman can be cast in a dramatically compelling leading role as a servant does not intervene on racist/sexist stereotypes, it reinscribes them. Hollywood awarded its first Oscar to a black person in 1939 when Hattie McDaniel won as Best Supporting Actress in *Gone With the Wind.* She played the maid. Contemporary films like *Fried Green Tomatoes* and *Passion Fish,* which offer viewers progressive visions of white females, still image black women in the same way—as servants. Even though the black female "servant" in *Passion Fish* comes from a middle-class background, drug addiction has led to her drop in status. And the film suggests that working secluded as the caretaker of a sick white woman redeems the black woman. It was twenty-four years after McDaniel won her Oscar that the only black man to ever receive this award won Best Actor. Sidney Poitier won for his role in the 1960s film *Lilies of the Field.* In this film he is also symbolically a "mammy" figure, playing an itinerant worker who caretakes a group of white nuns. Mass media consistently depict black folks either as servants or in subordinate roles, a placement which still suggests that we exist to bolster and caretake the needs of whites. Two examples that come to mind are the role of the black female FBI agent in *The Silence of the Lambs,* whose sole purpose is to bolster the ego of the white female lead played by Jodie Foster. And certainly in all the *Lethal Weapon* movies Danny Glover's character is there to be the buddy who because he is black and therefore subordinate can never eclipse the white male star. Black folks confront media that include us and subordinate our representation to that of whites, thereby reinscribing white supremacy.

2   While superficially appearing to present a portrait of racial social equality, mass media actually work to reinforce assumptions that black folks should always be cast in supporting roles in relation to white characters. That subordination is made to appear "natural" because most black characters are consistently portrayed as always a little less ethical and moral than whites, not given to rational reasonable action. It is not surprising that it is those black characters represented as didactic figures upholding the status quo who are portrayed as possessing positive characteristics. They are rational, ethical, moral peacemakers who help maintain law and order.

3   Significantly, the neo-colonial messages about the nature of race that are brought to us by mass media do not just shape whites' minds and imaginations. They socialize black and other non-white minds as well. Understanding the power of representations, black people have in both the past and present challenged how we are presented in mass media, especially if the images are perceived to be "negative," but we have not sufficiently challenged representations of blackness that are not obviously negative even though they act to reinforce white supremacy. Concurrently, we do not challenge the representations of whites. We were not outside movie theaters protesting when the white male lead character in *Paris Trout* brutally slaughters a little black girl (even though I can think of no other image of a child being brutally slaughtered in a mainstream film) or when the lead character in *A Perfect World* played by Kevin Costner terrorizes a black family who gives him shelter. Even though he is a murderer and an escaped convict, his character is portrayed sympathetically, whereas the black male father is brutally tortured presumably because he is an unloving, abusive parent. In *A Perfect World* both the adult white male lead and the little white boy who stops him from killing the black man are shown to be ethically and morally superior to black people.

4   Films that present cinematic narratives that seek to intervene in and challenge white supremacist assumptions, whether they are made by black or white folks, tend to receive negative attention or none at all. John Sayles's film *The Brother from Another Planet* successfully presented a black male character in a lead role whose representation was oppositional. Rather than portraying a black male as a sidekick of a more powerful white male, or as a brute and sex fiend, he offered us the image of a gentle, healing, angelic black male spirit. John Waters's film *Hairspray* was able to reach a larger audience. In this movie, white people choose to be anti-racist, to critique white privilege. Jim Jarmusch's film *Mystery Train* is incredibly deconstructive of racist assumptions. When the movie begins we witness a young Japanese couple arriving at the bus station in Memphis who begin to speak Japanese with a black man who superficially appears to be indigent. Racist stereotypes and class assumptions are challenged at this moment and throughout the film. White privilege and lack of understanding of the politics of racial difference are exposed. Yet most viewers did not like this film and it did not receive much attention. Julie Dash's film *Daughters of the Dust* portrayed black folks in ways that were radically different from Hollywood conventions. Many white viewers and even some black viewers had difficulty relating to these images. Radical representations of race in television and movies demand that we be resisting viewers and break our attachment to conventional representations. These films, and others like them, demonstrate that film and mass media in general can challenge neo-colonial representations that reinscribe racist stereotypes and perpetuate white supremacy. If more attention were given these films, it would show that aware viewers long for mass media that act to challenge and change racist domination and white supremacy.

5   Until all Americans demand that mass media no longer serve as the biggest propaganda machine for white supremacy, the socialization of everyone to subliminally absorb white supremacist attitudes and values will continue. Even though many white Americans do not overtly express racist thinking, it does not

mean that their underlying belief structures have not been saturated with an ideology of difference that says white is always, in every way, superior to that which is black. Yet so far no complex public discourse exists that explains the difference between that racism which led whites to enjoy lynching and murdering black people and that wherein a white person may have a black friend or lover yet still believe black folks are intellectually and morally inferior to whites. . . .

6   When black psyches are daily bombarded by mass media representations that encourage us to see white people as more caring, intelligent, liberal, etc., it makes sense that many of us begin to internalize racist thinking.

7   Without an organized resistance movement that focuses on the role of mass media in the perpetuation and maintenance of white supremacy, nothing will change. Boycotts remain one of the most effective ways to call attention to this issue. Picketing outside theaters, turning off the television set, writing letters of protest are all low-risk small acts that can become major interventions. Mass media are neither neutral nor innocent when it comes to spreading the message of white supremacy. It is not far-fetched for us to assume that many more white Americans would be anti-racist if they were not socialized daily to embrace racist assumptions. Challenging mass media to divest of white supremacy should be the starting point of a renewed movement for racial justice. ◆◆

THE MATTER OF WHITENESS*

Richard Dyer

Richard Dyer is professor of film studies at the University of Warwick in England. The following piece is an excerpt from Dyer's book White: Essays on Race and Culture, *which was published in 1997. Here Dyer explores the representation of white people in Western culture.*

1   Racial[1] imagery is central to the organisation of the modern world. At what cost regions and countries export their goods, whose voices are listened to at international gatherings, who bombs and who is bombed, who gets what jobs, housing, access to health care and education, what cultural activities are subsidised and sold, in what terms they are validated—these are all largely inextricable from racial imagery. The myriad minute decisions that constitute the practices of the world are at every point informed by judgements about people's capacities and worth, judgements based on what they look like, where they come from, how they speak, even what they eat, that is, racial judgements. Race is not the only factor governing these things and people of goodwill everywhere struggle to overcome the prejudices and barriers of race, but it is never not a factor, never not in play. And since race in itself—insofar as it is anything in itself—refers to some intrinsically insignificant geographical/physical differences between people, it is the imagery of race that is in play.

*Richard Dyer, *White: Essays on Race and Culture* (London: Routledge, 1997), pp. 1–4.

2   There has been an enormous amount of analysis of racial imagery in the past decades, ranging from studies of images of, say, blacks or American Indians in the media to the deconstruction of the fetish of the racial Other in the texts of colonialism and post-colonialism. Yet until recently a notable absence from such work has been the study of images of white people. Indeed, to say that one is interested in race has come to mean that one is interested in any racial imagery other than that of white people. Yet race is not only attributable to people who are not white, nor is imagery of non-white people the only racial imagery.

3   [I write] about the racial imagery of white people—not the images of other races in white cultural production, but the latter's imagery of white people themselves. This is not done merely to fill a gap in the analytic literature, but because there is something at stake in looking at, or continuing to ignore, white racial imagery. As long as race is something only applied to non-white peoples, as long as white people are not racially seen and named, they/we function as a human norm. Other people are raced, we are just people.

4   There is no more powerful position than that of being "just" human. The claim to power is the claim to speak for the commonality of humanity. Raced people can't do that—they can only speak for their race.[2] But non-raced people can, for they do not represent the interests of a race. The point of seeing the racing of whites is to dislodge them/us from the position of power, with all the inequities, oppression, privileges and sufferings in its train, dislodging them/us by undercutting the authority with which they/we speak and act in and on the world.

5   The sense of whites as non-raced is most evident in the absence of reference to whiteness in the habitual speech and writing of white people in the West. We (whites) will speak of, say, the blackness or Chineseness of friends, neighbours, colleagues, customers or clients, and it may be in the most genuinely friendly and accepting manner, but we don't mention the whiteness of the white people we know. An old-style white comedian will often start a joke: "There's this bloke walking down the street and he meets this black geezer," never thinking to race the bloke as well as the geezer. Synopses in listings of films on TV, where wordage is tight, none the less squander words with things like: "Comedy in which a cop and his black sidekick investigate a robbery," "Skinhead Johnny and his Asian lover Omar set up a laundrette," "Feature film from a promising Native American director" and so on. Since all white people in the West do this all the time, it would be invidious to quote actual examples, and so I shall confine myself to one from my own writing. In an article on lesbian and gay stereotypes,[3] I discuss the fact that there can be variations on a type such as the queen or dyke. In the illustrations which accompany this point, I compare a "fashion queen" from the film *Irene* with a "black queen" from *Car Wash*—the former, white image is not raced, whereas all the variation of the latter is reduced to his race. Moreover, this is the only non-white image referred to in the article, which does not however point out that all the other images discussed are white. In this, as in the other white examples in this paragraph, the fashion queen is, racially speaking, taken as being just human.

6   This assumption that white people are just people, which is not far off saying that whites are people whereas other colours are something else, is endemic to

white culture. Some of the sharpest criticism of it has been aimed at those who would think themselves the least racist or white supremacist. bell hooks, for instance, has noted how amazed and angry white liberals become when attention is drawn to their whiteness, when they are seen by non-white people as white.

> Often their rage erupts because they believe that all ways of looking that highlight difference subvert the liberal belief in a universal subjectivity (we are all just people) that they think will make racism disappear. They have a deep emotional investment in the myth of "sameness," even as their actions reflect the primacy of whiteness as a sign informing who they are and how they think.[4]

7   Similarly, Hazel Carby discusses the use of black texts in white classrooms, under the sign of multiculturalism, in a way that winds up focusing "on the complexity of response in the (white) reader/student's construction of self in relation to a (black) perceived 'other.'" We should, she argues, recognise that "everyone in this social order has been constructed in our political imagination as a racialized subject" and thus that we should consider whiteness as well as blackness, in order "to make visible what is rendered invisible when viewed as the normative state of existence: the (white) point in space from which we tend to identify difference."[5]

8   The invisibility of whiteness as a racial position in white (which is to say dominant) discourse is of a piece with its ubiquity. When I said above that [I am not] merely seeking to fill a gap in the analysis of racial imagery, I reproduced the idea that there is no discussion of white people. In fact for most of the time white people speak about nothing but white people, it's just that we couch it in terms of "people" in general. Research—into books, museums, the press, advertising, films, television, software—repeatedly shows that in Western representation whites are overwhelmingly and disproportionately predominant, have the central and elaborated roles, and above all are placed as the norm, the ordinary, the standard.[6] Whites are everywhere in representation. Yet precisely because of this and their placing as norm they seem not to be represented to themselves *as* whites but as people who are variously gendered, classed, sexualised and labeled. At the level of racial representation, in other words, whites are not of a certain race, they're just the human race.

9   We are often told that we are living now in a world of multiple identities, of hybridity, of decentredness and fragmentation. The old illusory unified identities of class, gender, race, sexuality are breaking up; someone may be black *and* gay *and* middle class *and* female; we may be bi-, poly- or non-sexual, of mixed race, indeterminate gender and heaven knows what class. Yet we have not yet reached a situation in which white people and white cultural agendas are no longer in the ascendant. The media, politics, education are still in the hands of white people, still speak for whites while claiming—and sometimes sincerely aiming—to speak for humanity. Against the flowering of a myriad postmodern voices, we must also see the countervailing tendency towards a homogenisation of world culture, in the continued dominance of US news dissemination, popular TV programmes and Hollywood movies. Postmodern multiculturalism may have genuinely opened up a space for the voices of the other, challenging the authority of the white West,[7] but it may also simultaneously function as a side-show for white people who look on with delight at all the differences that surround them.[8]

We may be on our way to genuine hybridity, multiplicity without (white) hegemony, and it may be where we want to get to—but we aren't there yet, and we won't get there until we see whiteness, see its power, its particularity and limitedness, put it in its place and end its rule. This is why studying whiteness matters.

10   It is studying whiteness *qua* whiteness. Attention is sometimes paid to "white ethnicity,"[9] but this always means an identity based on cultural origins such as British, Italian or Polish, or Catholic or Jewish, or Polish-American, Irish-American, Catholic-American and so on. These however are variations on white ethnicity (though . . . some are more securely white than others), and the examination of them tends to lead away from a consideration of whiteness itself. John Ibson, in a discussion of research on white US ethnicity, concludes that being, say, Polish, Catholic or Irish may not be as important to white Americans as some might wish.[10] But being white is. ◆◆

NOTES

1. I use the terms race and racial . . . in the most common though problematic sense, referring to supposedly visibly differentiable, supportedly discrete social groupings.
2. In their discussion of the extraordinarily successful TV sitcom about a middle-class, African-American family, *The Cosby Show*, Sut Jhally and Justin Lewis note the way that viewers repeatedly recognise the characters' blackness but also that "you just think of them as people"; in other words that they don't only speak for their race. Jhally and Lewis argue that this is achieved by the way the family conforms to "the everyday, generic world of white television," an essentially middle-class world. The family is "ordinary" *despite* being black; because it is upwardly mobile, it can be accepted as "ordinary," in a way that marginalises most actual African-Americans. If the realities of African-American experience were included, then the characters would not be perceived as people." Sut Jhally and Justin Lewis, *Enlightened Racism: 'The Cosby Show,' Audiences and the Myth of the American Dream* (Boulder: Westview Press, 1992).
3. Richard Dyer, "Seen to Be Believed: Problems in the Representation of Gay People as Typical," in *The Matter of Images: Essays on Representation* (London: Routledge, 1993), pp. 19–51.
4. bell hooks, "Representations of Whiteness in the Black Imagination," in *Black Looks: Race and Representation* (Boston: South End Press, 1992), p. 167.
5. Hazel V. Carby, "The Multicultural Wars," in *Black Popular Culture*, ed. Gina Dent (Seattle: Bay Press, 1992), p. 193.
6. . . . The research findings are generally cast the other way round, in terms of non-white under-representation, textual marginalisation and positioning as deviant or a problem. Recent research in the US does suggest that African-Americans (but not other racially marginalised groups) have become more represented in the media, even in excess of their proportion of the population. However, this number still falls off if one focuses on central characters.
7. See, for example, Craig Owens, "The Discourse of Others: Feminists and Post-modernism," in *The Anti-Aesthetic: Essays on Postmodern Culture*, ed. Hal Foster (Port Townsend, Wash.: Bay Press, 1983), pp. 57–82.
8. *The Crying Game* (GB, 1992) seems to me to be an example of this. It explores with fascination and generosity, the hybrid and fluid nature of identity: gender, race, national belonging, sexuality. Yet all of this revolves around a bemused but ultimately unchallenged straight white man—it reinscribes the position of those at the intersection of heterosexuality, maleness and whiteness as that of the one group which does not need to be hybrid and fluid.

9. See, for example, Richard D. Alba, *Ethnic Identity: The Transformation of White America* (New Haven, Conn.: Yale University Press, 1990).
10. John Ibson, "Virgin Land or Virgin Mary? Studying the Ethnicity of White Americans," *American Quarterly* 33 (1981): 284–308.

DOCUMENTED/UNDOCUMENTED*

Guillermo Gómez-Peña

Guillermo Gómez-Peña is a writer and performance artist whose work explores life on the "border" and the relationship among race, culture, and identity in America.

1   I live smack in the fissure between two worlds, in the infected wound: half a block from the end of Western civilization and four miles from the beginning of the Mexican/American border, the northernmost point of Latin America. In my fractured reality, but a reality nonetheless, there cohabit two histories, languages, cosmologies, artistic traditions, and political systems which are drastically counterposed. Many "deterritorialized" Latin American artists in Europe and the United States have opted for "internationalism" (a cultural identity based upon the "most advanced" of the ideas originating out of New York or Paris). I, on the other hand, opt for "borderness" and assume my role: my generation, the *chilango* (slang term for a Mexico City native), who came to "El Norte" fleeing the imminent ecological and social catastrophe of Mexico City, gradually integrated itself into otherness, in search of that other Mexico grafted into the entrails of the et cetera . . . became Chicano-ized. We de-Mexicanized ourselves, to Mexi-understand ourselves, some without wanting to, others on purpose. And one day, the border became our house, laboratory, and ministry, culture (or counterculture).

2   Today, eight years after my departure from Mexico, when they ask me for my nationality or ethnic identity, I can't respond with one word, since my "identity" now possesses multiple repertories: I am Mexican but I am also Chicano and Latin American. At the border they call me *chilango* or *mexiquillo;* in Mexico City it's *pocho* or *norteño;* and in Europe it's *sudaca.* The Anglos call me "Hispanic" or "Latino," and the Germans have, on more than one occasion, confused me with Turks or Italians. I walk amid the rubble of the Tower of Babel of my American postmodernity.

3   The recapitulation of my personal and collective topography has become my cultural obsession since I arrived in the United States. I look for the traces of my generation, whose distance stretches not only from Mexico City to California, but also from the past to the future, from pre-Columbian America to high technology, and from Spanish to English, passing through "Spanglish."

---

*Guillermo Gómez-Peña, *Warrior of Gringostroika* (St. Paul, Minn.: Graywolf Press, 1993), pp. 37–38, 40–41.

4   As a result of this process I have become a cultural topographer, border-crosser, and hunter of myths. And it doesn't matter where I find myself, in Califas or Mexico City, in Barcelona or West Berlin; I always have the sensation that I belong to the same species: the migrant tribe of fiery pupils.

5   My work, like that of many border artists, comes from two distinct traditions, and because of this has dual, or on occasion multiple, referential codes. One strain comes from Mexican popular culture, the Latin American literary "boom," and the Mexico City counterculture of the 1970s. . . . The other comes directly from Fluxus (a late-1960s international art movement that explored alternative means of production and distribution), concrete poetry, conceptual art, and performance art. These two traditions converge in my border experience and they fuse together.

6   In my intellectual formation, Carlos Fuentes, Gabriel García Márquez, Oscar Chávez, Felipe Ehrenberg, José Agustín, and Augusto Boal were as important as William Burroughs, Michel Foucault, Rainer Werner Fassbinder, Jacques Lacan, Vito Acconci, and Joseph Beuys.

7   My "artistic space" is the intersection where the new Mexican urban poetry and the colloquial Anglo poetry meet; the intermediate stage somewhere between Mexican street theatre and multimedia performance; the silence that snaps in between *corrido* and punk; the wall that divides "neográfica" (a 1970s Mexico City art movement involved in the production of low-budget book art and graphics) and graffiti; the highway that joins Mexico City and Los Angeles; and the mysterious thread of thought and action that puts Pan–Latin Americanism in touch with the Chicano movement, and both of these in touch with other international vanguards.

8   I am a child of crisis and cultural syncretism, half-hippie and half-punk. My generation grew up watching movies about *charros* (Mexican cowboys) and science fiction, listening to *cumbias* and tunes from the Moody Blues, constructing altars and filming in Super-8, reading *El Corno Emplumado* and *Artforum,* traveling to Tepoztlán and San Francisco, creating and de-creating myths. We went to Cuba in search of political illumination, to Spain to visit the crazy grandmother, and to the United States in search of the instantaneous musico-sexual paradise. We found nothing. Our dreams wound up getting caught in the webs of the border.

9   Our generation belongs to the world's biggest floating population: the weary travelers, the dislocated, those of us who left because we didn't fit anymore, those of us who still haven't arrived because we don't know where to arrive at, or because we can't go back anymore.

10   Our deepest generational emotion is that of loss, which comes from our having left. Our loss is total and occurs at multiple levels: loss of our country (culture and national rituals) and our class (the "illustrious" middle class and upper-middle); progressive loss of language and literary culture in our native tongue (those of us who live in non-Spanish-speaking countries); loss of ideological meta-horizons (the repression against and division of the left) and of metaphysical certainty.

11   In exchange, what we won was a vision of a more experimental culture, that is to say, a multifocal and tolerant one.

◆◆◆◆

12   Our experience as Latino border artists and intellectuals in the United States fluctuates between legality and illegality, between partial citizenship and full. For the Anglo community we are simply "an ethnic minority," a subculture, that is to say, some kind of pre-industrial tribe with a good consumerist appetite. For the art world, we are practitioners of distant languages that, in the best of cases, are perceived as exotic.

13   In general, we are perceived through the folkloric prisms of Hollywood, fad literature, and publicity; or through the ideological filters of mass media. For the average Anglo, we are nothing but "images," "symbols," "metaphors." We lack ontological existence and anthropological concreteness. We are perceived indiscriminately as magic creatures with shamanistic powers, happy bohemians with pretechnological sensibilities, or as romantic revolutionaries born in a Cuban poster from the 1970s. All this without mentioning the more ordinary myths, which link us with drugs, supersexuality, gratuitous violence, and terrorism; myths that serve to justify racism and disguise the fear of cultural otherness.

14   These mechanisms of mythification generate semantic interference and obstruct true intercultural dialogue. To make border art implies to reveal and subvert said mechanisms.

15   The term Hispanic, coined by techno-marketing experts and by the designers of political campaigns, homogenizes our cultural diversity (Chicanos, Cubans, and Puerto Ricans become indistinguishable), avoids our indigenous cultural heritage, and links us directly with Spain. Worse yet, it possesses connotations of upward mobility and political obedience.

16   The terms Third World culture, ethnic art, and minority art are openly ethnocentric and necessarily imply an axiological vision of the world at the service of Anglo-European culture. Confronted with them, one can't avoid asking the following questions: Besides possessing more money and arms, is the "First World" qualitatively better in any other way than our "underdeveloped" countries? Aren't the Anglos themselves also an "ethnic group," one of the most violent and antisocial tribes on this planet? Aren't the 500 million Latin American mestizos that inhabit the Americas a "minority"?

17   Among Chicanos, Mexicans, and Anglos, there is a heritage of relations poisoned by distrust and resentment. For this reason, my cultural work (especially in the camps of performance art, radio art, and journalism) has concentrated upon the destruction of the myths and the stereotypes that each group has invented to rationalize the other two.

18   With the dismantling of this mythology, I look, if not to create an instantaneous space for intercultural communication, at least to contribute to the creation of the groundwork and theoretical principles for a future dialogue that is capable of transcending the profound historical resentments that exist between the communities on either side of the border.

19   Within the framework of the false amnesty of the Immigration Reform and Control Act and the growing influence of the North American ultra-right, which seeks to close (militarize) the border because of supposed motives of "national security," the collaboration among Chicano, Mexican, and Anglo artists has become indispensable.

20   Anglo artists can contribute their technical ability, their comprehension of

the new media of expression and information (video and audio), and their altruist/internationalist tendencies. In turn, Latinos (whether Mexican, Chicano, Caribbean, Central or South American) can contribute the originality of their cultural models, their spiritual strength, and their political understanding of the world.

21   Together, we can collaborate in surprising cultural projects without forgetting that both should retain control of the product, from the planning stages up through distribution. If this doesn't occur, then intercultural collaboration isn't authentic. We shouldn't confuse true collaboration with political paternalism, cultural vampirism, voyeurism, economic opportunism, and demagogic multiculturalism.

22   We should clear up this matter once and for all: We (Latinos in the United States) don't want to be a mere ingredient of the melting pot. What we want is to participate actively in a humanistic, pluralistic, and politicized dialogue, continuous and not sporadic, and we want this to occur between equals who enjoy the same power of negotiation.

23   For this "intermediate space" to open, first there has to be a pact of mutual cultural understanding and acceptance, and it is precisely to this that the border artist can contribute. In this very delicate historical moment, Mexican artists and intellectuals as well as Chicanos and Anglos should try to "recontextualize" ourselves, that is to say, search for a "common cultural territory," and within it put into practice new models of communication and association. ◆◆

ON BEING A CONCEPTUAL ANOMALY*

Dorinne K. Kondo

Dorinne K. Kondo, a Japanese American professor of anthropology, is the author of Crafting Selves: Power, Gender, and Discourses of Identity in a Japanese Workplace. *In this excerpt from her book she relates her experiences in visiting Japan, where she looked Japanese but acted like an American.*

1   As a Japanese American,[1] I created a conceptual dilemma for the Japanese I encountered. For them, I was a living oxymoron, someone who was both Japanese and not Japanese. Their puzzlement was all the greater since most Japanese people I knew seemed to adhere to an eminently biological definition of Japaneseness. Race, language, and culture are intertwined, so much so that any challenge to this firmly entrenched conceptual schema—a white person who speaks flawlessly idiomatic and unaccented Japanese, or a person of Japanese ancestry who cannot—meets with what generously could be described as unpleasant reactions. White people are treated as repulsive and unnatural—*hen na gaijin,* strange foreigners—the better their Japanese becomes, while Japanese Americans

*Dorinne K. Kondo, Crafting Selves: Power, Gender, and Discourses of Identity in a Japanese Workplace (Chicago: University of Chicago Press, 1990), pp. 11–17.

and others of Japanese ancestry born overseas are faced with exasperation and disbelief. How can someone who is racially Japanese lack "cultural competence"?[2] During my first few months in Tokyo, many tried to resolve this paradox by asking which of my parents was "really" American.

2　　Indeed, it is a minor miracle that those first months did not lead to an acute case of agoraphobia, for I knew that once I set foot outside the door, someone somewhere (a taxi driver? a salesperson? a bank clerk?) would greet one of my linguistic mistakes with an astonished "Eh?" I became all too familiar with the series of expressions that would flicker over those faces: bewilderment, incredulity, embarrassment, even anger, at having to deal with this odd person who looked Japanese and therefore human, but who must be retarded, deranged, or—equally undesirable in Japanese eyes—Chinese or Korean. Defensively, I would mull over the mistake of the day. I mean, how was I to know that in order to "fillet a fish" you had to cut it "in three pieces"? Or that opening a bank account required so much specialized terminology? Courses in literary Japanese at Harvard hadn't done much to prepare me for the realities of everyday life in Tokyo. Gritting my teeth in determination as I groaned inwardly, I would force myself out of the house each morning.

3　　For me, and apparently for the people around me, this was a stressful time, when expectations were flouted, when we had to strain to make sense of one another. There seemed to be few advantages in my retaining an American persona, for the distress caused by these reactions was difficult to bear. In the face of dissonance and distress, I found that the desire for comprehensible order in the form of "fitting in," even if it meant suppression of and violence against a self I had known in another context, was preferable to meaninglessness. Anthropological imperatives to immerse oneself in another culture intensified this desire, so that acquiring the accoutrements of Japanese selfhood meant simultaneously constructing a more thoroughly professional anthropological persona. This required language learning in the broadest sense, mastery of culturally appropriate modes of moving, acting, and speaking. For my informants, it was clear that coping with this anomalous creature was difficult, for here was someone who looked like a real human being, but who simply failed to perform according to expectation. They, too, had every reason to make me over in their image, to guide me, gently but insistently, into properly Japanese behavior, so that the discrepancy between my appearance and my cultural competence would not be so painfully evident. I posed a challenge to their senses of identity. How could someone who *looked* Japanese not *be* Japanese? In my cultural ineptitude, I represented for the people who met me the chaos of meaninglessness. Their response in the face of this dissonance was to *make* me as Japanese as possible. Thus, my first nine months of fieldwork were characterized by an attempt to reduce the distance between expectation and inadequate reality, as my informants and I conspired to rewrite my identity as Japanese.

4　　My guarantor, an older woman who, among her many activities, was a teacher of flower arranging, introduced me to many families who owned businesses in the ward of Tokyo where I had chosen to do my research. One of her former students and fellow flower-arranging teachers, Mrs. Sakamoto, agreed to take me in as a guest over the summer, since the apartment where I was scheduled to move—owned by one of my classmates in tea ceremony—was still under construction. My proclivities for "acting Japanese" were by this time firmly established. During my stay with the Sakamotos, I did my best to conform to what I thought their expectations of a guest/daughter might be. This in turn seemed to please them and reinforced my tendency to behave in terms of what I perceived to be my Japanese persona.

5   My initial encounter with the head of the household epitomizes this mirroring and reinforcement of behavior. Mr. Sakamoto had been on a business trip on the day I moved in, and he returned the following evening, just as his wife, daughter, and I sat down to the evening meal. As soon as he stepped in the door, I immediately switched from an informal posture, seated on the *zabuton* (seat cushion), to a formal greeting posture, *seiza*-style (kneeling on the floor) and bowed low, hands on the floor. Mr. Sakamoto responded in kind (being older, male, and head of the household, he did not have to bow as deeply as I did), and we exchanged the requisite polite formulae, I requesting his benevolence, and he welcoming me to their family. Later, he told me how happy and impressed he had been with this act of proper etiquette on my part. "Today's young people in Japan," he said, "no longer show such respect. Your grandfather must have been a fine man to raise such a fine granddaughter." Of course, his statements can hardly be accepted at face value. They may well indicate his relief that I seemed to know something of proper Japanese behavior, and hence would not be a complete nuisance to them; it was also his way of making me feel at home. What is important to note is the way this statement was used to elicit proper Japanese behavior in future encounters. And his strategy worked. I was left with a warm, positive feeling toward the Sakamoto family, armed with an incentive to behave in a Japanese way, for clearly these were the expectations and the desires of the people who had taken me in and who were so generously sharing their lives with me.

6   Other members of the household voiced similar sentiments. Takemi-san, the Sakamotos' married daughter who lived in a distant prefecture, had been visiting her parents when I first moved in. A few minutes after our initial encounter, she observed, "You seem like a typical Japanese woman" (*Nihon no josei, to iu kanji*). Later in the summer, Mrs. Sakamoto confided to me that she could never allow a "pure American" (*junsui na Amerikajin*) to live with them, for only someone of Japanese descent was genetically capable of adjusting to life on *tatami* mats, using unsewered toilets, sleeping on the floor—in short, of living Japanese style. Again, the message was unambiguous. My "family" could feel comfortable with me insofar as I was—and acted—Japanese. . . .

7   My physical characteristics led my friends and coworkers to emphasize my identity as Japanese, sometimes even against my own intentions and desires. Over time, my increasingly "Japanese" behavior served temporarily to resolve their crises of meaning and to confirm their assumptions about their own identities. That I, too, came to participate enthusiastically in this recasting of the self is a testimonial to their success in acting upon me. . . .

8   The more I adjusted to my Japanese daughter's role, the keener the conflicts became. Most of those conflicts had to do with expectations surrounding gender,

and, more specifically, my position as a young woman. Certainly, in exchange for the care the Sakamotos showed me, I was happy to help out in whatever way I could. I tried to do some housecleaning and laundry, and I took over the shopping and cooking for Mr. Sakamoto when Mrs. Sakamoto was at one of the children's association meetings, her flower-arranging classes, or meetings of ward committees on juvenile delinquency. The cooking did not offend me in and of itself; in fact, I was glad for the opportunity to learn how to make simple Japanese cuisine, and Mr. Sakamoto put up with my sometimes appalling culinary mistakes and limited menus with great aplomb. I remember one particularly awful night when I couldn't find the makings for soup broth, and Mr. Sakamoto was fed "*miso* soup" that was little more than *miso* dissolved in hot water. He managed to down the tasteless broth with good grace—and the trace of a smile on his lips. (Of course, it is also true that although he was himself capable of simple cooking, he would not set foot in the kitchen if there were a woman in the house.) Months after I moved out, whenever he saw me he would say with a sparkle in his eye and a hint of nostalgic wistfulness in his voice, "I miss Dōrin-san's salad and sautéed beef," one of the "Western" menus I used to serve up with numbing regularity. No, the cooking was not the problem.

9   The problem was, in fact, the etiquette surrounding the serving of food that produced the most profound conflicts for me as an American woman. The head of the household is usually served first and receives the finest delicacies; men—even the sweetest, nicest ones—ask for a second helping of rice by merely holding out their rice bowls to the woman nearest the rice cooker, and maybe, just maybe, uttering a grunt of thanks in return for her pains. I could never get used to this practice, try as I might. Still, I tried to carry out my duties uncomplainingly, in what I hope was reasonably good humor. But I was none too happy about these things "inside." Other restrictions began to chafe, especially restrictions on my movement. I had to be in at a certain hour, despite my "adult" age. Yet I understood the family's responsibility for me as their guest and quasi-daughter, so I tried to abide by their regulations, hiding my irritation as best I could.

10   This fundamental ambivalence was heightened by isolation and dependency. Though my status was in some respects high in an education-conscious Japan, I was still young, female, and a student. I was in a socially recognized relationship of dependency vis-à-vis the people I knew. I was not to be feared and obeyed, but protected and helped. In terms of my research, this was an extremely advantageous position to be in, for people did not feel the need to reflect my views back to me, as they might with a more powerful person. I did not try to define situations; rather, I could allow other people to define those situations in their culturally appropriate ways, remaining open to their concerns and their ways of acting in the world. But, in another sense, this dependency and isolation increased my susceptibility to identifying with my Japanese role. By this time I saw little of American friends in Tokyo, for it was difficult to be with people who had so little inkling of how ordinary Japanese people lived. My informants and I consequently had every reason to conspire to re-create my identity as Japanese. Precisely because of my dependency and my made-to-order role, I was allowed—or

rather, *forced*—to abandon the position of observer. Errors, linguistic or cultural, were dealt with impatiently or with a startled look that seemed to say, "Oh yes, you are American after all." On the other hand, appropriately Japanese behaviors were rewarded with warm, positive reactions or with comments such as "You're more Japanese than the Japanese." Even more frequently, correct behavior was simply accepted as a matter of course. *Naturally* I would understand, *naturally* I would behave correctly, for they presumed me to be, *au fond*, Japanese.

◆◆◆◆

11   Identity can imply unity or fusion, but for me what occurred was a fragmentation of the self. This fragmentation was encouraged by my own participation in Japanese life and by the actions of my friends and acquaintances. At its most extreme point, I became "the Other" in my own mind, where the identity I had known in another context simply collapsed. The success of our conspiracy to re-create me as Japanese reached its climax one August afternoon.

12   It was typical summer weather for Tokyo, "like a steam bath" as the saying goes, so hot the leaves were drooping limply from the trees surrounding the Sakamotos' house. Mrs. Sakamoto and her married daughter, Takemi, were at the doctor's with Takemi's son, so Mr. Sakamoto and I were busy tending young Kaori-chan, Takemi-san's young daughter. Mr. Sakamoto quickly tired of his grandfatherly role, leaving me to entertain Kaori-chan. Promptly at four P.M., the hour when most Japanese housewives do their shopping for the evening meal, I lifted the baby into her stroller and pushed her along ahead of me as I inspected the fish, selected the freshest-looking vegetables, and mentally planned the meal for the evening. As I glanced into the shiny metal surface of the butcher's display case, I noticed someone who looked terribly familiar: a typical young housewife, clad in slip-on sandals and the loose, cotton shift called "home wear" (*hōmu wea*), a woman walking with a characteristically Japanese bend to the knees and a sliding of the feet. Suddenly I clutched the handle of the stroller to steady myself as a wave of dizziness washed over me, for I realized I had caught a glimpse of nothing less than my own reflection. Fear that perhaps I would never emerge from this world into which I was immersed inserted itself into my mind and stubbornly refused to leave, until I resolved to move into a new apartment, to distance myself from my Japanese home and my Japanese existence.

13   For ultimately this collapse of identity was a distancing moment. It led me to emphasize the *differences* between cultures and among various aspects of identity: researcher, student, daughter, wife, Japanese, American, Japanese American. In order to reconstitute myself as an American researcher, I felt I had to extricate myself from the conspiracy to rewrite my identity as Japanese. Accordingly, despite the Sakamotos' invitations to stay with them for the coming year, I politely stated my intentions to fulfill the original terms of the agreement: to stay just until construction on my new apartment was complete. In order to resist the Sakamotos' attempts to re-create me as Japanese, I removed myself physically from their exclusively Japanese environment. ◆◆

NOTES

1. See Edward Said, *Orientalism* (New York: Pantheon, 1978). The issue of what to call ourselves is an issue of considerable import to various ethnic and racial groups in the United States, as the recent emphasis on the term "African American" shows. For Asian Americans, the term "Oriental" was called into question in the sixties, for the reasons Said enumerates: the association of the term with stereotypes such as Oriental despotism, inscrutability, splendor, exoticism, mystery, and so on. It also defines "the East" in terms of "the West," in a relationship of unequal power— how rarely one hears of "the Occident," for example. Asian Americans, Japanese Americans included, sometimes hyphenate the term, but some of us would argue that leaving out the hyphen makes the term "Asian" or "Japanese" an adjective, rather than implying a half-and-half status: i.e., that one's loyalties/identities might be half Japanese and half American. Rather, in the terms "Asian American" and "Japanese American," the accent is on the "American," an important political claim in light of the mainstream tendency to see Asian Americans as somehow more foreign than other kinds of Americans.

2. Merry White, *The Japanese Overseas: Can They Go Home Again?* (New York: Free Press, 1988) offers an account of the families of Japanese corporate executives who are transferred abroad and who often suffer painful difficulties upon reentering Japan.

CULTURE BY THE CAMPFIRE*

Esther Pan and Sherry Keene-Osborn

Esther Pan and Sherry Keene-Osborn explore the world of culture camps, where children and parents deal with the issues of raising children in mixed-race families.

1   Hidden Valley looks a lot like the dozens of other camps that dot the woods of central Maine. There's a lake, some soccer fields and horses. But the campers make the difference. They're all American parents who have adopted kids from China. They're at Hidden Valley to find bridges from their children's old worlds to the new. Diana Becker of Montville, Maine, watches her 3-year-old daughter Mika dance to a Chinese version of "Twinkle, Twinkle Little Star." "Her soul is Chinese," she says, "but really she's growing up American."

2   Hidden Valley and a handful of other "culture camps" serving families with children from overseas reflect the huge rise in the number of foreign adoptions, from 7,093 in 1990 to 15,774 last year [1998]. Most children come from Russia (4,491 last year) and China (4,206), but there are also thousands of others adopted annually from South America, Asia and Eastern Europe. After cutting through what can be miles of red tape, parents often come home to find a new dilemma. "At first you think, 'I need a child,'" says Sandy Lachter of Washington, D.C., who with her husband, Steve, adopted Amelia, 5, from China in 1995. "Then you think, 'What does the child need?'"

3   The culture camps give families a place to find answers to those kinds of questions. Most grew out of local support groups; Hidden Valley was started last year

Newsweek, October 4, 1999, p. 75.

by the Boston chapter of Families with Children from China, which includes 650 families. While parents address weighty issues like how to raise kids in a mixed-race family, their children just have fun riding horses, singing Chinese songs or making scallion pancakes. "My philosophy of camping is that they could be doing anything, as long as they see other Chinese kids with white parents," says the director, Peter Kassen, whose adopted daughters Hope and Lily are 6 and 4.

4   The camp is a continuation of language and dance classes many of the kids attend during the year. "When we rented out a theater for *Mulan,* it was packed," says Stephen Chen of Boston, whose adopted daughter Lindsay is 4. Classes in Chinese language, art and calligraphy are taught by experts, like Renne Lu of the Greater Boston Chinese Cultural Center. "Our mission is to preserve the heritage," Lu says.

5   Kids who are veteran campers say the experience helps them understand their complex heritage. Sixteen-year-old Alex was born in India and adopted by Kathy and David Brinton of Boulder, Colo., when he was 7. "I went through a stage where I hated India, hated everything about it," he says. "You just couldn't mention India to me." But after six sessions at the East India Colorado Heritage Camp, held at Snow Mountain Ranch in Estes Park, Colo., he hopes to travel to India after he graduates from high school next year.

6   Campers say the sessions help them feel more "normal," especially if they live in communities where there are no other families like theirs. Gina Gruelle, 19, who was also adopted from India, grew up in the tiny town of Gresham, Ore. "It's important to go someplace where people do look and feel like you," she says of her time at Snow Mountain. Last summer, she returned as a volunteer counselor. "Some of the new kids, you could tell they had never been around other people from India," she says.

7   Snow Mountain is run by a volunteer group, Colorado Heritage Camps, founded by adoptive parent Pam Sweetser in 1992. They have sessions for kids from Korea, Vietnam, India, Latin America and the Philippines. "As adoptive parents, we have to realize they're the ones who deal with being a minority; we don't," says Sweetser. "We have to give them the skills to deal with that."

8   Camp can be a learning experience for the whole family. Whitney Ning, 23, a counselor for four years, says the Korea Heritage Camp helped her become closer to her parents. "They were hesitant at first," she says, "but when they saw how much it meant to me, they became very supportive." Sometimes the most direct route around the world is across a campfire. ◆◆

B. TO WHAT EXTENT SHOULD INDIVIDUALS ALLOW THEIR CULTURAL HERITAGE TO BE ASSIMILATED?

QUESTIONS TO CONSIDER BEFORE YOU READ

Have you ever known anyone who was forced to give up a sense of his or her own history, culture, or language for the sake of adjusting to a new social situation or country? What changes take place within an individual whose past or heritage conflicts with the ways of living in the dominant culture? Should people preserve their identities? Should they discard them? If you suddenly found yourself living in another country, how do you think you would respond to the new situation and how would that affect your sense of being American? Are you from another country? What difficulties concerning your identity do you currently face?

ASIAN IDENTITY CRISIS*

Yahlin Chang

Yahlin Chang writes for Newsweek *and, like the other authors in this section, raises the question about assimilating one's ethnic identity with the dominant group. Do you agree that it is good for Eric Liu to give up his Chinese heritage for an American identity? What is the author's position on this question?*

1   Eric Liu has spent most of his life climbing up the social ladder without looking back. The son of Chinese immigrants from Taiwan, he grew up learning to play down his ethnic identity in the mostly white community of Wappingers Falls, N.Y. Then he went on to amass a heap of power credentials: he graduated from Yale, at 25 he wrote speeches for President Clinton, and now he's at Harvard Law School. In his provocative, wonderfully honest new book, *The Accidental Asian*, Liu, 29, finally pauses long enough to reflect on his assimilationist's guilt, on the feeling that he's left something behind without knowing exactly what it is. Half cultural commentary, half memoir, *Accidental* is a remarkable accomplishment—both a defense of assimilation and an intense recounting of personal loss.

2   Though he's one of Asian America's biggest stars, Liu doesn't act or feel particularly Asian-American. He married a white woman—half of all Asian-Americans intermarry, he points out. He says he cannot escape the feeling that the Asian-American identity is "contrived" and "unnecessary." "Asian Americans are only as isolated as they want to be," he writes. "They—we—do not face the levels of discrimination and hatred that demand an enclave mentality. . . . The choice to invent and sustain a pan-Asian identity is just that: a choice, not an imperative." His book, which just hit stores, is already infuriating Asian-Americans who have a fierce sense of ethnic pride. "Liu has been totally co-opted by the white mainstream," says Bert Wang, who works on labor issues and anti-Asian violence, and christened his rock band Superchink. "But would he be where he is today if he weren't Asian? They love him because he's this novelty who's pro-assimilation." Jeff Yang, the founder of *A. Magazine*—a sort of Asian *Vanity Fair*—finds Liu's view misguided and a bit naive. "Race is an obsession in our society," he says. "To be out of the racial equation takes us away from the table of dialogue completely. But we're creating a culture out of our common experiences: immigration, being perceived as strangers in our own land, serving as a bridge between East and West."

Newsweek, June 22, 1998, p. 68.

3   But even the most militant Asian-Americans admit to an identity crisis. Chinese, Koreans, Filipinos and other "Asians" have not only different cultures and languages but deep historical antagonisms toward one another. More than anything, what binds them together in America is what they look like—the exact basis for their stigmatization. The Asian-American "race" is just three decades old, born with the immigration boom in 1965. "Race is fundamentally an invention," says Liu. "And just as something can be invented, so it can be dismantled. If you believe in the identity, I can respect that. I'm just not sure it'll last another generation."

4   The economic success many Asian-Americans have achieved may only further weaken that identity. They account for 4 percent of the population, and have the highest median income of all races, including whites. A higher percentage of them earn advanced degrees than of any other group. But those statistics hide the growing number of poor immigrants who feel increasingly alienated from upper-class Asians. "The poor are an embarrassment to professionals who don't want to be seen as peasants," says Peter Kwong, head of Asian-American Studies at New York's Hunter College. "You're taught to be ashamed of your parents," says Chinatown labor activist Trinh Duong, whose mother works in a garment factory. Some activists, who say they have a hard time drawing attention to the plight of those immigrants, try to play down the achievements of upper-class Asians and chafe at the "model minority" stereotype. "That label is clearly part of a hostile discourse between whites and blacks," says Kwong. "Whites are basically saying to blacks, 'We're not racist, and the reason you're not as successful is because you're not working as hard as Asians.'"

5   Yet the abstract debate over assimilation can't do justice to the complex emotional acrobatics of dealing with your own ethnicity. While Liu grew up trying to fit in to white America, that was the last thing I wanted. I was taught that Asians were smarter and harder-working than everyone else and that explained their success—when the truth is that immigration laws favored professionals, a highly selective group to begin with. There seemed to be no way to have ethnic pride without ethnocentrism. The only solution, it seemed, was to try and transcend race—to erase racial concerns by ignoring them. I started to think a lot like Liu.

6   But something always comes along to jolt me out of this colorblind slumber. The rising number of incidents of anti-Asian violence. College-admission quotas against us. Coverage of the campaign-finance scandals, filled with "shadowy" Orientals creeping into power, practicing the ancient Chinese art of *guanxi,* a scarily exotic word for "connections." And why do so many articles on race neglect to mention us? Why do so many reports from the Census Bureau include only blacks, whites and Hispanics?

7   Is racial identity formed only through racial persecution? I was once berated by a white classmate for claiming I had never been persecuted—which made me wish that I had. But I can't help feeling that it would be contrived to suddenly become passionate about my ethnicity, or to dredge up racial scars that don't exist. Liu says, "Race for people of color should be as much of an option as ethnicity is for whites." But in America, trying to forget about being a minority can still get you in as much trouble as being one. ◆◆

EDUCATING OURSELVES INTO COEXISTENCE*

Anouar Majid

Author of Unveiling Traditions: Postcolonial Islam in a Polycentric World, *Anouar Majid is a member of the English department at the University of New England. As the title of this article suggests, Majid argues the necessity of a humanities curriculum in schools to help people from different backgrounds understand one another. What do you think? Can a multicultural curriculum help heal the wounds between Islam and America in a post-9/11 world?*

1   Many years ago, a devout Muslim man who was a friend of mine, an avid reader of Islamic medieval theological texts and a bright scientist completing an engineering doctorate at an American university, discovered a secret about the United States that had eluded him in all the years he had lived in this country. He had always found Americans hospitable, but to him they were still Christian, Jewish, or even worse, atheist, and would do better if they could be guided to Islam, God's final revealed religion. It was a sincerely held belief, felt without malice or condescension. He wanted his hosts—and me, too, because although I was born Muslim, I wasn't as observant as I could have been—to share his joy.

2   Knowing me to be a student of American literature, he talked about ideas and science in the Koran. Once he froze me on the spot by citing two or three verses that unambiguously showed that time was relative in the eyes of Allah. I had an interest in notions of time (having just read Stephen Hawking's *A Brief History of Time*) and was working my way through the second law of thermodynamics, having just read Thomas Pynchon's *The Crying of Lot 49*. The Koran also described in moving poetic detail the rotation of heavenly bodies; it even suggested that the sun was not stationary but drifting away at a slow pace.

3   All of that impressed me tremendously. I read the Koran chapter by chapter and took notes. We continued our conversation, now going on to Islamic jurisprudence and poetry. Yet our daily lives could not have been more different. While I went for long periods without thinking about the Koran or my religious beliefs, my pious interlocutor focused on every detail of daily life: He ate only halal food; averted his eyes from women; didn't watch much TV; played soccer with long, baggy pants; and prayed regularly and often.

4   Then, one day, he announced that the United States was a Muslim country. He had read the Declaration of Independence and was stunned to find that it—as well as the U.S. Constitution—embodied the Islamic tenets that he had spent his life promoting. Resistance to oppression, the ideals of social justice and good government, and the freedom of worship are what all committed Muslims want to see established in their home countries. Much like Jefferson and his revolutionary peers warned against the destructive effects of tyranny, the Koran recounts dozens of tales about rulers and nations who transgressed the limits of divine justice, and the horrible punishments that befell them. Now America's secular manifestoes appeared imbued with the same divine intent. Why don't more Muslims know about this part of American history and culture?

Chronicle of Higher Education, April 12, 2002, pp. B10+.

5   With the same zeal he had used to try to convert Americans, my friend now started explaining to perplexed fellow Muslim students his new thesis about the U.S. government. What a shame that Muslims, Allah's intended inheritors of such a wise political system, should be deprived of it. That was an old idea I had heard constantly while growing up in Tangier, a liberal city dismissed as hopelessly corrupt by conservative Muslims and Westerners alike. The idea is basic: Europeans and Americans are the true Muslims because they have justice and democracy, whereas Muslims are infidels because their behavior contradicts their proclaimed faith.

6   I recall the experience of the pious Muslim engineering student at this tragic moment in the world's history because we are, once again, misdiagnosing underlying causes of conflict and missing new opportunities to bring human cultures closer to one another. For I do consider that Muslim student, who had wanted to guide Americans to the truth, to have been guided by his reading of the founding documents of American democracy. His discovery disabused him of the misperceptions he had accumulated over the years—that nice, unsuspecting Americans (and Westernized Muslims) were a new people in desperate need of some uncorrupted, ancient truth.

7   Quite often, people like him wonder how such a permissive society could at the same time be a superpower. How could a just God allow infidels to rule the world while faithful Muslims suffered all sorts of indignities? Now he had the answer. The Declaration and the Constitution were the nation's moral compasses. That's why God allowed it to prosper, for God does not allow the unjust to flourish. The United States was doing something right.

◆◆◆◆

8   In my almost 20 years of living here, studying and teaching American literature and culture, I have come to realize that the United States, the groundbreaking social and political experiment of modern history, somehow remains totally unknown to much of the rest of the world. If Muslims were to study the making of the United States, they would quickly realize that the country taken to be superficial and new has a history and culture as rich and tragic as any that they know. If the Muslim engineering student reacted so positively to the Declaration, how would he have reacted had he read Jonathan Edwards and the texts of other early American writers about the varied religious movements in American history, all struggling to establish the ideal society on earth? That classic American struggle, pitting pure faith against worldly success, is something Muslims could learn from, particularly educated youth looking for answers to their own cultural frustrations and identity crises.

9   In the aftermath of September 11, commentators wrote that the attack on the World Trade Center was an attack on capitalism, America's ultimate expression of freedom. Capitalism is certainly one of the key words that explains much of the present conflict, for consumer cultures invariably frustrate the religious life passionately sought by believers of all faiths. Mundane activities like banking, restaurant dining, reading magazines, watching TV, and traveling become emotionally charged undertakings loaded with meaning, since they all challenge the piety of devout Muslims. And because we live in environments that are always luring us

into never-ending cycles of consumerism, the faithful's anxieties are constantly being renewed, sparking an ever-mutating cycle of tension.

10   Many Americans, in some ways, share the Muslims' predicament. Granted, the U.S. Constitution (like Islam) never explicitly separated the unhindered flow of commerce from political freedom, but one still wonders whether Jeffersonian democracy is truly compatible with the dictates of the prevailing economic ethos. Jefferson's enlightened Republicanism, with its stress on agrarian virtues, is obscured by the glaring lights of corporate logos, the blaring sounds of commercials, and the dizzying proliferation of franchises. Similarly, the Koran encourages trade but contains economic activity within the higher imperative of spiritual and social obligations.

11   The question then is, how do religious and even truly enlightened secular cultures preserve themselves while they are fully inserted into the machinery of laissez-faire capitalism? Since a bland deculturing process is making all of us unrecognisable to ourselves (both as human beings and as communities), a strong consciousness of the corrosive powers of the reigning global economy is a necessary first step toward a cultural dialogue and a true multicultural human civilization. Education can play a vital role in this process, yet our educational systems, increasingly geared to accommodate the needs of the marketplace, are perpetuating that destructive tendency, not alleviating it. To restore the balance, we must reinvigorate the humanities as the central component of all academic curriculums.

12   Last fall, Lynne V. Cheney challenged educators to teach more American history and not spend so much time on efforts to devise a dubious multicultural agenda. In many ways, she is right. American students ought to know their history first, just as Muslims ought to know theirs. But what kind of history are students being exposed to?

13   Critics seem to suggest that multiculturalism weakens the national resolve and produces a breed of weak, uncertain citizens unfit to defend the nation in times of crisis. I'd like to suggest the opposite: that the problem with multiculturalism is that we educators haven't invested the concept with solid substance, or expanded it broadly enough. A required multicultural education solidly based in the humanities could do more for U.S. national security than all the resources of the military. It would allow students to realize how other nations and cultures are made up of human communities wrestling with familiar issues, how all people are ultimately influenced by local dogmas, and that no one society holds the monopoly on a universal truth. Once we begin to see others not as others but as ourselves, the inclination to inflict injury on them diminishes; to humanize members of different cultures through education is to begin forging ties of sympathy with them.

◆◆◆◆

14   By virtue of its diverse population representing every part of the globe, the United States has the unique opportunity of incorporating various experiences and points of view into its curriculums. Much of this is already being carried out through the globalizing of Western-civilization courses and the inclusion of indigenous, non-Western and female perspectives in the literary canon. All it needs now is to strengthen the process by making it more rigorous, and then modeling the idea to Muslims who resist incorporating the study of other cultures and

religions into their academic programs. Of course, not all Muslim countries are the same. Some, like Morocco, have fairly advanced bilingual—or even tri-lingual—curriculums that do a good job preparing students for higher education at home or abroad. For example, I studied Western literature and philosophy, Islamic thought, and the history and economy of the United States and other Western countries in high school.

15   Other Muslim countries load their curriculums with heavier doses of Islamic studies and neglect the study of other cultural and religious communities. Foreign students also miss out on opportunities to study the histories and cultures of their host countries, which is why many Muslim students in the United States and Eu-rope know so little about Western philosophy and literature. A well-designed multicultural education that puts one's community in global perspective is good for everyone. Just as American students are encouraged by many educators to question their own cultural assumptions, Muslims would benefit from asking such questions as whether Islam is the "only" true religion, or whether women and members of minority groups enjoy their God-given rights in Islamic states. Muslims who censor such questions to protect their faith are in fact impoverish-ing their intellectual heritage. Even major prophets, according to the Koran, chal-lenged God to prove his existence.

16   A multicultural curriculum that showcases the contributions of other cultures is certainly consistent with Islamic teachings. The Koran states that God's will is to have a world made up of many different nations, and that the challenge for Mus-lims and others is to know one another and compete in the performance of good deeds. Such an education would allow students to see civilization as a mosaic of traditions ultimately sharing the same cosmic destiny. Even while Muslims and non-Muslims must do their utmost to preserve a world of diversities, we should all remember that our human civilization—as embattled and fragmented as it is—needs to be understood as a common venture. For better or worse, we are one another's keepers.

17   A solid education in the humanities is the answer to the post-September 11 world. Such an education would allow us to distinguish the essence of Islamic and U.S. cultural traditions from the proliferating dogmas and rampant commer-cialism that have come to replace them. A dialogue of cultures begins here. Every other strategy of containment will most likely make things worse. ◆◆

AMERICAN JEWS AND THE PROBLEM OF IDENTITY*

Edward S. Shapiro

History professor at Seton Hall University, Edward Shapiro is author of A Time for Healing: American Jewry Since World War II. *In the following essay, Shapiro wonders what it*

---

means to be Jewish. Is Jewish identity a question of religion, culture, race, history or a combination of these? How does one know?

1   The question of identity has been more problematic for Jews than for any other American subgroup. This is due in the first place to the perplexing nature of what it means to be Jewish. The issue of "Who is a Jew?" has vexed American Jews just as it has Jews in Israel. Thus the most contentious issue within American Jewish religious circles during the past two decades was the decision of the American Reform movement in the early 1980s to cast aside the definition of Jewishness that had delineated the Jewish community for thousands of years. According to this definition, a Jew had to have a Jewish mother or to have been converted according to Jewish law. Matrilineal descent was used to determine Jewish identity since the identity of one's mother, in contrast to one's father, was never in doubt.

2   The Reform movement, however, broadened the definition of Jewish identity to include patrilineal descent if intermarried parents, for their part, involved their children in the Jewish community through such things as participation in religious services or enrollment in a religious school. This move was taken not because of any theological revelation but because of the rapid increase in intermarriage between Jews and non-Jews beginning in the 1960s. This resulted in hundreds of thousands of families in which there were doubts about the Jewishness of the children since their mothers had never undergone even a minimal conversion. Leaders from the Orthodox and Conservative wings of American Judaism strongly protested this decision of the Reform movement. They claimed that it would result in a schism within American Judaism since Reform Jews could no longer be automatically considered as appropriate marriage partners for Jews who accepted the traditional definition of who is a Jew and who wished to avoid intermarriage. But the problem of Jewish identity goes beyond this intramural conflict over the religious definition of who is a Jew. It encompasses the broader and more important question of whether Jewishness is a matter of religion, history, culture, or ethnicity.

3   The identity of other groups is not so muddled. There is no confusion, for example, over the fact that the ethnicity of Irish-Catholics is Irish while their religion is Roman Catholicism. A lapsed Irish-Catholic remains Irish although he or she is no longer a Catholic in good standing. But such clarity of religious and ethnic identity does not exist among Jews. A Jewish atheist or agnostic, such as an Albert Einstein or a Sidney Hook, remains a Jew in good standing. In fact, many of the fiercest critics of Judaism have been Jews, and modern-day Jewish movements such as Jewish socialism and Labor Zionism have opposed traditional Judaism. Jews also do not constitute a language group. Few Jews speak Hebrew, Yiddish, or Ladino (Spanish-Jewish). Nor are Jews defined by being the victims of prejudice and discrimination. This might have been true in Europe and the Arab countries, but it certainly is not true in the United States, where the income, occupational mobility, and social status of Jews is far higher than that of the general population.

4   This ambiguity regarding the nature of Jewishness is particularly confusing to Americans, who tend to see Jews as comprising a religious group comparable to

that of Protestants and Catholics. Books such as Will Herberg's *Protestant-Catholic-Jew* (1995) reinforced this disposition to see religion as the essence of Jewishness. One of the reasons that anti-Semitism has never been as strong in America as elsewhere is that Americans place a high value on religion and because they equate Jewishness with Judaism. This conflating of Jewishness with Judaism is also seen in academia, where courses in Jewish Studies, even when they are concerned with sociology and history, are often located in departments of religion.

5   Complicating the definition of American Jewish identity is the relationship of Jews to America. Traditional Judaism emphasized the obligation of Jews to be good citizens and to defer to those in power, even if they were anti-Semitic. Thus in the early years of Nazi Germany, Orthodox rabbis in Germany told their followers to respect the edicts of the political authorities. Traditional Judaism, however, also taught that Jews were in exile and would eventually return to the Promised Land. But the nationalistic and religious impulses encouraging Jews in the late nineteenth and early twentieth centuries to settle in Palestine were not as powerful as the social and economic opportunities of America. For every Jew who left Europe for Palestine in these years, forty emigrated to the United States. Here was a land in which the government did not encourage or tacitly accept anti-Semitism, in which the property and lives of Jews were protected by the local and national governments, and in which there were not official barriers to the social and economic advancement of Jews. As George Washington noted in his famous letter of 1790 to the synagogue of Newport, Rhode Island, in America Jews as well as Christians will "possess alike liberty of conscience and immunities of citizenship."

6   If America was not the Promised Land, this "novus ordo seclorum" was certainly the land of promise for Jews, and they were fiercely loyal to their new country. "This synagogue is our temple, this city our Jerusalem, this happy land our Palestine," Rabbi Gustavus Poznanski told the congregants of Beth Elohim, the Charleston, South Carolina, synagogue, prior to the Civil War. Mary Antin, a Jewish immigrant raised in Boston, also saw America as the new Israel, with Boston being the New Jerusalem. The title of her 1911 autobiography is *The Promised Land*. Another Jew, Irving Berlin, wrote "God Bless America," while a third, Emma Lazarus, wrote "The New Colossus," the sonnet placed at the base of the Statue of Liberty celebrating America as the refuge for the "huddled masses yearning to be free." Lazarus, who was involved in efforts to ameliorate the conditions of eastern European immigrants in New York City, was undoubtedly thinking of her co-religionists when she wrote her poem.

7   Eager to become part of America, American Jews were skeptical of ideologies and movements that impeded their movement into the American mainstream. Zionism, for example, was unpopular among America's Jews until the 1930s, when it became obvious that a Jewish homeland was necessary for Europe's beleaguered Jews. But American Jews had no intention themselves of migrating to Palestine or, later, to Israel. They feared that the Zionism movement would raise doubts among Americans as to their political loyalties. Rather than rejecting Zionism, American Jews transformed it to conform to American realities. For them, Zionism was not a nationalistic movement encompassing all Jews but rather a

philanthropy to succor other Jews. This gave rise to the quip that American Zionism was a program in which one group of Jews gave money to another group of Jews to bring a third group of Jews to the Middle East. For Israelis, most notably David Ben-Gurion, the first prime minister of Israel, American Zionism was not truly Zionist since it downplayed the fundamental Zionist principles of the negation of the Diaspora and the in-gathering of all exiles to Israel. With the establishment of a Jewish state, American Zionism seemed to be an anachronism to the Israelis. How could one claim to be a Zionist and yet not settle in the Jewish state? The Israeli statesman Abba Eban joked that American Zionism demonstrated the truth of one religious principle: that there could be life after death.

8   Traditional Judaism suffered the same fate as Zionism in America. The dietary and other restrictions in Judaism that promoted a sharp separation between Jews and Gentiles and discouraged the movement of Jews into the American economic and cultural mainstream fell by the wayside. New religious ideologies, such as Reform Judaism, Conservative Judaism, and Reconstructionism, partially filled the vacuum created by the diminished appeal of Orthodoxy. As one wag put it, Jews gave up Orthodoxy at the drop of a hat. This refusal to cover one's hair or to refrain from eating forbidden foods or to observe the Sabbath was symptomatic of a deeper problem: the fact that only a small minority of American Jews believed that they were a chosen people, elected by God to serve a distinctive purpose. The Bible talks about the Jews being a "peculiar people," and for thousands of years there had been no doubt among Jews as to the source of their distinctiveness. Every morning religious Jews had blessed God for having "chosen us among all peoples and given us thy Torah" and for not having "made me a heathen."

9   Jews were anxious to be thought of as no different than other Americans. In June 1952, *Look* magazine published Rabbi Morris Kertzer's article "What Is a Jew?" The thrust of Kertzer's piece was that Jews and Christians "share the same rich heritage of the Old Testament. They both believe in the fatherhood of one God, in the sanctity of the Ten Commandments, the wisdom of the prophets and the brotherhood of man." If Kertzer was correct that Jews were like everyone else, then what reason was there for them to maintain their distinctiveness? Why should they choose to remain Jewish if they were not different from their Christian neighbors? Had not the type of thinking expressed by Kertzer deprived Jews and Judaism of the raison d'etre for any peculiarity?

10   In 1960, the sociologist Erich Rosenthal used the phrase "acculturation without assimilation" to describe the process of social adaptation of Jews in America. Jews, he argued, had adopted the values and lifestyles of the general society, but they separated themselves from the rest of America in choosing marriage partners, friends, and places to live. In America even this limited sense of separation could not long be maintained, not when many Jews were attending colleges in which they were a minority and were rapidly moving up the social and economic ladder. Life was simply too attractive and open for Jews to isolate themselves. Yeshiva University could not compete with Columbia or Harvard, nor could the dense Jewish neighborhoods of New York City, Philadelphia, and Chicago compete with the beckoning suburbs. In the case of Kerri Strug, who captivated the country when she won the gold medal for the American women's gymnastic

team at the Atlanta Olympics despite having an injured leg, Jewish identity lost out to the attraction of the uneven bars and the balance beam. Jewish newspapers informed their readers that Strug's parents were active in a Tucson synagogue but that their daughter had been too busy with her athletic development to be involved in anything Jewish.

◆◆◆◆

11   David Gelernter, the polymath Yale professor, protested against this tendency to recast Judaism in order to conform with the latest sociological or intellectual fad. "Like most American Jews," he wrote in 1996,

> I find myself able to observe only a tiny fraction of the Torah's commandments. Unlike some, I believe that the commandments are binding. When I fail to perform a religious obligation, I do not want a soothing Reform or Conservative authority to tell me I am in luck—that particular obligation has been dropped from the new edition and I am free to ignore it. I am not free to ignore it and commit a sin when I fail to do it. I acknowledge my failings and recall that God is merciful. . . . This infantile insistence that religious ritual conform to you rather than the other way around is the essence of modern American culture, and is strangling Judaism.

Gelernter's view of American Jewry's future is bleak. Being Jewish, he predicted, will come to mean what "'being Scottish in America' means: nothing. Certain family names will suggest Jewish or Scottish origins." That is all.

12   Reinforcing the centrifugal nature of American Jewish identity was the absence of any official rabbinate or politically recognized communal officials with the power to determine who is and is not Jewish and what being Jewish entails. The result was a Jewish community of incredible religious and cultural diversity. America has been the birthplace of new religious ideologies such as Conservative Judaism, Reconstructionist Judaism, the Havurot movement, and Jewish feminism. Though "We Are One," the motto of the United Jewish Appeal in America, might have been an effective fund-raising slogan, it certainly was not an accurate description of the reality of American Jewry. This Jewishness without barriers has had its bizarre side effects as well. Thus there is even a group of "Messianic Jews" or "Jews for Jesus" who claim that they are good Jews despite their belief in the divinity of Jesus.

13   The enigmatic nature of American Jewish identity is responsible for the curious fact that the three major interpretations of what it means to be an American were provided by Jews. Emma Lazarus's "The New Colossus" argued for integrating the "wretched refuse yearning to be free," and her own assimilated life was a model of what she hoped the immigrants from Europe, and particularly the Jewish immigrants, would conform to. Two decades after the Statue of Liberty was dedicated in 1886, Israel Zangwill published his play *The Melting Pot*. This tale of an intermarriage in New York City between David, a Russian Jew, and Vera, the daughter of a Christian Russian responsible for a pogrom in David's hometown, reflected Zangwill's belief in the beneficence of the ethnic amalgamation that he believed was taking place in America. The glory of America, he emphasized, lay in the ability of Americans, native-born and immigrant alike, to put aside ancient rivalries and to create a new nationality combining the best traits of the various ethnic groups peopling America. Zangwill did not regret the fact that in America

the Jew would disappear, as would the Italian, the Irishman, and the Yankee. Zangwill himself had married the daughter of a Protestant clergyman and did not rear his children as Jews.

14   The most important answer to the melting pot idea was Horace Kallen's 1915 essay "Democracy versus the Melting Pot." Kallen, the son of an Orthodox Jew who had settled in Boston, argued that the most accurate metaphor for the process of Americanization was not a melting pot but an orchestra. Just as each instrument in an orchestra made a distinctive contribution to the symphony, so each ethnic group made a distinctive contribution to American life. And just as it would be foolish to melt down the instruments of the orchestra, so it would be equally foolish to melt down America's ethnic groups. Out of this ethnic diversity, Kallen predicted, there was emerging a new "symphony of civilization" in which "each nationality would have its emotional and involuntary life, its own peculiar dialect or speech, its own individual and inevitable esthetic and intellectual forms." And just as a democratic government was obligated to safeguard the rights of the citizens to join whatever religious and social groups they chose, so a democratic government should encourage the people to preserve their ethnic identities, which, Kallen mistakenly believed, were inalienable: "There are human capacities which it is the function of the state to liberate and to protect in growth," Kallen said, "and the failure of the state as a government to accomplish this automatically makes for its abolition."

15   The pluralism expressed by Horace Kallen has been American Jewry's greatest strength and its greatest potential weakness. Elaine Marks, a professor of European literature at the University of Wisconsin, recently showed just how far a Jewishness without boundaries can be stretched: "I am Jewish precisely because I am not a believer," she said paradoxically, "because I associate from early childhood the courage not to believe with being Jewish." For Marks, choosing to deny Judaism is thus a quintessential Jewish act; and the Jew who rejects Judaism is transformed into the most committed Jew.

16   With Jewish identity increasingly a matter of prescription rather than ascription, what guarantee is there that a sufficient number of Jews will ever choose the same things? What will be the source of Jewish communal affiliation when many Jews have come to believe that Judaism sanctions whatever they believe or wish to do? What is the lowest common denominator of Jewish belief and practice that can act as the cement of Jewish identity? Certainly traditional Judaism no longer fills that role. No more than one-quarter of American Jews observe the dietary laws, less than 10 percent keep the Sabbath as a day of rest, and over half do not light Sabbath candles (90 percent even think that a Jew could be religious without being observant). These same persons claim that being Jewish was very important to them and that they consider themselves to be "very good" Jews. For them, being Jewish has little to do with practicing Judaism. In their own minds, they are very good Jews because their version of Jewishness demands nothing of them. It is a Jewishness without content.

◆◆◆◆

17   The question of Jewish identity is particularly important today when it can no longer be assumed that Jewishness, however it might be defined, is being

automatically passed on from one generation to the next. In his 1959 apologia, *This Is My God,* the novelist Herman Wouk, an Orthodox Jew, described a mythical Mr. Abramson, a Jewish amnesiac, "pleasantly vanishing down a broad highway at the wheel of a high-power station wagon, with the golf clubs piled in the back." When his amnesia clears "he will be Mr. Adamson, and his wife and children will join him, and all will be well. But the Jewish question will be over in the United States."

18   For Jewish survivalists, the most troubling aspect of American life was the rapid increase in intermarriage beginning in the 1960s. The 1990 National Jewish Population Survey, an important demographic study of contemporary American Jewry, reported that 52 percent of Jews were then choosing non-Jewish marriage partners. But could anything be done to reverse this development, or would Jews have to learn to live with it? In other words, was intermarriage a problem for which there was a solution, or was it a condition that could not be changed? For Conservative Rabbi Robert Gordis it was the latter. In *Judaism in a Christian World* (1966), Gordis argued that "intermarriage is part of the price that modern Jewry must pay for freedom and equality in an open society." This was scant comfort for Jewish survivalists.

✦✦✦✦

19   In *The Ambivalent American Jew* (1973), the sociologist Charles Liebman noted that American Jews were "torn between two sets of values—those of integration and acceptance into American society and those of Jewish group survival." Jerold A. Auerbach, a historian at Wellesley College, agreed with Liebman. In *Rabbis and Lawyers: The Journey from Torah to Constitution* (1990), Auerbach argued that American Jews were heirs to two disparate and, at times, contradictory traditions—Jewish and American—and that committed American Jews were fated to live in two competing and discordant worlds. "The synthesis of Judaism and Americanism," he said, was "a historical fiction." The symposium in the August 1996 issue of *Commentary* magazine on "What Do American Jews believe?" indicated that a significant number of America's leading Jewish religious thinkers agree.

20   If the buzzwords of the 1930s and 1940s for American Jews were "survival" and "anti-Semitism," the buzzwords of the 1980s and 1990s have been "continuity" and "identity." While Jews do not fear for their physical safety, they are concerned about the viability of a Jewish population that is experiencing major demographic hemorrhaging due to religious apathy, a low birth rate, a high rate of exogamy, and the lure of a secular culture emphasizing individual autonomy and personal gratification rather than religious obligations and communal commitment. History should instill caution on the ability to predict the future. Who could have predicted in 1988 the demise of the Soviet Union, a peace treaty between Israel and the Palestine Liberation Organization, and the election of an obscure governor of Arkansas as president? In May 1964, *Look* magazine published an article entitled "The Vanishing American Jew." Well, the American Jew did not vanish, but *Look* soon did. But whether the editors of *Look* will have the last laugh remains to be seen. The experience of Jews, more than that of America's other ethnic groups, "is the supreme test of how far acculturation can go without eroding the sense of distinctiveness," Stephen J. Whitfield wrote recently. "So far

American Jewry as a whole has not flunked this test of an open society. Sometimes they are in the dark, however." ◆◆

QUESTIONS TO HELP YOU THINK AND WRITE ABOUT RACE, CULTURE, AND IDENTITY

1. Using your own experiences and observations, test bell hooks's claims about how black and white relationships are depicted on film and television. Is she right or not? Give examples that prove or disprove her theory.

2. Demographers predict that whites will become a minority race sometime in the first half of the twenty-first century. Consider Dyer's idea that the concept of "whiteness" be racialized. What effect might that have now, at the beginning of the twenty-first century? What effect might it have later in the century, if white people become a "racial minority"?

3. Gómez-Peña writes about the conflicts in cultural identity that come from living on the Mexican-American border. How does he characterize his own cultural identity? How would he compare it with Anglo culture, which he describes as "violent and antisocial"? What does he recommend at the end of his article to reduce conflict? What is your reaction to his ideas about reducing conflict?

4. Imagine Kondo and the family she lived with in Japan attending the camp in Colorado described by Pan and Keene-Osborn to help them better understand and accept one another's cultural differences. Would that interaction work? Why or why not?

5. Imagine going to live in another country where the race, culture, and language are different from your own. What aspects of your culture would you want to keep? What would you be willing to give up? Do you think you would experience the cultural identity crisis Kondo describes? How might your own sense of personal identity be affected by such a relocation?

6. Suppose that hooks, Dyer, Gómez-Peña, and Kondo have been invited to participate in a television talk show, and the subject for discussion is how members of their respective races are depicted on film and television. What might their positions be on the following three issues?

    a. Racial stereotyping: Does it exist on film and television, or not? Give evidence.
    b. Relationships among the races: Are they depicted as equal or unequal? Give evidence.
    c. Racial colorblindness: Does it exist? Should it exist? Explain your answers.

7. In "Educating Ourselves into Coexistence" Majid suggests that education can help to create a more peaceful world. Reread the last four paragraphs of his article and paraphrase his recommendations. What is your reaction to them?

8. Chang, Majid, and Shapiro all discuss the problems of assimilation. Go back over each essay. Make notes on the ways each author sees assimilation as necessary or beneficial to living in America for the ethnic groups represented in each article. Then make notes on the ways each author sees assimilation as something to be resisted. Discuss your findings with a classmate. What conclusions can you draw about what people from other cultures should do?

9. The historical perspective Shapiro offers is a good place to begin research on a larger topic concerning what it means to be Jewish. Review Shapiro's essay and pick one historical event in Jewish history you would like to learn more about. What kind of information does Shapiro give? What kind of information would you still like to know? How do you think you can add to the discussion?

⫸ Section V ⫷

Issues Concerning Freedom

THE ISSUES

A. HOW RIGOROUSLY SHOULD WE PROTECT OUR CIVIL LIBERTIES?

Richard Posner in "Security versus Civil Liberties" points out that civil liberties have been compromised in the past in times of war and that safety is sometimes more important than protecting civil liberties. Peter Lewis also looks at the conflict between freedom and security and concludes that even though some safety measures are tolerable, losing fundamental liberties is not.

B. HOW CAN WE BALANCE SECURITY AGAINST PRIVACY IN A TECHNOLOGICAL AGE?

In "How Private Is Your Life?" Peter Maas demonstrates how computer technology makes information we have traditionally considered private readily available to people who know how to access it. Lisa Guernsey in "Living under the Electronic Eye" agrees with Maas and asks whether the government should be given the authority to use this information. Finally, Dana Hawkins writes about some of the problems associated with biometrics, a way of identifying individuals through biological characteristics, and Eric Cohen comments on the political positions taken on privacy issues by liberals and conservatives and conjectures about the privacy wars of the future.

C. HOW DOES PROFILING THREATEN CIVIL LIBERTIES?

Jeffrey Goldberg in "The Color of Suspicion" describes racial profiling: he discusses why it has been used by police, especially in the war against drugs, and why it is controversial. Lynette Clemetson and Keith Naughton examine the racial profiling of Muslims that followed the terrorist attacks in America, and Fareed Zakaria describes an alternative to racial profiling which he calls "smart profiling." See also "Letter from Birmingham Jail" (page 277).

D. WEB SITES FOR FURTHER EXPLORATION AND RESEARCH

Government Security	http://govtsecurity.securitysolutions.com
The Biometric Consortium	http://www.biometrics.org
Government Technology	http://www.govtech.net
ACLU Freedom of Information Act	http://www.aclu.org/library/foia.html
Electronic Privacy Information Center	http://www.epic.org/open_gov
Internet Freedom	http://www.netfreedom.org

E. FILMS AND LITERATURE RELATED TO FREEDOM

Films: Minority Report, 2002; *Total Recall,* 1990; *Enemy of the State,* 1998.
Literature: novels: *A Brave New World* by Aldous Huxley; *1984* by George Orwell; *Fahrenheit 451* by Ray Bradbury; *The Handmaid's Tale* by Margaret Atwood; *The Giver* by Lois Lowry; *Utopia* by Thomas More; short story: "The Ones Who Walk Away from Omelas" by Ursula K. Le Guin; plays: *Enemy of the People* by Henrik Ibsen; *Antigone* by Sophocles; political document: "The Declaration of Independence" by Thomas Jefferson.

THE RHETORICAL SITUATION

Americans have traditionally regarded their civil liberties—freedom of the press, protection of privacy, protection of the rights of criminal suspects, freedom of religion, freedom to assemble, freedom of speech—as rights that are guaranteed by the Constitution and that are thus inviolable. These civil liberties represent the foundational values of this country. Following the terrorist attacks of September 11, 2001, however, some of these liberties were compromised and curtailed by the government in an effort to improve national security. September 11 has provided a fresh exigency for arguing about the guarantees of civil liberties. Basically, individuals disagree on the degree to which various liberties should be changed or even abandoned in an effort to assure greater national security.

Besides the terrorist attacks, however, other exigencies exist in American society that prompt argument about how important it is to protect the basic freedoms, particularly when weighed against the perceived requirements of national security. Long before September 11, law enforcement was often criticized for the racial profiling of possible criminals and also for violating individuals' privacy rights in the war on drugs.

This section presents perspectives on the present conflicts between maintaining everyone's basic civil liberties and maintaining national security. The civil liberties Americans traditionally enjoy also provide terrorists with precisely the opportunities they need to move through the country and engage in destructive events. The basic question of how important it is to guard our civil liberties is the first issue considered. Then the protection or dissolution of two basic freedoms—the right to privacy and the right to freedom from racial profiling—is argued by the authors of the remaining articles.

One way to develop your own perspectives on the issues raised by these topics is to try to understand both the exigencies and the constraints that cause people to contemplate abandoning their basic freedoms. Then you can compare these with the importance of maintaining the freedoms themselves. Value warrants figure strongly in arguments about basic freedoms. You may find that you will have to prioritize your values and assign relatively greater value to some desirable courses of action than to others, even when, under other circumstances, you may regard all of them as of equal value.

A. HOW RIGOROUSLY SHOULD WE PROTECT OUR CIVIL LIBERTIES?

QUESTIONS TO CONSIDER BEFORE YOU READ

What civil liberties do you particularly value? How would you live differently if you could no longer rely on these liberties? What liberties are you willing to sacrifice in order to feel safer in America? What might be the final effect on the quality of life in the country?

SECURITY VERSUS CIVIL LIBERTIES*

Richard A. Posner

Richard A. Posner argues in favor of curtailing our civil rights when that is necessary and provides historical comparisons to justify that practice at present. Consider what would happen if we all adopted that view.

1   In the wake of the September 11 terrorist attacks have come many proposals for tightening security; some measures to that end have already been taken. Civil libertarians are troubled. They fear that concerns about national security will lead to an erosion of civil liberties. They offer historical examples of supposed overreactions to threats to national security. They treat our existing civil liberties— freedom of the press, protections of privacy and of the rights of criminal suspects,

*Atlantic Monthly, December 2001, pp. 46–48.

and the rest—as sacrosanct, insisting that the battle against international terrorism accommodate itself to them.

2   I consider this a profoundly mistaken approach to the question of balancing liberty and security. The basic mistake is the prioritizing of liberty. It is a mistake about law and a mistake about history. Let me begin with law. What we take to be our civil liberties—for example, immunity from arrest except upon probable cause to believe we've committed a crime, and from prosecution for violating a criminal statute enacted after we committed the act that violates it—were made legal rights by the Constitution and other enactments. The other enactments can be changed relatively easily, by amendatory legislation. Amending the Constitution is much more difficult. In recognition of this the Framers left most of the constitutional provisions that confer rights pretty vague. The courts have made them definite.

3   Concretely, the scope of these rights has been determined, through an interaction of constitutional text and subsequent judicial interpretation, by a weighing of competing interests. I'll call them the public-safety interest and the liberty interest. Neither, in my view, has priority. They are both important, and their relative importance changes from time to time and from situation to situation. The safer the nation feels, the more weight judges will be willing to give to the liberty interest. The greater the threat that an activity poses to the nation's safety, the stronger will the grounds seem for seeking to repress that activity, even at some cost to liberty. This fluid approach is only common sense. Supreme Court Justice Robert Jackson gave it vivid expression many years ago when he said, in dissenting from a free-speech decision he thought doctrinaire, that the Bill of Rights should not be made into a suicide pact. It was not intended to be such, and the present contours of the rights that it confers, having been shaped far more by judicial interpretation than by the literal text (which doesn't define such critical terms as "due process of law" and "unreasonable" arrests and searches), are alterable in response to changing threats to national security.

4   If it is true, therefore, as it appears to be at this writing, that the events of September 11 have revealed the United States to be in much greater jeopardy from international terrorism than had previously been believed—have revealed it to be threatened by a diffuse, shadowy enemy that must be fought with police measures as well as military force—it stands to reason that our civil liberties will be curtailed. They *should* be curtailed, to the extent that the benefits in greater security outweigh the costs in reduced liberty. All that can reasonably be asked of the responsible legislative and judicial officials is that they weigh the costs as carefully as the benefits.

5   It will be argued that the lesson of history is that officials habitually exaggerate dangers to the nation's security. But the lesson of history is the opposite. It is because officials have repeatedly and disastrously underestimated these dangers that our history is as violent as it is. Consider such underestimated dangers as that of secession, which led to the Civil War; of a Japanese attack on the United States, which led to the disaster at Pearl Harbor; of Soviet espionage in the 1940s, which accelerated the Soviet Union's acquisition of nuclear weapons and emboldened Stalin to encourage North Korea's invasion of South Korea; of the installation of

Soviet missiles in Cuba, which precipitated the Cuban missile crisis; of political assassinations and outbreaks of urban violence in the 1960s; of the Tet Offensive of 1968; of the Iranian revolution of 1979 and the subsequent taking of American diplomats as hostages; and, for that matter, of the events of September 11.

6   It is true that when we are surprised and hurt, we tend to overreact—but only with the benefit of hindsight can a reaction be separated into its proper and excess layers. In hindsight we know that interning Japanese-Americans did not shorten World War II. But was this known at the time? If not, shouldn't the Army have erred on the side of caution, as it did? Even today we cannot say with any assurance that Abraham Lincoln was wrong to suspend habeas corpus during the Civil War, as he did on several occasions, even though the Constitution is clear that only Congress can suspend this right. (Another of Lincoln's wartime measures, the Emancipation Proclamation, may also have been unconstitutional.) But Lincoln would have been wrong to cancel the 1864 presidential election, as some urged: by November of 1864 the North was close to victory, and canceling the election would have created a more dangerous precedent than the wartime suspension of habeas corpus. This last example shows that civil liberties remain part of the balance even in the most dangerous of times, and even though their relative weight must then be less.

7   Lincoln's unconstitutional acts during the Civil War show that even legality must sometimes be sacrificed for other values. We are a nation under law, but first we are a nation. I want to emphasize something else, however: the malleability of law, its pragmatic rather than dogmatic character. The law is not absolute, and the slogan *Fiat iustitia ruat caelum* ("Let justice be done though the heavens fall") is dangerous nonsense. The law is a human creation rather than a divine gift, a tool of government rather than a mandarin mystery. It is an instrument for promoting social welfare, and as the conditions essential to that welfare change, so must it change.

8   Civil libertarians today are missing something else—the opportunity to challenge other public-safety concerns that impair civil liberties. I have particularly in mind the war on drugs. The sale of illegal drugs is a "victimless" crime in the special but important sense that it is a consensual activity. Usually there is no complaining witness, so in order to bring the criminals to justice the police have to rely heavily on paid informants (often highly paid and often highly unsavory), undercover agents, wiretaps and other forms of electronic surveillance, elaborate sting operations, the infiltration of suspect organizations, random searches, the monitoring of airports and highways, the "profiling" of likely suspects on the basis of ethnic or racial identity or national origin, compulsory drug tests, and other intrusive methods that put pressure on civil liberties. The war on drugs has been a big flop; moreover, in light of what September 11 has taught us about the gravity of the terrorist threat to the United States, it becomes hard to take entirely seriously the threat to the nation that drug use is said to pose. Perhaps it is time to redirect law-enforcement resources from the investigation and apprehension of drug dealers to the investigation and apprehension of international terrorists. By doing so we may be able to minimize the net decrease in our civil liberties that the events of September 11 have made inevitable. ◆◆

THE TOOLS OF FREEDOM AND SECURITY*

Peter Lewis

Peter Lewis allows that collecting information is important in winning the war on terror, but he also points out that some of that information may be about you. You will learn from this article about information technology currently in use. What are the implications for the personal freedoms you have come to value?

1 The personal freedoms that we take for granted in the U.S. also make more possible the acts of terrorism that have traumatized the country. As a result, an urgent conflict has emerged between the legitimate needs of law enforcement and the long-established protections of privacy and the ability to move freely about the country. Some people argue that, paradoxically, Americans must surrender some freedoms in order to enjoy the ones we cherish.

2 Technology plays a central role in this conflict. Many of the proposals to fight terrorism focus on personal technology as both a tool and a target. When it comes to technology, it's hard to get more personal than a biometric scan, a wiretap on a cell phone, a surveillance camera, the interception of private e-mail, a shared database of sensitive personal information, or a "smart" national identification card.

3 One thing is clear: In a war like the one we're now engaged in, timely information is more valuable in saving lives than guns or missiles. The issue is how to gather that information efficiently without adopting the draconian methods of the cultures we're fighting. Terrorists and the regimes that support them are not constrained by concerns over abuse of personal freedoms. We must be. The first step in reconciling the need for security with the principles of our democracy is to understand the various technological approaches being proposed to fight terrorism and how they might affect us as citizens.

REGULATING THE ELECTRONIC WORLD

4 Why are law-abiding citizens likely to be touched by the investigations into terrorism? Billions of messages are exchanged every day over digital networks, in e-mail, and in land line and cellular voice calls; by radio and wireless messaging; by digital file transfers; and by satellite. Criminals use the same communications systems. The digital nature of modern communications, as well as the vast amount of traffic, makes it more difficult to conduct wiretaps for criminal investigations.

5 Meanwhile, computer databases store the most intimate details of our daily lives, including medical records, banking and investment transactions, credit reports, employment records, credit card purchases, photographs, fingerprints, and so on.

6 Surveillance cameras are ubiquitous at ATMs, airports, and other public places. The courts and lawmakers have, over the years, sought to protect this private information from unnecessary disclosure and to enact strict guidelines on

---

Fortune, October 29, 2001, pp. 195–199.

the interception and gathering of such information by government agencies. At press time debate was still under way in Congress on House and Senate actions to expand the powers of law-enforcement and intelligence agencies to conduct electronic surveillance and searches. The Bush Administration initially proposed authorizing law-enforcement agencies' access to business, telephone, e-mail, bank, and credit records of people in the course of an anti-terrorism investigation without judicial review or a requirement for "probable cause." It would also expand the ability of foreign and domestic investigative agencies to share information, which is currently restricted by law. Congressional leaders are seeking less sweeping restrictions. One concern is that new powers granted to law enforcement in time of war not be abused when the threats abate.

ENCRYPTION

7   There are many legitimate reasons for citizens to use powerful data-encryption technology, which allows individuals to send confidential e-mail, operate ATMs, conduct online banking and shopping, protect personal files, gain access to private computer systems, and guarantee the privacy and confidentiality of phone calls. Easily available "strong" encryption tools, like the Pretty Good Privacy (PGP) program, render messages unreadable except to those who have the proper key or pass phrase. Without those keys, messages encoded using strong encryption would take years or decades to decipher, even with the most powerful computers in the world. Law-enforcement officials believe that criminals, including terrorists, may be using strong encryption methods to communicate, thwarting the effectiveness of wiretaps and message interception. For the past decade, each successive President has sought legislation that would require all encryption methods to have a "back door" accessible to law enforcement to decipher intercepted communications quickly.

8   Civil liberties advocates say such back-door facilities will not only weaken personal privacy but also jeopardize the security of business transactions. Strong encryption technology, already available worldwide, would continue to work effectively regardless of U.S. legislation. Not even the dumbest terrorist would choose an encryption program that allowed the U.S. government to hold the key.

BIOMETRICS

9   Fingerprints and other unique physical and chemical characteristics allow security officials to determine with great accuracy the identities of individuals, but such tests are slow and impractical for widespread use. New scanners have been developed that recognize physical attributes like retina patterns, voice characteristics, facial structures, and hand geometries (including fingerprints) in real time and with reasonably high accuracy. Law-enforcement officials believe the widespread use of biometric scanners could be more effective than current identification methods in determining the identities of people trying to use an ATM, gain access to a computer network, or board an aircraft. The obvious problem is that the biometrics of foreign terrorists will be difficult if not impossible to obtain, and they're not likely to volunteer them. In some cases, a photograph can be used in conjunction with a facial scanner, which analyzes dozens of structural features, creates a unique algorithm, and compares it with a database of known criminals.

10   The technology has been used at major sporting events and will soon be installed at some airports. But in recent tests, the false-positive identification rate has been troublesome. The growing use and increasing sophistication of biometric scanners will certainly retard unauthorized access to secure areas in both the physical and virtual worlds, but it also erodes the concept of anonymity. Moreover, the possibility of someone's hacking and stealing a biometric identity raises grave security concerns. . . .

CARNIVORE AND ECHELON

11   Government and law-enforcement agencies have deployed new technologies to scan and capture private communications, analyzing the contents and headers of e-mail messages, listening for keywords in phone conversations, and identifying patterns in data transmissions. In the U.S. a computer system formerly known as Carnivore, now named DCS1000, can be attached to the servers of an Internet service provider to give the FBI the ability to monitor the e-mail messages, file transfers, Web-surfing activities, and instant messages of everyone who uses the ISP—potentially millions of law-abiding people. The FBI asserts that it will use the system only to target individuals involved in an investigation, but it has provided no independently verifiable information on how it will safeguard the privacy of other users of the ISP. Internationally, a system known as Echelon, developed by the U.S. and deployed in Europe, allows the interception of all digital and electronic forms of global communications, including cellular and satellite calls. Coupled with new technologies for sifting these billions of messages for keywords and suspicious patterns—words like "bomb" or sudden flurries of messages to people suspected of illegal activity—these sniffing systems allow law-enforcement agencies to spy on both individual and corporate communications. What's more, some governments have even relayed sensitive business communications to favored companies, giving them a competitive advantage.

PUBLIC SURVEILLANCE

12   It is now virtually impossible to walk the streets of New York City, buy a hamburger, rent a car, enter a major building, or drive from Raleigh to Atlanta without being captured on videotape or closed-circuit TV. The terrorist attacks will lead to greater use of surveillance cameras in public spaces. The courts have held that citizens have a limited expectation of privacy in public spaces, but the capturing of their images in databases, and the potential use and sharing of those images among various agencies, raise serious privacy concerns.

SMARTCARD IDS

13   Widely used in Europe, ID cards with embedded microprocessors allow large amounts of personal information to be stored in a wallet. Smartcards are increasingly common in the U.S. to hold medical or welfare-benefits data, or to gain access to secure workplace areas. Since Sept. 11 there have been calls from government and law enforcement to require all citizens to carry smart IDs in the interest of public security. Such cards could replace a driver's license and also hold a passport, criminal records, medical histories, photos and biometric data, and other sensitive information. The lack of an ID would not necessarily prevent

people from moving about freely, but it could lead to police interrogation or delays in transit. While smart IDs could lessen the ability of foreign terrorists to assume false identities and move about the country, they also effectively weaken the concept of anonymity.

14   Other personal technologies might also be affected (laptops, for instance, could be banned on airplanes). Such safety measures are tolerable; the loss of fundamental liberties is not. ◆◆

B. HOW CAN WE BALANCE SECURITY AGAINST PRIVACY IN A TECHNOLOGICAL AGE?

QUESTIONS TO CONSIDER BEFORE YOU READ

Has your privacy ever been invaded by a family member or a friend? What happened? How did you feel when you discovered the transgression? How do you think you would react if you found out that large companies or the government were spying on your computer and communications activities?

HOW PRIVATE IS YOUR LIFE?*

Peter Maas

Peter Maas is a contributing editor for Parade *and the author of* The Valachi Papers, Serpico, Killer Spy, *and* Underboss. *Maas's article claims that advancing computer technology compromises citizens' right to privacy, which is guaranteed by the U.S. Constitution.*

1   I have an acquaintance named Fred P. Smith. Actually, that's not his real name. I'm not using his real name because, as I have discussed in preparing this article, it is about the only shred of privacy he has left. And Fred Smith just as easily could be you or me.

2   The concept of the right to privacy was a treasured hallmark of the American way of life, institutionalized early on, indeed, by our Founding Fathers in the Fourth and Fifth Amendments to the U.S. Constitution. But that was long before the present hordes of private investigators and rapacious marketeers in an era of advanced computer technology that today draws on heretofore private information contained in vast databases that most Americans don't even know exist.

3   As a result, there are at this writing some 80 different patchwork bills pending in Congress aimed at restricting the flow of intimate personal data in cyberspace, now available to anyone browsing through the World Wide Web. Unfortunately, as the saying goes, the horse appears already to have departed the barn.

4   To learn precisely what was what, I visited the offices of Sutton Associates, located on New York's Long Island, which specialized in investigative services. Its

*Parade, April 19, 1998, pp. 4–6.

president is James F. Murphy, a retired FBI agent. (As an agent, Murphy once had been a heroic headline figure. He had shot and killed one of two bank robbers holding a number of hostages at gunpoint as they tried to make their escape. The dramatic moment was later portrayed in the movie *Dog Day Afternoon*.)

5   As one of the most reputable firms of its sort in the nation, Sutton Associates limits itself primarily to background screenings for potential employment hirings and "due diligence" probes on behalf of corporate clients involved in buyouts, mergers, acquisitions and divestitures, all of which are considered quite legitimate. Sutton will not, on the other hand, accept divorce or criminal defense cases.

6   Recently, a company asked Sutton to locate a female consultant, now retired, who was urgently needed for a new project. The only information supplied was her name and that she was believed to reside somewhere in the vicinity of Washington, D.C. She wasn't listed in any phone books. It took no more than five minutes to come up with seven candidates with the same name, one of whom— the right one—met the appropriate retirement age of 64. But she had moved from her home in northern Virginia. So it took perhaps another five minutes to get a correct updated South Carolina address from one of the three major credit bureaus—Equifax, Experian and Trans Union—whose data banks record anyone who ever used a credit card.

7   My agreement with Jim Murphy was that Sutton Associates would demonstrate *how* a dossier could be compiled on an individual (not necessarily a job it actually would undertake). On occasion, a corporate client will ask Murphy if he can find out thus-and-such about someone. If Murphy considers the information beyond the bounds of propriety or legality, his standard reply is, "Yes, but I won't."

8   I supplied Murphy with the name of "Fred P. Smith." The only other information I provided was that he resided in the U.S. and was in the securities business. Sutton Associates had 72 hours to find out whatever it could about him.

9   The search began with what is called a "surname scan," which can be done nationally, regionally or locally based on data banks that have been compiled from such public source documents as voter registrations, motor-vehicle records (some states, like Maryland, actually sell these records) and real property listings.

10   Given the severe time constraints I had imposed and the fact that "Fred" was in the securities business, which could likely mean a Wall Street brokerage house, Sutton Associates elected to start with the greater New York City area. His middle initial helped narrow the field to 27 possibilities.

11   A so-called "credit header" search was then used to establish his occupation. These headers—essentially bare-bones I.D. reports maintained by credit agencies—list not only occupations but also Social Security numbers, dates of birth and residential addresses. This information is also instantly available, for a modest fee, to subscribers to commercial databases, such as one called DBT-Online. An executive name search, using Dun & Bradstreet's *Dun's Market Identifiers*, confirmed that Smith was an officer in his brokerage firm.

12   A Cole's directory—actually a reverse directory in which phone numbers and addresses are cross-referenced for the whole country—is contained on sets of CD-ROMs. Once an address is known, the names of every other resident in that

building or neighbors on a suburban block can be ascertained, opening the door to more intensive field investigations of any designated target.

13   A property search, such as those available from a Lexis-Nexis service, showed Fred Smith's previous residences, charting his rise from an apartment in a lower-middle-class neighborhood in one of the city's outer boroughs to a condominium on Manhattan's Upper East Side with a purchase price of more than $2 million. It also revealed that he owned a luxury sedan and a sport-utility vehicle, as well as another condo at a ski resort. Such information would come into play if he were subject to bankruptcy proceedings, tax liens or civil judgments. As it happened, his record was clear in these areas, nor was there any criminality.

14   It was revealed, however, that Fred—in his late 40s and married with two children—had a separate apartment in the city. Surveillance indicated that a young, attractive woman was in residence there. While adultery generally is not a financial factor in a divorce settlement, it could come into play if child custody became an issue. It might leave him open to blackmail as well.

15   Jim Murphy stopped Sutton Associates short of delving deeply into the lifestyle of Fred Smith. But if he had wanted to, Murphy could have learned about the restaurants Fred frequented, his airline travel, hotels he stayed at, his salary, ownership of stocks and bonds, his phone records, any evidence of addiction to drugs or alcohol (such as DWI arrests) or gambling, where his wife shopped and what she bought, how much money she spent, what schools their children attended, even the current state of their marriage.

16   But, in addition to circumspect firms like Sutton, there are other avenues open in the explosion of available personal information, chief among them "information wholesalers" that cater to private investigators, bill collectors, insurance agents and similar interested parties, such as business competitors.

17   One is Advanced Research Inc., located in Stroudsburg, Pa. It offers a range of intimate data that includes detailed credit-card activity, long-distance and intrastate toll calls, bank account numbers, deposits and balances, wire transfers, a beeper trace, a cellular phone trace, an employment history, business client lists, life insurance policies and a medical treatment history going back as much as 10 years.

18   I decided to offer myself up as a guinea pig. I allotted Advanced Research 48 hours to come up with an unlisted phone number, a month's worth of toll calls and information about any bank accounts I had, either separate or held jointly with my wife. (I skipped a request for my medical treatment history when I learned that this would take four to six weeks. But I have no doubt that the firm would have delivered, based on its performance in other areas.)

19   As promised, it quickly came up with my unlisted number—not especially surprising, since I've had to include it on applications for various utility services and cable TV as well as warranties for purchases I had made (naïvely supposing it would not be disseminated elsewhere).

20   But two *other* unlisted numbers, which I have never given out, also were included. So were the toll calls I had made on all three lines, which, when matched with my phone bills, were right on the money. All my bank-account information—the account numbers, the banks involved, balances and deposits for the previous month—also was disturbingly accurate.

21   Michael Martin, who heads up Advanced Research, was coy about how this information was gathered. "These are well-guarded trade secrets," he told me. He said that he had specialists on call throughout the country who are allowed "to pursue their own methods." Defending his operation, he added: "In finding dead-beat dads, getting key evidence in child-custody cases, locating hidden assets in court-ordered judgments, why pay high attorney fees when we can do the job a lot quicker, a lot better and a lot cheaper?"

22   Jim Murphy of Sutton Associates said he was concerned about other (un-named) companies, who engage in unscrupulous privacy incursions. "This is a business where you can't be partially pregnant," he said. "If you have people who don't care, you're asking for regulations that will hurt all legitimate private investigators." . . .

23   Still, as alarm over the invasion of privacy grows, 14 of the largest database companies—fearful of restrictive legislation—recently agreed to attempt to regulate themselves by adopting guidelines that would limit access to personal information by the general public.

24   The rub is that private investigators are an exception to the rule. According to *P.I. Magazine*, there are about 60,000 licensed private eyes operating in the U.S. The qualifications vary from state to state. Some states—like Colorado, Alabama, Mississippi, Idaho and South Dakota—don't require licenses at all.

25   There remain certain steps an individual can take to protect against unwarranted privacy invasions. The great irony is that a fundamental building block in creating a personal dossier is your Social Security number. Yet when the Social Security Act of 1935 was originally passed by Congress, an individual's number was not to be used as an identifier for other than Social Security purposes.

26   Who could have imagined what would subsequently happen? Today, to apply for just about anything, you are required to give the number up. ◆◆

LIVING UNDER THE ELECTRONIC EYE*

Lisa Guernsey

Lisa Guernsey writes for the New York Times. *Guernsey shows that after the terrorist attacks of September 11, 2001, Americans were willing to sacrifice personal freedom for security. How willing are they now?*

1   In 1928 Justice Louis D. Brandeis made a prediction. Someday, he wrote in a dissent to a Supreme Court decision on wiretapping, the government may find ways to reproduce documents in court without removing them from "private drawers." Such methods, he warned, will expose "the most intimate occurrences of the home."

---

*New York Times, September 27, 2001, pp. D6+.

2   The dawn of computer technology, especially the Internet, has proved him right. With so much public and personal business being carried out electronically, it has become technically feasible for government agencies—or anyone with the proper tools—to find private electronic correspondence without ever breaking into secret drawers, or even entering a person's home or office.

3   And not just e-mail can be seized. The most mundane aspects of a person's life are now recorded digitally, often in databases beyond their control. With each new technology, more details of people's daily activities can potentially be scooped up by law enforcement officials and later presented in a courtroom.

4   But with such surveillance capabilities on tap, the question inevitably arises: Should the government be given the authority to use them?

5   In reaction to the terrorist attacks of Sept. 11, lawmakers and many of their constituents are saying yes. Several bills are being considered this week that would expand the ways in which the federal government could use technology not only as a law enforcement tool to track down terrorists or anyone suspected of committing a crime but also as a crime prevention tool to monitor suspicious activity and possibly anticipate any future attacks.

6   Officials, for example, are asking for broad authority to inspect logs of Internet use and the address fields of e-mail messages, which in addition to revealing the senders and the recipients could also divulge the messages' content through their subject lines. And they are seeking more latitude in listening to conversations of people on the move as they communicate by cellphone or other wireless technologies.

7   A wealth of new electronic information is already available to law enforcement agencies. With a court order, agents can retrieve records of credit-card purchases, peruse the logs kept by automated toll booths to determine which cars drove through, listen to voice mail left in databases, gather lists of library books checked out by patrons, watch videos recorded by public surveillance cameras and find out which television shows a subscriber has ordered on pay-per-view services.

8   "The problem that Brandeis feared is amplified," said Jeffrey Rosen, an associate professor of law at George Washington University and the author of *The Unwanted Gaze,* which traces the erosion of privacy. "The fact that so much more of our lives can be recorded and monitored in cyberspace makes the problem greater in degree and scope."

9   It is an open question, however, whether people view digital surveillance as intrusive, especially given their new fears about terrorism. By reviewing some of those seemingly mundane electronic records, investigators have been able to retrace the movements of terrorists who carried out the attacks on Sept. 11. Agents have searched computers at a public library and a Kinko's shop in Florida that appear to have been used by the hijackers to buy airline tickets. Videotape of automobile traffic at Logan Airport in Boston revealed that one of them, Mohamed Atta, drove through the area at least five times before the attacks, perhaps making dry runs.

10   A year ago, during the presidential election campaign, political pollsters were finding that voters seemed increasingly wary of privacy invasions by companies or by the government. Today, concerns about security are trumping such wariness. In a poll conducted on Sept. 13 and 14 by *The New York Times* and CBS News, respondents were asked whether they believed that Americans would have to "give up some personal freedoms in order to make the country safe from terrorist attacks." "Yes" was the response of 74 percent. A week later that number rose to 79 percent.

11   The same poll showed a strengthening of support for governmental monitoring of e-mail and phone conversations of ordinary Americans on a regular basis. About 45 percent said they would be willing to allow such monitoring, up from 39 percent the week before; 56 percent of people also favored the idea of national electronic ID cards.

12   Steve and Paula Baumgardner, from Jacksonville, Fla., who visited New York City last week as tourists, echo the prevailing sentiments. "Freedom is not free," said Mr. Baumgardner, a business manager. "I'm not for Big Brother, but I don't mind paying a price for security and safety."

13   In national crises in the past, Americans have often declared their willingness to sacrifice some privacy in the name of security. When fears of Communism were running high in the 1950's, 65 percent of American adults surveyed in a Gallup poll said that the government should have the right to listen in on private telephone conversations.

14   After the bombing of the Oklahoma City federal building in 1995, *The Los Angeles Times* asked people if they thought that it would be necessary for the average person to give up some civil liberties to curb terrorism. Nearly half—49 percent—answered yes. When the Pew Research Center revisited the security question in 1997 (using the same methodology as the 1995 *Times* poll), that figure had dropped to 29 percent.

15   It is difficult to gauge whether the support for governmental monitoring will outlast the immediate trauma of the Sept. 11 attacks. Nor have the recent polls determined exactly what kinds of freedoms most people would be willing to forgo.

16   Congress is considering several anti-terrorism measures, some of which involve eavesdropping on the Internet. Attorney General John Ashcroft has asked that the words "electronic communications" be added to existing laws governing telephone surveillance. His proposal implies the wider use of Carnivore, an Internet surveillance system that is used by the Federal Bureau of Investigation, although the system is not named in the proposal.

17   If the proposal becomes law, government agencies would be allowed to trace Web use under the same laws that govern their tracing of telephone numbers. Those laws call for less judicial oversight than laws for wiretaps, which involve the content of phone conversations.

18   But is a Web address equivalent to a telephone number? Some privacy advocates argue that Web addresses reveal far more information because some of them are made up of the words that a person keyed into a search engine. If the user enters

the search terms "bomb" and "recipe" at Google, for example, the search yields the Web address <www.google.com/search?q=bomb+recipes&btnG=Google+Search>.

19   Similar concerns may apply to e-mail. The Ashcroft proposal appears to treat a message's addressing and routing information as if it were no more than a phone number, retrievable with the same low level of judicial oversight. But if that information were to include a message's subject line—a matter that is still up in the air—the government would essentially be peeking at personal correspondence, some privacy advocates say.

20   "We're not saying that law enforcement should not be able to gain access to that information," said Barry Steinhardt, associate director of the American Civil Liberties Union. What the A.C.L.U. is arguing, he said, is "that the information is content and that law enforcement should meet a higher standard to prove their need for it."

21   The changing technology of the telephone has also altered the politics of the wiretap. Mr. Ashcroft has proposed what analysts are calling "roving wiretaps," in which the government would have the authority to tap into a suspect's telephone calls regardless of what jurisdiction he was in or what phone he was using at a given moment. Before now, a criminal investigator had to get a separate court order for every jurisdiction in which a phone was tapped, which becomes more difficult as cellphones proliferate and can be used across borders.

22   "We need to be able to have the court authority to monitor not the phone but the telephone communications of a person," Mr. Ashcroft said at a recent news conference, "and to have that authority stay with the person."

23   Cellphones can also be used to locate people within a few city blocks. As long as a phone is turned on, it is communicating with the closest cell towers, sending signals about its whereabouts. If those signals are considered addressing or routing information, analysts say, they could easily be part of the records requested in a wiretap.

24   Aside from the legal questions, it is unclear how effective these forms of electronic surveillance may prove to be. For example, while some electronic information about the Sept. 11 terrorists has come to light via computer searches and video records, it is not known whether increased digital tracking would have helped head off the plot, since so few of the terrorists had come to the attention of the Central Intelligence Agency before the attacks.

25   Marc Rotenberg, director of the Electronic Privacy Information Center, said he wondered if law enforcement and intelligence agents might be better served by old-fashioned techniques like infiltrating suspected groups and code-breaking. "It may turn out that the problem was that we had too much electronic surveillance," he said.

26   Winn Schwartau, a security consultant in Seminole, Fla., and the author of the books *Information Warfare* and *Cybershock,* agrees that electronic surveillance should not be a substitute for proven labor-intensive techniques.

27   "We need human intelligence—a live human being on the ground, being a spy," Mr. Schwartau said. "And we've given up a huge amount of it." ◆◆

BODY OF EVIDENCE*

Dana Hawkins

Dana Hawkins is a writer for U.S. News & World Report. *As Hawkins notes, biometric technology is far from perfect, but what problems would still exist if it were? What could be done if rather than stealing credit card numbers, criminals began stealing fingerprints and iris scans?*

1   "Please-move-forward . . . a little," a robotic yet oddly sultry female voice commands. A camera whirs to focus on the eyeball of a visitor to Thales Fund Management, on the 45th floor of an ebony tower in Lower Manhattan. "We-are-sorry. You-are-NOT-identified," says the disembodied voice. "We like the *Star Trek* feel," grins Laurel Galgano, who manages the automated security system. "And it impresses the investors."

2   They're not the only ones taken with biometrics. Iris scanners are among the sexiest of these technologies, which convert distinctive biological characteristics, such as the patterns of the iris or fingertip or the shape of a hand or face, into a badge of identity. Even before the September 11 terrorist attacks, the industry was growing sharply as scanners and software became cheaper and more accurate. The International Biometric Industry Association estimates that sales reached $170 million in 2001, a 70 percent jump over the previous year. Now, the IBIA predicts that sales will rise to $1 billion by 2004, propelled in part by new security worries at airports and other critical facilities. Thousands of systems are being tested or are already up and running. Employees at some businesses punch in and out by placing their hand on a reader, and digital finger-scan devices verify thousands of schoolchildren's enrollment in lunch programs. At a handful of airports, face scanners are scrutinizing passengers, and the New York State lottery uses iris scanners for employee access to a secured room containing its data system.

3   Nothing's perfect. Yet biometrics experts and even some vendors worry about promising too much, too soon. In theory, when your fingerprint or face structure becomes your identity card, you no longer have to worry that it will be lost or stolen—nor does an employer, a government agency, or anyone else with a stake in knowing who you are. But biometrics systems, like traditional ID cards, can be fooled, and some, like hand and face scans, are less accurate in practice than in theory. "The people who say biometrics provides foolproof, fail-safe, positive identification are just wrong," says Jim Wayman, director of biometric research at San Jose State University. What's more, face scanning can be done without people's permission, raising privacy concerns and prompting calls for laws that would regulate how biometric data could be collected and used.

4   Some biometric systems have been a hit, providing a real boost in security and convenience. At a Gristedes grocery store in Manhattan, a hand reader has

*U.S. News & World Report, February 18, 2002, pp. 60+.

replaced the time clock. "You can't cheat the boss, and he can't accuse you of buddy punching," says a store clerk. It takes just minutes for New York State to enroll an applicant for public assistance in a digital fingerprint system, which has boosted arrests for attempted fraud. To allay privacy concerns, legislation prohibits the state from sharing the data with the FBI unless it is subpoenaed. And travelers laud INSPASS. The program allows over 65,000 passengers who regularly fly abroad to breeze by immigration lines at nearly a dozen airports by passing through a hand-scan reader, linked to a database of known travelers. There's an appealing backup system, too. When a hand reader fails, the passenger gets to cut to the front of the customs line.

5   But the technology has glitches. Digital fingerprint readers can draw a blank on some people, such as hairdressers who work with harsh chemicals, and the elderly, whose prints may be worn. Recent tests by the independent research and consulting firm International Biometric Group showed that some systems are unable to collect a finger scan from up to 12 percent of users. And the IBG found that the performance of face-scanning systems can be dismal. Six weeks after test subjects had "enrolled" with an initial face scan, some systems failed to recognize them nearly one third of the time—and that was under ideal conditions. The companies say they've since upgraded their software.

6   Yet an increasing number of airports, including Boston's Logan, Fresno, St. Petersburg–Clearwater, Palm Beach, and Dallas–Fort Worth, are testing or deploying the face-scan technology—in some cases at security checkpoints but also for covert crowd scanning. The systems compare passing faces against a database of images from FBI lists of suspected terrorists and wanted felons. Independent privacy and security expert Richard M. Smith, who has studied these systems, says that because they are so easily fooled by changes in lighting, viewing angle, or sunglasses, they serve merely as a deterrent. "The camera in the ceiling is like the man behind the curtain in the Wizard of Oz. It's all for show," says Smith. "Crowd scanning can be problematic," says Tom Colatosti, CEO of Viisage Technology, a face-scan company. "If you're talking about an airport, you need a chokepoint" for scanning people one by one.

7   *Gummy dummies.* Many systems can be deliberately fooled. A new study form Yokohama National University in Japan shows that phony fingers concocted from gelatin, called "gummy dummies," easily trick fingerprint systems. Manufacturers of some systems claim to guard against such tactics by recording pupil dilation, blood flow in fingers, and other evidence that the biometric sample is "live." And although some makers assert that biometrics solves the problem of identity theft—no one can steal your iris or hand, after all—many experts disagree. A hacker who broke into a poorly designed system might be able to steal other people's digital biometric templates and use them to access secure networks. This trick, called "replay," could take identity theft to a whole new level. "Your fingerprint is uniquely yours, forever. If it's compromised, you can't get a new one," says Jackie Fenn, a technology analyst at the Gartner Group.

8   Privacy concerns—although they seem less pressing to many these days—may also slow public acceptance of the technology. Yet in some cases, biometrics can actually enhance privacy. A finger-scan system for controlling access to medical records, for example, would also collect an audit trail of people who

viewed the data. But face scanning, with its potential for identifying people without their knowledge, has alarmed privacy advocates.

9   Last month, for example, Visionics Corp.'s face-scanning system was redeployed as an anticrime measure in a Tampa, Fla., entertainment district. Detective Bill Todd says the system had been taken down two months into its 12-month trial because of a bug in the operating system, but it has been upgraded and is now back in use. The 36-camera system is controlled by an officer at the station, who can pan, tilt, and zoom the cameras to scan faces in the crowd so that the software can compare them with faces in a database.

10   While Todd says the database contains only photographs of wanted felons, runaways, and sexual predators, police department policy allows anyone who has a criminal record or might provide "valuable intelligence," such as gang members, to be included. So far, according to a report by the American Civil Liberties Union, the technology has produced many false matches. And Todd confirms that it hasn't identified any criminals. "We have our limitations," says Frances Zelazny, spokesperson for Visionics. "It's an enhancement to law enforcement, not a replacement."

11   At times, the privacy problem is more perception than reality. The Lower Merion school district near Philadelphia had installed finger-scan devices for school lunch lines. Students would place their finger on a pad to verify their identity, and money would be deducted from their account. The optional program was instituted to make lines move faster, and to spare embarrassment to students entitled to free or discounted meals. But even though the system did not capture a full fingerprint image, but rather a stripped-down digital version, some parents felt that it came uncomfortably close to traditional fingerprinting. After a spate of bad press, the program was killed last year. Forty other school districts still use the system.

12   *Bioprivacy.* Such privacy dust-ups are causing some biometrics experts and vendors to call for laws to govern the fledgling industry. Samir Nanavati, a partner at IBG, says his company stresses "bioprivacy" rules: Tell people what data you're collecting and why; minimize the amount gathered; use the data only for the purpose originally stated; and give users a chance to correct their records.

13   Nanavati also worries that the technology is not always used to best advantage. On a recent, informal tour of biometric installations in Manhattan, where the dapper consultant lives, it was easy to see what he meant. At a New York University dorm, the hand-scan access system seemed to offer little security benefit. Fewer than half the students used it. The others gained entry the old-fashioned way, slightly faster and a lot less secure—by casually flashing an ID card to the friendly security guard. And at New York–Presbyterian Hospital, where long queues sometimes form at hand-scan readers, frustrated employees smashed machines two weeks in a row last month. Yet Joe Salerno of New York–Presbyterian says every building has a hand reader. He speculates that employees may be upset about the rigorous timekeeping.

14   The real trick, says Nanavati, is to choose the right biometric system and design it with both security and convenience in mind. And sometimes that means no system. One client, who desired the cachet of owning the most secure, high-tech residence in Manhattan, hired IBG to set up an iris-reader system for tenants of his

24-hour doorman building. "I told him it was already very secure," Nanavati laughs. "Biometric access would've only cost money and annoyed people."

15   Sometimes, *Star Trek* just isn't the answer. ◆◆

THE REAL PRIVACY WARS ARE JUST OVER THE HORIZON*

Eric Cohen

Former managing editor of the Public Interest, *Eric Cohen is a resident fellow at the* New America Foundation. *Cohen argues that the concern over privacy is really a political and moral issue. What do you think? Do politics shape our thinking about the way we allow privacy to shape our lives?*

1   Scott McNealy, the chief executive officer of Sun Microsystems, made waves a few years ago when in response to a question about whether one of his products adequately protected consumer privacy, he snapped: "You have zero privacy, anyway. Get over it."

2   Clearly, America is not over it. The number of books and articles on privacy in the last few years are too many to count—all with foreboding titles like *The End of Privacy, The Limits of Privacy, The Destruction of Privacy in America* and *The Death of Privacy in the 21st Century.*

3   In a recent *Wall Street Journal*–NBC poll, Americans named privacy as their No. 1 concern for the 21st century.

4   Protecting privacy is quickly becoming a big industry—what the market gurus call "the new privacy space." Companies with names like Anonymizer and Privacy X are rushing to offer high-technology cloaking devices that promise to return to individuals some of the privacy that technology has taken away. Other technologies would allow individuals to profit from selling their personal information to the highest bidders.

5   But while the nation may highly value privacy, it is also clear that many Americans value invasions of other people's privacy—made all too evident by the remarkable, almost cult-like success of "reality" television shows.

6   When it comes to privacy, America speaks with multiple voices—both because different people want different things and because the same people want irreconcilable things.

7   This war will not go away. The stakes will only heighten, especially with the coming revolutions in genetics that will allow us to uncover, with scientific precision, the mysteries of our being. Today's culture wars will be tomorrow's privacy wars, just as bitter and just as marked by ideological confusions and political expediency among both liberals and conservatives.

Fort Worth Star-Telegram, April 22, 2001, p. 5E.

8   For the fact is that most privacy issues are really moral issues in disguise, with the two major political parties defining privacy in accordance with their own most cherished ideals or using it as a club to attack their chosen enemies as anti-privacy. But these ideals and interests, liberal and conservative alike, are not always consistent, which makes either party's claim to be the "party of privacy" sometimes hard to swallow.

9   The liberal commitment to "privacy activism" is clear. Democrats have taken the lead in passing privacy legislation to protect individuals' medical records against "big pharmaceutical and insurance companies." They have taken the lead in pushing legislation to protect consumer information from being sold without the customer's consent. They have worked to uphold the Miranda rights of those who are arrested and to limit the search and seizure powers of police and investigators. Perhaps most passionately, they have defended what might be called the "privacy of the body"—the rights to contraception, abortion and sexual autonomy.

10   Yet when other liberal ideals are at stake—safety, the environment, health and self-esteem—liberals have been willing to disregard or greatly limit the right to privacy. They have encroached on the privacy rights of gun owners with extensive restrictions on guns. They have attempted, with some success, to regulate people who work at home with restrictions on occupational safety, as part of the so-called ergonomics movement. They have limited the privacy of homeowners and landowners with environmental restrictions. They have fought against private-school vouchers, which would use some taxpayer dollars to allow parents to send their children to private schools.

11   Perhaps on no issue is the contradiction within liberalism about privacy more clear than in sexual harassment law where, in stark opposition to their usual views on respecting accused criminals, liberals have subordinated the rights of the accused to the rights of the accuser.

12   Similarly, conservatives have their own ideological commitments to privacy—for example, the privacy of gun owners to own guns, landowners to develop their land, workers to have their own private retirement accounts. Above all, conservatives are committed to the rights of business "to be let alone."

13   Like liberals, conservatives have their own moral ideals that often radically conflict with or limit their commitment to privacy, central among them the belief in the right to life of the unborn. The problem is that as capitalism increasingly becomes genetic capitalism—dependent as it soon will be on a ready supply of human embryos for research and development—it will become much harder, perhaps impossible, to be both pro-business and pro-life.

14   Even in areas where there is widespread agreement that privacy must be protected—banning the use of genetic screening to discriminate against people applying for health insurance and jobs, for instance—the pro-privacy consensus will soon shatter. A buyer would never purchase a house without a full inspection for problems. Why should a health insurance company accept a client without an equivalent "inspection" once science gives us the power to conduct one?

15   The comparison may seem crass and dehumanizing—and it is—but so is the science that made such great genetic powers possible in the first place: a science

that dissects human bodies, clones human embryos, tests placebos in Third World countries and, in general, reduces human beings to spiritless subjects for experiment.

16   With genetic screening, the American desire for privacy will reach an impasse: We will either allow insurance companies to discriminate, or we will socialize medicine to make discrimination impossible. But, as Andrew Sullivan has argued, even if we socialize medicine, the state will have to make decisions about how much treatment it gives individuals or whether it allows them to get their own genetic tests in the private market and then use their positive results, like SAT scores, to buy their own private insurance at reduced rates. Whatever path we choose, our healing powers will be increased, but our privacy and our ideals will be significantly compromised.

17   Ultimately, there is no easy remedy for our privacy problems—only the hard fact that Americans desire irreconcilable things with equal passion. We are a privacy-obsessed nation that entertains itself with voyeurism; we demand tailor-made services and economic efficiency but resent having private information mined by corporate interests; we want safety from cyber-terrorism but resent cyber-intelligence; we assert all the rights to privacy but usually accept none of the responsibilities; we demand the powers of technology but often dislike the consequences, which may already be too far out of the box to rein in or repair.

18   But at least we can begin by owning up to the inconsistency of our desires and the inadequacies of our politics. At least it's a start.

19   As in all things American, we look to autonomy and choice—"informed consent," as the professional ethicists call it—as the bedrock principles upon which to navigate the privacy shoals. In other words, as long as individuals themselves sell their personal information, family stories, love lives and whatever else the market for titillating confessions and tailor-made services can bear, there is no problem. But if a third party does the selling, it is an infringement on the right to privacy, a cause for outrage.

20   But as in all things moral and economic, autonomy and choice alone cannot guide us. Privacy is often a public matter and, therefore, requires criteria beyond personal choice to balance private interests and the common good, whether the issue is drugs, smoking, land development or sex. ◆◆

C.   HOW DOES PROFILING THREATEN CIVIL LIBERTIES?

QUESTIONS TO CONSIDER BEFORE YOU READ

Have you or anyone you have ever known been a victim of racial profiling? Think about that time, what went through your mind, what the events were. What were some of the thoughts and feelings you had while it was happening? Conversely, have you ever suspected someone of being a threat to you based on his or her appearance? What made you act or feel the way you did? Were there other factors than simply the way the person looked? How do you feel now about those events?

THE COLOR OF SUSPICION*

Jeffrey Goldberg

Jeffery Goldberg explores the issue of racial profiling. Is profiling a form of racism or a legitimate tool for fighting crime?

1   Sgt. Lewis of the Maryland State Police is a bull-necked, megaphone-voiced, highly caffeinated drug warrior who, on this shiny May morning outside of Annapolis, is conceding defeat. The drug war is over, the good guys have lost and he has been cast as a racist. "This is the end, buddy," he says. "I can read the writing on the wall." Lewis is driving his unmarked Crown Victoria down the fast lane of Route 50, looking for bad guys. The back of his neck is burnt by the sun, and he wears his hair flat and short under his regulation Stetson.

2   "They're going to let the N.A.A.C.P. tell us how to do traffic stops," he says. "That's what's happening. There may be a few troopers who make stops solely based on race, but this—they're going to let these people tell us how to run our department. I say, to hell with it all. I don't care if the drugs go through. I don't."

3   He does, of course. Mike Lewis was born to seize crack. He grew up in Salisbury, on the Eastern Shore—Jimmy Buffett country—and he watched his friends become stoners and acid freaks. Not his scene. He buzz-cut his hair away and joined the state troopers when he was 19. He's a star, the hard-charger who made one of the nation's largest seizures of crack cocaine out on Route 13. He's a national expert on hidden compartments. He can tell if a man's lying, he says, by watching the pulsing of the carotid artery in his neck. He can smell crack cocaine inside a closed automobile. He's a human drug dog, a walking polygraph machine. "I have the unique ability to distinguish between a law-abiding person and an up-to-no-good person," he says. "Black or white." All these skills, though, he's ready to chuck. The lawsuits accusing the Maryland State Police of harassing black drivers, the public excoriation—and most of all, the Governor of New Jersey saying that her state police profiled drivers based on race, and were wrong to do so—have twisted him up inside. "Three of my men have put in for transfers," he says. "My wife wants me to get out. I'm depressed."

4   What depresses Mike Lewis is that he believes he is in possession of a truth polite society is too cowardly to accept. He says that when someone tells this particular truth, his head is handed to him. "The superintendent of the New Jersey State Police told the truth and he got fired for it," Lewis says.

5   This is what Carl Williams said, fueling a national debate about racial profiling in law enforcement: "Today, with this drug problem, the drug problem is cocaine or marijuana. It is most likely a minority group that's involved with that." Gov. Christine Todd Whitman fired Williams, and the news ricocheted through police departments everywhere, especially those, like the Maryland State Police, already accused of racial profiling—the stopping and searching of blacks because they are black.

---

*New York Times Magazine, June 20, 1999, pp. 51–56.

6   The way cops perceive blacks—and how those perceptions shape and mis-shape crime fighting—is now the most charged racial issue in America. . . .

7   Neither side understands the other. The innocent black man, jacked-up and humiliated during a stop-and-frisk or a pretext car stop, asks: Whatever happened to the Fourth Amendment? It is no wonder, blacks say, that the police are so wildly mistrusted.

8   And then there's the cop, who says: Why shouldn't I look at race when I'm looking for crime? It is no state secret that blacks commit a disproportionate amount of crime, so "racial profiling" is simply good police work.

9   Mike Lewis wishes that all this talk of racial profiling would simply stop.

10   As we drive, Lewis watches a van come up on his right and pass him. A young black man is at the wheel, his left leg hanging out the window. The blood races up Lewis's face: "Look at that! That's a violation! You can't drive like that! But I'm not going to stop him. No, sir. If I do, he's just going to call me a racist."

11   Then Lewis notices that the van is a state government vehicle. "This is ridiculous," he says. Lewis hits his lights. The driver stops. Lewis issues him a warning and sends him on his way. The driver says nothing.

12   "He didn't call me a racist," Lewis says, pulling into traffic, "but I know what he was thinking." Lewis does not think of himself as a racist. "I know how to treat people," he says. "I've never had a complaint based on a race-based stop. I've got that supercharged knowledge of the Constitution that allows me to do this right."

13   In the old days, when he was patrolling the Eastern Shore, it was white people he arrested. "Ninety-five percent of my drug arrests were dirt-ball-type whites—marijuana, heroin, possession-weight. Then I moved to the highway, I start taking off two, three kilograms of coke, instead of two or three grams. Black guys. Suddenly I'm not the greatest trooper in the world. I'm a racist. I'm locking up blacks, but I can't help it."

14   His eyes gleam: "Ask me how many white people I've ever arrested for cocaine smuggling—ask me!"

15   I ask.

16   "None! Zero! I debrief hundreds of black smugglers, and I ask them, 'Why don't you hire white guys to deliver your drugs?' They just laugh at me. 'We ain't gonna trust our drugs with white boys.' That's what they say."

17   Mike Lewis's dream: "I dream at night about arresting white people for cocaine. I do. I try to think of innovative ways to arrest white males. But the reality is different."

◆◆◆◆

WHY A COP PROFILES

18   This is what a cop might tell you in a moment of reckless candor: in crime fighting, race matters. When asked, most cops will declare themselves color blind. But watch them on the job for several months, and get them talking about the way policing is really done, and the truth will emerge, the truth being that cops, white and black, profile. Here's why, they say. African-Americans commit a disproportionate percentage of the types of crimes that draw the attention of the police. Blacks make up 12 percent of the population, but accounted for 58 percent of all carjackers between 1992 and 1996. (Whites accounted for 19 percent.) Victim

surveys—and most victims of black criminals are black—indicate that blacks commit almost 50 percent of all robberies. Blacks and Hispanics are widely believed to be the blue-collar backbone of the country's heroin- and cocaine-distribution networks. Black males between the ages of 14 and 24 make up 1.1 percent of the country's population, yet commit more than 28 percent of its homicides. Reason, not racism, cops say, directs their attention.

19   Cops, white and black, know one other thing: they're not the only ones who profile. Civilians profile all the time—when they buy a house, or pick a school district, or walk down the street. Even civil rights leaders profile. "There is nothing more painful for me at this stage in my life," Jesse Jackson said several years ago, "than to walk down the street and hear footsteps and start thinking about robbery—and then look around and see somebody white and feel relieved." Jackson now says his quotation was "taken out of context." The context, he said, is that violence is the inevitable by-product of poor education and health care. But no amount of "context" matters when you fear that you are about to be mugged.

20   At a closed-door summit in Washington between police chiefs and black community leaders recently, the black chief of police of Charleston, S.C., Reuben Greenberg, argued that the problem facing black America is not racial profiling, but precisely the sort of black-on-black crime Jackson was talking about. "I told them that the greatest problem in the black community is the tolerance for high levels of criminality," he recalled. "Fifty percent of homicide victims are African-Americans. I asked what this meant about the value of life in this community."

21   The police chief in Los Angeles, Bernard Parks, who is black, argues that racial profiling is rooted in statistical reality, not racism. "It's not the fault of the police when they stop minority males or put them in jail," Parks told me. "It's the fault of the minority males for committing the crime. In my mind it is not a great revelation that if officers are looking for criminal activity, they're going to look at the kind of people who are listed on crime reports."

◆◆◆◆

PROFILING IN BLACK AND WHITE

22 "Some blacks, I just get the sense off them that they're wild," Mark Robinson says. "I mean, you can tell. I have what you might call a profile. I pull up alongside a car with black males in it. Something doesn't match—maybe the style of the car with the guys in it. I start talking to them, you know, 'nice car,' that kind of thing, and if it doesn't seem right, I say, 'All right, let's pull it over to the side,' and we go from there."

23   He is quiet and self-critical, and the words sat in his mouth a while before he let them out. "I'm guilty of it, I guess."

24   Guilty of what?

25   "Racial profiling."

26   His partner, Gene Jones, says: "Mark is good at finding stolen cars on the street. Real good."

27   We are driving late one sticky Saturday night through the beat-down neighborhood of Logan, in the northern reaches of Philadelphia. The nighttime commerce is lively, lookouts holding down their corners, sellers ready to serve the addict traffic. It's a smorgasbord for the two plainclothes officers, but their

attention is soon focused on a single cluster of people, four presumptive buyers who are hurrying inside a spot the officers know is hot with drugs.

28 The officers pull to the curb, slide out and duck behind a corner, watching the scene unfold. The suspects are wearing backward baseball caps and low-slung pants; the woman with them is dressed like a stripper.

29 "Is this racial profiling?" Jones asks. A cynical half-smile shows on his face.

30 The four buyers are white. Jones and Robinson are black, veterans of the street who know that white people in a black neighborhood will be stopped. Automatically: Faster than a Rastafarian in Scarsdale.

31 "No reason for them to be around here at this time of night, nope," Jones says.

32 Is it possible that they're visiting college friends? I ask.

33 Jones and Robinson, whose intuition is informed by experience, don't know quite what to make of my suggestion.

34 "It could be," Jones says, indulgently. "But, uhhhh, no way."

35 Are you going to stop them?

36 "I don't know what for yet, but I'm going to stop them."

◆◆◆

"DRIVING WHILE BLACK," AND OTHER EXAGGERATIONS

37 Here's the heart of the matter, as Chief Greenberg of Charleston sees it: "You got white cops who are so dumb that they can't make a distinction between a middle-class black and an under-class black, between someone breaking the law and someone just walking down the street. Black cops too. The middle class says: 'Wait a minute. I've done everything right, I pushed all the right buttons, went to all the right schools, and they're jacking me up anyway.' That's how this starts."

38 So is racism or stupidity the root cause of racial profiling?

39 Governor Whitman, it seems, would rather vote for stupidity.

40 "You don't have to be racist to engage in racial profiling," she says. We are sitting in her office in the State House in Trenton. She still seems a bit astonished that her state has become the Mississippi of racial profiling.

41 Whitman, though burned by the behavior of her state troopers, is offering them a generous dispensation, given her definition of racial profiling. "Profiling means a police officer using cumulative knowledge and training to identify certain indicators of possible criminal activity," she told me. "Race may be one of those factors, but it cannot stand alone."

42 "Racial profiling," she continues, "is when race is the only factor. There's no other probable cause."

43 Her narrow, even myopic, definition suggests that only stone racists practice racial profiling. But the mere sight of black skin alone is not enough to spin most cops into a frenzy. "Police chiefs use that word 'solely' all the time, and it's such a red herring," says Randall Kennedy, Harvard Law professor and author of the book *Race, Crime, and the Law.* "Even Mark Fuhrman doesn't act solely on the basis of race."

44 The real question about racial profiling is this: Is it ever permissible for a law-enforcement officer to use race as one of even 5, or 10, or 20 indicators of possible criminality?

45   In other words, can the color of a man's skin help make him a criminal suspect?

46   Yes, Whitman says. She suggests she doesn't have a problem with the use of race as one of several proxies for potential criminality. "I look at Barry McCaffrey's Web site," she says, referring to the Clinton Administration's drug czar, "and it says certain ethnic groups are more likely to engage in drug smuggling."

47   It is true. . . . The Office of National Drug Control Policy's Web site helpfully lists which racial groups sell which drugs in different cities. In Denver, McCaffrey's Web site says, it is "minorities, Mexican nationals" who sell heroin. In Trenton, "crack dealers are predominantly African-American males, powdered cocaine dealers are predominantly Latino."

48   The link between racial minorities and drug-selling is exactly what Whitman's former police superintendent, Carl Williams, was talking about. So was Williams wrong?

49   "His comments indicated a lack of sensitivity to the seriousness of the problem."

50   But was he wrong on the merits?

51   "If he said, 'You should never use this solely; race could be a partial indicator, taken in concert with other factors'"—she pauses, sees the road down which she's heading, and puts it in reverse—"but you can't be that broad-brushed."

52   "Racial profiling" is a street term, not a textbook concept. No one teaches racial profiling. "Profiling," of course, is taught. It first came to the public's notice by way of the Federal Bureau of Investigation's behavioral-science unit, which developed the most famous criminal profile of all, one that did, in fact, have a racial component—the profile of serial killers as predominantly white, male loners.

53   It is the Drug Enforcement Administration, however, that is at the center of the racial-profiling controversy, accused of encouraging state law-enforcement officials to build profiles of drug couriers. The D.E.A., through its 15-year-old "Operation Pipeline," finances state training programs to interdict drugs on the highway. Civil rights leaders blame the department for the burst of race-based stops, but the D.E.A. says it discourages use of race as an indicator. "It's a fear of ours, that people will use race," says Greg Williams, the D.E.A.'s operations chief.

54   Cops use race because it's easy, says John Crew, the A.C.L.U.'s point man on racial profiling. "The D.E.A. says the best profile for drug interdiction is no profile," he says. "They say it's a mistake to look for a certain race of drivers. That's their public line. But privately, they say, 'God knows what these people from these state and local agencies do in the field.'"

55   The A.C.L.U. sees an epidemic of race-based profiling. Anecdotes are plentiful, but hard numbers are scarce. Many police officials see the "racial profiling" crisis as hype. "Not to say that it doesn't happen, but it's clearly not as serious or widespread as the publicity suggests," says Chief Charles Ramsey of Washington. "I get so tired of hearing that 'Driving While Black' stuff. It's just used to the point where it has no meaning. I drive while black—I'm black. I sleep while black too. It's victimology. Black people commit traffic violations. What are we supposed to say? People get a free pass because they're black?" ◆◆

PATRIOTISM VS. ETHNIC PRIDE: AN AMERICAN DILEMMA*

Lynette Clemetson and Keith Naughton

Lynette Clemetson and Keith Naughton discuss the new form of profiling after the terrorist attacks on the World Trade Center and the Pentagon and raise an important question: How should Americans and Muslims alike handle this new dilemma?

1   Hasson Awadh grew up in a part of the world scarred by terrorism, but he never stared down the barrel of a rifle until last week. At 2:25 A.M. last Wednesday, a man wearing a white rubber mask and a black hooded coat walked into Awadh's Marathon gas station in Gary, Ind., and, with no evident purpose other than vengeance, opened fire with a high-powered assault rifle. The 43-year-old native of Yemen dived for cover behind his cash register, as a fusillade of bullets pierced the one-inch-thick supposedly bulletproof glass he stood behind. Awadh crawled to a back room and prayed to Allah to spare his life. "I still hear the sound of the bullets," says Awadh, whose assailant is still at large. "That scary mask. It is still in front of my eyes."

2   As America reels from last week's deadly terrorist attacks, Muslims and Arab-Americans are experiencing an isolating terror all their own. In Washington, D.C., Muslim women have had hijab scarves snatched from their heads. A mosque in San Francisco was splattered with pig's blood. A bomb threat at a mostly Arab school in Dearborn, Mich., sent frightened teens running into the streets. Times have certainly changed since Pearl Harbor, when the government fueled ethnic hatred by interning Japanese-Americans. Last week political leaders from President George W. Bush to New York Mayor Rudolph Giuliani urged tolerance. But these socially evolved messages may be little match for today's equally evolved high-tech networks of intolerance, the often faceless, underground nature of which leaves many Arab-Americans fearing payback around every corner. Even as law enforcement promises them extra protection, Arab-Americans are targeted for suspicion and detainment. The paradox has left many with an uncomfortable struggle—in a forever altered America, how do they show both their patriotism and their ethnic pride?

3   The instant and anonymous connectivity of the Internet and talk radio became a hothouse for hate. "You are the true coward now sand n——r. Police won't protect Muslims now," raged one e-mail to a Muslim organization in Florida. Radio jocks are amping up callers with comments like, "Death to ragheads." Even legitimate journalists have vented rage. Political analyst Ann Coulter wrote in an op-ed: "We should invade their countries, kill their leaders and convert them to Christianity." Many Muslims are confronting the vitriol with a careful retort that being a good Muslim and a good American are not incompatible. When caught off guard by insults last week, Rashad Hussein, a legislative

---

*Newsweek, September 24, 2001, p. 1C.

aide, reminded his accuser that Islam is about peace. Arab groups urged members to show patriotism by donating blood and raising money for victims.

4   Still, in some places it is a perilous time to openly display Muslim identity. Virginia college student Faiza Mohammed has avoided going out in public since a police officer asked her last week to take off her head scarf—which, to a devout Muslim woman, is like asking her to take off her clothes. When the officer asked to search her car, she first asked if he had a search warrant, but quickly relented under his intimidating stare. "There's a line between our desire for security and for civil liberties," says Faisil Gill, of the American Muslim Council. "Right now none of us knows where that line is."

5   The cruel irony is that many of those bearing the brunt of the fallout came to this country to escape terrorism. Mariam Bakri, 47, whose family fled to the United States from Lebanon, says she feels, at moments, as if she is without a country. She was sickened as she watched televised images of West Bank Arabs celebrating the attack on America. She is equally sickened when she hears of her Arab neighbors being spit on. "Now people are going to think that if you're Arabic, you are a terrorist," says Bakri. Contemplating the national mood as collective grief turns to desire for vengeance, she says: "And the worst is yet to come." The best parts of America hope she's wrong. ◆◆

FREEDOM VS. SECURITY*

Fareed Zakaria

In the following excerpt from a Newsweek *article originally published in 2002, Fareed Zakaria describes the racial profiling that occurred after September 11, 2001, and makes recommendations for the future. How far have we come since then?*

1   The one area where America—government and people—has vastly improved on its past is in its treatment of a threatened minority during war. From the start [after September 11, 2001], President Bush, New York's Mayor Rudolph Giuliani and almost all other national leaders sounded the call for tolerance and asked Americans not to vent their anger on people who were (or looked like) Arabs. There were many attacks on such people—by some counts, more than 400—but the government has been vigorous in prosecuting the offenders. A district attorney in Indiana told me that in one such case he was pressed by the federal government to ask for the most severe punishment possible to send a signal that such behavior was unacceptable. Considering the nature of the September 11 attacks and the size of this country, we should be proud that for the most part America lived up to its ideals.

---

*Newsweek, July 8, 2002, pp. 26+.

2   One thing bothers some Americans: the airport searches. I have heard commentator after commentator angrily wonder why 80-year-old white women are being thoroughly searched while swarthy young men with exotic names walk freely onboard. "Stop those men," they thunder. Relax. As a swarthy young man with an exotic name, trust me, we're being checked. I don't know what the system is and how much discretion is allowed the security guards at the gates, but I've taken more than 50 flights all over the country since September 11, and I've been searched about 60 percent of the time. Either they are checking me out or I'm the unluckiest man alive.

3   What's more, I don't object to it. At least not on ethical grounds. If the pool of suspects is overwhelmingly of a particular ethnic/racial/religious group, then it only makes sense to pay greater attention to people of that background. But were this one factor to trigger a search, I'd be opposed, not on moral grounds but because it's stupid. Here the homeland-security crowd could learn something from local police. Racial profiling is less and less used by police departments, and not because it's increasingly being outlawed but rather because it doesn't work.

4   It's not that there isn't a racial profile that one could compose. After all, in most major American cities, young black and Latino men are still overwhelmingly the most likely perpetrators of many kinds of crime. But police forces have found that racial profiling doesn't work. David Harris, an authority on racial profiling who has interviewed hundreds of cops, explains that race is too broad a category to be useful. "Every cop will tell you what's important is suspicious behavior," Harris says. "If you focus on race, the eye is distracted from behavior and moves to what is literally skin deep." Customs Service agents have also learned this lesson. They used to stop blacks and Latinos at vastly disproportionate rates to whites. Then they switched and began using information and behavior as their criteria. They looked at where and how tickets were bought, did background checks, watched whether you stuck to your bags at all times. As a result, they searched fewer people and found twice as many blacks and whites, and five times as many Latinos, who were running drugs.

5   The key to the information revolution is that good information, properly used, is the most effective weapon any organization can have. Vincent Cannistraro, former head of counterterrorism at the CIA, explains that racial profiling is bad information. "It's a false lead. It may be intuitive to stereotype people, but profiling is too crude to be effective. I can't think of any examples where profiling has caught a terrorist." With this particular enemy, racial profiling would be pointless. Consider the four most famous accused terrorists in custody today: John Walker Lindh, a white American; Zacarias Moussaoui, an African with a French passport; Richard Reid, a half–West Indian, half-Englishman with a British passport; Jose Padilla, a Hispanic American. They are all Muslim, but that broadens the category to the point of uselessness. There are 1.2 billion Muslims in the world, and even in the United States there are several million. "If you're looking for a needle in a haystack, adding hay isn't going to help," says the Arab-American activist James Zogby.

6   What we need is not profiling but smart profiling. Stephen Flynn of the Council on Foreign Relations is among the leading homeland-security experts in

the country. Flynn argues that you start with reverse profiling. People who are low risk should be "precleared." When you buy your ticket, the airline asks the FBI to run your name through its database. If you come out clean, you go through a "green line." That way the inspections process can focus on the much smaller group of people about whom the government has either suspicions or too little information—the "red line." (Every one of the September 11 hijackers would have had to go through such a red line had it been in place.) "That narrows the field," says Flynn, "not in a dumb way as race or religion would, but in a smart way." Flynn argues that above all else, interrogation and intuition are what works. "The Feds need to be able to observe and talk to the small number of suspicious people rather than doing broad or random searches," he says. "Behavior is usually the giveaway, in terrorism as in crime."

7 Overly broad, ethnically based profiling has one other practical problem. It hurts the government's ability to form good relations with these groups, get information and recruit double agents. If there are Al Qaeda sympathizers within the American Arab or Muslim communities—and there surely are—the best way to find out is to gain allies within the communities. That's why Cannistraro believes the FBI's decision to round up 5,000 Arabs for questioning is "counterproductive. It alienates the very community whose cooperation you need to get good intelligence." And consider how some of these interrogations take place. An Arab artist living in Brooklyn—who asked that his name be withheld—was taken in for questioning by two FBI agents. He was put in a lower-Manhattan cell where guards told him to shut up and an FBI agent muttered, "They'll let any of you sorry motherf——ers in this country now?" Two agents interrogated him for three hours and then threw him in jail for the night. After being given a Snickers bar for dinner, he slept on a concrete floor with two other Arab-immigrant men. In the morning they informed him that they now "liked him," and asked if he would like to join the FBI's fight against terrorism and help translate during other interviews such as the one he went through. Guess what: he declined.

8 Unlike many European countries where immigrants live a bitter, resentful life outside the mainstream, in America new minorities have tended to integrate into the broader community. There are doubtless elements within Muslim or Arab communities here that are sympathetic to Al Qaeda. But finding out who they are requires gaining the trust of the vast majority who are in America because they want the American dream.

9 In 1942, eight Nazi agents—all German-Americans or Germans who had lived in the United States for long stretches—landed on New York's Long Island with instructions to destroy American power plants, factories and bridges. They were captured by the FBI, President Roosevelt declared them enemy combatants and they were tried and convicted by a military tribunal. This case—*Ex parte Quirin*—is the model often cited to explain how we should fight the war on terror bluntly and robustly. But it leaves out one part of the story. The FBI had no idea that these men had landed and knew nothing of their plans. The terrorists were discovered only because one of the eight men was an American patriot. He had set off on the mission with the intention of divulging the plot to the

authorities. America must change a great deal as it fights this new and strange war on terror. But let us ensure it always remains the kind of country for which people will make such sacrifices. ◆◆

QUESTIONS TO HELP YOU THINK AND WRITE ABOUT FREEDOM ISSUES

1. Imagine that Posner and Lewis are being interviewed on television and these questions are posed to them: How important is it to protect our civil liberties? Are there ever circumstances that might cause us voluntarily to sacrifice our civil liberties? If there are, what do we sacrifice and for how long a time? How do you think these authors would respond to these questions? How would each of them conclude his remarks?

2. How does Posner use historical analogy in his essay? What point are his historical comparisons used to prove? How effective is this proof?

3. Lewis suggests that a line needs to be drawn somewhere between freedom and security. Where do you think he would draw it? Where would you draw it?

4. Guernsey's article states: "It is difficult to gauge whether the support for governmental monitoring will outlast the immediate trauma of the Sept. 11 attacks." Take a poll in class similar to the one that appears in Guernsey's article. Ask the following questions: Are you willing to give up your personal freedoms to make the country safe from terrorist attacks? Do you support governmental monitoring of your e-mail, mail, and phone conversations? Compare your results with the results of the polls taken after 9/11 and discuss your findings with your class.

5. After reading the article by Hawkins, what is your opinion concerning the implementation of biometric technologies? What are some of the benefits and drawbacks? If you could design your own biometric scanning system, what would it be, and how would it work?

6. Cohen's essay argues that privacy issues largely come down to our own political and moral beliefs. Using his essay as a way of understanding warrants, apply his thinking to the articles by Maas, Guernsey, and Hawkins. What moral and political warrants would you ascribe to these other authors on the basis of their writings? What about Cohen's warrants? What do you speculate they are?

7. Identify the warrants of police who use racial profiling in fighting crime, as described by Goldberg. Then contrast these warrants with your own. If you and the police officers described by Goldberg were to have a dialogue on this issue, how might you achieve common ground? How might you resolve your differences?

8. Compare the articles written by Zakaria and Goldberg. Given what is said about the effectiveness of profiling in Goldberg's article, do you agree that police officers find profiling to be ineffective, as suggested by Zakaria? How do you account for this contradiction? What would Sgt. Lewis in Goldberg's article think of Zakaria's idea of "smart profiling"?

⋙ Section VI ⋙

Issues Concerning the Future

THE ISSUES

A. WHAT ARE SOME POSSIBLE ISSUES FOR THE FUTURE?

"Looking Back on Tomorrow" by David Brooks will get you started thinking about some of the possible issues for the twenty-first century. Brooks provides a historical perspective by identifying what he thinks were the most pervasive issues in the nineteenth and twentieth centuries and then nominates the four issues he believes will most occupy people's attention in the next century. He provides other possible issues at the end of his article. This article is presented first so that you will begin to think about some issues for the future yourself. If you had written this article, what issues would you have identified?

B. WHAT MIGHT AFFECT THE FUTURE OF HUMAN BEINGS?

The authors of the articles in this section raise issues associated with the future use of existing technologies that could change the nature of the human race. Silver projects futurist and imaginative scenarios that could result from the genetic engineering of human beings, Kurzweil discusses computers and the issues that could arise when they are finally able to outsmart human beings, and Stolberg writes about creating genetically altered animals that can be used to supply vital organs and medicines for human beings. Wood examines the implications of these technologies and cautions others to do the same. See also "The Road to Unreality" (page 86), "Gene Tests: What You Know Can Hurt You" (page 178), "Human Cloning: An Annotated Bibliography" (page 338), and "Human Cloning: Is It a Viable Option?" (page 257).

C. WHAT MIGHT AFFECT THE FUTURE OF THE PLANET?

In excerpts from his book *The Future of Life,* Edward O. Wilson spells out the key elements of a plan to protect the future of the ecosystems and species on the planet. Kluger and Dorfman identify other specific areas in which nations need to work to save the planet. Louria examines recent science that extends the normal life span of human beings and projects the effects of an increased population of older people on the future resources of the planet.

D. WEB SITES FOR FURTHER EXPLORATION AND RESEARCH

The Hastings Center (Ethics and the Future)	http://www.thehastingscenter.org
Cybersociology.com	http://www.cybersociology.com
Internet Studies Resource Center	http://www.isc.umn.edu/read.html
Center for Literary Computing	http://www.clc.wvu.edu
Genetic Science Learning Center	http://gslc.genetics.utah.edu
Guardian Unlimited	http://www.guardian.co.uk/genes
National Institute of Health/Bioethics on the Web	http://www.nih.gov/sigs/bioethics

E. FILM AND LITERATURE RELATED TO ISSUES ABOUT THE FUTURE

Films: *Gattaca*, 1998; *Minority Report*, 2002; *TRON*, 1982; *Johnny Mnemonic*, 1995; *The Net*, 1995; *Strange Days*, 1995; *You've Got Mail*, 1999.

Literature: novels: *When the Wind Blows* by James Patterson; *The Third Twin* by Ken Follett; *Chromosome 6* by Robin Cook; *Brave New World* by Aldous Huxley; *Frankenstein* by Mary Shelley; *The Experiment* by John Darnton; *Alchemist* by Peter James; *Society of the Mind* by Eric L. Harry; *Mona Lisa Overdrive* and *Neuromancer* by William Gibson.

THE RHETORICAL SITUATION

At the turn of each new century, people like to speculate about the future. A new century prompts us to revisit the issues of the previous one and then to predict what might be the important issues during the new century. The authors of the essays in this section of "The Reader" include professors, journalists, and a medical doctor. All these authors have areas of expertise they draw on to make educated guesses about the issues in their areas in the twenty-first century. It is all guesswork, of course. Some of their projections will turn out to be accurate and some will not. As you read these essays, you will find yourself both agreeing and disagreeing with the future conditions and issues that these authors imagine.

As you read this section of "The Reader," you will be invited specifically to think about the issues that cluster around the future of the human race and the future of the planet. To be sure, the turn of the century provides some of the exigency for examining such issues. Other exigencies motivate an interest in these issues as well. Modern scientific technologies may soon make it possible to genetically engineer human beings, harvest animal parts to transplant into humans, and create computers that will be more intelligent than people. During the next century, everyone will need to consider the implications of these technologies and participate in debate and discussion to decide not only how they can best be used, but also how they can be controlled. All of them, as you can imagine, could have a profound effect on the future of the human race.

The future of the planet will also generate issues and discussion in the twenty-first century. Most authors writing on this subject warn that natural resources are being depleted at an alarming rate and that we are in danger of creating a planet that will no longer be hospitable to humans. We can change this pattern, but we will have to start now and be diligent in our efforts. A turn-of-the-century World Summit on Sustainable Development met in Johannesburg, South Africa, in August 2002 to assess the status of the environment at that time and to develop a plan of action. That summit, along with the usual concerns that most people have about conservation, population control, and the preservation of natural resources, provides additional motivation for an interest in the issues associated with the future of the planet.

Certainly the future of humans and the planet is important in anyone's scheme of future projections. You are encouraged to consult what you know and to make some projections of your own. Do you have an area of expertise? What issues do you think will be generated in your area during the twenty-first century? You can try your hand at looking into the future, particularly in the areas you know something about. For that matter, you can look over the other issue areas in "The Reader" and try making some predictions about them regarding the next 100 years. Marriage and families, education, crime and criminals, race and culture, freedom, and war and peace will all continue to generate issues in the future just as they have in the past. Can you take a guess at what some of these issues in these various areas might be? Can you begin to imagine the positions you are likely to take in regard to them?

A. WHAT ARE SOME POSSIBLE ISSUES FOR THE FUTURE?

QUESTIONS TO CONSIDER BEFORE YOU READ

Think about what issues in the world seem most important today and jot them down. Based on what you know, how do you think these current issues might develop in the future? What other issues might become important?

LOOKING BACK ON TOMORROW*

David Brooks

David Brooks writes for the Atlantic Monthly *and poses a startling question: If the century ahead turns out to have a theme, what will it be?*

1   What are we going to do with our lives? I don't mean that question in any small, personal sense; whether or not you decide to retire early to open a bed-and-breakfast is of no interest to me. I mean it in the biggest sense. Which issues will dominate the twenty-first century? What debates and controversies will roil our children's lives? In other words, what will the twenty-first century be about?

2   If forced to sum up nineteenth-century America in one sentence, I'd say that it was about national union. The century opened with the Louisiana Purchase and continued with the acquisition and settling of the West. Then came efforts to link our vast space with networks of canals, railroads, towns, and telegraph wires. The Civil War was, of course, an all-out fight for political and cultural union. And the century ended with the consolidation of the national economy.

3   The twentieth century, in America and elsewhere, was about the size of government. The main debate was between those who wanted to preserve limited government and those who wanted a bigger and more active government, whether the latter were Progressives, New Deal liberals, democratic socialists, or totalitarians. Two of the great conflicts of the century, World War II and the Cold War, were fought against ideologies—fascism and communism, respectively—that held that the state should control economic and social life. In the United

*Atlantic Monthly, April 2002, pp. 20+.

States election after election revolved around the question of small versus big government.

4   It is hard to believe that the debate about the right size of government will dominate the coming century. Most nations have reached a rough consensus on the matter. In the United States federal expenditures now equal about one fifth of GDP, as they have for many years; there is no sign that that figure will change much anytime soon. In 1993 Hillary Clinton tried to expand the scope of government by offering an enormous proposal to reform health care, and in 1995 the speaker of the House, Newt Gingrich, tried to shrink it. Both failed. Democrats and Republicans still attack each other on the issue, but their fight has become a sort of petty trench warfare on familiar terrain, marked by tired arguments and no significant movement one way or the other.

5   Which project or controversy, then, will define the coming century? Here are a few nominees:

REMAKING HUMAN NATURE

6   We are experiencing a biotechnological revolution. In his book *Life Script* (2001), Nicholas Wade, a science reporter for *The New York Times,* predicts that the revolution will wash over us in three overlapping waves. First will come what has been called individualized medicine. Doctors will match drugs to our specific genotypes and will even introduce "regenerative medicine": instead of fixing diseased organs, they will grow and implant new ones. The second wave will bring breakthroughs in gene therapy as it applies to reproduction. Fertilized eggs will be treated in vitro with selected genes to increase the future person's height or intelligence, for example, or to prevent depression or other illnesses. The result of these advances will be a third wave: a radical increase in how long people live. Wade suggests that we may eventually regard 320 years as a normal life-span.

7   Breakthroughs of this sort would certainly reduce disease and suffering. But they would also raise many doubts, which can be boiled down to two questions: Is there more to life than maximizing pleasure and minimizing pain? Do we improve our bodies at the cost of our souls?

8   Critics of the drive toward such technologies argue that we take on a terrible burden when we try to redesign human nature and human beings. Parents who try to implant "improvements" in their prospective children, they contend, will be perverting parenthood. They will be assessing their children in consumerist terms, not regarding them as intrinsically holy creations. . . . And parenthood will become despotism as parents refuse to accept limits on their control over another human life.

9   Regarding the third wave of Wade's revolution, would a radically longer life necessarily be a better life? "Teach us to number our days," the Psalmist says, "that we may apply our hearts unto wisdom." We seek to live according to God's word, the critics argue, precisely because we are aware that our time on earth is short.

10   The forces of science say that they are attempting to master nature in order to improve man's estate, in the spirit of the Baconian tradition. The forces of religion say that at some point the domination of the flesh becomes the death of the spirit.

GLOBALIZATION

11 Before the terrorist attacks in New York and Washington, most social scientists would have predicted that the economics and politics of globalization would dominate the twenty-first century. One of the classic texts in this debate is *The End of the Nation-State* (1995), by the French intellectual Jean-Marie Guéhenno. Guéhenno begins with the familiar argument that nations are too big to solve some problems and too small to solve others. However, he deepens the discussion when he writes that certain concepts associated with the nation-state, such as democracy, politics, and liberty, continue to define our horizons but no longer mean what they once did.

12 According to Guéhenno, power is now diffused to markets, multinational companies, and nongovernmental organizations. Geographic space has become less important. The world will soon consist of a number of overlapping networks, with a "universal empire" that contains them all (think of the interlocking rings of the Olympic symbol). No single power structure will be able to exercise all the dimensions of sovereignty, which will instead be fluid and open.

13 This basic idea has been fleshed out and endorsed or condemned in dozens of books. One left-wing critique is Michael Hardt and Antonio Negri's *Empire* (2000), which has attracted a cult following—in part, one suspects, because it is written in the obscure style that is taken in certain academic circles as a sign of oracular brilliance. Another book is Paul A. Cantor's *Gilligan Unbound* (2001). Using television shows of the past several decades, from *Star Trek* to *The Simpsons*, Cantor argues that globalization has washed away certain basic assumptions. People no longer assume that they live in a world of centrally directed nation-states, which may eventually converge into a single global authority. They no longer assume that politics reigns over commerce. Instead, authority is decentralized. The world is no longer a coherent place that we can shape; rather, the shadowy force of globalization exerts its will on us.

14 Should we fight to preserve our system of nation-states or embrace the postnational future? If we are no longer defined by our national identities, do we fall back on racial or religious identities, or do we invent new ones? And what about this notion of a global "empire"? Will such an empire be just? Or will it be a machine that runs by itself, crushing human beings in its gears?

INEQUALITY

15 In the early 1990s a story floated around Russia about a Japanese steel executive who was invited to tour a Russian steel plant. The Russians took him around, showed him their machines and processes, and then asked him, "How far behind you are we? Are we five years behind, or ten?" The Japanese executive responded, "Forever. You are forever behind." He meant that the Russian plant was not only backward but also falling further behind every year, because its rate of progress was slower than that of those ahead of it.

16 A similar dynamic could prove to be a feature of the information age. The rich countries and people may not only maintain their lead but also increase it year after year, because they are better equipped to take advantage of fresh opportunities. This widening inequality occurs in both international and domestic realms.

The European and Asian tiger nations could roar ahead of the rest of the world, leaving behind whole continents in poverty and disorder, which would inevitably lead to shame and rebellion among those left behind. The historian Bernard Lewis has argued persuasively . . . that such a sense of failure has helped to fuel the anti-Western radicalism that has swept through the Muslim world and endangered our own.

17   Within many nations the gap between those in the top income decile and those in the bottom appears to be widening. This has been happening in the United States, Germany, Britain, and Japan, regardless of what sort of political party or philosophy holds sway. If widening inequality is inherent in the structure of the information-age economy, will nasty class warfare necessarily follow? Or will the people lagging behind, who will form a majority, eventually come up with their own economic system—some updated neo-Marxist vision, perhaps—to replace democratic capitalism and its perceived unfairness?

THE AMERICAN CENTURY REDUX

18   On the other hand, why be so gloomy? Perhaps the United States will emerge from the war on terrorism more powerful and influential than before. Perhaps it will continue the task that occupied it for so much of the twentieth century: spreading the gospel of the Declaration of Independence—the idea that all human beings (and not just a few lucky ones in North America and Western Europe) are born with certain unalienable rights.

19   Perhaps over the coming decades democracy and freedom will take root in Africa, in the Middle East, in China. Already it is striking that many people in the former Soviet Union and the Arab world say they just want their countries to be "normal"—by which they mean contented, bourgeois nations, in which politics is a series of compromises, religious tolerance is the rule, and shopping is a prime leisure activity. They have internalized our Founders' vision.

20   A survey of the social science of the past century shows it to be, by and large, an insanely pessimistic field. Intellectuals are always predicting decline. So perhaps it's time to try to compensate for our tendency to see problems instead of progress. To achieve a new American Century the United States would have to solve some of its problems—for example, how to preserve our distinctive identity even as our nation is demographically transformed; how to retain our character and sense of national mission in the face of mass affluence and commercial pressures; how to remain a dynamic economic power. American leaders will have to rebut dour standpatters, including the professor of government Samuel Huntington, who argues that civilizations are practically inviolable and that Western civilization should generally not try to project its image of right and wrong onto others' turf. But the task of championing democracy has never been easy. And it is not unrealistic to think that the United States will continue on the trajectory that it followed in the past two centuries, and that this will have positive, world-shaping effects.

21   There are, of course, many other issues that could dominate the coming years: global warming, the global spread of feminism, a worldwide religious revival, a militant secular revival, ethnic balkanization. But these four are my

finalists. And I'm betting that issue No. 4—the American Century redux—will emerge at the top of the list. ◆◆

B. WHAT MIGHT AFFECT THE FUTURE OF HUMAN BEINGS?

QUESTIONS TO CONSIDER BEFORE YOU READ

What are your opinions about cosmetic surgery? Do you think people should medically change their physical appearance? What about their genes? Should people change their genetic structure? Do you have an interest in computers? What are the advantages of computers? Do you think there are any disadvantages to computers? How do you think these advantages and disadvantages could affect the future?

REPROGENETICS: A GLIMPSE OF THINGS TO COME*

Lee M. Silver

Lee M. Silver is a professor at Princeton University, where he teaches and conducts research in genetics, evolution, reproduction, and developmental biology. He has also written and lectured on the social impact of biotechnology. The following excerpt is from his book Remaking Eden: Cloning and Beyond in a Brave New World.

DATELINE BOSTON: JUNE 1, 2010

1   Sometime in the not-so-distant future, you may visit the maternity ward at a major university hospital to see the newborn child or grandchild of a close friend. The new mother, let's call her Barbara, seems very much at peace with the world, sitting in a chair quietly nursing her baby, Max. Her labor was—in the parlance of her doctor—"uneventful," and she is looking forward to raising her first child. You decide to make pleasant conversation by asking Barbara whether she knew in advance that her baby was going to be a boy. In your mind, it seems like a perfectly reasonable question since doctors have long given prospective parents the option of learning the sex of their child-to-be many months before the predicted date of birth. But Barbara seems taken aback by the question. "Of course I knew that Max would be a boy," she tells you. "My husband Dan and I chose him from our embryo pool. And when I'm ready to go through this again, I'll choose a girl to be my second child. An older son and a younger daughter—a perfect family."

2   Now, it's your turn to be taken aback. "You made a conscious choice to have a boy rather than a girl?" you ask.

3   "Absolutely!" Barbara answers. "And while I was at it, I made sure that Max wouldn't turn out to be fat like my brother Tom or addicted to alcohol like Dan's

---

*Lee M. Silver, *Remaking Eden: Cloning and Beyond in a Brave New World* (New York: Avon Books, 1997), pp. 1–4, 7–11.

sister Karen. It's not that I'm personally biased or anything," Barbara continues defensively. "I just wanted to make sure that Max would have the greatest chance for achieving success. Being overweight or alcoholic would clearly be a handicap."

4   You look down in wonderment at the little baby boy destined to be moderate in both size and drinking habits.

5   Max has fallen asleep in Barbara's arms, and she places him gently in his bassinet. He wears a contented smile, which evokes a similar smile from his mother. Barbara feels the urge to stretch her legs and asks whether you'd like to meet some of the new friends she's made during her brief stay at the hospital. You nod, and the two of you walk into the room next door where a thirty-five-year old woman named Cheryl is resting after giving birth to a nine-pound baby girl named Rebecca.

6   Barbara introduces you to Cheryl as well as a second woman named Madelaine, who stands by the bed holding Cheryl's hand. Little Rebecca is lying under the gaze of both Cheryl and Madelaine. "She really does look like both of her mothers, doesn't she?" Barbara asks you.

7   Now you're really confused. You glance at Barbara and whisper, "Both mothers?"

8   Barbara takes you aside to explain. "Yes. You see Cheryl and Madelaine have been living together for eight years. They got married in Hawaii soon after it became legal there, and like most married couples, they wanted to bring a child into the world with a combination of both of their bloodlines. With the reproductive technologies available today, they were able to fulfill their dreams."

9   You look across the room at the happy little nuclear family—Cheryl, Madelaine, and baby Rebecca—and wonder how the hospital plans to fill out the birth certificate.

DATELINE SEATTLE: MARCH 15, 2050

10   You are now forty years older and much wiser to the ways of the modern world. Once again, you journey forth to the maternity ward. This time, it's your own granddaughter Melissa who is in labor. Melissa is determined to experience natural childbirth and has refused all offers of anesthetics or painkillers. But she needs something to lift her spirits so that she can continue on through the waves of pain. "Let me see her pictures again," she implores her husband Curtis as the latest contraction sweeps through her body. Curtis picks the photo album off the table and opens it to face his wife. She looks up at the computer-generated picture of a five-year-old girl with wavy brown hair, hazel eyes, and a round face. Curtis turns the page, and Melissa gazes at an older version of the same child: a smiling sixteen-year-old who is 5 feet, 5 inches tall with a pretty face. Melissa smiles back at the future picture of her yet-to-be-born child and braces for another contraction.

11   There is something unseen in the picture of their child-to-be that provides even greater comfort to Melissa and Curtis. It is the submicroscopic piece of DNA—an extra gene—that will be present in every cell of her body. This special gene will provide her with lifelong resistance to infection by the virus that causes AIDS, a virus that has evolved to be ever more virulent since its explosion across

the landscape of humanity seventy years earlier. After years of research by thousands of scientists, no cure for the awful disease has been found, and the only absolute protection comes from the insertion of a resistance gene into the single-cell embryo within twenty-four hours after conception. Ensconced in its chromosomal home, the AIDS resistance gene will be copied over and over again into every one of the trillions of cells that make up the human body, each of which will have its own personal barrier to infection by the AIDS-causing virus HIV. Melissa and Curtis feel lucky indeed to have the financial wherewithal needed to endow all of their children with this protective agent. Other, less well-off American families cannot afford this luxury.

12   Outside Melissa's room, Jennifer, another expectant mother, is anxiously pacing the hall. She has just arrived at the hospital and her contractions are still far apart. But, unlike Melissa, Jennifer has no need for a computer printout to show her what her child-to-be will look like as a young girl or teenager. She already has thousands of pictures that show her future daughter's likeness, and they're all real, not virtual. For the fetus inside Jennifer is her identical twin sister—her clone—who will be born thirty-six years after she and Jennifer were both conceived within the same single-cell embryo. As Jennifer's daughter grows up, she will constantly behold a glimpse of the future simply by looking at her mother's photo album and her mother.

◆◆◆◆

DATELINE PRINCETON, NEW JERSEY: THE PRESENT

13   Are these outrageous scenarios the stuff of science fiction? Did they spring from the minds of Hollywood screenwriters hoping to create blockbuster movies without regard to real world constraints? No. The scenarios described under the first two datelines emerge directly from scientific understanding and technologies that are already available today. . . . Furthermore, if biomedical advances continue to occur at the same rate as they do now, the practices described are likely to be feasible long before we reach my conservatively chosen datelines.

14   It's time to take stock of the current state of science and technology in the fields of reproduction and genetics and to ask, in the broadest terms possible, what the future may hold. Most people are aware of the impact that reproductive technology has already had in the area of fertility treatment. The first "test tube baby"—Louise Brown—is already eighteen years old, and the acronym for in vitro fertilization—IVF—is commonly used by laypeople. The cloning of human beings has become a real possibility as well, although many are still confused about what the technology can and cannot do. Advances in genetic research have also been in the limelight, with the almost weekly identification of new genes implicated in diseases like cystic fibrosis and breast cancer, or personality traits like novelty-seeking and anxiety.

15   What has yet to catch the attention of the public at large, however, is the incredible power that emerges when current technologies in reproductive biology and genetics are brought together in the form of *reprogenetics*. With reprogenetics, parents can gain complete control over their genetic destiny, with the ability to guide and enhance the characteristics of their children, and their children's children as well. But even as reprogenetics makes dreams come true, like all of the

most powerful technologies invented by humankind, it may also generate night-mares of a kind not previously imagined.

16   Of course, just because a technology becomes feasible does not mean that it will be used. Or does it? Society, acting through government intervention, could outlaw any one or all of the reprogenetic practices that I have described. Isn't the *nonuse* of nuclear weapons for the purpose of mass destruction over the last half century an example of how governments can control technology?

17   There are two big differences between the use of nuclear technology and reprogenetic technology. These differences lie in the resources and money needed to practice each. The most crucial resources required to build a nuclear weapon—large reactors and enriched sources of uranium or plutonium—are tightly controlled by the government itself. The resources required to practice reprogenetics—precision medical tools, small laboratory equipment, and sim-ple chemicals—are all available for sale, without restriction, to anyone with the money to pay for them. The cost of developing a nuclear weapon is billions of dollars. In contrast, a reprogenetics clinic could easily be run on the scale of a small business anywhere in the world. Thus, even if restrictions on the use of re-progenetics are imposed in one country or another, those intent on delivering and receiving these services will not be restrained. But on what grounds can we argue that they should be restrained?

18   In response to this question, many people point to the chilling novel *Brave New World* written by Aldous Huxley in 1931. It is the story of a future worldwide political state that exerts complete control over human reproduction and human nature as well. In this brave new world, the state uses fetal hatcheries to breed each child into a predetermined intellectual class that ranges from alpha at the top to epsilon at the bottom. Individual members of each class are predestined to fit into specific roles in a soulless utopia where marriage and parenthood are pre-vented and promiscuous sexual activity is strongly encouraged, where universal immunity to diseases has been achieved, and where an all-enveloping state prop-aganda machine and mood-altering drugs make all content with their positions in life.

19   While Huxley guessed right about the power we would gain over the process of reproduction, I think he was dead wrong when it came to predicting *who* would use the power and for what purposes. What Huxley failed to understand, or refused to accept, was the driving force behind babymaking. It is individuals and couples who want to reproduce themselves in their own images. It is individ-uals and couples who want their children to be happy and successful. And it is in-dividuals and couples—like Barbara and Dan and Cheryl and Madelaine and Melissa and Curtis and Jennifer, *not governments*—who will seize control of these new technologies. They will use some to reach otherwise unattainable reproduc-tive goals and others to help their children achieve health, happiness, and suc-cess. And it is in pursuit of this last goal that the combined actions of many individuals, operating over many generations, could perhaps give rise to a polar-ized humanity more horrific than Huxley's imagined Brave New World.

20   There are those who will argue that parents don't have the right to control the characteristics of their children-to-be in the way I describe. But American

society, in particular, accepts the rights of parents to control every other aspect of their children's lives from the time they are born until they reach adulthood. If one accepts the parental prerogative after birth, it is hard to argue against it before birth, if no harm is caused to the children who emerge.

21   Many think that it is inherently unfair for some people to have access to technologies that can provide advantages while others, less well-off, are forced to depend on chance alone. I would agree. It is inherently unfair. But once again, American society adheres to the principle that personal liberty and personal fortune are the primary determinants of what individuals are allowed and able to do. Anyone who accepts the right of affluent parents to provide their children with an expensive private school education cannot use "unfairness" as a reason for rejecting the use of reprogenetic technologies.

22   Indeed, in a society that values individual freedom above all else, it is hard to find any legitimate basis for restricting the use of reprogenetics. And therein lies the dilemma. For while each individual use of the technology can be viewed in the light of personal reproductive choice—with no ability to change society at large—together they could have dramatic, unintended, long-term consequences.

23   As the technologies of reproduction and genetics have become ever more powerful over the last decade, most practicing scientists and physicians have been loath to speculate about where it may all lead. One reason for reluctance is the fear of getting it wrong. It really is impossible to predict with certainty which future technological advances will proceed on time and which will encounter unexpected roadblocks. This means that like Huxley's vision of a fetal hatchery, some of the ideas proposed here may ultimately be technically impossible or exceedingly difficult to implement. On the other hand, there are sure to be technological breakthroughs that no one can imagine now, just as Huxley was unable to imagine genetic engineering, or cloning from adult cells, in 1931.

24   There is a second reason why fertility specialists, in particular, are reluctant to speculate about the kinds of future scenarios that I describe here. It's called politics. In a climate where abortion clinics are on the alert for terrorist attacks, and where the religious right rails against any interference with the "natural process" of conception, IVF providers see no reason to call attention to themselves through descriptions of reproductive and genetic manipulations that are sure to provoke outrage.

25   The British journal *Nature* is one of the two most important science journals in the world (the other being the American journal *Science*). It is published weekly and is read by all types of scientists from biologists to physicists to medical researchers. No one would ever consider it to be radical or sensationalist in any way. On March 7, 1996, *Nature* published an article that described a method for cloning unlimited numbers of sheep from a single fertilized egg, with further implications for improving methods of genetic engineering. It took another week before the ramifications of this isolated breakthrough sank in for the editors. On March 14, 1996, they wrote an impassioned editorial saying in part: "That the growing power of molecular genetics confronts us with future prospects of being able to *change the nature of our species* [my emphasis] is a fact that seldom appears to be addressed in depth. Scientific knowledge may not yet permit detailed

understanding, but the possibilities are clear enough. This gives rise to issues that in the end will have to be related to people within the social and ethical environments in which they live. . . . And the agenda is set by mankind as a whole, not by the subset involved in the science."

26   They are right that the agenda will not be set by scientists. But they are wrong to think that "mankind as a whole"—unable to reach consensus on so many other societal issues—will have any effect whatsoever. The agenda is sure to be set by individuals and couples who will act on behalf of themselves and their children. . . .

27   There is no doubt about it. For better *and* worse, a new age is upon us. And whether we like it or not, the global marketplace will reign supreme. ◆◆

AN INEXORABLE EMERGENCE: TRANSITION TO THE TWENTY-FIRST CENTURY*

Ray Kurzweil

This is an excerpt from Ray Kurzweil's book The Age of Spiritual Machines: When Computers Exceed Human Intelligence, *published in 1999. Kurzweil is also the author of* The Age of Intelligent Machines, *which won the Association of American Publishers' award for the Most Outstanding Computer Science Book of 1990.*

1   Computers today exceed human intelligence in a broad variety of intelligent yet narrow domains such as playing chess, diagnosing certain medical conditions, buying and selling stocks, and guiding cruise missiles. Yet human intelligence overall remains far more supple and flexible. Computers are still unable to describe the objects on a crowded kitchen table, write a summary of a movie, tie a pair of shoelaces, tell the difference between a dog and a cat (although this feat, I believe, is becoming feasible today with contemporary neural nets—computer simulations of human neurons),[1] recognize humor, or perform other subtle tasks in which their human creators excel.

2   One reason for this disparity in capabilities is that our most advanced computers are still simpler than the human brain—currently about a million times simpler (give or take one or two orders of magnitude depending on the assumptions used). But this disparity will not remain the case as we go through the early part of the next century. Computers doubled in speed . . . every two years in the 1950s and 1960s, and are now doubling in speed every twelve months. This trend will continue, with computers achieving the memory capacity and computing speed of the human brain by around the year 2020.

3   Achieving the basic complexity and capacity of the human brain will not automatically result in computers matching the flexibility of human intelligence.

*Ray Kurzweil, *The Age of Spiritual Machines: When Computers Exceed Human Intelligence* (New York: Viking, 1999), pp. 2–6.

The organization and content of these resources—the software of intelligence—is equally important. One approach to emulating the brain's software is through reverse engineering—scanning a human brain (which will be achievable early in the next century)[2] and essentially copying its neural circuitry in a neural computer (a computer designed to simulate a massive number of human neurons) of sufficient capacity.

4   There is a plethora of credible scenarios for achieving human-level intelligence in a machine. We will be able to evolve and train a system combining massively parallel neural nets with other paradigms to understand language and model knowledge, including the ability to read and understand written documents. Although the ability of today's computers to extract and learn knowledge from natural language documents is quite limited, their abilities in this domain are improving rapidly. Computers will be able to read on their own, understanding and modeling what they have read, by the second decade of the twenty-first century. We can then have our computers read all of the world's literature—books, magazines, scientific journals, and other available material. Ultimately, the machines will gather knowledge on their own by venturing into the physical world, drawing from the full spectrum of media and information services, and sharing knowledge with each other (which machines can do far more easily than their human creators).

5   Once a computer achieves a human level of intelligence, it will necessarily roar past it. Since their inception, computers have significantly exceeded human mental dexterity in their ability to remember and process information. A computer can remember billions or even trillions of facts perfectly, while we are hard pressed to remember a handful of phone numbers. A computer can quickly search a database with billions of records in fractions of a second. Computers can readily share their knowledge bases. The combination of human-level intelligence in a machine with a computer's inherent superiority in the speed, accuracy, and sharing ability of its memory will be formidable.

6   Mammalian neurons are marvelous creations, but we wouldn't build them the same way. Much of their complexity is devoted to supporting their own life processes, not to their information-handling abilities. Furthermore, neurons are extremely slow; electronic circuits are at least a million times faster. Once a computer achieves a human level of ability in understanding abstract concepts, recognizing patterns, and other attributes of human intelligence, it will be able to apply this ability to a knowledge base of all human-acquired—and machine-acquired—knowledge.

7   A common reaction to the proposition that computers will seriously compete with human intelligence is to dismiss this specter based primarily on an examination of contemporary capability. After all, when I interact with my personal computer, its intelligence seems limited and brittle, if it appears intelligent at all. It is hard to imagine one's personal computer having a sense of humor, holding an opinion, or displaying any of the other endearing qualities of human thought.

8   But the state of the art in computer technology is anything but static. Computer capabilities are emerging today that were considered impossible one or two

decades ago. Examples include the ability to transcribe accurately normal continuous human speech, to understand and respond intelligently to natural language, to recognize patterns in medical procedures such as electrocardiograms and blood tests with an accuracy rivaling that of human physicians, and, of course, to play chess at a world-championship level. In the next decade, we will see translating telephones that provide real-time speech translation from one human language to another, intelligent computerized personal assistants that can converse and rapidly search and understand the world's knowledge bases, and a profusion of other machines with increasingly broad and flexible intelligence.

9   In the second decade of the next century, it will become increasingly difficult to draw any clear distinction between the capabilities of human and machine intelligence. The advantages of computer intelligence in terms of speed, accuracy, and capacity will be clear. The advantages of human intelligence, on the other hand, will become increasingly difficult to distinguish.

10   The skills of computer software are already better than many people realize. It is frequently my experience that when demonstrating recent advances in, say, speech or character recognition, observers are surprised at the state of the art. For example, a typical computer user's last experience with speech-recognition technology may have been a low-end freely bundled piece of software from several years ago that recognized a limited vocabulary, required pauses between words, and did an incorrect job at that. These users are then surprised to see contemporary systems that can recognize fully continuous speech on a 60,000-word vocabulary, with accuracy levels comparable to a human typist.

11   Also keep in mind that the progression of computer intelligence will sneak up on us. As just one example, consider Gary Kasparov's confidence in 1990 that a computer would never come close to defeating him. After all, he had played the best computers, and their chess-playing ability—compared to his—was pathetic. But computer chess playing made steady progress, gaining forty-five rating points each year. In 1997, a computer sailed past Kasparov, at least in chess. There has been a great deal of commentary that other human endeavors are far more difficult to emulate than chess playing. *This is true.* In many areas—the ability to write a book on computers, for example—computers are still pathetic. But as computers continue to gain in capacity at an exponential rate, we will have the same experience in these other areas that Kasparov had in chess. Over the next several decades, machine competence will rival—and ultimately surpass—any particular human skill one cares to cite, including our marvelous ability to place our ideas in a broad diversity of contexts.

12   Evolution has been seen as a billion-year drama that led inexorably to its grandest creation: human intelligence. The emergence in the early twenty-first century of a new form of intelligence on Earth that can compete with, and ultimately significantly exceed, human intelligence will be a development of greater import than any of the events that have shaped human history. It will be no less important than the creation of the intelligence that created it, and will have profound implications for all aspects of human endeavor, including the nature of work, human learning, government, warfare, the arts, and our concept of ourselves.

13   This specter is not yet here. But with the emergence of computers that truly rival and exceed the human brain in complexity will come a corresponding ability of machines to understand and respond to abstractions and subtleties. Human beings appear to be complex in part because of our competing internal goals. Values and emotions represent goals that often conflict with each other, and are an unavoidable by-product of the levels of abstraction that we deal with as human beings. As computers achieve a comparable—and greater—level of complexity, and as they are increasingly derived at least in part from models of human intelligence, they, too, will necessarily utilize goals with implicit values and emotions, although not necessarily the same values and emotions that humans exhibit.

14   A variety of philosophical issues will emerge. Are computers thinking, or are they just calculating? Conversely, are human beings thinking, or are they just calculating? The human brain presumably follows the laws of physics, so it must be a machine, albeit a very complex one. Is there an inherent difference between human thinking and machine thinking? To pose the question another way, once computers are as complex as the human brain, and can match the human brain in subtlety and complexity of thought, are we to consider them conscious? This is a difficult question even to pose, and some philosophers believe it is not a meaningful question; others believe it is the only meaningful question in philosophy. This question actually goes back to Plato's time, but with the emergence of machines that genuinely appear to possess volition and emotion, the issue will become increasingly compelling.

15   For example, if a person scans his brain through a noninvasive scanning technology of the twenty-first century (such as an advanced magnetic resonance imaging), and downloads his mind to his personal computer, is the "person" who emerges in the machine the same consciousness as the person who was scanned? That "person" may convincingly implore you that "he" grew up in Brooklyn, went to college in Massachusetts, walked into a scanner here, and woke up in the machine there. The original person who was scanned, on the other hand, will acknowledge that the person in the machine does indeed appear to share his history, knowledge, memory, and personality, but is otherwise an impostor, a different person.

16   Even if we limit our discussion to computers that are not directly derived from a particular human brain, they will increasingly appear to have their own personalities, evidencing reactions that we can only label as emotions and articulating their own goals and purposes. They will appear to have their own free will. They will claim to have spiritual experiences. And people—those still using carbon-based neurons or otherwise—will believe them.

17   One often reads predictions of the next several decades discussing a variety of demographic, economic, and political trends that largely ignore the revolutionary impact of machines with their own opinions and agendas. Yet we need to reflect on the implications of the gradual, yet inevitable, emergence of true competition to the full range of human thought in order to comprehend the world that lies ahead. ◆◆

NOTES

1. For an excellent overview and technical details on neural-network pattern recognition, see the "Neural Network Frequently Asked Questions" Web site, edited by W. S. Sarle, at <ftp://ftp.sas.com/pup/neural/FAQ.html>. In addition, an article by Charles Arthur, "Computers Learn to See and Smell Us," from *Independent*, January 16, 1996, describes the ability of neural nets to differentiate between unique characteristics.

2. As will be discussed . . . , destructive scanning will be feasible early in the twenty-first century. Noninvasive scanning with sufficient resolution and bandwidth will take longer but will be feasible by the end of the first half of the twenty-first century.

COULD THIS PIG SAVE YOUR LIFE?*

Sheryl Gay Stolberg

Sheryl Gay Stolberg often writes about medicine and health policies. In this article she describes how pig-to-human transplants may soon save thousands of lives a year, make lots of money for the technique's developers, and raise a host of medical and ethical problems. What is your reaction?

1   In an unmarked warehouse in the middle of a wheat field in central Ohio, a hulking 300-pound pig lies on her back, her legs tethered to a crude iron gurney in a bare, well-lighted room. The animal has been sedated into a light state of sleep, and the pale pink expanse of her belly rises and falls rhythmically with each breath. A young man in green hospital garb has just sliced a six-inch incision between the sow's nipples; now he pokes around her innards with latex-gloved hands.

2   The pig on the table is pregnant. The young man, a veterinary technician named Bruce Close, is about to remove her newly fertilized eggs. At 26, Close is an old hand at pig surgery; he has performed this operation more than 600 times in the two years he has been employed by Nextran, the Princeton, N.J., biotechnology company that runs this warehouse as a breeding center. This, however, is no ordinary pig farm. For the past decade, Nextran has been locked in a high-stakes race to build the perfect pig: an animal with human genes, whose organs can be transplanted into people. In the medical lexicon, this is known as xeno-transplantation, and it has been an elusive dream of scientists for nearly 100 years.

3   Today, despite fears that pig-to-human transplants could unleash a deadly new virus, the dream is closer than ever to reality. In August, a long-awaited safety study conducted by Nextran's chief competitor, Imutran Ltd., of Cambridge, England, found no evidence of active infection in 160 people who had

---

New York Times Magazine, October 3, 1999, pp. 46–51.

been treated with pig tissue for a variety of conditions. The findings come as the companies are laying the groundwork to begin testing transplanted organs in people. Sometime within the next few years, and possibly as soon as the end of the next year, either the British or the Americans will grab the brass ring: approval from a regulatory agency, either the United States Food and Drug Administration or its equivalent in Britain, to perform the world's first animal-to-human transplant using a heart or a kidney from a genetically engineered pig.

4   Nobody expects cross-species transplants to be successful overnight. But with time, xenotransplantation could solve the most pressing crisis in medicine—the organ shortage. It could also make the companies very rich. Unlike human organs, which are donated, pig organs will be sold, and in a climate in which demand far outstrips supply, the seller will name the price. By greatly expanding the donor pool, pigs could make transplants possible for tens of thousands of people who, because of the current rationing system, never even make the list, not to mention those in some Asian nations, where taking organs from the dead is culturally taboo. Imagine a therapy as revolutionary as penicillin and as lucrative as Viagra rolled into one.

5   In Ohio, Bruce Close is working toward that day. Moving quickly and in silence, he tears at layers of pig fat until he can feel the pig's uterus. Gently, he extracts the slippery pink-and-purple mass, palpating it until his fingers reach a cluster of 10 blood-rich pustules—"the ovulation points." Each contains a single egg so recently joined with a sperm, through artificial insemination, that it has not yet divided from one cell into two. This is the optimal moment for creating "transgenic" piglets—animals that, at least in a genetic sense, look ever so slightly like people.

6   It is a bizarre, almost creepy sight, this big, fat pig upside down on an operating table, her head dangling backward over a bucket in case she vomits, her insides splayed out on a blue-paper surgical drape as a scientist rearranges the DNA of her unborn young. In a moment, the animal's eggs will be flushed out of the ovaries, collected in a tiny vial and smeared onto a glass slide; then a "microinjectionist" will examine them under a high-powered microscope and, with a needle finer than a strand of hair, insert a single human gene into each.

7   Later this afternoon, Close will return to the operating room to implant the growing embryos into a foster mother sow. In roughly 114 days, if all goes as Nextran hopes, she will deliver a litter that includes at least one transgenic piglet. Yet if Close sees anything Frankensteinian in this, he does not admit it. "What I'm doing right now," he says, "may someday save people's lives."

8   Across the Atlantic Ocean, at an undisclosed location in the English countryside, Imutran is running its own transgenic pig farm. Like Nextran, which was purchased several years ago by Baxter International, one of the world's largest medical-products manufacturers, Imutran is owned by a drug industry powerhouse, the Swiss-based Novartis Pharma AG, a company with three times the annual revenue and nearly seven times the research budget that Baxter has. While Nextran has been testing its pig hearts and kidneys in baboons, Imutran has been running tests in monkeys and baboons, and reporting longer survival

times. Like Nextran, Imutran is facing mounting criticism as it moves closer to testing its organs in people.

9   Animal rights advocates, predictably, lament the fate of the poor pigs that will be used as spare-part factories, a change the companies shrug off by pointing to refrigerators stuffed with bacon and pork chops. What they cannot shrug off, however, are the very real safety concerns. The Campaign for Responsible Transplantation, a coalition of scientists and public-health professionals, has asked for a ban on cross-species transplant research. And one prominent xenotransplant expert, Dr. Fritz Bach, of Harvard University, who is a paid consultant to Novartis, has called for a national commission to study the risks.

10   And so the companies are proceeding quietly, insisting that there is no rush to the clinic. "I don't believe that there is a race in the sense of, 'Oh, let's be first,'" says David White, Imutran's chief scientist. Says John S. Logan, Nextran's scientific director, "What we all want to be is the first to be *successful.*"

11   But there is a race, and in science, as in life, being first counts. "Clearly," says Jeffrey L. Platt, a transplant immunologist at the Mayo Clinic, in Rochester, Minn., "there is a competition between the two companies to enter the clinical arena." The first "whole organ" xenotransplant will attract intense press coverage, giving whoever conducts it free publicity, not to mention a spot in the medical history books. And if being first means earning the confidence of regulators and the public, then being first may well be tantamount to being successful.

12   Platt, for one, says that if xenotransplants could be made as safe and effective as human transplants, they would replace them. "Metaphorically speaking," he says, "it will be like the automobile repair industry. Nobody makes much effort to rebuild parts, because it is cheaper and better for your car to have a brand-new part."

13   If it sounds like science pushing itself to the edge of science fiction, it is. And like all good science-fiction stories, this one has the potential to end in disaster.

◆◆◆◆

14   At a time when biological tinkering has invaded every aspect of modern life, the sight of swine with human DNA should probably not seem alarming. Still, it is difficult to look at Nextran's pigs without wondering if there is an element of hubris to Logan's work, if porcine-people aren't better left to Greek mythology, or at least George Orwell, than to modern medicine. Clearly, in 1999, some pigs really are more equal than others.

15   Harold Vanderpool, a medical ethicist at the University of Texas Medical Branch, in Galveston, has a term for the visceral reaction these pigs evoke. "I call it 'the gag factor,'" he says. "We are thinking across a barrier that should never be crossed." And in point of fact, there may be very good reason—the viruses—it should not be. Pigs have become the animal of choice in xenotransplant research for a variety of reasons. They are plentiful, and they breed easily. They are physiologically similar enough to humans. And pigs and people have lived side by side, in relative health and harmony, for centuries. Virologists say most disease-causing germs can be eliminated through careful selection and breeding. But over the past two years, they have focused their attention on one obscure organism that cannot

be bred out, the porcine endogenous retrovirus, abbreviated in the medical literature as PERV.

16   Of all viruses, retroviruses are the most feared. They integrate their genetic code into the cells they infect, which means they multiply along with the cells. Retroviruses last for life. They are typically spread through blood or sexual contact, and they can lurk in the body for years, even decades, before causing any symptoms. "It's like a ghost virus, a stealth virus," says Jonathan S. Allan, a virologist at the Southwest Foundation for Biomedical Research, in San Antonio. "Once it splices itself into the host genome, it is virtually impossible to get it back out."

17   If this scenario sounds familiar, it's because over the past two decades, another retrovirus, H.I.V., believed to have originated in apes, has cut a devastating swath around the world. Most scientists, Allan included, do not believe that xenotransplants will unleash the next AIDS epidemic. But no one, not even the companies, argues that the transplants will be risk-free. While there is thus far no evidence that PERV makes people sick, it can infect human cells in the test tube. And some experts theorize that the virus could mutate into a deadly form, as H.I.V. did, and then spread through sexual contact, infecting untold numbers before causing any symptoms. While the recent Imutran study is a comfort, it looked at only 160 patients, who had been treated in hospitals around the world and were later tracked down by Novartis. What will happen when people are getting xenotransplants by the tens of thousands?

18   The danger may not be limited to PERV. In January 1997, a pig farmer in Ipoh, a Malaysian village about 200 miles north of Kuala Lampur, became ill with what appeared to be encephalitis. The following year, 258 Malaysian pig farmers became sick; 101 of them died. It took until March of this year for the Centers for Disease Control and Prevention to identify the cause: a brand-new virus named Nipah.

19   This is a point that Allan, who serves on a panel of scientific experts convened by the Food and Drug Administration to plan for its first xenotransplant clinical trial, has made repeatedly. For all the focus on PERV, he says, there may be other viruses, about which much less is known, that in the end will pose a greater danger to the public health. To justify any human experiment, the scientists conducting it must show that the benefits to the patient outweigh the risk. But xenotransplants defy that calculation: the patient benefits while society takes the risk. "The individual," Allan warns, "can sign a consent form and say, 'I'll take the risk because I'm going to die anyway.' But that person is signing a consent form for the whole population, the whole human race."

20   Still, there are good reasons to proceed. More than 62,000 Americans are now waiting to receive donated hearts, lungs, livers, kidneys and pancreases, according to the United Network for Organ Sharing. A new name is added to the list every 16 minutes, and every day 11 people die waiting. Increasing donations will not solve the problem; surgeons need young, healthy organs for transplants, so even if every dead person donated, there would still not be enough.

21   There is another reason, of course: money. In 1996, Salomon Brothers predicted that the global market for transgenic organs could reach $6 billion by the year 2010, a figure that explains why big pharmaceutical companies are involved.

Novartis manufactures cyclosporine, an anti-rejection drug; the market for it would skyrocket if xenotransplants became common. Baxter's interest is self-preservation; it makes dialysis machines, which would be relegated to the medical junk heap if people with failing kidneys were given pig organs instead.

22   Hospitals and surgeons stand to gain as well. Transplants are expensive, and they make a good living for those who perform them. Three years ago, the Institute of Medicine calculated that if animal organs made it possible to offer a transplant to everyone in the United States who needed one, annual expenditures would rise to $20.3 billion, from $2.9 billion. Already, the Mayo Clinic has entered into what its director of heart and lung transplantation, Dr. Christopher McGregor, calls a "strategic alliance" with Nextran. McGregor is busy testing pig hearts in baboons, and the company has built a state-of-the-art breeding facility not far from the clinic so Mayo doctors can have a ready supply of pigs in the event that xenotransplantation takes off.

23   While the medical world is gearing up, so, too, is the Government. Donna E. Shalala, the Secretary of Health and Human Services, will soon appoint a special committee to advise her on medical, ethical and social issues surrounding xenotransplants. As the infrastructure grows, so does critics' frustration. The Campaign for Responsible Transplantation, the group pressing for a research ban, has lately been threatening to sue Shalala if she does not respond to its petition. "The prospect of a global health pandemic doesn't seem to be concerning anybody," warns Alix Fano, the campaign's director. "And the people that are voicing their concerns are either being silenced or ignored." ◆◆

BETTER LIVING THROUGH GENETICS*

James Wood

James Wood wrote this article for Liberty *magazine. What dangers to personal liberty does Wood see in the development of technology?*

1   Utopia beckons. Its promises are already beginning to come to fruition.

2   Genetic analysis during in vitro ("test tube") fertilization enables couples to eliminate sickle cell anemia and a host of other diseases from their offspring. Gene therapy experiments have reversed brain deterioration in aged monkeys and show great promise for humans with Alzheimer's disease. The unprecedented convenience of Internet shopping has caused some shoppers to go overboard, at great risk to their credit standing.

3   But we should be neither worried nor judgmental: addiction to binge shopping, as well as to sex or gambling, is (according to many scientists) linked to genes, rather than to weakness of character. A little more research, and we will

---

*Liberty, April 2000, pp. 23, 25–28.

know how to tweak the genetic makeup to cure or avoid such problems. On other fronts, we are informed that Global Positioning Satellite technology will enable insurance companies to refine premiums to reflect when, how much, where, and under what circumstances each insured's car is driven. Sophisticated analyses of Internet messages and computer hard drives enable police to catch criminals who thought they were safely anonymous. Thus the miracles of genetic and cybernetic technology are said to be carrying us toward a crime-free, disease-free, ultra-convenient, well-regulated utopia.

4   The people I've drawn on for coherent descriptions of the coming utopia are responsible academics, often holding directorships or chaired positions, and specialist journalists. They include, among others, Nicholas Negroponte at MIT, Gregory Stock at UCLA, Kevin Kelly, formerly executive editor of *Wired* magazine, and Lee Silver at Princeton. These people predict a swift and radical shift into a new global culture, a shift which goes beyond biological evolution. Though varying in some particulars, their descriptions of the world to come show remarkable commonality. These visions ensue from careful consideration of technological advances in genetics and cybernetics, advances commonly reported in major newspapers. Perhaps most telling is the fact that even forceful critics of the emerging utopia—Jeremy Rifkin and Bryan Appleyard, for example—accept most of the assumptions on which these predictions are based.

5   The most fundamental new technologies will control the genes which determine the nature of humans and all other living organisms. "Bad genes" can be detected and eliminated, and "good genes" can be fostered. Current practices of combining genes from different sorts of organisms will be expanded to create entirely new species and to modify humans. In the new utopia, humans and computers will combine into a global system to reverse planetary warming, prevent famine in sub-Saharan Africa, or resolve ethnic clashes in the Balkans.

6   Presumably, such social and economic problems will be too complex for human direction and too important to be left to short-sighted, self-interested human deliberation in the marketplace of ideas. Air traffic control and management of electric power grids, already slipping beyond human control, are trivial challenges compared with integrating a global economy while preserving a livable environment. The Internet is a crude prototype of this entity's nervous system. Individual humans will function much as cells in the human body do now. We humans will scarcely understand bits of what's going on, much less control anything of importance. For this global organism, Gregory Stock coined the useful, if somewhat melodramatic, term "Metaman." Kevin Kelly parallels Stock with his own notion of a "whole world wired into a human/machine mind."

7   Will we face overpowering incentives to abandon individual autonomy and meld into Metaman? Kelly, for one, thinks so; he suggests that our chief psychological task in the coming century will be "letting go with dignity." We may want to explore our situation and options more fully before "letting go."

8   It's easy either to dismiss the projected future as science fiction or to accept it as inevitable. But it is neither fiction nor inevitable. It is a genuine threat to our autonomy as humans, grounded in the eugenics implicit in genetic research, the narrowing views of what is acceptably normal for both humans and cultures, and the erosion of personal identity and moral responsibility.

GENETIC RESEARCH AND EUGENICS

9   The vast sums spent on basic research in human genetics, most evident in the project to map the human genome, are based on an underlying assumption of genetic determinism: the significant characteristics of a person, both mental and physical, are determined by that person's genetic makeup. Genetic testing can detect potential defects. The meaning of "defect" will become very elastic: today it usually refers to catastrophic congenital diseases, but in the future it is liable to include wrong eye color or lack of athletic prowess.

10   To prevent children from having precisely predictable defects, parents will have the current options of embryo selection during in vitro fertilization (IVF) procedures or abortion when defects are detected after normal conception. In the emerging utopia they will add far more powerful options for actually altering genes in early-stage embryos to achieve what biotechnologist Lee Silver calls "designer children." Alterations in germ-line cells will determine traits to be carried down through generation after generation.

11   Such genetic engineering in pursuit of improved humans *is* eugenics. It doesn't really matter much for purposes of definition whether it's market-driven or government-ordered. Genetic engineering does seem a more humane procedure than genocide to remove "impurities" and to "improve" the ethnic group or society. It is also a much more precise means for controlling human evolution. The prospect of changing—"designing"—the genetic makeup of human embryos to control evolution did raise enough ethical issues to cause a meeting of concerned scientists at UCLA in 1998. As reported in *The New York Times* (March 20, 1998), several scientists present expected to see the process in use within twenty years, at least by parents who can afford it.

12   Would ready availability of the technology place irresistible pressure on parents-to-be to use genetic testing and act on the results? Or to put it differently, would substantial portions of the population find themselves participating in eugenics, even without storm troopers at the door? Several reasons suggest that the answer is yes. Lee Silver provides the most direct argument: some parents will use these procedures, including genetic modification in IVF, to give their offspring advantages, and other parents will have to follow suit in order to have kids who will be competitive.

13   I have yet to read an informed author who disagrees with Silver's line of reasoning here. The strength of parental ambition is illustrated by past examples, as from northern India in which use of amniocentesis had the unfortunate side effect of leading to abortion of large numbers of embryos whose only defect was that they were female. The greatest pressure will be on parents who find themselves in a dilemma: revolted by the notion of interfering in natural evolution but driven by responsibility to give their offspring a competitive edge in, for instance, memory capacity, stature, or good looks.

14   Another factor driving parents to practice eugenic control begins with the inclination of insurance companies and employers to discriminate against those who may be genetically risky. In a free market, who can object to the insurance company which refuses health insurance to a family in which one member has been diagnosed with Huntington's disease? Who can blame the oil refinery

manager who declines to invest time and money training a highly effective engineer because her family history shows several emotionally unstable individuals? As genetic testing of individuals becomes more refined, such discrimination should become more rational. Inaccurate predictions for individuals will continue, however, as many decisions are made on the basis of statistical probability that certain combinations of gene-forms will produce certain characteristics. The point is that parents-to-be will feel compelled to have embryos tested—and if necessary, "corrected"—in order to make sure their progeny do not face these sorts of discrimination.

15   Defensive eugenics goes beyond merely avoiding discrimination in the marketplace. If a couple insists on having a child without use of readily available genetic testing, then society can hold them responsible for any ensuing problems with that child, whether it's mild social maladjustment or catastrophic illness. What once would have been cause for sympathy and financial support from society now becomes cause for social stigma.

16   Governments will be sorely tempted by the benefits of applying genetics. Genetic determinism provides a very attractive theoretical basis to planners for solving such problems as homelessness, poverty, and crime: mandatory testing can isolate the genetic predispositions toward such sad states, and then the state can terminate at least the capacity of such individuals to reproduce. Involuntary sterilization is rather coercive! If this seems implausibly extreme, reflect on the fact that by 1931 some thirty states had sterilization laws, many of which were being actively applied to reduce undesirable classes. Then Hitler gave eugenics a bad name. Memories pale. Now the miracles promised by genetic research reinforce a growing faith in genetic determinism, laying the groundwork for a new eugenics.

A NARROWER RANGE OF ACCEPTABLE NORMALCY

17   How much deviation from an ideal norm will be acceptable in utopia? Less than we might initially expect. Medicine's job is to cure diseases. Obesity, alcoholism, and clinical depression are diseases; at least, some people consider some of these to be diseases. At the minimum, the propensities toward such defects are found in the genes, so corrections at that level will be sought. Most people consider cynicism and pessimism to be less conducive to a cheerful life than optimism; so presumably these qualities will be identified as defects in want of correction through genetic engineering. Rifkin gives short stature as one current example of the shift from acceptable personal characteristic to an "illness" that doctors can now treat with hormones. How far will the trend go to purge departures from a social concept of "normal"?

18   The philosopher Philip Kitcher, certainly one of the more conservative writers on the subject, provides a hypothetical depiction of the scene a couple of generations hence: genetic medicine, practiced in a culture of "reproductive responsibility," has virtually eliminated such congenital defects as Tay-Sachs and Down's syndrome, and has gone on to eliminate obesity and homosexuality; now the issue is whether to eliminate left-handedness.

19   A subtler and often unjust constriction on acceptable normalcy will stem from increasing reliance by parents, physicians and officials on statistical probabilities.

At the present time, to avoid congenital illnesses genetics relies on selection from a couple's embryos in vitro, and is based on equations of single defective genes with virtual certainty of specific diseases, such as Tay-Sachs. It is unlikely, however, that the cause of, say, colon cancer or clinical depression will be confidently linked to a single defective gene. Rather, the geneticist will be looking at complicated patterns of causation involving several genes and environmental factors. The solution will almost certainly be to link propensities toward specific defects to combinations of specific gene-forms on the basis of statistical probability, e.g., someone with such and such combination of genes has an 83% probability of exhibiting violent criminal behavior. Lack of complete reliability may seem a small price to pay for preventing cancer deaths, suicidal depressives, and serial killers.

20   But there is a problem. We must wonder about early-stage embryos whose suspect genetic combination would condemn them, by a shake of the statistical dice, to nonexistence even though these particular individuals would have grown up innocent of the feared defect. In reflecting on an actual instance from the mid-1970s, Kitcher wonders how many mothers did the "responsible" thing and aborted male embryos which were found, through amniocentesis, to carry an extra Y chromosome. It was then believed that such offspring were highly likely to become violent criminals. Later, of course, this belief was found to stem from an error in statistical inference.

21   As the technology improves, parents and doctors will be able conveniently to achieve relatively trivial, even cosmetic, results. Preventing serial killers may justify some gambling on statistical probability and some narrowing of the human genetic pool. Preventing hyperactive or introverted children does not justify that. But both advocates and critics of the new genetic engineering agree that if the technology is available some parents will use it and others will feel compelled to follow suit, until the eschewed characteristic, whether shyness or shortness, is banished from the range of acceptable normalcy.

22   Thus we have an irony. The promise of genetic engineering is to give parents greater choice in designing their offspring. Actually, in the long run, economic and social pressures to use a ready technology will reduce parents' options to a narrower range of conformity.

◆◆◆◆

TECHNOLOGY AND PERSONAL IDENTITY

23 The notion that each of us is a complexly integrated being with a unique identity is under attack, partly in the form of a double-barreled reductionism. One type of reductionism views each human as essentially an information-processing system, arguing that we differ from other information-processing systems, whether organic, social, or mechanical, only in our brain's greater capacity to contain and internally arrange information. This capacity marks our superiority over the amoeba and the orangutan—and our presumed future inferiority to new generations of supercomputers. The other type of reductionism splinters the individual into a conglomerate of discrete characteristics, each of which can be defined by DNA analysis and be subjected to manipulation by genetic engineering. As the

technology becomes more reliable, transgenic engineering could combine genes from other species into human embryonic cells, thus "improving" the human species, at least for those individuals and their progeny. After all, in this view, there is nothing significantly unique about humans, either as individuals or as a species.

◆◆◆◆

24   Intuitively, we reject this ultimate attack on our identities as autonomous individuals. We insist that morality exists. Genetic determinists have a ready answer: A central theory of evolutionary psychology tells us that "morality" is what has over time proven to be the most effectual means for genes to assure their continued survival generation after generation. Philosophy, religion, serious literature, and political idealism, all are merely subterfuges to conceal a genetic determinism which can theoretically be described with mathematical precision. Francis Crick . . . warns, "The development of biology is going to destroy to some extent our traditional grounds for ethical beliefs, and it is not easy to see what to put in their place."

25   Substitution of genetic determinism for free will has unpleasant consequences beyond demeaning the human spirit. The notion that an individual is responsible for his or her actions—free will—is a central assumption in our legal and moral systems. But in utopia individuals can hardly be held responsible for their genes or for actions deterministically flowing from those genes. Nevertheless, society will still have to protect itself from criminals. The only practical solution, until defects are purged from the species, is mandatory genetic testing and preemptive action, including preventive incarceration. Recall that many of the links between genes and criminal traits are based on statistical probabilities. The notion of political agitation as a sign of criminal defect opens still further possibilities for controlling large societies in the name of the greater good. Some readers may feel secure that preemptive incarceration on the basis of a likelihood, or even a possibility of criminal behavior, is impossible in America. They should recall the preventive detention in internment camps for Japanese-Americans during World War II.

26   In sum, the new technologies invite conceptualizing future humans as information-processing systems genetically pre-set to fit narrowly defined ranges of acceptable normalcy. Decisions of any importance will be made, as for example they are now in an increasing number of major investment houses, by machine intelligences with minor roles for human input. Denied significantly unique identity and free will, the individual can appropriately be subordinated to the welfare of the global society, to Metaman. Those few hardy souls who resist utopia will, like recalcitrant cultures, be banished to the fringes; they will cease to matter.

◆◆◆◆

27   Acceptance of the coming utopia takes place incrementally and on several fronts at once. So the critic must select which aspects to accept and which to oppose. One can, for example, agitate against manipulation of the human germ cells which control evolution, while accepting use of transgenic animals to produce medicines for human use. Or one can oppose making cybernetic technology central in public education, while accepting the Internet as one communication tool.

28   Almost every one of the myriad incremental steps toward utopia appeals to some value such as competitive advantage or convenience. Unintended, long-term, or more fundamental effects are often ignored. Thus, those who feel ethically responsible to oppose some technological innovation are challenged to persuade others to see beyond the temptations of short-term appeals.

29   The rhetorician Richard Weaver advised that the strongest foundations for arguments are to be found in what he called first principles. For critics of utopia these would be fundamental assumptions, such as the need to preserve moral autonomy and to value the identity of humans as both individuals and species. The raw material from which to dialectically refine first principles is found in the humanities—history, serious literature, philosophy—not in the data of science. ◆◆

C. WHAT MIGHT AFFECT THE FUTURE OF THE PLANET?

QUESTIONS TO CONSIDER BEFORE YOU READ

What do you see as some of the most pressing environmental issues today? Why? If you could do one thing to make the environment better, what would it be? On the basis of your own experiences, do you think the health of the planet is better or worse now than five years ago? Why?

THE FUTURE OF LIFE*

Edward O. Wilson

The following excerpts are taken from Edward O. Wilson's book The Future of Life. *Wilson, a well-known authority on science and conservation, is a professor at Harvard University. According to Wilson, the exigency to save the world from human intervention is imminent. But what are the ethics involved in making the tough choices that are necessary for accomplishing this all-important goal?*

1   The natural world in the year 2001 is everywhere disappearing before our eyes—cut to pieces, mowed down, plowed under, gobbled up, replaced by human artifacts. . . .

2   Now, more than six billion people fill the world. The great majority are very poor; nearly one billion exist on the edge of starvation. All are struggling to raise the quality of their lives any way they can. That unfortunately includes the conversion of the surviving remnants of the natural environment. Half of the great tropical forests have been cleared. The last frontiers of the world are effectively

---

*Edward O. Wilson, *The Future of Life* (New York: Knopf, 2002), pp. xxii–xxiii, 151–152, 160–164, 189.

gone. Species of plants and animals are disappearing a hundred or more times faster than before the coming of humanity, and as many as half may be gone by the end of this century. An Armageddon is approaching at the beginning of the third millennium. But it is not the cosmic war and fiery collapse of mankind foretold in sacred scripture. It is the wreckage of the planet by an exuberantly plentiful and ingenious humanity.

3   The race is now on between the technoscientific forces that are destroying the living environment and those that can be harnessed to save it. We are inside a bottleneck of overpopulation and wasteful consumption. If the race is won, humanity can emerge in far better condition than when it entered, and with most of the diversity of life still intact.

4   The situation is desperate—but there are encouraging signs that the race can be won. Population growth has slowed, and, if the present trajectory holds, is likely to peak between eight and ten billion people by century's end. That many people, experts tell us, can be accommodated with a decent standard of living, but just barely: the amount of arable land and water available per person, globally, is already declining. In solving the problem, other experts tell us, it should also be possible to shelter most of the vulnerable plant and animal species.

5   In order to pass through the bottleneck, a global land ethic is urgently needed. Not just any land ethic that might happen to enjoy agreeable sentiment, but one based on the best understanding of ourselves and the world around us that science and technology can provide. Surely the rest of life matters. Surely our stewardship is its only hope. We will be wise to listen carefully to the heart, then act with rational intention and all the tools we can gather and bring to bear.

◆◆◆◆

6   And everyone has some kind of environmental ethic, even if it somehow makes a virtue of cutting the last ancient forests and damming the last wild rivers. Done, it is said, to grow the economy and save jobs. Done because we are running short of space and fuel. *Hey, listen, people come first!*—and most certainly before beach mice and louseworts. I recall vividly the conversation I had with a cab driver in Key West in 1968 when we touched on the Everglades burning to the north. Too bad, he said. The Everglades are a wonderful place. But wilderness always gives way to civilization, doesn't it? That is progress and the way of the world, and we can't do much about it.

7   Everyone is also an avowed environmentalist. No one says flatly, "To hell with nature." On the other hand, no one says, "Let's give it all back to nature." Rather, when invoking the social contract by which we all live, the typical people-first ethicist thinks about the environment short-term and the typical environmental ethicist thinks about it long-term. Both are sincere and have something true and important to say. The people-first thinker says we need to take a little cut here and there; the environmentalist says nature is dying the death of a thousand cuts. So how do we combine the best of short-term and long-term goals? Perhaps, despite decades of bitter philosophical dispute, an optimum mix of the goals might result in a consensus more satisfactory than either side thought possible from total victory alone. Down deep, I believe, no one wants

a total victory. The people-firster likes parks, and the environmentalist rides petroleum-powered vehicles to get there.

◆◆◆◆

8   During the past two decades, scientists and conservation professionals have put together a strategy aimed at the protection of most of the remaining eco-systems and species. Its key elements are the following:

9   ◆ Salvage immediately the world's hotspots, those habitats that are both at the greatest risk and shelter the largest concentrations of species found nowhere else. Among the most valuable hotspots on the land, for exam-ple, are the surviving remnants of rainforest in Hawaii, the West Indies, Ecuador, Atlantic Brazil, West Africa, Madagascar, the Philippines, Indo-Burma, and India, as well as the Mediterranean-climate scrublands of South Africa, southwestern Australia, and southern California. Twenty-five of these special ecosystems cover only 1.4 percent of Earth's land sur-face, about the same as Texas and Alaska combined. Yet they are the last remaining homes of an impressive 43.8 percent of all known species of vascular plants and 35.6 percent of the known mammals, birds, reptiles, and amphibians. The twenty-five hotspots have already been reduced 88 percent in area by clearing and development; some could be wiped out entirely within several decades by continued intrusion.

10   ◆ Keep intact the five remaining frontier forests, which are the last true wildernesses on the land and home to an additional large fraction of Earth's biological diversity. They are the rainforests of the combined Amazon Basin and the Guianas; the Congo block of Central Africa; New Guinea; the tem-perate conifer forests of Canada and Alaska combined; and the temperate conifer forests of Russia, Finland, and Scandinavia combined.

11   ◆ Cease all logging of old-growth forests everywhere. For every bit of this habitat lost or degraded, Earth pays a price in biodiversity. The cost is especially steep in tropical forests, and it is potentially catastrophic in the forested hotspots. At the same time, let secondary native forests recover. The time has come—rich opportunity shines forth—for the timber-extraction industry to shift to tree farming on already converted land. The cultivation of lumber and pulp should be conducted like the agribusiness it is, using high-quality, fast-growing species and strains for higher productivity and profit. To that end, it would be valuable to forge an international agreement, similar to the Montreal and Kyoto Protocols, that prohibits further destruction of old-growth forests and thereby pro-vides the timber-extraction economy with a level playing field.

12   ◆ Everywhere, not just in the hotspots and wildernesses, concentrate on the lakes and river systems, which are the most threatened ecosystems of all. Those in tropical and warm temperate regions in particular possess the highest ratio of endangered species to area of any kind of habitat.

13   ◆ Define precisely the marine hotspots of the world, and assign them the same action priority as for those on the land. Foremost are the coral reefs, which in their extremely high biological diversity rank as the rainforests

of the sea. More than half around the world—including, for example, those of the Maldives and parts of the Caribbean and Philippines—have been savaged variously by overharvesting and rising temperatures, and are in critical condition.

14 ◆ In order to render the conservation effort exact and cost-effective, complete the mapping of the world's biological diversity. Scientists have estimated that 10 percent or more of flowering plants, a majority of animals, and a huge majority of microorganisms remain undiscovered and unnamed, hence of unknown conservation status. As the map is filled in, it will evolve into a biological encyclopedia of value not only in conservation practice but also in science, industry, agriculture, and medicine. The expanded global biodiversity map will be the instrument that unites biology.

15 ◆ Using recent advances in mapping the planet's terrestrial, fresh-water, and marine ecosystems, ensure that the full range of the world's ecosystems are included in a global conservation strategy. The scope of conservation must embrace not only the habitats, such as tropical forests and coral reefs, that harbor the richest assemblages of species, but also the deserts and arctic tundras whose beautiful and austere inhabitants are no less unique expressions of life.

16 ◆ Make conservation profitable. Find ways to raise the income of those who live in and near the reserves. Give them a proprietary interest in the natural environment and engage them professionally in its protection. Help raise the productivity of land already converted to cropland and cattle ranches nearby, while tightening security around the reserves. Generate sources of revenue in the reserves themselves. Demonstrate to the governments, especially of developing countries, that ecotourism, bioprospecting, and (eventually) carbon credit trades of wild land can yield more income than logging and agriculture of the same land cleared and planted.

17 ◆ Use biodiversity more effectively to benefit the world economy as a whole. Broaden field research and laboratory biotechnology to develop new crops, livestock, cultivated food fish, farmed timber, pharmaceuticals, and bioremedial bacteria. Where genetically engineered crop strains prove nutritionally and environmentally safe upon careful research and regulation . . . they should be employed. In addition to feeding the hungry, they can help take the pressure off the wildlands and the biodiversity they contain.

18 ◆ Initiate restoration projects to increase the share of Earth allotted to nature. Today about 10 percent of the land surface is protected on paper. Even if rigorously conserved, this amount is not enough to save more than a modest fraction of wild species. Large numbers of plant and animal species are left with populations too small to persist. Every bit of space that can be added will pass more species through the bottleneck of overpopulation and development for the benefit of future generations. Eventually, and the sooner the better, a higher goal can and should be set.

At the risk of being called an extremist, which on this topic I freely admit I am, let me suggest 50 percent. Half the world for humanity, half for the rest of life, to create a planet both self-sustaining and pleasant.

19   ◆ Increase the capacity of zoos and botanical gardens to breed endangered species. Most are already working to fill that role. Prepare to clone species when all other preservation methods fail. Enlarge the existing seed and spore banks and create reserves of frozen embryos and tissue. But keep in mind that these methods are expensive and at best supplementary. Moreover, they are not feasible for the vast majority of species, especially the countless bacteria, archaeans, protistans, fungi, and insects and other invertebrates that make up the functioning base of the biosphere. And even if somehow, with enormous effort, all these species too could be stored artificially, it would be virtually impossible to reassemble them later into sustainably free-living ecosystems. The only secure way to save species, as well as the cheapest (and on the evidence the only sane way), is to preserve the natural ecosystems they now compose.

20   ◆ Support population planning. Help guide humanity everywhere to a smaller biomass, a lighter footstep, and a more secure and enjoyable future with biodiversity flourishing around it.

21   Earth is still productive enough and human ingenuity creative enough not only to feed the world now but also to raise the standard of living of the population projected to at least the middle of the twenty-first century. The great majority of ecosystems and species still surviving can also be protected. Of the two objectives, humanitarian and environmental, the latter is by far the cheaper, and the best bargain humanity has ever been offered. For global conservation, only one-thousandth of the current annual world domestic product, or $30 billion out of approximately $30 trillion, would accomplish most of the task. One key element, the protection and management of the world's existing natural reserves, could be financed by a one-cent-per-cup tax on coffee.

◆◆◆◆

22   The central problem of the new century, I have argued, is how to raise the poor to a decent standard of living worldwide while preserving as much of the rest of life as possible. Both the needy poor and vanishing biological diversity are concentrated in the developing countries. The poor, some 800 million of whom live without sanitation, clean water, and adequate food, have little chance to advance in a devastated environment. Conversely, the natural environments where most biodiversity hangs on cannot survive the press of land-hungry people with nowhere else to go.

23   I hope I have justified the conviction, shared by many thoughtful people from all walks of life, that the problem can be solved. Adequate resources exist. Those who control them have many reasons to achieve that goal, not least their own security. In the end, however, success or failure will come down to an ethical decision, one on which those now living will be defined and judged for all generations to come. I believe we will choose wisely. A civilization able to envision God and to embark on the colonization of space will surely find the way to save the integrity of this planet and the magnificent life it harbors. ◆◆

THE CHALLENGES WE FACE*

Jeffrey Kluger and Andrea Dorfman

Jeffrey Kluger and Andrea Dorfman write for Time *magazine. Here they write about the environmental issues discussed at the 2002 World Summit in Johannesburg, South Africa. What do you think is the best way to cure the ills that are harming our planet?*

1   For starters, let's be clear about what we mean by "saving the earth." The globe doesn't need to be saved by us, and we couldn't kill it if we tried. What we do need to save—and what we have done a fair job of bollixing up so far—is the earth as we like it, with its climate, air, water and biomass all in that destructible balance that best supports life as we have come to know it. Muck that up, and the planet will simply shake us off, as it's shaken off countless species before us. In the end, then, it's us we're trying to save—and while the job is doable, it won't be easy.

2   The 1992 Earth Summit in Rio de Janeiro was the last time world leaders assembled to look at how to heal the ailing environment. Now, 10 years later, Presidents and Prime Ministers are convening at the World Summit on Sustainable Development in Johannesburg next week to reassess the planet's condition and talk about where to go from here. In many ways, things haven't changed: the air is just as grimy in many places, the oceans just as stressed, and most treaties designed to do something about it lie in incomplete states of ratification or implementation. Yet we're oddly smarter than we were in Rio. If years of environmental false starts have taught us anything, it's that it's time to quit seeing the job of cleaning up the world as a zero-sum game between industrial progress on the one hand and a healthy planet on the other. The fact is, it's development—well-planned, well-executed sustainable development—that may be what saves our bacon before it's too late.

3   As the summiteers gather in Johannesburg, *Time* is looking ahead to what the unfolding century—a green century—could be like. In this special report, we will examine several avenues to a healthier future, including green industry, green architecture, green energy, green transportation and even a greener approach to wilderness preservation. All of them have been explored before, but never so urgently as now. What gives such endeavors their new credibility is the hope and notion of sustainable development, a concept that can be hard to implement but wonderfully simple to understand.

4   With 6.1 billion people relying on the resources of the same small planet, we're coming to realize that we're drawing from a finite account. The amount of crops, animals and other biomatter we extract from the earth each year exceeds what the planet can replace by an estimated 20%, meaning it takes 14.4 months to replenish what we use in 12—deficit spending of the worst kind. Sustainable development works to reverse that, to expand the resource base and adjust how we use it so we're living off biological interest without ever touching principal.

---

*Time, August 26, 2002, pp. A7+.

"The old environmental movement had a reputation of élitism," says Mark Mal-loch Brown, administrator of the United Nations Development Program (UNDP). "The key now is to put people first and the environment second, but also to re-member that when you exhaust resources, you destroy people." With that in mind, the summiteers will wrestle with a host of difficult issues that affect both people and the environment. Among them:

5   ◆ Population and Health: While the number of people on earth is still rising
           rapidly, especially in the developing countries of Asia, the good news is
           that the growth rate is slowing. World population increased 48% from
           1975 to 2000, compared with 64% from 1950 to 1975. As this gradual
           deceleration continues, the population is expected to level off eventually,
           perhaps at 11 billion sometime in the last half of this century.

6   Economic-development and family-planning programs have helped
           slow the tide of people, but in some places, population growth is moder-
           ating for all the wrong reasons. In the poorest parts of the world, most
           notably Africa, infectious diseases such as AIDS, malaria, cholera and
           tuberculosis are having a Malthusian effect. Rural-land degradation is
           pushing people into cities, where crowded, polluted living conditions
           create the perfect breeding grounds for sickness. Worldwide, at least
           68 million are expected to die of AIDS by 2020, including 55 million in
           sub-Saharan Africa. While any factor that eases population pressures may
           help the environment, the situation would be far less tragic if rich nations
           did more to help the developing world reduce birth rates and slow the
           spread of disease.

7   Efforts to provide greater access to family planning and health care
           have proved effective. Though women in the poorest countries still have
           the most children, their collective fertility rate is 50% lower than it was in
           1969 and is expected to decline more by 2050. Other programs targeted at
           women include basic education and job training. Educated mothers not
           only have a stepladder out of poverty, but they also choose to have fewer
           babies.

8   Rapid development will require good health care for the young since
           there are more than 1 billion people ages 15 to 24. Getting programs in
           place to keep this youth bubble healthy could make it the most produc-
           tive generation ever conceived. Says Thoraya Obaid, executive director of
           the U.N. Population Fund: "It's a window of opportunity to build the
           economy and prepare for the future."

9   ◆ Food: Though it's not always easy to see it from the well-fed West, up to a
           third of the world is in danger of starving. Two billion people lack reliable
           access to safe, nutritious food, and 800 million of them—including
           300 million children—are chronically malnourished.

10   Agricultural policies now in place define the very idea of unsustain-
           able development. Just 15 cash crops such as corn, wheat and rice pro-
           vide 90% of the world's food, but planting and replanting the same crops
           strips fields of nutrients and makes them more vulnerable to pests.

Slash-and-burn planting techniques and overreliance on pesticides further degrade the soil.

11   Solving the problem is difficult, mostly because of the ferocious debate over how to do it. Biotech partisans say the answer lies in genetically modified crops—foods engineered for vitamins, yield and robust growth. Environmentalists worry that fooling about with genes is a recipe for Frankensteinian disaster. There is no reason, however, that both camps can't make a contribution.

12   Better crop rotation and irrigation can help protect fields from exhaustion and erosion. Old-fashioned cross-breeding can yield plant strains that are heartier and more pest-resistant. But in a world that needs action fast, genetic engineering must still have a role—provided it produces suitable crops. Increasingly, those crops are being created not just by giant biotech firms but also by home-grown groups that know best what local consumers need.

13   The National Agricultural Research Organization of Uganda has developed corn varieties that are more resistant to disease and thrive in soil that is poor in nitrogen. Agronomists in Kenya are developing a sweet potato that wards off viruses. Also in the works are drought-tolerant, disease-defeating and vitamin-fortified forms of such crops as sorghum and cassava—hardly staples in the West, but essentials elsewhere in the world. The key, explains economist Jeffrey Sachs, head of Columbia University's Earth Institute, is not to dictate food policy from the West but to help the developing world build its own biotech infrastructure so it can produce the things it needs the most. "We can't presume that our technologies will bail out poor people in Malawi," he says. "They need their own improved varieties of sorghum and millet, not our genetically improved varieties of wheat and soybeans."

14 ◆ Water: For a world that is 70% water, things are drying up fast. Only 2.5% of water is fresh, and only a fraction of that is accessible. Meanwhile, each of us requires about 50 quarts per day for drinking, bathing, cooking and other basic needs. At present, 1.1 billion people lack access to clean drinking water and more than 2.4 billion lack adequate sanitation. "Unless we take swift and decisive action," says U.N. Secretary-General Kofi Annan, "by 2025, two-thirds of the world's population may be living in countries that face serious water shortages."

15   The answer is to get smart about how we use water. Agriculture accounts for two-thirds of the fresh water consumed. A report prepared for the summit thus endorses the "more crop per drop" approach, which calls for more efficient irrigation techniques, planting of drought- and salt-tolerant crop varieties that require less water and better monitoring of growing conditions, such as soil humidity levels. Improving water-delivery systems would also help, reducing the amount that is lost en route to the people who use it.

16   One program winning quick support is dubbed WASH—for Water, Sanitation and Hygiene for All—a global effort that aims to provide water

services and hygiene training to everyone who lacks them by 2015. Already, the U.N., 28 governments and many nongovernmental organizations (NGOs) have signed on.

17 ◆ Energy and Climate: In the U.S., people think of rural electrification as a long-ago legacy of the New Deal. In many parts of the world, it hasn't even happened yet. About 2.5 billion people have no access to modern energy services, and the power demands of developing economies are expected to grow 2.5% per year. But if those demands are met by burning fossil fuels such as oil, coal and gas, more and more carbon dioxide and other greenhouse gases will hit the atmosphere. That, scientists tell us, will promote global warming, which could lead to rising seas, fiercer storms, severe droughts and other climatic disruptions.

18   Of more immediate concern is the heavy air pollution caused in many places by combustion of wood and fossil fuels. A new U.N. Environment Program report warns of the effects of a haze across all southern Asia. Dubbed "Asian brown cloud" and estimated to be 2 miles thick, it may be responsible for hundreds of thousands of deaths a year from respiratory diseases.

19   The better way to meet the world's energy needs is to develop cheaper, cleaner sources. Pre-Johannesburg proposals call for eliminating taxation and pricing systems that encourage oil use and replacing them with policies that provide incentives for alternative energy. In India there has been a boom in wind power because the government has made it easier for entrepreneurs to get their hands on the necessary technology and has then required the national power grid to purchase the juice that wind systems produce.

20   Other technologies can work their own little miracles. Micro-hydroelectric plants are already operating in numerous nations, including Kenya, Sri Lanka and Nepal. The systems divert water from streams and rivers and use it to run turbines without complex dams or catchment areas. Each plant can produce as much as 200 kilowatts—enough to electrify 200 to 500 homes and businesses—and lasts 20 years. One plant in Kenya was built by 200 villagers, all of whom own shares in the cooperative that sells the power.

21   The Global Village Energy Partnership, which involves the World Bank, the UNDP and various donors, wants to provide energy to 300 million people, as well as schools, hospitals and clinics in 50,000 communities worldwide over 10 years. The key will be to match the right energy source to the right users. For example, solar panels that convert sunlight into electricity might be cost-effective in remote areas, while extending the power grid might be better in Third World cities.

22 ◆ Biodiversity: More than 11,000 species of animals and plants are known to be threatened with extinction, about a third of all coral reefs are expected to vanish in the next 30 years and about 36 million acres of forest are being razed annually. In his new book, *The Future of Life,* Harvard

biologist Edward O. Wilson writes of his worry that unless we change our ways half of all species could disappear by the end of this century.

23   The damage being done is more than aesthetic. Many vanishing species provide humans with both food and medicine. What's more, once you start tearing out swaths of ecosystem, you upset the existing balance in ways that harm even areas you didn't intend to touch. Environmentalists have said this for decades, and now that many of them have tempered ecological absolutism with developmental realism, more people are listening.

24   The Equator Initiative, a public-private group, is publicizing examples of sustainable development in the equatorial belt. Among the projects already cited are one to help restore marine fisheries in Fiji and another that promotes beekeeping as a source of supplementary income in rural Kenya. The Global Conservation Trust hopes to raise $260 million to help conserve genetic material from plants for use by local agricultural programs. "When you approach sustainable development from an environmental view, the problems are global," says the U.N.'s Malloch Brown. "But from a development view, the front line is local, local, local."

25   If that's the message environmental groups and industry want to get out, they appear to be doing a good job of it. Increasingly, local folks act whether world political bodies do or not. California Governor Gray Davis signed a law last month requiring automakers to cut their cars' carbon emissions by 2009. Many countries are similarly proactive. Chile is encouraging sustainable use of water and electricity; Japan is dangling financial incentives before consumers who buy environmentally sound cars; and tiny Mauritius is promoting solar cells and discouraging use of plastics and other disposables.

26   Business is getting right with the environment too. The Center for Environmental Leadership in Business, based in Washington, is working with auto and oil giants including Ford, Chevron, Texaco and Shell to draft guidelines for incorporating biodiversity conservation into oil and gas exploration. And the center has helped Starbucks develop purchasing guidelines that reward coffee growers whose methods have the least impact on the environment. Says Nitin Desai, secretary-general of the Johannesburg Summit: "We're hoping that partnerships—involving governments, corporations, philanthropies and NGOs—will increase the credibility of the commitment to sustainable development."

27   Will that happen? In 1992 the big, global measures of the Rio summit seemed like the answer to what ails the world. In 2002 that illness is—in many respects—worse. But if Rio's goal was to stamp out the disease of environmental degradation, Johannesburg's appears to be subtler—and perhaps better: treating the patient a bit at a time, until the planet as a whole at last gets well. ◆◆

SECOND THOUGHTS ON EXPANDING LIFESPANS*

Donald B. Louria

According to Donald B. Louria, there is a good chance that by the year 2100, the world's population will be between 15 and 30 billion people. How will future generations be able to accommodate such an enormous number of people? What can be done now to prevent an overpopulation catastrophe?

1   We are in the midst of an age of fantastic discoveries. The human lifespan at the beginning of the twentieth century was about 49 years. At the start of the twenty-first century, in countries like the United States, it is approaching 80 years. What if, by the end of this century, we could more than double the average lifespan to between 160 and 180 years?

2   A concerted scientific attack on the aging process is already well under way. The world population is now more than 6 billion people. At the dawn of the next century, or the one after that, if these scientific endeavors are successful, there could be four or five people on this planet for every one we have now. More than one-half the population then could be over 65 or even 80 years old.

3   Given that possibility, these are the issues that should be thoroughly discussed and debated:

4   At some point, the number of people may become so large that it exceeds the carrying capacity of the planet, making life miserable for the vast majority of humans (and impossible for many other species), even sowing the seeds for our own destruction.

5   The quality of life for very old people may be severely diminished if changing the boundaries of aging is not accompanied by reasonably good health. Certain tissues and organs may deteriorate even as lifespan is markedly prolonged, so people may live 140 years with ever-worsening sight, hearing, mental function, and musculoskeletal function.

6   Meanwhile, we might be expected to work, support ourselves, and pay taxes until age 80, 90, 110, or older. Some of us will outlive our resources and spend our extended years living in poverty. This would likely create intense adversarial relations between younger and older persons as they compete for limited jobs and resources.

7   Thus, the overriding question is, Where is the research on aging going, where do we want it to go, and what limitations, if any, do we want to impose on it?

ANTIAGING FORCES

8   Health professionals focused on prolonging human life can be divided into two groups: (1) those attempting to allow individuals to live their maximum lifespans with current physiological and biochemical boundaries and (2) those who are determined to actually change the boundaries of aging.

9   The first group of professionals intend to achieve their goals by controlling major diseases (such as cancer and coronary heart disease) or by reducing some of

---

Futurist 36.1 (2002), pp. 44–49.

the deterioration accompanying the aging process that can promote certain diseases (for example, using nutritional supplements to slow or reverse the decline in our immune systems that characterizes the aging process). If the goals of preventing or ameliorating disease are achieved, thereby permitting individuals to live until their biological time clocks in essence turn off physiological and biochemical processes that sustain life, we might anticipate that life expectancy at birth would increase to perhaps 100 to 110 years (even to 120 years), roughly a three- to four-decade increase for the "developed" world (average lifespan currently 76 years) and a four- to five-decade increase for the "less developed" world (average lifespan currently 66 years).

10   The second group of health professionals want to slow or halt the aging process. These scientists, as well as nonscientists, now talk of average life expectancies of 120 years to 180 years. Indeed, there are now articles and books on optional dying, and this topic is no longer science fiction. There are multiple promising approaches to changing the boundaries of aging, including administration of pharmacological agents, use of the enzyme telomerase, control of oxidant stress (free radicals) by antioxidants, and finding genes that are responsible for either aging or prolonged survivorship.

ALTERNATIVES TO DEATH

11   In each of our cells, at the ends of our chromosomes, are sticky areas called telomeres. These telomeres control cell life; the more often the cells divide, the shorter the telomeres get. Eventually, the telomere shortening results in cells being unable to divide, and they die. The telomeres appear to serve as the biological clock that determines our maximum physiological lifespan. If the enzyme telomerase is added to cells in the test tube, it prevents telomere shortening, so cells stay young and keep dividing, potentially indefinitely. The telomere fantasy is that, at appropriate intervals during our adult lives, we will drink a telomerase cocktail, the telomerase will miraculously go to all our cells, keep them young—and we will live for an incredibly long time.

12   A decade ago, researchers concurred that aging was such a complex phenomenon that multiple interacting genes would be involved and we would be unlikely to find single controlling genes that could be manipulated. That notion has changed dramatically. In one form of premature aging, called Werner syndrome—characterized by very early hair loss, cataracts, blood vessel calcification, coronary heart disease, diabetes, and cancers—a single gene mutation appears to be responsible for the disease manifestations, causing death at an average age of 47 years. Naturally occurring mutations of single genes called *age-1* and *daf-2* result in an extraordinary prolongation of lifespan in earthworms.

13   A variety of other single-gene candidates are now being investigated that may control critical pathways or may be the controlling factor in a cascade of events that define the aging process. If single genes can be found that play a controlling or dominant role in the aging process, their proteins can be characterized and, with our pharmaceutical cornucopia, pharmacological agents can be created that either mimic gene products considered desirable or interfere with gene products that are considered undesirable.

14   Genetic manipulation to control oxidant stress has already prolonged life in fruit flies. Reducing the number of calories in the diet has resulted in similar extension of life in mice and rats. It now appears that the extension of lifespan in calorie-restricted rodents may be related to the behavior of a single gene called *SIR2*. In this regard, a recent study of fruit flies found that slight modification of a single gene called *Indy* ("I'm not dead yet") doubled lifespan. The gene, also present in humans, appeared to work by changing metabolism so that the fruit flies ate normally, but behaved as if they had their caloric intake reduced; they appeared to be using energy differently.

15   Like calorie-restricted mice and rats, these fruit flies appeared to retain their vitality and normal function, even with extended lifespans; they were actually able to reproduce for a longer time than normal fruit flies. Eventually, "it may be possible to design a drug that can extend life," says the senior investigator on that extraordinary study, Stephen Helfand of the University of Connecticut School of Medicine. The drug he envisions would also be used to prevent or treat obesity, so it would be very widely used.

16   Some urge us not to worry about moving the boundaries of aging because these "very old" fruit flies, earthworms, and rodents are at least as "healthy" as their younger counterparts. But at this early stage in the research, such conclusions are very premature. Furthermore, what happens in mice, rats, or fruit flies may not apply to humans. If the optimists, whose statements are based on no human experience, are wrong, we would then have unstoppable technologies that create huge numbers of very, very old people who will cause extraordinary physical, emotional, and economic burdens on families and society.

17   Thus, there is now a concerted attack not only on diseases and abnormalities accompanying chronological aging, but also on the aging process itself. The scientific advances in this area are stunning, and progress in both areas (maximizing physiologic lifespan and changing the boundaries of aging) is so spectacular that the possibility for human application of these animal, insect, and test-tube studies in the not-too-distant future by responsible scientists and physicians is very real. Another danger has emerged, as might have been expected: Enthusiastic and often irresponsible entrepreneurs are hawking various pharmacological aging antidotes to the gullible.

HOW MANY MORE PEOPLE?

18   If we are able to delay death markedly by creating average lifespans of 120, 140, 160, or 180 years, there will inevitably be a lot more people living on planet Earth at any given time, but, surprisingly, demographers have thus far virtually ignored the possibility of profound extensions of lifespans. I have been unable to find any relevant published projections that focus on this issue. The population experts all use maximum average lifespans of less than 100 years. That is scary. Uncertain as such projections may be, we need them to guide discussions and public policy. I asked Robbert Associates Ltd. of Ottawa, Canada, a future-oriented company, to use their "what if" software program to provide information on world population in the year 2100 if life expectancy increased to an average of 90 years by the year 2040 (a two-decade increase in life expectancy). Their model projects a

2.5-billion-person increase for every 10-year increase in life expectancy. Using different assumptions for ultimate world population projections, an expert demographer at the International Program Center of the U.S. Census Bureau estimated a 1.3-billion-person increase in eventual world population for every decade increase in average life expectancy from 90 to 120 years.

19   Using those two projections—a 1.3-billion or 2.5-billion increase in eventual world population for every decade increase in average life expectancy—the following would be the anticipated world population as life expectancy increases beyond 80 years:

Average Life Expectancy at Birth	Eventual World Population
100 years	12.6–15 billion
120 years	15–20 billion
140 years	17.6–25 billion
180 years	23–35 billion

20   Obviously, catastrophic events could modify these projections, such as the deaths of hundreds of millions of people from emerging disease epidemics, bioterrorism, nuclear war, or other overwhelming events. The calculations are also based on equal longevity increases around the world. That, of course, would not happen initially. The lifespan prolongation will first take place in the developed world (Europe, North America), where the technologies are likely to be available earlier. Asia and Latin America would be expected to follow in a matter of decades. In Africa, where the aging of the population is occurring much more slowly, the emphasis will continue to be largely on reducing infant mortality; technologies to markedly prolong lifespans will probably be utilized much later.

21   Whatever the sequence of adoption of life-extending technologies, whatever calculations and assumptions are used, marked extension of lifespan would have a profound effect on world population. At some point, population growth and population size are likely to have substantial adverse effects on the planet and its inhabitants (see box, "Potential Consequences of Excessive World Population Growth").

22   The potential negative effects of population growth are magnified by global warming. Indeed, population growth and warming are inextricably interconnected: The greater the number of people on the planet, the more severe the global warming will be, because at least some portion of global warming is man-made. Global warming, in turn, exacerbates many of the problems created by excessive population growth. For example, there are currently about 40 million people who are either refugees outside their own countries or internally displaced. In a world hotter by several degrees centigrade and with a population of 10 billion or more, the devastating effects of floods, drought, and wars could create hundreds of millions of refugees and internally displaced persons. That would most likely create a situation beyond our coping capacity.

23   Common sense would suggest that excessive population growth could have some very unpleasant consequences, so ensuring the health and prosperity of humankind (as well as other creatures that share the planet with us) is likely to

POTENTIAL CONSEQUENCES OF EXCESSIVE WORLD POPULATION GROWTH

- ◆ Greater likelihood of global warming.
- ◆ Increase in war within or between nations.
- ◆ Major increases in internally displaced persons and refugees.
- ◆ More crowding in urban slums.
- ◆ Severe malnutrition and hunger (newer technologies could prevent or minimize).
- ◆ Rainforest destruction.
- ◆ Species loss.
- ◆ Inadequate potable water supply (new technologies could prevent or minimize).
- ◆ Increase in poverty (some insist this can be avoided by world economic growth).
- ◆ Increased potential for disease spread.
- ◆ Perceptions that quality of life is diminished.

require us to stabilize population at some reasonable level (e.g., 10 to 12 billion people). If that notion is accepted, then it follows that the greatest threat to achieving population stability at reasonable levels will not be a failure to control birthrates but rather the extension of adult lifespan. That, in turn, invites the conclusion that the greatest threat to planetary stability is within the scientific community.

GUIDING SCIENCE

24   Some 40 years ago, author Archibald MacLeish argued that the loyalty of science is not to humanity, but to its own truth, and that the law of science is not the law of the good but the law of the possible.

25   We are now more than ever in an era of scientific domination—a period of unfettered technology that has [produced] and will produce many stunning discoveries that will benefit humankind, but some that are likely to harm our global society. As philosopher-scientist René Dubos put it, "We must not ask where science and technology are taking us, but rather how we can manage science and technology so they can help us get where we want to go." Today, there is no evidence that we are following Dubos's admonition and first figuring out where we want to go, rather than reacting sometime in the future to the consequences of scientific discoveries that lengthen lifespans profoundly.

26   For starters, we need biologists, ethicists, philosophers, demographers, theologians, historians, and others to become a lot more interested in the potential consequences of our astounding and accelerating technological achievements in the area of aging.

27   I would submit that we need to create thoughtful guidelines. We need to initiate thorough discussions both inside and outside the scientific community. We

need vigorous debate and analysis to define our goals, and we need to establish sensible regulations and laws consistent with those goals. If we do not do this, the consequences of the technological and scientific achievements that markedly lengthen adult lifespans will be imposed upon us. That could be a very unpleasant scenario.

28   I suggest that we concentrate on conquering diseases and slowing the aging process so people can live out their maximum physiological lifespan. That will benefit individuals. It will also challenge the global society, as average life expectancy increases by 20 or 30 years, but we can cope with those changes with a reasonable amount of thought and planning.

29   On the other hand, we should approach changing the boundaries of aging with great caution, insisting on debate and requiring that any attempt to change the boundaries in human beings be kept experimental. Such attempts should be accompanied by rigorous long-term assessment that includes evaluating the quality of life of these very old persons.

30   In sum, my view is: Maximizing physiological lifespan—full speed ahead. Changing the boundaries of human aging—go slow, with extreme caution. The research into aging is spectacular, but the implications and potential consequences are so profound that we cannot afford to leave it solely in the hands of the scientific community. We had better figure out where we are going or we may find some unpleasant surprises when we get there.

31   Let the debate begin. ◆◆

QUESTIONS TO HELP YOU THINK ABOUT ISSUES CONCERNING THE FUTURE

1. In "Looking Back on Tomorrow," Brooks identifies four areas of potential controversy for the twenty-first century: remaking human nature, globalization, inequality, and the "American century redux." In a group of four, have one student take each section and attempt to persuade the group why his or her issue has the most potential for being the major issue of this century. By group vote, determine who was most successful. Then, switch issues and attempt to persuade the audience of the new topic.

2. Basing your reasoning on the articles by Silver, Wood, and Stolberg, consider the advantages and disadvantages of genetically altering human beings. Divide a sheet of paper down the middle and on one side, list all the advantages of this technology; on the other, list the disadvantages. If you were on a national committee to decide future policy on genetically altering human beings, what policies would you recommend? Why?

3. Think about the changes in computer technology since the early 1980s. Read Kurzweil's article and list items from it that describe the state of computer technology now and in the future. What can you conclude about Kurzweil's projected changes? How do you react to these changes?

4. Kurzweil postulates that in the next twenty years or so, computers will be able to read massive amounts of material and share what they have learned from their reading with other computers. What advantages do you see in such technology? How might human beings use and benefit from this technology?

5. Why is the situation for saving the planet, according to Wilson, desperate? Give as many reasons as you can. On the basis of your reading of the articles in this section and any outside readings, how desperate do you think the situation is?

6. Imagine Wilson and Louria in a conversation about the future of the planet. How might they agree? How might they disagree? With which of them would you be more likely to agree?

7. The last three articles on the future of the planet mention the immediate problems facing the world to improve upon the planet's condition. What are these problems? What are the ways the different authors suggest for solving these problems? For practical purposes, with whom do you agree the most? Why?

8. Kluger and Dorfman suggest that we can solve the earth's problems by taking one step at a time. If you were participating in a summit geared at solving the planet's problems, what might you suggest as the best method?

⇒ Section VII ⇒

Issues Concerning War and Peace

THE ISSUES

A. IS WAR INEVITABLE?

In this section, three authors, two of whom are major figures in American philosophy and anthropology, provide competing perspectives on the relationships between war and biology, culture, and history. William James, a self-avowed pacifist, believes that people, and young men in particular, have a need for warfare, and he offers a way to transfer that aggression to other, more productive outlets. Margaret Mead does not agree that the need to fight is a natural condition. Basing her work on research that shows some cultures do not understand the concept of war, Mead argues that war is neither a biological given nor a necessary condition of the nature of history, but is instead an invention. Victor Davis Hanson's essay fits keenly between Mead's and James's. Hanson, who argues against the thinking of the "elites," claims that war is inevitable for seemingly different reasons. As you read these selections, you will want to think about the relationship of war with biology, culture, and history.

B. HOW DO PEOPLE JUSTIFY WAR?

The three essays here focus on why people are willing to go to extremes to do violence to others. The first piece, written by Eyad Sarraj, discusses why Arab men and women choose to die for the sake of combating national and personal shame. William J. Bennett advocates the use of war when it is "moral." Nobel Prize–winning author Elie Wiesel seeks to understand the minds of fanatics and offers a look into the nature of their hatred. As you read this section, it is important to keep in mind all sides of all arguments. What can one offer as a way of solution when different parties think their actions are justified, moral, and even religiously sanctioned?

C. WHAT MIGHT HELP ESTABLISH PEACE?

The essays in this section offer three different perspectives on ways to achieve peace. William L. Ury shows how opposing parties can move from a "lose-lose" situation to a "both-gain" situation. Richard Rhodes provides a historical account of the atomic bomb and shows how its creation has benefited the modern world. In the final essay, Bruce Hoffman shows how terrorism can be combated in imaginative and creative ways that do not involve warfare. As you read these articles, keep in mind all that must be given up in order to achieve peace. Ask yourself how much liberty you would be willing to relinquish for peace. See also the essays by James and Mead (pages 671 and 675).

D. WEB SITES FOR FURTHER EXPLORATION AND RESEARCH

Institute for War and Peace Reporting	http://www.iwpr.net
The Global Beat	http://www.nyu.edu/globalbeat
Department of Defense–Homeland Security	http://www.defenselink.mil/specials/homeland
United Nations	http://www.un.org
The Electronic Intifada	http://electronicintifada.net/news.html
Jews Against the Occupation	http://www.jewsagainsttheoccupation.org
The War in Context	http://www.warincontext.org
The Stockholm International Peace Research Institute	http://www.sipri.se
The Carnegie Endowment for International Peace	http://www.ceip.org
The United States Institute of Peace	http://www.usip.org

E. FILMS AND LITERATURE RELATED TO CRIME

Films: Operation Enduring Freedom, 2002; *Black Hawk Down,* 2002; *Pearl Harbor,* 2001; *The Patriot,* 2000; *Saving Private Ryan,* 1999; *Braveheart,* 1995; *Schindler's List,* 1993; *The Dogs of War,* 1991; *Apocalypse Now,* 1979; *War Games,* 1983; *Bananas,* 1971; *Mein Kampf,* 1961.

Literature: poetry anthology: *The Oxford Book of War Poetry* edited by Jon Stall-
worthy; short story: "On the Rainy River" by Tim O'Brien; novels: *War and
Peace* by Leo Tolstoy; *Heart of Darkness* by Joseph Conrad; *Red Badge of
Courage* by Stephen Crane; *A Rumor of War* by Philip Caputo; *Going After
Cacciato* and *If I Die in a Combat Zone, Box Me Up and Ship Me Home* by Tim
O'Brien; *From Here to Eternity* and *For Whom the Bell Tolls* by Ernest Heming-
way; *The Naked and the Dead* by Norman Mailer; *The Thin Red Line* by James
Jones.

THE RHETORICAL SITUATION

Few issues are more controversial than whether or not a country should go to
war. In the United States, nationalism and patriotism remained strong for World
Wars I and II and for almost all of the other smaller wars this country has been
engaged in, but Vietnam, like the Civil War one hundred years earlier, tore this
country in half, changing the face of politics and conceptions about warfare.

In hindsight, the Persian Gulf War against Iraq in 1991 did not turn out to be
such an easy win for America as was first believed. The occupation of American
military in the Gulf and America's support for Israel in the Israeli–Palestinian conflict fueled an already established antipathy for America by many living in the
Middle East. On September 11, 2001, a new kind of war emerged in full light
when four passenger planes were hijacked, three of which were flown into New
York's famous Twin Towers of the World Trade Center and Washington's Pentagon; the final plane, believed to be destined for either the White House or the
Capitol, crashed in Pennsylvania after its passengers and crew fought the hijackers for control of the aircraft. With the collapse of the Twin Towers, symbols of
American power and freedom, and the loss of thousands of American lives, a new
exigency was created for how people of this country and all over the world will
deal with a "war on terror." Actual wars in Afghanistan in 2002 and Iraq in 2003
were fought as part of the war on terror.

At issue for citizens of the world is what to do, but attached to that question
is always the risk of more mothers, fathers, brothers, sisters, and children being
lost. The central question, then, is the nature of war itself. The essays first presented question the origins of war and explore its connection to society and
history. In the wake of terror, it is helpful to try to understand the minds of those
who are considered terrorists and the cultures that help shape who they become. Why are certain people willing to sacrifice their own lives to kill innocent
people? When, if ever, is war just? Can we ever hope to have a lasting peace?
What sacrifices would we be willing to make for peace? What sacrifices would
others be willing to make? Is compromise even possible?

The current state of national affairs and recent history will largely affect
the way you and others think about the nature of war. Answers to some of these
questions may be found and others may seem elusive, but by understanding the
nature of war and peace in their various forms, we might have the hope of solving some of these very important problems.

A. IS WAR INEVITABLE?

QUESTIONS TO CONSIDER BEFORE YOU READ

Think about a destructive argument you have had with a friend or family member. Could it have been prevented, or was it inevitable? Think about other arguments of this type you have had. Could they have been prevented? Do you think war is something we have in our "blood"? Or do you think it is something people learn from culture and history? Do you think that people will become more and more civilized, moving toward the elimination of war?

THE MORAL EQUIVALENT OF WAR*

William James

The philosopher William James (1842–1910), brother of novelist Henry James, advanced pragmatic philosophy through his famous writings The Will to Believe and Other Essays in Popular Philosophy *(1897) and* The Varieties of Religious Experience *(1902). In the following essay, James claims that it is necessary to get the desire to fight out of men rather than going to war and proposes a solution. What is that solution? How pragmatic for civil life do you think his solution would be?*

1   The war against war is going to be no holiday excursion or camping party. The military feelings are too deeply grounded to abdicate their place among our ideals until better substitutes are offered than the glory and shame that come to nations as well as to individuals from the ups and downs of politics and the vicissitudes of trade. There is something highly paradoxical in the modern man's relation to war. Ask all our millions, north and south, whether they would vote now (were such a thing possible) to have our war for the Union expunged from history, and the record of a peaceful transition to the present time substituted for that of its marches and battles, and probably hardly a handful of eccentrics would say yes. Those ancestors, those efforts, those memories and legends, are the most ideal part of what we now own together, a sacred spiritual possession worth more than all the blood poured out. Yet ask those same people whether they would be willing in cold blood to start another civil war now to gain another similar possession, and not one man or woman would vote for the proposition. In modern eyes, precious though wars may be, they must not be waged solely for the sake of the ideal harvest. Only when forced upon one, only when an enemy's injustice leaves us no alternative, is a war now thought permissible.

2   It was not thus in ancient times. The earlier men were hunting men, and to hunt a neighboring tribe, kill the males, loot the village and possess the females, was the most profitable, as well as the most exciting, way of living. Thus were the

---

*First published by the Association for International Conciliation in 1910 and in *McClure's*, 1910. From *The Best American Essays of the Century*, Joyce Carol Oates, ed., and Robert Atwan, coed. (New York: Houghton Mifflin, 2000), pp. 45–49, 52–55.

more martial tribes selected, and in chiefs and peoples a pure pugnacity and love of glory came to mingle with the more fundamental appetite for plunder.

3   Modern war is so expensive that we feel trade to be a better avenue to plunder; but modern man inherits all the innate pugnacity and all the love of glory of his ancestors. Showing war's irrationality and horror is of no effect upon him. The horrors make the fascination. War is the *strong* life; it is life *in extremis:* war-taxes are the only ones men never hesitate to pay, as the budgets of all nations show us.

4   History is a bath of blood. The *Iliad* is one long recital of how Diomedes and Ajax, Sarpedon and Hector *killed*. No detail of the wounds they made is spared us, and the Greek mind fed upon the story. Greek history is a panorama of jingoism and imperialism—war for war's sake, all the citizens being warriors. It is horrible reading, because of the irrationality of it all—save for the purpose of making "history"—and the history is that of the utter ruin of a civilization in intellectual respects perhaps the highest the earth has ever seen.

◆◆◆◆

5   Such was the gory nurse that trained societies to cohesiveness. We inherit the warlike type; and for most of the capacities of heroism that the human race is full of we have to thank this cruel history. Dead men tell no tales, and if there were any tribes of other type than this they have left no survivors. Our ancestors have bred pugnacity into our bone and marrow, and thousands of years of peace won't breed it out of us. The popular imagination fairly fattens on the thought of wars. Let public opinion once reach a certain fighting pitch, and no ruler can withstand it. In the Boer war both governments began with bluff, but couldn't stay there, the military tension was too much for them. In 1898 our people had read the word WAR in letters three inches high for three months in every newspaper. The pliant politician McKinley was swept away by their eagerness, and our squalid war with Spain became a necessity.

6   At the present day, civilized opinion is a curious mental mixture. The military instincts and ideals are as strong as ever, but are confronted by reflective criticisms which sorely curb their ancient freedom. Innumerable writers are showing up the bestial side of military service. Pure loot and mastery seem no longer morally avowable motives, and pretexts must be found for attributing them solely to the enemy. England and we, our army and navy authorities repeat without ceasing, arm solely for "peace," Germany and Japan it is who are bent on loot and glory. "Peace" in military mouths to-day is a synonym for "war expected." The word has become a pure provocative, and no government wishing peace sincerely should allow it ever to be printed in a newspaper. Every up-to-date Dictionary should say that "peace" and "war" mean the same thing, now *in posse,* now *in actu.* It may even reasonably be said that the intensely sharp competitive *preparation* for war by the nations *is the real war*, permanent, unceasing; and that the battles are only a sort of public verification of the mastery gained during the "peace"-interval. . . .

7   In my remarks, pacificist tho' I am, I will refuse to speak of the bestial side of the war-regime (already done justice to by many writers) and consider only the higher aspects of militaristic sentiment. Patriotism no one thinks discreditable; nor does any one deny that war is the romance of history. But inordinate ambitions are the soul of every patriotism, and the possibility of violent death the soul

of all romance. The militarily patriotic and romantic-minded everywhere, and especially the professional military class, refuse to admit for a moment that war may be a transitory phenomenon in social evolution. The notion of a sheep's paradise like that revolts, they say, our higher imagination. Where then would be the steeps of life? If war had ever stopped, we should have to reinvent it, on this view, to redeem life from flat degeneration.

8 Reflective apologists for war at the present day all take it religiously. It is a sort of sacrament. Its profits are to the vanquished as well as to the victor; and quite apart from any question of profit, it is an absolute good, we are told, for it is human nature at its highest dynamic. Its "horrors" are a cheap price to pay for rescue from the only alternative supposed, of a world of clerks and teachers, of co-education and zoophily, of "consumer's leagues" and "associated charities," of industrialism unlimited, and feminism unabashed. No scorn, no hardness, no valor any more! Fie upon such a cattleyard of a planet!

9 So far as the central essence of this feeling goes, no healthy minded person, it seems to me, can help to some degree partaking of it. Militarism is the great preserver of our ideals of hardihood, and human life with no use for hardihood would be contemptible. Without risks or prizes for the darer, history would be insipid indeed; and there is a type of military character which every one feels that the race should never cease to breed, for every one is sensitive to its superiority. . . .

10 This natural sort of feeling forms, I think, the innermost soul of army-writings. Without any exception known to me, militarist authors take a highly mystical view of their subject, and regard war as a biological or sociological necessity, uncontrolled by ordinary psychological checks and motives. When the time of development is ripe the war must come, reason or no reason, for the justifications pleaded are invariably fictitious. War is, in short, a permanent human *obligation*. General Homer Lea, in his recent book *The Valor of Ignorance,* plants himself squarely on this ground. Readiness for war is for him the essence of nationality, and ability in it the supreme measure of the health of nations.

◆◆◆◆

11 . . . All the qualities of a man acquire dignity when he knows that the service of the collectivity that owns him needs them. If proud of the collectivity, his own pride rises in proportion. No collectivity is like an army for nourishing such pride; but it has to be confessed that the only sentiment which the image of pacific cosmopolitan industrialism is capable of arousing in countless worthy breasts is shame at the idea of belonging to *such* a collectivity. It is obvious that the United States of America as they exist to-day impress a mind like General Lea's as so much human blubber. Where is the sharpness and precipitousness, the contempt for life, whether one's own, or another's? Where is the savage "yes" and "no," the unconditional duty? Where is the conscription? Where is the blood-tax? Where is anything that one feels honored by belonging to?

12 Having said thus much in preparation, I will now confess my own utopia. I devoutly believe in the reign of peace and in the gradual advent of some sort of a socialistic equilibrium. The fatalistic view of the war-function is to me nonsense, for I know that war-making is due to definite motives and subject to prudential checks and reasonable criticisms, just like any other form of enterprise. And when whole nations are the armies, and the science of destruction vies in

intellectual refinement with the sciences of production, I see that war becomes absurd and impossible from its own monstrosity. . . .

13   All these beliefs of mine put me squarely into the anti-militarist party. But I do not believe that peace either ought to be or will be permanent on this globe, unless the states pacifically organized preserve some of the old elements of army-discipline. A permanently successful peace-economy cannot be a simple pleasure-economy. In the more or less socialistic future towards which mankind seems drifting we must still subject ourselves collectively to those severities which answer to our real position upon this only partly hospitable globe. We must make new energies and hardihoods continue the manliness to which the military mind so faithfully clings. Martial virtues must be the enduring cement; intrepidity, contempt of softness, surrender of private interest, obedience to command, must still remain the rock upon which states are built—unless, indeed, we wish for dangerous reactions against commonwealths fit only for contempt, and liable to invite attack whenever a centre of crystallization for military-minded enterprise gets formed anywhere in their neighborhood.

14   The war-party is assuredly right in affirming and reaffirming that the martial virtues, although originally gained by the race through war, are absolute and permanent human goods. Patriotic pride and ambition in their military form are, after all, only specifications of a more general competitive passion. They are its first form, but that is no reason for supposing them to be its last form. Men now are proud of belonging to a conquering nation, and without a murmur they lay down their persons and their wealth, if by so doing they may fend off subjection. But who can be sure that *other aspects of one's country* may not, with time and education and suggestion enough, come to be regarded with similarly effective feelings of pride and shame? Why should men not some day feel that it is worth a blood-tax to belong to a collectivity superior in *any* ideal respect? Why should they not blush with indignant shame if the community that owns them is vile in any way whatsoever? Individuals, daily more numerous, now feel this civic passion. It is only a question of blowing on the spark till the whole population gets incandescent, and on the ruins of the old morals of military honour, a stable system of morals of civic honour builds itself up. What the whole community comes to believe in grasps the individual as in a vise. The war-function has graspt us so far; but constructive interests may some day seem no less imperative, and impose on the individual a hardly lighter burden.

15   Let me illustrate my idea more concretely. There is nothing to make one indignant in the mere fact that life is hard, that men should toil and suffer pain. The planetary conditions once for all are such, and we can stand it. But that so many men, by mere accidents of birth and opportunity, should have a life of *nothing else* but toil and pain and hardness and inferiority imposed upon them, should have *no* vacation, while others natively no more deserving never get any taste of this campaigning life at all,—*this* is capable of arousing indignation in reflective minds. It may end by seeming shameful to all of us that some of us have nothing but campaigning, and others nothing but unmanly ease. If now—and this is my idea—there were, instead of military conscription a conscription of the whole youthful population to form for a certain number of years a part of the army enlisted against *Nature*, the injustice would tend to be evened out, and numerous

other goods to the commonwealth would follow. The military ideals of hardihood and discipline would be wrought into the growing fibre of the people; no one would remain blind as the luxurious classes now are blind, to man's real relations to the globe he lives on, and to the permanently sour and hard foundations of his higher life. To coal and iron mines, to freight trains, to fishing fleets in December, to dish-washing, clothes-washing, and window-washing, to road-building and tunnel-making, to foundries and stoke-holes, and to the frames of skyscrapers, would our gilded youths be drafted off, according to their choice, to get the childishness knocked out of them, and to come back into society with healthier sympathies and soberer ideas. They would have paid their blood-tax, done their own part in the immemorial human warfare against nature, they would tread the earth more proudly, the women would value them more highly, they would be better fathers and teachers of the following generation.

16 Such a conscription, with the state of public opinion that would have required it, and the many moral fruits it would bear, would preserve in the midst of a pacific civilization the manly virtues which the military party is so afraid of seeing disappear in peace. We should get toughness without callousness, authority with as little criminal cruelty as possible, and painful work done cheerily because the duty is temporary, and threatens not, as now, to degrade the whole remainder of one's life. I spoke of the "moral equivalent" of war. So far, war has been the only force that can discipline a whole community, and until an equivalent discipline is organized, I believe that war must have its way. But I have no serious doubt that the ordinary prides and shames of social man, once developed to a certain intensity, are capable of organizing such a moral equivalent as I have sketched, or some other just as effective for preserving manliness of type. It is but a question of time, of skillful propagandism, and of opinion-making men seizing historic opportunities.

17 The martial type of character can be bred without war. Strenuous honour and disinterestedness abound elsewhere. Priests and medical men are in a fashion educated to it, and we should all feel some degree of it imperative if we were conscious of our work as an obligatory service to the state. We should be *owned*, as soldiers are by the army, and our pride would rise accordingly. We could be poor, then, without humiliation, as army officers now are. The only thing needed henceforward is to inflame the civic temper as past history has inflamed the military temper. ◆◆

WARFARE: AN INVENTION—NOT A BIOLOGICAL NECESSITY*

Margaret Mead

A leading cultural anthropologist, Margaret Mead (1901–1978) became a household name in the United States because of her best-selling Coming of Age in Samoa, *about her field*

*Asia 40.8 (August 1940): 402–405.

research on sexuality among adolescents in Samoa. She went on to write forty-four books. In the following article, Mead argues against the traditional notion that warfare is a biological, not cultural, drive. While you read, you will want to consider whether you think war is something we inherit from genetics or from society.

1   Is war a biological necessity, a sociological inevitability, or just a bad invention? Those who argue for the first view endow man with such pugnacious instincts that some outlet in aggressive behavior is necessary if man is to reach full human stature. It was this point of view which lay back of William James's famous essay, "The Moral Equivalent of War," in which he tried to retain the warlike virtues and channel them in new directions. A similar point of view has lain back of the Soviet Union's attempt to make competition between groups rather than between individuals. A basic, competitive, aggressive, warring human nature is assumed, and those who wish to outlaw war or outlaw competitiveness merely try to find new and less socially destructive ways in which these biologically given aspects of man's nature can find expression. Then there are those who take the second view: warfare is the inevitable concomitant of the development of the state, the struggle for land and natural resources of class societies springing, not from the nature of man, but from the nature of history. War is nevertheless inevitable unless we change our social system and outlaw classes, the struggle for power, and possessions; and in the event of our success warfare would disappear, as a symptom vanishes when the disease is cured.

2   One may hold a compromise position between these two extremes; one may claim that all aggression springs from the frustration of man's biologically determined drives and that, since all forms of culture are frustrating, it is certain each new generation will be aggressive and the aggression will find its natural and inevitable expression in race war, class war, nationalistic war, and so on.

3   All three positions are very popular today among those who think seriously about the problems of war and its possible prevention, but I wish to urge another point of view, less defeatist perhaps than the first and third, and more accurate than the second: that is, that warfare, by which I mean organized conflict between two groups as *groups*, in which each group puts an army (even if the army is only fifteen Pygmies) into the field to fight and kill, if possible, some of the members of the army of the other group—that warfare of this sort is an invention like any other of the inventions in terms of which we order our lives, such as writing, marriage, cooking our food instead of eating it raw, trial by jury, or burial of the dead, and so on. Some of this list any one will grant are inventions: trial by jury is confined to very limited portions of the globe; we know that there are tribes that do not bury their dead but instead expose or cremate them; and we know that only part of the human race has had a knowledge of writing as its cultural inheritance. But, whenever a way of doing things is found universally, such as the use of fire or the practice of some form of marriage, we tend to think at once that it is not an invention at all but an attribute of humanity itself. And yet even such universals as marriage and the use of fire are inventions like the rest, very basic ones, inventions which were perhaps necessary if human history was to take the turn it has taken, but nevertheless inventions. At some point in his

social development man was undoubtedly without the institution of marriage or the knowledge of the use of fire.

4   The case for warfare is much clearer because there are peoples even today who have no warfare. Of these the Eskimo are perhaps the most conspicuous example, but the Lepchas of Sikkim are an equally good one. Neither of these peoples understands war, not even the defensive warfare. The idea of warfare is lacking, and this lack is as essential to carrying on war as an alphabet or a syllabary is to writing. But whereas the Lepchas are a gentle, unquarrelsome people, and the advocates of other points of view might argue that they are not full human beings or that they had never been frustrated and so had no aggression to expend in warfare, the Eskimo case gives no such possibility of interpretation. The Eskimo are not a mild and meek people; many of them are turbulent and troublesome. Fights, theft of wives, murder, cannibalism occur among them—all outbursts of passionate men goaded by desire or intolerable circumstance. Here are men faced with hunger, men faced with loss of their wives, men faced with the threat of extermination by other men, and here are orphan children, growing up miserably with no one to care for them, mocked and neglected by those about them. The personality necessary for war, the circumstances necessary to goad men to desperation are present, but there is no war. When a traveling Eskimo entered a settlement he might have to fight the strongest man in the settlement to establish his position among them, but this was a test of strength and bravery, not war. The idea of warfare, of one *group* organizing against another *group* to maim and wound and kill them, was absent. And without that idea passions might rage but there was no war.

5   But, it may be argued, isn't this because the Eskimo have such a low and undeveloped form of social organization? They own no land, they move from place to place, camping, it is true, season after season on the same site, but this is not something to fight for as the modern nations of the world fight for land and raw materials. They have no permanent possessions that can be looted, no towns that can be burned. They have no social classes to produce stress and strains within the society which might force it to go to war outside. Doesn't the absence of war among the Eskimo, while disproving the biological necessity of war, just go to confirm the point that it is the state of development of the society which accounts for war, and nothing else?

6   We find the answer among the Pygmy peoples of the Andaman Islands in the Bay of Bengal. The Andamans also represent an exceedingly low level of society: they are a hunting and food-gathering people; they live in tiny hordes without any class stratification; their houses are simpler than the snow houses of the Eskimo. But they knew about warfare. The army might contain only fifteen determined Pygmies marching in a straight line, but it was the real thing none the less. Tiny army met tiny army in open battle, blows were exchanged, casualties suffered, and the state of warfare could only be concluded by a peacemaking ceremony.

7   Similarly, among the Australian aborigines, who built no permanent dwellings but wandered from water hole to water hole over their almost desert country, warfare—and rules of "international law"—were highly developed. The

student of social evolution will seek in vain for his obvious causes of war, struggle for lands, struggle for power of one group over another, expansion of population, need to divert the minds of a populace restive under tyranny, or even the ambition of a successful leader to enhance his own prestige. All are absent, but warfare as a practice remained, and men engaged in it and killed one another in the course of a war because killing is what is done in wars.

8   From instances like these it becomes apparent that an inquiry into the causes of war misses the fundamental point as completely as does an insistence upon the biological necessity of war. If a people have an idea of going to war and the idea that war is the way in which certain situations, defined within their society, are to be handled, they will sometimes go to war. If they are a mild and unaggressive people, like the Pueblo Indians, they may limit themselves to defensive warfare; but they will be forced to think in terms of war because there are peoples near them who have warfare as a pattern, and offensive, raiding, pillaging warfare at that. When the pattern of warfare is known, people like the Pueblo Indians will defend themselves, taking advantage of their natural defenses, the *mesa* village site, and people like the Lepchas, having no natural defenses and no idea of warfare, will merely submit to the invader. But the essential point remains the same. There is a way of behaving which is known to a given people and labeled as an appropriate form of behavior. A bold and warlike people like the Sioux or the Maori may label warfare as desirable as well as possible; a mild people like the Pueblo Indians may label warfare as undesirable; but to the minds of both peoples the possibility of warfare is present. Their thoughts, their hopes, their plans are oriented about this idea, that warfare may be selected as the way to meet some situation.

9   So simple peoples and civilized peoples, mild peoples and violent, assertive peoples, will all go to war if they have the invention, just as those peoples who have the custom of dueling will have duels and peoples who have the pattern of vendetta will indulge in vendetta. And, conversely, peoples who do not know of dueling will not fight duels, even though their wives are seduced and their daughters ravished; they may on occasion commit murder but they will not fight duels. Cultures which lack the idea of the vendetta will not meet every quarrel in this way. A people can use only the forms it has. So the Balinese have their special way of dealing with a quarrel between two individuals; if the two feel that the causes of quarrel are heavy, they may go and register their quarrel in the temple before the gods, and, making offerings, they may swear never to have anything to do with each other again. Under the Dutch government they registered such mutual "not-speaking" with the Dutch government officials. But in other societies, although individuals might feel as full of animosity and as unwilling to have any further contact as do the Balinese, they cannot register their quarrel with the gods and go on quietly about their business because registering quarrels with the gods is not an invention of which they know.

10   Yet, if it be granted that warfare is after all an invention, it may nevertheless be an invention that lends itself to certain types of personality, to the exigent needs of autocrats, to the expansionist desires of crowded peoples, to the desire for plunder and rape and loot which is engendered by a dull and frustrating life. What, then, can we say of this congruence between warfare and its uses? If it is a

form which fits so well, is not this congruence the essential point? But even here the primitive material causes us to wonder, because there are tribes who go to war merely for glory, having no quarrel with the enemy, suffering from no tyrant within their boundaries, anxious neither for land nor loot nor women, but merely anxious to win prestige which within that tribe has been declared obtainable only by war and without which no young man can hope to win his sweetheart's smile of approval. But if, as was the case with the Bush Negroes of Dutch Guiana, it is artistic ability which is necessary to win a girl's approval, the same young man would have to be carving rather than going out on a war party.

11   In many parts of the world, war is a game in which the individual can win counters—counters which bring him prestige in the eyes of his own sex or of the opposite sex; he plays for these counters as he might, in our society, strive for a tennis championship. Warfare is a frame for such prestige-seeking merely because it calls for the display of certain skills and certain virtues; all of these skills—riding straight, shooting straight, dodging the missiles of the enemy, and sending one's own straight to the mark—can be equally well exercised in some other framework and, equally, the virtues—endurance, bravery, loyalty, steadfastness—can be displayed in other contexts. The tie-up between proving oneself a man and proving this by a success in organized killing is due to a definition which many societies have made of manliness. And often, even in those societies which counted success in warfare a proof of human worth, strange turns were given to the idea, as when the Plains Indians gave their highest awards to the man who touched a live enemy rather than to the man who brought in a scalp—from a dead enemy—because killing a man was less risky. Warfare is just an invention known to the majority of human societies by which they permit their young men either to accumulate prestige or avenge their honor or acquire loot or wives or slaves or sago lands or cattle or appease the blood lust of their gods or the restless souls of the recently dead. It is just an invention, older and more widespread than the jury system, but none the less an invention.

12   But, once we have said this, have we said anything at all? Despite a few instances, dear to the hearts of controversialists, of the loss of the useful arts, once an invention is made which proves congruent with human needs or social forms, it tends to persist. Grant that war is an invention, that it is not a biological necessity nor the outcome of certain special types of social forms, still, once the invention is made, what are we to do about it? The Indian who had been subsisting on the buffalo for generations because with his primitive weapons he could slaughter only a limited number of buffalo did not return to his primitive weapons when he saw that the white man's more efficient weapons were exterminating the buffalo. A desire for the white man's cloth may mortgage the South Sea Islander to the white man's plantation, but he does not return to making bark cloth, which would have left him free. Once an invention is known and accepted, men do not easily relinquish it. The skilled workers may smash the first steam looms which they feel are to be their undoing, but they accept them in the end, and no movement which has insisted upon the mere abandonment of usable inventions has ever had much success. Warfare is here, as part of our thought; the deeds of warriors are immortalized in the words of our poets; the toys of our children are modeled upon the weapons of the soldier; the frame of reference within

which our statesmen and our diplomats work always contains war. If we know that is it not inevitable, that it is due to historical accident that warfare is one of the ways in which we think of behaving, are we given any hope by that? What hope is there of persuading nations to abandon war, nations so thoroughly imbued with the idea that resort to war is, if not actually desirable and noble, at least inevitable whenever certain defined circumstances arise?

13   In answer to this question I think we might turn to the history of other social inventions, inventions which must once have seemed as firmly entrenched as warfare. Take the methods of trial which preceded the jury system: ordeal and trial by combat. Unfair, capricious, alien as they are to our feeling today, they were once the only methods open to individuals accused of some offense. The invention of trial by jury gradually replaced these methods until only witches, and finally not even witches, had to resort to the ordeal. And for a long time the jury system seemed the one best and finest method of settling legal disputes, but today new inventions, trial before judges only or before commissions, are replacing the jury system. In each case the old method was replaced by a new social invention; the ordeal did not go out because people thought it unjust or wrong, it went out because a method more congruent with the institutions and feelings of the period was invented. And, if we despair over the way in which war seems such an ingrained habit of most of the human race, we can take comfort from the fact that a poor invention will usually give place to a better invention.

14   For this, two conditions at least are necessary. The people must recognize the defects of the old invention, and some one must make a new one. Propaganda against warfare, documentation of its terrible cost in human suffering and social waste, these prepare the ground by teaching people to feel that warfare is a defective social institution. There is further needed a belief that social invention is possible and the invention of new methods which will render warfare as out-of-date as the tractor is making the plow, or the motor car the horse and buggy. A form of behavior becomes out-of-date only when something else takes its place, and in order to invent forms of behavior which will make war obsolete, it is a first requirement to believe that an invention is possible. ◆◆

WAR WILL BE WAR: NO MATTER THE ERA, NO MATTER THE WEAPONS, THE SAME OLD HELL*

Victor Davis Hanson

Victor Davis Hanson wrote this article for the National Review. *Is war something that we will always be doomed to suffer through, no matter what the age, no matter what the society?*

1   War is eternal. It is part of the human condition; it is, as Heraclitus wrote, "the father of us all." This is the first thing we must remember whenever

---

National Review, May 6, 2002, pp. 35+.

discussion turns to "revolutions in military affairs." Some things will change, but the underlying laws and lessons that have shown themselves over millennia of warfare remain true about wars today—and wars tomorrow.

2   One of these key truths is that culture largely determines how people fight. The degree to which a society embraces freedom, secular rationalism, consensual government, and capitalism often determines—far more than its geography, climate, or population—whether its armies will be successful over the long term. Israel today is surrounded by a half-billion Middle Eastern Muslims—and has little to fear from their conventional militaries. Kuwait and Saudi Arabia have some of the most sophisticated weapons in the world; Saddam Hussein's Iraq still fields one of the largest armies; Iran boasts of spirited and fiery warriors. Israel—not to mention the United States—could vanquish them all. This appraisal is simply a statement of fact; it is neither triumphalist nor ethnocentric. It recognizes that if—for example—Iraq were to democratize, establish a Western system of free speech and inquiry, and embrace capitalism, then Iraq too, like Taiwan or South Korea, might well produce a military as good as Israel's. Another key truth is that overwhelming force wins. Much has been made of the latest epidemic of terror and suicide bombing—as if hijackers with tiny budgets could overcome opponents who spend trillions on defense. But history proves otherwise: Frightful terrorists such as the Jewish sicarii of Roman times, the ecorcheurs of the Hundred Years' War, and the Mahdi's dervishes in 19th-century Sudan usually petered out when they were faced with an overwhelming military force that was fighting for attractive ideas. Guerrillas, after all, require money, modern weapons, and bases in countries with friendly governments. Superpowers—such as imperial Rome and contemporary America—have the wherewithal to deny the terrorists access to much of this necessary support. September 11 revealed the complacency and carelessness of a democratic and affluent United States; but the relative absence of follow-up attacks—as America systematically eradicates al-Qaeda 7,000 miles away from its shores—suggests that a powerful state can more than handle stateless terrorists.

3   It can do so because a Green Beret fighting terrorists in a cave can rely on a multibillion-dollar carrier battle group to bomb the terrorists; all he has to do is call in his GPS coordinates. This is the West's edge; and a chief military challenge of the 21st century, therefore, will be not terrorists per se, but the degree to which globalization brings the Western way of war to the much larger non-West.

4   During the Clinton administration, it was feared that exported weapons and pilfered expertise might soon bring China technological parity with America. But no one is yet sure whether the simple possession of sophisticated arms amounts to military equivalence—without the accompanying and more fundamental Western notions of discipline, market logistics, free-thinking command, and civilian supervision.

5   An F-16 fighter jet does not exist in a vacuum: A literate middle class is needed to produce mechanics who can service and modify it; freedom of scholarship is required if designers are going to update it; and an open society is necessary if the plane's sophisticated controls are going to be operated by competent, motivated, and individualistic pilots. As a rule, Israeli pilots proved deadly against

Syrian jets in Lebanon—but Iraqis in advanced Russian aircraft would fly into Iran rather than fight American planes during the Gulf War.

6   Another example: There are probably plenty of Stinger missiles still hidden away in Afghanistan, but it has been nearly two decades since they were built—and Afghans have not modified or updated them to meet the intervening efforts to neutralize their effectiveness. In the short term, such subtle differences don't seem important. But in the long run—as we have seen in the Falklands, the Arab-Israeli wars, the Gulf War, and Afghanistan—they can trump numerical superiority, tactical genius, and heroism itself. There is a reason that Arafat, not Sharon, was surrounded in his bunker. It is not terrorists, but tanks—and the quality of men in them—that decide the preponderance of strength in the Middle East.

7   This is true not just in the Middle East but everywhere. The education system, therefore, and the preservation of an open society with a common Western culture are as valuable for our national security as our impressive military hardware. If the degree of Westernization in the next few years will often determine which armies win and lose, history also teaches us that with affluence and personal freedom comes a sense of laxity. The fact that a society can, in theory, defeat its enemies does not ensure that it will indeed do so. The unwillingness of affluent individuals to accept the responsibilities of defense is a common theme in Roman authors as diverse as Livy and Juvenal.

8   We see evidence of this sort of smugness in today's Europe, whose elites snicker at America's muscular response to September 11, whose taxpayers are unwilling to shoulder defense expenditures that might imperil their lavish social spending, and whose society has embraced a utopian view that war itself is simply outdated and can be eliminated by properly educated diplomats. (This is in stark contrast to such powerful countries as China and India, which have lately begun to adopt elements of the Western way of war: They maintain large defense establishments and have highly nationalistic citizenries that are not yet affluent or secure enough to trust that war is a relic of the past.)

9   The U.S. doesn't share Europe's anti-military bias, but it has its own problems. In a society in which a $50,000, three-ton, gas-guzzling monstrosity is required to transport safely a soccer mom and her twelve-year-old a few blocks to the practice field, it should come as no surprise that the military, too, has an "SUV syndrome": the embrace of expensive gadgetry and machines to ensure at all costs the safety of the individual combatant. The more that technology and science can ameliorate the human condition of the average American citizen, and prolong life by conquering the age-old banes of accident, disease, and famine, the more our cultures expect that our soldiers, too, will avoid wounds and death. The anticipation that we shall die at 90 in our sleep—peacefully and without pain—results in an array of social and cultural limitations placed upon the conditions of battle. Societies that are affluent and free expect their soldiers to be able to kill thousands of enemies who are neither—and without incurring any deaths in the process. In Afghanistan, our military has chosen repeatedly to be wary about exposing our own men to danger—even when it meant that dozens of dangerous al-Qaeda and Taliban would escape.

◆◆◆◆

10   Another eternal law of war is that the advantage keeps shifting, back and forth, between defense and offense. For centuries the methods of defense—whether stout ashlar-stone walls in the pre-catapult era, or knights in the age before the crossbow—trumped the effectiveness of most attackers. Today, however, destruction is easy—thanks to automatic weapons, precision bombing, and nuclear arsenals. But we may be witnessing the beginning of a shift back toward the defense: Breakthroughs in impenetrable light plastic and composite materials may well make our infantrymen as well protected against projectiles as yesterday's hoplites. We have seen this already in Afghanistan, where unharmed American soldiers have found spent slugs in their ultramodern flak vests.

11   For all the lethality of bunker-busters, daisy-cutters, and thermobaric bombs, reinforced caves—outfitted with space-age communications and supplies—seemed to protect al-Qaeda warriors well enough to force our designers back to the drawing boards to discover new ordnance that might bore through yards of such rock. On the intercontinental level, the once ridiculed concept of missile defense is no longer so ridiculous, and only a few years rather than decades away—raising the eerie and once inconceivable thought that a missile exchange might not result in horrendous carnage.

12   Tomorrow's wars will also prove that other historical rules remain valid. In the 1970s, for example, it was popular to scoff that carriers were simply floating targets that would "last about a minute" in a war with the Soviet Union. But any weapons system that is mobile, capable of sending out dozens of planes either to attack any type of enemy or to defend their mother ship, has timeless value. Despite its massive size, nuclear propulsion, electronics, and superior design, today's *Enterprise* is not all that different in form and function from its eponymous ancestor that fought at Midway. Why? Because a floating airstrip is a perfect and timeless weapon, one not dependent on volatile host countries; it is forever mobile, lethal at great distances, and eternally useful because it can be updated to reflect new technologies.

13   By the same token, submarines that twenty years ago were deemed the wave of future naval warfare have played a less prominent role in the post–Cold War era; their nuclear arsenals and near-miraculous stealth have proved of little value in the asymmetrical Gulf War or the air campaign against Serbia. It would, however, be a mistake to dismiss as superfluous any weapon that can strike without being seen: An array of conventionally armed submarines has already been modified to fire dozens of cruise missiles at distant inland targets, and there's no reason submarines could not be posted off the coast of Iran or North Korea with a full arsenal of anti-ballistic missiles to ensure that any nukes launched from those countries would be shot down a few thousand feet from their launch pads.

14   The conventional wisdom of the pundits will always be evanescent. We must not be hoodwinked by their presentism into thinking that a new weapon or a new theory has "reinvented" war. It cannot happen. There will be new technologies and new approaches to fighting—but we need to see how they fit into age-old military realities.

15   The first such reality is that war will not be outlawed or made obsolete. This idea is a spasm of utopian thinking on the part of elites; its only result is to get millions of less educated and less affluent innocents killed. War cannot be eliminated entirely, only avoided by deterrence. "He who wishes peace should prepare for war," runs the ancient wisdom—and it remains true today. When America had a "Department of War," no more Americans were killed overseas than in the period after its name was changed to the less bellicose "Department of Defense"—reminding us that we can repackage and rename conflict through euphemism and good intentions, but never really alter its brutal essence.

16   The second key reality is that war is not merely a material struggle, but more often a referendum on the spirit. No nation has ever survived once its citizenry ceased to believe that its culture was worth saving. Themistocles' Athens beat back hundreds of thousands of Persians; yet little more than a century later Demosthenes addressed an Athens that had become far wealthier—and could not marshal a far larger population to repulse a few thousand Macedonians. Rome was larger, far more populous, and wealthier in A.D. 400 than in 146 B.C.—but far more unsure about what it meant to be a Roman, and confused about whether being Roman was better than, or merely different from, being German or Persian. France, which stopped the Germans at Verdun, a quarter-century later let them romp through the Ardennes in six weeks. The more complex, expensive, and lethal our weapons become, the more we must remember that they are still just tools, whose effectiveness depends on the discipline, training, and spirit of their users.

17   If the United States continues to believe that its culture is not only different from, but better than, those of the rest of the world—and if it believes that its own past pathologies were symptoms of the universal weaknesses of men, rather than lasting indictments of our civilization—we will remain as strong as we were during the wars of the 20th century. In contrast, if we ever come to believe that we are too healthy, too sophisticated, and too enlightened ever to risk our safety in something as primitive as war, then all the most sophisticated weapons of the 21st century will not save us when our hour of peril comes. And, as September 11 reminds us, that hour most surely will come. ◆◆

B. HOW DO PEOPLE JUSTIFY WAR?

QUESTIONS TO CONSIDER BEFORE YOU READ

Think back on a time when you were in an argument with another person and both participants believed they were right. What was your reason? The other person's? Reflecting back on it now, would you change anything in the way you handled the situation if it were to occur again? How do you think religious fanatics become fanatics? What forces can you imagine that go into making certain people that way? It is considered ethically acceptable to retaliate against someone who strikes against you; would you say that it is acceptable to begin a transgression against another? Why or why not?

WHY WE BLOW OURSELVES UP*

Eyad Sarraj

Eyad Sarraj, a Palestinian doctor, wrote the following piece for Time *discussing why martyr-dom is something his people want to achieve. What cultural and religious forces create a need for people to find honor in their own deaths?*

1   A few weeks ago, my sister, a professional and a mother of four, was visibly shaken as she watched, on television, Israeli tanks torturing the streets of a refugee camp and soldiers raping its homes. She shocked us all when she declared that she would like to become a martyr. A few hours later, a young Palestinian woman stunned the world when she turned herself into a human bomb and ex-ploded in Jerusalem, killing one Israeli and wounding 150 others. In the weeks after, more women joined the queue of suicide bombers as the world stood alarmed and bewildered.

2   To understand why Palestinian men, and now women, are blowing them-selves up in Israeli restaurants and buses is to understand the Arab-Israeli conflict. Ours is a nation of anger and defiance. The struggle today is how not to become a suicide bomber. We are told that there are long queues of people willing to join the road to heaven, and I believe it.

3   What propels people into such action is a long history of humiliation and a desire for revenge that every Arab harbors. Since the establishment of Israel in 1948 and the resultant uprooting of Palestinians, a deep-seated feeling of shame has taken root in the Arab psyche. Shame is the most painful emotion in the Arab culture, producing the feeling that one is unworthy to live. The honorable Arab is the one who refuses to suffer shame and dies in dignity.

4   The 35 years of Israeli military occupation of the West Bank and the Gaza Strip has served as a continuous reminder of Arab weakness. But it was the de-struction of the P.L.O. in Lebanon by Ariel Sharon that decisively shifted the Palestinian-Israeli confrontation to the occupied territories and Israel. Helpless-ness and shame gave way to anger that later poured into the streets as defiance. That was the first *intifadeh.*

5   Suddenly Palestinians felt that they were restoring their honor by fighting the aggressor, by not being helpless victims. Facing a superior Israeli army with its formidable arsenal, they felt morally victorious as the children of the stones be-came heroes of defiance. While that sense of victory served Arafat as a psycholog-ical platform to launch his peace initiative and recognition of Israel, it was the Oslo agreement and the peace process that followed that disillusioned the Pales-tinians and threw them into a new episode of confrontation. The reluctance of Is-raeli governments to implement promised withdrawals from Palestinian land, and then the catastrophic failure of the Camp David talks, prepared the fertile soil for a new breed of militants and suicide bombers.

6   It was the re-entry of Sharon to the political scene that sparked the new

---

intifadeh. Scores of Palestinians were killed and maimed as Sharon declared his intention to cause as many casualties as possible. This time around, however, Israeli soldiers were not on foot and not even visible as they shot from their tanks. Palestinian militants shifted their target to the exposed Israeli civilians in markets and cafés. For the extremist militant, there is no difference between Israelis. They are the enemy; they are all the same.

7   In every case of martyrdom, there is a personal story of tragedy and trauma. A curious journalist once asked me to introduce him to a potential martyr. When the journalist asked, "Why would you do it?" he was told, "Would you fight for your country or not? Of course you would. You would be respected in your country as a brave man, and I would be remembered as a martyr."

8   This is the influence of the teaching of the Koran, the most potent and powerful book in Arabia for the past 14 centuries. In the holy book, God promised Muslims who sacrificed themselves for the sake of Islam that they would not die. They would live on in paradise. Muslims, men and women, even secularists, hold to the promise literally. Heaven is then the ultimate reward of the devout who have the courage to take the ultimate test of faith.

9   What the young man did not say was that he was burning with a desire for revenge. He was a tearful witness, at the age of six, to his father's beating by Israeli soldiers. He would never forget seeing his father taken away, bleeding from the nose.

10   As Sharon was taking Arafat hostage and grinding the salt of humiliation into the sour wounds, he was taking us into a new horrific level of madness. Another Palestinian girl blew herself up in Jerusalem last week, killing two Israelis and wounding more. She will not be the last. ◆◆

WHY WE FIGHT*

William J. Bennett

These excerpts come from a chapter titled "The Morality of Anger" in William J. Bennett's book Why We Fight: Moral Clarity and the War on Terrorism. *First Bennett explains the concept of a "just war" and describes its historical origins. Then he describes the problems he personally has with pacifism. What would you say is his final claim about conducting war?*

1   Nowhere in the New Testament do we find force itself held up for explicit praise—that would be all but unthinkable. But neither are the Gospel writers so unworldly as to posit that the answer to every human conflict is to turn the other cheek; in certain circumstances and for certain purposes, force would seem to be forbidden, in other cases allowed (even if never encouraged for its own sake). Indeed, it was to elaborate the why and how and wherefore of the latter

---

*William J. Bennett, *Why We Fight: Moral Clarity and the War on Terrorism* (New York: Doubleday, 2002), pp. 27–30, 39–43.

case that the Church, over the centuries, developed the doctrine of "just war," a theory that received its first extended treatment in the late fourth century at the hands of St. Augustine and was significantly modified nine centuries later by St. Thomas Aquinas.

2   "A great deal," Augustine wrote in *Contra Faustum*, "depends on the causes for which men undertake wars, and on the authority they have for doing so." Aquinas, specifying, named three main criteria for determining if one could initiate war. (This part of just-war doctrine was called by the medieval scholastics *jus ad bellum*, the right to go to war, as distinct from *jus in bello*, the proper conduct of war.) The three were: whether war is declared by a legitimate sovereign; whether it is for a just cause—that is, a cause that avenges wrongs or rights an injustice; and whether the belligerents "intend the advancement of good, or the avoidance of evil." To those who argued that Christians should always seek peace, Aquinas responded that those who wage war justly do, in fact, aim at true peace, being opposed only to an "evil peace." Indeed, Christians would be shirking their religious duty were they not to struggle against an unjust peace, including by taking up arms.

◆◆◆◆

3   Did American military action in the wake of September 11 satisfy these three criteria? That it was waged by a legitimate authority is patent: that authority being the duly elected and sworn president, acting with the virtually unanimous approval of the elected representatives of the American people. Likewise, it was clearly waged in a just cause, against terrorists who sought and still seek to destroy us, as well as to avoid future evil.

4   True, even when a war is waged by a legitimate authority, for a legitimate reason, and for a legitimate end, other factors must weigh heavily. Implicitly referring to the tradition of *jus in bello*, the letter of the U.S. Conference of Catholic Bishops to the president warned: "Any military response must be in accord with sound moral principles, . . . such as probability of success, civilian immunity, and proportionality." Although war is certainly hell (in the pithy observation of General William Sherman), our conduct of it must nevertheless be appropriate. We may be unable to avoid injuring innocent civilians in the course of fighting, but we must not target them. Likewise, we must not kill or mistreat prisoners of war. And we must always be wary of producing, even unintentionally, evils commensurate with those we are seeking to eliminate.

5   Obviously there is a fine moral line here. As the scholar Jean Bethke Elshtain has pointed out, Augustine, in developing the idea of the just war, struggled with the fact that the weight of Scripture challenges the use of force. But he recognized, as most Christians have, that there are times when *not* resorting to force leads to evils far greater than the one we oppose. And as for whether we have fought a war justly (in contrast to fighting a just war), any proper assessment requires careful analysis based on specific facts—and often on the outcome of the hostilities themselves. To quote the Anglican theologian Patrick Comerford, "It is only long after a war is over that we have the time and the luxury to determine whether all conditions [of a just war] have been met."

6   By all these standards, both the military campaign in Afghanistan and our conduct of that campaign qualify unreservedly as just. In light of its aims and its

achievements, in consideration of our extraordinary sensitivity to the avoidance of civilian casualties, and in light of our vast efforts of humanitarian relief for the suffering people of Afghanistan, I would not be surprised if, in historical retrospect, the Afghanistan campaign were to qualify as one of the most just wars ever fought.

◆◆◆◆

7   Why has the critique of violence taken such hold among us, and why does it exercise such influence? The answer is paradoxical. Contrary to the myth of our nation as violence-prone, Americans are in fact a peaceful people, averse to conflict. That is the larger truth about us. Our habits are the habits of a commercial society, resting on rich deposits of social trust and on laws that regulate and protect transactions of every kind. Our outlook is the outlook of a democratic polity, guided by the spirit of accommodation and compromise, superintended by guarantees of due process and judicial review.

8   It is exactly these same habits and this same outlook, I believe, that make so many of us susceptible to arguments of the give-peace-a-chance kind. I don't mean that we necessarily buy those arguments, but something in them appeals to something good in our nature, and though we may know they are wrong we often do not know quite how to answer them. That is precisely why I have been at such pains to take them seriously on their own terms. But I also want to be clear about where they come from.

9   It is theoretically true that one can espouse nonviolence *and* support the war effort. As Scott Simon reminds us, some genuine pacifists and conscientious objectors have done just that in past conflicts. The trouble with many of today's pacifists is that, in the name of the higher morality of nonviolence, they have not only declined to support the war effort but have actively tried to hamper it, loudly warning about cycles of violence, accusing us of an unseemly lust for vengeance, invoking the supposedly dark record of our past, sowing doubts about our intentions, impugning our right to defend ourselves.

10   In short, many in the "peace party" who cloak their arguments in moral objections to war are really expressing their hostility to America, and it does the cause of clarity no good to pretend otherwise. That hostility—in more than a few cases, hatred is a more accurate word—is many-sided and has a long history, and we shall be encountering facets of it in our discussion. But where armed conflict is concerned, the arguments of today's "peace party" are basically rooted in the period of the Vietnam war and its aftermath. It was then that the critique of the United States as an imperialist or "colonialist" power, wreaking its evil will on the hapless peoples of the third world, became a kind of slogan on the Left. This same critique would, in due course, find a home in certain precincts of the Democratic party and, in more diluted form, would inform the policy preferences of the Carter and Clinton administrations, and it is with us still.

11   It is especially prevalent in our institutions of higher learning. At a teach-in at the University of North Carolina immediately after the [September 11, 2001] attack, one speaker remarked that, were he the president of the United States, his first act would be not to avenge the infamy but to apologize to "the widows and orphans, the tortured and impoverished, and all the millions of the other victims of American imperialism." For a professor at Rutgers, whatever the "proximate

cause" of September 11, "its ultimate cause is the fascism of U.S. foreign policy over the past decades." Like the character in Molière's *Le Bourgeois gentilhomme* who was astonished to learn that he had been speaking prose all his life, these two seemed unconscious of the fact that they were speaking clichés, and clichés with a certain identifiable provenance.

12   Allied to the political critique of America that developed in the 1960s and 1970s was a cultural and psychological critique. Not just imperial ambition but a sort of deranged, Wild West machismo was said to be driving our activities abroad, impelling us to drop bombs on innocent people and/or to force upon them our uniquely rapacious model of economic activity. At home, this same derangement was said to lie behind everything from our alleged obsession with guns to our alleged obsession with order and the perverse way in which we brought up our children, especially our boys. Out of this critique there arose the by-now standard counterwisdom that I have already discussed: that conflict is always a product of misunderstanding, and that violence is always wrong.

13   In the past decades, since Vietnam and especially since our defeat there, our culture has undergone a process that one observer has aptly termed *debellicization*. Military virtues have been devalued and shunned, and along with them the very idea that war solves anything or is ever justified. Generations of schoolchildren have been taught that conflict is something to be avoided. Parents and teachers have been cautioned by psychologists and feminists alike that male aggression is a wild and malignant force that needs to be repressed or medicated lest it burst out, as it is always on the verge of doing, in murderous behavior. The 1999 shooting spree by two teenagers at Columbine High School in Colorado is taken to be all too horridly typical; in the meantime, the Boy Scouts of America, an irreplaceable institution that has always known how to channel the healthy impulses of male aggression, and to inspire male idealism, is derided as irrelevant, "patriarchal," and bigoted.

14   What you get in the end is that eleven-year-old schoolboy, dutifully repeating his mantra: "We learned that you should always find a peaceful way to solve your problems because you should never be violent."

◆◆◆◆

15   "You should never be violent." In this world, a world in which, to the best of my knowledge, the lion has yet to lie down with the lamb, teaching children this lesson does an unforgivable injury both to them and to the adult community of which they are about to become a part. It renders them vulnerable to abuse and injury, and leaves them without moral or intellectual recourse when abuse and injury are inflicted upon them. If no distinction is made among kinds of "peace," children are deprived of the tools they require to distinguish a just from an unjust peace, peace with honor from the peace of the grave. They are robbed of the oldest and most necessary wisdom of the race, which is that some things are worth fighting and dying for.

16   Are we to tell our children that, because "you should always find a peaceful way to solve your problems," the brave men who fought in the Revolutionary War, the Civil War, the two World Wars, and every other conflict in our history were acting immorally? That way lies a generation prepared only for accommodation, appeasement, and surrender. If, heaven forbid, they should ever be faced

in their turn with the need to respond to aggression and evil, better by far for them to have learned, understood, and taken to heart the words of John Stuart Mill:

> War is an ugly thing, but not the ugliest of things. The decayed and degraded state of a moral and patriotic feeling which thinks that nothing is worth war is much worse. A man who has nothing for which he is willing to fight—nothing he cares about more than his own safety—is a miserable creature who has no chance of being free, unless made and kept so by the exertions of better men than himself.

17   What term shall we reserve for those who in the current instance have preached to us that, given who we are, and what we have done in the world, nothing of ours is worth fighting for? "Much of what is passing for pacifism," wrote the characteristically blunt columnist Michael Kelly, "is not pacifism at all but only the latest manifestation of a well-known pre-existing condition." That condition, that plague, is anti-Americanism. ◆◆

HOW CAN WE UNDERSTAND THEIR HATRED*

Elie Wiesel

Nobel Prize winner and author of Night *and numerous other novels and essays, Elie Wiesel explores religious fanaticism and finds a place for hope. Where is this hope located? How effective do you think Wiesel's solution is to combat the hate that fuels fanatics?*

1   Fanaticism today is not a nice word; it carries an unpleasant connotation. But in ancient times, fanatics enjoyed a more favorable reaction from the public. They were linked to religion and, more specifically, to religious experience. In the Bible, Pinhas was praised for slaying a sinner. The Prophet Elijah was admired as an extreme opponent of the wicked Queen Jezebel. Later, in Islam, *fana* (meaning the annihilation of the will) described the Sufi's desire to attain ecstasy in his union with the divine.

2   Today, in our modern language, fanaticism refers to excessive behavior, uncritical political opinions, ethnic zeal and religious bigotry. How did this come to be?

3   Previous centuries suffered from tribal and religious wars and from national extremism, but our last century was ravaged mainly by ideological and secular hatred. Nazism and communism moved fanaticism to unprecedented dimensions—dimensions future historians may term as absolute. Stalin used Terror just as Hitler used Death to oppress tens of millions of people: Never have man-made ideologies introduced so much evil into society: never have they given Death so much power.

4   Early in my own life, I experienced the consequences of fanaticism. On Sept. 11, like so many others throughout the world, I saw its terrible consequences again. Glued for days to the television, I witnessed unthinkable acts of

---

*Parade, April 7, 2002, pp. 4–5.

terror. How, I asked myself, after the last century's horrors, could fanaticism still hold sway?

♦♦♦♦

5   On reflection, I believe that fanaticism appeals to people for a variety of reasons. But on the deepest level, fanaticism is seductive because it makes the fanatic feel less alone.

6   The fanatic fails to understand that the tragedy of man is that, in essential matters, we are each condemned to be alone—we can never break out of the "self." How does one cease being one's own jailer? By becoming each other's prisoner. The fanatic thinks he can tear down the walls of his cell by joining other fanatics. No need to think—the Party does the thinking for him, and the deciding for him.

7   The fanatic is stubborn, obstinate, dogmatic: Everything for him is black or white, curse or blessing, friend or foe—and nothing in between. He has no taste for or interest in nuances. Does he seek clarity? Driven by irrational impulses, he wants everything to be visible and necessarily clear.

8   The fanatic simplifies matters: He is immune to doubt and to hesitation. Intellectual exercise is distasteful, and the art and beauty of dialogue alien to him. Other people's ideas or theories are of no use to him. He is never bothered by difficult problems: A decree or a bullet solves them . . . immediately. The fanatic feels nothing but disdain toward intellectuals who spend precious time analyzing, dissecting, debating philosophical notions and hypotheses. What matters to the fanatic is the outcome—not the way leading there.

9   And more: The fanatic derides and hates tolerance, which he perceives as weakness, resignation or submission. That is why he despises women: Their tenderness is to him a sign of passivity. The fanatic's only interest is domination by fear and terror. Violence is his favorite language—a vulgar language filled with obscenities: He doesn't speak, he shouts; he doesn't listen, he is too busy yelling; he doesn't think, he doesn't want *anyone* to think.

10   In other words, the fanatic, intoxicated with hatred, tries to reduce everybody to his own size.

11   He has a goal and is ready to pay any price to achieve it. Or more precisely: He is ready to make *others* pay any price in order to achieve it.

12   The fanatic feels important, for he presumes being capable of altering—and dominating—the course of history. Using the obscure power of hatred, he feels he can—and must—take charge of man's fate. Working in the dark, forever involved in plots and counterplots, he thinks his mission is to abolish the present state of affairs and replace it with his own system. No wonder that he, the human failure, now feels proud and superior.

13   The fanatic who kills in God's name makes his God a murderer.

♦♦♦♦

14   Let me conclude with this thought:

15   Of all the "isms" produced by the past centuries, fanaticism alone survives. We have witnessed the downfall of Nazism, the defeat of fascism and the abdication of communism. But fanaticism is still alive. And it is spreading fast. As horrible as it may sound, racial hatred, anti-Semitism and bin Laden terrorism are popular and still glorified in certain communities.

16   How can the fanatics be brought back to moral sanity? How can the killers and suicide warriors be disarmed?

17   If there is a simple answer, I do not know it. All I know is that, as we embark on this newest century, we cannot continue to live with fanaticism—and only we ourselves can stem it.

18   How are we to do this?

19   We must first fight indifference.

20   Indifference to evil is the enemy of good, for indifference is the enemy of everything that exalts the honor of man. We fight indifference through education: we diminish it through compassion. The most efficient remedy? Memory.

21   To remember means to recognize a time other than the present; to remember means to acknowledge the possibility of a dialogue. In recalling an event, I provoke its rebirth in me. In evoking a face, I place myself in relationship to it. In remembering a landscape, I oppose it to the walls that imprison me. The memory of an ancient joy or defeat is proof that nothing is definitive, nor is it irrevocable. To live through a catastrophe is bad; to forget it is worse.

22   And so, as we move forward from Sept. 11, let us continue to remember. For memory may be our most powerful weapon against fanaticism. ◆◆

C. WHAT MIGHT HELP ESTABLISH PEACE

QUESTIONS TO CONSIDER BEFORE YOU READ

Recall a time when you and another person reached a compromise. What was the compromise over? How did you feel afterward? Some people consider compromise to be a sign of weakness. What do you think? Do you think that all people are willing to compromise? When there is a lot at stake, is compromise always a better solution than conflict? Aside from fighting or compromise, do you think there are other ways in which peace between two parties can be achieved?

GETTING TO PEACE*

William L. Ury

The following excerpt by William L. Ury comes from his book The Third Side. *Ury advocates moving from a situation of conflict to one of compromise. What would you be willing to give up in order to have peace in the world?*

FROM WIN-LOSE TOWARD LOSE-LOSE

1   A "win-lose" mentality can wreak havoc in any domain of human life. When husbands and wives seek to control each other, the result is often a bitter divorce. When quarreling neighbors take each other to court, they frequently lose their

---

*William L. Ury, *The Third Side* (New York: Penguin, 2000), pp. 87–92.

time and money. When unions and companies fight, everyone can lose their jobs—permanently. Voltaire put it best of all: "I was never ruined but twice: once when I lost a lawsuit and once when I won one."

2 The Knowledge Revolution only sharpens the "lose-lose" logic of conflict. Partly because the spread of knowledge tends to equalize power, partly because destructive weaponry is increasingly accessible, it is becoming harder to win a dispute in a decisive and enduring fashion.

3 Consider the history of warfare in the twentieth century. In August 1914, the nations of Europe went to war confident their soldiers would be home by Christmas with a clear victory over the enemy. When the war ended four years later, even the victors had lost. France, the principal battleground, was ravaged, and the British Empire had suffered a blow from which it was never to recover. Even worse, the victory proved to be a mere truce until an even more devastating war erupted twenty years later.

4 The logic of "no one wins" was clearest during the Cold War. The governments of the United States and the Soviet Union spent hundreds of billions of dollars trying to find a way to make a nuclear war winnable. They came up with weapon system after weapon system, from MIRVs to the neutron bomb, and doctrine after doctrine, from decapitation to first strike. Each weapon and doctrine was designed to make it credible that nuclear weapons could be used to win a war. Some of the best scientific minds of a generation tried to crack this puzzle—to no avail. What became clear over time was that a nuclear war would bring only losers.

5 Even smaller wars proved hard to win for the powerful nations on earth. The Vietnam War became a cruel education for the United States, as did the war in Afghanistan for the Soviet Union. The spread of advanced weaponry and new ideas of freedom and self-determination, both fruits of the Knowledge Revolution, have made it ever more costly to impose control over others.

6 This change was driven home for me when I was facilitating peace discussions between Russian and Chechen leaders in the spring and fall of 1997. The vaunted Red Army, which the United States had spent a trillion dollars seeking to contain, had failed to impose its will on tiny Chechnya in almost two years of barbaric warfare. The opposing force that had compelled the Red Army to withdraw consisted, as the Chechen vice president explained, of fewer than seven thousand determined fighters. They obtained much of their weaponry from Russian soldiers and listened in on Russian military radio frequencies to learn their opponents' plans. Thanks to independent media, only recently established, the war became intensely unpopular in Russia; mothers of Russian soldiers traveled to Chechnya to take their sons home. The Chechens' dramatic seizure of hundreds of Russian civilian hostages and the Russian military's violent and ineffectual responses, captured on television, forced the Russian government into negotiations. Unable to fight effectively in an age of information, Moscow withdrew from a devastated Chechnya.

7 The Knowledge Revolution has accentuated the "all-lose" nature of destructive conflict. One statistic about warfare is particularly telling. In 1900, the ratio of civilian to military casualties in war ranged from ten to fifty percent. Now the average figure is over ninety percent. As in Chechnya, nine out of ten deaths are not

soldiers but civilians. It is mostly the innocent who die—elderly shoppers in the marketplace, young children playing in the street, and women huddled in their houses with their babies.

8   We are all vulnerable. From personal life to business to world politics, people are going through a painful reeducation about the nature of conflict, just as American and Soviet leaders did during the Cuban Missile Crisis. "An eye for an eye" was the old law. The new realization is, in Mahatma Gandhi's words, "An eye for an eye and we all go blind."

FROM WIN-LOSE TOWARD BOTH-GAIN

9   If the Knowledge Revolution makes it possible for both to lose, it also makes it easier for both to "gain." "Both-gain" does not mean that both parties get everything they want, but rather that they each benefit more than they probably would by fighting. It usually means, furthermore, that the most basic human needs of the parties are met.

10   Consider the essential need for food. For the last five or ten millennia, food has been an item of scarcity in virtually every agricultural society on earth. Famine and hunger were normal and accepted occurrences. My generation in the United States was admonished to eat all the food on our plates because "children were starving in India and China." Our image of India and China at the time was of teeming millions of people, for whom there would never be enough food. Since the 1950s, however, despite a doubling of their population, India and China have both acquired the ability to feed their own peoples. The Knowledge Revolution in the form of machinery, fertilizers, and genetic breeding has transformed the practice of agriculture. The malnutrition that tragically remains in the world results from economic and political inequity, not from lack of capacity to produce food.

11   In the global economy, a "both-gain" logic is making more and more sense. Companies are finding it to their advantage to pool their resources for research and development, to share production facilities, and to learn from each other. They are forging strategic alliances and joint ventures, sometimes with their most ardent competitors. The largest company in the world, General Motors, created an alliance with its competitor Toyota; IBM did the same with Fujitsu. Benetton's success comes from its cooperative relationships with its more than seven hundred small entrepreneurial subcontractors. Benetton concentrates on what it does best, buying raw materials, creating colors, and marketing the clothes, while the suppliers do what they do best, making clothes; as Benetton grows, everyone benefits. Increasingly in today's marketplace, a business's ability to compete depends on its ability to cooperate.

12   The Knowledge Revolution makes possible new solutions to old conflicts. The war between Israel and Egypt, for example, came to an end in a negotiation over the Sinai Peninsula, occupied by Israel during the 1967 Six-Day War. Egypt demanded the return of the entire peninsula, but Israel insisted on retaining a third of the peninsula as a security buffer. No simple compromise was acceptable. It turned out, however, that what Israel really needed most was not the land itself, but knowledge—early warning of attack. Thanks to new technology, both sides

were able to agree to demilitarize the Sinai and establish electronic detectors to monitor any threatening movement. Egypt received all its land back and Israel obtained even more of a security buffer than it had been demanding. A negotiated both-gain solution replaced an unstable win-lose solution.

13   Even an expanded pie, however, still needs to be divided up. Who will get what part? Opposed interests remain. A buyer wants to get a certain product for less; the seller insists on more. An ethnic group wants more autonomy; the state insists on less. While a both-gain logic does not imply an end to the win-lose aspect of conflict, it does sharpen the incentive to handle these opposed interests through negotiation rather than force.

THE EXAMPLE OF SOUTH AFRICA

14   Nowhere has the shift in the underlying logic of human conflict been more dramatically illustrated than in the case of South Africa. In early 1995, I heard Nelson Mandela and F. W. de Klerk, separately, describe the journey each had taken from war to peace. De Klerk spoke about how he had come to realize that, politically and militarily, the white minority could not hold on to power indefinitely in the face of strong black resistance armed with the fruits of the Knowledge Revolution: ideas of equality, modern means of communication, weapons, and international support. South Africa's economy was suffering from international trade and financial sanctions. Only by reaching a peace accord could the white minority hope to retain its quality of life and the Afrikaner tribe protect its identity.

15   Mandela talked about seeing the country descending into civil strife and economic ruin. While he was confident that the black majority would prevail in the long term, he wondered what kind of country would be left in the end for the blacks to inherit. Only by prospering in the new global economy could they put an end to their poverty and deprivation—and that prosperity could be achieved only by cooperating with the white minority with their technical skills and business experience. The vision of the African National Congress, moreover, had always been a democratic multiracial society. With every passing year of ethnic violence, that vision was fading out of reach.

16   Both leaders, in other words, realized that the conflict was stalemated. Continuing the violence would spell defeat for everyone. Only through negotiation could both sides hope to meet their needs. If both sides could lose through a spiral of violence, then perhaps both sides could win through a spiral of dialogue. As Mandela put it, "I never sought to undermine Mr. de Klerk, for the practical reason that the weaker he was, the weaker the negotiations process. To make peace with an enemy one must work with that enemy, and the enemy must become one's partner."

17   To test this theory, de Klerk and other white leaders met with Mandela while he was still in prison, and came away feeling personal respect for the man. Each side came to realize that the people on the other side were not the monsters they had imagined. Gradually, during the course of the negotiations, as Roelf Meyer, the chief negotiator for the white Nationalist government, explained to me, both sides came to believe in the possibility of a new alternative, neither a white victory nor a black victory nor even a split-the-difference compromise. The new

alternative they envisioned was a victory for both sides—a peaceful, democratic, and prosperous South Africa that could compete in the new global economy.

18   Through a process of laborious and continuous conflict resolution, war gradually turned to peace. This peace was not harmony but an ongoing, often conflictual process of seeking to address the basic needs of people for adequate food and shelter, safety, identity, and freedom. For the problems facing South Africa remained enormous. Poverty, malnutrition, and illiteracy were widespread. The economic inequalities were perhaps greater than in any other nation on earth. Crime was rising. Violence between Zulus and other tribes continued. Immigrants from other parts of Africa poured in by the millions. Meeting these challenges depended on harnessing the full potential of the Knowledge Revolution.

19   None of these problems, however, could detract from the extraordinary political transformation that had taken place. Thanks to the wisdom of the leadership in realizing that neither side could win without the other, what had seemed impossible proved not to be. Irreconcilable confrontation gave way to peaceful cooperation. ◆◆

THE ATOMIC BOMB*

Richard Rhodes

Richard Rhodes, a Pulitzer Prize winner, wrote this article for Newsweek. *What is the importance of the nuclear bomb for the modern world?*

1   The first nuclear reactor on earth went critical 2 billion years ago in western Africa when groundwater seeped into a rich vein of uranium ore. It controlled itself elegantly, its water moderator boiling off to regulate its fissioning, ran for a hundred thousand years and shut itself down. Its nuclear waste didn't wander and has long since decayed to lead.

2   French mining experts discovered the remains of several such natural reactors in Gabon in 1972. By then, science imitating nature, workers in many countries were pouring concrete for water-moderated, man-made nuclear reactors to generate electricity, and six nations were stockpiling atomic and hydrogen bombs.

3   Two German chemists studying uranium, Otto Hahn and Fritz Strassmann, discovered nuclear fission in Nazi Germany in December 1938, nine months before the beginning of World War II in Europe. When the chemists published their finding the following month, the scientific community was amazed. No one had ever seen such an energetic reaction: fire one low-energy neutron into a uranium atom and the atom split apart and released a burst of energy 10 million times as intense.

4   Such ferocious output made it immediately obvious to physicists everywhere that the discovery could lead to a vastly destructive new kind of bomb.

*Newsweek, Special Issue, Winter 1997–98, Vol. 130, Issue 22, pp. 56–60.

Jewish physicists in England and America who had escaped Nazi Germany were horrified. Fearing a German head start, Hungarians Leo Szilard, Eugene Wigner and Edward Teller, plus Albert Einstein, an earlier arrival, alerted Franklin Roosevelt. The president, realizing that possession of such a weapon would be the only defense against an enemy similarly armed, gave the go-ahead for a top-priority research effort. The British, already at war, contributed a detailed proposal, and in October 1941 the Manhattan Project was born.

5 　　It cost as much to make the first three bombs as it would cost two decades later to send men to the moon. What began on a benchtop in Germany in 1938 became an industry comparable in scale to the U.S. automobile industry of the day. Vast secret factories went up in Tennessee that drew megawatts of TVA electricity and employed tens of thousands of workers. The Columbia River was partly diverted to cool powerful graphite-and-uranium production reactors in the state of Washington. Tons of uranium ore entered one end of the system; a few grams of pure uranium and the new man-made element plutonium came out the other. Once a week an army security man carried the week's output in an ordinary suitcase by passenger train to a new secret laboratory high on a mesa at Los Alamos, N.M., where the first bombs were to be built. "Gadgets," lab director J. Robert Oppenheimer dubbed them when the laboratory set up shop behind barbed wire in April 1943.

6 　　Oppenheimer, a charismatic theoretical physicist, guided a crack team of world-class scientists at Los Alamos. The two different bombs they devised over the next 28 months, Little Boy and Fat Man, fissioned baseball-size cores of uranium or plutonium to deliver explosions equivalent to thousands of tons of TNT. Designing such awesome weapons required inventing whole new technologies: electrical detonators with microsecond timing, high explosives shaped into lenses that focused shock waves to compress solid metal, diagnostic cameras spinning a million frames a second, plutonium's bizarre metallurgy.

7 　　The first Fat Man exploded on a tower in a barren stretch of New Mexican desert before dawn on July 16, 1945, confirming the success of this immense commitment of people and resources. "There was an enormous ball of fire which grew and grew and it rolled as it grew," Columbia University physicist I. I. Rabi remembered. "It looked menacing. It seemed to come toward one." Rabi saw the test's deeper portents as well: "A new thing had just been born; a new control; a new understanding of man, which man had acquired over nature."

8 　　To recruit his remarkable team, Oppenheimer had whispered that the bombs they would build would not only end World War II but might also end war itself. Certainly they ended the Pacific war. Of the 76,000 buildings in the Japanese port city of Hiroshima, bombed on Aug. 6, Little Boy damaged or destroyed 70,000— 48,000 of them totally. Ninety percent of all Hiroshima's medical personnel were disabled or killed. At least 70,000 people died by the end of the month; more died later of the effects of fire, blast and radiation. A second Fat Man, twice as powerful as Little Boy, similarly decimated Nagasaki on Aug. 9. A third Fat Man was waiting in the wings; Oppenheimer thought he could produce six a month beginning in October. Japanese Emperor Hirohito specifically cited "a new and most cruel bomb" in his historic broadcast of Aug. 15, when he ordered his people to lay down their arms.

9   Was Oppenheimer right? Did the development of nuclear weapons put an end to war? Not all war, obviously, but world-scale war became increasingly unthinkable after those brutal August shocks. Across the second half of the century—an era one historian has called the "long peace"—tens of thousands of bombs would be built and stockpiled, but in all those years not one was ever exploded in anger.

10   Why such unprecedented restraint? Because a proliferating balance of terror made nuclear war suicidal. A Soviet scientific team under physicist Igor Kurchatov started small-scale development of an atomic bomb in Moscow early in 1943, after spies in England and the United States alerted Stalin to the Manhattan Project. The Soviet dictator suspected a hoax, but the evidence of Hiroshima and Nagasaki two years later persuaded him to order an all-out Russian effort. By then, two Los Alamos physicists, German émigré Klaus Fuchs and an American, Theodore Alvin Hall, had independently passed detailed plans to the KGB. The British began a bomb project immediately after the Japanese surrendered. France under Charles de Gaulle soon weighed in. Even Sweden launched a small bomb program in those early days but eventually shut it down.

11   The United States temporized for two years before beginning to improve and stockpile nuclear weapons in earnest: as late as April 1947 there were no working atomic bombs in the American arsenal, though the cold war had begun dividing the world by then and Soviet conventional forces in Europe were expanding. Harry Truman, determined to pay off the war deficit and judging that the world's only nuclear power could afford to reduce its conventional forces, cut the defense budget to the bone. When the Pentagon realized in 1948 that the civilian Atomic Energy Commission was legally required to build as many bombs as the military certified it needed—and that the commission would bear the expense—official military requirements soared from a few hundred bombs to, eventually, tens of thousands. The Soviet Union was a serious threat, but "overkill," as it came to be called—making the rubble bounce—had more to do with interservice rivalry in both the United States and the U.S.S.R. than with military reality.

12   When U.S. "sniffer" planes picked up fallout from the first Soviet atomic-bomb test, on Aug. 29, 1949, two years ahead of CIA predictions, Washington panicked: suddenly Russia had nuclear potential to go with its massive conventional advantage. A few wise heads, including Rabi, saw that nuclear parity might make the Soviets amenable to international control and called for renewed diplomacy. But hawks, encouraged by an ambitious Edward Teller, clamored for a new, unique capability: the hydrogen bomb. The Joint Chiefs heard about the hydrogen bomb for the first time on Oct. 13 and decided on the spot that the United States had to build it before the Russians did. Truman concurred, announcing his decision on Jan. 31, 1950. "I never forgave Truman," Rabi would say bitterly. "For him to have alerted the world that we were going to make a hydrogen bomb at a time when we didn't even know how to make one was one of the worst things he could have done." Teller had sold Washington a pig in a poke.

13   Inventing the hydrogen bomb turned out to be a far harder job than the atomic bomb had been. Calculations on some of the earliest digital computers proved that the design Teller had banked on was a dud. He was near despair

when an urbane Polish mathematician at Los Alamos, Stanislaw Ulam, showed him the way to a breakthrough. The two-stage design that resulted, tested on the Pacific atoll of Eniwetok on Nov. 1, 1952, yielded a terrifying 10.4 megatons—a thousand times the power of the Hiroshima bomb. The Soviets worked out multiple staging in 1955 and tested a 58-megaton monster in 1961, the largest ever exploded. British, French and Chinese hydrogen bombs followed. Israel, India, Pakistan and South Africa developed more modest atomic capabilities.

14   The motive for going nuclear was always defensive, though national prestige also figured in. The United States built the bomb because it feared a German lead, Soviet Russia to counter the United States, Britain and France to acquire an independent anti-Soviet deterrent, China to counter the United States and the U.S.S.R., India to counter China, Pakistan to counter India, Israel because it was surrounded by hostile Arab states, apartheid South Africa to ward off black Africa. Before it gave up power, the white South African government dismantled its small nuclear arsenal, the only act of unilateral nuclear disarmament yet recorded.

15   Every U.S. president since Truman and every Soviet leader after Stalin said publicly that using nuclear weapons was inconceivable, and so it has proved to be. Not deadlock, as in Korea, nor even defeat, as in Vietnam and Afghanistan, would ever justify escalation. The danger was too great. "In the real world of real political leaders," John Kennedy's and Lyndon Johnson's national-security adviser, McGeorge Bundy, wrote in 1969, "a decision that would bring even one hydrogen bomb on one city of one's own country would be recognized in advance as a catastrophic blunder; ten bombs on ten cities would be a disaster beyond history; and a hundred bombs on a hundred cities are unthinkable."

16   Small, cheap and portable, with essentially unlimited destructive capacity, nuclear weapons deny advantage to aggressor and defender alike. Lesser wars continue and will continue until the world community is sufficiently impressed with their futility to forge new instruments of protection and new forms of citizenship. But world war has at least been revealed to be a historical interlude in human history that began when the industrial capacity of entire nations could be mobilized for war and ended when a few hundred bombs could destroy that capacity in a matter of hours. In the long history of human slaughter that is no small achievement.

17   An equal achievement has been the application of nuclear fission to peaceful purposes. Nuclear power plants in 32 countries today supply more than 17 percent of the world's electricity. Americans have been taught to fear nuclear power, but the United States has more installed capacity than any other country. France is second—75 percent of French electricity is nuclear, which has reduced French air pollution fivefold—followed by Russia and Japan. Chernobyl was an anomaly: a flawed design, illegal in the West, recklessly mishandled by a criminal regime.

18   Air pollution, increasing demand and depletion of fossil fuels make it a sure bet that natural gas and nuclear power will be the prime sources of energy in the 21st century: China, South Asia and the industrializing Third World have already begun ambitious nuclear power programs. Nuclear reactors breed plutonium as they burn uranium; the "spent" fuel that affluent America calls nuclear waste and

prepares to bury is a nearly unlimited source of energy that other nuclear nations value and recycle. (U.S. recycling was halted in 1979 to discourage weapons proliferation, but no nuclear power makes bombs from reactor-grade plutonium, and no terrorist group could—it's unreliable.) Like the natural reactors of Gabon, power reactors can transmute nuclear waste—including the tons of plutonium removed from the tens of thousands of nuclear weapons that the United States and Russia are dismantling as the arms race winds down—to less dangerous forms.

19   "The physicists have known sin," Robert Oppenheimer once famously said. He meant their pure science had fallen into a world of hard consequences. So long as civilization continues, we will have knowledge of how to destroy ourselves in nuclear war. But a world without nuclear weapons isn't a pipe dream; the time will come when deterrence means mothballed factories capable of delivering warheads in three months rather than nuclear submarines capable of delivering warheads in half an hour. Self-interest will dictate the stand-down, because nations growing more prosperous in a nuclear-powered world will have ever more to lose. That prospect and all this history, taken together, mean that the release of nuclear energy was arguably the most important human discovery since fire. ◆◆

ALL YOU NEED IS LOVE*

Bruce Hoffman

The following article by Bruce Hoffman first appeared in the Atlantic Monthly. *In it, Hoffman explores ways of stopping terrorism other than combat. What are those other ways? How effective do you think they would be?*

1   "Do you want to know how to eliminate terrorism? I'll tell you. In fact, I'll tell you about something that no one else knows. Something that has never been written about. You will be amazed, but it is true. Listen."

2   The speaker knew what he was talking about. Just a few years before, he had been a terrorist—a senior commander of al-Fatah, the largest constituent element of the Palestine Liberation Organization and the group that was founded, in 1959, and has been led ever since by Yasir Arafat, the chairman of the PLO. The speaker was now a brigadier general in one of the Palestine Authority's myriad security and intelligence services. He was an Arafat loyalist: his fidelity as much as his competence led to his appointment to this critically important post. We spoke when an uneasy peace still reigned between Israel and the Palestinians, and in fact there was a degree of cooperation between the Israeli intelligence and security agencies and their Palestinian counterparts, which was superintended by the CIA.

3   Ironically, the general's job was hunting down and rooting out terrorists. He was the archetypal poacher turned gamekeeper. His nemeses were neither the

Atlantic Monthly, May 2001, pp. 34–37.

Jews nor their Zionist benefactors but his brother Palestinians: men who, unlike him, had refused to swear allegiance to *al Rais* ("the head," as Arafat is often known among Palestinians) and the governing Palestine Authority. These men, moreover, were imbued with religious fervor and the unswerving belief that armed struggle was decreed by Allah and justified by the Koran. They belonged to a new generation of Palestinians, who had joined more-recently established terrorist groups such as Hamas (the Arabic acronym for the Islamic Resistance Movement) and the Palestine Islamic Jihad, and whose struggles were directed as much against what they saw as the corrupt and reprobate Palestine Authority as against their most reviled enemy, Israel.

4   We had been sitting in the general's office, above a sweltering prison in Gaza City, talking and drinking sweet coffee. The general was in mufti. He wore a blue suit, a light-blue shirt, and a blue-and-gold necktie. He looked like a middle-class businessman or an avuncular pharmacist. His office was sparsely decorated. On the wall behind his desk was a photograph of Arafat with his familiar stubble, attired in green military fatigues and wearing his trademark black-and-white *kuffiyeh* (Arab head scarf). On the desk was a picture of the general himself, standing beside Arafat and looking very serious. Along the wall, on a side table, were framed photographs of each of the general's children, greeting or being hugged by Arafat, who appeared the kindly, elderly patron paying a surprise visit to commemorate a birthday or celebrate some other noteworthy family event.

5   "Arafat and the PLO," the general said, "had a big problem in the 1970s. We had a group called the Black September Organization. It was the most elite unit we had. The members were suicidal—not in the sense of religious terrorists who surrender their lives to ascend to heaven but in the sense that we could send them anywhere to do anything and they were prepared to lay down their lives to do it. No question. No hesitation. They were absolutely dedicated and absolutely ruthless."

6   Black September was at the time among the most feared terrorist organizations in the world. It had been formed as a deniable and completely covert special-operations unit of al-Fatah by Arafat and his closest lieutenants following the brutal expulsion of the Palestinians from Jordan in September of 1970—the event from which the group's name was derived. Black September's mission, however, was not simply to exact retribution on Jordan but to catapult the Palestinians and their cause onto the world's agenda.

7   Black September's first operation was the assassination, in November of 1971, of Jordan's Prime Minister Wasfi al-Tal, who was gunned down as he entered the lobby of the Sheraton Hotel in Cairo. While Tal lay dying, one of the assassins knelt and lapped with his tongue the blood flowing across the marble floor. That grisly scene, reported in *The Times* of London and other major newspapers, created an image of uncompromising violence and determination that was exactly what Arafat both wanted and needed.

8   He doubtless succeeded beyond his expectations in September of 1972, when Black September perpetrated one of the most audacious acts of terrorism in history: the seizure of Israeli athletes at the Munich Olympic Games. That incident is widely credited as the premier example of terrorism's power to rocket a cause

from obscurity to renown. The operation's purpose was to capture the world's attention by striking at a target of inestimable value (in this case a country's star athletes) in a setting calculated to provide the terrorists with unparalleled exposure and publicity. According to Abu Iyad, the PLO's intelligence and security chief, a longtime Arafat confidant, and a co-founder of al-Fatah, the Black September terrorists "didn't bring about the liberation of any of their comrades imprisoned in Israel as they had hoped, but they did attain the operation's other two objectives: World opinion was forced to take note of the Palestinian drama, and the Palestinian people imposed their presence on an international gathering that had sought to exclude them." Just over two years later Arafat was invited to address the UN General Assembly, and shortly afterward the PLO was granted special observer status in that international body.

9   The problem, however, was that Black September had served its purpose. The PLO and its chairman had the recognition and acceptance they craved. Indeed, any continuation of these terrorist activities, ironically, now threatened to undermine all that had been achieved. In short, Black September was, suddenly, not a deniable asset but a potential liability. Thus, according to my host, Arafat ordered Abu Iyad "to turn Black September off." My host, who was one of Abu Iyad's most trusted deputies, was charged with devising a solution. For months both men thought of various ways to solve the Black September problem, discussing and debating what they could possibly do, short of killing all these young men, to stop them from committing further acts of terror.

10   Finally they hit upon an idea. Why not simply marry them off? In other words, why not find a way to give these men—the most dedicated, competent, and implacable fighters in the entire PLO—a reason to live rather than to die? Having failed to come up with any viable alternatives, the two men put their plan in motion.

11   They traveled to Palestinian refugee camps, to PLO offices and associated organizations, and to the capitals of all Middle Eastern countries with large Palestinian communities. Systematically identifying the most attractive young Palestinian women they could find, they put before these women what they hoped would be an irresistible proposition: Your fatherland needs you. Will you accept a critical mission of the utmost importance to the Palestinian people? Will you come to Beirut, for a reason to be disclosed upon your arrival, but one decreed by no higher authority than Chairman Arafat himself? How could a true patriot refuse?

12   So approximately a hundred of these beautiful young women were brought to Beirut. There, in a sort of PLO version of a college mixer, boy met girl, boy fell in love with girl, boy would, it was hoped, marry girl. There was an additional incentive, designed to facilitate not just amorous connections but long-lasting relationships. The hundred or so Black Septemberists were told that if they married these women, they would be paid $3,000; given an apartment in Beirut with a gas stove, a refrigerator, and a television; and employed by the PLO in some nonviolent capacity. Any of these couples that had a baby within a year would be rewarded with an additional $5,000.

13   Both Abu Iyad and the future general worried that their scheme would never work. But, as the general recounted, without exception the Black Septemberists fell in love, got married, settled down, and in most cases started a family. To make sure that none ever strayed, the two men devised a test. Periodically, the former terrorists would be handed legitimate passports and asked to go to the organization's offices in Geneva or Paris or some other city on genuine nonviolent PLO business. But, the general explained, not one of them would agree to travel abroad, for fear of being arrested and losing all that they had—that is, being deprived of their wives and children. "And so," my host told me, "that is how we shut down Black September and eliminated terrorism. It is the only successful case that I know of."

14   In the years since, as terrorism has itself become more egregiously lethal and destructive, seemingly more intractable and unrelenting, I have thought often of that story, and I suspect that it is a less far-fetched plan for combating terrorism than it at first seems. The authorities in Northern Ireland, for example, pursued a somewhat similar strategy during the years before the current cease-fire. Hard-core IRA and Loyalist terrorists serving long prison sentences were often given brief furloughs during holiday periods. The men to whom this privilege was accorded were carefully selected. They were mostly in their thirties, and therefore at a time in their lives when the perceived immortality of youth has been superseded by the dawning realization of death's inevitability, if not for themselves, then certainly for their parents.

15   Once at home with their families, these men, as the authorities had correctly calculated, developed a keen appreciation of elderly parents whom they might never see again once they were returned to prison, and also of children growing up too fast and of still young and attractive wives wasting their lives waiting. When the men returned to prison, they were asked if they would be interested in an expedited release. The Northern Ireland Office relied on a combination of factors to wean these men from terrorism: family pressure to forsake violence and secure an early release and the men's having seen with their own eyes how much the province had changed. To qualify for this form of parole, the men were required to move out of segregated prison wings (where they lived with only fellow IRA or Loyalist prisoners) and into fully integrated cell blocks, where Protestants and Catholics mixed freely—and nonviolently. This was a critical first step on the road to parole, followed by vocational training (not provided in segregated wings), counseling, and more-frequent family visits and furloughs. No one who had taken advantage of this opportunity for early parole ever returned to violence or to prison. The program was so successful that the option could be offered to only a limited number of prisoners, lest the terrorist organizations, fearing the loss of too many senior veterans and commanders, forbid their members to participate in the program. To a great extent, accordingly, the climate of peace that emerged in Northern Ireland in the mid-1990s may have owed as much to the creativity and foresight of the Northern Ireland Prison Service as to the political dexterity and visions of Gerry Adams and David Trimble or Martin McGuinness and Senator George Mitchell.

16   The lesson here is not that the United States should host a series of mixers in the Arab world in hopes of encouraging the young men of al Qaeda or other terrorist organizations to forsake violence and embrace family life. Rather, the lesson is that clever, creative thinking can sometimes achieve unimaginable ends. Indeed, rather than concentrating on eliminating organizations, as we mostly do in our approach to countering terrorism, we should perhaps focus at least some of our attention on weaning individuals from violence. It could hardly be any less effective than many of the countermeasures that have long been applied to terrorism—with ephemeral, if not often nugatory, results. ◆◆

QUESTIONS TO HELP YOU THINK AND WRITE ABOUT WAR AND PEACE

1. James calls for rethinking military service for young men. He claims that young men required to do civic instead of military duty will get the desire to fight out of their systems. As a result, men will become more contemplative and less aggressive after their training. Do you agree or disagree with James's claim? Identify the reasons for your answer. What are the benefits of adopting James's plan? What are the drawbacks? In your opinion, is there a "moral equivalent of war"?

2. What is your response to Hanson's ideas that war will always be war, no matter the time, no matter the form? Does this conception of war achieve what society hopes to achieve in terms of its own defense? How do you react to this position? Why?

3. After reading Mead's essay, explain how she intellectually justifies her belief that war is an invention. How do you respond to her justification? If you read this essay along with the argument by Hanson, how do you think Hanson would react to Mead's conclusion?

4. Compare "A Moral Equivalent of War" with Mead's essay. If these two authors were having a conversation on the "nature" of war, what do you imagine they might say to each other? In pairs, have one person play the role of Mead and the other James. Using the essays for support, attempt to persuade the other person of the "nature" of war. Whose arguments were more convincing? Why?

5. Sarraj and Wiesel are concerned with the reasons fanatics kill themselves and innocent people. Notice the difference between the two accounts. Sarraj is Palestinian, and Wiesel, although he is a Holocaust survivor, still writes from an outsider's perspective. Write down the reasons each gives for the behavior of fanatics. Whose reasons do you think are more helpful in understanding how to prevent further atrocities? Why?

6. Imagine Ury having a conversation with Sarraj and Wiesel. After reading Ury's essay, what do you think he would have to say about solving the problems of fanatics pointed out by the other two authors? What do you think they might say in response? Would the outcome, in your estimation, be productive? Why?

7. Read Bennett and Ury together. Divide a notebook page into two columns. In one column write down all the reasons Ury gives for peace, and in the other list the reasons Bennett gives for going to war. Whose reasons are more persuasive? Why?

8. After reading Rhodes's essay, do you agree that the nuclear bomb has been the greatest tool for achieving peace? Write down your reasons for agreeing or disagreeing.

9. After reading Hoffman's essay, brainstorm with some classmates and try to come up with parallel scenarios that could help curb terrorism. How many can you come up with? Which seem the most practical? Then, using Hoffman's essay as a model, write an argument showing why one of your ideas should be implemented.

Credits

Jerry Adler, "Building a Better Dad" from *Newsweek* (June 17, 1996). Copyright © 1996 by Newsweek Inc. All rights reserved. Reprinted with permission.

Lois Agnew, "Special Education's Best Intentions." Reprinted with permission of the author.

Taryn Barnett, "Dear Mom." Reprinted with permission of the author.

William J. Bennett, "Why We Fight" from *Why We Fight: Moral Clarity and the War on Terrorism*. Copyright © 2002 by William J. Bennett. Used by permission of Doubleday, a division of Random House, Inc.

Angela A. Boatwright, "Human Cloning: Is It a Viable Option?" and "Human Cloning: An Annotated Bibliography." Reprinted with permission of the author.

Judy Brady, "Why I Want a Wife" from *Ms.* (December 31, 1971). Copyright © 1971 by Judy Brady. Reprinted with permission of the author.

David Brooks, "Looking Back on Tomorrow" from *The Atlantic Monthly* (April 2002). Reprinted with permission of David Brooks.

Suzette Brewer, "One of Our Own: Training Native Teachers for the 21st Century" from *Native Peoples* (March–April 2002). Reprinted with permission of Suzette Brewer.

Beth Brunk, "Toulmin Analysis of 'What's Happened to Disney Films?'" Reprinted with permission of the author.

Jeff Burkholder, "Rogerian Paper." Reprinted with permission of the author.

Madelyn Cain, "The Childless Revolution" from *The Utne Reader* (July–August 2002). Reprinted with permission of Basic Books, a member of Perseus Books, LLC.

Campaign for Tobacco-Free Kids, advertisement ["Meet the Philip Morris Generation"] from *The New York Times* (April 20, 1999). Reprinted with permission of the National Center for Tobacco-Free Kids.

Yaraslana (Lada) Carlisle, "Issue Proposal." Reprinted with permission of the author.

Yahlin Chang, "Asian Identity Crisis" from *Newsweek* (June 22, 1998). Copyright © 1998 by Newsweek, Inc. All rights reserved. Reprinted with permission.

Lynette Clemetson and Keith Naughton, "Patriotism vs. Ethnic Pride" from *Newsweek* (September 24, 2001). Copyright © 2001 by Newsweek, Inc. All rights reserved. Reprinted with permission.

Eric Cohen, "The Real Privacy Wars Are Just Over the Horizon" from *Fort Worth Star-Telegram* (April 22, 2001). Reprinted with permission of Eric Cohen.

Stephanie Coontz, "The Future of Marriage" from *The Way We Really Are: Coming to Terms with America's Changing Families*. Copyright © 1997 by Basic Books, a division of HarperCollins Publishers, Inc. Reprinted with permission of Basic Books, a member of Perseus Books, LLC.

Susan Dentzer, "Paying the Price of Female Neglect" from *U.S. News & World Report* (September 11, 1995). Copyright © 1995 by U.S. News & World Report, Inc., L.P. Reprinted with permission.

Kelly Dickerson, "Minor Problems?" Reprinted with permission of the author.

Richard Dyer, "The Matter of Whiteness" from *White: Essays on Race and Culture*. Copyright © 1997. Reprinted with permission of Taylor & Francis, Ltd.

Barbara Ehrenreich and Frances Fox Piven, "Without a Safety Net" from *Mother Jones* (May–June 2002). Copyright © 2002 by Foundation for National Progress. Reprinted with permission.

Abby Ellin, "The Laptop Ate My Attention Span" from *The New York Times* (April 16, 2000). Copyright © 2000 by The New York Times Company. Reprinted with permission.

Elizabeth Elsberg, "Color Visual Argument." Reprinted with permission of Elizabeth Elsberg.

John Evans, "What's Happened to Disney Films?" from *The Dallas/Fort Worth Heritage* (August 1995). Copyright © 1995 by John Evans. Reprinted with permission of Movie Morality Ministries.

Alan Feuer, "Out of Jail, into Temptation: A Day in a Life" from *The New York Times* (February 28, 2002). Copyright © 2002 by The New York Times Company. Reprinted with permission.

Lyla Fox, "Hold Your Horsepower" from *Newsweek* (March 25, 1996). Copyright © 1996 by Newsweek, Inc. All rights reserved. Reprinted with permission.

Paulo Freire, "The Banking Concept of Education" from *Pedagogy of the Oppressed*. Copyright © 2001. Reprinted with permission of The Continuum International Publishing Group, Inc.

Michael Gazzaniga, "Zygotes and People Aren't Quite the Same" from *The New York Times* (April 25, 2002). Copyright © 2002 by The New York Times Company. Reprinted with permission.

James Gilligan, "Pictures of Pain" (excerpt) from *Behind the Razor Wire: Portrait of a Contemporary American Prison System*, edited and with photographs by Michael Jacobson-Hardy; text by Angela Davis, John Edgar Wideman, Marc Maurer, and James Gilligan (New York: New York University Press, 1998). Reprinted with permission of Dr. James Gilligan. Published also as "Reflections from a Life Behind Bars: Build Colleges, Not Prisons" from *The Chronicle of Higher Education* (October 16, 1998).

"Girls and Computers" from *The New York Times* (October 19, 1998). Copyright © 1998 by The New York Times Company. Reprinted with permission.

Chris Glaser, "Marriage As We See It" from *Newsweek* (September 16, 1996). Copyright © 1996 by Newsweek, Inc. All rights reserved. Reprinted with permission.

Index

TOPIC

AUTHOR–TITLE